Learning and Development for Managers
Perspectives from Research and Practice

Learning and Development for Managers

Perspectives from Research and Practice

Eugene Sadler-Smith

Blackwell
Publishing

BLACKWELL PUBLISHING
350 Main Street, Malden, MA 02148-5020, USA
9600 Garsington Road, Oxford OX4 2DQ, UK
550 Swanston Street, Carlton, Victoria 3053, Australia

First published 2006 by Blackwell Publishing Ltd

1   2006

Library of Congress Cataloging-in-Publication Data

Sadler-Smith, Eugene.
Learning and development for managers : perspectives from research and practice /
Eugene Sadler-Smith.
p. cm.
Includes bibliographical references and index.
ISBN-13: 978-1-4051-2981-7 (hardcover : alk. paper)
ISBN-10: 1-4051-2981-6 (hardcover : alk. paper)
ISBN-13: 978-1-4051-2982-4 (pbk. : alk. paper)
ISBN-10: 1-4051-2982-4 (pbk. : alk. paper)   1. Executives — Training of.
2. Organizational learning.   I. Title.
HD30.4.S22   2006
658.4'07124 — dc22
2005019822

A catalogue record for this title is available from the British Library.

Set in 10 on 12.5 pt Palatino
by SNP Best-set Typesetter Ltd, Hong Kong
Printed and bound in Great Britain
by T J International, Padstow, Cornwall

The publisher's policy is to use permanent paper from mills that operate a sustainable
forestry policy, and which has been manufactured from pulp processed using acid-free
and elementary chlorine-free practices. Furthermore, the publisher ensures that the text
paper and cover board used have met acceptable environmental accreditation standards.

For further information on
Blackwell Publishing, visit our website:
www.blackwellpublishing.com

Contents

Figures

Tables

Abbreviations

AC	abstract conceptualization
ACTA	applied cognitive task analysis
AE	active experimentation
ASTD	American Society for Training and Development
BITE	business improvement tool for entrepreneurs
BTRSPI	*Belbin Team-Role Self-Perception Inventory*
CBL	computer-based learning
CBT	computer-based training
CDT	cognitive demands table
CE	concrete experience
CEML	Council for Excellence in Management and Leadership
CIPD	Chartered Institute of Personnel and Development
CLT	cognitive load theory
CoP	community of practice
CPD	continuing professional development
CSF	critical success factors
CST	cognitive schema theory
CTA	cognitive task analysis
CVT	continuing vocational training
DIF	difficulty, importance and frequency
EEG	electroencephalography
EI	emotional intelligence
ELT	experiential learning theory
ENTO	Employment National Training Organization
ELM	experiential learning model
FMRI	functional magnetic resonance imaging
HPWS	high-performance work system

HR   human resources
HRD   human resource development
HRM   human resource management
HTA   hierarchical task analysis
ICT   information and computing technology
IDT   instructional design theory
IIP   Investors in People
IPISD   Inter-services Procedures for Instructional Systems Development
IOMA   Institute of Management and Administration, New York
ISD   instructional systems design
IT   information technology
KSA   knowledge, skill and/or attitude
LPP   legitimate peripheral participation
LSD   learning systems design
LSI   *Learning Styles Inventory*
LSQ   *Learning Styles Questionnaire*
LTM   long-term memory
LTSI   *Learning Transfer System Inventory*
MIS   management information systems
MRF   multi-rater feedback
MSC   Management Standards Centre
NLP   neuro-linguistic programming
NOS   National Occupational Standard
NTOs   National Training Organizations
NVQ   National Vocational Qualification
OB   organizational behaviour
OD   organizational development
ODL   open and distance learning
OJT   on-job training
PDP   personal development plan
PESTLE   political, economic, social, technological, legal and environmental
PL   programmed learning
PM   performance management
RBV   resource-based view
RO   reflective observation
ROI   return on investment
SEM   structural equation modelling
SHRD   strategic human resource development
SHRM   strategic human resource management
SMART   **s**pecific or stretch; **m**easurable; **a**greed or achievable; **r**ealistic; and
                  time-bound
SMEs   small and medium-sized enterprises
SOPs   standard operating procedures
SPC   statistical process control
SWOT   strengths, weaknesses, opportunities and threats

T&D	training and development
THRM	technical HRM
TQM	total quality management
TWI	Training Within Industry
VET	vocational education and training
VLEs	virtual learning environments
WICs model	wisdom-intelligence-creativity
ZPD	zone of proximal development

Preface

Learning and Development for Managers: Perspectives from Research and Practice aims to describe, analyse and synthesize a wide range of contemporary issues in the field of individual and collective workplace learning. It aims to provide an introduction to learning and development (L&D) and human resource development (HRD) both for students in higher educational programmes and for managers who are engaged in professional development. The book takes a broad view of learning as encompassing both explicit and implicit and individual and collective processes, and it explores these issues from a variety of perspectives and through the use of examples from academic research and business and organizational practice.

The book is intended for students on a range of courses including: Masters-level students on specialist programmes in human resource management, human resource development, and management and organizational learning; those studying for the CIPD Diploma in Personnel and Development; other managers in professional development programmes in HR and related areas; and undergraduate students of specialist modules in human resource management, human resource development, or aspects of organizational psychology.

The author wishes to acknowledge a debt of gratitude to a number of individuals: to Michael K. Hawes (formerly Manager of the British Gas Distance Learning Unit) who enabled me to move from the world of education into the world of business in 1987; to Dr R. J. Riding (formerly Director of the Assessment Research Unit at the School of Education, University of Birmingham) for taking me on as a part-time PhD student in 1988 and supervising me through to completion in 1992; and to Beryl Badger (Principal Lecturer in Human Resources Studies at the University of Plymouth Business School), who enabled my move from business back into education in 1994. Each of these individuals gave me the freedom and encouragement to learn and develop. Without the support of these individuals, and of course many other colleagues whom I could name, over many years it would not have been possible for me to undertake the endeavour of writing this book. I am also grateful to Rosemary Nixon at Blackwell Publishing for taking the project on and for her subsequent forbearance. Any inaccuracies, errors or omissions in the book are, of course, attributable solely to the author.

Eugene Sadler-Smith

CHAPTER 1
Introduction to Learning and Development

Key Concepts

Learning; training; education; development; human resource development; management development; learning and development (L&D); rigour and relevance; role of theory

---

Knowledge Outcomes

After studying this chapter you should be able to:

- define each of the key concepts listed above;
- explain the relationships between learning, training, education, development, human resource development, management development and learning and development (L&D);
- explain the individual and collective purposes of learning and development;
- explain the role of theory in L&D and the significance of rigour and relevance in L&D research.

Introduction

If the challenge of the past has been to 'get organised', the challenge of the future is to find ways in which we can remain open to continuous self-organisation: so that we can adapt and evolve as we go along.

Gareth Morgan, *Imaginization,* **p. 17**

Learning is at the heart of *organization*. Learning has the power to enable individuals and organizations to fulfil their personal and collective goals and ambitions. Individuals may be transformed by their learning, but also through learning they may gain the power to transform the context in which they find themselves or to create new contexts for themselves. Learning potentially is transformative and emancipating. It is through learning that we can acquire new knowledge, skills and attitudes that may enable us to function and perform more efficiently and effectively and exercise greater choice in our working and personal lives. The position adopted in this book is that managed learning has the potential to contribute to the development of individuals and organizations, to enhance their performance in worthwhile and meaningful ways, and that the benefits to be accrued by the individual, the organization and wider society can be significant and mutually reinforcing. For these reasons it is argued that learning and the ability to manage the processes of learning and development are key capabilities for individuals and organizations in the information age.

Learning is the focal point of this book. For students and practitioners of learning and development an understanding of learning is a vital aspect of professional education, development and practice, but of itself learning and the ability to learn also play crucial roles in one's personal growth and one's intellectual and professional development. The overarching aim of this book is to provide an introduction to the concept of learning and development in the context of work and organizations. If the book achieves this aim readers may come to be able to understand and explain learning and development in its many and various manifestations and also, in the context of a professional role, be able to manage it in the pursuit of enhanced organizational and individual effectiveness. The first step on this journey requires that we attempt to define learning and to distinguish it from related concepts. In order to do this we will begin by examining various perspectives on learning and then consider what learning means in relation to concepts such as training, development, education and human resource development (HRD).

Learning

Learning and development (L&D) as a field of management research and practice (and within this context learning per se) is concerned with how individuals (either singly or as groups) acquire (in the sense of getting something that already exists) or create (in the sense of making something completely new) knowledge and skills which enable them to perform and grow in their current or future occupational role. Definitions of learning abound in the literature; Table 1.1 summarizes a selection of these from some of the various fields that this book draws upon.

It is clear from the table that learning is an elusive phenomenon that may be interpreted in diverse ways when viewed from different perspectives; however, it

Table 1.1 Some definitions of learning

Field or sub-field	Description	Source
Andragogy	The process of gaining knowledge and/or expertise	Knowles et al. (1998: 17)
Behaviourist psychology	Learning can be understood in terms of environmental events (stimuli) and their effect upon behaviour without recourse to internal mental processes	Schwartz and Reisberg (1991: 14)
Cognitive psychology:	Learning is best understood in terms of the events taking place inside the learner and the role of mental processes in the acquisition of knowledge	Schwartz and Reisberg (1991: 2)
Education	It has the quality of personal involvement (both of feelings and cognitive aspects), of being self-initiated (the impetus comes from within), of being pervasive (making a difference in the behaviour, attitudes and even personality of the learner), of being evaluated by the learner (who knows if it is meeting a need) and of having the essence of meaning	Rogers (1985: 121–2).
Experiential learning	The process whereby knowledge is created through the transformation of experience	Kolb (1984: 38)
Instructional design	A change in human disposition or capability that persists over a period of time and is not simply ascribable to processes of growth	Gagne (1965)
Knowledge management	The creation of new knowledge, dissemination of it throughout the whole organization and embodiment of it in new technologies, products and services	Nonaka (1991)
Organization science	A process of detecting and correcting error	Argyris (1977)
Organizational behaviour	A relatively permanent change in behaviour, or potential behaviour, that results from experience	Rollinson and Broadfield (2002: 172)
Situated learning	For individuals it is an issue of engaging in and contributing to the practice of their communities, for communities it is an issue of refining their practice and ensuring new generations of members; for organizations it is an issue of sustaining the interconnectedness of communities of practice	Wenger (1998: 7–8)
Training	The systematic acquisition of skills, rules, concepts or attitudes that result in improved performance in another environment	Goldstein (1993: 3)

is possible to synthesize a definition that may be useful for the purposes of this chapter and for the remainder of the book:

> Learning is a longer-term change in the knowledge possessed by an individual, their type and level of skill, or their assumptions, attitudes or values, which may lead to them having increased potential to grow, develop and perform in more satisfying and effective ways.

Offering a definition of learning begs questions about how it relates to or differs from associated terms such as 'education' and 'training', which are also concerned with knowledge and skill acquisition, and also raises the question of why couple together 'learning' and 'development'? Many authors (for example, Buckley and Caple 1992) have attempted to differentiate the various concepts that have at their core the issue of learning whilst others have concluded that to attempt to make any such distinction is potentially futile (see Stewart 1999). There is also a more fundamental question of how learning may itself be conceptualized and perceived. The view of learning that was stated at the outset was essentially an optimistic, positive and humanistic one; however, as Holton (2000) has argued, learning may be seen in a number of ways, not all of which are positive:

1. Positively (as a humanistic endeavour): learning helps individuals to grow, aspire towards and realize higher-level needs; it enhances human potential individually and collectively for employees, organizations, society and humanity (see Holton 2000).
2. Neutrally (as the value-neutral transmission of information and knowledge): this is a narrower technical-rationalist and instrumentalist view of learning which sees it as a means to solve everyday problems through the effective transferring of information and knowledge (see Holton 2000).
3. Negatively (as a tool for societal oppression): the assumption that learning is by nature good or at least neutral may be a naïve one since, as Holton (2000: 63) argued, learning can also be a tool for oppression particularly outside organizational settings (he cites certain political, religious and educational examples to illustrate the potential that learning can have as a means for repression and control).

The assumption that learning is a 'good thing' has also been questioned by certain theorists who espouse critical perspectives of management (for example, Contu et al. 2003). In their view, the stance taken by some which asserts that 'learning is the only sustainable source of competitive advantage' makes it difficult to take up a position which is 'against learning' but such an uncritical position may overlook problematic L&D issues and practices. The potentially negative connotations of learning are a matter to which we shall return in our discussion of the relationship between learning and training.

L&D FACTS AND FIGURES

Here are some dictionary definitions of key concepts: (a) learn: to gain knowledge or understanding of or skill in by study, instruction or experience; (b) train: teach a specified skill especially by practice; (c) education: give intellectual and moral instruction, especially as a prolonged process; (d) develop: bring to or come to an active state or to maturity. (Source: *Oxford Encyclopaedic English*)

PERSPECTIVE FROM PRACTICE: HIGH-PERFORMANCE LEARNING PRACTICES

Based on the following source: J. C. Meister, 2005. Learning that leads to high performance, *Chief Learning Office*r, January 2005: 58.

A survey of senior executives in 285 organizations revealed an apparently simple association between productivity, growth and income and L&D practices. In the high-performing organizations L&D activity was characterized by:

- an alignment of L&D with strategic goals to the extent that many executives viewed the L&D function as a key to accomplishing the company's goals;
- a focus upon developing competencies for key occupational groups ('strategic workforces'), some of which had their own profession-specific L&D team;
- an integration of L&D with related HR (human resources) activities and to other areas such as knowledge management;
- a blending of L&D methods so that traditional classroom-type approaches were integrated with alternatives such as e-learning;
- a focus upon leadership development to the extent that some participants in the survey had developed their own stand-alone leadership institutes (such as Johnson & Johnson's School of Leadership).

Training

Training, especially in the traditional view or from a non-L&D perspective, is often equated with learning and development. However, L&D is much broader than the provision of training courses for employees (although the latter may, of course, be part of planned L&D interventions in organizations). Training is undoubtedly of value to individuals and organizations, but it is by no means the whole story. It is concerned with a tactical approach to the acquisition of predefined knowledge and skills rather than the more strategically aligned perspective that characterises human resource development (HRD) and the integrated view of L&D presented in this book. In this sense training is instrumental (i.e. it is a tool or a means to an end). The distinctive features of training may be described and explained in terms of its process and effects, and also by looking at what it is not (for example by comparison with contrasting concepts such as education). For example, Buckley and Caple (1992: 19) described the *process of training* as mechanistic; whereas that of education, for example, is more 'organic' (though the authors are not specific as to the meaning of this, but which presumably means more amorphous, less constrained and more unpredictable); and the *effects of training* as specific, predictable and uniform, whereas those of education are more general, less predictable and variable (see Figure 1.1).

This distinction is helpful in that L&D practitioners may be concerned with enhancing performance in organizational and business environments that are uncertain, rich and complex. Therefore to concern ourselves solely with training is too narrow a view since for one thing it may focus too much upon the learning content (i.e. the subject of the particular training) but may ignore learning processes (i.e. how the content is acquired) and also may overlook the unplanned, incidental, informal and implicit learning that is inevitable in any organizational or social context. The process of learning is important because the ability to engage in learning and to manage learning more effectively may present a generic competence that can help an organization to differentiate itself from its competitors. Content may be comparatively easy to acquire (it may be bought in or copied comparatively easily from the public domain of knowledge); process is more difficult to emulate (and hence of greater competitive value as a means of differentiation). Learning-how-to-learn may be as important as learning itself for individuals and organizations. Boxall and Purcell (2003: 143) noted that training is often predicated upon a deficit assumption (that is, there is a performance gap that needs to be filled). However, not all training needs to be predicated upon this assumption

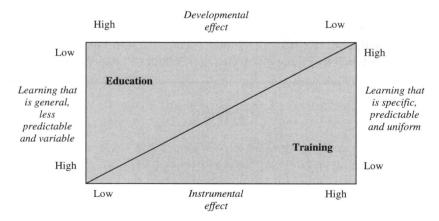

Figure 1.1   The relationship between education, training and development (after Buckley and Caple 1992: 19)

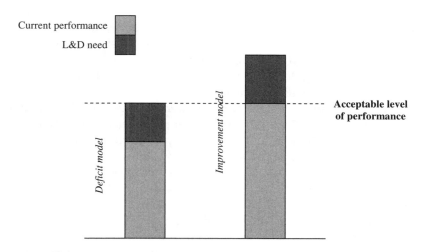

Figure 1.2 Deficit and improvement assumptions for L&D

and by going beyond the deficit assumption we can postulate an improvement assumption in which there is a level of satisfactory performance that can be enhanced or exceeded through L&D. Specifying demanding or 'stretch' goals is one way in which employees' learning can be extended beyond the minimum required in order to perform (Figure 1.2).

L&D FACTS AND FIGURES

In an employer survey in the UK published in 2002, 82 per cent of employers had provided on-the-job training, 62 per cent of employers had provided off-the-job training. Of the small number of employers that did not provide any training the reasons included: (a) existing skills meeting the needs (66 per cent); (b) employees learning adequately from experience (13 per cent); (c) new recruits being sufficient to obtain the skills required by the firm (12 per cent). (*Source*: Learning and training at work 2002, Department for Education and Skills SFR 02/2003.)

PERSPECTIVE FROM RESEARCH: THE NATURE OF DIFFERENCES BETWEEN TRAINING AND LEARNING IN THE UK BANKING SECTOR

Based on the following source: E. P. Antonacopoulou, 2001. The paradoxical nature of the relationship between training and learning, *Journal of Management Studies*, 38(3): 328–50.

Antonacopoulou's starting point is her argument for a more critical analysis of the relationship between training and learning. She defined the latter

Continued

as the liberation of knowledge through self-reflection and questioning. An implication of her argument is that progress in understanding this issue has been hampered by the limitations of reductionist approaches which assume linear cause-and-effect relationships and straightforward associations between training, learning and performance. The dilemmas faced by individuals and the dualities that we observe in L&D may be one way in which we can explain why development interventions have the potential to be counter-productive (2001: 331). One example of such a duality might be the identification of training needs ostensibly as an indicator of a development need or an opportunity to learn and grow, but which also may be perceived as an indication of an individual weakness that could have ramifications for wider matters such as individual reward. The conclusion that Antonacopoulou draws from this argument is that training and the activities associated with it (such as training needs identification and analysis) may not be assumed always to produce learning, nor can learning be assumed to be an integral part of training (because transfer of learning from the training situation to the job situation may not occur). *Note*: Antonacopoulou's perspective is somewhat different from the one outlined in the preceding discussion, where the learning process (lower order) was postulated as underlying training events (higher order). For her the training process is seen as leading (sometimes) to the occurrence of learning.

To investigate the paradoxical and dualistic relationships between training and learning Antonacopoulou employed a variety of data collection methods (interview, questionnaire, observation and critical incident review) longitudinally in three case study organizations in the retail banking sector of the UK. The type of questions asked of managers ranged from the specific and operational (for example, 'Give examples of the best learning experiences you came across so far') to the general and aspirational (for example, 'What do you think training should be able to do?'). The paradoxes are illustrated by some of the quotations from the participants in the study and are perhaps indicative of what she termed the 'strong' and 'weak' relationships that may exist between training and learning:

> Training can help shape ideas and aspirations because it involves learning new things. Depending on the type of training, it can be the most effective way of learning. (2001: 336)

> Some needs are not easily fulfilled by on-going training. They are continuous and part of the unexpected day-to-day procedures that a [training] course cannot resolve. (2001: 337)

The contradictions apparent between participants' responses were taken as indicative of a disjunction between training and learning. Some of the distinguishing and contradictory features of each are shown in Table 1.2 as a further means of comparison between the two.

The relationship between training and learning is often portrayed as uni-directional – for example, training produces learning which in turn has an effect upon performance; training is often portrayed as serving organizational priorities (enhanced performance); and as mechanistic (superficially perceived and rarely existing as an interaction between training and learning) (2001: 339). Antonacopoulou's study presents a thoroughly described and comprehensive analysis in a sub-sector (retail banking) of the financial services industry in the UK. Clearly the generalizability of these case study findings is limited but they articulate a fundamental tension and paradox between two terms (learning and training) that are sometimes used synonymously. Antonacopoulou's research suggested that it may be fallacious to attribute learning as an outcome of all training. One interpretation of this argument is that training may have at least three possible outcomes: an increase in an employee's capacity for effective action (the latter is based upon Senge's 1990 definition of learning); no change in an employee's capacity for effective action; or a dysfunctional outcome in which there is a reduction in an employee's capacity for effective action. This concurs to some extent with the views put forward by Holton (2000), and which were discussed earlier, of the potential positive, neutral and negative outcomes of learning.

Table 1.2 Differences between training and learning based on Antonacopoulou's research (2001)

Training	Learning
Conditioning and control of individuals' understanding	Broadening and liberating understanding
An 'event'	Ongoing
Teaching cultural norms of the organization and enforcing the organization's definitions and perspective	Questioning and experimentation with freedom to learn and unlearn
Prediction of outcomes	Unpredictability of outcomes
Consistent with single-loop learning (incremental change) (see Chapter 5)	Conducive to double-loop learning (radical change) (see Chapter 5)

L&D FACTS AND FIGURES

The 2004 American Society for Training and Development (ASTD) survey revealed that the annual number of hours of formal learning per employee averages about 28 hours across a broad cross-section of US organizations. In the UK, in a report published in 2002, the average amount of off-the-job training provided was 1.8 days per employee. (*Sources*: ASTD State of the Industry Report 2004; Learning and training at work 2002, Department for Education and Skills SFR 02/2003.)

Discussion Point

As Antonacopoulou's research suggests, the distinctions and relationships between terms we sometimes take for granted, like learning and training, are not always so clear-cut. What are the relationships as you see them between learning as defined earlier in this chapter and training? Is learning an outcome of all training? How might the 'no change' or 'reduced capacity for effective action' outcomes of training arise in practice?

Development and Education

Development is an increase over the longer term of the capacity that an individual has to live a more effective and fulfilling professional and personal life as a result of learning and the acquisition of knowledge, skills and attitudes. It is a directional shift towards a higher condition or state of being and in this sense is concerned with an outcome. Development in the L&D context should be considered distinct from development as a biological process of maturation (though of course aging may have an impact upon a number of L&D-related matters). Development occurs as a result of learning and can happen in any number of ways: for example, through training events (such as training courses) or via the methods of coaching, mentoring, planned and unplanned experiences in the workplace and so forth. Some training may be highly focused and job specific (such as learning how to use a new piece of software), whereas other training may contribute to a broader and longer-term development programme (such as undertaking training in team-working skills as a part of a management development programme). In this sense training (and to the same extent education also) may be seen as but one type of input into the developmental process (Table 1.3).

Individuals may differ in their motivations to engage in learning and development. Maurer (2002) argued that the notions of the actual self and the possible self are critical aspects of an individual's orientation towards their development. Taking Alderfer's notion of growth needs as a starting point, Maurer asserted that successful involvement in learning and development activities may strengthen an individual's orientation towards the attainment of what the self might become. A virtuous cycle may thereby operate where development-oriented individuals maintain or increase their interests in learning activities and projects. The building of learners' self-efficacy (the belief that one can perform tasks or behaviours) may be a crucial precondition for many individuals because as they become more effective as learners – and since learning often gives valuable payback – a positive feedback loop may operate. A related aspect of self-efficacy is the ability to learn how to learn and how to successfully engage in developmental and career planning activities. In one respect a 'learning-to-learn' capacity is likely to be founded upon individuals' understanding of their own personal learning preferences, styles and processes (i.e. what works for them and how this may be improved). Meta-cognition (defined here as thinking about and coming to under-

Table 1.3 The relationships between learning and training, development and education (K, knowledge; S, skill; A, attitude)

Outcome	What?	When?	Where?
Trained employee	KSAs that are specific and uniform and that may lead to enhanced job performance	Before or during employment	On-job and off-job
Developed employee	KSAs that are variable and more general and	Usually during employment	On-job and off-job
Educated employee	that may lead to professional and personal growth	Usually before employment	Usually non-work contexts

stand one's own thinking and learning processes) is an important aspect of a developmental and life-long learning orientation.

Managerial decisions to develop individual employees or groups of employees are not unproblematical. For example, if we examine the management of careers and the psychological contract we find that tensions and issues of organizational power and politics may become more focused through issues relating to L&D policy and practice. One such tension is with respect to where the boundaries of development are – these may be different from each particular stakeholder's perspective. For example, is development, when viewed from the individual's viewpoint, for career purposes (and perhaps beyond the organization), or is it, from the organization's perspective, for employment in the organization or employability in the wider labour market? As far as the management of L&D is concerned these tensions may raise policy-related questions such as 'development of whom and for what purposes?' These questions are important from the point of view not only of developing fair and equitable L&D plans and policies, but also for how L&D is perceived, understood and implemented in an organization, and in relation to L&D's political role and its relationships with the power exercised by specific occupational groups (such as managers). These issues may have ramifications for other organizational matters such as employee relations, employee involvement, workforce satisfaction and commitment, and may have a knock-on effect on human resource (HR) issues such as recruitment and retention.

L&D FACTS AND FIGURES

The UK's Chartered Institute of Personnel and Development's (CIPD) Annual Training Survey 2004 found that a third of respondents said that over 75 per cent of the training in their organizations was informal. At the other end of the scale, only a tenth of respondents said that less than one-quarter of their training was informal. (*Source*: Training and Development 2004: Survey Report (April 2004). London: CIPD.)

Like training, education is an input to the developmental process and has been defined as the 'long term acquisition of valid and usable bodies of knowledge and intellectual skills and the development of the ability to think critically, systematically and independently' (Ausubel 1985: 71). The aims and effects of education are broader and deeper than training since its concern is with the whole person over a longer period. From an organizational point of view, Ausubel's attributes of an 'educated individual' (critical, systematic and independent) are likely to be those that some employees might be expected to bring with them when selected for employment. The attributes are likely to vary in their level since what constitutes 'educated' will vary between occupations and contexts. Nonetheless, critical, systematic and independent individuals ought to be products of an effective educational system. An organization's policy may be to recruit educated employees and develop job-specific skills and thus enable the individual to apply her or his generic abilities to think independently, systematically and critically to workplace issues (this is especially true of professional and management occupations) and thus develop them further in situ into a unique set of difficult-to-imitate attributes.

L&D FACTS AND FIGURES

Many countries are facing significant challenges in their patterns of skills requirements and labour supplies. In the USA the Department of Labor estimated that the number of jobs requiring a degree is likely to grow by 31 per cent and that 160 million US jobs will have only 154 million American workers to fill them by 2008 (the population of the USA in 2005 was around 300 million). In the EU (European Union) on average the number of students enrolled in tertiary education has more than doubled in the last 25 years. (*Sources*: American Council on Education, http://www.acenet.edu; CEDEFOP, 2003. *Key Figures on Vocational Education and Training*, http://www.cedefop.eu.int)

Through the human resource (HR) activities of recruitment and selection educated employees can be hired or 'bought in'. Education also has a role to play during employment as part of L&D through which attempts may be made to develop, 'make' or 'grow' employees in particular ways. Those educational processes and their outcomes which take place before employment (at school, college or university) are likely to be of lesser immediate and direct relevance to a task or job than are L&D activities which are engaged in as a response to identified learning needs. However, the indirect and longer-term impact of educational experiences and background upon ongoing development and performance may be significant. Education may also occur after an individual becomes an employee (for example, through a part-time evening class as part of a management development programme, through a distance learning course and so forth). Hence, education may be considered to be more developmental and less instrumental in its effects than is training, though both contribute to an individual's development.

L&D FACTS AND FIGURES

As a general rule the unemployment rates for people with higher qualifications tends to be lower than for those without such qualifications. For example, in the EU on average in 2000 the unemployment rates for people with a tertiary qualification was 4 per cent against 7 per cent for those with secondary but not tertiary qualifications and 11 per cent for those with at most a secondary qualification. In the UK the figures were 2.2, 4.4 and 8.5 per cent respectively. (*Source*: CEDEFOP, 2003. *Key Figures on Vocational Education and Training*, http://www.cedefop.eu.int)

Education and training are tangible 'events' (for example, a training course or an educational programme). Development, on the other hand, is less tangible and is not an 'event' or an input as such; rather it is a trajectory of an individual or an organization. It takes place as a result of the process of learning and may be a naturalistic process (for example through experience) or supported by training, education and other workplace-based activities (inputs to the process). Education (including vocational education) often takes place pre-employment, but also may continue during employment with employer support (for example, as part of a company-sponsored management development programme) or without the sanctioning and support of the employer (for example, where an individual undertakes self-development activities that may or may not be work-related or career-related). One of the aims of training or education is to bring about learning, but training may be considered to be more instrumental in its effects (in the sense of being for a well-defined, and usually organizational, purpose) than is the ongoing professional education of managers and other employees.

Woodall and Winstanley (1998) approached the semantic issues relating to education and training from the perspective of management development and asked the question: why not 'management education' or 'management training'? For them 'education' is too tainted with notions of formalized learning in educational institutions that are far removed from the informal and workplace-contextualized learning that is a productive form of knowledge creation in organizations. Similarly, 'training' has connotations of vocationally oriented education guided by formal or structured means. For Woodall and Winstanley management development may include one or both of these but 'is used more comprehensively to encapsulate all types of learning which enable an individual to develop their skills and understanding to meet current and future organisational needs' (1998: 9). Woodall and Winstanley acknowledged an overlap between management development and human resource development (HRD), but the former is seen as being concerned more with learning and development at the strategic level whereas the latter may have more of a functional and specialist emphasis. They argue that the two concepts overlap in the areas of competence, appraisal, coaching and team-building skills. As we shall see in a later chapter, a further dimension is added when one considers leader and leadership development – an area seen by many as crucial in enhancing individual and organizational performance.

Human Resource Development (HRD)

The formal origins of the term HRD may be traced at least as far back as Nadler's work in the 1970s (see Nadler 1970). He defined it as 'a series of organised activities, conducted within a specified time and designed to produce behavioural change' (Nadler 1979: 3). Later it was defined by Davis and Mink in the 1990s as: 'a wide range of interacting, integrating processes aimed at developing greater purpose and meaning, higher levels of performance and achievement and greater capacity for responding to an ever-changing environment leading to more effective individuals, teams and organisations' (1992: 201). As usage of the term HRD has grown, so, it appears, has its remit – for example, more recently McLean and McLean (2001: 4) defined it as:

> any process or activity that, either initially or over the long term, has the potential to develop adults' work-based knowledge, expertise, productivity and satisfaction, whether for personal or group/team gain or for the benefit of an organisation, community, nation, or ultimately the whole of humanity.

Since its inception and growth in the USA in the 1970s and 1980s the term HRD appears to have migrated to the UK, mainland Europe and beyond and in many cases has supplanted references to 'training and development' (T&D) and 'employee development'. The field of HRD is undergoing strenuous attempts at self-definition and debates about HRD's precise meaning are continuous and ongoing (see Lee 2004). For example, HRD has been described as 'planned interventions in organisational and individual learning processes' (Stewart 1999: 19). The latter implicates HRD as being concerned with the more manageable aspects of learning. This does not mean that HRD is merely concerned with training, since clearly it is possible to have a managed learning process that goes beyond the instrumentality of training interventions and into broader issues of individual and organizational development (including, for example, action learning and action science). Grieves and Redman argued that the distinguishing characteristics of HRD are that it is a strategic intervention where there is some devolvement of responsibility to line managers and which assumes a positive set of attitudes to learning with an emphasis on the workplace as a context for learning (1999: 89–90). However, as we shall see in this regard, some have proffered the specific term 'strategic HRD' (SHRD), which begs the question of what HRD per se means given the implication in Grieves and Redman's assertion that all HRD is strategic. An alternative view is to consider HRD (or L&D for that matter) to have both strategic and operational facets. To this extent HRD has subsumed T&D (perhaps there are parallels between this and the relationship of HRM – human resource management – to personnel management). To be strategic in an effective manner HRD must have an operational component which is concerned with the day-to-day implementation of strategy (any HRD strategy is only as good as its implementation); however, it is also possible for L&D to be operational (i.e. concerned with the day-to-day activities of identifying and analysing learning needs, implementing and evaluating L&D) without having a strategic focus (this has been one of the perceived weaknesses of training and development in the past). The issue of strategic L&D will be returned to in the next chapter.

PERSPECTIVE FROM PRACTICE: THE ORIGINS OF HRD

Source: W. E. A. Ruona, 2001. The foundational impact of the Training Within Industry project on the HRD profession, *Advances in Developing Human Resources*, 3(2): 119–26.

The term human resource development (HRD) has gained significant currency and impact in academic and practitioner circles in recent years. The origins of contemporary HRD practice may be traced to the Training Within Industry (TWI) Service of the US government in the period 1940 to 1945, which had two objectives: to help contractors to the US government's war effort pursue faster production and reduce the costs of production of war materials (Ruona 2001: 121). Rather than training being viewed as an end in itself it was seen instrumentally as a means to achieving the desired objectives (increased production of resources to support the war effort). The ethos and method of the TWI approach were described by Ruona (2001: 122–25) and may be summarized thus:

1. Strategic and business focus: training is a business tool whose aim should be to solve production problems and whose results should be evaluated accordingly (i.e. the focus should be upon performance improvement).
2. Roles and responsibilities: training professionals should be business partners, supervisors should be the 'central conduits' (Ruona 2001: 124) for training, employee coaching and performance, and management is ultimately responsible for maximizing the impact of training (i.e. line managers have an important role).
3. Systematic approach: training should be based upon the sound analysis of tasks and work processes and be structured to provide opportunity for demonstration, practice and feedback (i.e. training should be based upon assessed needs and implemented in a workplace climate that is conducive to facilitating the transfer of learning from the training situation to the job situation).

Continued

4. Systems perspective: training should reach beyond the scope of the individual (for example, through a multiplier approach in which trainees train others and so forth) and should recognize the broader linkages, interactions and opportunities for integration between job, process, worker and supervisor (i.e. there should be integration with other aspects of HR and job design).

The TWI as described by its author, Dooley (1945; 2001), and reviewed by Ruona (2001) and Swanson (2001), may be seen as representing the birth over half a century ago of a systematic approach to L&D. The latter is discussed more fully in Chapter 2, but for now it is enough to note that it is a method that has an inherent logic and business focus and which, in spite of its acknowledged limitations and the changes and elaborations that it has undergone over the intervening decades, is still recognizable as providing the foundation of much HRD (or L&D) practice to this day.

The lack of consensus in terminologies (including the more recent usage in the UK of the term 'learning and development') may be seen as characteristic of a dynamic, emergent and rapidly evolving and practice-focused sub-field of management theory and practice. Ruona (2000: 1) asserted that that the work, values and paradigms of HRD are not yet well understood even by those within the field; as a result of this HRD (or the managed aspects L&D) often faces challenges in differentiating itself from related areas such as HR. For example, in the UK L&D practitioners may face difficulties in distinguishing themselves as a discrete body with their own identity from the mainstream of the HRM function; the same may be true in other national contexts with regard to L&D and adult and vocational educational practice in general. For our purposes we will argue that HRD (or L&D) should be considered as a set of practices that should be integrated with other relevant HRM practices.

L&D FACTS AND FIGURES

On average 62 per cent of countries in the EU provided continuing vocational training (CVT) (ranging from 96 per cent in Denmark to 18 per cent in Greece; the figure for the UK was 87 per cent). The figures were higher for larger enterprises (250 employees or more): 96 per cent compared to medium (50 to 249 employees), 81 per cent, and small firms (10 to 49 employees), 56 per cent. On average the percentage of employees participating in CVT was 40 per cent (for the UK the figure was 49 per cent). (CEDEFOP, 2003. *Key Figures on Vocational Education and Training*, http://www.cedefop.eu.int)

Learning and Development

The issue of the semantics of L&D terminology is not irrelevant. It needs to be seen in a historical context wherein may be detected clear changes in the emphases placed upon the different activities and processes associated with learning in organizations. A useful summary of the UK historical context is provided by Pedler et al. (1997: 12–14), who argued that there has been an evolution away from an education and training emphasis. For example, in the UK large public organizations often had their own workforce education departments, and even nowadays 'training departments' are not uncommon and job advertisements frequently appear for the post of 'Head of Training' or 'Training Manager'. According to Pedler et al. the approach to planned learning in organizations has evolved through a systematic training model (1950s, 1960s and 1970s), through self-development and action-based approaches (1980s) up to the decades in which the approach in their book (*The Learning Company*) was conceived (the 1980s and 1990s) and the advent of the much vaunted 'learning organization' movement. They argued that we never actually 'get there' (to the ideal approach) because as one problem is solved by the latest method (for example, systematic training) another emerges (for example, lack of transfer of learning from the training room to the work environment) because 'the seeds of [the next problem] were sown by the previous solution' (1997: 12). This chain of developments could be seen as accretions to extant practices in which newer ideas, tools and techniques are added to and embedded in older established ones rather than being replacements for them via a wholesale paradigm shift (in the same way that HRD as a field of practice subsumed T&D).

So, for example, even though the systematic approach (a 'plan-design-do-check' cycle) was limited by its very reductionism (the splitting or reducing of jobs into tangible micro skills was not universally applicable, especially to managerial and creative job roles), the systematic approach is not irrelevant simply because of this inherent (but non-fatal) limitation or because it happened to be developed in the 1950s and 1960s. The systematic approach is still alive and well (for example, in elements of the UK's national occupational standard for L&D practitioners and in many L&D and HR job descriptions and workplace practices). Newer developments in L&D practice (such as action learning) have been added to older ones thus enriching the L&D field as a whole (Figure 1.3). What has not been witnessed is any kind of major 'revolution' in L&D theory and method in which a wholesale paradigm shift has taken place. One reason that this has not occurred is perhaps because in practical terms traditional methods are not wholly incommensurate with newer ones and they also have an inertia which embeds them in practice, whilst newer ones (such as e-learning) have some undoubted utility but are not the panaceas that many of their proponents might have wished for or led us to believe.

Professional bodies also play a role in this evolutionary process by driving or reflecting changes in the occupational and organizational contexts of the practice

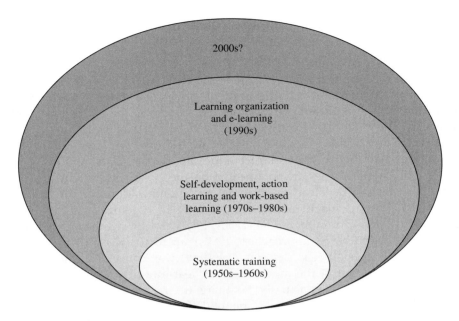

Figure 1.3   An accretionary model of the development of L&D practices (after Pedler et al., 1997: 12–14)

of L&D. For example, in the UK there used to be an Institute of Training and Development (ITD), which was subsumed in the 1990s by the Institute of Personnel Management, which itself became the Institute of Personnel and Development (and latterly the Chartered Institute of Personnel and Development, the CIPD). 'Training and development', gave way to 'employee development' and then 'HRD', and, as noted, the most recent shift in the UK has been to the use of the term 'learning and development'. Gibb suggested that a simple pragmatic reason for the adoption of the term 'learning and development' might be because in the UK the highly influential CIPD now calls what was 'employee development' by a new name, 'learning and development' (2002: 5). However, as outlined above there are valid conceptual reasons for using the term 'learning and development', not least because of increasing interest in and recognition of the processes of informal learning, including the role of implicit learning and tacit knowledge, in organizations. Learning and development represent processes that may be supported by events such as training, education or working. There are also national cultural differences in aspects of terminology. For example in the USA the term 'instruction', 'instructor' and the associated concept of instructional design is not uncommon; indeed the classic 1979 text for learning design by Gagné and Briggs is called *Principles of Instructional Design* (see Gagné et al. 1992). The equivalent term in the UK would have been 'training design' or more latterly 'learning design'. In some practitioner circles the term 'training and development' (T&D) appears, at the time of writing, to be holding up. Terminologies in the field are diverse.

L&D FACTS AND FIGURES

The American Society for Training and Development (ASTD) describes itself as a leading association of workplace learning and performance professionals, forming a world-class community of practice some 70,000 members strong. The ASTD has a membership structure, publishes magazines and books, runs conferences and sponsors research. The ASTD traces its development back to a meeting in New Orleans in 1942, when there was especial emphasis on training since this was essential in meeting increased production needs and for quickly replacing workers who had gone to fight overseas in the Second World War (for example, the USA's Training Within Industry initiative; see Dooley 1945). In 2004 the ASTD celebrated its 60th birthday (see: http://www.astd.org).

Whilst human resource development (HRD) is often concerned with the tactical and strategic management of organized learning and development processes in organizations (see Dooley 1945; Nadler 1970; Davis and Mink 1992; Grieves and Redman 1999), L&D, as defined for the purposes of this book, takes a broader view of learning as occurring in both explicit and implicit ways. To this extent L&D has two facets. Firstly, it is concerned with describing, explaining and understanding the informal and formal, planned and unplanned learning processes that occur in organizations. Secondly, it is concerned where possible with enabling, facilitating and managing these processes also. To this extent L&D is implicated in the management of explicit learning and planned interventions, but also is concerned with the interpretation and understanding of naturalistic learning processes that occur in social systems such as workplaces (even when they cannot be controlled or managed). Hence, from our perspective L&D may be defined as an area of management enquiry and practice which is concerned with the understanding and, where possible, management of learning in the workplace in order to maximize its impact upon the achievement of work goals, the development of the individual and the enhancement of collective performance.

Purposes and Practice of L&D

These discussions raise questions about the purposes of planned interventions such as those implied by the term HRD when it is described as 'planned interventions in organisational and individual learning processes' (see Stewart 1999: 19). Planned activities, such as training and formalized learning experiences, are most often concerned with the achievement of individual and organizational objectives. The latter are by definition predetermined (often on the basis of a needs analysis). Stewart offers another perspective in arguing that HRD is not necessarily bound up with achieving organizational objectives that are predetermined. He sees the purpose of HRD as being the changing of individual and collective behaviour, with concomitant questions about what is 'desirable behaviour' and for whom? There are implicit unitarist assumptions in many models of HRD and planned L&D of the congruence of individual and organizational motives and agendas. Such a conception of L&D, it may be argued, assumes that the vast majority of – if not all – employees are eager learners who are willing to buy in to the organizational and business purposes of L&D. This may overlook the agency of the individual. Moreover, it may gloss over political issues and the impact of organizationally driven change on the individual employee, for example through downsizing and delayering and the effects that these may have upon motivations, career development trajectories and even the very meaning and purpose of the term 'learning and development'.

There is a danger that in a changed organizational context a unitary, managerially driven or externally driven (for example, from professional or governmental bodies) conception of L&D may result in a partial and perhaps uncritical view. Such a perspective may fail to acknowledge the tensions and paradoxes, the role of emotions, the significance of power and hidden and conflicting agendas (wherein individual and organizational priorities may compete), which may be manifestations of political, cultural and contextual factors. Moreover, to focus wholly upon predetermined objectives assumes a rational planning process in which there is a natural sequence from business goals, through strategic planning, to HR planning and ultimately to L&D policies and plans and their execution and evaluation. However, the limits of rationality in management have been widely recognized (see, for example, Simon, 1989). Planned 'learning' and 'organization' are not unproblematic; indeed the conjunction of the two (learning and organization) may, as Weick and Westley (1999) have suggested, represent an oxymoron itself.

The label 'L&D practitioner' will be used, but it is not ideal (not least because it is cumbersome); nonetheless it is a useful blanket term intended to encompass those individuals whose role engages them in the formal planning, implementation, evaluation or management of activities which are intended to enable and assist:

- employees in acquiring new knowledge, skills or attitudes (for example by providing planned L&D);
- the collective learning process in organizations (for example, by facilitating or supporting organizational development and change).

The term 'L&D practitioner' is preferred as being less contentious than the term 'L&D professional'. As such it is not intended to encompass other groups of stakeholders such as line managers since for these groups, although they may have some key L&D responsibilities, L&D is not the main part of their job role. It has been argued that for the L&D practitioners' role to be sustained, grow and gain continued recognition L&D practitioners or the L&D profession (if it is such) must take learning seriously and strategically in an organizational context in which learning is inclusive and built into the ethos of practice (Gold et al. 2003: 447). The enhanced esteem and professional status to which Gold et al. allude is important if planned L&D interventions are to be successful in supporting organizational strategy and enhancing business performance by getting the 'buy-in' of senior managers. From a US perspective Kuchinke concurred with this view, namely that one potential difficulty in this regard is the ill-defined professional status of the field of L&D, with (in some instances) low entry barriers to L&D positions and often a location within organizational units that may have little power or influence (he cites the example of HR units) (2000: 281). Professional qualification and certification schemes such as that of the Chartered Institute of Personnel and Development (CIPD) in the UK represent one attempt by a national professional body to raise the entry level to HR and L&D roles.

L&D FACTS AND FIGURES

The Chartered Institute of Personnel and Development (CIPD) is the main professional body for human resource (HR) specialists in the UK. By 2001 it had over 100,000 members. Its roots and evolution can be traced back to the Welfare Workers Association in 1913, the Welfare Workers Institute (1919), Institute of Labour Management (1931), the Institute of Personnel Management (1946) and its merging with the Institute of Training and Development (ITD), formerly the British Institute of Training Officers (1964), in 1994. *Source*: I. Beardwell, 2002. In T. Redman and A. Wilkinson, *The Informed Student Guide to Human Resource Management*. London: Thomson Learning. (see also: http://www.cipd.co.uk).

The term 'intervention' used in some of the foregoing discussions is relevant and significant in that it implies a conscious act with the intention of enabling or managing the learning process in a planned (and perhaps systematic) way. This can apply equally to those instances where learning occurs away from a formal setting, for example in a workplace context, as much as it can to formal classroom-based learning (for example, it is entirely feasible to intervene in workplace settings to facilitate learning by methods such as job instruction training or coaching). The L&D practitioner's strategic as well as practical day-to-day concerns are likely to include managing learning in organizations through organized activities (Nadler 1970), and how such activities (whether formal or informal) may actually be organized is one of the themes of this book. In pursuit of this goal it is important for the student of L&D to understand the learning processes in organizations in order that they may be managed more effectively. A useful starting point, therefore, is to examine the process of learning as it occurs in organizational settings since it is this which underpins the higher-order concepts and processes such as training, development and HRD.

Theory, Rigour and Relevance in L&D

As part of a social scientific endeavour L&D research and practice must be grounded upon a strong theoretical base, which requires a cognizance of extant and emerging theories in the base disciplines. Weinberger (1998: 77–9) argued that L&D (or HRD) is underpinned by the disciplines of psychology and economics, system theories (see Swanson 1995; 2001) and philosophy (including ethics), and to which may be added sociology, anthropology and political science (see Kuchinke 2001). There are contributions from organizational behaviour (OB) and organizational development (OD) also. What is also required is a theory-building endeavour within L&D itself. Lynham (2002: 223) described theory building as the purposeful process of generating, verifying and refining coherent descriptions, explanations, and representations of observed or experienced phenomena, which results in:

- process knowledge in the form of increased understanding of how something works;
- outcome knowledge in the form of explanative and predictive knowledge (Dubin 1978; Lynham 2002).

Torraco (2002: 358–9) summarized the methods available to the researcher in pursuit of building a methodologically robust L&D as including quantitative approaches, grounded theory, meta-analysis, social-constructionist approaches and case study method. The knowledge thus produced should possess the qualities of rigour and relevance. In management more generally in the UK, recent years have witnessed a debate regarding these twin issues (some have referred to it as the 'double hurdle') of rigour (i.e. both in terms of underlying theories and the research design, method and analyses used) and relevance (i.e. the significance and importance of the research to managers and management practice). Tranfield and Starkey (1998) and more recently Anderson et al. (2001) have outlined a number of scenarios and consequences of the various permutations of rigour (high or low) and relevance (high or low). This gives rise to a number of possible scenarios for research in management, described by Anderson and his colleagues as:

1. Puerile science carried out by misguided researchers, lacking scientific rigour and of low practical relevance.
2. Popularist science based upon popular ideas, which gives high exposure and impact on managers but has weak theory.
3. Pedantic science, which has high methodological rigour, tends to dominate the academic journals but may be incomprehensible to the majority of managers.
4. Pragmatic science that produces knowledge that is scientifically valid but also of practical relevance to managers in their work (Anderson et al. 2001).

Discussion Point

As you become more familiar with specific examples of L&D research and practice you might ask the question, 'Where might they each fit within the typology suggested by Anderson et al. (2001)?' If you undertake any L&D or other management research of your own, how might you try to ensure that it occupies the most desirable category in Anderson et al.'s typology?

So, where does the preceding discussion leave us as we prepare to embark on a consideration of the concepts, models, theories, research and practice that might help us to understand and enable L&D at the individual and collective levels in the contemporary workplace? A central concern in any scholarly endeavour is the role of theory. In very simple terms, a theory explains what a phenomenon is and how it works (Torraco 1997). A field of management, such as L&D, may be said to be theoretical when it draws upon a set of conceptually coherent explanations for, or predictions of, real-world phenomena. Thus, goal-setting theory may be used as a means by which the effectiveness or otherwise of objective-setting in L&D may be described and explained; and in similar ways we might think, for example, of equity theory and expectancy theory and the ways in which they enable L&D practitioners to describe and explain relevant phenomena such as motivation and engagement in L&D. A field is, on the other hand, atheoretical when it does not have any scholarly or scientific basis for the ideas and principles that embody it (see Swanson 2001).

Sound theory is, according to Swanson, valuable to scholars and practitioners for a number of reasons: firstly, it results in models and principles which can provide powerful and practical explanations by which practitioners may carry out their work. But why should a practitioner necessarily be interested in erudite explanations? Swanson's second point is that without theory every problem has to be reinvented anew, new strategies have to be developed to cope with each challenge, and the pressure to perform may be such that 'trial and error' or 'if it works, use it' becomes the modus operandi. Ultimately such an approach may be inefficient (the wheel may need to be constantly reinvented) and intellectually impoverished, as well as intellectually impoverishing of the field itself. The question of whether there is a theory of L&D (or HRD) per se is an open question, answers to which are beginning to emerge from the various attempts at theoretically based enquiry and theory-building research (for example Lynham 2000, 2002; McGoldrick et al. 2001). The question that will be considered here, since it is more pertinent to the ambition of a practical text, is that of the nature of the theories in use in L&D and the value that they may add for practice.

There is no question (for the reasons outlined above) that L&D practice needs theories if it is to be intellectually rigorous and scientifically founded, and if its various interventions are to be executed with any degree of confidence in their likely outcomes. The question then arises of which theories and why? Swanson has argued that HRD (and we might add as a corollary L&D) relies upon theories from three base disciplines in order to understand, explain and engage in practice, and these are: psychology, because it captures the core human elements; economics, because of its concern with resources; and systems theory, because it captures the complexity and dynamism of organizations and their work processes at the individual and the organizational levels (2001: 304–5). As has already been noted above, these three theories are perhaps augmentable by the inclusion of others from areas such as philosophy (including ethics), sociology, anthropology and political science (see Kuchinke 2000, 2001). A slightly different perspective is offered by DeWolfe-Waddill and Marquardt (2003), who identified what they termed five major adult learning orientations (behaviourist, cognitive, humanist, social and constructivist). They start from the position of andragogy and its concerns with how adults learn, and they disaggregate this into the five major schools of thought (what might be termed theoretical traditions) referred to above. Hence, DeWolfe-Waddill and Marquardt are concerned with theories in L&D and the explanatory and predictive power they add to practice (their principal concern was with action learning). This is the stance that will be taken in this book, i.e. there will be a concern with the theories in L&D that may be used to describe, explain and make predictions about individual and collective learning in the workplace and hence inform L&D decision making. The main schools of thought that will be used as our foundation (and which correspond broadly with those of DeWolfe-Waddill and Marquardt) will be:

1. Behaviourist theory (because of its historical significance and concern with behavioural change).
2. Cognitive information processing theory (for its concern with the internal mental processes of learning).
3. Social learning theory (because of its concern with the significance of the human model and reciprocation with the environment).
4. Situated learning (for its concern with the role of participation in practice and the significance in learning of shared sets of assumptions, norms and language).
5. Cognitive constructivism (because of its concern with the significance of schema change).

Several theoretical traditions coalesce in the domains of experiential learning and andragogical learning and these are often called upon in attempts to theorize L&D practice. In the UK L&D practice has been dominated by models predicated upon the assumptions that adults 'learn through experience'. For example, Megginson et al. argued that the experiential learning model provides the trainer, manager or others involved in managing learning with 'a methodology that can be used to support learning covering a wide variety of situations and participants' (1993: 85). Downs (1995: 103) recommended the use of reflective 'ponder periods' after learning as part of an experiential learning cycle, with the latter sometimes represented as 'trial-and-error learning'. In recent decades, with the various exhortations to organizations to 'innovate or die', the 'trial and error' interpretation of learning is sometimes condoned and legitimized in the pursuit of the laudable goals of experimentation and creativity. Clearly, there are learning episodes in any workplace that are unplanned, unpredictable and even unintentionally hazardous; these can lead to creative breakthroughs which may ultimately translate into the invention of new products and processes and their eventual commercial exploitation as an innovation. Experiential learning is more complex than simple trial and error or learning from the mistakes that one makes. Furthermore, it is not enough to theorize adults' workplace learning largely in terms of the results of such experiences; L&D needs a comprehensive and coherent theoretical base. The experiential-type approaches alluded to above might also be interpreted as suggesting that adults have the resources and skills to be naturally reflective (whereas not all adults may have the skills or motivations to be reflective learners), and that formalized experiences have comparatively little to contribute in comparison to the experience of solving day-to-day problems (whereas formal learning experiences, when integrated with practice, have a significant and often unique contribution to make to managers' learning). None of this is to deny the value of error-based learning per se; errors may be beneficial in that they can elicit attention, uncover incorrect assumptions and force increased mental processing (Russ-Eft 2002: 52), but error-based learning is more than giving free reign to mistake making.

L&D FACTS AND FIGURES

'Learning is the major process of human adaptation . . . One's job as an educator is not only to implant new ideas but also to modify or dispose of old ones. In many cases, resistance to new ideas stems from their conflict with old beliefs that are inconsistent with them. The learning process will be facilitated . . . by bringing out the learner's beliefs and theories, examining and testing them and then integrating new, more refined ideas into the person's belief systems.' (*Source*: D. A. Kolb, 1984, *Experiential Learning*. Englewood Cliffs, NJ: Prentice Hall, 32, 28)

Alas, there is no 'grand theory' of learning; hence there is a necessity to consider a range of theories derived from the base disciplines (such as psychology and organizational behaviour). The experiential learning model is, undeniably, of central importance to the study of L&D and to L&D practice, but other viewpoints are also needed. Our endeavour also requires that we consider other perspectives from the domains of education, educational psychology and adult education (which themselves draw upon and interpret particular base disciplines in specific ways). None of these theories or perspectives is sufficient in itself to give as full a picture as possible of L&D as an applied field of management practice that is often highly complex and where outcomes can be causally ambiguous. Hence there may be a need at times to at least consider and draw upon, if not ascribe to, what may be seen by some as epistemologically incommensurate ways of seeing the world. Furthermore, it is impossible to ignore the important issue of the conditions under which certain forms of L&D (such as that which occurs away from the workplace, for example in training courses) are likely to prove effective in transferring back to the workplace setting, and hence the extent to which they may have the potential to impact upon performance. Some of the most conceptually rich and exciting theory-building efforts in human resource development are currently to be found in the area of learning transfer and the specification of the workplace conditions that may promote transfer. Deeper conceptual, philosophical and ethical issues are also raised relating to the nexus of learning and working. Where, for example, within a broad perspective of performance-oriented L&D, does work begin and learning end? Is there such a thing as 'learning' as formally understood or is there only the changing participation in the culturally designed settings of everyday organizational life (see Lave and Wenger 1991)?

Conclusion: the Plan of the Book

The focal point of this chapter and the underpinning concept of the book is learning. The definitions of learning that exist in the literature are diverse, and whilst it is well-nigh impossible to produce an all-encompassing definition that is likely to be valid across all contexts and perspectives, for our purposes learning involves a longer-term change in the knowledge, skill and attitudes that guide thought and action. Furthermore, from the perspective of the performance improvement mission of L&D these changes in knowledge, skill or attitude (KSA) should lead to employees either individually or collectively having an increased potential to perform in more effective ways. Within this paradigm enhanced or effective performance is often defined in terms of productivity; more of the latter is assumed to be 'good' and, furthermore, the contribution of the individual employee is taken to be meaningful in these terms. In the L&D field the question of what constitutes 'good' or 'meaningful' work or learning is not often held up to scrutiny.

One challenge for L&D theory and practice is the weaving together and reconciliation of some of the various themes and issues that were highlighted in this chapter so that learning in the workplace can be managed in more effective ways in order that individuals and organizations may acquire the knowledge and skills which may enable them to develop and grow and thereby achieve the goals that are important to them. This challenge in its various guises is the theme of the remainder of the book. Our journey will begin with an exploration of the business context for L&D and the purposes of learning from a performance perspective. From there we will examine in Chapter 3 a selection of theories that may help managers and L&D practitioners understand and explain learning in their own contexts. Not all learning occurs through explicit processes and the outcomes of learning may be tacit to the extent that, in the words of Polanyi, we may actually

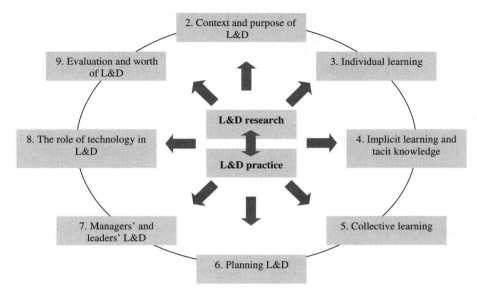

Figure 1.4 The plan of the book

'know more than we can tell'. The issues of implicit learning and tacit knowledge and its codification will be the subject of Chapter 4. The concept of individual learning is crucial but so is the notion of collective learning (Chapter 5), especially in those organizations for which the creation of knowledge assets is an important source of competitive advantage. L&D is not a process that can be left to chance and serendipity (although there is much learning in organizations that is incidental and unplanned); the bedrock of the L&D planning process is needs assessment, and this is covered in Chapter 6. Managers and leaders are crucial stakeholders in modern organizations and they have a dual role as learners themselves and as players in the L&D process more broadly (for example as clients of the L&D function) – we look at this in Chapter 7. L&D is an applied field and as such it has always drawn upon technology as a supporting mechanism for learning; therefore the role of technology in L&D (for example e-learning) and the notion of the technology of L&D (for example, instructional design) will be the subject of the Chapter 8. Finally, we will explore the concept of evaluation and issues of return on investment (ROI) in L&D, and the question of L&D's ultimate contribution and purpose in organizations (see Figure 1.4).

Concept Checklist

Can you now define each of the Key Concepts listed below, and are you now able to achieve the other Knowledge Outcomes specified at the beginning of the chapter?

- Learning
- Training
- Education
- Development
- Human resource development (HRD)
- Learning and development (L&D)
- Rigour and relevance
- Role of theory.

CHAPTER 2
The Strategic and Organizational Contexts of Learning and Development

---

Key Concepts

Core competence; strategic human resource management (SHRM); resource-based view (RBV); HR goals; external fit and internal fit; needed behaviours; performance management; L&D strategy and strategic L&D; vertical alignment and horizontal integration; stakeholders; balanced scorecard approach; systematic approach (needs identification; needs analysis; learning design; implementation; evaluation); systems approach; inputs; outputs; L&D roles and responsibilities; L&D function; outsourcing; L&D marketing mix; L&D costs; L&D budgets; profit centre; cost centre

---

Knowledge Outcomes

After studying this chapter you should be able to:

- define each of the key concepts listed above;
- identify the stakeholders in and characteristics of a strategic approach to learning and development (L&D);
- distinguish between systematic and systems approaches to L&D, and describe the stages in the L&D cycle and the elements of the L&D system;
- explain the significance of the role orientation of the L&D practitioner;
- describe some of the activities carried out by the L&D function;
- critically appraise the systematic and systems approaches to L&D.

The Global Context for L&D

Existing managerial personnel provide services that cannot be provided by personnel newly hired from outside the firm, not only because they make up the administrative organization which cannot be expanded except by their own actions, but also because the experience they gain from working within the firm and with each other enables them to provide services that are uniquely valuable for the operations of the particular group with which they are associated.

Edith T. Penrose, *The Theory of the Growth of the Firm*

Many businesses now operate in a knowledge economy that is networked, digital, virtual, fast-moving, global and uncertain. In such an environment managers may look inside their firm for 'rare, valuable and costly-to-imitate resources, and then exploit these resources through their organisation' (Barney 1999: 139). The learning of an organization's employees is a rare, valuable and costly-to-imitate form of capital. The process of learning is a core competence for success. But what is meant by a core competence in an L&D context? For our purposes, a core competence may be defined in terms of four of the characteristics proposed by Hamel and Prahalad (1994). It:

- provides benefits to customers;
- is not product-specific nor is it an asset (in the accounting sense);
- is competitively unique;
- represents an opportunity or gateway to the future.

The core L&D competence of an organization is one that:

- enables employees to acquire and create the knowledge, skills and attitudes necessary for them to provide value to stakeholders;
- is generic and transferable and is as much concerned with the process of learning as it is with the content of learning (and hence is not necessarily tied to a specific product or service);
- is complex and situated in a context and hence is difficult to imitate or transfer between organizations;
- empowers and emancipates employees in ways that enable them to engage in learning in a critical and reflective way, in order that they may create the products and services that will secure the continued existence and future success of an organization in which they themselves may develop and grow.

Those organizations for which L&D is a core strategic competence can be recognized by their:

External face: this reflects a sensitivity to the changes that are occurring or may be likely to occur in the organization's operating environment, and the capability to be agile in response to any such changes.

Internal face: this displays the qualities of reflection, inquiry and sharing which underpin the individual and collective learning of the organization's members and whereby new knowledge and new and better products and services may be created (Sugarman 2001: 62).

The L&D competence of an organization enables it to face outwards to the threats and challenges posed by the external environment. As well as having an inward face with respect to how L&D creates new knowledge and how it interfaces with the knowledge creation process, L&D's inward face also needs to be integrated with other elements of the organizational and HR systems, for example in the design of work, the selection of employees, reward and incentive systems and the culture and climate of the organization. For example, Leonard (1998), in discussing the case of Chaparral Steel in the USA (a highly equipment- and plant-intensive steel milling company), argued that:

1. Competitively advantageous equipment can be installed, used and improved only if the workforce is highly skilled.
2. Continuous learning is only a reality if employees are selected for their willingness to learn.
3. Scanning the external environment is only advantageous if employees are empowered (and, it might be added, incentivized) to apply the new knowledge to production problems (Leonard 1998: 16).

Where these different elements are integrated in a complex way the L&D competence of an organization is a difficult-to-imitate source of competitive advantage that may foster creativity, innovation and entrepreneurship and differentiate a business from the competition (Figure 2.1). The knowledge and knowledge-creating processes that L&D may leverage is an intangible resource which competitors may find difficult to imitate and hence is a core competence upon which an organization can build a lasting competitive advantage (Garcia and Vano 2002).

But why do organizations need L&D as a core competence? Organizations in the twenty-first century face particular challenges: for example, globalization, changes in the external labour market, changes in employees' expectations and values, the need to be adaptable and flexible and to anticipate and respond to emergent issues. Boxall and Purcell (2003: 19) identify a number of factors that have put greater pressure on cost structures and increased the need for flexibility, adaptability and business renewal:

1. For example, in the UK the deregulation of product, capital and labour markets has exposed organizations and employees to increased levels of competition.

INTERNAL
'Downsizing' and flatter st ructures
Increased performance expectations
Employee involvement in quality enhancement
Premium placed upon knowledge work and knowledge workers, etc.

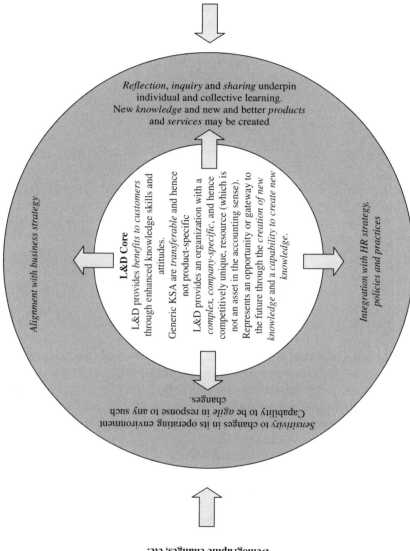

Figure 2.1 L&D as a core competence

2. Rapid pace of technological change, often producing discontinuities, offered new ways of improving production, distribution and communication processes. These presented organizations simultaneously with opportunities and challenges.

3. Regionalization and globalization of business has similarly created new opportunities for larger markets, but also exposed organizations to competitive threats from across the globe.

The effects of these pressures include: the need to 'downsize' (by making jobs redundant), increased performance expectations (for example, for employees to take on wider job roles), a drive for employee involvement in quality enhancement processes (such as TQM or total quality management) and the premium that is placed upon knowledge work and knowledge workers (Boxall and Purcell 2003). Against this backcloth it is worth bearing in mind that many commentators anticipate that even with the unparalleled productivity improvements in service activities in the world economy in general that the past few decades have witnessed, 'the real gains are yet to come; electronic commerce in particular offers the potential for massive efficiency gains' (Grant 2000: 34). This will create a demand for management and L&D practices that will facilitate the creation and management of knowledge and new ideas so that 'incentives will be introduced and disincentives eliminated to promote innovation, effective knowledge exchange, learning . . . [and] . . . cultural drivers will be changed to create environments of trust and efforts to find root causes of problems without assigning blame' (Wiig 2000: 14).

PERSPECTIVE FROM PRACTICE:
L&D IN THE PEOPLE'S REPUBLIC OF CHINA

Based on the following source: J. Xie and G. Wu, 2001. Training and development in the People's Republic of China, *International Journal of Training and Development*, 5(3): 223–32.

In simple numerical terms, China as the world's most populous nation has a huge human resource base (around 1.3 billion people) but its demographic characteristics are such that with the lowered birth rate the population will in proportionate terms have more older people. This aging population may create labour and skill issues for Chinese enterprises. China's economy has undergone a transformation. The extent to which VET (vocational education and training) systems are responsive to the change has been examined by a number of researchers. Xie and Wu argue that even though China has witnessed an annual GDP (gross domestic product) increase of the order of 10

Continued

per cent over the past two decades, its economic development has been negatively influenced by weaknesses in its VET system, which has resulted in a lack of development of its human resource base. They attribute this, in part at least, to a cultural tradition that attaches more importance to general academic education than to vocational education. This attitude appears to be rooted in historically founded perceptions of craft and technological work as being of lower status and even as being 'looked down upon' (Xie and Wu 2001: 229).

In terms of the legal framework that supports VET, Xie and Wu singled out a number of initiatives including: (a) the Compulsory Education Law of 1986 which states that people should follow at least nine years of compulsory education; (b) the Vocational Education Law of 1996 which states that a vocational education fee equivalent to 1.5 per cent of an employee's salary must be levied; (c) the Labour Reserve System which provides one to three years of vocational education or training for those who do not enter higher education; (d) the Vocational Ability Appraisal System and the Vocational Qualification Certificate System – over 50 million people joined the appraisal scheme in 1996 and half of them passed and obtained the certificate (2001: 226). Nonetheless problems remain; for example, Xie and Wu quote some estimates which suggest that only 3 per cent of the workforce is highly skilled and only about half a percent are at technician level. According to Xie and Wu, two of the main L&D issues that face China are:

1. VET activity and integration: little is being done to encourage vocational education in companies and there is a lack of integration between different types and stages of VET. Also, there is no complete system for investment in training and development.
2. L&D knowledge, skills and expertise: demand for VET teachers has outstripped the supply of competent and skilled VET teachers and there appears to be a lack of training in L&D for staff that are expected to deliver and facilitate learning in Chinese companies. There may be a 'training the trainers' need in many Chinese enterprises to facilitate the processes of learning and workforce development.

At the sub-national level, the question arises of how the human resources of an organization can be configured and managed in order to bring about the learning that is required if organizations are to survive, remain competitive and, over and above this, become increasingly efficient (i.e. 'do things right') and effective (i.e. 'do the right things'). One answer to this question lies in the strategic management of organizations' human resources (HR) and their L&D practices, and it is to these strategic people management and learning issues that we now turn our attention.

The Strategic Context of L&D

Our discussion of the strategic context of learning and development requires a consideration of two important issues:

1. Firstly, human resource management (HRM) and the way in which HRM may be configured to enhance business performance and learning.
2. Secondly, how learning and development (L&D) relates to HRM and to business strategy, and how L&D can be strategic and thereby enhance its utility as a core competence of an organization.

Strategic Human Resource Management

Human resource management is the term used to refer to those activities that are concerned with the management of the employment relationship between employees and the organizations that use their skills. A strategic approach to HRM (SHRM) involves the design and implementation of a set of organizational HR policies and practices that are themselves internally consistent, and also attempts to ensure that the human resources in an organization contribute to the achievement of business objectives (Huselid et al. 1997). An underlying assumption of this approach is that the appropriate configuration of human resources, policies and practices will have a positive effect upon performance. The human resources of an organization and their knowledge and skills are a unique source of competitive advantage provided that they cannot be easily copied or transferred between organizations. This latter view is typical of the resource-based view (RBV) of the firm (see Penrose 1959; Barney 1991). The non-imitability of HRM practices comes through the social complexity and causal ambiguity inherent in activities such as team working, empowerment and L&D (Huselid et al. 1997: 173). The overriding question of 'does SHRM lead to enhanced performance?' is one that has occupied researchers in varying ways over a number of decades. From the late 1980s through the 1990s a considerable number of studies were conducted in the USA and elsewhere that used cross-sectional studies (where a slice of the population is taken and surveyed at a particular point in time, see Haslam and McGarty 1998: 106) and longitudinal research (taking a sample of participants and following them over a period of time, see Haslam and McGarty 1998) in order to explore the links between HRM and performance. The aim was to identify if there was a link between HRM practices and firm performance, and also to identify the ways in which various types of HRM practices affected performance (and what the size of the effect was).

PERSPECTIVE FROM RESEARCH: TECHNICAL AND STRATEGIC HRM AND FIRM PERFORMANCE IN THE USA

Based on the following source: M. A. Huselid, S. E. Jackson and R. S. Schuler, 1997. Technical and strategic human resource management effectiveness as determinants of firm performance, *Academy of Management Journal*, 40(1): 171–88.

The research by Huselid, Jackson and Schuler built upon previous work in this area (for example, Schuler and Jackson's 1987 paper in the *Academy of Management Executive* that theorized the link between different types of business strategies, so-called 'needed behaviours' and HRM practices). In the 1997 paper Huselid et al. surveyed senior executives in 293 US firms. In their theoretical model they made a distinction between four independent variables (these are the causal variables which the researchers believe are responsible for particular effects, see Haslam and McGarty 1998):

1. Technical HRM activities: for example, recruitment, selection, performance measurement, training and the administration of compensation and benefits. This, like the other variables (2–3 below), was measured by means of self-report questions (items) in a survey. When using such measures it is important that the set of items which aim to assess the same construct (in this case technical HRM) are themselves consistent with what they intend to measure (Hair et al. 1998: 90). One test for how internally consistent a group of self-report items are is to compute the Cronbach α statistic (Cronbach 1951) using software packages such as SPSS. The value of Cronbach's α measure of reliability may range from zero to one and values in the range 0.60 to 0.70 are deemed by some researchers to be the lower limit of acceptability (Hair et al. 1998: 88). The value of Cronbach α for the technical HRM (THRM) measurement scale was 0.85. This suggests that the THRM scale is internally consistent as this value is above the more stringent threshold of acceptability of Cronbach $\alpha \geq 0.70$ that was suggested by Nunnally (1978).
2. Strategic HRM activities: a set of policies that encompass more sophisticated practices such as team working, flexible job roles, empowerment and management and executive development (Cronbach $\alpha = 0.75$).
3. Professional HRM effectiveness: a set of HR professional competencies or capabilities in areas such as leadership of HR function, ability to demonstrate financial impact of HR, defining and communicating and HR vision, educating line managers on HR issues and so forth (Cronbach $\alpha = 0.66$).

4. Business-related capabilities: general and line management experience in other non-HR business areas (Cronbach $\alpha = 0.61$).

Note that two of the Cronbach α's (3 and 4) failed to reach Nunnally's threshold value of 0.70. Some have argued that for exploratory research a value of 0.60 for Cronbach α is acceptable; however, many researchers would dispute this (see Hair et al. 1998). These four independent variables were measured using a total of 41 self-report items scored on a five-point scale. They aimed to address four research hypotheses:

1. Hypothesis 1 (H1): Firms have higher levels of technical HRM (THRM) than strategic HRM (SHRM) activities.
2. H2: THRM and SHRM activities will be positively related to firm performance.
3. H3: HR staff will have higher levels of professional HR capabilities than business-related capabilities.
4. H4: THRM activities will be positively related to professional HR capabilities whilst SHRM activities will be positively related to professional HR and business-related capabilities.

Their dependent variable (this is the outcome variable on which the researchers are interested in monitoring effects, see Haslam and McGarty 1998: 45), firm performance, was measured using publicly available financial performance data (i.e. productivity, rate of return on assets and Tobin's q – the latter reflects a firm's current and anticipated profitability and is a 'measure of the value added by management' [Huselid et al. 1997: 178]). Their data were analysed using factor analysis (to objectively check the validity of the four scales which were used to measure the four independent variables), correlational analysis (to measure the nature and strength of the relationship between pairs of variables, see Haslam and McGarty 1998) and multiple regression analyses (used to predict changes in a single metric dependent variable in response to changes in two or more metric independent variables, see Hair et al. 1998: 14). Their results supported the view that:

1. The firms were more proficient in THRM than SHRM (this finding was statistically significant at the 1 per cent level, i.e. $p < 0.01$). One implication of this that they drew was that as levels of proficiency in THRM generally rise (i.e. THRM becomes institutionalized) this may impose a ceiling upon the effect that THRM can have as a source of competitive advantage (and perhaps indicating that firms need to consider SHRM as a further means of leveraging competitive advantage through HR to differentiate themselves from the competition) – see below.

Continued

2. SHRM activities were positively related to firm performance ($0.10 \geq p \geq 0.05$) whereas THRM activities were not. Note that the level of significance was between the 5 per cent level and the 10 per cent level; the significance in this case might be described as marginal. According to Huselid et al., in real terms these findings suggested that on a per employee basis a one-standard-deviation increase in overall HRM effectiveness corresponds to a 5.2 per cent increase in sales per employee (employee productivity) and to an increase in cash flow of 16.3 per cent (the dollar value of this increase at the time was $9,673 per employee).

3. The professional HR capabilities of HR staff were higher than their business-related capabilities ($p < 0.01$). If HR capabilities by themselves are insufficient for SHRM (see (4) below) this may suggest an L&D need on the part of HR practitioners (i.e. for them to gain a wider experience of general business issues beyond their immediate HR function).

4. THRM activities were related to professional HR capabilities ($p < 0.001$), whereas SHRM activities were related to professional HR capabilities ($p < 0.001$) and business-related capabilities ($p < 0.10$).

One key finding of their research relates to the institutionalization (i.e. the general and widespread adoption) of HRM activities. Once HRM activities become institutionalized across firms (as in the case of THRM), they no longer provide a distinctive means for differentiating a firm from its competitors (and hence conferring competitive advantage). Therefore any future gains through HRM may need to be via another type or level of HRM, i.e. through SHRM activities. The effectiveness of SRM activities appears to be boosted by the professional capabilities of HR staff and to a lesser extent their business-related capabilities.

The relationships between HRM and performance are further expounded in conceptual (as opposed to empirical) terms by Boxall and Purcell (2003), who presented a taxonomic model of organizational goals that distinguishes between HR goals (such as desired type and level of labour productivity, flexibility and social legitimacy – the latter refers to the standing of an organization as an employer in terms of the norms of the wider society) and non-HR goals (for example, sales, market share, return on investment, etc.). Boxall and Purcell disaggregated these goals at successively finer levels of resolution, for example a second-tier HR goal is enhancing workforce capability and motivation, which itself may then be served by third-tier goals such as recruitment and selection goals, pay and promotion goals and L&D goals (2003: 13). Although not part of the Boxall and Purcell taxonomy, the L&D goal itself may be comprised of fourth-tier goals such as identifying the learning needs, providing learning opportunities, evaluating the contribution of L&D to the higher-order goals and so forth. Other third-tier goals (such as recruitment and selection) could of course be similarly further disaggregated.

Although a reductionist approach such as that described above and depicted in Figure 2.2 is a useful analytical device, what this particular diagram may run the risk of obscuring are the links between elements of the HR sub-system and the wider system. Any discussion of HR and goals cannot overlook the crucial importance of integration and at the level of the HR system such integration can be interpreted as operating in two ways:

1. Firstly, in terms of external fit – the HR strategy fits with the requirements of the business strategy (i.e. it may be vertically aligned).
2. Secondly, by internal fit whereby the HR policies and activities (including L&D) fit together so that they form a coherent whole (Torrington et al. 2002: 37) through horizontal integration.

A simple model of external fit is shown in Figure 2.3a. Its strengths are that it provides a very simple framework to show how the HR activities (selection, appraisal, reward and L&D) in an organization need to be configured in ways to support enhanced performance in pursuit of the business's goals. This type of model was used as the basis for a very influential work of HR theory – the concept of needed behaviours (Schuler and Jackson 1987) – in which it was argued that performance will improve when HR practices reinforce the firm's predetermined choice of strategy (for example, cost reduction, product differentiation or innovation strategies), where different strategies demand different kinds of employee behaviour (needed behaviours) (Boxall and Purcell 2003: 52).

The approach is not without its critics; for example, the model of Fombrun et al. (1984) that underpins Schuler and Jackson's work (and other related research) has been criticized as being oversimplistic, dependent upon a rationalist model, lacking in sophistication with respect to competitive strategy, and being overtly unitarist (Torrington et al. 2002; Boxall and Purcell 2003) and ignoring the role of employee relations. HRM policies and practices should themselves be internally coherent and reciprocating. For example, where sophisticated and expensive selection policies are used they should be complemented by other practices that minimize labour turnover (and hence minimize the need for further recruitment and selection); team working should be complemented by an appraisal system that rewards collective as well as individual efforts (so that collective behaviour is promoted and reinforced through HRM). To be internally coherent, an organization's HRM policies should avoid so-called deadly combinations (Delery 1998). For example, team working alongside an exclusively individually focused appraisal and reward system might counteract and cancel each other out. Similarly, expensive recruitment and selection policies coupled with poor promotion and L&D systems (which are therefore likely to increase labour turnover) might work to cancel each other out.

In this broader HR context Boxall and Purcell argued that an organization's decisions to 'buy' (i.e. recruit and select) people and 'make' (i.e. train and develop)

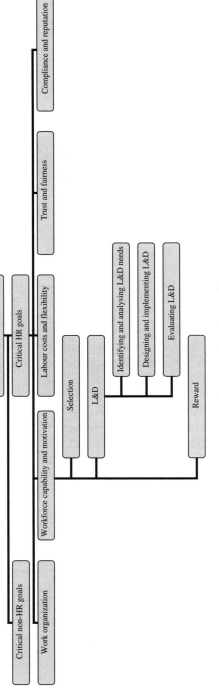

Figure 2.2　Part of a taxonomy of HR and L&D goals (after Boxall and Purcell 2003)

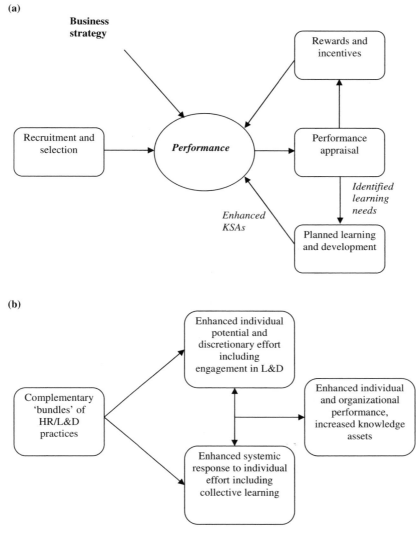

Figure 2.3 (a) HR system and (b) HPWS (high-performance work system) (adapted from Fombrun et al. 1984; Boxall and Purcell 2003: 21)

should be seen as complementary activities where long-term development of employees is used to build capacity through a judicious mix of on-job and off-job learning opportunities. There may also be a need for HR efficiency (executing HR policies and practices well) and HR effectiveness (critically appraising HRM practices and, where necessary, revising, replacing or reinventing them). This aspiration for multiple themes in an HR strategy is not without its tensions, as Boxall and Purcell noted: 'it is important [for an organization] to learn how to balance

HR practices that reinforce the execution of a given strategy with practices that help the firm to conceive of a completely different one' (2003: 245). More recently, in many UK organizations the concept of performance management (PM) appears to have taken centre stage in much of HR practice. There is no one generally accepted definition of what performance management is. Common characteristics include the emphasis upon strategic goals, a shared and well-communicated vision and a systemic and integrated approach to the management of performance that reflects the external environment. In an attempt to provide some further clarity, Mabey et al. (1998: 127) singled out the following elements of a systematic PM cycle:

- clarify performance requirements by setting objectives;
- review individual performance and measure outcomes;
- give feedback on results and link rewards to assessed outcomes;
- make on-going amendments to objectives and activities to continuously improve performance.

To this list one might add the need to agree on the support needed for individuals to achieve requisite levels of performance and any remedial, maintenance or developmental action including the appropriate L&D activities, such as induction training, job-related training, personal development (Harrison 2002). The relationship between performance management programmes and business performance in 437 public companies was investigated by McDonald and Smith (1995). Their research suggested that firms with performance management systems (including, for example, existence of specific job goals, incentives and feedback mechanisms and learning opportunities) tended to perform at or above the industry average (see Jacobs and Washington 2003).

The various elements of a high-performance work system (HPWS) (such as more rigorous selection, better L&D, more comprehensive incentives and participative structures) are hypothesized as functioning synergistically to the extent that attending to one element of the system (for example, selection or L&D) is unlikely to have as great an effect as an integrated response (see Boxall and Purcell 2003: 20). A comparison of a HPWS with an L&D emphasis and a traditional HR system is shown in Figure 2.3.

Research in the Netherlands (Hartog and Verburg 2004) into a HPWS comprising an overarching philosophy of mission statement, HRM strategy, strict selection, internal promotions and emphasis on L&D found that there was a positive relationship between HPWS and a number of dependent variables (perceived economic outcomes, working beyond contract and absenteeism). The question of a correlational fallacy (the mistaken belief that because two variables are related one must cause the other, see Haslam and McGarty 1998: 243) is sometimes a problem with cross-sectional research in general and in studies of this nature (for example, firms with better economic performance may have more resources to commit to HR practices). Nonetheless the results of the Hartog and Verburg study and other similar research carry high face validity, are explicable in theoretical

terms and are intuitively appealing. If the assertion that HRM and the L&D practices that are part of a coherent bundle of HRM practices that contribute to
enhanced individual and organizational performance is accepted, the question
arises of how the strategic L&D components of this system can be configured and
managed. It is to the strategic role of L&D that we now turn our attention.

Strategic Learning and Development

One of the fundamental assumptions of SHRM discussed above was that it is a
means of differentiating an organization and thereby gaining advantage over competitor organizations in the marketplace. The argument is not confined to for-
profit organizations: SHRM may be posited as leading to the delivery of better
value generally for an organization's stakeholders and in the same way a strategic approach to L&D is concerned with enhancing performance and value for
stakeholders. Three main issues will be considered in our examination of strategic learning and development:

1. Why do organizations need to have an L&D that is strategic?
2. What are the characteristics of a strategic L&D?
3. Who are the stakeholders responsible for ensuring that L&D is strategic?

Before considering these questions, a distinction will be drawn between strategic L&D and L&D strategies. Stewart's discussion of employee development
strategies (1999: 201–18) is concerned with particular L&D methods that have a
long-term orientation and a 'significant rather than marginal consequence' and
that go beyond an individual focus. Under the heading of 'employee development
strategies' he included the issues of the internationalization of employee development, the method of action learning, the philosophy of the learning organization and the practice of management development (1999: 219–39). At a more
mundane level, Reid and Barrington (1999) described training strategies as
methods chosen for their appropriateness in relation to objectives, likelihood of
transfer of learning to the workplace, resource availability and trainee-related
factors. In their menu of training strategies Reid and Barrington included on-job
training, planned experience (inside and outside the organization), in-house training courses, external training courses and self-managed learning (1999: 237). The
Stewart and Reid & Barrington discussions focused upon specific methods and
practices. In this book such L&D methods and practices will be considered from
the point of view of learning theories (Chapter 2), collective learning (Chapter 5),
planning learning (Chapter 6) and management and leader development (Chapter
7). The term of 'strategy', on the other hand, will be used in the context of L&D
to refer to macro-level features of the organization and the ways in which these
are configured so that L&D methods and practice can support the achievement of
overall business goals in ways that are mutually reinforcing with other elements

of the organizational system (such as HRM, work and organizational design, knowledge management, IT and so forth).

WHY DO ORGANIZATIONS NEED STRATEGIC L&D?

The arguments for why a strategic approach to L&D is needed have already been rehearsed earlier in this and the preceding chapter in the context of learning, the global business environment and the need for a strategic HRM. The general set of forces for change include new technology and the threats and opportunities that it presents, competition and the need for continuous improvement, internationalization and its effects on the employment relationship and the levels of uncertainty and ambiguity that confront many organizations. At the outset of this chapter L&D as a core competence was posited as a way in which an organization may be equipped with a generic and adaptable internal process that enables it to deal with these issues in a flexible and agile way.

What might a manager or L&D practitioner look for as indicators that a strategic approach to L&D is needed? Garavan et al. (1995) suggested that indicators or symptoms of the need for a more strategic approach might include difficulties in recruiting skilled employees, the need to develop a more adaptable and flexible skill base, a demand for management and leadership at all levels in a organization, a greater emphasis on performance management and evaluation, and an increased need for HR and succession planning. These are all issues that collectively may be difficult to address effectively by an ad hoc and piecemeal approach but which require an integrated and holistic solution and a proactive rather than reactive stance on the part of the L&D practitioner.

L&D FACTS AND FIGURES

The UK's Chartered Institute of Personnel and Development's (CIPD) Annual Training Survey 2004 found that the two most important factors in helping employees to learn effectively were ensuring that the organizational culture is supportive of L&D and ensuring managers have the skills and are committed to supporting L&D. (*Source*: Training and Development 2004: Survey Report (April 2004). London: CIPD)

WHAT ARE THE CHARACTERISTICS OF A STRATEGIC L&D?

One starting point for describing strategic L&D is by considering what it is not. A lack of strategic focus in L&D might be typified by an approach in which:

1.   There are numerous, unconnected and fragmented L&D initiatives which may appear to be appropriate from a tactical and operational perspective (and

which may be effective at this level) but which run the risk of duplication of effort; they may be supplier driven, subject to 'fad and fashion', reactive and lacking in longer-term focus.

2. Managers and L&D practitioners may often 'do their own thing' without reference to what is happening in the rest of the organization, stakeholders' views and needs, how it will impact on practice, how it relates to best practice and the extent to which their practices are justified on the basis of evidence or theory.

3. There are competing political agendas which are self-serving and defensive and do not promote critical self-reflection and analysis nor do they encourage the surfacing and sharing of knowledge between different factions and stakeholders (see Garavan et al. 1995; Walton 1999).

The outcomes of such an approach may include wasted efforts, poor use of resources, defensiveness, convergent and myopic thinking, the reinforcement of outmoded working practices and stifling of creativity and innovation. This may be contrasted with a strategic L&D which is coherent and holistic, corporate-wide, promotes collective learning through internal integration of activities, aligned with strategy, involves stakeholders and configures functional activities in order that they contribute to corporate strategy (Walton 1999: 87). A number of researchers have attempted to define the characteristics of strategic L&D, and three different perspectives are summarized in Table 2.1.

From these and other contributions it is possible to synthesize a number of features of strategic L&D:

1. Active commitment to and shared ownership of learning from managers and other employees.

2. Vertical alignment with strategy and horizontal integration of learning-related and other activities (including HRM and L&D).

3. Openness of communication channels within and beyond the organization.

4. Supportive culture and climate that enables learning, creativity and innovation.

5. Systemic and systematic planning processes that take account of the integration of L&D activities with the organizational mission.

6. Focused and prioritized L&D practices that support the strategic intent of the business and that will add value.

7. Proactive L&D functional stance that is open to evaluation and self-reflection and continuous improvement.

On the basis of these discussions strategic L&D may be defined as:

A coherent and vertically aligned and horizontally integrated set of L&D activities which are the outcome of proactive planning processes, which address the overall goals of the organization, acknowledge the

Table 2.1   The characteristics of strategic L&D

Garavan (1991: 17–23)	Horwitz (1999: 183)	Walton (1999: 117)
Integration with organization mission and goals: systemic linkage to goals though planning process that is integrated with corporate plan. L&D may help to shape strategy.	*Integration* into HR strategy and corporate strategy.	*Organization commitment* to learning expressed in core values or mission statements.
Senior management support: actively support L&D; the L&D of senior managers may help them to manage and lead.	Competency-based L&D derived from *systemation analysis* of needs.	Commitment supports *policies, systems* and *resource provision*.
Environmental scanning: up-to-date knowledge of the organization's external environment; interpret the results of scanning in terms of the L&D implications.	*Line management* responsibility for L&D is part of performance expectations of line manager.	Coherent *interaction* between various *L&D strategies* (team development, training, individual development, learning climate interventions and organization-wide initiatives).
L&D plans and policies: flow from organization's strategic plan (conversely, L&D plans developed in isolation will remain short-term and operational).	L&D practitioner and line managers work in *partnership*.	L&D strategies focus upon a *range of interventions* from macro to micro level, for example strategic awareness, creativity, innovation, flexibility, responsiveness to customers and task-related skills.
Line manager commitment and involvement: best placed to assess L&D needs; can have a legitimate input to plans and policies; role in providing instruction, coaching and mentoring.	Organizational *culture* of continuous learning.	
Complementary HRM activities: for example HR plans and forecasts, L&D implications of appraisal, career development, and so forth.	Measuring and *evaluating* effects of L&D on performance.	The outcome is *learning* being perceived as one of the *core competencies* of the organization that contributes towards its strategic intent.
Transformed L&D practitioner role: from passive to active; peripheral to central; L&D technical to L&D strategic.	Targeting interventions on specific areas that will *add value*.	
Recognition of the role of culture: supportive of feedback, open communication, mentoring roles, participation, tolerance and learning.	Integration of organizational and work processes across units and functions and the sharing of knowledge *across boundaries*.	
Emphasis on evaluation: asks how suitable, feasible and acceptable are L&D policies, plans and practices?		

needs of stakeholders, are future-oriented and which help to differentiate an organization from its competitors in a unique and non-imitable way.

PERSPECTIVE FROM RESEARCH: THE VERTICAL ALIGNMENT AND HORIZONTAL INTEGRATION OF L&D IN DUTCH COMPANIES

Based on the following source: A. A. M. Wognum, 2001. Vertical integration of HRD policies within companies, *Human Resource Development International*, 4(3): 407–21; I. Wognum and J. Fond Lam, 2000. Stakeholder involvement in strategic HRD aligning: the impact on HRD effectiveness, *International Journal of Training and Development*, 4(2): 98–110.

The question of the extent to which vertically integrated (the preferred term in this book is for vertical alignment and horizontal integration) strategic L&D actually occurs in companies is not an issue that has been well explored in the research literature (although there are many case study descriptions in the practitioner literature). Wognum (2001) and Wognum and Fond Lam (2000) investigated this question in 44 Dutch companies. Their conclusions were that in the companies they studied the vertical alignment of L&D activities was 'not really strategic and hardly interactive [in the sense that stakeholders were involved and consulted]'. The researchers distinguished three levels of L&D activity:

1. Strategic: executives are the prime stakeholders and the concern is with the L&D implications of the corporate mission.
2. Tactical: middle managers are the prime stakeholders and a concern at this level is the coordination and cooperation between units and departments.
3. Operational: lower level managers and employees who are concerned with identifying performance problems in the operating core of the business.

Of concern was that L&D goals and objectives were formulated mainly at the operational level and with little emphasis on the importance of any newly acquired knowledge and skills for the company as a whole. Also the absence of vertical alignment also inhibited effective horizontal integration. Their overall conclusion was that companies need to involve all relevant stakeholders and that L&D practitioners need to fulfil the role of consultant in the process in order to support the other stakeholders who are not L&D specialists. The perception of L&D effectiveness appears to be higher when stakeholders are involved in the process (Wognum and Fond Lam 2000: 98).

Continued

Involvement therefore appears to be a key process for engaging stakeholders; it may also have the effect of enhancing stakeholders' perception of, and
commitment to, L&D more generally. This may go some way to raising the
credibility and status of L&D and hence potentially extend and deepen its
influence.

WHO ARE THE STAKEHOLDERS IN STRATEGIC L&D?

Five groups of key stakeholders are identifiable in the strategic approach to L&D
outlined thus far: senior managers, line managers, learners, L&D specialists
(and HR practitioners) and others outside the organization (for example, external
providers of L&D services such as educational institutions and consultants, as
well as customers). For L&D to be strategic the commitment on the part of
these stakeholder groups is to ownership (of L&D issues), participation (in
L&D activities) and feedback (on L&D impacts). The contribution of each of the
groups with respect to ownership, participation and feedback is summarized in
Table 2.2.

PERSPECTIVE FROM PRACTICE: STRATEGIC L&D IN INDIA

Based on the following source: B. Pattanayak, 2003. Gaining competitive advantage and business success through strategic HRD: an Indian experience,
Human Resource Development International, 6(3): 405–11.

The case study described by Pattanayak (2003) concerned L&D-related
changes that were implemented in a large steel-manufacturing organization
in India (the Essar company). The company's declared aim was to align L&D
strategies with corporate strategy and this entailed some 'reformulation' of
the L&D function. The starting point for the project was an analysis of the
L&D and general organizational issues that confronted the company. In
order to assess these issues a questionnaire survey was conducted amongst
employees working at a managerial level ($N = 700$). Two of the main issues
identified in the results of the survey were, firstly, that employees reported
a lack of organizational clarity in terms of the company's overall mission
and, secondly, they did not feel that their efforts were recognized and
rewarded positively. Furthermore the culture was bureaucratic and author-
itarian but this appeared to be at odds with the preferred style and expectations of the managers (the mean age was only 27 years). Managers' prime
concern did not appear to be job security; rather they were more interested
in a job role in which there was freedom, flexibility and autonomy with high
performance expectations. In response to these and other issues the L&D

function in the organization implemented a number of strategically focused initiatives:

1. Workforce skills audit: the entire workforce was audited to identify the competencies of each employee and the requirements of the organization. One outcome of this was that some employees were asked to leave the organization.
2. Culture of continuous learning: management training opportunities were provided through workshops, 'learning rooms' were provided with advanced multimedia audiovisual systems, and there was professional knowledge updating through the regular dissemination of information.
3. Open communication: an 'open house' system was introduced where employees could air problems with supervisors, managers and directors with the aim of building transparency and trust.
4. Executive leadership development: a 'leadership camp' was held for young executives that exposed participants to a range of activities including yoga, meditation, workshops, outdoor activities and the opportunity to interact in a social occasion with senior executives.
5. Reward scheme: a financial reward scheme was introduced for suggestions that could result in cost savings, workplace improvements and enhanced productivity.
6. Compulsory training: each employee was required to undergo at least seven days' training per year on issues identified through an L&D needs identification and analysis.
7. Priority issues: learning needs that were identified and analysed as having a high priority (for example, those relating to the production process) were singled out for special attention and extensive training was provided.
8. Value enhancement programme: in addition to the above a special programme was introduced that aimed to raise employees' potential to enhance shareholder value through capacity enhancement (upgrading competencies), contribution enhancement (motivational issues) and the awareness of the value of intangibles (such as ethics, human value, transparency and ethos).

The author makes claims for the direct impact of the programme on production and downtime (although the attribution of these solely to the programme is perhaps a little problematical). As well as examining financial and production data the programme evaluation also incorporated feedback sessions with departmental heads, who were able to offer their views on the effects of the programme.

Table 2.2 Stakeholders' commitments in a strategic approach to L&D

| Role | Inside organization | | | | Outside organization |
	Senior managers	Line managers	Learners	L&D practitioners	Providers, customers, etc.
Ownership	Articulate a clear vision Value learning's contribution to strategy	'Buy in' to organizational goals Value L&D's contribution to enhancing job performance	Preparedness to engage in learning Commitment to continuous maintenance and/or improvement of job-related knowledge and skills	'Buy in' to an L&D role that is proactive and transformative Share ownership with other stakeholders Outsource where necessary	Share ownership with internal stakeholders (external providers of L&D) Articulate and prioritize own needs (customers)
Participation	Resource provision to support learning Participate as learners in manager and leader development	Articulate own and subordinates' L&D needs Engage in coaching and mentoring Create opportunities for learning and transfer of learning Support evaluation	Self-direction and motivation Engagement in learning and application in the workplace Capture and share knowledge	Exhibit role flexibility: for example, provider; internal consultant; change agent Integrate L&D activities vertically and horizontally	Provide company-specific solutions (external providers of L&D)
Feedback	Stipulate requirement for L&D to be evaluated Give feedback and listen to findings See learning as a means to shape strategy	Listen to feedback Act on feedback	Engage in evaluation Give constructive and forthright feedback	Elicit feedback and evaluation Be open to criticism Exhibit competence in evaluation techniques and methods	Continuously improve (external providers) Give feedback on individual and collective performance (customers)

Discussion Point

Do you feel that the Indian case study describes L&D strategies or strategic L&D? Justify your reasoning. What factors need to be in place in organizations in general if L&D is to have a strategic impact?

Organizational Context of L&D

The preceding discussion has aimed to set the strategic context into which L&D may be located. The main concerns were with the vertical alignment of L&D with overall vision and corporate goals of an organization and the horizontal integration with other elements of the organizational system (principally the HR system). Having considered L&D from this top-level analysis, it is now appropriate to focus our attention at the level of the organization itself and the ways in which L&D may be:

- better understood in the organizational context;
- managed in order to realize its value as a core competence.

The discussion will begin by drawing a distinction between L&D from a systemic perspective and L&D as a systematic process.

Learning and Development as a Systematic Process

In a world that we assume to be rational, one way to avoid ending up in a place where one does not want to be is by being systematic. The term 'systematic' is used in this context simply to mean doing things according to a plan or system, and in a way that is defensible on the grounds of reason, rationality or logic. The systematic approach is a general approach to problem solving and is by no means unique to L&D; it can be found in many areas of human endeavour, such as engineering, medicine, the social sciences. In the context of L&D the systematic process tends to follow the sequence outlined below (steps 1 to 5). Note that for the sake of simplicity the term 'L&D practitioner' is used, but the activities could be carried by more than one individual and by persons other than those with an L&D functional role (for example, line managers), and might include external providers such as consultants.

1. The systematic approach to L&D may be thought of as commencing with a Needs Identification stage in which the L&D practitioner (in an investigator role) begins with her or his attempts to identify whether the available evidence suggests that a performance problem actually exists (for example, to enquire if the desired level of performance is not being met). If the observable

'symptoms' are enough to convince the analyst that there is a current or a potential performance problem that can be addressed through L&D, he or she may proceed to the next stage. The outcome of this stage constitutes the identified learning need.

2. In the second step (Needs Analysis) the L&D practitioner (in an analyst role) attempts to analyse the precise nature of the learning need. For example, data may be collected through observation, interview, questionnaire, performance records and other sources; this is then collated and analysed in the most appropriate way (for example, the statistical analysis of survey data, content analysis of interview transcripts and so forth). On the basis of the results of these investigations the precise nature of the learning need and the potential solution may become more apparent. The outcome of this stage can be expressed in many different ways, most typically as a statement of what the learning outcomes of any L&D programme devised in response to the identified need might be at the individual, team, departmental or organizational level, along with some specification of critical success factors (see the balanced scorecard approach discussed below). The outcome of this stage is an analysed learning need. Note that steps 1 and 2 may be grouped together as a more general needs assessment phase.

3. By the third step (Learning Design) the L&D practitioner (in designer role) will, on the basis of the evidence and her or his professional knowledge, skills, experience and judgement, be ready to devise or design the best solution to address the learning outcomes specified in the preceding stage. This could be anything from recommending that an individual attend a training course on a specific subject to a team-building event for a group of employees, or an e-learning solution for a large section of the workforce to a whole organizational development programme. The outcome of this stage is likely to be some form of learning design specification (which can include methods, media, assessment strategy, implementation plan and so forth).

4. In the fourth step (L&D Implementation) the L&D practitioner (in provider or facilitator role) might implement the solution or provide guidance for others (for example, trainers, coaches, mentors, line managers, consultants and so forth) in how to implement the proposed plan (i.e. the learning design specification from the preceding stage) in order that the identified learning needs be met. The outcome of this stage will be some overt attempt to change the knowledge, skill or attitudes of the learners.

5. Finally, in the fifth stage the L&D practitioner (in evaluator role) is likely to be interested in evaluating whether or not the solution implemented in the preceding stage has achieved the outcomes that were set (on the basis of the needs identification and needs analysis). In this evaluation stage the L&D practitioner is validating not only the L&D solution itself (for example, by asking questions such as: was the 'best' decision taken with regard to learning methods and media, was the learning design implemented effectively, how did the learners react?) but the decisions made at the earlier stages as well, along with broader issues of impact (for example, did the learning have

any impact in the workplace, how does the project stack up in terms of costs and benefits, does it fit with the corporate and related HR practices?). Questions might be asked about the efficacy of the process and its outcomes, for example whether or not the learning need was analysed correctly, and even further back to ascertain if the nature of the problem was identified correctly in the first place. In a spirit of continuous improvement the lessons learned through the reflection and evaluation may then be enacted in subsequent projects.

Each stage of the process depends on the preceding one. If the results of the preceding stages are invalid (for example, because of misdiagnosis) the subsequent stages of the process will by definition have limited validity also. Ongoing formative evaluation and checking is advisable at each stage to enable adjustments and modifications to be made and to maximize the overall effectiveness of the process. Within this very simplified description for the systematic process there are five stages that proceed in a reasoned and rational (logical) sequence and form an L&D cycle. The five stages are: identify; analyse; design; implement; and evaluate (Figure 2.4). They represent a systematic process that is applicable across a whole range of human endeavour, from medical diagnoses, to engineering design to the L&D process within organizations and much more besides. Note that the L&D practitioner fulfils a variety of roles (investigator, analyst, designer, implementer and evaluator) on the basis of her or his professional knowledge, skills and expertise. It may call for a team-based approach and for some elements

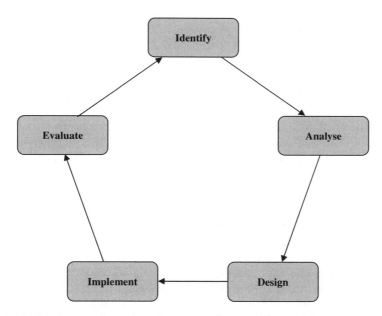

Figure 2.4 A simple generic systematic approach to problem solving

of the work to be contracted out to specialists (for example, e-learning designers, specialist consultants and so forth).

This is one version of a general set of approaches that are known variously as the systematic approach to L&D, the training cycle, the L&D cycle, learning systems design (LSD) model or instructional systems development model. They exist in various degrees of elaboration and complexity, for example the Inter-services Procedures for Instructional Systems Development (IPISD) model has 19 discrete steps (Branson et al. 1977), Briggs and Wager's 1981 model has 15 stages, whilst Patrick's Learning Systems Development model has three main phases that are further subdivided (Patrick 1992: 117–22). For our purposes five stages will be sufficient, especially since enough complexity and choice is introduced within each stage when the L&D practitioner is confronted with decisions about the various tactics available for needs analysis, implementation and so forth.

On the face of it, each element of the process cannot be in any other position within the sequence, and there are clear parallels with areas such as total quality management and continuous improvement. In an L&D context the findings of the analytical phase can be evaluated by verifying the findings of the research. The design phase can be evaluated by means of pilot testing, and the implementation phase can be evaluated by formative ongoing evaluation. The evaluation becomes a summative activity once the implementation stage is complete and it is at this point that overall issues can be addressed (by asking questions such as: 'Were the objectives achieved?', 'Was there an impact on job performance?' and 'Was there a bottom-line pay-back?'). Hence some of the flows are unidirectional (from analyse to design) whilst others are bidirectional (evaluate and design) (see Figure 2.5).

It can be argued that the approach is based upon a rational mode of thinking predicated on the assumptions that organizations are ordered, regular and pre-dictable places where plans once formulated only need be followed through if they are to be successfully executed. But, as we know, the world is complex, uncertain and unpredictable; strategies and plans can be thrown off course by a whole host of known and unknown factors. Hence we can contrast this rational school of thought with a more emergent approach in which organizations are acknowledged as complex and uncertain places where processes may be subject to experimentation, failure and learning-by-doing. The cool, calm and clear-headed logic of the systematic approach may not always run as smoothly as the discussions thus far may have implied that it will.

This should not necessarily be taken as undervaluing or invalidating the systematic approach (or its rational precepts); it does, however, alert us to the fact that things do not always turn out as planned and that very often managers end up justifying their strategies and plans after the event (post hoc). For example, the nature of the problem may change part way through an L&D project, and this might entail radical changes to its design; a financial crisis in the company may precipitate the abandonment of an L&D project; and so forth. The overall process may be more emergent and less deterministic than it has been depicted. One way of developing an arguably deeper and less process-driven insight into L&D is by

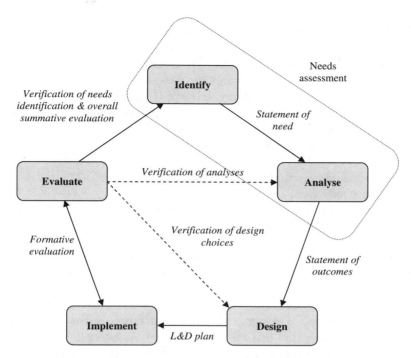

Figure 2.5   A more complex generic systematic approach to L&D (the L&D cycle)

examining the issues from a systems rather than systematic perspective. The ideal situation is one in which there is constant checking back by cross-referral to the preceding stages in order to ensure the validity of analysed needs, objectives, assessment, design and implementation. It should be borne in mind, however, that an L&D decision may appear to be the right one at the time; its true validity, however, may only become apparent after the event.

PERSPECTIVE FROM RESEARCH: THE RHETORIC AND THE REALITY OF ANALYSING L&D NEEDS IN NEW ZEALAND

Based on the following source: M. P. O'Driscoll and P. J. Taylor, 1992. Congruence between theory and practice in management training needs analysis, *The International Journal of Human Resource Management*, 3(3): 593–603.

O'Driscoll and Taylor's main aim was to explore the gap between the framework for L&D needs analysis propounded in the academic literature and the
Continued

methods actually used by organizations to make decisions about planned L&D. The framework they put to the test was that of the systematic approach as embodied in the work of Goldstein (1993) and others, which advocates a systematic analysis at an appropriate level (individual, job and organizational). They addressed these issues by means of a cross-sectional postal questionnaire survey to the human resource (HR) director of 153 organizations in New Zealand that employed over 300 employees (a total of 99 responses were obtained). Respondents were asked, with respect to a recent management L&D programme, to describe:

- who had been involved in the planning decisions;
- how the needs were assessed;
- how the content of the L&D programme was decided and by whom;
- who decided who would participate in the programme.

The answers to these open-ended questions were coded and checked by means of content analyses involving independent assignation of responses to categories by the principal researchers and research assistants. Their findings revealed that most L&D decisions rested with CEOs (chief executive officers) and general managers, that informal mechanisms were used to make L&D decisions, that L&D practitioners themselves played a relatively minor role in the decision-making process and their prime responsibility was for the implementation of decisions once they had been made at higher levels.

The implications drawn from this by O'Driscoll and Taylor were that organizations do not appear to adhere to the idealized systematic approach and that the framework as described in the academic literature of the early 1990s does not appear to reflect the reality in their sample of companies. From areas of weakness identified in the research, the authors argue for stronger links between:

- performance appraisal and L&D;
- strategic planning and planned L&D activities through a matching of organizational goals and L&D goals.

Although the findings are of limited generalizability, the research findings parallel or prefigure the moves towards strategic integration of L&D as discussed earlier.

In recent years there have been attempts to move on from what are seen as primarily process-driven approaches (such as the systematic approach). Pedler, Burgoyne and Boydell (1997) attribute this to the fact that although the systematic approach was very effective in solving problems that existed half a century ago (for example, lack of skilled workers in the USA in the Second World War or in post-Second World War Britain), the very processual nature of the model, its behaviourist elements and the limits of reductionist analyses when applied to complex work (for example, the job of manager), problems with the transfer of learning and the formal 'training' emphasis led to the systematic approach being superseded by self-development, action-based, experiential and work-based methods (1997: 12–13). An alternative view was offered in Chapter 1; namely that rather than being superseded, the systematic approach (albeit in a more modified form) is still is an important tool in the L&D portfolio along with the newer methods. Whilst moves to reject the systematic approach may be justifiable as a reaction to what might have been an over-reliance on its reductionist elements (with the danger that L&D could become the organizational equivalent of 'painting by numbers'), L&D practitioners need to be mindful of throwing the baby out with the bath water. The limitations of the systematic approach are not necessarily fatal ones. On the positive side, it does require an analytical discipline, logic and rigour allied to a methodologically sound research-based method, and whilst it can be a good servant, it can also be a bad master if taken to extremes. Irwin Goldstein, in *Training in Organisations: Needs Assessment, Development and Evaluation* (first published in 1974 and which has gone into several editions), identified the beneficial features of the systematic approach as:

1. Feedback: uses feedback to continually modify the L&D process, hence from this perspective the L&D project is never finished; even when a specific intervention is concluded the lesson learned can be applied to new projects.
2. Complexity: recognizes the complex interactions between components of the system.
3. Framework: provides an invaluable reference for planning, monitoring and remaining on target (all of which resonate with current trends towards performance management), and, most importantly, Goldstein states explicitly that 'a research approach is necessary' (1993: 19).
4. Holistic: L&D system and its processes are part of a bigger whole of corporate policies.
5. Proven: it does not provide a 'magic wand' but it is a tried and tested tool for the establishment of needs, expectations, processes and outcomes in L&D.

One of the problems of L&D in the past was not necessarily its systematic nature (which arguably is a necessary but insufficient condition on its own for effective, and especially strategic, L&D), rather it lay in the over-reliance upon behaviouristic and pedagogically driven learning. The utility of the systematic approach is perhaps best evidenced by the proliferation of models. It has been estimated that between 50 and 100 different versions of this approach have been presented over the past 50 years (see for example: Andrews and Goodson 1980). Patrick (1992: 123–4) concluded that the use of any one systematic model does not guarantee the development of good L&D but their use does provide an important framework and is of benefit for the following reasons:

1. Transferable and generalizable: they are generic functions of L&D in organizations and hence are transferable between organizations and are generalizable across contexts.
2. Tool for non-experts: they are helpful to those who do not have an L&D functional background, for example, general managers and line managers.
3. Enable specialization: the approach enables the division of labour amongst specialists (such as analysts, designers and evaluators) and the coordination of L&D activities. This makes the approach valuable especially to large organizations (such as educational institutions and large public and private organizations).
4. Theory relevant: psychological concepts, theories and principles can be bolted on to the various stages.
5. Evaluative: it provides a framework for evaluation of outcomes (for example by enabling the question 'Were the learning objectives achieved?' to be formulated and answered) and processes (for example, 'Were the learning needs identified correctly?') (see Patrick 1992).

Patrick also singles out two main drawbacks: the approach presents a top-down view which assumes a rational linear process with little or no deviation; it tends to specify 'what to do' rather than 'how to do it'. It is left to the L&D practitioner's professional skill, judgement and expertise to put some flesh on the bones.

L&D FACTS AND FIGURES

The UK's Chartered Institute of Personnel and Development's (CIPD) Annual Training Survey 2004 found that the most frequently cited benefits of training to employers were higher employee competence and improved behavioural and technical skills. The least frequently cited benefits were staff retention, raised commitment and reduced absenteeism. (*Source*: Training and Development 2004: Survey Report (April 2004). London: CIPD.)

Learning and Development as an Organizational Sub-system

A system is a complex whole comprising a set of connected elements linked together by processes. One of the simplest forms that a system can take comprises inputs, processes and outputs (Figure 2.6). A system can be understood and analysed in terms of its elements and the flows (for example, energy resources, matter and information) between the various components. There are biological systems (the human body is one example of such a system with inputs, processes and outputs), environmental systems (like the hydrological cycle with rainfall inputs, water processes on land and outputs into the sea) and computer systems.

Figure 2.6   A generic system model

If we take the latter as our analogy, it can be argued that it has these three elements:

1. Inputs are the data that go into the computer via the keyboard or mouse.
2. Processes are those various operations that are performed on these inputs inside the computer itself (effectively treated as a 'black box').
3. Outputs are the transformed data that appear on the screen of the monitor, as hard copy through the printer or as data files saved to the computer's memory or other storage device.

From a systems perspective it is possible to choose different levels of resolution; for example, as indicated above the computer itself can be treated as a 'black box' with little consideration for what goes on inside it and merely focusing on what goes in and what comes out. One of the drawbacks of this approach is that it ignores the processes inside the black box. An example of this 'black box'-type approach is familiar from learning theory; the behaviourists such as Pavlov, Skinner and Thorndike at one level treated humans as black boxes subject to stimuli (inputs) and exhibiting behaviours (outputs). Such approaches are useful simplifications but may ultimately be self-limiting. One impetus behind the cognitive movement in psychology was precisely to take a look inside the 'black box'.

A further advantage of a systems perspective is that it provides a potentially powerful tool for identifying cause-and-effect relationships. In the highly popular book on organizational learning, *The Fifth Discipline*, Peter Senge (1990) identifies a number of 'disciplines' (team learning, personal mastery, shared vision and mental models), which are linked together by the fifth discipline of 'systems thinking'. Before considering an L&D systems approach, the first point to emphasize is that the organizational system is immensely complex and the concern of this chapter is the organizational context of L&D; hence the discussions will be confined to a consideration of the various elements of a system conceived in such a way as to help managers to understand the L&D's place in this overall context.

As defined in the terms set out above, the L&D system has its own inputs, processes and outputs. If the processes are put to one side for the moment, we can ask ourselves what are the inputs of the L&D system? These inputs may be seen as operating at two levels – internal inputs and external inputs.

1. External inputs of the L&D system are those factors in the organization's external environment that can impact upon L&D by triggering its occurrence (for

example, the development of a new technology outside of the organization, such as the internet, may create a learning need amongst employees) or influencing it in some other way. Political change is one instance of an external factor that can cause organizations to undertake planned L&D projects. For example, in the UK the privatization drives of the Conservative government in the 1980s meant that public utilities (water, gas and electricity) experienced organizational change which had huge implications for learning and development (a whole range of new L&D needs surfaced as a result of an external political factor). Other external triggers include political, environmental, social, technical, legal and economic factors (these so-called PESTLE factors which provide managers with a useful framework to analyse and anticipate changes).

2.   Internal factors can also be inputs to the L&D process; for example, job redesign may precipitate L&D needs at the job and individual levels with concomitant needs for the retraining of whole cohorts of employees. Similarly, the introduction of team working will bring with it the requirement for team building or end-user training. Note that the internal factors themselves cannot always be seen in isolation from external factors. For example, the introduction of a new initiative inside the organization (such as increased job flexibility) may be triggered by an external stimulus (such as a drive to reduce the costs of production as a result of increased competition).

The outputs of the system may be seen as operating at three levels: the individual, the collective and the organizational.

1.   Some L&D projects are focused very much at the individual level. For example, the personal development plan (PDP) of a manager may result in him or her gaining an additional qualification, such as a company-sponsored MBA – in this sense the individual's qualification is the output.

2.   The collective outputs are those that are at the level of groups of individuals but not at the level of the whole organization. As a result of learning (or organizational learning – see Chapter 5 for a more detailed discussion), groups of individuals may develop shared mental models, which may be considered a component of the organization's knowledge assets. Other collective outcomes of L&D might include socialization in the organization's norms and values (perhaps through induction training) and participation in collaborative working and learning.

3.   Other L&D projects may be focused at the organizational level. For example, attempts to develop entire sections of the workforce with respect to a changed set of organizational practices (such as cross-functional working) would have the intention of resulting in an output (changed working practices) at the level of the organization (and would in all likelihood trigger the need to develop new knowledge, skills and attitudes at the level of a substantial section of the workforce).

The benefits to the L&D practitioner of a systems approach (Figure 2.7) are that it provides an integrated and integrating perspective; causal and predictive relationships may be identified; and key variables that may need to be controlled or managed may be singled out (Anderson 1993: 19).

Discussion Point

What are the main differences between systematic approaches and systems approaches in learning and development? In your view, which one adds greater value to planned L&D from a practitioner's perspective? To what extent are the two perspectives compatible?

Integrating Systematic and Systems Approaches in L&D

The two perspectives which have been outlined above are not necessarily mutually exclusive, and indeed when combined they may offer a synergy which affords opportunities for greater insight and a more integrated perspective on the strategic and operational aspects of L&D than each does on its own (Figure 2.8). Perhaps

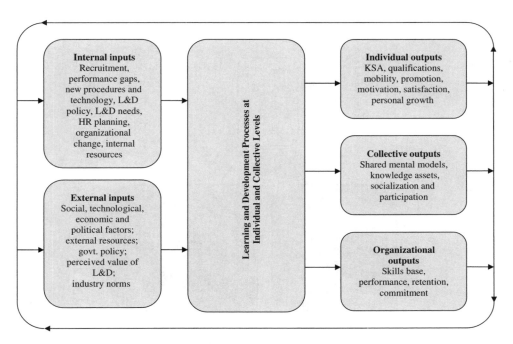

Figure 2.7   A generic L&D system model

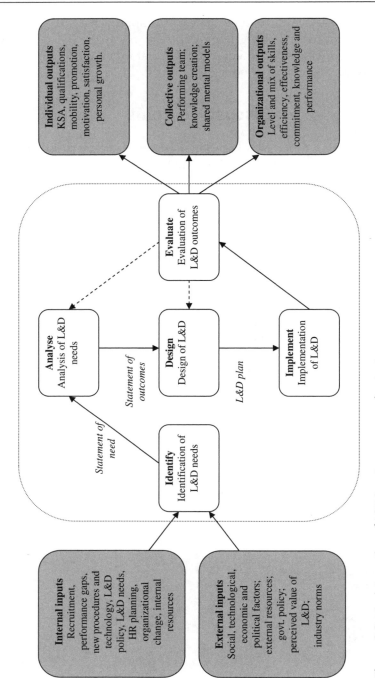

Figure 2.8 An integration of L&D inputs, process and outputs

the simplest way to integrate the two is by considering the systematic approach as one way of describing the processes that may occur within the 'black box'. The resultant model is more integrative and hints at some of the complexities of L&D within the organization; for example:

1. L&D processes are driven by inputs and affect the outputs (for example various factors trigger L&D, and L&D results in enhanced levels of knowledge and skill of the workforce and in the labour market more generally).
2. The outputs of L&D themselves may in turn affect the inputs (for example, enhanced flexibility, adaptability and competitive advantage as a result of L&D may affect the operating environment more generally as competitor organizations respond).
3. The development of L&D as a core competence may itself shape strategy (for example, the human resource of the organization may be a 'bottom-up' driver of strategy).

The value of each approach (systems and systematic) lies in the different and complementary perspectives of each: the systematic perspective brings a linear, processual perspective that may miss the bigger picture; the systems perspective brings a holistic perspective that may overlook details. The planning of effective L&D within an organization entails examining problems and making decisions with each viewpoint in mind – it is not an 'either or' question, and both perspectives are needed ultimately.

L&D Roles and Responsibilities

The discussion of the role of the L&D practitioner has a long history in L&D theory and research. Kirkpatrick, almost four decades ago, asked the question 'Whose responsibility is training?' He framed his discussion in terms of whether it is the training manager or the line manager who is responsible. An important distinction he drew was that of responsibility and authority, when he argued that:

- training managers have the responsibility to see that training is carried out effectively in all departments;
- line managers have the authority to make final decisions regarding the training activities of subordinates.

Inevitably, any lack of authority on the part of the L&D manager has the potential to create difficulties and tensions, for example in terms of convincing sometimes sceptical managers of the benefits of L&D. Managers are important stakeholders since they are likely to have the authority to sanction training for their subordinates and they can also play a significant role in the creation of opportunities to apply new learning. Line managers have considerable control over the potential effects and the impact of L&D (especially with regard to the climate or conditions for learning transfer that may or may not exist in the workplace). Kirkpatrick's conclusion was that the secret for continued success for L&D practitioners is the promotion of L&D and provision of practical help that will be 'enthusiastically received by line managers' (1967: 25). The debates about the role of line managers in L&D and exhortations for them to have a greater involvement appear to have continued unabated over almost 40 years.

PERSPECTIVE FROM PRACTICE: LINE MANAGEMENT RESPONSIBILITY IN L&D IN IRELAND

Based on the following source: N. Heraty and M. Morley, 1995. Line managers and human resource development, *Journal of European Industrial Training*, 19(10): 31–7.

Strategic models of L&D make strong claims that line managers should be involved in L&D, but the question remains of what is the extent of line managers' actual involvement in L&D. There have been a number of studies that have sought to address this question. Heraty and Morley (1995) surveyed 58 organizations based in Ireland in order to answer the question of where the responsibility for L&D activities rested (was it with L&D specialists, with line managers or with both?). Their results for four key areas of L&D activity (identification of needs, selection of methods, delivery of L&D and evaluation of L&D) are summarized in Figure 2.9.

These results suggest that there is a degree of shared responsibility between L&D specialists and line managers in the identification of needs and in the delivery of L&D. In the more specialized and technical areas of the selection of learning methods and the evaluation of L&D, the prime responsibility appears to be that of the L&D practitioner. Moreover, there was no area of L&D activity for which the line mangers had the overall responsibility. This paints a picture of direct partnership between line managers and L&D practitioners in some areas but clear ownership by L&D in others. No distinction was drawn between the firms in the study in terms of the extent to which L&D was strategically focused. The extent to which a different pattern of results may have been obtained if an independent variable of organizational type (strategic orientation to L&D) had been included is not clear.

In parallel with these discussions and over the intervening years the notion of the 'training and development (T&D) professional' emerged. The historical roots of this research stretch back over two decades on both sides of the Atlantic. The issue of what constitutes professional practice in the area of T&D was investigated by the American Society for Training and Development (the ASTD) in the 1970s and

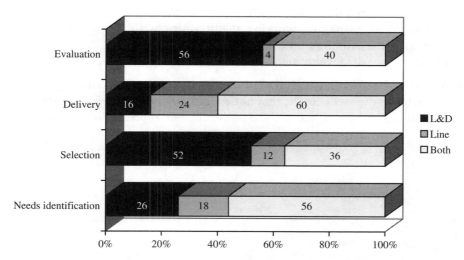

Figure 2.9 Responsibility for key L&D activities. (*Source*: Heraty and Morley 1995: 35)

reported by Pinto and Walker (1978). Their research was based upon the development by an expert panel of a set of performance categories including professional competence, consulting competence, managing, developing and administering training programmes, facilitating learning and general skills (such as problem solving). These formed the basis of a questionnaire survey of all ASTD members (Pinto and Walker received 2,790 responses, which represented approximately a 20 per cent response rate). The large number of items (questions) in the survey made interpretation cumbersome and hence they attempted to reduce the items down to a smaller number of manageable groups. The underlying pattern of responses to the items on the questionnaire was identified through factor analysis. Factor analysis is a technique that condenses the information contained in a larger number of original variables into a smaller set of variates called factors (Hair et al. 1998: 14). It provides an objective, as opposed to subjective, means for creating groupings based upon participants' responses. This analysis and subsequent interpretation of the statistical findings resulted in the identification of eight groups of activities:

1. Needs analysis and diagnosis.
2. Determining appropriate training approach.
3. Programme design and development.
4. Training resources: develop material resources; manage internal resources; manage external resources.
5. Training and development activities: individual development planning and counselling; job/performance-related training; conducting classroom training; group and organization development.

6. Training research (including evaluation).
7. Management: managing working relationships with managers and clients; managing the training and development function.
8. Professional self-development.

Aside from a detailed consideration of the content of the eight clusters, Pinto and Walker point to the facts: firstly, that not every L&D practitioner can fulfil each of the roles at all times, and, secondly, that the clusters represent a flow of activities

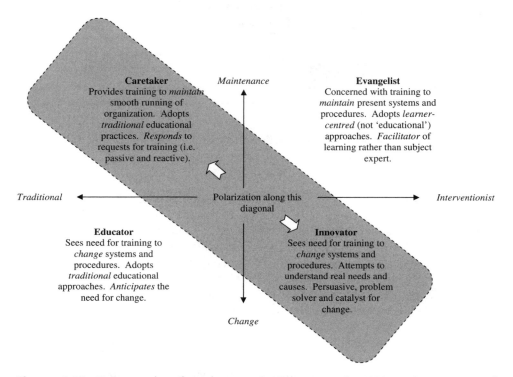

Figure 2.10 Trainer roles (based upon Pettigrew et al. 1982 and Bennett and Leduchowicz 1983). Note: the training manager role is excluded from the diagram

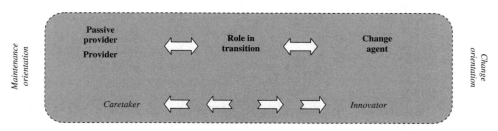

Figure 2.11 The maintenance change dimension in trainer roles: Pettigrew et al. (1982) roles in **bold**; Bennett and Leduchowicz (1983) roles in *italics*. Note: the training manager, educator and evangelist roles are excluded from this diagram

from diagnosis and analysis of needs through to research and data gathering on the effectiveness of a specific training programme. In the UK in the 1980s there was some research activity that aimed to identify the roles fulfilled by trainers. For example, Pettigrew, Jones and Reason (1982) surveyed trainers in the chemical industry and identified five trainer roles:

1. Passive provider: adopts a 'sit back and wait for clients to come forward' approach and then provides training aimed at maintenance and improvement but not major change.
2. Provider: concerned with the maintenance and improvement of performance but without major change.
3. Role in transition: in between the role of provider and change agent, no longer content to provide courses but desires to have more proactive and influential role.
4. Change agent: main concern is organizational development (OD) and complex issues of cultural change.
5. Training manager: concerned with the smooth running of the training function.

Other research in the UK in the 1980s by Bennett and Leduchowicz (1983) suggested that trainers occupy four roles that vary according to two dimensions: a traditionalist versus an interventionist orientation, and maintenance versus a change orientation. The various roles are mapped out in Figures 2.10 and 2.11. Bennett and Leduchowicz noted some polarization of roles along the diagonal corresponding to the continuum that is implicit in the Pettigrew et al. framework (from passive provider to change agent).

At the present time there are a number of efforts to describe the L&D practitioner's role in terms of competencies (i.e. the knowledge, skills, abilities and behaviours required for effective performance). There have been parallel developments in this regard in the UK and the USA and these are described below.

PERSPECTIVE FROM PRACTICE: THE AMERICAN SOCIETY FOR TRAINING AND DEVELOPMENT'S 2004 COMPETENCY STUDY

Based on the following source: W. Rothwell and R. Wellins, 2004. Mapping your future: putting new competencies to work for you, *Training & Development*, 58(5): 1–8.

The ASTD has developed a competency model for L&D practitioners which it hopes will provide a model for a learning and performance profession. The model is research-based and was derived from:

- interviews with 75 'thought leaders' and practitioners during 2003;
- literature review of existing models;
- telephone interviews and focus groups with 60 thought leaders, experts and practitioners (Davis et al. 2004: 31).

Continued

The model has three cumulative elements. At the base of the model are the foundational competencies (such as the interpersonal competence of communicating effectively, the management competence of thinking strategically and the personal competence of adaptability). Altogether there are 12 foundational competencies across these three areas. At the next level in the model are the areas of expertise that represent the technical and professional activities that the L&D practitioner is likely to engage in (for example, designing learning, coaching, measuring and evaluating and so forth). Altogether there are nine areas of expertise, which also are supported by, and themselves 'leverage' (make use of), learning technologies. The final components of the model are the four roles (learning strategist, business partner, project manager and professional specialist). Roles are broad areas of professional responsibility that are flexible depending upon the nature of the L&D project. The roles are not job titles: for example, an L&D manager's job may encompass the strategist and business partner roles, whilst an L&D adviser role might encompass the specialist and project manager roles. A full description of the model may be found in Davis et al. (2004). Figure 2.12 summarizes its main elements and their interrelationships.

Rothwell and Wellins (2004) identified the following applications of the 2004 ASTD Competency Model:

1.   Certification: the model may be used for professional certification as a standard against which competence may be assessed.
2.   Self-development: the model may be used by individuals as the basis for self-development whereby an L&D practitioner may assess the competencies that are important in their current job, those that will be important in the future and their current levels of performance in these areas.
3.   PDPs: as the basis for a Personal Development Plan (PDP) for an L&D practitioner.
4.   Professional Standard: as a standard for entry to the profession.
5.   L&D Professional Education: as a means for guiding the design of the curriculum in L&D professional education.

PERSPECTIVE FROM PRACTICE: THE UK'S NATIONAL STANDARD FOR LEARNING AND DEVELOPMENT

Based on the following source: http://www.ento.co.uk/

In the UK the government has established National Training Organizations (NTOs), which have the brief to be the national representative bodies for vocational education and training (VET) and to develop national occupational standards. There are a large number of NTOs, each of which represents the interests of particular sectors of industry. The Employment NTO (ENTO) represents the areas of training and development and personnel (as well as trade unions and health and safety), i.e. occupations that deal primarily with people and employment issues (part of its declared main objective is the enhancement and improvement of the performance of people involved in the development and management of people in the workplace).

The qualification structure that underpins the standard is the UK's National Vocational Qualification (NVQ) system. The aim of these qualifications is for them to be used to show that an individual is competent in a particular occupational area. As such, NVQs are qualifications for work and intended to provide the evidence that a person can perform a task or job. NVQs are made up of 'units' that describe the skills and knowledge needed to do a job effectively (http://www.dfes.gov.uk/nvq). The UK's national occupational standard for learning and development comprises a total of 24 units. These are shown in Table 2.3. The units have been classified here into seven categories for ease of interpretation (*note*: these are not official ENTO categories). Based upon these units, NVQs in learning and development are available at three levels, from the lowest (NVQ Level 3) to the highest (NVQ Level 5). The levels and their descriptors are:

Level 3: involves the 'application of knowledge in a broad range of varied work activities performed in a wide variety of contexts, most of which are complex and non-routine. There is considerable responsibility and autonomy and control or guidance of others is often required' (http://www.dfes.gov.uk/nvq/example).

Level 4: involves the 'application of knowledge in a broad range of complex, technical or professional work activities performed in a variety of contexts and with a substantial degree of personal responsibility and autonomy. Responsibility for the work of others and the allocation of resources is often present' (http://www.dfes.gov.uk/nvq/example).

Level 5: involves the 'application of a range of fundamental principles across a wide and often unpredictable variety of contexts. Very substantial personal autonomy and often significant responsibility for the work of others and for the allocation of substantial resources features strongly, as do personal accountabilities for analysis, diagnosis, design, planning, execution and evaluation' (http://www.dfes.gov.uk/nvq/example).

So, for example, at Level 3 the mandatory L&D units are L3, 5, 6, 9, 16 and 18 (see: http://www.ento.co.uk/standards). The assessment is on the basis of competence and therefore usually judged on candidates' actual behaviours. However, there are certain areas in which it is permissible for an assessor to use a hypothetical context (for example when assessing the management of group dynamics, L13.1). We will meet again the concepts of competence and levels in our discussions of manager L&D in a later chapter.

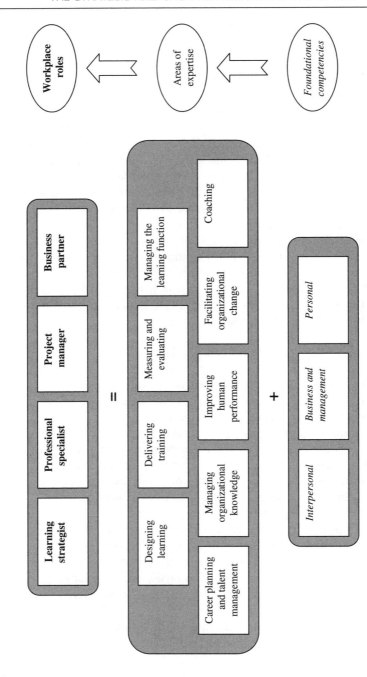

Figure 2.12 The 2004 ASTD Competency Model. (*Source:* Davis et al. 2004)

Table 2.3 The UK's national occupational standard for learning and development (based upon: http://www.ento.co.uk/standards)

Extract from the UK's National Occupational Standard for Learning and Development	
Areas	**Units**
1. Identifying L&D needs	Developing a strategy for learning and development
	Identifying the learning and development needs of the organization
	Identifying individual learning aims and programmes
2. Designing and developing L&D programmes	Designing learning programmes
	Agreeing learning programmes with learners
	Developing training sessions
	Preparing and developing resources to support learning
3. Enabling L&D	Managing the contribution of other people to the learning process
	Creating a climate that promotes learning
	Enabling learning through presentations, demonstrations, instruction, coaching and group learning
4. Supporting learners	Supporting learning by mentoring in the workplace
	Supporting and advising individual learners
	Monitor and review progress with learners
	Supporting competence achieved in the workplace
5. Continuously improving L&D	Evaluating and improving L&D programmes
	Respond to changes in L&D
6. Providing L&D for international settings	Identifying, designing and producing L&D programmes for international settings
7. Planning, introducing and supporting basic skills acquisition (for example, literacy and numeracy)	Planning how to provide basic skills in the workplace
	Introducing training for basic skills in the workplace
	Supporting how basic skills are delivered in the workplace
	Supporting people learning basic skills in the workplace

Discussion Point

Compare and contrast the ASTD and the ENTO frameworks. To structure your comparison you could consider questions such as: what are the similarities and differences? In your view does either one have greater theoretical rigour than the other? Does either one have greater practical relevance and utility than the other? Justify your reasoning.

The approach embodied in the ENTO standards has attracted critical comment. For example, Harrison (writing in 2003) expressed the view that the most worrying aspects of the approach taken in developing such standards is the lack of sufficient emphasis on the 'need for a holistic and integrative approach to L&D as an organisational process' and also an inadequate attention to the ways in which L&D can cross functional boundaries (beyond HR for example) and organizational levels (the same L&D function may be performed by managers at quite different levels in an organization) (2003: 163). Currie and Darby (1995), in their critical review of management competencies, raise a number of more general issues, namely that complex behaviours are non-generic, context specific and subject to individual variability. These comments, it may be argued, apply equally to L&D competence as to management competence:

1. L&D practice is not generic: one may question the extent to which it is possible to produce a list of generic managerial competencies that can be carried around like a 'tool kit'.
2. L&D practice is context specific: the implication that L&D skills are of a general nature is at odds with the view that even if an L&D practitioner functions well in one context this does not necessarily transfer to other contexts.
3. There is individual variability in L&D practice: producing 'identikit' lists of competencies can hide important variations in how the individual practitioner operates (1995: 13); this may be especially true in the case of the expert performer who might have developed idiosyncratic but effective ways of carrying various complex tasks.

L&D FACTS AND FIGURES

A survey by the ASTD published in 2004 examined the proportion of time (as a percentage) that a sample of L&D practitioners in the USA spent on various activities. The findings revealed that L&D practitioners in the sample on average spent: 19 per cent of their time on designing learning; 17 per cent on delivering training; 11 per cent on managing the L&D function; and 11 per cent of their time on coaching. The remaining time was spent on miscellaneous activities including measuring and evaluating. (*Source*: P. Davis, J. Naughton and W. Rothwell, 2004. New roles and new competencies for the professional, *Training & Development*, 58(4): 26–36.)

The L&D Function

The term 'L&D function' refers to the activities that take place in an organization to support, facilitate and enable L&D; this is L&D's internal face. However, L&D must also face outwards and take into account the structural arrangements of the L&D function in relation to other areas (such as finance, engineering, manufacturing and so forth) within the organization (see Stewart 1999: 82). This in its simplest and most traditional sense might refer to the L&D-related activities of a Training Department or Human Resources Department within an organization; in a more complex sense it might refer to the apportionment of responsibility for L&D between the different stakeholders, where an L&D department might be more virtual than real (see Figure 2.13).

In terms of its historical context in the UK, according to Reid and Barrington (1999), what might now be referred to as the L&D Function first began to appear on a significant scale in large UK organizations as Training Departments in the 1960s. These existed along a spectrum from a token presence to meet minimal needs to high-status and high-influence units within large well-resourced organizations (Reid and Barrington 1999: 120). Reid and Barrington paint a somewhat 'bleak house' picture of the era of the 1970s in the UK where, in their view, there was a limited stock of training expertise, with low-calibre staff coupled with unrealistically high expectations of training departments. The structure was often one in which a training manager presided over training officers (often subject specialist instructors drawn from the relevant function such as engineering) and training administrators to deal with the day-to-day matters of organizing and running training courses. The role performed by L&D practitioners was typically that of the provider of training courses often founded upon an educational model (see the discussion above of Pettigrew et al.'s work). Reid and Barrington paint a rosier picture for the L&D function in the 1980s, during which period of time many of the employee relationship problems that had occupied personnel (or, as they were coming to be known, HR) departments had ameliorated, which often meant that more effort and resources could be devoted to employee training and development (Reid and Barrington 1999: 121). In parallel with this, considerable effort was also devoted to improving the knowledge and skills of UK managers in the light of identified shortcomings. Drives towards a more strategic role for HR in general (including L&D) emerged in the late 1980s and the 1990s. By the beginning of the twenty-first century debate and practice has shifted away from an administratively driven provider ethos to one that emphasizes the role that L&D can play in collective learning and in the effective management of knowledge assets within newer and more virtual organizational forms.

L&D FACTS AND FIGURES

The UK's Chartered Institute of Personnel and Development's (CIPD) Annual Training Survey 2004 found that 60 per cent of respondents felt that HR or the training department has the main responsibility for training; 18 per cent of respondents felt that line managers have the main responsibility for training. (*Source*: Training and Development 2004: Survey Report (April 2004). London: CIPD.)

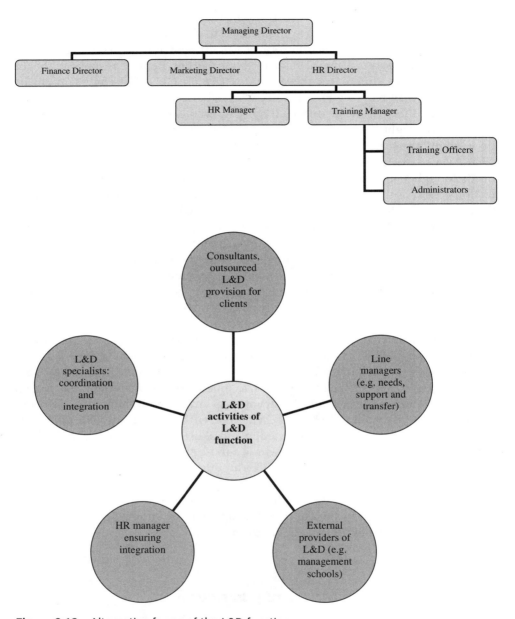

Figure 2.13 Alternative forms of the L&D function

The question of the position within the organization that an L&D function occupies in relation to a central HR function is an important one both in terms of day-to-day operations (for example, how does L&D interface with other HR activities?) and also in terms of the strategic role played by L&D and how L&D is perceived. Stewart argued that the 'people focus' of L&D might imply that it sits naturally with personnel or HR but sees a number of advantages (mostly in terms of horizontal integration) and disadvantages (mostly in terms of lack of vertical alignment):

Advantages: If L&D is located within HR there is an increased opportunity for HR planning to feed directly into the forecasting of L&D requirements; recruitment and L&D may be planned in tandem; performance appraisal and L&D stand a greater chance of being integrated; succession and promotion decisions taken by HR may be linked more easily to L&D plans; and it avoids duplication of effort in employee record keeping (Stewart 1999).

Disadvantages: Stewart (1999) couched the disadvantages of a tight coupling between HR and L&D in terms of the knock-on effect upon L&D if HR itself has little or no influence, credibility or esteem. He further argued that a senior executive should have responsibility for L&D, that L&D might be aligned with the other functions directly (such as engineering, finance, marketing, customer service, and so forth – in effect L&D becomes an arm of the function).

Whether L&D is better placed being tightly coupled or loosely coupled to its HR partner depends upon the context, history and culture of L&D and HR in the organization. For L&D to have a secure foothold in an organization Reid and Barrington identified three conditions that should be met: firstly, line managers should have some responsibility for L&D; secondly, L&D should be appropriately structured (in terms of its internal and external face); and, finally, L&D practitioners within an organization should have, and be seen to have, professional competence. The time factor may also be significant in determining the degree of acceptance, trust and respect accorded to the L&D function, and it might be the case that the L&D function has to go through a number of stages leading to acceptance, trust and respect. The question of how L&D is aligned in practice is likely to depend upon a number of factors including:

1. The historical pattern of relationships between 'training' and the rest of the organization.
2. The culture and context of the organization in terms of the importance attached to learning, buy-in to L&D by senior managers, general significance attached to L&D in the organization and the extent to which L&D has a strategic role to play.
3. The level of professional and specialist knowledge amongst L&D practitioners and the extent to which L&D is outsourced to consultants and other providers.

There are strong arguments for a middle way in which L&D specialists are aligned to specific departments, for example in the role of L&D adviser to departments such as manufacturing with the responsibility to proactively seek to define problems and provide solutions, but who for line management purposes are located within a coherent and central L&D function (which may or may not be part of corporate HR) in which the broader issues of leveraging change through

L&D may be addressed collectively and with a distinct L&D identity. The former gives leverage within a function, the latter provides the synergy and overall perspective required if L&D is to have strategic impact. The type of matrix structure that might be used is illustrated in Table 2.4. The relevant L&D adviser works in partnership with the function's project manager (whose own line of reporting is to the manager of the function) for the duration of the project but reports herself or himself to the L&D manager. For example, Adviser A is working with a project manager in Function X (which could be for front-line staff in the telesales department) on a project to enhance performance in delivering higher-quality customer service. Adviser A and Project Manager X work together for the duration of the project, but their working relationship may cease on completion of the project. Adviser A might bring process skills to the project (for example in terms of identification, analysis, design, implementation and evaluation), whilst Project Manager X might bring content knowledge and skills (since Project Manager X is located close to the learning need within the function). The structure gives flexibility in that advisers may work on more than one project and with more than one function. The function may buy in L&D expertise from the organization's L&D function or it may buy in external expertise to suit the project. In terms of reporting, the client for the project is the X's manager who may be the senior person (i.e. the director) within the function. Ownership of the project is with the function; the L&D input is a means to an end.

Table 2.4 Matrix management structure for L&D projects. *Note*: Current L&D projects in italics

			Function X	**Function Y**	**Function Z**
			Manager X (L&D's client)	Manager Y (L&D's client)	Manager Z (L&D's client)
	L&D function		Project Manager X (L&D's project partner)	Project Manager Y (L&D's project partner)	Project Manager Z (L&D's project partner)
L&D Manager		L&D Adviser A	*Customer care for front-line staff*		*Assessing customer satisfaction*
		L&D Adviser B		*Finance for non-financial managers*	
		L&D Adviser C	*Basic IT skills*		
		L&D Adviser D	*Organizational change*	*Organizational change*	*Organizational change*
		L&D Adviser E			*Quality assurance and control*

PERSPECTIVE FROM PRACTICE: L&D AND STRATEGY AT AVAYA

Based on the following source: T. Kraack, 2003. Turning the aircraft carrier, *Training & Development*, November 2003: 60–4.

A vexing question for L&D practitioners can relate to the organizational arrangements that need to be in place to forge the all-important links between strategy and L&D (thus supporting effective implementation). Kraack reports a consultancy project at Avaya, a global business communications company, which appears to have recognized the need to link L&D and business strategy, has put the structures in place to make it happen and has evaluated the results. As part of their approach to securing this link the organization appointed a Chief Learning Officer and created a Corporate Learning Council in order to ensure that:

- Avaya's strategic objectives are interpreted and articulated within L&D;
- an approach to learning that was commensurate with this strategic stance was enacted through the corporate Avaya University;
- L&D needs were prioritized;
- there was reporting back to the Corporate Governance Team on the alignment between L&D and strategy.

The Corporate Governance Team guided the Corporate Learning Council's actions by determining the L&D needs of Avaya based upon its strategic outlook; it also kept a watching brief on the impact of L&D projects by assessing learners' levels of satisfaction and their learning performance, both of which increased over the duration of the project. Amongst the observed benefits have been that employee time-to-competence has been significantly reduced (i.e. the time needed to train employees to reach an acceptable level of performance has gone down) and concomitantly L&D efficiency has increased. The business benefit of these increased levels of performance and efficiency have meant that in a highly competitive market place Avaya was able to achieve better new product roll-outs, which was aligned with the corporate goals of productivity enhancement, new product launches and organizational agility.

Managing the L&D Function

In our consideration of the management of the L&D function we will concern ourselves with the key issues of the resourcing (including outsourcing), marketing and costing of L&D activities.

RESOURCING L&D

The resourcing of the L&D function is a key decision for the management of L&D since this will determine:

- the level of expertise and professional knowledge recruited to (i.e. 'bought in') or developed within ('home-made') the L&D function and available to the organization more widely;
- the degree of flexibility that can be achieved within the L&D function from its internal resources or from outsourcing from external providers of L&D products and services.

The expertise and professional knowledge of the L&D practitioner is now well defined through the conceptual, functional and empirical analyses used to derive the various national and international frameworks such as that of the ASTD in the USA, and of ENTO and the Chartered Institute of Personnel and Development (CIPD) in the UK. Such frameworks and the associated qualification schemes (as in the case of the CIPD) now mean that it is easier for employers to recruit and select L&D practitioners who will have a predefined level of knowledge and skill. Furthermore, some professional bodies (such as the CIPD) make demands upon their members for continuing updating and professional L&D (for example, continuing professional development or CPD). Frameworks such as those of the ASTD, ENTO and CIPD provide the bases for a standard for entry into the L&D profession and selection criteria for employers. This has resulted in a general rise in the standard for entry to L&D roles. Flexibility of staff within the L&D function has a number of dimensions including:

1. Numerical flexibility: this allows the organization to respond quickly in terms of the numbers of people who can employed in a particular task.
2. Temporal flexibility: enabling flexibility in the pattern of hours worked by employees.
3. Functional flexibility: giving the capacity amongst the workforce to undertake a variety of tasks (see Torrington et al. 2002: 142–4).

A related notion is that of core and peripheral workers. The former group have firm-specific competencies and are generally highly regarded by the employer; the latter group include those not employed by the firm who provide work for the organization and those who are employees of the firm but are engaged in routine and single-skill work and whose status is tangential to the organization (Boxall and Purcell 2003: 133). The implications of flexibility for L&D are:

1. Numerical flexibility may be required in the L&D functions to cope with peaks of demand for L&D projects, for example when an organization-wide learn-

ing need surfaces and has to be met with consistency and within a relatively short time-frame (for example, health and safety training in the wake of an incident might demand a rapid and company-wide response).

2. Similarly, temporal flexibility may be advantageous if L&D practitioners are required to work outside normal working hours in order to meet the needs of a particular project, when dealing with a globally dispersed workforce operating remotely in different time zones and so on. Temporal flexibility may also be a means by which the employment requirements of individuals can be met in order to accommodate personal circumstances.

3. One implication for L&D of functional flexibility is that individuals may be required to become multi-skilled in order to undertake a broader range of tasks (for example in the skills of needs analysis, design, implementation and evaluation and other related HR issues). In addition to the latter (which may be described as horizontal flexibility), L&D practitioners may also need to undertake work previously carried out by superiors or subordinates (Torrington et al. 2002) (i.e. vertical flexibility).

4. Whether or not L&D is seen as a core activity may influence the extent to which senior mangers within an organization choose to keep an activity within its boundaries or engage in distancing strategies such as subcontracting to external providers (Walton 1999: 281).

OUTSOURCING L&D

In L&D there has always been a tendency to subcontract some aspects of projects, especially where expertise is required from outside of the organization. For example, certain aspects of selection or needs analysis such as psychometric testing are routinely outsourced (as assessors may need to be licensed by professional bodies), as are the high levels of technical and scientific knowledge such as that which is available in universities or research organizations and which is bought in on an occasional basis. Organizational size may also have a role to play in resourcing L&D, since small firms often lack the expertise in specialized areas such as HR and L&D and therefore may have little choice but to buy in the provision of such activities. Moves to encompass the numerical, temporal and functional facets of flexibility in the wake of downsizing and reorganizing have meant that there have been increased tendencies towards outsourcing and subcontracting L&D activities and projects. The need for organizations to develop and change in the light of competitive pressures has provided an additional impetus in this regard and in projects such as organizational development and evaluation consultants are often used (see below for some of the advantages of using consultants).

L&D FACTS AND FIGURES

'You will work with senior managers to carefully assess business needs, and devise and deliver the programmes that enable employees to fulfil their potential. You'll therefore be instrumental in shaping learning and development initiatives, as well as providing one-to-one coaching, organizing assessments and evaluating development activities against business objectives. We are looking for someone with the drive to make things happen in a fast-paced environment, a team player with self-confidence, good interpersonal skills and an analytical mind.' Job advertisement for an L&D Specialist, Toyota Motor Manufacturing (UK). (*Source*: *People Management*, January 2005: 84.)

PERSPECTIVE FROM RESEARCH: OUTSOURCING L&D IN THE USA

Based on the following source: T. W. Gainey and B. S. Klaas, 2002. Outsourcing the training function: results from the field, *Human Resource Planning*, 25(1): 16–22.

Gainey and Klaas used a cross-sectional survey of training managers in the USA in order to explore outsourcing practices in training. They surveyed a cross-sector sample of 1,361 managers in firms of all sizes (mean size was 2,370 employees) and received 323 responses (a response rate of 24 per cent). Their main findings were in three areas:

1. Type of training: outsourced training appeared to be concentrated in the areas of management development and technical training.
2. Level of outsourcing: the level of outsourcing was quite modest, about half of the respondents outsourced less than 25 per cent of their training, with less than 10 per cent outsourcing more than 75 per cent of their training. As might be expected, this pattern was mirrored in expenditure on outsourced training – only 5 per cent of respondents reported spending more than 75 per cent of their budget on outsourced training.
3. Outcomes: in terms of the outcomes of outsourcing a majority of respondents felt that there had been performance improvements (64 per cent), more effective training design (62 per cent) and greater overall satisfaction (60 per cent). Only 29 per cent felt that there had been costs savings as a result of outsourcing.

The pattern that emerged was of outsourcing of training for quality-related purposes rather than as a means primarily to achieve cost savings. The authors offered some guidelines for making the outsourcing of L&D more effective:

1. Establishment of trusting relationships with suppliers by sharing information and building long-term relationships.
2. Making clear and comprehensive contractual agreements with suppliers, with goals, expectations and penalties articulated clearly.
3. Maintaining close working relationships with suppliers for the duration of a project and not assuming that outsourcing will provide a simple 'turn-key' solution.
4. Outsource for the right reasons and not simply in anticipation of costs savings (recall that the majority of respondents in the survey outsourced for quality-related rather than cost-related reasons).

The L&D function has proved to be one of the most vulnerable to being downsized or dispensed with in times of financial hardship (Walton 1999: 229). There may be a variety of justifiable reasons for outsourcing L&D projects (especially those concerned with change rather than maintenance of organization norms and practices). Consultants and other external providers are sometimes used in this regard since they may be seen by managers as providing (Torrington et al. 2002: 165):

• specialized knowledge and skills (especially in environments that are technologically complex and volatile);
• an independent perspective and demonstrable impartiality;
• a catalyst for change, a means to achieve consensus or to justify potentially unpleasant or unpopular decisions;
• numerical and temporal flexibility in the L&D resource available to the organization.

They may also help to reduce costs through economies of scale when the same L&D product has to be provided for a number of organizations (the up-front development costs are therefore spread and hence a lower-cost product may be offered more cheaply than a one-off in-house design). There are, however, disadvantages to the use of external providers as summarized by Gainey and Klaas (2002); for example, by continually relying upon outsiders an organization may inhibit the development of its own in-house expertise; furthermore, outsiders may not understand an organization's culture well, and the insider's tacit knowledge of this is difficult to articulate to outsiders.

PERSPECTIVE FROM PRACTICE: A PSYCHOLOGIST'S DIATRIBE?

Based on the following source: A. Furnham, 1997. Fire the training department, *Across the Board*, 34(3): 9–10.

Outsourcing is certainly a challenge for L&D. More than most, the function has to be explicit about the value that it adds; and indeed the L&D function may be sometimes faced with the challenge of justifying its very existence. For this reason L&D practitioners need to be forewarned of this possibility and forearmed in rebutting some of the assertions that may be levelled at L&D. Furnham argued that training in organizations can be improved by nothing less than getting rid of in-house training departments and bringing in trainers from outside the organization who can be 'hired when required and fired when tired', and who might bring in valuable expertise and experiences from outside the company. Furnham's reasons for this position are stated as:

1. To be cost-effective the trainers need to be 'in the classroom' 70 per cent of the time, which might be difficult to achieve because of peaks and troughs in business cycles. Furnham does not give any justification for the notional figure of 70 per cent and the point appears to be predicated on a set of educational or pedagogical assumptions of trainers as providers that may not be all that relevant in many modern organizations.
2. 'Trainers burn out easily' because they need to be entertainers, monitors, enthusiasts and educators and under such demands even the best can become 'tired, flat and boring' – perhaps a gross generalization and based upon a set of assumptions about what L&D actually is (and which begs the question of whether the same applies to other professional groups, such as university lecturers, for example).
3. Managing trainers is like 'herding cats'; they are difficult to manage because of personal idiosyncrasies and foibles. Even if this were true it might equally apply to other professional groups.
4. Over time trainers become too inwardly focused and 'organo-centric' (as Furnham describes it), with a lack of external perspective. This is easily solved, if it is a justifiable criticism, by development activities for L&D practitioners themselves as part of their ongoing continuous professional development through job rotation, special projects, secondments and so forth.

Discussion Point

If Furnham's diatribe against training departments were to be heard and taken seriously by budget holders, might it pose a potential threat to L&D? Do you think that managers and executives should take Furnham's reasons for outsourcing L&D seriously? How would you react to such criticisms if they were levelled at you as an L&D practitioner? Justify your reasoning.

MARKETING L&D

L&D in organizations can often be a contradictory area. One the one hand, it is often espoused by managers as a key means of enabling learning and hence providing a sustainable source of competitive advantage. Balance this, on the other hand, with the fact that (in the UK at least) L&D has been one function that often has been placed under threat in times of restructuring and downsizing. This leaves the proactive L&D practitioner with the need to market the function in order to maximize L&D's impact and justify its continued existence. This raises the question of what 'marketing' for L&D actually is. The Chartered Institute of Marketing defines marketing as 'The management process responsible for identifying, anticipating and satisfying customer requirements profitably'. More specifically, this is likely to involve:

- identifying what the customer wants;
- developing products and services to satisfy those wants;
- establishing a price that is consistent with the requirements of the supplier and the perceptions of the customer;
- distributing products and services effectively and efficiently to the customer;
- agreeing on the exchange (i.e. selling) (Hannagan 2002: 94–5).

From an L&D perspective the first two stages in this process may already be familiar from our discussion of needs analysis. However, there is an important and subtle distinction between the language used from our L&D perspective and from the marketing perspective offered above; this distinction is customers' 'wants' (their wishes and desires) and customers' 'needs' (what is required to solve a problem or give some benefit). Perhaps rather than looking at the issue in terms of needs or wants it may be more productive to think of the marketing of L&D in terms of the benefits to be accrued by learners and to organizations, which may involve a shift in mind-set from what can be produced by L&D to what can be sold to clients by L&D (see Hannagan 2002: 95 for the produced-versus-sold distinction). However, the question of wants versus needs still remains, to some extent. A professional dilemma that the L&D practitioner may be faced with is whether he or she provides managers with what they want (and which can be sold to them and from which managers may anticipate benefits) or do L&D practitioners provide managers with what in their professional judgement they need (the benefits of which may not yet be fully appreciated by clients)? One approach to resolving this dilemma is through the notion of partnership between L&D (the supplier) and managers (the clients). Harrison argued that this partnership is one which is concerned more with collaborative working with stakeholders to provide the right kind of products for the organization than with 'branding' and public relations aspects of the marketing process (2002: 201). Two of the precepts of the matrix model described previously were the importance of the client relationship and the partnership between L&D and the client function in meeting business needs.

Walton (1999: 237–50) approaches the issue of marketing L&D from the perspective of the marketing mix, which in an L&D context he argued might consist of:

1. Product (for example, learning materials) or service (a needs analysis or evaluation): Walton argues that it is important to reflect on the attributes and benefits of L&D products and services in terms of their importance to the customer (will they meet a need?) and the customer's perception of them (how well such products have in the past, or might in the future, meet their needs).

2. Promotion: Walton describes this as the process of communicating effectively with existing or potential clients in order to create a favourable image of L&D and its products and services. Promotion of L&D may be through personal selling or advertising to make L&D more visible (1999: 245).

3. Price: based upon Nagle's work on the tactics and strategies of pricing Walton (1999: 248) argued that L&D practitioners need to be aware of a number of issues that may influence the sensitivity of clients to the price of L&D products and services: (a) buyers become less price sensitive the more distinctive a product is (unique value effect), the more difficult it is to make a direct comparison (difficult comparison effect) and the lower the expenditure is as a proportion of income or budget (total expenditure effect); (b) buyers become more price sensitive as they become more aware of substitute products (substitute awareness effect).

4. Place: it is important that L&D products and services are available to clients (managers) and learners. Efforts at implementing flexible and technology-based learning (e-learning) are one attempt to provide an L&D product or service that is sensitive to the wants and needs of clients in terms of place.

The partnership approach to L&D should take account of this mix but also at a more general level ought to configure L&D in such a way that it supports the achievements of business goals in order that L&D is seen as a core activity which can contribute to the core competence of learning. Harrison suggested that a marketing plan for L&D that takes this strategic perspective must:

1. Specify how L&D fits in the organization value chain (the collection of activ- ities used to design, produce, market, deliver and support the company's product or service; Porter 1985).
2. Indicate how L&D will work collaboratively with clients to explore their needs and how they may be met in pursuit of overall business goals (see Figure 2.14 for an example of this).
3. Show the value added of its products and services and how they will be the most appropriate and cost effective to meet the identified need.
4. Indicate in operational terms how the products and services offered by L&D will be implemented, monitored and evaluated (2002: 201).

PERSPECTIVE FROM PRACTICE: MARKETING e-LEARNING AT LUBRIZOL FLUID TECHNOLOGY WORLDWIDE

Based on the following source: B. Mosher, 2003. Marketing enterprise learning, *Chief Learning Officer*, November 2003: 24–8.

Lubrizol provides high-performance chemicals, systems and support serv- ices but has a workforce that is geographically dispersed. To meet the L&D needs of its workforce, Lubrizol used e-learning (using computers and com- munications technology to deliver and facilitate learning online). Lubrizol recognized that to be successful, its e-learning project had to be marketed in the right way. To do this the company:

1. Created quiet spaces where people could learn and made e-learning available to employees from home and work all day, every day (i.e. 24/7).
2. Identified a group of pioneer users, who tested the products before final roll-out and who also became advocates for the new e-learning system in order to create local ownership.
3. Linked the e-learning to wider organizational initiatives and projects such as new product roll-outs and the introduction of organization-wide ethics policies.
4. Promoted the new system with presentations as well as gimmicks such as mouse mats and screen savers.

In spite of the reported successes of the project, Lubrizol also recognized that barriers still exist in the areas of cultural differences (some countries accepted e-learning more readily), individual differences (some learners were better at self-study than others) and the workload pressures on middle managers that limited the extent to which this key group could champion and implement the project.

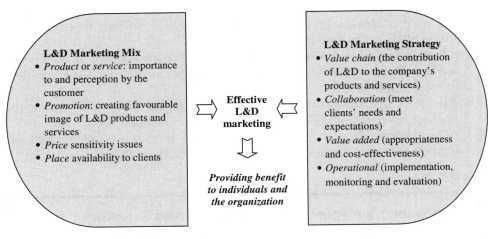

Figure 2.14   A marketing strategy/marketing mix for L&D

Discussion Point

Which aspects of the marketing mix/strategy mix outlined above were present in Lubrizol? Where did deficiencies appear to exist in their marketing approach?

COSTS OF L&D

The costs and benefits of L&D will be discussed when we examine the issue of evaluation (see Chapter 9). However, the issue of costs more broadly is worthy of a brief consideration in our discussion of the management of L&D. One of the themes that runs through this book is the relationship between learning and working, and more specifically between informal learning (such as that which occurs in the workplace) and formal learning (such as that which occurs away from the workplace in planned, formalized L&D activities, for example training courses or developmental programmes for managers). The former should not be perceived as a zero-cost option; both the informal and formal approaches have associated costs, which Reid and Barrington (1999: 192–3) summarized thus:

Informal learning: incurs costs related to payments to employees whilst learning on the job, the costs of less than optimal performance during learning (for example, wastage, lower output, mistakes and so forth), additional supervision and management costs, etc.

Formal learning: the costs associated include: (a) people costs, e.g. instructor costs, downtime costs, fees, travel, subsistence accommodation, etc.; (b) equipment and materials costs, for example computers, consumables, tools, learning resources, etc.; (c) administration costs, for example office costs, setting-up and running administrative systems, premises, etc.

Furthermore, costs may be fixed (such as the costs of salaries for L&D staff) or variable according to the project (such as materials and equipment). As far as L&D is concerned, there are a number of cost-related issues that L&D practitioners need to be mindful of:

1. The hidden costs of carrying out L&D, especially through informal and work-place methods.
2. The potential costs of not meeting identified L&D needs in both tangible and intangible terms.
3. The opportunity costs of alternative activities that must be given up if L&D is to be undertaken and the interference costs (i.e. of disrupting work patterns) (Reid and Barrington 1999: 199).
4. The development of a clear L&D plan that is linked to organizational goals, thereby providing a strategic justification for L&D projects.
5. The priorities attached to different L&D needs and the recognition that in the real world it may not be possible to meet every need.
6. The inclusion of the costs of evaluation in project budgets (otherwise evaluation may be glossed over at the end of a project or left out altogether).

L&D FACTS AND FIGURES

The 2004 American Society for Training and Development (ASTD) survey revealed that the average annual expenditure on training per employee across a broad cross-section of US organizations was $820. The same survey revealed that across a broad cross-section of US organizations the average amount of payroll invested in training was 2.52 per cent. (*Source*: ASTD State of the Industry Report 2004.)

The basis upon which the L&D function within an organization is configured is also important from a budgeting point of view; for example, if the L&D function operates as a cost-recovery centre (i.e. full recovery of the financial costs of L&D projects by re-charging internal client departments), or as a profit centre (i.e. operating more like an independent organization that sells its services to internal and external clients in competition with external providers). Carliner (2004) described each of these models thus:

1. Internal profit centre: offers a wide range of L&D products and services, reports to an internal manager or executive and funded either by charging for participation in classroom-based activities (a cost recovery fee) or on a project-by-project basis, but expected to generate a profit. The market arrangements within the organization may be such that potential internal clients may have the choice of whether or not to use the internal profit centre. As far as the L&D practitioner is concerned issues of marketing, the marketing mix and price sensitivity issues are likely to be to the fore in such a scenario.
2. Internal cost centre: provide training courses and related learning design services along with performance consulting. Reporting arrangements may be to an L&D or HR manager or executive where the group is centralized within corporate L&D or corporate HR, or in the decentralized model the group reports to the area that they serve (such as manufacturing for manufacturing L&D). Finance may be through the form of an internal levy in proportion to the amount of the L&D group's services that will be drawn upon (for example if engineering uses 20 per cent of the L&D services it pays 20 per cent of the budget). The cost centre operates from a position of power and departments may not have a choice of L&D provider (Carliner 2004: 285).

In an entrepreneurial or intrapreneurial culture the shift from cost centre to a profit centre may be seen as a revitalizing and incentivizing move since it may give tighter controls, enhance efficiency, provide a 'layoff defence' and a way to keep organizations customer-focused (Zeinstra 2004: 32).

L&D FACTS AND FIGURES

The UK's *Learning and Training at Work* survey, published in 2002, reported that 60 per cent of respondents had a training plan and 46 per cent had a training budget. There were wide variations between the smallest employers and the largest ones. (*Source*: Learning and training at work 2002, Department for Education and Skills SFR 02/2003.)

PERSPECTIVE FROM PRACTICE: SECURING A TRAINING BUDGET

Based on the following source: $9^1/_2$ Steps to winning training budgets, *IOMA Report on Managing Training & Development*, August 2002: 10–14.

The competition for financial resources within an organization can sometimes be fierce. In those environments in which L&D is perceived as peripheral a strong justification is sometimes required for the allocation of financial resources to L&D projects. IOMA (Institute of Management and Administration, New York) offer some simple rules of thumb for practitioners to help them in their attempts to secure financial resources for L&D from senior managers and executives. To be successful in this L&D practitioners are likely to need two types of knowledge and skill:

- analytical skills in the basics of finance;
- process skills in communicating the needs for an L&D budget and negotiating the best deal possible (since power, people and politics are likely to be important factors).

Some of the necessary skills in these two domains are summarized in Table 2.5.

L&D FACTS AND FIGURES

The UK's Chartered Institute of Personnel and Development's (CIPD) Annual Training Survey 2004 found that the average training budget was £156,667 for government/non-profit organizations ($N = 45$), £473,656 for public-sector organizations ($N = 81$) and £672,484 for private-sector organizations ($N = 194$). (*Source*: Training and Development 2004: Survey Report (April 2004). London: CIPD.)

Table 2.5   Analytical and process skills for L&D budgeting (based on IOMA 2002)

Analytical skills	Process skills
Formulating clear goals and objectives that speak directly to managers: for example, 'The L&D project will result in enhanced customer satisfaction.'	*Identify a project 'champion'*: for example, get a senior person on board with the project; 'sound out' their support early on.
Specifying realistic and deliverable metrics: for example, 'The L&D project will reduce production line errors by 5 per cent.'	*Communicate* the project effectively, for example by:
Inputs and resources: for example, clear specification of the people, equipment and finance required to deliver on the metrics.	<ul><li>showing the big picture;</li><li>outlining a number of possible cost options;</li><li>give evidence of past successes;</li></ul>
Being realistic about the parameters: for example, identify factors that might drive the project off course.	<ul><li>specify the results clearly and unambiguously;</li><li>assure clients of L&D's expertise, competence and professionalism;</li></ul>
Time-scales: for example: set a realistic delivery date and stick to it.	<ul><li>be realistic and credible.</li></ul>

Conclusion: Evaluating Learning at the Strategic Level – A Balanced Scorecard Approach

A consistent feature of the models of strategic L&D that were presented earlier in the chapter was a commitment to evaluation. It is with this issue that we conclude our discussions of L&D and strategy. Evaluation of L&D (which is treated in more detail Chapter 9) more often than not focuses upon the operational level of analysis. However, one of the potential problems with this approach is that it may be at too fine a level of resolution, with the risk that the bigger picture may be inadvertently overlooked. Analytical tools are required that enable organizations to examine the extent to which L&D has had a strategic impact (traditional frameworks do tend to focus on the 'results' level of analysis) and which enable managers to understand and evaluate the links between L&D practices and the organization's strategy. Within a framework of strategic L&D there is a need to ask the question 'What has been the strategic impact of L&D?' In this regard Walton (1999: 47) discussed the use of the balanced scorecard as a means to evaluate business strategy; he considered it to be especially relevant in an L&D perspective since it gives particular emphasis to individual and collective learning.

The balanced scorecard approach was developed and popularized in the 1990s in an attempt to suggest ways of reshaping strategic management. One of the central tenets of the balanced scorecard approach as put forward by Kaplan and Norton (1996; 2001) is that it is executed strategy that is most important. To put it another way: poor execution is a limiting factor on any strategy and, moreover, good implementation of a well-formulated strategy is rare (Boxall and Purcell 2003: 235–6). The traditional balanced scorecard has four elements:

1. Financial: this is concerned with the question of 'to succeed financially how should we appear to our shareholders?'
2. Customers: 'to achieve our vision, how should we appear to our customers?'
3. Internal business processes: 'to satisfy our shareholders and customers, what business processes must we excel at?'
4. Learning and growth: 'to achieve our vision, how will we sustain our ability to change and improve?' (from: Kaplan and Norton 1996, in Boxall and Purcell 2003: 236).

It is the fourth element that is of the greatest significance to the L&D practitioner, firstly because it flags up the significance of L&D in the strategic development of an organization, but secondly it gives macro-level pointers to what the organizational level L&D needs might be. Indeed, Kaplan and Norton describe the learning and growth strategy in terms of the strategic skills and knowledge required by the workforce to support the strategy, which itself may be allied to:

1. The strategic technologies (and recall that these can produce discontinuities), which themselves may surface L&D needs.

2. Climate for action, which embraces the cultural shifts needed to motivate, empower and align the workforce to achieve the business' goals.

Kaplan and Norton asserted that the learning and growth strategy of an organization is the starting point for sustainable long-term change. Each element (1–4 above) may be articulated in terms of four criteria: objectives, measures, targets and initiatives.

L&D need not be confined to the learning and growth aspect of the scorecard since the other strategic perspectives may themselves have L&D implications. For example, how the company appears to customers may raise issues related to customer service L&D; what processes the company excels at may raise operational L&D issues, and so on. This type of analysis is a comprehensive and powerful tool for articulating the strategic learning needs, but more than that it enables a specification of L&D outcomes that need to be achieved if the strategy is to be successfully implemented (recall that it is the implementation of a strategy which imposes an upper limit on its effectiveness). The ways in which these issues might be integrated into a balanced scorecard approach are illustrated in Table 2.6. The shaded regions represent areas where L&D strategy and planning may make an input, and represents one means by which L&D may be aligned with overall strategy and organizational goals.

Table 2.6 The balanced scorecard approach applied to L&D (adapted from Kaplan and Norton 1992, 1996, 2001; Walton 1999: 47). *Note*: shaded area represents L&D contribution to process

Our vision of the future is:				
If our vision succeeds, how will we differ in terms of:	*Shareholder perspective*	*Customer perspective*	*Internal business processes*	*Learning and growth*
The critical success factors are:				
The critical measurements are:				
The learning needs that have to be met to support the achievement of these measured targets are:				
We will know these learning needs have been met when:				

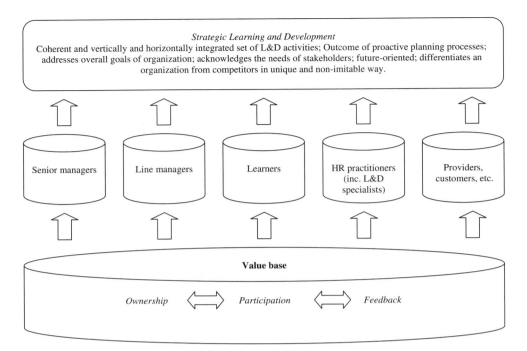

Figure 2.15   Strategic learning and development

This type of evaluation takes a very top-level view with a particular emphasis upon the vision and strategy of the organization and how this may be achieved. As was noted earlier, evaluation is a feature that is common to a number of the models of strategic L&D; what has been suggested here is a means of analysis at this strategic level. The concept of strategic L&D in terms of the value base (ownership, participation and feedback) that underpins the actions of the internal stakeholders (senior managers, line managers, learners and L&D specialists) and external stakeholders (for example, providers of L&D and customers) is summarized in Figure 2.15.

Table 2.7 presents an audit tool that may be used with specialized audiences to assess the extent to which L&D in an organization is perceived as having a strategic orientation ('strongly agree' scores five, 'strongly disagree' scores one: tick one response for each item and sum the scores to give a total out of 100). The wording of the items is such that this questionnaire should be used *only* with a specialized audience, such as L&D or HR practitioners. It can be used as an audit of the degree to which specialists perceive L&D in an organization to be strategic. A high score indicates a more strategic approach to L&D. The questionnaire contains a mix of positively and negatively worded items – note that the negative items (i.e. the non-strategic ones) are reverse-scored ('strongly disagree' scores five, 'strongly agree' scores one).

Table 2.7 Auditing strategic L&D. *Note*: Items 2, 3, 7, 8, 9, 11, 12, 13, 14, 19 and 20 are reverse scored

Question	Strongly disagree	Disagree	Neutral	Agree	Strongly agree
1. There is active commitment to, and shared ownership of, L&D from managers and other employees.	☐	☐	☐	☐	☐
2. Critical self-reflection and analysis are lacking in this organization.	☐	☐	☐	☐	☐
3. There are numerous, unconnected and fragmented L&D initiatives in this organization.	☐	☐	☐	☐	☐
4. L&D activities in this organization support the strategic intent of the business.	☐	☐	☐	☐	☐
5. L&D in this organization is integrated with other HR activities.	☐	☐	☐	☐	☐
6. L&D activities in this organization are the outcome of a proactive planning process.	☐	☐	☐	☐	☐
7. L&D in this organization is reactive and lacking in longer-term focus.	☐	☐	☐	☐	☐
8. L&D in this organization is subject to 'fad and fashion'.	☐	☐	☐	☐	☐
9. L&D is supplier-driven (often by people selecting from training course brochures).	☐	☐	☐	☐	☐
10. L&D practices in this organization help us to stand out from the competition.	☐	☐	☐	☐	☐
11. Managers in this organization act without reference to stakeholders' views and needs.	☐	☐	☐	☐	☐
12. Managers and L&D practitioners in this organization 'do their own thing', often independently of what anyone else is doing.	☐	☐	☐	☐	☐

Table 2.7 *Continued.*

Question	Strongly disagree	Disagree	Neutral	Agree	Strongly agree
13. Managers in this organization fail to act on the basis of acknowledged 'best practice' in L&D.	☐	☐	☐	☐	☐
14. There is duplication of effort in L&D in this organization.	☐	☐	☐	☐	☐
15. There is openness of communication within and beyond the organization.	☐	☐	☐	☐	☐
16. On the whole L&D practitioners in this organization adopt a proactive role.	☐	☐	☐	☐	☐
17. There is a culture and climate in this organization that supports and enables learning and development.	☐	☐	☐	☐	☐
18. Planning processes in this organization take account of the integration of L&D with the organizational mission.	☐	☐	☐	☐	☐
19. There are competing political agendas in this organization which are self-serving and defensive.	☐	☐	☐	☐	☐
20. There is little which encourages the surfacing and sharing of knowledge between different factions and stakeholders in this organization.	☐	☐	☐	☐	☐

Concept Checklist

Can you now define each of the Key Concepts listed below, and are you now able to achieve the other Knowledge Outcomes specified at the beginning of the chapter?

- Core competence
- Strategic human resource management (SHRM)

- Resource-based view (RBV)
- HR goals
- External fit and internal fit
- Needed behaviours
- Performance management
- L&D strategy and strategic L&D
- Vertical alignment and horizontal integration
- Stakeholders
- Balanced scorecard approach
- Systematic approach (needs identification; needs analysis; learning design; implementation; evaluation)
- Systems approach
- Inputs and outputs
- L&D roles and responsibilities
- L&D function
- Outsourcing
- L&D marketing mix
- L&D costs and budgets
- Profit centre and cost center

CHAPTER 3
Individual Learning and Development

Key Concepts

Behaviourism; classical conditioning; objectives; assimilation; accommodation; cognitive (information processing) theory; short-term memory; working memory; long-term memory; schema; cognitive load theory (CLT); episodic LTM; semantic LTM; insight; cognitive schema theory (CST); limbic system; social learning theory; modelling; self-efficacy; motivation; goal-setting theory; reciprocal determination; situated learning; cognitive social interpretations; andragogical model of learning; experiential learning theory (ELT); learning transfer; identical elements; transfer through principles; transfer climate

---

Knowledge Outcomes

After studying this chapter you should be able to:

- define each of the key concepts listed above;
- distinguish between behaviourist, cognitive and social learning theories;
- explain the concepts of situated learning and legitimate peripheral participation;
- explain the significance of schemas and schema change in individual and collective learning;

- describe the main features of the andragogical and experiential models and their significance for L&D;
- synthesize practical approaches to L&D that are based upon relevant theories of learning;
- critically evaluate the various concepts, models and theories presented in the chapter.

Introduction

Learning depends at least in part on conditions similar to those created in the studios and conservatories: freedom to learn by doing in a setting relatively low in risk, with access to coaches who initiate students into the 'traditions of the calling' and help them, by 'the right kind of telling', to see on their own behalf and in their own way what they need most to see.

Donald A. Schon, *Educating the Reflective Practitioner*

Homo sapiens is the learning species par excellence. More so than any other organism we are able to adapt to our environments and adapt our environments in spectacular ways to maximize our chances of surviving and thriving. Through learning individually and collectively humans are able to devise ways to solve problems, make decisions and engage in creative acts which allow us to meet our needs from the very basics of food, warmth and shelter through to our higher-order needs for accomplishment and self-fulfilment. In organizational life in the twenty-first century employees more than ever are being required to work smarter, make important decisions in fast-moving environments, learn and work collectively and collaboratively, solve problems in a complex and uncertain world and at the same time connect with their own innate needs for self-esteem, self-expression and self-worth. As far as L&D is concerned, a study of the ways in which human beings learn in organizations is essential for at least two reasons:

1. Theoretical reasons: deepening our understanding of the ways in which humans learn. L&D as an eclectic field of research and practice should endeavour to be theoretically comprehensive and coherent as well as methodologically sound.
2. Practical reasons: applying knowledge in order to make learning more effective both for individual employees and organizations as part of a broader project to make working life more productive and meaningful. L&D, as an applied field of study, should endeavour to be relevant as well as aspiring at the same time to being theoretically and methodologically rigorous.

For the L&D practitioner an understanding of the concepts and theories that underpin learning at the individual and collective levels is a key element of the knowledge that underpins professional competence and is a prerequisite for improved professional practice. Without theories of learning or with an over-

reliance on a single theory there is the danger that L&D practices may become isolated acts devoid of a rich conceptual explanation of how and why such practices
lead to the observed outcomes (see Ulrich 1997). The aim of this chapter is to:

1. Examine the concept of learning at the individual unit of analysis.
2. Explore some of the theories that psychologists and others over the past
   hundred years or so have used in order to explain how humans acquire new
   knowledge and skills.
3. Discuss how such an understanding can shed light on the process of learning
   in organizations, and ultimately on if and how learning can be managed more
   effectively and its outcomes improved.

In Chapter 5 we will examine the equally important issue of collective learning,
i.e. the creation and acquisition of knowledge at the supra-individual (for
example, group and organizational) levels.

L&D FACTS AND FIGURES

The UK's Chartered Institute of Personnel and Development's (CIPD)
Annual Training Survey 2004 found that 56 per cent of respondents agreed
or strongly agreed that people learn primarily through training whereas 24
per cent of respondents agreed or strongly agreed that training is not particularly effective at promoting learning. (*Source*: Training and Development
2004: Survey Report (April 2004). London: CIPD.)

L&D Theories and Models

In this chapter we will consider a number of theories of learning, principally from
the discipline of psychology. However, before embarking upon this it will be
worth saying a few words about concepts and theories in L&D. Many of the theories that inform practice in L&D draw upon learning-related research in the field
of psychology, including cognitive psychology, developmental psychology, clinical psychology, educational psychology, social psychology and organizational
behaviour, as well as those emergent fields such as evolutionary psychology and
cognitive neuroscience. As was noted in Chapter 1, concepts from other social
science base disciplines such as economics and sociology also underpin L&D, but
since our concern in this chapter is with individual learning per se the psychological view is to the fore. With this in mind a number of primary theories can be
distinguished in the field of L&D, for example: behaviourist theory; cognitive
information processing theory; social learning theory and so forth. In addition
there are a number of higher-order models or theories that draw upon and synthesize various theories such as cognitive information processing theory and
social learning theories (and their underpinning concepts) to provide workable

models of the learning process (for example, the experiential model), or knowledge of the conditions which may promote learning (for example, the andragogical model). This knowledge may then be used to directly inform the practice of L&D in the workplace. Furthermore, there are a number of areas of actionable knowledge that do not fit neatly into any of these theories or models but instead draw upon them and are of direct relevance to the day-to-day practice of L&D. These areas of actionable knowledge are not mutually exclusive and include applications such as instructional design, which synthesizes cognitive information processing, aspects of behaviourism and social learning theory as well as concepts from the andragogical learning model. The relationships between the various disciplines, theories and models are shown in Figure 3.1.

The various theories, models and actionable knowledge, and the associated concepts, principles and frameworks, have a useful contribution to make to L&D research and practice. However, each presents only a partial insight into human learning in the workplace, and to appreciate L&D as a field of practice demands an eclectic and integrated approach across a variety of perspectives. We will now turn our attention to a more detailed discussion of a selection of theories that may be used to inform our understanding of L&D and the ways in which it is practised in organizations. No one theory of itself provides a complete and compre-

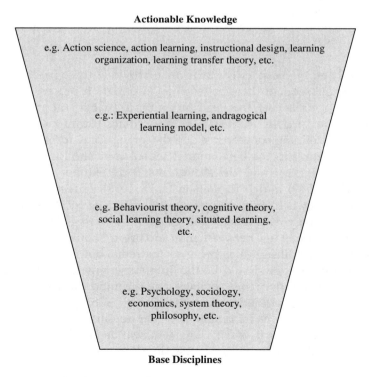

Figure 3.1 Some of the disciplines, theories and models that underpin actionable knowledge in L&D practice

hensive explanation of learning in the workplace; some are of more historical interest than others (such as behaviourism), and some may not sit all that comfortably alongside each other, but nevertheless each has its own unique insights, historical relevance and practical utility from an L&D perspective.

Behaviourist Theories of Learning

For the first half of the twentieth century, and prior to the 'cognitive revolution' of the 1960s, theories of learning in the training and development (T&D) literature as it was then known tended to be dominated by behaviourism. Behaviourism is important historically but also its influence can still be felt in some limited aspects of L&D practice. Behaviourism in its educational manifestation frames the learning process as the communication of predetermined, presequenced information to learners with feedback, reinforcement and remediation (Borthick et al. 2003). Amongst the fundamental assumptions of behaviourism were:

1. Much of human behaviour is determined by factors outside of the person, and thoughts, feelings and intentions play little role in determining what we do.
2. Humans are biological machines that react to stimuli.
3. Learning cannot be observed directly but only inferred from behaviour (Gregory 1987).

Whilst in L&D and many other contexts the first two of these precepts have been superseded by subsequent theories (such as information processing theory and other cognitive approaches), the third precept is arguably still influential and of practical utility in L&D in areas such as prescribing learning outcomes in performance terms, defining competence and designing some forms of assessment.

The leading figures in the behaviourist school were the Russian physiologist Ivan Pavlov (1849–1936) and the Americans B. F. Skinner (1904–2001), E. L. Thorndike (1874–1949) and J. B. Watson (1878–1958). Indeed, the behaviourist school in psychology is seen by many as being instigated by Watson in 1913 with his paper, 'Psychology as the behaviourist views it' (Gregory 1987). His views (such as that no dividing line between 'man and brute' should be recognized) were seen by some of his colleagues as being too extreme, but nevertheless his declaration was that behaviour should be the only subject matter of psychology and that a study of introspection, consciousness and the mind was likely to prove fruitless. Similarly, other behaviourists such as Skinner (1938) and Hull (1943) considered human processes to be automatic and that any higher-order cognition, if it was present at all in the form of consciousness, was an epiphenomenon of behaviour and feelings, that is, not a cause of actions but a mere consequence (Kirsch et al. 2004).

The antecedent of much of this is to be seen in Pavlov's work, which began in the 1870s on the physiology of digestion and specifically the reflex action of salivation. The earlier stages of this work were founded on the incidental observations of what was termed 'psychic' salivation wherein a dog would begin to produce saliva not by being fed, but merely by the stimulus of the presence of the food container or the human attendant who normally carried out the feeding. The essence of the subsequent work is that after experiencing a number of pairings of a stimulus, for example a bell tone, and a reinforcer, for example food, the dogs salivated to the bell tone stimulus as they did to the food stimulus. An important point to note about classical conditioning is that it explains passive or reflexive learning and hence is limited in the extent to which it can explain human learning since it is concerned primarily with biological reflexes. It was dissatisfaction with the over-reliance upon the reflex that led Skinner to develop the notion that the passive response of organisms to the environment was not explanation enough (Gregory 1987). It seemed to Skinner that through its behaviour an organism can also be active in operating on the environment to generate consequences. For example, an animal learning to press a lever to obtain food is in effect operating upon its environment (an experimental apparatus) to generate an outcome (Gregory 1987: 73). Key concepts from operant conditioning are:

1. Reinforcement, defined as the means by which the probability of the organism behaving in a desired way may be increased by positive reinforcement, in which the organism is rewarded (for example, with food) for a particular response (for example, for pressing a lever), or negative reinforcement, in which the organism may act to remove an aversive stimulus in a way that results in increased frequency (strengthening) of a particular behaviour.
2. Negative reinforcement should not be confused with punishment: the latter is intended to eliminate particular behaviours through punishment by application (the administering of an adverse stimulus following undesirable behaviour) or punishment by removal (removal of a positive reinforcer following undesirable behaviour).
3. The use of reinforcers is a means by which animal behaviour can be shaped in successive small steps; for example, Skinner 'taught' pigeons to play a rudimentary form of ping-pong.

Whilst classical conditioning has limited applications in L&D because it is concerned with reflexes, some elements of operant conditioning arguably were evident in aspects of practice such as the design of programmed learning materials (which was one of the forerunners of 'self-teach' books and manuals, open learning packages, computer-based learning and e-learning). In programmed learning the learning sequence was shaped in a series of small steps, with checks on learning (behaviour) at each stage and immediate reinforcement (in the form of praise for a correct answer, for example 'That's correct. Well done', and feedback on a wrong answer, such as 'That's not quite correct, did you think to . . .?') as a response to the learning. Many open learning or distance learning materials display similar features.

L&D FACTS AND FIGURES

The concept of 'behaviourism' was introduced by John Broadus Watson (1878–1958) as a reaction against the techniques of introspection that were prevalent in psychology at the time. Watson's interest was in the study of objective and tangible entities such as the relationships between visible stimuli and visible responses, and for this reason behaviourist psychology is sometimes referred to as 'stimulus-response psychology'. (*Source*: A. Huczynski and D. Buchanan, 2001. *Organizational Behaviour: An Introductory Text*. Harlow: Pearson, p. 113.)

Some elements of behaviourism have a powerful appeal in explaining aspects of human learning and behaviour (such as reinforcement); however, behaviourism has severe limitations in a number of respects. Some have argued that the lower levels of learning, such as the acquisition of factual knowledge, could, with sufficient patience, be learned through some form of operant conditioning in a programmed learning fashion (small steps, feedback and reinforcement) (Rollinson and Broadfield 2002: 180). The shaping aspect of Skinnerian behaviourism fails to take into account sufficiently the intentions, feelings, motives and desires of the learner. This provocative but simplistic behaviourist conception of learning 'crumbles' in the face of the realities of learning in the classroom and workplace, where the individual is a 'purposeful participant in the making of knowledge and is a social being whose purposes and strategies are influenced by what he or she perceives' in her or his social and organizational environment (Rowntree 1982: 16).

Objectives in L&D

Learning outcomes, usually phrased as 'objectives', loom large in L&D practice (for example, it might not be untypical for a time management training course to begin with a statement such as, 'By the end of this course you will be able to manage your time more effectively') and also in education in general (for example, 'By the end of this chapter you will be able to describe and explain the major theories that underpin L&D practice'). Behaviourism is arguably one theory (along with goal-setting theory) that underpins the use of learning objectives (they are sometimes even called 'behavioural objectives' because they specify what the learner will be able to do after learning has taken place – the so-called 'terminal performance'). One potential source of tension in the use of behavioural objectives is the various dimensions of individual difference that can exist between learners which strict behaviourism can overlook. For example, people can differ in terms of the rate at which they learn, the methods they prefer to learn by and the ways in which they think and process information. The use of performance statements that specify outcomes in very precise terms may fail to take into account these differences.

Tennant (1988) argued that not all learning outcomes are specifiable in behavioural terms and he cited Bruner's notions of specific transfer (for example, the behaviour of hammering nails in one context transfers readily to another, which holds with simple behaviourism) and non-specific transfer, or the transfer of principles that consist of general and widely applicable ideas that are difficult to specify in terms of terminal performance (because they are a high level of abstraction). Furthermore, the conditions under which they will be performed can vary greatly because the more abstract abilities are broad areas of human capability that are difficult to define in narrow behaviourist terms (Bruner 1957).

From the broad array of theory that contributes to our understanding of learning the L&D practitioner has to be able to select those elements that are both theoretically sound ('do they make sense?') and have practical utility ('do they work?'). In spite of their limitations behavioural approaches do appear to have some value for L&D practice. People's behaviour (what they say or do) is often the kind of evidence that is permissible in workplaces that are concerned with performance. Employees' behaviours and actions may be the only evidence that managers have to hand as to what an employee knows or thinks (as it is not possible to access their minds directly).

Skinner is said to have declared provocatively that, 'The question is not whether machines think, but whether men [sic] do.' In a response to this, Pinker (1997: 62) argued that stimulus-response theory turned out to be wrong because it failed to take into account human beings' desires and beliefs. He argued that what does predict behaviour, and predict it well, are our beliefs which are, admittedly, related to the stimuli in the environment but in a somewhat tortuous and circuitous way that is mediated by perceptions and conceptions about the world and the way it works:

> In our daily lives we all predict and explain other people's behaviour from what we think they know and what we think they want. Beliefs and desires are the explanatory tools of our own *intuitive psychology*, and intuitive psychology is still the most useful and complete science of behaviour there is. (1997: 63, emphasis added)

In spite of these problems, the emphasis accorded to behavioural objectives in theories of instructional design (Gagné and Briggs 1974; Mager 1984; Gagné 1985) has been an important element of L&D practice over the past 40 years or so. By expressing what we would like the learner to be able to do or to say, and by inferring what lies behind their actions or words (written or spoken) we are, as L&D practitioners, in a better position to be able to assess the extent to which learning has taken place (Rowntree 1982: 16). We are also in a better position to be able to present evidence for this to managers and the organization. However, we should not allow our thinking to be dominated by this approach since difficult to articulate and codify knowledge is as important as overt behaviours in many learning situations.

Discussion Point

Stop and reflect upon what you have learned from reading thus far in this chapter. What can you now do as a result of what you have learned? (For example, you may be able to list the base disciplines that underpin L&D – what else can you actually now do that you couldn't do before?) How valuable do you feel a behaviourist approach is in this regard?

PERSPECTIVE FROM PRACTICE: PREPARING LEARNING OBJECTIVES – VIEWS FROM THE USA AND THE UK

Based on the following sources: R. F. Mager, 1984, *Preparing Instructional Objectives*, Belmont, CA: David S. Lake Publishers; D. Rowntree, 1990, *Teaching through Self-Instruction*, London: Kogan Page; G. Sanderson, 1995, Objectives and evaluation. In S. Truelove (ed.), *The Handbook of Training and Development*, Oxford: Blackwell.

An important skill for the L&D practitioner is the ability to specify learning outcomes, since these are key deliverables of the needs assessment phase of the L&D cycle. It is often the case that such outcomes need to be expressed in terms that are amenable to assessment. One way of specifying outcomes that are readily assessable is by stipulating terminal (in the sense of 'at the end') performance, i.e. what the learner will be able to do after learning takes place. Often it may be tempting to specify a learning outcome in terms of broad phrases such as, 'by the end of this course the learners will be able to understand theories of learning', or 'upon completion of this module learners will appreciate the learning theories that underpin L&D practice'. But the question then arises of how would we know if the learner 'understood' or 'appreciated', especially if we were faced with the task of assessing if learning had actually occurred and were required to produce some form of objective evidence in this regard?

One answer to this question is that we might ask the learners to 'describe the main learning theories' or 'explain the main learning theories'. If more precise performance terms such as 'describe' or 'explain' are used, vague abstract words like 'understand' or 'appreciate' become redundant. The difference lies in the fact that 'describe' and 'explain' are verbs ('doing' words); we could actually observe someone 'describing' or 'explaining' (for example, they could write or speak a description or explanation). The learner's ability to describe or explain could be taken as an indicator of understanding or appreciation (the latter may reflect the teacher's or trainer's aims but they are not observable performances on the part of the learner). Mager (1984: 29) makes a distinction between:

- 'doing' words (these are performances) such as 'solving'; and
- 'being' words (these are abstractions) such as 'understand'.

An important part of the L&D planning process is the specification of learning outcomes or learning objectives. The key to specifying these in behavioural terms is for the L&D practitioner to ask herself or himself the question, 'Does the objective I have written specify a state of being or a performance?' – in other words, 'Could I observe someone doing it?' From a behaviourist stance performances (which are open to fewer interpretations) are to be favoured when writing objectives over abstractions (which are open to many interpretations). A number of writers have produced useful lists of words that may be used when writing learning objectives (for example, Mager 1984; Rowntree 1990; Sanderson 1995). Table 3.1 summarizes some of these. A complementary approach is to formulate so-called SMART objectives (**s**pecific or **s**tretch; **m**easurable; **a**greed or **a**chievable; **r**ealistic; and **t**ime-bound).

It should be noted that in contrast to the dominance of the behaviourists in North America, in Europe the gestalt psychologists, including Max Wertheimer (1880–1943) and Wolfgang Kohler (1887–1967), had not abandoned the study of the mind. Their study of phenomena such as insight problem solving examined and proposed theories about the structural relationships in mental processes. Also in Europe the Swiss psychologist Jean Piaget (1896–1980) pioneered the study of cognitive development in children and the notion of the dynamic development of the mind wherein the learner is seen as an active explorer of the world through

Table 3.1 Examples of performances and abstractions for use in the specification of learning outcomes/objectives and aims

Performances (useful for writing objectives)	Abstractions (useful for writing aims)
Draw; Label; List; Name; Recall; Recite; State; Select; Write down	Appreciate; Be aware of; Believe; Comprehend; Know; Understand
Describe; Distinguish between; Explain; Summarize	
Apply; Carry out; Construct; Demonstrate; Operate; Repair; Solve	
Analyse; Integrate; Synthesize Assess; Critique; Evaluate	

assimilation (modification of perceptual inputs by existing knowledge structures) and accommodation (modification of knowledge structures to adapt to the input). Other later developments in Europe and the USA, including advances in cybernetics, the invention of the first digital computer and the recognition that there was what appeared to be at the time striking similarities between the way computers and the human brain process information, paved the way for cognitivism. These developments and others led to the 'rehabilitation of the mind' in psychology (Johnson-Laird 1988: 23) and are sometimes referred to as the 'cognitive revolution'.

Cognitive (Information Processing) Approaches to Learning

The development of cognitive psychology can be seen in some ways as a reaction against the behaviourists' view that the study of the processes of the mind was likely to prove fruitless. To the behaviourists the mind was a 'ghost in the machine' and what was important for an objective, scientific psychology was the study of behaviour and its prediction and control. Behaviourism could explain performance on predetermined tasks, but it was 'silent on explaining conceptual change in learners' (Borthick et al. 2003: 108). Hence, one of the problems with this approach was the lack of explanatory power. A scientific psychology should aim to explain phenomena as well as describe them in ways that invoke no more causes than are needed to account for observable facts (that is, by means of parsimonious laws) (Johnson-Laird 1988: 18). Unlike research that attempted to outline general laws which described learning based on principles of conditioning, cognitive psychology attempted to explain learning in terms of memory and the associated cognitive processes. This required an information processing model to represent the necessary memory structures and memory processes and from which predictions could be made. From a computer-inspired information processing approach the cognitivists viewed learning as the acquisition of knowledge and the development of problem-solving skills that transfer to new tasks and situations (Borthick et al. 2003). How this information processing approach contrasted with the behaviourist position is shown in Figure 3.2. Modern information processing theory focuses on the modelling of general problem-solving capabilities as well as the development of domain-specific expertise and general cognitive architectures (Derry 1996).

Components of Memory

Contemporary theories of human information processing draw upon the work of Broadbent (1958), Norman (1968), Tulving (1972) Baddley and Hitch (1974), Neisser (1976), Anderson (1990) and others. Information processing theories postulate a number of cognitive structures within the brain and a series of corresponding and interrelated cognitive functions. More specifically, such theories

Behavioural

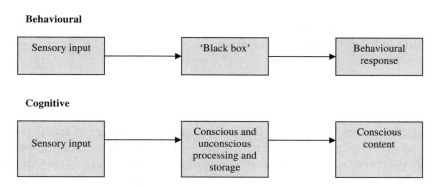

Cognitive

Figure 3.2 Comparison of behavioural and cognitive approaches to mind and behaviour (adapted from Le Doux 1996: 26)

propose that when a stimulation is encountered it is processed firstly in the registration of the event, secondly by its transitory storage in a temporary (short-term memory or working memory) store, and thirdly by its encoding and assimilation into long-term storage. Hence, viewed processually, cognition may be divided into a number of stages:

1. Input processing (i.e. attention and pattern recognition in the sensory register).
2. Temporary storage and active processing (i.e. in a short-term or working memory).
3. Encoding and more-or-less permanent storage (i.e. in long-term memory).
4. Output (i.e. manifested in problem solving, reasoning and language).

The German experimental psychologist Hermann Ebbinghaus (1850–1909) was one of the first modern scientists to attempt to formulate fundamental laws of human memory. Ebbinghaus's research focused on the memorization of nonsense syllables comprising two consonants and a vowel (for example, LAQ). He found that most of the loss of these syllables in a memorization task occurred within the first few minutes after training. Once a memory had got through a crucial early period (in a temporary storage) it appeared to have much more stability, presumably having been transferred to a long-term storage system. The research can be criticized on the grounds that the tasks used were somewhat meaningless (nonsense syllables); nonetheless it represented a step forward in the scientific study of cognition. Classic research by Miller (1956), which may be seen as an extension of Ebbinghaus's work, revealed the capacity of the temporary storage to be restricted to approximately seven items (plus or minus two), giving rise to the classic '7 ± 2 rule' of short-term memory. However, as far as the temporary component of the system is concerned, the idea of short-term memory per se was limiting and has been superseded by the concept of working memory. Short-term memory was conceived of as 'a simple storage component', whereas working memory is 'a system consisting of [a] storage component as well as an attention component' (Engle et al. 1999: 105) and is a more powerful conceptual tool for explaining human information processing.

It was the psychologist Alan Baddeley who in the 1970s reformulated the notion of short-term memory (conceived of as a temporary storage system) with the notion of a more active working memory (a 'workspace'). Hence, working memory may be seen as a more recent theoretical development of the concept of short-term memory. The working memory system, which has a limited (and short-term) capacity, may be modelled as comprising three components: the central executive, and two 'slave' systems, the phonological loop that stores verbal information and the visuo-spatial sketchpad for visual information (see Baddeley and Hitch 1974; Baddeley 1997):

The *central executive* is responsible for control and integration of information from the phonological loop and visuo-spatial sketchpad (Baddeley 1997).
The *working memory* is a mental 'workspace' where our awareness of the present moment resides (indeed some cognitive scientists assert that consciousness itself is the awareness of what is in the working memory).

Rehearsal and simultaneous processing are examples of processes that may take place in this workspace. The components of working memory are shown in Figure 3.3.
    Working memory is defined as being where conscious processing occurs, yet it can hold maybe only two or three novel interacting elements, which is far below

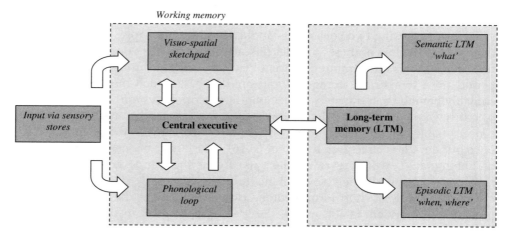

Figure 3.3 Components of a memory system (adapted from Baddeley 1997)

the number that appear to be used in intellectual functioning (Paas et al. 2003). One of the perceived problems with the concept of working memory as it was originally set out is the apparent contradiction that it has limited capacity but can cope with very complex forms of thinking and performance. The paradox is: how can it hold the amount of information needed if its capacity is so limited? Newer conceptualizations of the notion of working memory reject the 'all-or-nothing' storage concept and postulate that information is available to working memory from long-term storage on a gradient with some information at any one time being more available than other information (Woltz 2003: 100).

Some have also argued that the seat of human intellectual skill may not be working memory but rather long-term memory and specifically in relation to the role of schemas. A schema is defined as a cognitive construct that organizes information. Particular schemas may organize information in a variety of ways, for example according to the manner in which it will be dealt with. A problem-solving schema characterizes or represents problems according to solution mode (and so can be used to generate solutions), whereas a schema for 'recognizes an animal' allows us to categorize the animal concerned despite our only seeing some features of it (Sweller and Chandler 1994: 187). Schemas are important firstly because they provide a mechanism for knowledge organization; but secondly, they reduce working memory load by acting as a single (schematic) element (Sweller et al. 1998: 255) that may be drawn upon by the central executive during processing. Some psychologists are of the view that it is possible that most knowledge is encapsulated in schemas.

L&D FACTS AND FIGURES

The duration of the trace of a stimulus in the sensory register is about one second. The duration in short-term (working) memory is between six and 12 seconds and its capacity is about seven items (plus or minus two). The duration in long-term memory is indefinite and its capacity is potentially limitless. (*Source*: Rollinson and Broadfield 2002: 170.)

A further development in theories of working memory has been the concept of cognitive load (the amount of information in working memory at any one time). Some researchers in this area see an important aim of learning design as being the reduction of the cognitive load placed upon the learner's working memory. The temporary storage elements of this system act in a similar way to the buffers in a computer system. The reduction in cognitive load may facilitate more effective encoding of new information into extant schemas and hence into long-term storage. Cognitive information processing theorists argue that one reason schemas are crucial in the learning process is because they reduce the load placed upon the system. Schemas enable us to ignore much of the information that swamps our senses and our limited-capacity working memory, and draw upon our long-term memories and the schemas contained therein (Sweller and Chandler 1994: 226).

One of the aims of effective learning design should be to assist the learner in the construction of schemas, for example by helping learners to build a cognitive architecture based upon experience, prior learning and the like and to which new ideas maybe linked. Cognitive load researchers make a number of suggestions as to how L&D practitioners may go about achieving this aim (see below). The construction of elaborate schemas (which may serve as a single reference point) through extensive experience of, exposure to and immersion in knowledge may represent one way in which the cognitive load placed upon working memory may be reduced. The existence of elaborate schemas may used to account for expert–novice difference, in that experts have a large repertoire of schemas and associated action scripts, which give the impression of effortlessness and an almost intuitive judgement in the execution of a task or decision (Klein 2003).

The recognition or interpretation of a stimulus is determined to a large extent by the repertoire of structural frames or schemas that represent an individual's knowledge of any experience. Our perceptual or recognition processes determine the appropriate schema to which a stimulus can be matched. If there are too many discrepancies, a new schema must be selected or the current one reorganized to accommodate the stimulus (Norman and Bobrow 1975). Each individual will have unique schema for a given concept. For example, the formal definition of 'aircraft' belongs to a more general class of 'modes of transport'; it has properties such as wings and engines; it has similarities to other modes of transport or flying objects (such as birds). However, the personal definition of this schema will link to the individual's past experiences of aircraft and is unlikely to match wholly with that of another person. When we move away from concrete to more abstract concepts like 'culture' or even 'learning', each individual's conceptualization is likely to be quite unique. Moreover, the way in which individuals take action is driven by how they interpret their world (that is, how they perceive it), which is itself shaped by past experiences and learning (Hodgkinson and Sparrow 2002: 13). Kelly's personal construct theory argues that entrenched and central schemas are unlikely to be discarded even in the face of contradictory evidence. For example, if the construct of 'teacher-centred versus learner-centred' is part of the L&D practitioner's constructive system, he or she will have difficulty thinking in terms that do not fit within this frame of reference (Reger et al. 1994: 570).

There is an important distinction to be made between the ways in which long-term memory and short-term memory interact in the process of encoding, perception and interpretation of stimuli and events. Psychologists distinguish between:

Top-down processing: for example, when watching a football game memories of previous football games are activated and bias our perceptions towards picking up external information relevant to football games (Le Doux 1996: 272).

Bottom-up processing: this, by contrast, is when incoming stimuli influence memory without reference to past memories (Hodgkinson and Sparrow 2002).

Schemas may simplify reality and can help to reduce the amount of cognitive effort that we have to put into solving a previously encountered problem. This may free up processing capacity to deal with tasks which, because of their novelty, difficulty or significance, are more taxing in their information processing demands. Le Doux (1996) described working memory as sitting at the crossroads of the bottom-up and top-down processing systems, thus making possible the high-level thinking and reasoning that require temporary storage and interplay between information stored temporarily and a larger body of knowledge from long-term storage.

L&D FACTS AND FIGURES

Baddeley and Hitch asked participants to remember a series of digits (for example, 523) while carrying out a reasoning task in which they had to judge the truth of statements with which they were presented (for example 'A is not preceded by B'). The time taken to complete the reasoning task increased as the participants were given more digits to remember but nevertheless they were able to complete it. They argued that if there was just one phonetically based store it should not be possible to do both things. This was presented as evidence in favour of the phonological component of working memory. (*Source*: M. M. Smyth, P. E. Morris, P. Levy and A. W. Ellis, 1987. *Cognition in Action*. LEA Associates: London.)

LONG-TERM MEMORY

As far as long-term storage is concerned, human evolution has placed two very different demands on our memory system: one is to remember personally unique events or episodes (like our experiences of particular people) and the other is to remember more generic knowledge about the world (Pinker 1997: 124). Psychologists such as Tulving (1972) suggested that there are two types of long-term memory (LTM) storage. Past events and narratives are stored as episodic long-term memory, whilst words and their meanings are held in semantic long-term memory:

Episodic LTM is sometimes referred to as 'autobiographical memory' and is dependent upon the spatial and temporal context of the event. Episodic LTM has been described as the re-experiencing of an event that has occurred in the past (akin to 'mental time travel') with recall of the specific time ('when') and place of the event ('where') (http://www.mrc-cbu.ac.uk). A test of episodic memory might be to ask someone to 'describe what happened to them on Christmas day last year'.

Semantic LTM is abstract and is independent of the context. It is made up of knowledge of words and their meanings, objects, concepts and facts (memory of 'what') with no explicit re-experiencing of the initial encoding episode (http://www.mrc-cbu.ac.uk). A test of semantic memory might be to ask someone to 'name three of the founders of the behaviourist school of psychology'.

More recent research suggests that the simple fractionation of LTM into these two systems is something of a simplification, as they appear to interact with each other (http://www.mrc-cbu.ac.uk). Cues are important in facilitating the retrieval of information from long-term storage and they can be contextualized in the form of coincidences that stimulate memories of experienced events from episodic LTM (such as an image) or other types of decontextualized cues such as those employed in mnemonics for the retrieval of information from semantic LTM. A further aspect of the cognitive model of memory is the distinction that may be drawn between its declarative and procedural (skill) components of knowledge (Anderson 1990). Derry (1996: 165) distinguished between them thus:

Declarative knowledge is represented as propositional networks, and the dominant learning mechanisms include the elaboration and organization of the contents of the declarative components of memory.
Procedural knowledge is represented as complex collections of if '... then' statements learned through processes of composition and proceduralization of skills.

PERSPECTIVE FROM PRACTICE: MEMORY TRICKS

Based upon the following source: R. N. Carney, J. R. Levin and M. E. Levin, 1994. Enhancing the psychology memory by enhancing the memory of psychology, *Teaching of Psychology*, 21(3): 171–4.

'Mnemonics' (pronounced 'ne-mon-ics') originated from the Greek word *mneme* which means 'to remember'. Mnemonics work by putting labels and hooks (often in a visual mode) on knowledge in order to enable its recall at a later time. Mnemonics encompass a range of techniques for improving recall. Research supports their use as an effective method for facilitating storage and retrieval in a range of contexts (Carney et al. 1994: 171). There is a variety of approaches that may be employed to help learners remember lists, associated concepts and labels which they may need to use in situations where they might not have access to written information or where there is too much information to hold at one time in short-term or working storage. Although seemingly trivial, there are likely to be tasks in the workplace which demand memorization, notwithstanding the need to memorize and recall information from semantic LTM in formal assessments that aim to test the acquisition of knowledge (one need only think of the knowledge element of the driving test in the UK and other countries).

1. *Acronyms* are a way of forming a word from the initial letters of the list of words to be remembered. The word can be real or made up, but the important thing is that it is memorable to the individual. For example, a simple acronym for three types of learning is MUD (i.e. **m**emorizing, **u**nderstanding and **d**oing).
2. *Acrostics* are words that make some grammatical sense when formed from the initial letters of the word sequence or list to be remembered. For example, in England children are sometimes taught to remember the colours of the rainbow with the acrostic, '**R**ichard **o**f **Y**ork **g**ave **b**attle **i**n **v**ain' (red, orange, yellow, green, blue, indigo, violet).
3. *Method of loci* is often used by skilled speechmakers to remember their script. In this technique a sequence of locations (loci) and visual memory are used to create an imaginary journey along which the objects to be remembered are located. The visualization of the journey enables the list of items to be recalled in sequence.
4. *Pegword* method uses the pegwords ('one is a bun', 'two is a shoe', 'three is a tree', etc.) and visual hooks upon which items to be remembered can be hung. Remembering the pegword sets off a train of connections to the objects.

The images used in mnemonics can be bizarre, humorous and even vulgar. Many of these approaches are useful for rote learning but arguably do not add much to understanding. They may form a foundation for higher-order and more complex cognitive operations where there is a need to reduce the load on working memory.

Cognitive Schema Theory

From the information processing perspective a schema is simply a term used to denote a memory structure. As noted previously, a schema is stored in long-term memory and activated in working memory in response to an environmental input. The schema provides a framework for interpreting experience and assimilating new knowledge (Derry 1996). Derry identified three different types of schema in the cognitive information processing literature with which cognitive schema theory (CST) is concerned:

1. Memory objects: various types of representations (for example, declarative knowledge, pictorial information, sounds, emotions and so on) that are combined into a single memory object, which can be activated by a stimulus and may cohere with other memory objects (Derry 1996: 167).
2. Mental models: the building blocks for mental models are previously learned memory objects that are combined to produce situational understandings that are context-dependent. The process of mental modelling involves the con-

struction, testing and adjusting of mental representations (Derry 1996: 168). The construction of a mental model may be thought of as a problem-solving or sense-making process for the understanding of a task or situation. One L&D implication of the mental model component of CST is that in order for two individuals to communicate as effectively as possible, they must each have or construct (for example, by surfacing and sharing) a similar mental model of the object of interest.

3. Cognitive fields: Derry defined a cognitive field as 'a distributed pattern of memory activation that occurs in response to a particular event or problem' and which results in certain memory objects being more available for use in working memory than others (1996: 168). The process is one whereby experience triggers the activation of the cognitive field, which in turn delineates relevant memory objects that are then available for modelling the experience and the construction of new schemas or the elaboration of extant schemas. There are surface similarities between this process and that suggested by Klein (2003) in the activation of action scripts in the intuitive solving of problems in time-pressured situations.

Derry argued that CST is one interpretation of a modern cognitive information processing theory (the three components of CST are shown in Figure 3.4), which itself is but one aspect of a broad cognitive constructivist approach. The theoretical significance of schemas and schema change lies in the fact that they are impor-

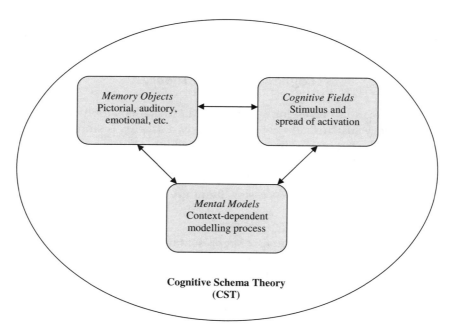

Figure 3.4   Three components of cognitive schema theory (adapted from Derry 1996)

tant both in cognitive information processing theories and other more radical constructivist interpretations of learning (1996: 163) and hence provide a conceptual bridge between these two ideas.

Context, Emotion and Memory

The emotions are increasingly seen as important for a whole range of issues in the workplace, including learning. For this reason some understanding of the limbic system is necessary since it is this part of the central nervous system that is implicated in important functions relating to anger and aggression (the amygdala), learning and memory (hippocampus) and anger and fear (septum) (Sternberg 1999). The amygdala (for reasons that will be outlined below) can respond before the overlying 'higher' structures of the brain have time to react; for this reason it has been described by Goleman (one of the popularizers of 'emotional intelligence') as the 'emotional sentinel' (1996: 17), which can 'hi-jack' the higher-order cognitive system. Research using neuro-imaging (fMRI scanning), reported by Whalen and his colleagues at the University of Wisconsin in 2004, suggested that cues as small as the appearance of the whites of someone's eyes can trigger an extremely rapid response in the amygdala without provoking any conscious awareness of the process (Stafford 2005). The connections to the cortex allow the amygdala to influence attention, perception and memory in situations where danger is faced (Le Doux 1996: 285). The amygdala has been described as the 'storehouse' of emotional memories and the part of the brain that generates the feelings that can override the brain's cerebral and more rational functions (Goleman 1996: 15, 28). There appear to be specialized neural circuits (a 'white-hot route') in this sub-cortical region of the human brain to deal with fear (Stafford 2005).

The hippocampus and the surrounding structures play a crucial role in the formation of long-term memory. Because of the way in which memory appears to work, learning tends to be state dependent to the extent that learning which takes place under one set of conditions is generally better remembered under the same sets of conditions (Le Doux 1996: 211). State-dependent learning has implications for L&D and especially for the transfer of learning from the learning situation to the work situation since recall may be better if it takes place in the same place as the learning. This presents design challenges for the L&D practitioner in ensuring that learning occurs under optimum sets of conditions that will aid encoding into long-term memory structures and facilitate recall. Memories for past events are stored in associative networks, the individual elements of which have particular weights attached to them (see LeDoux 1996). Scientists such as Le Doux have proposed that in order to enter consciousness memories have to reach a certain level of activation, based upon: (a) the number of components activated and (b) the weights or significance attached to those components. One of the components of a memory is the emotional implication of the experience; hence any emotional cues in the new situation that match those in the learning situation will act to raise the level of activation and bring the memory into conscious awareness (Le Doux 1996: 212). Le Doux draws our attention to the distinction between emotional memories (like the arousal of fear on the basis of a past experience – he terms this an implicit emotional memory) and memories of emotions (the emotional memory of the situation in which the fear arose – he terms this an explicit memory about an emotional situation). Through experiments with animals and studies of human patients it has been possible to attribute the implicit memories to the amygdala system and the explicit memories to the hippocampal system.

Memory and Learning

It was the psychologist George Miller, over half a century ago, who demonstrated that the capacity of working memory is limited to about seven items (plus or minus two). The learning implications of this are that by 'chunking' information the capacity limitations of working memory can be overcome to a certain extent. We need only to introspect about our own cognitive strategies for remembering a telephone number – when we tend to group digits together – to attest to the positive impact of chunking upon memory processes. From a practical point of view it is also important:

- not to overload working memory and to allow sufficient time for information to be processed;
- that the relevant prior learning and experience is evoked from long-term storage in order that the content of working memory may be processed in relation to existing knowledge.

Hence, a further implication for L&D is that long-term memory structures need to be activated in order that they become readily accessible to the learner, thus serving as a reminder of, and a structure into which, new information may fit (Gagné 1985: 60). This notion is commensurate with Ausubel's theory of meaningful learning (Ausubel 1968), in which it was proposed that the learning of new ideas becomes meaningful through their being subsumed into an extant cognitive structure. The extant structure may be activated by means of some form of advance organizer (for example, the Key Concepts at the beginning of each of the chapters of this book or the use of analogies to introduce an unfamiliar topic), which is at a higher level of abstraction than the material to be learned (Gagné 1985). As well as advance information helping to give some structure to new information, the act of inserting questions into a learning sequence can aid mental organization by 'forcing' some form of encoding on the material in a meaningful way. The various Discussion Points interspersed throughout this book are an attempt to facilitate or enable some form of processing and elaboration and hence encoding into LTM. The basic principle is that the activation of extant cognitive structures and the incorporation of new information into these structures may be facilitated by the use of advance information and an appropriate sequence of questioning.

The way in which problems and tasks are presented can also have an important influence over the effectiveness and efficiency of learning. It was noted earlier that some have argued that one of the aims of learning design should be the reduction of cognitive load, thereby freeing up working memory capacity. The question is, what strategies are available for reducing cognitive load? One such strategy is by managing the modalities (for example text, speech, pictures) by which new information is presented. It will be recalled that the working memory system as originally hypothesized by Baddeley consisted of the central executive with a verbal sub-system (the phonological loop) and a visual sub-system (the visuo-spatial sketchpad). Mayer and Moreno (2003) argued that meaningful learning requires a substantial amount of processing to take place in the visual and verbal channels; furthermore, such processing should be generative in that it incorporates new information into existing schemas through attention, mental organization and reorganization and integration (Wittrock 1989). Mayer and Moreno suggested several ways in which cognitive overload of these channels can be avoided. Their suggestions are likely to be pertinent to many forms of structured L&D, but especially so in the design of textual or electronic media for learning (such as job aids, distance learning materials or e-learning programmes).

1. Off-loading: presenting words as narration rather than as written text, thereby reducing the demands on the visual channel.
2. Segmenting: breaking the learning up into segments with sufficient time between each segment for processing to take place.
3. Pre-training: Mayer and Moreno use this term to refer to the pre-learning of concepts (for example, the components of a car braking system) in advance of the learning of the causal model (how the car braking system works).
4. 'Weeding': making the presentation of the information as sparse as possible to include only the essential elements.
5. Signalling: using typographical (such as *italicization*) and other presentational cues and devices to point out to the learner important facts or relationships.
6. Alignment: where words and pictures are presented they should be aligned to avoid scanning and eye movement between the word and the relevant part of a picture or diagram (2003: 46–9).

These issues are all the more important if one accepts that modern cognitive information processing theories and recent developments in instructional design suggest that there should be an emphasis upon 'real life' tasks such as cases, projects and problem solving with their inherent complexity and fidelity (Van Merrienboer et al. 2003).

PERSPECTIVE FROM PRACTICE: SOME PRINCIPLES FOR THE DEVELOPMENT OF e-LEARNING MATERIALS

Based on the following source: G. P. Maul and D. S. Spotts, 1993. Developing computer-based instructional courses, *Information Management*, November/December: 9–11.

A number of the principles from the cognitive information processing approach outlined above have direct L&D applications in a number of areas but in particular to the design of instructional media or e-learning materials. The guidelines for developing computer-based learning materials (what used to be called computer-based training or CBT) have been well documented in the instructional design literature (for example, Allesi and Trollip 2001). Maul and Spotts (1993) summarized some principles for the design of computer-based learning that are commensurate with many of the concepts that have been discussed thus far in this and the previous section:

1. Gain the learner's attention (for example, through the quality of the mode of presentation).
2. Inform the learner of the objectives (i.e. state what they should be able to do on completion of the 'lesson').
3. Stimulate recall of prior learning (for example, through an advance organizer).
4. Guide the learner's progress (for example, by using appropriate sequencing guided by structure, logic and difficulty).
5. Elicit participation and performance (for example, through appropriate level and sequence of questioning).
6. Provide feedback (for example, on their standard of performance in relation to the learning objectives).
7. Assess performance (for example, through testing).

Clearly, many of these guidelines apply equally to other forms of L&D and not exclusively to computer-based learning; they provide helpful theory-based rules of thumb for the design of structured L&D more generally.

Bandura's Social Learning Theory

Like the information processing approaches, social learning theory overcomes some of the perceived limitations of behaviourism by examining internal processes and explaining, for example, how new responses may be learned through observation, example and imitation. The theory is concerned with understanding how social influences can alter the individual's thoughts, feelings and actions through cognitive, vicarious (through the experiences of others), self-regulative and self-reflective processes. The theory is interactive in that it recognizes that the environment influences an individual's learning but also that the individual can exert control over their environment. The researcher credited most often as the pioneer of social learning theory is Alfred Bandura, whose argument was that learning would be effortful, laborious and potentially hazardous if individuals had to rely solely upon their own actions; without any reference to the actions of others the likelihood would be that learning would be severely retarded, not to say tedious. Much of his research focused on child development.

It may be recalled from earlier discussions that one definition of learning is 'a change in behaviour or potential behaviour as a result of direct experience'. The argument of social learning theory is that as well as learning through direct experiences, individuals can learn through observing another individual make a particular action or response and witnessing the outcomes of that action or response. In other words, through observation and interpretation we can profit from the successes and mistakes of others. As a general rule, we are more likely to do things that we have seen others succeed with, and avoid those actions that we have seen to fail (Bandura 1996: 577). Social learning theory does not imply learning simply by imitation; the role of reinforcement and rewards are also important. Moreover, behaviours can be learned but not necessarily displayed until circumstances present themselves where it will be rewarding for the individual to display, or refrain from displaying, the particular learned behaviour. Socially learned behaviours become, therefore, part of the individual's repertoire of potential behaviours. The fact that courses of action produce mixed effects and that they may not be temporally contiguous opens up ample scope for complexity, misinterpretation and misjudgement (Bandura 1996).

L&D FACTS AND FIGURES

Role plays are widely used for interpersonal skill development. The role players act out characters assigned to them in a scenario. The technique is based on the assumption that active experience, human modelling (either real or presented on video) and practice are better than passive methods for the learning of conflict management, negotiation, active listening, giving and receiving feedback and so forth. (*Source*: M. E. Gist and D. McDonald-Mann, 2000. Leadership training and development. In C. L. Cooper and E. A. Locke. (eds), *Industrial and Organisational Psychology*. Oxford: Blackwell, p.62–3.)

In observational learning a single model can transmit new ways of thinking and behaving, sometimes simultaneously to large numbers of people, thus giving observational learning great multiplicative power (Bandura 2003: 169). This type of learning requires a human model (for example, a person who might be perceived as having credibility or status) who is observed making certain behaviours or taking certain action choices. The behaviours may be desirable or undesirable and accompanied by rewards or punishments as appropriate, depending upon whether or not the actions are deemed good or bad. Humans have evolved an advanced capacity for observational learning, and the acquisition of new knowledge and skills through modelling is seen as vital for survival (Bandura 1996). Hill, writing in the context of leader development, made the point succinctly when she said that because people are 'social learners, they need others to provide them with candid feedback and coaching' (2004: 122). Some of the classic research in social learning was conducted in experiments with children whose levels of aggression were raised or lowered by manipulating the behaviours which they observed and the reinforcements that they were given for those behaviours. The children could be made to act more or less aggressively depending upon the actions of an adult model and the rewards or punishments administered (Bandura 1996). Moreover, the model need not be a direct experience: it could be described (verbally or textually) or otherwise witnessed second hand (for example in a video) (Gagné 1985: 234). The role of mass media in social learning should not be underestimated, especially since this is one way in which an individual's perception (their symbolic environment) of their physical and social environment can be greatly expanded (Bandura 1996). The observational learning process involved in modelling consists of:

1. Attention (determining what is to be attended to from a profusion of potential models) and cognitive representation (encoding what has been observed).
2. Behavioural production (appropriate courses of action are identified).
3. Motivation (the consequences the learner observes for others, or which the learner experiences or anticipates for themselves).

A further influence on this process is the role that emotion plays, for example vicarious emotional arousal can result in long-lasting attitudes or dispositions towards people, places or objects from positive or negative emotional experiences (Bandura 1996: 578).

PERSPECTIVE FROM RESEARCH: LEARNING MORE THAN WE CAN TELL THROUGH OBSERVATION

Based on the following source: J. Nadler, L. Thompson and L. van Boven, 2003. Learning negotiation skills: four models of knowledge creation and transfer, *Management Science*, 49(4): 529–40.

The view has already been expressed that the simple act of having an experience may not be enough for effective learning to occur. Nadler, Thompson and van Boven (2003: 537) argued that in the absence of other supporting techniques (such as the acquisition of principles), simply having an experience is a largely ineffective way to learn. They argued that for the learning of complex skills, such as the ability to negotiate, the method of observational learning produces efficient and effective learning. Moreover, the process occurs not by simple mimicry; rather observers are active processors of the information provided by the model's behaviour (though the extent to which this processing is conscious is not clear – a point to which we will return shortly). Consistent with Bandura's theory, they suggest that the observational learning process is facilitated when the observer:

1. Pays attention to the human model (in this case the skilled negotiator).
2. Retains the information (an integrative 'picture' of the skills required).
3. Has the capacity to enact the model's behaviour (to apply it in a similar situation).
4. Is motivated to behave in the way depicted by the model (Nadler et al. 2003).

Nadler et al. (2003) compared experience alone as a learning condition with four other methods: didactic learning (essentially 'teacher-tell'); information revelation (revealing information in the task scenario to help with the completion of the required task); analogical learning (using analogy to reveal the deep structure of the task); and observational learning. They used an experimental approach with 122 participants to test the efficacy of each of these methods in a predefined negotiating task. An experiment in this context is a piece of research in which one or more independent variables (the treatment in this case is the learning method) are manipulated (i.e. different methods were used with different groups) and others are controlled in order to assess the impact of the manipulated variable on the relevant outcome (dependent variable – in this case performance in the negotiating task) (Haslam and McGarty 1998: 46). Nadler et al.'s results suggested that observational learning and analogical learning led to better outcomes compared to the baseline condition of experience only (with observation scoring highest). One interesting outcome was that although the participants in the observational learning group showed the largest increase in performance they were unable to explicitly articulate the learning principles that they used to achieve the enhanced performance. The researchers speculated that the observational learners had acquired a tacit form of knowledge that helped them to perform but they were unable to articulate why or how (in a sense they 'knew more than they could say').

Social learning theory may be seen as a broad theory that emphasizes the roles played by vicarious (i.e. obtained through another person's experiences) as well as self-regulatory processes in psychological functioning (Bandura 1996). A further important feature of Bandura's theory is that of reciprocal determination, whereby an individual has an effect upon her or his environment, but reciprocally the environment has an effect upon the individual. In this regard cognitive, behavioural and environmental factors interact to the extent that:

> This conception of human functioning then neither casts people into the role of powerless objects controlled by environmental forces nor free agents who can become whatever they choose. Both people and their environments are *reciprocal determinants* of each other. (Bandura 1977: vii, emphasis added)

The notion of reciprocal determinism is not incommensurate with aspects of the cognitive conceptions of learning discussed previously: for example, our genetic make-up predisposes us to develop and behave in particular ways and places limits on our capabilities; however, it is the complex interaction of this genetic predisposition with our environment that is the ultimate determinant of outcomes and that can shape the form that our cognitive structures and behaviours ultimately take. Bandura argues that a distinctive characteristic of humans is their 'endowed plasticity', which depends upon specialized neurophysiological mechanisms and structures that have evolved over time to aid survival but which manifest themselves in modern humans as forethought, symbolic communication, evaluative self-regulation and reflective self-consciousness (Bandura 1996: 580).

Two further concepts are relevant to L&D in the context of this learning theory:

1. Development of an individual's beliefs in his or her own capabilities – their self-efficacy.
2. Enhancement of an individual's motivation through the use of expectations and goals (see Goldstein 1993).

Self-efficacy (the belief that one can perform specific tasks and behaviours) is a powerful predictor of outcomes, and it has been shown on repeated occasions to lead to better learning and performance (Salas and Cannon-Bowers 2001: 478). When self-efficacy is perceived to be high the individual will set higher goals and have firmer commitment to those goals (Wood and Bandura 1989). Goals provide a sense of purpose and direction because individuals seek self-satisfaction by fulfilling goals; self-efficacy therefore is an important part of the motivational process (Locke and Latham 1990). Individuals motivate themselves and guide their actions by:

- setting themselves challenging goals (discrepancy production);
- mobilizing the necessary internal and external resources to achieve the set goal (discrepancy reduction) (Bandura 1996).

If individuals believe they possess the capacity for learning it is more likely that they will make the extra effort required to acquire new knowledge and skills. Encouragement from others as a form of social persuasion can be important in this regard since it may help an individual to overcome self-doubts. Training in self-efficacy may be an underexploited area of L&D practice; furthermore, it is important that individuals have the opportunity to pursue goals that are commensurate with their perceived capacity to fulfil these goals. It is also important that individuals achieve success and are not put off by failure. On the other hand, L&D experiences should be such that individuals can learn to overcome failure (Goldstein 1993: 95) as this can provide a boost to self-efficacy and the motivation to engage in further learning. The achievement of appropriate goals is one way in which an individual satisfies higher-level needs such as personal growth.

Expectancy theory states that in order for an individual to make an effort in a task, he or she must believe that exerting the effort will increase the probability of getting the desired reward (Vroom 1964) and it may provide one explanation for why an individual may choose to engage or not engage in learning. An L&D implication of the expectancy model is the significance that perceptions (subjective probabilities) can have upon motivation to learn. The attitudes, beliefs and values an individual brings with them to the learning situation can be crucial in deciding the extent to which they will engage in learning, thus adding further weight to the assertion that to ignore individuals' beliefs and internal states (as behaviourism did) presents a very limiting view.

Social learning theory (and related concepts, such as self-efficacy, expectancy and motivation) has had an important influence upon L&D practice in areas such as the self-developmental and action-based approaches as well as the use of learning contracts. For example, Bandura argued (admittedly from a clinical setting) that:

1. The self-selection of well-defined intermediate and longer-term goals is an essential aspect of any self-directed programme of change.
2. Participants should make contractual agreements to practise self-controlling behaviours.
3. Self-directing behaviours need to be instituted with positive consequences arranged to act as self-arranged reinforcements to facilitate the achievement of goals.

One of the strengths of social learning theory is the way in which it integrates internal factors (such as self-efficacy) and external factors (such as rewards); however, one of the problems with self-efficacy judgements is that they are subjective assessments of an internal process and therefore have inherent limitations (Eysenck 1996: 321). Combining self-perception and others' perceptions of an individual's competence may provide a more reliable and objective form of assessment.

Discussion Point

How might L&D practitioners implement some of the principles of social learning theory in order to enhance the effectiveness and efficiency of learning in organizations?

Situated Learning

The concept of situated learning was developed in educational theory as an alternative to cognitive and related information processing approaches (the limitations of which have been alluded to earlier). The main difference between the two is that in the information processing approach the individual is the unit of analysis and learning 'takes place' in the mind of the individual as he or she acquires knowledge and skill. In the situated learning approach, on the other hand, learning takes place within a social framework of participation whereby individuals construct their own meaning through collaboration and interaction with others. The origins of the approach can be traced back to the work of Vygotsky, in which the learning activity was the unit of analysis and in which social (especially peer) interaction was crucial (Borthick et al. 2003). Constructionism itself is a philosophical stance that, from the perspective of L&D through the notion of social constructionism, holds that socio-cultural processes dominate learning. The core activity of participation need not be confined to face-to-face interactions but instead 'all individual actions may be viewed as elements or aspects of an encompassing system of social practices' in which individuals participate even when they act in physical isolation from each other (Cobb and Bowers 1999: 6). One of the main analytical concepts of this approach is that of legitimate peripheral participation (LPP), which is a label for the process by which individuals may gradually become part of a community of practice through access and exposure to a community's activities. Before inclusion into the community potential new members gain a sense of how the community operates (for example, as in a traditional apprenticeship). LPP contends that learners are participating in interactional contexts (communities of practice), that learning and meaning are defined in relation to the action-in-context and that this is the locus of the learning, (Elkjaer 1999). From this stance learning is not seen merely as the mind filling up like an empty vessel (this is one way in which social constructionists might characterize the locus of learning from an information processing perspective).

PERSPECTIVE FROM RESEARCH: CONSTRUCTIVIST LEARNING IN ACTION

Based on the following source: B. Elkjaer, 1999. In search of a social learning theory. In M. Easterby-Smith, L. Araujo and J. Burgoyne (eds), *Organisational Learning and the Learning Organisation: Developments in Theory and Practice*. London: Sage.

If learning is seen as being the active and social construction of meaning in situ there are implications for the role of the L&D practitioner which may entail a shift in emphasis from provider role to one of facilitation and guidance. In broad terms, what principles might an approach to L&D have from situated learning perspective? Elkjaer's (1999) commentary on the relationship between situated learning and organizational learning offers a number of glimpses of this:

1. Learning is not created by the mere participation in practice; learning occurs where is there is reflection upon actions.
2. Learning involves both action and cognition, and a continuous process of reflection which reorganizes and reconstructs experience to generate new meanings.
3. Reflection, reorganization and reconstruction are intentional and effortful activities.
4. Reflection requires a shared language acquired in situ whereby the learner can reorganize and reconstruct experiences and engage in meaningful dialogue.
5. The language for dialogue is in the form of both internal thought processes and external processes of communication with others.
6. The point of departure for learning is a problem that causes the individual or the organization to stop and engage in purposeful enquiry.
7. Purposeful enquiry may lead individuals and organizations to change their mental models and their actions.

One role of the L&D practitioner is to enable the process of dialogue and enquiry to occur through appropriate means such as the action-based approaches of Argyris, Schon and Revans (see Chapter 5).

The situated learning approach often appeared to have adopted a stance that was the antithesis of the individual approach embodied in a strict interpretation of cognitive information processing theories. The situated learning theorists themselves have not been without their critics. Anderson et al. (1996) offered a critique of constructivist approaches on a number of grounds. For example, one claim of constructivism is that knowledge is specific to the context in which it was acquired and that to 'teach' more general knowledge is in a sense futile since it cannot transfer to real-world situations. Anderson et al. argued that the kind of knowledge being acquired will determine how tightly it is bound to a specific context and that knowledge learned in one context (such as the school or training room) can generalize to workplace performance. Psychological research on the transfer of learning presents clear and compelling evidence that learning may transfer between situations and tasks (see for example Baldwin and Ford 1988; Rouillier and Goldstein 1997). Secondly, a corollary of the claims for the legitimacy and primacy of contextualized learning (such as apprenticeships and coaching) is a challenge to the legitimacy of more abstracted and formalized methods of learning (such as those that take place in the training room or lecture hall). As

Anderson et al. noted, however, classroom-based instruction can be ineffective if what is taught in the classroom is not what was required on the job (there is further discussion of this point in Chapter 5 in respect of Orr's ethnographical research from the 1980s). On the other hand, classroom-based instruction can be highly effective if it is designed and implemented appropriately by combining the teaching of abstract and general principles with concrete examples and opportunities to practise (indeed there are learning contexts for which this type of 'abstract' learning may be the only safe place for learning to take place). The final substantive issue that Anderson et al. address in their critique is that of complexity. Situated learning theorists have argued that learning should take place in complex social settings. Anderson et al. argued that whilst there are legitimate reasons why it is necessary to practise some skills in their own complex setting, it can in other situations be more effective to abstract parts of a complex task and teach these separately in order to reduce their complexity and to use procedures that involve 'whole tasks and components and individual training and training in social settings' (Anderson et al. 1996: 10). The use of part tasks is consistent with cognitive load theory (CLT), which suggests that it is important when designing instruction to take the limits of human information processing capacity into account (van Merrienboer et al. 2003).

Cognitive-Social Interpretations of Learning

One of the dilemmas in making sense of learning in the workplace is the extent to which learning may be seen as an individual-focused or a socially situated process. This tension sometimes goes unresolved and theorists and practitioners often prefer to adopt a position in one or other camp. Cobb and Yackel resolved the dilemma in their own work by arguing that individual cognitive processes and socio-cultural ones are mutually implicative and cannot be studied in isolation (Cobb and Yackel 1996). In other words, the cognitive processes that are implicated in individual knowledge construction occur in a social context and hence through a cognitive constructivist lens individual cognitions need to be seen against the backcloth of the social context (Derry 1996: 164). A central element of this argument is that of schema change through reflection and dialogue. If one accepts a resolution of the theoretical tension between the individual and socially situated perspectives, as a practitioner one is then left with the practical matter of how learning experiences may be designed which reflect the cognitive and the social aspects of learning. Borthick et al. (2003) turned to the work of Vygotsky in an attempt to address this issue through the notion of a zone of interaction between a novice and an expert, in which the learner can participate in performance at a higher level of complexity that he or she could achieve alone (2003). This is derived from the Vygotskian notion of the zone of proximal development (ZPD); see Figure 3.5. The core represents performance that the learner can attain without assistance; and the zone is what the learner can only do with assistance. The activ-

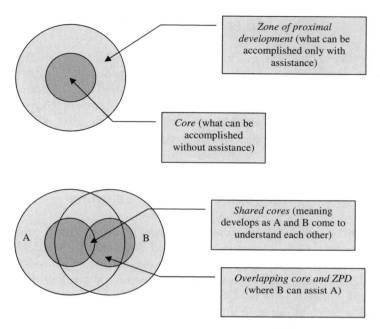

Figure 3.5 The zone of proximal development (ZPD) for an individual and a dyad (adapted from Borthick et al. 2003: 110, and based on Vygotsky)

ity in the zone is focused not on the transfer of skills to the learner but on a collaboration between an expert and the learner (such as A and B in Figure 3.5) that enables the development of a cognitive structure which internalizes some of the complexity of the system (Borthick et al. 2003: 111). Such an approach is likely to involve instruction, study, collaboration, practice, feedback, questioning and coaching through assistance from the expert via modelling, providing cognitive scaffolding, providing encouragement and fostering self-awareness and self-efficacy. Where an expert's core and learner's zone overlap the expert can assist the non-expert; moreover, individuals may be expert in different domains and the dialogue may produce schema change and insights which have the potential to be more complex that the individuals' conceptions alone, i.e. there may be a synergy from the construction of a shared mental model. Scaffolding is a term used to refer to devices or strategies to support learners (Rosenshine and Meister 1992). The function of a scaffold is to initially provide the support to enable a learner to achieve a goal not achievable without the support, and because excessive support can hinder learning the scaffold should be withdrawn (faded) until it is no longer needed (van Merrienboer et al. 2003).

L&D FACTS AND FIGURES

Lev Vygotsky (1896–1934) graduated from Moscow University with a degree in law. However, he also studied philosophy, psychology and literature. In 1919, he contracted tuberculosis and only later, in 1925, did he complete his dissertation *The Psychology of Art*. Vygotsky lectured, conducted research and published in the field of psychology until his death in 1934. His work was banned in the USSR for political reasons and was not published until 1956. (*Source*: http://web.archive.org/web/Vygotsky.html)

Andragogical Model of Learning

The andragogical model synthesizes a number of concepts and principles from other theories and applies them in the context of adult and workplace learning. The person most often credited with being the originator of the model is the adult educator Malcolm Knowles, whose work has been highly influential in the adult learning field – primarily in the USA but increasingly in Europe – as L&D practitioners seek a more integrative theoretical frame upon which to base their practice over and above that provided by the experiential learning model (see below). One of the basic premises of the model is that andragogy and pedagogy are fundamentally different; therefore, to build adult learning upon principles that have only been tried and tested in school education may be erroneous and fallacious. In a historical review of the field of adult education Knowles argued that historically two streams of inquiry may be distinguished: firstly, a scientific stream characterized by systematic and experimental investigation and exemplified in the work of Thorndike (1928) and others; secondly, an artistic/intuitive stream that is concerned with the discovery of new knowledge through intuition and analysis of experience, exemplified in the work of Lindeman (1926) (Knowles 1990: 28–9). It was the work of Lindeman that provided Knowles with a new way of thinking about adult learning and which constituted his basis for an adult learning (andragogical) model. Lindeman's assumptions were that:

- adults are motivated to learn as they experience needs and interests that motivate them to learn;
- adults' orientation to learning is life-centred;
- experience is the richest source for adults' learning;
- adults have a need to be self-directing in their learning;
- individual differences amongst learners widen with age, therefore adult education must take account of these differences (Knowles 1990: 31).

Knowles argued that by the 1940s all the conceptual and theoretical pieces were available to assemble a comprehensive framework of adult learning, with contributions from clinical psychology (for example, from Jung, Freud, Fromm and in particular Carl Rogers – who argued that we cannot teach another person directly, we can only facilitate her or his learning), developmental psychology, sociology, social psychology and philosophy. There was also an important contribution from the field of adult education itself, and Knowles singled out the work of Cyril Houle (and associated work by Alan Tough), who looked at what made a 'continuing learner' (in terms of 'why?' and 'how?' they engaged in continuing learning). The research by Houle (an in-depth study on a small sample, only 22 participants) identified three types of learner:

1. Goal-oriented learners, motivated by the need to achieve clear-cut objectives.
2. Activity-oriented learners, motivated by the 'amount and kind of human relationships it [the learning project] would yield' (1990: 47).
3. Learning-oriented learners, motivated by the need to seek knowledge for its own sake.

Knowles also acknowledged a debt to European colleagues for the actual term 'andragogy' (attributed by Knowles to the Yugoslav Dusan Saicevic); its usage may be traced back at least as far as the early nineteenth century. The features of pedagogy that Knowles uses as a foil against which to contrast andragogy are that the pedagogical model prevalent at the time invested full responsibility for making decisions about what and how learning will take place with the teacher. Pedagogy, Knowles argued, may be practised appropriately up to the age of around 18 years, but beyond this the practice of pedagogy produces tension, resistance, resentment and rebellion (1990: 55). The validity of this assertion itself is open to question (and perhaps extension), as such tensions are sometimes also manifest in learning before the age of 18 years.

L&D FACTS AND FIGURES

Malcolm Knowles (1913–97) used the term andragogy, derived from the Greek *aner*, meaning 'of the man [adult]' and *agogus*, meaning to 'lead or accompany' and signifying adult learning, in order to differentiate the theory and practice of adult learning from that of pedagogy (from the Greek *paid*, meaning 'of the child' and signifying 'youth learning'). Knowles was highly influential as a practitioner and author in the adult education field in the USA. He authored around 18 books and over 200 articles. He is identified with the practices of self-directed learning, learning contracts, and learning environments.

The term andragogy was first introduced into the American educational literature, according to Knowles in 1968 in his paper 'Andragogy, not pedagogy'. The concept as articulated by Knowles has a number of distinctive features drawn from the several traditions of psychology and education that he acknowledged (for example, Lindeman). The six assumptions of andragogy are:

1. Adults need to know why they need to learn something before undertaking it.
2. The adult's self-concept is one of being responsible for their own decisions.
3. Adults come into a learning experience with greater volume and variety of life experience than do younger learners.
4. Adults are ready to learn those things that they need to know to cope with their 'real life' situations.
5. Adults' orientation to learning is life-centred and there should be some form of potential pay-off in work or personal life.
6. The most potent motivators for the adult learner are internal pressures such as job satisfaction, self-esteem and quality of life (Knowles 1990).

Adult learning is seen as a process that is central to the fields both of adult education and human resource development (Knowles et al. 1998). But what are the direct implications of andragogy for L&D? They are far-reaching, and Knowles et al. chose to map the implications onto a systematic learning process of needs identification, creation of personal learning strategy, implementation of personal learning strategy and evaluation of the attainment of goals, summarized as: adults determine their own learning needs; adults create and implement their own learning; adults evaluate their own learning. Knowles et al. go on to suggest that one way of operationalizing this idealized process is through the use of a learning contract that specifies the process in eight steps (1998: 212–16) (Figure 3.6).

The application as set out above is somewhat processual (and might even be criticized as being overly mechanical) but, setting aside this rigid method of application, one of the main strengths of Knowles's set of assumptions about learning is that they provide the L&D practitioner with two interlinked guiding principles relating, firstly, to the role of motivation in adult learning (which is often overlooked in L&D), and, secondly, to the context-relatedness of adult learning (it is difficult to separate out the learning from the context in which it occurs since they are so interwoven). These two factors are reciprocal in the terms set out in Knowles's model in that if one assumes that adults in the workplace are motivated to perform (an assumption which may not by any means be universally accepted) then linking their learning to their performance needs is a powerful way for engaging adults in the learning process. This has practical implications for the planning, design and implementation of learning and development, and in particular for the ways in which learning needs are identified and analysed, and how they are met. It may also fit well within a performance management framework. The more effectively such an identification and analysis process can single out task-related issues that learners need to be able to solve in order to perform, then, theoretically at least, the stronger will be the link between the learning provided and the motivation to undertake the learning.

Another feature of Knowles's approach is that of the role of context in learning (a point of contact with the notions of situated learning and communities of practice). A logical conclusion from a number of Knowles's assumptions is that the more that learning is integrated with work or in work the more satisfying and

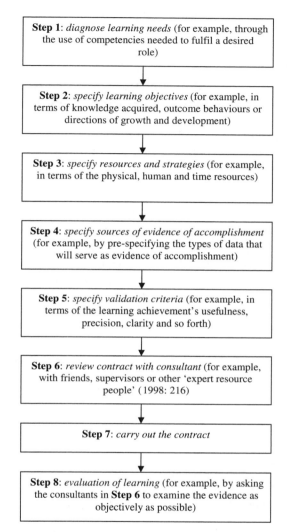

Step 1: *diagnose learning needs* (for example, through the use of competencies needed to fulfil a desired role)

Step 2: *specify learning objectives* (for example, in terms of knowledge acquired, outcome behaviours or directions of growth and development)

Step 3: *specify resources and strategies* (for example, in terms of the physical, human and time resources)

Step 4: *specify sources of evidence of accomplishment* (for example, by pre-specifying the types of data that will serve as evidence of accomplishment)

Step 5: *specify validation criteria* (for example, in terms of the learning achievement's usefulness, precision, clarity and so forth)

Step 6: *review contract with consultant* (for example, with friends, supervisors or other 'expert resource people' (1998: 216)

Step 7: *carry out the contract*

Step 8: *evaluation of learning* (for example, by asking the consultants in **Step 6** to examine the evidence as objectively as possible)

Figure 3.6 The application of learning contracts in the andragogical model. (*Source*: Knowles et al. 1998)

effective it is likely to be. This represents a return to an issue alluded to at the end of Chapter 1 relating to the distinction between learning and working (there are also links here to Kolb's experiential learning model, see below). In short the Knowles approach has high face validity and is readily applicable in an organizational context by those involved in the planning and delivering of L&D and in managing performance. It is also integrative in the sense that it draws upon notions of reinforcement, feedback, motivation and interaction with the environment. It synthesizes important ideas from behaviourist, cognitive and social theories of learning as well as sharing features with Kolb's experiential learning model.

PERSPECTIVE FROM PRACTICE: WESTINGHOUSE'S ANDRAGOGICAL EXECUTIVE FORUM

Based on the following source: M. S. Knowles, 1990. *The Adult Learner: A Neglected Species*. Houston: Gulf Publishing Company.

In his book *The Adult Learner: A Neglected Species* Knowles described the development of an executive development programme for Westinghouse Electric Corporation based on his andragogical principles. The need in Westinghouse was to develop a programme to overcome poor performance amongst managers and prepare general manager candidates for further development, with the important proviso from 'on high' that a generic programme was not what was needed. Senior executives within Westinghouse wanted something that was new, different and company specific (i.e. bespoke). The starting point was the development, in conjunction with senior executives, of a profile of the competencies needed for the role of a Westinghouse general manager in six functional areas (i.e. marketing, engineering, manufacturing, finance, personnel and general management). A set of assumptions and principles commensurate with andragogical learning theory were recognized and agreed with the key stakeholders in the organization:

1. Participants would be selected on their potential to be high flyers and their capacity to be self-directed as learners.
2. Participants had more exposure in some areas of management than in others.
3. Each participant had recognized L&D needs in some areas of management.
4. Support and resources would be made available to participants to help them in assessing their own needs and in planning a programme of self-development.

An element of human modelling (through coaching) was built in by bringing in experienced managers to demonstrate and communicate their philosophy and values through their participation in the programme as 'faculty resource people'. The basic design of the course consisted of pre-reading, self-assessment of competency, one-day orientation, four learning 'units' (using discussions, exercises, role plays and case studies) of between three and four-and-a-half days (organizational understanding; mission and planning; people management; division operations), development of an ongoing 'Continuing Personal Development Plan', planning of ongoing follow-up clinics, post-course self-assessment of competency and a follow-up survey to evaluate the impact of the programme on managerial knowledge and skill. Knowles (1990: 199–201) reported at length the comments made by the participants, and the description Knowles provides of the application of andragogy in Westinghouse is interesting and relevant for a number of reasons:

1. Firstly, it is an example of the way in which senior management involvement can create ownership of an L&D project right through from inception to implementation.
2. Secondly, the programme was Westinghouse specific and therefore met learning needs that were relevant to the managers' day-to-day jobs and hence could have an immediate potential payback in terms of enhanced ability to solve real and pressing problems (giving the proverbial 'quick win' that is sometimes expected from L&D).
3. Finally, there was a very strong element of self-direction to the programme, which made a number of assumptions about the participants' levels of self-efficacy and motivation.

Experiential Learning Model

The experiential paradigm in L&D is based upon the precept that learning is not something that is confined to the classroom or lecture hall; rather learning, in its broadest sense, is something that individuals are engaged in for a good proportion of their time every day both in their work and their personal lives. The experiential movement can be traced back to American educational philosophy in the first half of the twentieth century. The American educationalist John Dewey may be seen as one of the pioneers of experiential learning. He propounded the view that there is an intimate and necessary relation between the processes of actual experience and education (1938). One of the most passionate writers on the significance of experience-based learning has been Carl Rogers; he defined learning in terms of its having the quality of personal involvement (both of feelings and cognitive aspects), of being self-initiated (the impetus comes from within), of being pervasive (making a difference in the behaviour, attitudes and even personality of the learner), of being evaluated by the learner (who knows if it is meeting a need) and of having the essence of meaning (Rogers 1969; 1980). Like andragogy, the concept of 'learning from experience' has considerable face validity, and not surprisingly it has been formalized into a model with its own set of concepts and practical applications. Over the past 20 years experiential learning has been highly influential in L&D generally and in management education and development in particular (for example, in the UK through the work of Honey and Mumford 1992, and others).

The notion of learning though experience (and especially in the workplace) is most often associated with the work of the American psychologist David Kolb, whose experiential learning model continues to be one of the most influential frameworks in the whole of management learning and L&D, with over 1,500 studies, refereed articles, dissertations and papers conducted on it since 1971 (Kayes 2002). Central to the model is the view that learning is a process whereby 'knowledge is created through the transformation of experience' (Kolb 1984: 41). The experiential learning theory (ELT) has its theoretical origins in the work of Kurt Lewin, Jean Piaget and Carl Jung, as well as Dewey and Rogers. The model emphasizes the central role that experience plays in the learning process and distinguishes the ELT from cognitive learning theories, which emphasize cognition over affect, and behavioural learning theories, which deny any role for subjective experience in the learning process (Mainemelis et al. 2002). Mainemelis et al. described the ELT thus:

> Drawing on the works of Piaget, James and Freire, ELT suggests that adaptive flexibility is related to the degree that one integrates the dual dialectics of the learning process, conceptualizing/experiencing and acting/reflecting. (2001: 8)

Kolb et al. consciously attempt to distinguish the ELT from the theories that were considered earlier in this chapter, and it can be seen as synthesizing behaviourism and cognitivism. Kayes concurs with this view when he states that action, cognition, reflection and experience represent four interdependent facets of the learning process, each of which is required for a learning experience to be 'whole' and which are embodied in the ELT (2002: 139). Underpinning the model is a humanist, Rogerian conception that people have a natural capacity (not to say predisposition) to learn. Within the ELT learning is conceived as a four-stage process consisting of:

1. Immediate real-life experiences (Kolb called this 'concrete experience', CE).
2. Stepping back and observing and reflecting upon these experiences (reflective observation, RO).
3. Assimilating one's reflections and observations into general (abstract) concepts or rules (abstract conceptualization, AC).
4. Active testing of these general concepts or rules and using them as guides for creating or testing out new experiences (active experimentation, AE) (Kolb, Boyatzis and Mainemelis, 2001: 228).

L&D FACTS AND FIGURES

In his experiential learning model (ETM) Kolb asserted most famously that 'knowledge is created through the transformation of experience'. The theory rests on a diverse set of theoretical traditions including the work of major figures in education, learning and psychology such as John Dewey, Kurt Lewin, Jean Piaget, Carl Rogers and Abraham Maslow. Interest in the theory, model and its measurement continues unabated and research papers constantly appear in the psychology and education journals using the Kolb *Learning Style Inventory* in various construct validation studies (see, for example, Loo 2004).

In the UK Honey and Mumford (1992), in their application of the ELT, used terminology that is perhaps more 'user- or manager-friendly' in their version of the model, which consists of a four-stage model labelled: 'having an experience'; 'reviewing the experience'; 'concluding from the experience'; and 'planning the next step'. The dialectics of Kolb's model are not immediately apparent in the Honey and Mumford version, and we have to go back to Kolb's more explicit terminology to fully appreciate the conceptual nuances that underlie the ELT:

1. The creation of knowledge in the ELT occurs in two ways: 'grasping' experiences and 'transforming' those experiences.
2. Kolb suggested that pairs of the activities in the model (CE, RO, AC and AE) are the opposite ends of two dimensions that reflect these two fundamental activities: grasping (CE-AC) and transforming (RO-AE).
3. These two activities each contain polar opposites (see Figure 3.7), and individuals differ (perhaps through habitual preference or choice) in terms of how to grasp experiences (by CE or AC) and how to transform them (by RO or AE).

At the heart of experiential learning is a conflict between ways of dealing with the world (Kolb 1984: 29). Because these choices are at opposite ends of each dimension they have within them an inherent tension and hence Kolb argued that individuals have preferred learning styles that result from their habitual ways of grasping and transforming their experiences.

An integrated learning is one that involves the creative tension between the four learning modes where the learner touches all of the bases (Mainmelis et al. 2002). The integration comes from a resolution of the dialectic inherent in the model. The dialectic and the circular mode of representation resonates, according to Kolb, with the archetype of the mandala (meaning circle), which Jung defined as having a quadripartite structure (like a wheel, or flower or cross) wherein poles of light and darkness rotate and resolve. Hence within the model a non-Western tradition may be identified (via Jung) and also connections to Taoism and

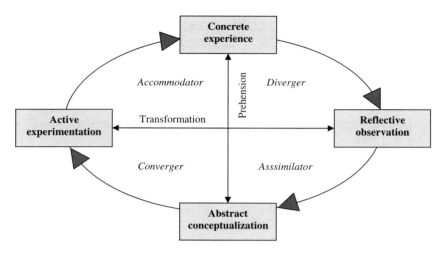

Figure 3.7   The experiential learning model (adapted from Kolb 1984)

Buddhist thinking and philosophy. Furthermore, Kolb recognizes similarities in the theoretical tradition provided by Jean Piaget (assimilation and accommodation), William James ('direct perception' and 'mediating perception') and Paolo Friere (an action–reflection dialogue). This emphasizes one of the most important attributes of experiential learning: the notion of adaptation through the resolution of conflicts. The conflicts are between acting and reflecting, and between being concrete and theoretical. It is the way in which these conflicts are resolved that determines the type of learning that results. Dominance by one mode or suppression of another will lead to learning that is specialized around the dominant mode. A higher form of adaptation and integration between the two modes can lead to a creative synthesis (Kolb 1984: 31) and Kolb himself cites the example of Wallas's (1926) four-stage model of creativity (he describes it as consisting of intelligence, incubation, insight and verification) wherein a number of contrasting modes give rise to an adaptive, complex and creative process which map onto ELT thus: concrete experience and intelligence (or expertise); reflective observation and incubation; abstract conceptualization and insight; and active experimentation and verification. As well as developing a model of the learning process, Kolb was also interested in making the ideas actionable for manager L&D. To this end he devised the *Learning Styles Inventory* (*LSI*), a self-report questionnaire that enables an individual to identify her or his preferred learning style quickly and easily in terms of one of the four learning-style types (assimilators, accommodators, divergers and convergers). The experiential learning cycle and the associated learning styles can be seen in Figure 3.7.

The ELT has links to other models of learning, such as Knowles's andragogical theory which asserts that as individuals develop and mature they change with respect to a number of characteristics; for example, they become more self-directing, make greater use of their experiences in learning, are able to identify more easily their own readiness to learn and organize learning around life problems (Knowles et al. 1998). One crucial aspect of the ELT that management education and development has made extensive use of is the notion that a wholly effective learner is one who has the capability to operate effectively at each stage of the cycle (the concept of 'integration'). As mentioned earlier, Honey and Mumford (1992) in the UK built upon the work of Kolb and developed their own model of the learning process (the learning cycle) and learning styles (activist, reflector, theorist and pragmatist) and also developed their own instrument – the *Learning Styles Questionnaire* (*LSQ*).

Woodall and Winstanley (1998) argued that the 1980s and 1990s witnessed a displacement of cognitive learning theory by experiential learning models as the emphasis in theory and practice shifted from management training to management learning. They see this as a move towards emphasizing the internal frame of reference of the individual and giving them the knowledge and skills to 'find the solution for themselves' (1998: 142). In this regard the ELT may be seen as operating at a number of levels. At one level it is interpreted as a model of process (akin to other similar problem-solving cycles), with the notion of preferences for the different stages (or styles) bolted on (for example in the learning cycle). At another level it is concerned with more complex issues of the tensions between different ways of coming to know the world. A deeper understanding at this level is helpful to learners in that they may better come to understand their own thinking and learning processes. Arguably this is an aspiration that is not wholly at odds with the understandings and insights that the cognitive information processing approach can reveal to the individual; hence ELT may be more a complement to rather than a displacement for cognitive learning theory. Alongside the theoretical debates (for example, Kayes 2002) there have been a number of more searching empirical critiques levelled at the *LSI* (for example: Freedman and Stumpf 1980). Also the notion of the 'complete learner' comes under a critical scrutiny by Tennant, who argued that this notion of psychological integration inherent in the underlying model is not 'worked out in detail' and is illustrative of a utopian conception of psychological development (1988: 102) with which he feels uncomfortable for three reasons:

1. Not every learning situation demands a balanced integration of the four stages and hence the model may be more suited as a scheme for the fourfold classification of learning experiences.
2. Kolb's questionnaire (the *LSI*) measures the individual's relative preference for one set of words over another and does not measure learning style competence per se.
3. There is the danger that individuals might be categorized into a privileged group (i.e. those who can integrate their experiences and construct knowledge) and a less privileged group (i.e. those who are unable to do so).

In spite of his criticisms Tennant recognized the approach embodied in the ELT as providing an excellent framework for planning teaching and learning activities. Other critics have expressed different sets of concerns. For example, Vince (1998) voiced concerns about the lack of attention accorded to psychodynamic issues such as power, anxiety, fear and doubt in Kolb's model. Reynolds (1997) argued that the individualistic conceptualization is itself limiting, and Holman et al. (1997) contended that the model fails to take into account the significance of social processes.

PERSPECTIVE FROM PRACTICE: MAKING SPACE AND TIME FOR REFLECTION TO HAPPEN

Based on the following source: A. Kransdorff, 1999. Applying experiential learning to work, *Knowledge Management Review*, 9: 12–15.

Nadler et al. (2003) argued that experience alone is not necessarily effective for learning. To be effective experiential approaches need to embrace reflection in a managed and systematic way Reflection requires an open and curious mind-set and constructive critiques from oneself and others; without these there is the danger that 'too many hard knocks can have a damaging psychological effect' (Woodall and Winstanley 1998: 154). One of the day-to-day problems with experiential and reflective approaches to learning that rely upon the conscious act of reflection is that in busy workplaces where speed is seen to be of the essence the temptation is to 'fly by the seat of one's pants' and move from problem to problem (if not crisis to crisis). Organizations may not be places that support experiential and reflective forms of learning (indeed there is the danger that the ill-informed may equate experiential learning with learning through mistakes and by trial and error). This can create real difficulties for the reflective stage of an experientially driven learning process. To expect reflection to occur naturally when employees are under continual pressure may be unrealistic; therefore organizations need to make time and space for reflection to occur. Kransdorff points to a further danger: the inability to reflect, and especially to reflect collectively, may lead to corporate amnesia with concomitant repetition of mistakes, 'reinvention of wheels' and other 'unlearned lessons, the expensive evidence of which litters industry' (1999: 13). He offered a number of suggestions for ways in which this tendency to 'corporate amnesia' may be obviated:

1. Use oral debriefings: interviews should be used to elicit knowledge from key employees during their tenure and especially shortly before they leave. Questioning should be open and honest; it should elicit constructive critiques and negative messages should not be glossed over. The knowledge elicited should be captured and stored in an accessible and flexible knowledge management system.

2. Write experiential learning histories by conducting interviews with principal decision makers and key employees immediately after a significant event to capture the lessons learned as soon as possible.
3. Write corporate histories: most corporate histories, rather than being written as celebratory events every few decades to record 'what' happened of significance, should be written more frequently and should concentrate upon the analysis of 'why' as well as 'what' significant events in a corporation's life cycle took place.

The passing on of these debriefings, experiential and corporate histories should be something that new generations of employees are exposed to routinely and systematically, otherwise they may be condemned to repeat the mistakes of their predecessors.

Transfer of Learning

The final issue that needs to be considered in our discussion of learning theories is the link between learning and job performance. L&D is concerned with how individuals (either singly or as groups) acquire or create knowledge and skills that enable them to perform and grow in their current or future occupational role. Therefore, as well as needing theories that help us to understand the learning process itself, we also need some understanding of how any learning that takes place may actually be applied to the job, i.e. how it may transfer from the learning situation to the work situation.

The transfer of learning may be most easily understood by reference to an example. Simulators (such as flight simulators) are often used for the acquisition of skills that might be difficult or dangerous to acquire in the real setting (flying a passenger aircraft). However, such learning is undertaken in the belief that the knowledge and skills acquired in the simulated situation will transfer to learning in the real situation. The assumption is that a transfer of learning will occur and the learner will be able to apply what she or he has learnt in the simulated setting when confronted by learning to deal with the same situation in the real world. Transfer of learning does not simply apply to learning that takes place in simulated situations (such as multi-million-dollar flight simulators), it applies to any learning that takes place in a non-work setting. The aim should be for the learning to be able to be applied effectively to the learner's job. From an economic perspective the expectation of any investment in planned L&D is that the learner will be able to apply their new knowledge or skill to the workplace.

Positive transfer occurs when the learning that has taken place on one task assists in the learning of another, for example learning to drive one type of car assists in learning to drive another (because the controls are basically the same) (Reid and Barrington 1999: 89). In this situation the knowledge and skills are directly transferable from the learning situation (for example, simulator or one model of car) to the work situation (for example, the flight deck of an aircraft or other models of cars). Learning transfer has been defined as the degree to which learners effectively apply knowledge, skills and attitudes gained during L&D in a generalized manner (generalization) to the job context over a period of time (maintenance) (Baldwin and Ford 1988). The degree to which generalization and maintenance occur depends upon learning and retention of knowledge, skills and attitudes, which themselves are likely to be a function of:

- learner characteristics: for example, ability, personality and motivation;
- learning design: for example, principle of learning, sequencing and content;
- work environment: for example, support and opportunity to apply (Baldwin and Ford 1988: 64–5).

Positive transfer is by no means automatic; for example, in some cases learning in one situation can have a detrimental effect upon behaviour and performance in another setting. Think of the case of driving in the UK: unlike much of the rest of the world, in the UK cars are driven on the left-hand side of the road and naturally drivers learn to drive in this way. When a driver who has learned to drive in the UK is confronted by the task of driving in Europe or the USA he or she can be perplexed and confused because the skills that were learned at home may not directly transfer to the new context. Even more than that, the skills learned in the original UK context may, for a short time at least, interfere with performance in the new context. That said, it does not take an individual long to adapt to driving on the right-hand side of the road and after a short time many English drivers report being comfortable with the new context and are able to drive competently. The interference described above is an example of negative transfer, and whilst it does occur it is normally only a problem in specific instances involving closely related tasks, such as transferring from one aircraft type to another or one industrial process to a similar one (Annett and Sparrow 1985: 119).

PERSPECTIVE FROM RESEARCH: MICRO-FEATURES OF THE LEARNING ENVIRONMENT TO PROMOTE EFFECTIVE TRANSFER

The practical question begged by these discussions of learning transfer is: what are the conditions necessary for transfer to occur efficiently and effectively? There is a considerable body of psychological research into the features of a learning environment that may promote transfer. Two theories have been developed that may aid the L&D practitioner in deciding how to design L&D in order to maximize the chances of transfer occurring:

1. The first of these is the identical elements theory, which posits that transfer will occur so long as there are identical elements in the learning and the work situations. The purpose of learning that takes place away from

the workplace is that it provides an environment that is (hypothetically at least) more conducive to learning; it is therefore important to develop learning environments that are as similar as possible to the work environment (Goldstein 1993: 125).

2. The second theory is transfer through principles, which states that learning should focus upon general principles so that the learner can apply these and generalize problems and solutions across a range of tasks and contexts (Goldstein 1993: 126), and in a meaningful way. It is important therefore that L&D assists learners in developing the necessary schemas from which general principles may be drawn and applied, and into which new learning and new examples may be assimilated.

Annett and Sparrow (1985) suggested that L&D practitioners can further promote transfer by:

- avoiding rote learning;
- making learning meaningful;
- integrating theory and practice (in order that underlying principles are clearly explicated);
- using varied examples;
- allowing time and opportunity for practice;
- providing the motivation both to learn and to transfer the learning.

To the latter we might add that managers have a role to play in enabling the right conditions to be created in the workplace for the application of new learning to the job. Hence line manager and organizational support are important higher-level features of the environment for learning transfer.

L&D FACTS AND FIGURES

The UK's Chartered Institute of Personnel and Development's (CIPD) Annual Training Survey 2004 found that 41 per cent of respondents rated on-the-job training as the most effective way in which people learn in organizations; 16 per cent of respondents rated formal training courses as the most effective way in which people learn in organizations. (*Source*: Training and Development 2004: Survey Report (April 2004). London: CIPD.)

In addition to the micro features of the learning environment outlined above, a further macro feature of the transfer process is having a climate in the organization that is conducive to the transfer of learning. Goldstein and his colleagues were concerned with those system-wide components of an organization that may impact upon the extent to which a learner arriving with newly acquired skills can apply them in the workplace. So, for example, a learner can arrive in a workplace with knowledge and skills acquired in a learning situation only to discover that the job may not be carried out in the way that he or she has been trained; the equipment that they anticipate being there may be sub-standard, different or absent and so on. Rouillier and Goldstein (1997) identified a series of features (referred to as situational cues) that facilitate transfer, including making sure that:

- learners have the opportunity to use their newly acquired skills;
- learners and experienced managers share their knowledge and skills;
- equipment in the learning situation is similar to that in the job situation;
- an experienced co-worker is assigned to a new recruit to give feedback and coaching on their application of the skills;
- managers ease the pressure, at least for a short time, on new recruits to enable them to get up to speed;
- job aids (such as checklists and protocols) are available to enable learners to accelerate their pace of learning and application of new skills to the job (Goldstein 1993: 42). The use of such devices is consistent with cognitive load theory, which stresses that support for learners must be fully embedded in the task for the learning environment to be effective (van Merrienboer et al. 2003).

Two additional factors are put forward by Reid and Barrington (1999) as ways to assist transfer: firstly, by practising a skill well beyond the minimum level of competence (over-learning) and, secondly, by associating and integrating new learning with learning that has already taken place (similar to Ausubel's concept of meaningful learning) and into extant cognitive structures.

PERSPECTIVE FROM RESEARCH: LEARNERS' PERCEPTIONS AND THE TRANSFER OF LEARNING IN KOREA

Based on the following source: D. H. Lim and S. D. Johnson, 2002. Trainee perceptions of factors that influence learning transfer, *International Journal of Training and Development*, 6(1): 36–48.

The authors studied the effects of various factors on learning in one of the largest Korean conglomerates, the SK Group. The L&D intervention was a three-week course for L&D practitioners in the company and covered concepts and characteristics of performance improvement technology. Lim and Johnson aimed to find out:

1. The extent to which trainees perceived their learning as transferring to their job.
2. What the relationship is between the degree of perceived learning and the resultant transfer to the job.
3. What the factors were that influenced the trainees' ability to transfer learning to the job.

They employed a case study method with ten L&D practitioners and data were gathered by means of interviews, questionnaires and document review. The researchers looked at, amongst other things, the reasons for high transfer to the job and the reasons for low transfer:

1. The most popular reason for high transfer was simple: it was the provision of the opportunity to use the learning on the job.
2. The three most popular reasons for low transfer included: lack of opportunity to apply on the job; undertaking L&D that is not directly related to the job; lack of understanding (i.e. low L&D effectiveness in promoting learning).

There appeared also to be specific work environment features that influenced transfer and these were categorized as being at the individual or the organizational level:

1. At the individual level they included: opportunity to discuss the new learning with supervisors; supervisors' involvement in the L&D; positive feedback from supervisors. A lack of a mentor or role model was seen as a negative factor, as were getting negative feedback and poor work design.
2. At the organizational level the features that promoted transfer included organizational commitment to L&D, the fit between departmental goals and the new learning and the supportiveness and openness of the climate in the organization.

The research suggests that the transfer of learning to the workplace depends upon the interaction of organizational and task factors (such as climate and work design) and management variables (such as support and feedback). Attention to these features of the transfer environment (the workplace) is essential if the time and money invested in training is to have any chance of having an impact upon organizational performance.

Holton and his co-researchers (for example Holton et al. 2000) have theorized and empirically tested the relationships between a number of elements in the L&D system which are theorized as impacting upon transfer. Holton's aim was to develop a robust theory and set of guidelines for practitioners that enable learning transfer to be maximized. The factors that were hypothesized as affecting whether learning transfer will take place or not included such things as learners' readiness, learners' self-efficacy, and learners' motivation to transfer. The features of the environment such as peer and managers' support, and the content validity of the programme are also important (Holton et al. 2000: 339). What Holton is proposing is a model whereby inputs to the L&D process are configured in such a way (i.e. by taking the relevant variables into account) that transfer of learning becomes less of a hit-or-miss affair. Their empirical study in the USA involving 1,616 participants revealed three higher-order factors which may facilitate transfer:

- the climate for transfer that exists in the workplace;
- the job-related utility of the learning;
- the payback or rewards for the learner of the learning.

One interpretation of these and findings from other research is that by attending to the features of the work environment (climate), the job-relatedness of the learning (utility) and by taking close heed of what is 'in it' for the learners (motivations), the transfer of learning from a non-workplace L&D context to the workplace stands a greater chance of success. Holton et al. argue that the time has come to move the transfer of learning from being the topic of research studies to a matter of intervention in L&D as it is practised in organizations. Attending to the crucial matter of learning transfer is an important way of enhancing the value added by L&D interventions.

PERSPECTIVE FROM RESEARCH: TAKING THE TEMPERATURE OF THE TRANSFER CLIMATE IN US ORGANIZATIONS

Based on the following source: E. F. Holton, R. A. Bates, and W. E. A. Ruona, 2000. Development of a generalised learning transfer system inventory, *Human Resource Development Quarterly*, 11(4): 333–60.

Holton and his colleagues have developed an instrument, the *Learning Transfer System Inventory* (*LTSI*), that practitioners can use in order to assess potential transfer problems that might be present in the environment or that might exist as a result of the way the L&D has been designed (Holton et al. 2000: 357). The *LTSI*, as reported by Holton et al. (2000), consisted of 16 factors, including learner readiness, motivation to transfer, support (peer and supervisor) and so forth. Each of these 16 factors can be assessed using multiple-item scales (between three and six items each). The internal consistency of the scales appears to be acceptable with only three of the scales having Cronbach α's below Nunnally's (1978) threshold value of 0.70 (those failing to reach the threshold returned values of 0.63, 0.68 and 0.69 – more than acceptable for exploratory research of this nature). They describe the *LTSI* as a 'pulse-taking diagnostic tool' that will enable L&D practitioners to engage in collaborative action planning to overcome areas of weakness. They cite the examples of overcoming low peer support through team building and enhancing supervisor support by providing supervisor training.

Conclusion: Theory and Practice in L&D

A perplexed student of L&D might ask, 'Why do we need so many theories and models?' Apart from the adage attributed to Kurt Lewin that 'there is nothing so practical as a good theory', a further response to this question might be that none of the theories or models on their own provides a comprehensive enough description and explanation of learning in the workplace. Furthermore, one's own personal ontological and epistemological stance also affects how relevant, valid and useful we might perceive the different theories to be. It can be argued that each of the theories has some explanatory power but they all also have their limitations.

Behaviourism illustrates the importance of feedback and reinforcement (positive and negative), and that reinforcement may need to be constantly topped up to remain effective. Behaviourist approaches are mechanistic; they focus only on behaviours and treat human beings as a 'black boxes' (with inputs and outputs). Behaviourism helps us to understand some of the antecedents of modern L&D theory and practice.

Cognitive information processing theories enable us to delve inside the black box in order to explain human memory and information processing. However, some aspects of information processing theory take rationality (that is, actions based on facts and logic) as a given and may ignore affect. However, as we are well aware, humans are not always rational – emotions and feelings can play an important part in how we think and behave, as does tacit knowledge and implicit learning. There seems to be scope for examining the ways in which feelings and the more automatic, unconscious and intuitive forms of thinking influence our judgements and actions.

Social learning theory offers further insights into cognition; for example, ways in which newcomers to organizations learn certain standards (such as how to interact at work, the dress code, and so forth) and the importance of observational learning and perhaps the implicit learning processes that may be at work. Informal socialization processes expose newcomers to models of behaviour, and experience allows them to practise the behaviours they perceive as important. In an L&D context formalized socialization may be achieved through induction training and mentoring. In an organizational setting there may also be informal reinforcements – for example, correct behaviour being given praise and encouragement and incorrect behaviour being ignored or ridiculed.

Situated learning emphasizes the idea that much of what is learned is specific to the social situation in which it was learned. Through this lens learning is seen as a social phenomenon and the product of participation in practice whereby individuals construct their own and shared meanings through collaboration and interaction with others. It is through legitimate peripheral participation that individuals may become part of a community of practice by gaining a sense of its language, norms and shared meanings. The locus of learning is action-in-context, hence the role of the L&D practitioner may be one of facilitator and guide to the community of practice and an enabler of the process of dialogue and enquiry.

The andragogical model emphasizes, amongst other things, the role that self-direction and experience have to play in adult learning. Moreover, it was emphasized that adults may not learn for the sake of learning but are driven by needs of enhancing their self-esteem, gaining recognition from peers, improving the quality of their life and achieving a sense of purpose and fulfilment. From an L&D perspective this may translate into participatory learning through projects and work-based assignments. Adult learners in the workplace are likely to need to see a 'payback' in the form of a direct application or a 'quick win' from any formal L&D activity. The adult learner is active agent rather than passive recipient (for example, in deciding what to learn). There are a number of difficulties that it is easy to overlook when adopting a self-directing stance with regard to learning; for example, individual and organizational learning agendas may not align or coincide and the andragogical model appears to assume that intrinsic motivation may be taken for granted (for example, that adults will undertake learning if it will help them with their job) whereas sometimes extrinsic motivation is needed.

The experiential learning model and the associated learning cycle emphasizes the importance of the dynamic between concrete experience and abstract conceptualization and between reflective observation and active experimentation. The model also recognizes the role that individual differences may play in the learning process. There have been critiques of the model and especially of the various measures of learning styles. If anything, the experiential learning model appears to be all too easily fallen back on by many researchers and practitioners as a universal framework for explanation and action. One of the problems with 'learning from experience' per se is that learning does not take place automatically by osmosis; sometimes the wrong lesson may have been learned or individuals may come away from potentially valuable learning experiences with nothing at all (McCall 2004: 128). There is a need to facilitate and structure the experiential learning process and capture and share the lessons learned.

So where does this leave the L&D practitioner when confronted with the task of designing and implementing L&D projects? We can draw a number of inferences from the theories and models discussed in this chapter in order to suggest some rules of thumb for practice that combines common sense with a theoretical rationale. The guidelines offered should not be taken as exhaustive or definitive, neither should they be adhered to in the absence of a recognition of the all-too-crucial role that local contextual factors may play in influencing the efficacy or otherwise of L&D. In summary, we can say that to be effective in workplace contexts planned L&D should endeavour to:

1.   Have a definite goal that is related to the learner's needs.
2.   Be linked to existing knowledge.
3.   Actively involve learners in the process and give feedback and reinforcement.
4.   Enable social interaction between learners and experts, who can present good model behaviour, with whom learners may develop a shared language and

meanings and with whom learners may reflect and share their knowledge and skills.

5. Attend to issues of intrinsic and extrinsic motivation.
6. Enhance learners' self-efficacy in relation to learning outcomes and learning performance.
7. Provide the time, space and resources for reflection upon experiences to occur.
8. Elicit, capture and share new knowledge and skills.
9. Attend to the micro features of the learning design and the macro features of the transfer environment if new learning is to translate into enhanced performance.
10. Enable, facilitate and guide the process of dialogue and enquiry.

Concept Checklist

Can you now define each of the Key Concepts listed below, and are you now able to achieve the other Knowledge Outcomes specified at the beginning of the chapter?

- Behaviourism
- Classical conditioning
- Objectives
- Assimilation and accommodation
- Cognitive (information processing) theory
- Short-term memory/working memory
- Long-term memory
- Schema
- Cognitive load theory (CLT)
- Episodic LTM and semantic LTM
- Insight
- Cognitive schema theory (CST)
- Limbic system
- Social learning theory
- Human modelling
- Self-efficacy, motivation and goal-setting theory
- Reciprocal determination
- Situated learning
- Cognitive social interpretations
- Andragogical model of learning
- Experiential learning theory (ELT)
- Learning transfer
- Identical elements and transfer through principles
- Transfer climate

CHAPTER 4
Implicit Learning and Tacit Knowledge

Key Concepts

Implicit learning; incidental learning; explicit learning; incubation; insight; procedural knowledge; declarative knowledge; tacit knowledge; intuition; action scripts; expert; novice; expertise; rationality; neuro-linguistic programming and focusing; knowledge creation; SECI-*ba* model; intuitive practitioner

---

Knowledge Outcomes

After studying this chapter you should be able to:

- define each of the key concepts listed above;
- explain the theoretical and practical significance of the concepts of implicit learning and tacit knowledge;
- explain how knowledge which is not explicit might be surfaced and codified;
- critically evaluate attempts to codify tacit knowledge;
- explain the meaning and significance of the concept of the 'intuitive practitioner' in an L&D context.

Introduction

We can know more than we can tell.

Michael Polanyi, *The Tacit Dimension*

By tradition, and perhaps by default, management theory and practice tends to draw upon rational forms of knowing. Being rational entails the acquisition of knowledge through the power of conscious reasoning and deliberative analytical thought. Within this rational paradigm information is collected, collated, analysed and interpreted; alternatives are formulated; and a logical choice, conclusion or judgement is consciously arrived at. The pre-eminence of the rational paradigm in business is often justified by the assumption that managers are rational decision makers who seek to maximize outcomes in a world where business environments are considered objective entities and successful strategies are the product of deliberate planning (Hodgkinson and Sparrow 2002; Sadler-Smith and Shefy 2004). This may be taken to imply a strategy of information search, acquisition and analysis wherein feelings and emotions are subjugated. Such a position raises a number of problems:

1. Being exclusively rational requires some agreement about goals since these determine what information should be collected and how it should be analysed. But goals are often difficult to formulate, are sometimes ambiguous and even when arrived at may remain contested.
2. Agreement about cause-and-effect relationships is also important since this may inform plans and predictions about future actions and their outcomes. But cause-and-effect relationships may also be ambiguous, and effects may be difficult to attribute and causes hard to isolate.
3. In some decisions emotions or affect may be as useful a form of data as are facts and figures (for example, if there is an information vacuum affect may be the only 'data' that a manager has at her or his disposal).

The assumption that knowledge may be recognized and valued only when it is explicit, untainted by emotions and open to conscious thought and introspection overlooks the potential importance of unconscious mental processes, tacit knowledge and the role of feelings. All of these may be important in the execution of expert performance. The L&D implications of this are, firstly, that there may need to be a recognition of this in learning needs assessment (for example, when eliciting expert performance as a benchmark standard), and, secondly, in the development of expert performance (for example, learners may be able to learn by participation with and observation of some of the more intuitive aspects of an expert's performance).

L&D FACTS AND FIGURES

'I believe sensitiveness about our intellects is often due especially to the fact that the part of behaviour of which we are most conscious is at least largely intellectual, whereas much of our most effective behaviour, such as reflects vitality, decisiveness and responsibility, is largely a matter of course, unconscious, responsive, and on the whole has to be so to be effective' (Barnard 1948).

In learning and development (L&D) theories of learning are more often than not concerned with describing and explaining those learning processes in which there is a conscious and overt attempt to acquire new knowledge or learn a new skill. Learning (and especially training) is often viewed from an instrumental perspective as an intentional process aimed at improving effectiveness (Huber 1996: 125). This is unsurprising since one of the aims of L&D is to enable, facilitate or provide organized activities designed to produce behavioural change (see Nadler 1979: 3). One of the L&D practitioner's roles is to offer some form of intervention (for example, a training course) in the anticipation that the outcome of the intervention will be more or less apparent (through an individual's changed behaviours, for example). The assumption in providing a tangible intervention, and which will produce a change in the learners that will be identifiable, is that both the L&D process and the outcomes are overt, conscious and explicit. Recall, however, that in the previous chapter we met the example of observational learning in which participants' negotiating skills improved but they were unable to articulate why or how (Nadler et al. 2003). The participants in the observational learning in Nadler et al.'s study may have been engaged in an implicit learning process that gave rise to the acquisition of tacit knowledge. The process by which the learning occurred appeared to be difficult for the participants to identify or articulate. This implicit type of learning is not confined to observational learning but occurs in a wide range of work and everyday settings and is important, therefore, for L&D theory and practice.

Implicit Learning

Implicit learning is the acquisition of knowledge that takes place largely:

- independently of conscious attempts to learn;
- without awareness of how learning took place;
- in the absence of explicit knowledge about what knowledge or skill was acquired (Reber 1993).

Educational, and by extension L&D, theory and practice has been concerned almost exclusively with the explicit and overt learning functions (Reber 1993).

However, in many learning situations (or life experiences more generally) implicit learning takes place with an inevitability, and the outcome of any learning experience or event may have both explicit and implicit facets. The balance between these components will depend upon the individual, context and process and, moreover, the outcome of such implicit learning is difficult to control or predict. From a practical point of view, it is important for the L&D practitioner to understand those processes which may be difficult to plan for (as well as being able to understand those processes that are more manageable), if the knowledge assets of an organization are to be utilized to their fullest extent. Organizations contain more knowledge than people can express and the latent knowledge is waiting to be transformed, voiced and interpreted (Starbuck and Hedberg 2001: 336). This can be crucial in a dynamic and turbulent business environment where learning and knowledge may be a source of differentiation and competitive advantage. Implicit learning and tacit knowledge provide a potentially valuable asset for which the L&D practitioner must be able to provide assistance in unlocking and leveraging to the advantage of individuals and organizations.

From a historical standpoint research and theorizing on the subject of implicit learning gathered pace in the 1960s. The term 'implicit' (which is broadly equivalent to incidental learning and learning-without-awareness) was chosen by the psychologist Arthur Reber to differentiate it from the explicit learning that various cognitive theorists and others at that time were focusing their thoughts and attentions upon. Some of the antecedents of this idea can be traced to the writings of the physical chemist turned social philosopher Michael Polanyi, who argued that there existed a tacit knowledge whose contents are not part of one's normal consciousness or open to introspection. He is most famously quoted as saying that 'we can know more than we can tell'. Subjective insights, intuitions and hunches fall into this category of knowing (Nonaka et al. 2001: 494). Tacit knowledge is personal, intuitive and context specific; it is difficult to verbalize, formalize and communicate to others (Child 2001: 660).

Dreyfus and Dreyfus (1986) proposed that the progress from being a novice, (defined as someone who tends to be reliant upon detached, context-free rules) to being an expert (i.e. someone who is able to draw upon involved, situation-specific, experience-based intuitions) involves learning through a number of levels of progression. Within Dreyfus and Dreyfus's model the highest level of skill acquisition is that of 'expertise', which is based upon mature and practised understanding and total, often intuitive, engagement in skilful performance. At this level experts (including expert managers or expert L&D practitioners), rather than solving problems and making decisions in a laborious manner, would 'do what normally works' (Dreyfus and Dreyfus 1986: 31), probably based wholly or in part upon their tacit reading of the cues that characterize a situation, and by drawing upon and executing previously learned and sometimes complex action scripts (Klein 2003). Expert performers are therefore intuitive practitioners, who base their actions upon an intuition developed through long exposure and 'apprenticeship' in practice rather than any innate 'sixth sense'.

Expert performers may not be able to provide a convincing rational verbal explanation for their intuitively derived decisions, but nonetheless well-honed intuitive expertise brings with it an agility and fluidity of performance based upon the ability to call upon a large repertoire of knowledge and understanding and discriminate across a large number and variety of situations. Against this back-cloth of an argument for the significance of tacit forms of knowing and the role of experience and expertise in learning and performing, intuition and rationality can be seen as parallel and perhaps mutually reinforcing ways of knowing. This assertion has a number of potential ramifications:

1. Being exclusively rational or exclusively intuitive brings with it a partial view of the world.
2. A more holistic approach to decision making, problem solving and learning involves uniting intuition and rationality into a third, hybrid mode of think-ing which capitalizes upon the strengths of each approach but also relies upon each one to off-set biases associated with the other (Sadler-Smith and Shefy 2004). This hybrid mode might be called *intuitive intelligence*.
3. As problems become more complex, the business environment more uncer-tain and dynamic ('white water' environments) and the limits of rationality recognized more widely, implicit learning and tacit knowledge may become increasingly important in management in general and in L&D theory and practice in particular.

Vince (2003: 559) noted that L&D practitioners are often searching for certain-ties in an uncertain world of contradictions. He argued that it might be more useful to search for contradictions as they are in more plentiful supply, and made a plea for L&D to get 'more complicated'. One way in which this complexity may be engaged with is by recognizing and acknowledging the ostensibly non-rational (such as intuition) as well as rational forms of knowing. The hypothesized rela-tionships between explicit learning, implicit learning and tacit knowledge are pre-sented in Figure 4.1.

L&D FACTS AND FIGURES

'Michael Polanyi's (1891–1976) philosophy of science argued that there is no scientific method that can be transmitted as a logical and rigorous method to be learned in textbooks. Science is learned by the practice that is trans-mitted from master to apprentice. A crucial part of scientific knowledge that is learned is tacit in character, so that it cannot be spoken, but only demon-strated and imitated' (Nye 2002).

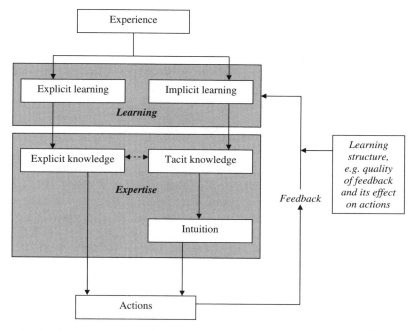

Figure 4.1   Explicit learning, implicit learning and tacit knowledge (based on Burke and Sadler-Smith 2006)

PERSPECTIVE FROM PRACTICE: TACIT TACTICS – IF TACIT KNOWLEDGE CANNOT BE CODIFIED HOW CAN IT BE MANAGED?

Based on the following source: R. M. Grant, 2000. Shifts in the world economy. In C. Despres and D. Chauvel (eds), *Knowledge Horizons: the Present and the Promise of Knowledge Management*. Boston: Butterworth Heinmann, pp. 27–54.

Compared to tacit knowledge, explicit knowledge is identifiable, codifiable and manageable and the various developments in management information systems, information technology and knowledge management systems are part of this endeavour. However, there is a fundamental paradox in the management of tacit knowledge. If tacit knowledge is largely inarticulable (it cannot easily be told), how can it be expressed, let alone codified and managed? Grant (2000: 51) offers three questions that may be asked by L&D practitioners in those organizations that confront the important issue of the management of their tacit knowledge assets:

Continued

Tacitness: firstly, what is the degree of tacitness of the knowledge? Tacit knowledge may be embedded in expertise to varying degrees. For example, a wine taster's tacit knowledge or artist's aesthetic sensibility (known only to him or her) may be considered to be a deeply embedded form of tacit knowledge (nonetheless people do attend wine-tasting training programmes). Other aspects of expertise, for example how to make a ceramic pot, although tacit (in the 'tips of the potter's fingers') are by no means untrainable, but such learning usually takes place through one-to-one teaching from an expert. Hence, from an L&D perspective some view needs to be taken of the extent to which the knowledge in question may be transmitted, if not articulated and codified. If, for example, the knowledge is something that rests upon the unique set of abilities, skills, experiences and talents of an individual, any attempt to codify it may prove fruitless. If it is inarticulable it may nonetheless be transferable by non-verbal means.

Context: secondly, what is the role of social context in the transfer of tacit knowledge? In the example of the potter above it was argued that learning can take place under the close guidance of an expert. The latter represents recognition that 'uncodifiable knowledge can be transferred, integrated and enriched within the appropriate social context' and within this context the main medium of communication is a narrative based upon a shared language and set of interests, and a common knowledge base (Grant 2000: 51).

Integration: finally, if tacit knowledge cannot be codified and transferred can its disparate elements be integrated in such a way as to leverage enhanced performance? Grant argued that a challenge for businesses is the integration of the knowledge bases that experts and specialists possess and might contribute. In other words, rather than attempt to replicate tacit knowledge, it may be better to efficiently integrate the different knowledge types without the cost of experts having to learn from each other. One way to achieve this is to modularize production – as in the case of Microsoft's approach to the production of its MS Office package, in which experts' knowledge was integrated by modularization of the efforts of several hundred different experts (Grant 2000).

Conscious and Unconscious Processing

Our discussion of learning in previous chapters was concerned mainly with conscious processing. However, as implied by the notions of implicit learning and tacit knowledge, there are unconscious as well as conscious aspects to cognition. Furthermore, a moment's introspection by the reader may reveal insights about the extent of the unconscious nature of much skilled performance. Take the act of speech, for example: when talking in one's native language the speaker is typically unaware of the rules of syntax and grammar that are being followed and he or she probably cannot describe the circumstances under which the rules were learned in spite of the fact that the rules are often obeyed almost flawlessly (Woltz 2003). The memory structures underlying much of skilled performance have been described as an implicit memory (Reber 1989; Woltz 2003) and are often procedural in their nature.

From an L&D perspective implicit learning and tacit knowledge are potentially useful concepts in a number of areas; for example, they can be used to explain how experts can perform tasks and skills without the same level of conscious effort required by novices. It may help to explain how 'intuitive' decisions come more easily to managers who have extensive experience, whose 'intuitions', rather than being some instinctual 'sixth sense', may be no more than past experiences which have become 'frozen' into habits of mind (Simon 1989). These may be stored as implicit memories which individuals are not generally consciously aware of (Davis and Davis 2003: 129).

The role of the unconscious in cognition is sometimes illustrated by the example of the phenomenon of incubation, which is often witnessed in the solving of complex problems. By taking a break from the problem or 'sleeping on it', our unconscious mental processes appear to work on the problem, the solution to which may then be revealed to our consciousness in the 'eureka!' or 'aha!' moment. Incubation is part of Wallas's (1926) theory, which depicts creativity as a four-stage process (recall that there have been attempts to map this onto the experiential model – see Chapter 3):

1. Preparation: creativity demands a familiarity with and an immersion in the topic of interest and the problem to hand. For example, Pasteur said, 'Chance only favours the prepared mind'.
2. Incubation: this is where the unconscious mind appears to come to our rescue in solving problems and generating creative solutions. For example, the scientist Kekule allegedly made a major breakthrough in his discovery of the ring structure of the chemical benzene when he dreamt of snakes swallowing their own tails (the benzene molecule is in the form of a ring of atoms joined together).
3. Illumination: this is the sudden flash of insight, as when Archimedes made his famous discovery and, so the story goes, leapt naked from his bath and ran down the street in ancient Greece shouting 'Eureka' (meaning 'I have found it!').
4. Verification: this is the time-consuming stage of proving the new idea and implementing it. Edison is often quoted as saying: 'Genius is 2 per cent inspiration and 98 per cent perspiration.'

Insight is a 'distinctive and sometimes seemingly sudden understanding of a problem, or of a strategy that aids the solving of the problem' (Sternberg 1999: 364). It is often characterized by a 'sudden flash', most often in the context of a well-defined task and sometimes after a period of unconscious incubation (Shirley and Langan-Fox 1996: 564). When an insight solution occurs the problem solver suddenly moves from a state of not knowing how to solve a problem to a state of knowing how to solve it (Mayer 1995). Insight relies upon unconscious processes and may be distinguished from intuition in that insight reveals the logical relations between the problem and the answer (insight solutions often appear to be disappointingly obvious after the fact).

L&D FACTS AND FIGURES

An example of an insight problem is the 'prisoner in the tower' problem, which goes as follows. The prisoner was trying to escape from a tower using a rope that was only half long enough to allow her to reach the ground safely. The prisoner divided the rope into two pieces, tied them together and was then able to escape successfully. How could this be?*

PERSPECTIVE FROM RESEARCH: SHEDDING LIGHT ON INCUBATION AND INSIGHT IN PROBLEM SOLVING

Based on the following source: M. Jung-Beeman, E. M. Bowden, J. Haberman, J. L. Frymiare, S. Arambel-Lui, R. Greenblatt, P. J. Reber, and J. Kounios, 2004. Neural activity when people solve verbal problems with insight, *Public Library of Science Biology* 2(4): 0500–0510. http://biology.plosjournals.org

Neurological research evidence has shed light upon the brain region that may be involved in the insight process. Jung-Beeman et al. (2004) devised a series of insight problems comprising words ('crab', 'pine' and 'sauce'** or 'fence', 'card' and 'master'***) for which participants were required to come up with a linking fourth word and to press a button when they experienced their 'eureka' moment. Subjects' brains were mapped using FMRI (functional magnetic resonance imaging) and EEG (electroencephalography). The laborious thinking activity appeared to be in the left hemisphere but a telltale sign of neural activity was identified in a small region of the right brain (the anterior superior temporal gyrus, aSTG) at the moment of insight. This region seems to be implicated in tasks that require the identification of broad associative semantic relationships. The researchers have discounted the effect as an emotional jolt at the moment of insight because activity in the same region was encountered when the problem was administered. The telltale sign was of high-frequency (γ band) activity that reflects complex cognitive processing which occurred 0.3 seconds before participants pressed the button.

---

*   The rope is untwined and the two lengths tied together to give a rope half as thin but twice as long.

**   Apple.

***   Post.

Jung-Beeman et al. concluded that general problem solving involves complex cortical networks to encode, retrieve and evaluate information but that their results show that insight problem solving is unique and involves at least one additional component over and above this (2004: 416) that appears to operate at an unconscious level. The research sheds important light on the growing role of cognitive neuro-psychology in explaining learning and emotion. From a practical perspective, it provides some objective evidence relating to the neurological processes that may underlie the practice of allowing certain problems to go away and 'cook' in the unconscious mind or be 'slept on' as a way to promote their solution.

Myers (2002: 57) noted that tacit knowledge is often procedural (a knowing about 'how' – a distinction made by Ryle in the 1940s), unlike explicit knowledge which is more often associated with 'knowing that'. This parallels the distinction between procedural knowledge (how) and declarative knowledge (what) (see Anderson 1990). It is important to note that not all procedural knowledge is tacit or acquired implicitly. Implicit learning is largely an inductive process (based on particular instances) in which complex information about the environment in which one is operating may be acquired independently of awareness of the process or the content of the learning. It is implicated in some of the most important and fundamental episodes of human learning including natural language learning and socialization (Reber 1993). In an organizational context Hodgkinson and Sparrow (2002: 52) noted that as a result of the 'tacitness' of knowing, much of managers' thinking, deciding and problem solving occurs through processes that may not necessarily take rational elements into account. This does not mean that managers are irrational actors, but what it does suggest is that their learning may be the result of unconscious or not explicitly rational processes. The precise role of tacit knowledge in the management field has been explored by Wagner and Sternberg in the USA, who used problem-solving scenarios in an attempt to measure the kind of practical 'know-how' that is rarely described formally or taught directly.

PERSPECTIVE FROM RESEARCH: THE ROLE OF TACIT KNOWLEDGE IN MANAGEMENT

Based on the following source: R. K. Wagner, 2002. Smart people doing dumb things: the case of managerial incompetence. In R. J. Sternberg (ed.), *Why Smart People Can Be So Stupid*. New Haven, CT: Yale University Press, pp. 42–63.

Tacit knowledge has been defined by Wagner (2002: 51) as 'practical know-how that is rarely described formally or taught directly' but which is used

Continued

to solve the ill-defined problems that we face in everyday life and for which there is often no one right answer. Measuring this type of tacit knowledge may sound like a contradiction in terms; however, there are researchers who have attempted to do just this. Wagner and his fellow researchers have devised tests which consist of scenarios derived from interviews with successful managers in which, for example, participants were asked to imagine they have been promoted to the post of head of an important department in the organization with the task of 'shaping it up' quickly, not in the light of glaring deficiencies but against a backcloth of 'so-so' performance. Each participant is then presented with a range of strategies (say, three) such as: 'buy time by taking quick but limited action whilst considering what needs to be done in the longer run'. Scoring was done in terms of how they performed relative to how an expert would react. The tacit knowledge measure of the type used by Wagner is a performance (rather than self-report) measure. There have been a number of studies using this approach and the findings that have emerged suggest that:

1. Individuals can be differentiated on the basis of tacit knowledge as measured using Wagner's test; for example, performance on the tacit knowledge task differed between experienced managers, MBA students and undergraduates (Wagner and Sternberg 1985).
2. There are correlations between tacit knowledge scores and various criterion measures of managerial performance including salary, position in the Fortune 500 list, merit pay awards, new business venturing success and leadership performance.
3. Tacit knowledge showed only low correlations with measures of ability such as verbal reasoning.

The Three I's (Incubation, Insight and Intuition)

In Wallas's classic model of creativity the early preparatory stage (in which the individual is immersed in the problem and its context) is succeeded by a period of incubation during which (it is argued) unconscious mental processes are at work and eventually yield a solution in the so-called 'aha' or 'eureka' moment of insight. When insight occurs the individual is able to explain the solution to the problem encountered. In intuition this is usually not the case; for example, Bowers et al.'s definition of intuition is as a 'preliminary perception of coherence (pattern, meaning, structure) that is at first not consciously represented but which nevertheless guides thought and inquiry towards a hunch or hypothesis about the nature of the coherence in question' (1990: 74). When intuition occurs there is the felt sense of a solution but this may be difficult or impossible to put into words. In their experimental work on problem solving with college students, Bowers et al. found that participants' guesses were indicative of accurate intuitive hunches and this led the researchers to conclude that the tacit unconscious understandings of the coherence of the problem guided participants to an explicit representation of the form that the solution to the problem might eventually take.

Intuition in Management

Reber (1993) equated the psychologist's notion of implicit learning with the layperson's understanding of intuition (i.e. coming to a judgement automatically without knowledge of the rules of inference involved). Intuition may be considered as having a number of components, namely cognitive, affective (emotions and feelings) and somatic (bodily). The cognitive component of intuition is distilled from learning and experience (Agor 1989; Behling and Eckel 1991; Shirley and Langan-Fox 1996; Burke and Miller 1999; Claxton 2000; Hogarth 2001; Klein 2003). Intuition is embodied in unconscious processes that manifest themselves in the apparently effortless and spontaneous solving of problems, but which in reality draw upon elaborate cognitive structures built up over many years of learning and experience (Behling and Eckel 1991). This expertise allows some individuals (for example, an expert instructor or an experienced CEO) to make a decision within seconds in situ. The cognitive explanation for intuition is most famously expressed in Simon's assertion that intuitive judgements are 'simply analyses frozen into habit and into the capacity for rapid response through recognition' (Simon 1989: 38). Klein summarized the process as a staged one in which:

- the situation generates cues;
- the cues let the individual recognize patterns;
- the patterns activate action scripts;
- the action scripts are implemented and affect the situation that generated the cues (2003: 13).

Whether an intuitive or a rational approach is taken depends to some extent upon the situation, problem and context. Klein (2003: 57) argued that intuition functions as a kind of peripheral (wide-angle) vision that keeps us oriented to and aware of our surroundings, whereas rationality is more attuned to a foveal (pinpoint) vision. The latter approach can be used to identify 'hard' facts and figures upon which to conduct logical analyses and from which predictions and plans about the future can be made. When the problems faced are simple and routine the necessary facts and figures are often readily available and can be drawn upon, interpreted and used in a rational manner. However, the solutions for many problems may be beyond knowledge that is explicit, immediately to hand or readily detectable. In this situation managers can acquire more facts and data to fuel their rational thinking processes; but this has a number of potential difficulties: firstly, the external knowledge may not be available; secondly, by accumulating more knowledge managers may inadvertently subject themselves to 'information overload' and be afflicted by 'analysis paralysis'; thirdly, by the time the extra knowledge needed to solve the problem is available the problem itself may have changed, disappeared or been solved by competitors (see Sadler-Smith and Shefy 2004). Klein (2003) argued that certain sets of conditions favour intuition whilst others favour rationality:

Conditions favouring intuition: time pressure; ill-defined goals; dynamic conditions; experienced participants.

Conditions favouring rationality: conflict resolution; optimization; justification; computational complexity.

The rapid recognition and response that characterizes intuition depends upon the availability of extensive and well-organized schemas and a correspondingly complex set of discrimination rules that allow for quick and accurate judgements to be made (Kaufmann 2001: 58). This would make the tacit knowledge that underpins an expert's intuition unique, complex and difficult to articulate as it consists of ingrained mental models, beliefs and perspectives (Cole 1998; Leonard and Sensiper 1998). It also makes it a difficult-to-imitate knowledge asset and hence a potentially useful way of differentiating one's human resource base from that of competitor organizations. For example, after years of experience a skilled craftsman develops a wealth of readily available expertise which is so entrenched that it tends to be taken for granted (Nonaka 1994) and which is often learned through participation in a community of fellow practitioners (Wenger 1998) who have shared language, interest and knowledge. For this reason tacit knowledge and intuition contribute to an organization's knowledge assets in ways that may be very difficult for competitors to imitate. Hence an individual's expertise produces an individual's capability to be intuitive as a result of implicit learning acquired over long periods and accumulated expertise in real-world contexts. The individual's accumulated expertise interacts with the local context to determine the most appropriate actions. Feedback upon those actions then informs the implicit and explicit learning process, but this feedback process itself may be affected by the environment and by how good the feedback is for building intuition (see Hogarth 2001).

L&D FACTS AND FIGURES

When a sample of US professionals and managers were asked, 'What does it mean to make decisions using your intuition?', the most popular responses were that these were experienced-based decisions (50 per cent) or affect-initiated decisions based on gut-feel and hunch (40 per cent). None of the respondents viewed intuition as a paranormal power. Forty-seven per cent of the sample said they often used intuition at work, whilst only 3 per cent said they rarely used it. (*Source*: L. A. Burke and M. K. Miller, 1999. Taking the mystery out of intuitive decision-making, *Academy of Management Executive*, 13: 91–9.)

These arguments support the definition of intuition as experientially established cognitive schemas that work to simplify individual decision making (Wally and Baum 1994; Burke and Miller 1999). In this way, intuition is viewed as a cognitive culmination or mental model of a person's life experiences (Simon 1987; Agor 1989; Behling and Eckel 1991; Shapiro and Spence 1997), and most certainly not as some type of mystical 'sixth sense' or paranormal power. Moreover, intuition is viewed as a precursor to creative thought (Bastick 1982) and is enabled by the human cognitive attributes of long-term memory, rapid retrieval and automatic rules of inference (Isenberg 1984). The unverbalized tacit managerial knowledge (intuition) that makes for success in areas such as motivating staff, delegation, how to 'read' people and how to promote one's own career appears to be associated with better performance ratings and higher salaries (Myers 2002: 57). It may serve as the base for conscious operations where we have the sense of the correct action or response but are incapable of articulating why this is the case (Raelin 2000: 58). Hence our implicitly acquired, tacit, unverbalizable knowledge may manifest itself in hunch or intuition. Often these 'gut feelings' can guide a person's creative, decision-making or problem-solving behaviours.

The dynamic between tacit and explicit ways of knowing in many ways reflects the supposed dichotomy of intuition versus rationality that some have argued is a fundamental aspect of managers' thinking style (for example, Allinson and Hayes 1996). Within this dichotomy individuals may be depicted as being either more or less of each of these and hence varying in their preferred way of thinking along a continuum from highly intuitive to highly rational. However, this has been challenged in empirical work by Hodgkinson and Sadler-Smith (2003), who argued that it makes more sense both theoretically and empirically to talk about intuition *and* rationality (they provided statistical evidence from over 1,000 participants in support of construct validity of their claim) rather than intuition *or* rationality. If we accept that intuition and rationality can coexist, this raises interesting, not to say challenging, possibilities from an L&D perspective: namely, how can we develop managers' intuitive awareness given that the majority of their management education is likely to have been devoted to the development of rational analysis? How can we develop managers' intuitive intelligence?

Discussion Point

Think of a situation in which you relied upon your intuition to make a decision. What was the issue, what was the context and what decision were you confronted with? What was the outcome of relying upon your intuition? Do you think your intuition served you well or badly in this case? Why? Do you think your intuition serves you well or badly in general? Why?

**PERSPECTIVE FROM PRACTICE: DEVELOPING
MANAGERS' INTUITIVE AWARENESS**

Based on the following source: E. Sadler-Smith, and E. Shefy, 2004. The intuitive executive: understanding and applying 'gut feel' in decision-making, *Academy of Management Executive*, 18(4): 76–91.

The argument put forward by Sadler-Smith and Shefy is that intuition is inevitable in that we are all the (perhaps at times unwilling) recipients of our own intuitions and that the gut feelings associated with intuition are a form of 'soft data'. A number of authors recognize that intuition can also be perilous to the inexperienced or unaware manager. Wind and Crook (2005: 178–81), for example, suggest that intuition can be wrong for a number of reasons:

1. When the world changes we may be left with an intuition that was highly developed but is out of 'sync' with the current environment.
2. Our intuitions have been developed in environments that give bad feedback, hence the intuitions that we may be subject to are themselves poor. This type of learning environment is termed a 'wicked' environment, as opposed to a 'kind' learning environment (Hogarth 2001).
3. When we do not communicate with others what we are going to do on the basis of our intuitions it makes it difficult for others to work with us (Wind and Crook 2005).

Similarly, Sadler-Smith and Shefy (2004) urged managers to be wary of blindly following intuition and instead suggested that an intelligent approach to intuition combines intuitive judgements with rational approaches to optimize the extent to which biases from one source (intuition or rationality) may be offset by the strengths of the other source. Intuitions may therefore be subject to the checks and balances of rational analysis, whilst rationally derived judgements may be scrutinized from the point of view of the question, 'How does this decision *feel* to me?' In order to assist managers in making better use of their intuitions, the authors suggested seven rules for the intelligent use of intuition These are summarized in Table 4.1.

Intuition is inevitable and often compelling and it can be handled well or badly. It is important, therefore, from an L&D perspective that individuals have the awareness and skills to handle their intuition. All too often the content of L&D is biased in favour of rational analysis, but given the significance of the tacit knowledge and expertise which underlie intuitive judgements, it is important that L&D embraces the tools and techniques for developing learners' intuitive awareness.

Table 4.1 Sadler-Smith and Shefy's seven recommendations for handling intuition (*Source*: Sadler-Smith and Shefy 2004)

Rule	Description
Opening up the 'closet'	Learners should ask themselves the question, 'To what extent do you: experience intuition; trust your feelings; count on intuitive judgements; suppress your hunches; covertly rely upon gut feel?
Not mixing up your I's	It is important to be able to distinguish between instinct, insight and intuition. To get a better feel for what intuition is learners should practise distinguishing between their instincts, insights and intuitions.
Eliciting good feedback	Feedback is crucial in developing good intuitive judgement skills, therefore learners should seek feedback on the intuitive judgements that they make and in this way they may build confidence in their gut feelings and also create a learning environment around them where they can develop better intuitive awareness.
Getting a feel for your 'batting average'	Benchmarking your intuitions is a good way to get a feel for how accurate they are and for getting a sense for how reliable they are and also asking 'How might my intuitive judgements be improved?'
Using imagery	Learners can be encouraged to use imagery rather than words; literally visualize potential future scenarios that take their gut feelings into account.
Playing devil's advocate	Learners can test out their intuitive judgements by raising objections to them, generating counter-arguments, probing just how robust their gut feel is when challenged.
Capturing and validating intuitions	By 'quieting the rational mind' learners can be trained to create the inner state that can allow the intuitive mind the freedom to roam. These intuitions can then be captured and logged before they are censored by rational analysis.

Telling What We Know

Implicit learning may present practical problems for managers and organizations. For example, tacit knowledge acquired through concrete experiences in one situation may not transfer easily to another situation. Managers who move between jobs may need to relearn a whole set of implicit knowledge that is not taught directly but only absorbed through practice in context. Hence, from an L&D perspective, these findings raise important questions of 'if?' and 'how?' tacit knowledge can be developed. Raelin (2000: 53) contended that even though much tacit knowledge may not be codifiable, it may be teachable through a competent instructor providing an observable model that a learner can imitate. There are clear links here to the observational elements of social learning theory (Bandura) and also to situated learning theory (Lave and Wenger) and to the theories of knowledge creation (especially those of Nonaka and his colleagues). In drawing a distinction between explicit and tacit forms of knowledge Raelin (2000) added a further dimension – that of modes of learning. He combines these into a typology of work-based learning at the individual level of analysis which shares some of the features of the experiential learning cycle (Kolb 1984). His framework yields four types of learning: conceptualization and reflection (explicit); and experimentation and experience (tacit). Like Kolb, Raelin agrees that individuals are predisposed to particular types of learning but that all four should be used to 'engender the most learning in the shortest amount of time' (2000: 55). The model is shown in Figure 4.2.

Central to the acquisition of implicit knowledge and the ability to respond intuitively is the individual's immersion in experience. However, the argument of Raelin and Nonaka and others is that this acquisition of knowledge is not enough and it has to be augmented with the process of reflection (either individual or collective). This raises the vexed question of what we mean by the term 'learning' in a work context. Scrutiny and reflection are seen by many as crucial for productive learning (for example in the work of Argyris, Schon and Senge – see Chapter 5). Unexamined or unreflected practice can quickly become rigidified into routines that may have outlived their usefulness to the extent that thinking becomes constrained and converges to a narrow groove. On the other hand, action that is

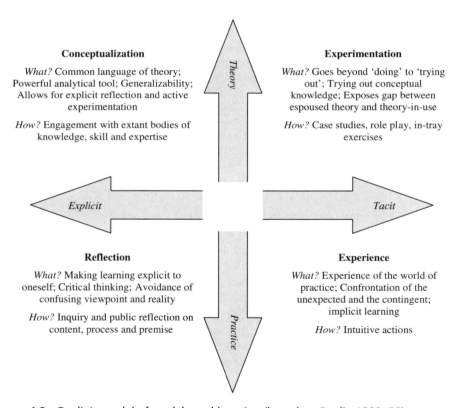

Figure 4.2   Raelin's model of work-based learning (based on Raelin 1999: 55)

subjected to critical scrutiny (for example, by using the methods of action learning and action science) constitutes reflective practice that opens the door for a more divergent form of thinking and learning that may enable individuals and organizations to go beyond their existing capabilities. Raelin argued that it is important for this reflective process to be 'public' or shared and brought into the open for a number of reasons:

1. Learners need to be aware of their own behaviours and the consequences of these.
2. There may be a gap between what we say either to ourselves or to others about what we propose to do and what we actually do.
3. Our untested assumptions, errors and biases need to be brought out into the open.
4. To test the validity of our actions that may be based upon past successes but which may no longer be effective under different or changed circumstances (2000: 103–4).

The issue of context is crucial when considering if and how tacit knowledge may be developed. Exposure to and immersion in context in the presence of role models and with the assistance of coaches and mentors is one way in which managers can learn from experience. Job rotation and secondment are classic cases in point: managers can develop effective skills in these new contexts often through implicit learning processes. However, the effectiveness of these experiences depends upon the role models, the context for learning, and the extent to which managers are able to reflect upon and process the knowledge and skills that are available to be learned. Without the opportunity to reflect contemplatively and critically, managers will know how to solve specific problems in depth but may have not learned sufficiently to decide when the implicit skills can or cannot be applied in new situations (see Raelin 2000: 19) and hence may have acquired technique but lack expertise (see Dreyfus and Dreyfus 1986 below).

Discussion Point

What tactics might be available to an L&D practitioner to extend her or his own personal tacit knowledge through implicit learning? Or do you think that 'tactics' and 'tacit' are a contradiction in terms?

The Acquisition of Expertise

The intuitive judgements that may characterize expert performance make considerable use of tacit knowledge. Even when the knowledge is capable of being explicitly described it may be used tacitly because that is usually quicker (Eraut

2000). Extensive and elaborate tacit knowledge takes time and, paradoxically, effort to acquire. It occurs through the deep and prolonged immersion in practice and develops in tandem with the acquisition of explicit forms of knowledge in the same and related domains. Wagner (2002), in summarizing the research on the acquisition of expertise, noted that expertise is not acquired cheaply; in his view even the most eminent individuals in arts and sciences require a decade or more of intense training. Expertise is more often than not domain specific; for example, chess grand masters have superior recall for the arrangement of the pieces on the board when they are in a meaningful configuration as opposed to a random one. The skill acquisition model of Dreyfus and Dreyfus (1986) brings together situational understanding, routinized action and decision making into a five-stage model of the development of expertise. The five stages are shown in Table 4.2.

This discussion began with a paradox: much of the learning that takes place in the workplace is implicit and may give rise to the acquisition (albeit unconsciously) of tacit knowledge. If this is the case, where does that leave the L&D practitioner whose role it is to facilitate learning and to improve the management of an organization's knowledge assets? How can she or he help the organization to surface, codify and store tacit knowledge? Eraut (2000) identified four reasons why we as practitioners might want to help individuals and organizations acquire tacit knowledge and make tacit knowledge more explicit:

- to improve of the quality of an individual's or a team's performance;
- to communicate knowledge to another person;
- for the critical (i.e. reflective) control of one's actions;
- to construct artefacts that can assist decision making or reasoning.

'Explicitness' is needed both for improving performance and for accountability (Eraut 2000). As we have seen, implicit learning, the acquisition of tacit knowl-

Table 4.2 Five stages of Dreyfus and Dreyfus's skill acquisition model (*Source*: Dreyfus and Dreyfus 1986)

Stage	Description
1 *Novice*	Characterized by, for example, rigid adherence to taught rules or plans.
2 *Advanced beginner*	For example, guidelines for action based on global characteristics of situations recognizable only after some prior experience.
3 *Competent*	For example, coping with the crowdedness of problem scenarios; sees actions at least partially in terms of longer-term goals.
4 *Proficient*	For example, situations are seen holistically rather than in terms of sets of separate aspects; and seeing what is most important in a situation.
5 *Expert*	For example, no longer relies on rules, guidelines or maxims; has an intuitive grasp of situations based on deep tacit understanding; analytic approaches are used only in novel situations; and when problems occur or when justifying conclusions the expert has a realistic vision of what is possible.

edge and the making of tacit knowledge explicit depend upon both experience and inquiry (ideally as public or collective reflection). Experience can be fostered in a number of ways: for example, by having an expert human model to emulate and learn from through narratives, imitation and practice (much like the master–apprentice relationship, in coaching, job-instruction training and mentoring). Experience can also be gained through job rotation and secondments, but the tacit knowledge thus acquired may have limited general application in the absence of reflection. In terms of practical recommendations, Eraut's research found that individuals were able to talk more explicitly about their knowledge at work when there was:

- some mediating object (for example, an X-ray image in health care, a video or diagram or a piece of equipment);
- a climate of regular mutual consultation;
- a formal relationship, for example through training or mentoring, in which explanations were expected;
- an informal relationship leading to work-related discussions of information out of hours, when more 'provisional' and 'riskier' comments might be made;
- a crisis, review or radical change in practice, which caused people to exchange opinions and experiences, and make their values more explicit.

A further factor in Eraut's view was the role of continuing education, which added to individuals' ability to think and talk about work by providing a *vocabulary* for verbalizing aspects of their experiences, and giving the necessary concepts and theories which helped them to understand issues and see alternative perspectives more quickly and clearly. This corresponded to the role played by explicit theory (conceptualization) in Raelin's model of work-based learning (2000: 55). Instructional technologies such as video may be one way of drawing learners' attention to features of a situation that are below-the-surface aspects of behaviour in order to convey both explicit and tacit knowledge. Eraut (2000) argued that a skilled coach can stop, scrutinize and repeat a video episode to ensure that observers and coach are looking at and talking about the same thing, and not be distracted by unimportant surface features. The expertise of the coach lies both in the comments provided as well as in the selection of scenes and episodes for closer observation.

Discussion Point

What are the skills and aptitudes that distinguish an expert L&D practitioner from a novice L&D practitioner? How might you recognize or measure expert L&D performance?

PERSPECTIVE FROM PRACTICE: NEURO-LINGUISTIC PROGRAMMING (NLP) AND FOCUSING

Based upon the following sources: J. O'Connor and J. Seymour, 1990. *Introducing NLP: Psychological Skills for Understanding and Influencing People*. London: Element; E. T. Gendlin, 1981. *Focusing*. New York: Bantam.

Techniques such as neuro-linguistic programming (NLP) build on notions of stage models of learning and expertise (unconscious incompetence, conscious incompetence, conscious competence and unconscious competence). NLP was developed in the 1970s by Bandler (mathematician and information scientist) and Grinder (a linguist) and synthesized concepts from cybernetics, linguistics, anthropology and psychoanalysis. Their book on the subject was entitled *Structure of Magic: A Book about Language and Therapy* (1975). The term NLP was derived from supposed links between three inter-related elements of a person's internal experience: mind (neuro), language (linguistic) and behaviour (programming). It is a form of interpersonal skill and communication training that concentrates upon the intrapersonal and intra-psychic processes of reality construction (Tosey and Mathison 2003: 383). NLP provides a range of techniques for developing *sensory acuity*, which trains individuals where to place their attention and how to change and enlarge their perceptual filters so that things are noticed that were previously overlooked or in the realm of the unconscious by noticing faint but crucial signals, for example in communicating with others (O'Connor and Seymour 1990: 8–9). Tosey and Mathison (2003) argued that its theoretical bases are in the work of Rogers (1969) and Bateson (1972) and others, and that there are two fundamental assumptions that underpin NPL. Firstly, a person's verbal reports may be literal accounts of their inner experience and that a verbal description represents an internal visual image ('the mind's eye') and that this is unique to each individual. Hence, in teaching, learning, therapy and counselling it is important to be aware of the structure of this imagery and each individual's 'map of the world'. Secondly, NLP is predicated upon the notion that an individual's pattern of language reveals something about their epistemological processes, and Tosey and Mathison made connections between this aspect of NLP and Vygotsky's learning theories, and the links between language and thought (2003: 380). Lyon (1996: 221) suggested that from these various precepts four basic elements of NLP may be singled out:

1. Having a specific goal or outcome.
2. Having the flexibility to change one's behaviour in order to attain the desired outcome (for example, if what you are doing isn't working try something else instead).

3. Having the sensory acuity to notice the effect of one's behaviour on others (for example, noting what works and what doesn't work).
4. Having a self-maintenance capability (for example, to be able to stay focused and on target).

Readers are referred to specialist texts for an exposition of the model, its methods and potential applications in psychotherapy and counselling (see for example, O'Connor and Seymour 1990). Some of the specific techniques of NLP include rapport (responsiveness in terms of physiology, voice, language and behaviour), anchoring (an anchor is a learned response which may be subconscious but that can be changed), outcomes (the desired result in terms of what is seen, heard or felt) and the role of the meta-model (a set of questions which allow one to specify someone's experience in order to understand it) (Lyon 1996: 222–30). In an L&D context NLP has potential applications in the areas of coaching, team working, interpersonal skills training, communication and developing self-awareness.

Another technique that has its origins in psychotherapy and related fields is 'focusing', developed E. T. Gendlin and his co-workers at the University of Chicago in the 1970s (Gendlin 1981). Focusing involves paying attention to the subtle sensations or felt senses in the body. To be able to 'focus' in this sense is an ability to 'listen' to one's body. The felt sense is the inner ground from which thoughts, feelings and images may emerge if they were given the time and attention (Claxton 1997: 171). There are three main principles that underpin focusing. Firstly, there is a bodily awareness (a felt sense) that profoundly influences our lives and that can help us to achieve personal goals. Secondly, the felt sense will shift if it is approached in the right way; and, thirdly, when the felt sense of a situation changes the person changes (Gendlin 1981: 32).

The manifestation of a felt sense may be an image or an evocative phrase which can then be used to solve a personal problem. The technique of focusing (in order to be able to identify the felt sense) is a teachable skill and one that professional learning and development could make use of (Claxton 1997). Focusing is relevant in the context of a discussion of tacit knowledge since its proponents argue that it enables individuals to access deeper levels of awareness in the body (as opposed to the mind) and thereby is a means to address unresolved issues and problems.

Nonaka's Theory of Knowledge Creation

Knowledge and other forms of intellectual capital have to be managed effectively if organizations are to compete successfully in the modern world. The successful management of knowledge depends upon the quality of the knowledge assets and their successful application to problems (Wiig 2000: 6). Knowledge management systems create, capture and share knowledge. The capturing and sharing of knowledge is an area that has been given a good deal of attention in the knowledge management literature from a systems-technical perspective. From an L&D perspective the management of knowledge assets is important since it may provide ways not only for the capturing and sharing of explicit knowledge, but also for the articulation, codification and replication of tacit knowledge. One of the most influential theories of knowledge creation, and one which provides a model of the process in both social and cognitive terms, is the theory of knowledge creation developed by Ikujiro Nonaka and his colleagues.

Nonaka and his colleagues argued that the most important aspect of any understanding of the knowledge-creating capabilities of an organization is a focus upon how it can 'create new knowledge from its existing capabilities and not [up]on the stock of knowledge, such as a particular technology, that a firm possesses at any one time' (Nonaka et al. 2001: 492, emphasis added). So how can an organization acquire new knowledge assets by internal generation ('make'), rather than by importing them in from outside ('buy in')? (Note: from an HRM perspective Boxall and Purcell (2003: 143) see 'buy in' and 'make' as complementary rather than mutually exclusive activities.) Nonaka and his colleagues proposed a comprehensive and holistic model in which process and platforms interact to create knowledge assets:

1. The process of knowledge creation through socialization (S), externalization (E), combination (C) and internalization (I) – referred to by the acronym SECI.
2. The platforms for knowledge creation (referred to by the term *ba* meaning 'place') (Nonaka et al. 2001).

The process of knowledge creation in the Nonaka model (Table 4.3) depends upon an understanding of the distinction outlined previously between tacit and explicit knowledge and also the transformations that occur between these two contrasting modes of knowing.

1. *Socialization* (from tacit to tacit): tacit knowledge by its nature is difficult to articulate; therefore the transfer from tacit to tacit involves individuals who possess the tacit knowledge sharing it with others in an appropriate context. The classic example is that of the learning of an apprentice by exposure, experience, observation, imitation and modelling. This relies on a social process of empathizing (Nonaka et al. 2001).
2. *Externalization* (from tacit to explicit): this transfer depends upon whether or not one accepts the notion that tacit knowledge can be made explicit or to what degree this transfer can actually happen (Stewart 1999). If one accepts that tacit knowledge can be made explicit, Nonaka et al. suggest that this may occur through the use of metaphors, analogies and models as proxies for the knowledge itself. They described this as the key to knowledge creation because this is when 'knowledge becomes crystallised' and at this point it can

Table 4.3 Summary of Nonaka's SECI-*ba* model of dynamic knowledge creation (based on Nonaka et al. 2000: 16–17; Nonaka et al. 2001)

What?	How?	Where?	Example
Socialization (Tacit-to-tacit)	Empathizing	Originating *ba*	Individual face-to-face interactions for sharing of experiences, feelings, emotions and mental models.
Externalization (Tacit-to-explicit)	Articulating	Dialoguing *ba*	Collective face-to-face interactions where individuals' mental models and skills are shared and converted into concepts. More consciously constructed than the originating *ba*.
Combination (Explicit-to-explicit)	Connecting	Systematizing *ba*	Collective virtual interactions whereby explicit knowledge is transmitted to a large number of people (for example through email and intranets).
Internalization (Explicit-to-tacit)	Embodying	Exercising *ba*	Individuals embody explicit knowledge communicated through media such as print or electronic documents.

be shared with others and also be a basis for new knowledge (2001: 495). This relies on a social process of articulation (Nonaka et al. 2001).

3. *Combination* (from explicit to explicit): Nonaka et al. described this as connecting disparate elements of explicit knowledge into a coherent whole. This may be through an exchange and an interpretation involving media, documents and personal interactions to create a shared mental model. The collection, dissemination and processing of information to create knowledge by combination can be:
   (a) Bottom-up integration (for example, collecting financial and other information to produce a company report).
   (b) Top-down analysis (for example, collecting information to identify the causes of a performance problem).
   It relies upon a social process of connecting (Nonaka et al. 2001).

4. *Internalization* (from explicit to tacit): Nonaka et al. argue that through learning by doing, training, experiments, simulations and other forms of experience a dynamic interaction is created between the individual and the explicit knowledge that exists 'out there'. This knowledge may then be interpreted, encoded and stored in the individual's mental model in a subjective fashion and become part of that individual's tacit way of knowing. This relies on a social process of embodying (Nonaka et al. 2001).

It will be recalled that the second element of Nonaka's model is the notion of a 'place' or *ba*, which signifies the context and its interactions in which knowledge creation can take place (the platform for learning). *Ba* is not a physical space, but it can be. *Ba* can be any combination of physical, virtual or mental spaces where interactions occur, knowledge is activated and new knowledge created (for example, via an intranet).

Capturing Learning

Having established the conceptual basis for the SECI-*ba* model, Nonaka et al. make a number of suggestions for how the process can be managed as a means by which knowledge might be captured and codified. A number of their ideas have a direct L&D application:

1. Knowledge leadership: senior managers with the support of learning and information specialists should take strategic and overall responsibility for the management of the knowledge creation process. As Nonaka et al. note, some organizations make formal appointments in pursuit of this goal, for example through the role of the 'chief knowledge officer'. Such a role may be consistent with the concept and aspirations of a strategic approach to L&D.
2. Resources: the provision of space such as meeting rooms and cyberspace for the creation of knowledge assets and opportunities for face-to-face interactions in meetings, project teams and seminars is important for the construction of the necessary platforms. The physical and temporal space for learning is an important aspect of an organization's L&D environment.
3. Knowledge redundancy: Nonaka et al. use the term 'redundancy' of knowledge in a specialized, subtle and positive way. Redundancy in this context means the intentional overlapping of information about an organization's activities which, it is argued, promotes knowledge creation by fostering sharing and common understanding, enabling individuals to invade others' boundaries in a meaningful and constructive way (Nonaka calls it 'learning by intrusion'). Redundancy of information also enables individuals to get a better grasp of the whole and their place in it. Learning specialists and managers may jointly map where redundancies might be built in to the information and knowledge structure of the environment.

It could be argued that one role of management (including the HR and L&D functions) is to promote overlapping information (redundancy) through job rotation, secondments, cross-functional working, 'fuzzifying' boundaries, promoting internal competition and action learning. The role of culture and context is crucial and it is important to promote a cultural change or realignment whereby knowledge creators are highly inspired, positive thinkers who are totally committed to their goals and express 'love, care, trust and commitment' in the organization (2001: 511). There are potential links between this aspect of knowledge creation, as articulated passionately by Nonaka et al., and the notions of organizational spirituality (in the non-religious sense, see for example Mitroff 2003). Indeed, according to Porth et al. (1999) some of the precepts of a knowledge-creating company or a learning organization (see Chapter 5) resonate with many aspects of spiritual teachings in a number of the following ways: the primacy of the human intellect; the emphasis upon the dignity of the individual and the whole person (intellectually, physically, emotionally and spiritually); the acknowledgement of multiple ways of knowing (Porth et al. 1999). The interface between organization and spirituality is an area that is beginning to be explored by scholars (see for example, Mitroff 2003).

L&D FACTS AND FIGURES

Competitive advantage is now located in learning and knowledge; for this reason the notions of 'learning organizations', 'brain-based organizations', 'intellectual capital', 'the economics of ideas' and 'knowledge management' are to the fore, as reflected in the fact that the number of new knowledge management articles registered on the ABI/INFORM database more than doubled each year from a mere three articles in 1988 to almost 700 in 1998. (*Source*: Despres and Chauvel (2000): 55–6)

Inevitably when one considers the management of knowledge an important issue is the role played by the collection of the learning that takes place (see Chapter 5). Through collective learning a number of system or organization-level factors (such as organizational routines) may be leveraged to enhance performance. This has the potential to add greater value than does the leveraging of individual performance offered by learning at the individual level (for example, through training). There are four direct implications of Nonaka's model in this regard for the L&D practitioner:

1. Experience and exposure: learning occurs through the social process of identifying oneself with a person or object of attention (empathizing) and by means of the learner's exposure to and experience, observation, imitation and modelling of appropriate behaviours (Nonaka et al. 2001). Opportunities need to be created that will allow exposure in appropriate domains and facilitate the acquisition of relevant experience.
2. Articulation and communication: knowledge requires articulation through analogies, models, metaphors and stories in order for tacit knowledge to become explicit (Nonaka et al. 2001). Forums should be created which allow analogies and metaphors to be articulated and for stories to be told and interpreted.
3. Integration and analysis: knowledge from disparate sources needs to be identified, connected and combined through integrative (bottom-up) or analytical

(top-down) processing (Nonaka et al. 2001). The organization and its activities should be viewed through a bottom-up and a top-down lens and managers should be trained both in integrative and analytical techniques of discovery and enquiry.

4. Encoding and assimilation: new knowledge has to be assimilated so that it may be embodied in individuals' mental models and thereby be part of a meaningful and coherent cognitive structure (Nonaka et al. 2001). Systems should be put in place that enable knowledge to be articulated, shared and accessed in all its various forms and modes (analogies, metaphors, stories, artefacts, human models, bottom-up, top-down etc.).

The perspective offered by Nonaka and his colleagues arguably places greater emphasis upon knowledge per se and its intangible features than does much traditional Western thinking in this area. No claim is being made that one set of culturally biased assumptions about knowledge and learning is 'better' than another. Indeed as Senge has noted, the way that Eastern cultures approach management issues makes sense, but so do the Western approaches. Unfortunately the two can lead to opposite conclusions; hence there are likely to be several equally valid, and quite possibly complementary, ways to look at complex organizational issues (1990: 185). What is not in doubt is that the knowledge acquired by an organization may be an invaluable asset. It may be held in shared mental models and be tacit to the extent that collectively the organization 'knows more than it can tell'. It is possible to manage the implicit learning process through individual and collective activities that facilitate gaining a greater depth and breadth of experience, engaging in experimentation and inquiry, practising sensitivity and observational skills, and becoming more contemplative, reflective and self-aware. One of the roles of the L&D practitioner is to assist managers and leaders to leverage the collective knowledge assets to the benefits of the organization and the individuals.

Knowledge management (KM) has been defined as the creating, acquiring, capturing, sharing and utilization of knowledge (Scarborough et al. 1999). Typically, it emphasizes the role of technology rather than people in the process. Gourlay (2001) argued that HRD managers have been engaged in knowledge management although they may not have used the term as such. He further stated that if people issues should be to the fore and if natural communities (of practice) are the best place for knowledge management, there is a potential role for the skills and knowledge of the HRD (L&D) practitioner in facilitating the KM process. In practice this means an understanding and recognition of the significance of informal and incidental learning, on-the-job training, on-site study and on-site practice as well as longer-term change in management and organizational development projects. Gourlay goes so far as to claim that irrespective of the perspective on knowledge used, 'HRD skills and knowledge are critical to the KM process' (2001: 40) and that HRD practices may need to shift their focus to the informal learning processes in organizations.

PERSPECTIVE FROM RESEARCH: THE PROBLEMS OF INFORMAL LEARNING IN GREEK SMALL AND MEDIUM-SIZED ENTERPRISES

Based on the following source: S. Zambarloukos and A. Constantelou, 2002. Learning and skills formation in the new economy: evidence from Greece, *International Journal of Training and Development*, 6(4): 240–53.

In the information society that we live in there is an ever-increasing demand for information and computing technology (ICT) skills. In many economies – for example, that of Greece which is dominated by SMEs (small and medium-sized enterprises) – there are often two problems in this area: firstly, firms often have to hire untrained personnel; and, secondly, they generally do not invest heavily in training. As a result, the level of organizational knowledge within such firms is often impoverished. In order to investigate these issues in the Greek context, Zambarloukos and Constantelou interviewed 23 ICT/web managers in firms from a variety of sectors in order to explore how ICT-related skills are created, learned and managed.

The results of Zambarloukos and Constantelou's interviews confirmed the importance of informal learning but they also found that many of the firms, especially the smaller ones, did not possess the necessary stock of ICT knowledge to enable formal or informal learning to take place. As a consequence, learning tended to be 'by doing' or by reading manuals, whereas learning through interaction with skilled peers was not cited as being significant, presumably because there were few if any skilled workers to provide coaching and expert guidance. Zambarloukos and Constantelou highlighted the important fact that the learning environment needs to have a critical mass of knowledgeable and skilled employees who could actually facilitate learning through cooperation and interaction. Without this, firms have to rely on experimentation and making mistakes, and on second-hand sources of knowledge such as that codified in manuals or external sources. These problems disadvantage small firms in particular. In the firms studied the use of outsourcing of ICT tasks was one way in which managers overcame the lack of knowledge, but this of itself would not necessarily enhance the internal stock of knowledge.

Discussion Point

Given the importance of ICT skills and the fact that they quickly become outdated, what are the problems associated with outsourcing of these skills for SMEs? Is the problem an intractable one?

Against a backcloth of globalization, increased competition, rapid technological change, and increased levels of information sophistication amongst employees and customers, L&D and management practices in general have to adapt in order to facilitate the more effective management of knowledge assets. A further aspect to this already complex picture is the uncertainty that organizations face. All of these things combined require L&D practices that promote learning through socialization, the articulation of knowledge through communication, the assimilation of new knowledge into extant schemas, the adaptation of those schemas to accommodate new knowledge and the leveraging of expertise, tacit knowledge and intuition. Wiig (2000: 16–17) suggests that in practical terms this requires:

1. New ways of working: collaboration, team working, assembling expertise through interdisciplinary project teams.
2. New roles for HR and for L&D: appropriate incentive and reward structures, succession planning for learning, the design of L&D programmes that facilitate collective learning.
3. New roles for information management: designing and implementing systems that capture knowledge, make knowledge available quickly and easily (for example, through intranets and personal homepages).

In one sense, the efforts at knowledge management are concerned with leveraging individual expertise, and to the extent that such expertise is tacit it may be thought of as a form of intuition. Indeed, Reber argued that the basic principles embodied in his characterization of implicit learning theory are close to the layperson's conception of intuition, i.e. a natural judgemental process that takes place without conscious thought and outside an awareness of the knowledge used as the basis for the thought (Reber 1993: 159). As far as the learning implications are concerned, Reber concluded that the content of learning should focus more upon the 'variations that a specific subject matter displays', and that we should experience for ourselves the complex patterns within a domain as learners rather than through explicit instruction and the specific tutoring of formulaic rules and procedures. As an afterword in his seminal book, Reber saw parallels between the principles that have emerged from studies of implicit learning and the Zen Buddhist philosophy of knowledge acquisition by attentive immersion in a context and refraining from conscious and strenuous attempts to fathom the nature of the world. The mindfulness that is the fundamental precept of this approach is a non-reactive bare awareness that is open to anything and may be achieved by setting aside a mental space to the here and now in order that the brain can 'register the bare perception, observe with detachment and notice without elaboration' (Austin 1999: 127).

Discussion Point

To what extent do you think it is possible for the L&D practitioner to enable individuals and organizations to engage in implicit learning in more effective ways? What suggestions would you make for practical techniques for making tacit knowledge more explicit?

Conclusion: the Intuitive L&D Practitioner

The complexities of the interaction of individual, task and context means that the role of the practitioner sometimes is as much an art as it is a science. The experienced and skilful L&D practitioner relies upon implicit learning, tacit knowledge and expertise to execute successful decisions. They may, nonetheless, find difficulty in explaining what they are actually doing and many of their actions may be considered to be intuitive. Indeed, one of the hallmarks of professional practice is the ability to trust one's intuitive judgements (Atkinson 2000). L&D practitioner intuition is a process in which they efficiently code, sort and access experientially conceived mental models for use in making decisions (Burke and Sadler-Smith 2006). Intuitive practitioners have cognitive schemas or mental models born of an immersion and experience that they can overlay on particular problems in order to detect an appropriate solution, and action scripts (below the level of conscious awareness) are activated by a particular set of cues and patterns (Klein 2003). As Atkinson and Claxton (2000) have noted, professional practice and professional development in a variety of fields are often discussed as if conscious understanding and deliberation are of the essence. In reality there is a good deal that is intuitive about professional practice, which then begs the question of how professional development might embrace intuition? How can practitioners deal with ambiguous, ill-defined and complex tasks in fast-moving environments, often in time-sensitive situations and under circumstances of considerable cognitive uncertainty and complexity? How can a novice L&D practitioner become an intuitive L&D practitioner? Confidence in one's expertise is a crucial issue. To develop an appropriate level of confidence in one's intuition, Atkinson (2000: 58) argued that the novice practitioner needs a nurturing environment, high level of support and not too much external direction. Burke and Sadler-Smith (2006) offered a number of suggestions for ways by which practitioners might extend their intuitive capabilities and build relevant expertise in a planned and deliberate way.

Firstly, L&D practitioners (especially novices to the profession) can extend their own experiences by immersion in the domain of L&D practice. This might be achieved by interacting with others in their community of practice in order to solicit insights, ideas, suggestions and model behaviours. The assistance of an expert practitioner as a coach for specific tasks or as a mentor for a longer-term development process (with a judicious mix of directed behaviour and freedom to act) may be a way in which the experiential wisdom of others may be drawn upon, applied and validated. Active engagement with the collective wisdom of others can enhance the individual's explicit and tacit knowledge base (Burke and Sadler-Smith 2006).

Secondly, the practitioner's intuitive capabilities may be more readily enhanced by their becoming increasingly reflective upon their own practice. The use of a practice-relevant diary, journal or learning log may be helpful in getting novices to think through dilemmas or in recording thoughts about approaches, methods and ideas that have worked or not, and why (Burke and Sadler-Smith 2006).

Thirdly, a quiet, relaxed mind that is focused upon the present moment and free of distracting fears and desires was described by Taggart (1997) as the sine qua non of intuitive experience. Reflection and contemplation may serve as a check and balance against a headlong rush to identify, analyse, design, implement and evaluate (haste may be a response to anxiety and the need to be seen to 'deliver', sometimes in a 'hare-brained' way). The expert may, through quiet contemplation, revert to a more centred and balanced state. The skills of mindfulness (i.e., an acute awareness), reflection and contemplation are means whereby an L&D practitioner can refine and reflect upon their knowledge and expertise and build intuitive skills. For the expert mental relaxation and quiet contemplation may be as likely to yield up a novel solution to a practical or professional dilemma as extreme effort and intense concentration (Burke and Sadler-Smith 2006).

Concept Checklist

Can you now define each of the Key Concepts listed below, and are you now able to achieve the other Knowledge Outcomes specified at the beginning of the chapter?

- Implicit learning
- Incidental learning
- Explicit learning
- Incubation and insight
- Procedural knowledge
- Declarative knowledge
- Tacit knowledge
- Intuition
- Action scripts
- Expert/novice differences
- Expertise
- Rationality
- Neuro-linguistic programming and focusing
- Knowledge creation
- SECI-*ba* model
- Intuitive practitioner
- Intuitive intelligence

CHAPTER 5
Collective Learning and Development

Key Concepts

Collective learning; knowledge creation; action; reflection; action science; action learning; espoused theories; theories-in-use; Model I behaviour; Model II behaviour; ladder of inference; team learning; communities of practice (CoP); legitimate peripheral participation; activity system; organizational learning; single-loop learning; double-loop learning; adaptive learning; generative learning; shared mental models; incomplete learning; critiquing organizational learning; learning organization; the competent organization

---

Knowledge Outcomes

After studying this chapter you should be able to:
- define each of the key concepts listed above;
- explain the significance of action-based methods for the L&D practitioner;
- distinguish between Model I and Model II behaviour and between single- and double-loop learning;
- describe some of the impediments to organizational learning that may be encountered in the workplace;
- distinguish between the learning organization and organizational learning;
- critically appraise the notion of the 'learning organization';

- explain the meaning and significance of the concept of the competent organization for L&D.

Introduction

Learning organisations are possible because, deep down, we are all learners. Learning organisations are possible because not only is it our nature to learn but we love to learn.

Peter M. Senge, *The Fifth Discipline*

Many companies do not appear to live for very long; indeed those that do live for more than a hundred years seem to be few and far between. So is there anything that characterizes those firms that do possess corporate longevity? This question was explored by a planning group at Royal Dutch Shell who were interested in this issue because as an oil company they were preoccupied with the question of, 'Is there life after oil? (see De Gues 1997; Van der Heijden et al. 2002). The view that the group at Shell came to was that most corporations seem to die prematurely from collective learning disabilities. In essence this meant that they failed to adapt as the world around them changed. In the survival of the fittest, the survivors were those who were able to flex and change in response to a dynamic and uncertain world. Shell's in-depth study of 27 firms found that long-lived companies:

- were sensitive to their environments;
- had strong cultures;
- financed conservatively;
- were tolerant of new and different ways of doing things.

From an L&D perspective the last point is crucial: it meant that long-lived companies had openness, which predisposed them to a collective learning that was a crucial strand in the 'DNA code' for corporate survival (de Gues 1997; Fulmer et al. 1998).

The term 'collective learning' is used here to distinguish between the learning that takes place at the individual and that which takes place at the supra-individual (i.e. above the individual) level. Collective learning can encompass dyads, teams, communities, networks, organizations and even whole societies. Inevitably there is overlap in a number of respects:

1. Firstly, individual learning cannot be considered in isolation – one only needs to think of Bandura's theories of social learning and the importance accorded to human modelling to appreciate the social and interactive nature of individual learning.
2. Secondly, individual learning is interactive in another way also: dyads, teams, groups, organizations and societies are all made up of individuals; hence it is

the learning of the individual members of such groups that may be considered a source of the collective learning.

Over and above this the significance of collective learning lies in the argument that a synergy (i.e. a combined effect) may operate whereby the knowledge of the group is greater than the sum of the individual members' knowledge (Senge 1990). It is sometimes remarked that if only organizations 'knew what they knew' they could be more effective. The synergistic nature of collective learning is something that is of immense potential significance to organizations as a source of differentiation and competitive advantage.

L&D FACTS AND FIGURES

Synergy is from the Greek word *synergos* meaning 'working together'. The dictionary definition of it is 'a mutually advantageous conjunction or compatibility of distinct business participants or elements (as resources or efforts)'. Synergism is the combined action or operation of these elements. Other ways of expressing it are as 'the whole is greater than the sum of its parts'. (*Source*: Merriam-Webster Online; http://www.m-w.com)

The collectiveness of learning inevitably also raises issues of the role of organizational structures and cultures, as well as emotions, power and politics in learning. It is these issues that can be turned to for a more critical and sobering assessment over and above the rhetoric that has surrounded organizational learning and the learning organization concept. In a sense, what lay at the root of the concept of the learning organization as proffered in the 1990s was the potential added value, which lay in:

1. A set of structural arrangements that could be put into place in order to enable the creation of knowledge assets.
2. The establishment of certain managerial processes whereby those assets could be harnessed and leveraged to enhance performance.

Like much of L&D practice and theory there is a performance improvement assumption that is implicit in the learning organization 'ideal'. The argument goes that once put into place within a particular context such knowledge creation processes and the assets thereby created (for example, technical know-how, an in-depth understanding of customers' needs and so forth) are a source of competitive advantage that is difficult for competitors to imitate and thereby provides a powerful mechanism for leveraging enhanced performance. This led to another famous rallying cry of the learning organization movement: 'learning is the only sustainable source of competitive advantage'. Turning to the reasons behind the rhetoric leads to an important realization which singles out collective learning from individual learning in terms of the locus of effect: collective learning has the potential to increase performance across multiple factors at the level of the organization and its systems (Boerner et al. 2001: 98).

PERSPECTIVE FROM PRACTICE: CONCEPTUAL AND OPERATIONAL LEARNING IN A BELGIAN MANUFACTURING FIRM

Based on the following source: M. A. Lapre and L. N. Van Wassenhove, 2002. Learning across lines: the secret to more effective factories, *Harvard Business Review*, October: 107–11.

Learning and the collective production of new knowledge is a means by which firms can enhance the quality of their products and services and their levels of productivity. The creation of new knowledge cannot, however, be left to chance; organizations need to be proactive in exploring ways in which viable knowledge that will have a broad impact upon quality and the bottom line can be realized. The Belgian firm NV. Bekaert is the one of the world's largest independent producers of steel wire; for example, their products are used in about one-third of the world's tyre cord. Both quality and productivity are crucial to the organization's success. Bekaert were interested in the conditions under which quality improvement projects produce scientifically valid knowledge which is actionable in the organization in order to impact upon performance. The research reported by Lapre and Van Wassenhove was based upon the analysis of reports of quality improvement projects in the Bekaert company archives. They examined 62 projects and devised a scheme for the classification of the type of learning that took place and the knowledge produced by the projects. Two types of learning were identified and projects could be classified as being high or low on each of these (thus giving a two-by-two typology of knowledge production). The two types of learning were:

1. *Conceptual learning*, which was defined as that which gave rise to knowledge of cause-and-effect relationships (for example, through the use of sophisticated data analysis techniques) and the development of explanatory theories. Conceptual learning yielded 'know-why'.
2. *Operational learning*, which was defined as the process that gave rise to knowledge about whether or not a solution actually worked and what the best way was to apply it in practice. Operational learning yielded 'know-how'.

Their classification gave about 15 projects in each of the four categories which they labelled as shown in Table 5.1. Each of the four groups of projects was analysed in terms of the extent to which there was transfer of usable knowledge which led to cost reductions which in turn impacted upon the bottom line.

The conclusion that the authors drew from these findings was that a central R&D facility may not always be the best place to conduct process improvement projects that will yield knowledge that is valid and applicable. Isolated researchers have difficulty in engaging in operational learning because they are divorced from the context in which the new knowledge will be applied. To deliver high levels of operational and conceptual learning Bekaert decided to relocate production improvement projects to its factory at Aalter in order to create an integrated production line. All production stages were at one site and multi-functional teams could work together in an integrated way and learn in a holistic fashion by combining both conceptual learning (to generate new ideas and theories) and operational learning (testing out whether they worked in practice). Knowledge and expertise from science, engineering, production and process control could be pooled and the result was that the learning of the integrated teams produced operationally validated theories that led to dramatic plant-wide improvements in productivity and quality. The key finding from this research, from an L&D perspective, is that effective learning about how to improve quality and enhance productivity occurred in integrated teams who operated in real time in the workplace.

Table 5.1 Operational and conceptual learning at Bekaert. (*Source*: Lapre and Van Wassenhove (2002)

		Conceptual learning	
		Low	High
Operational learning	High	*Artisan skills*: work for problem at hand; understanding of 'why'; causal ambiguity; lack of transfer of solution to other problems	*Operationally validated theories*: draw on scientific insights to produce replicable results; enhance the company-wide rate of quality enhancement
	Low	*Fire fighting*: trying to solve the immediate problem; lack of insight; minor improvements; dealing with symptoms	*Unvalidated theories*: highly scientific solutions; impact on results are unverified; persuasive science; developed in R&D facilities

Knowledge Creation

The root of knowledge creation is learning. Knowledge is more than mere data or information; it is integrated into and embedded within a particular field or context. It may be defined as information acquired through implicit or explicit learning means and in the process combined with experience, context, interpretation and reflection (Davenport and Prusak 1998). It can be categorized in a number of ways (or as varying along a number of dimensions), for example:

- as *declarative knowledge* ('what' something is) or *procedural knowledge* ('how' something is done);
- as *tacit knowledge* (personal, subjective, unconscious, ineffable and intuitive – or, in the words of Polanyi 1966, a knowledge that means we can know 'more than we can tell') or *explicit knowledge* (public, objective, in conscious awareness, communicable and rational);
- as *individual knowledge* (helped in an individual's schema or mental model) or *shared knowledge* (held in an abstract way as a shared schema or shared mental model).

An oft-quoted example of tacit knowledge is the ability to tie one's shoelaces or ride a bicycle – skills that have been learned through experience and are executable but which are hard to put into words. A more sophisticated example in an L&D context would be the feel that a potter has in his or her fingers for the working of the clay. This type of knowledge (oftentimes manifested as a skill) is developed through experience and learning, more often than not in the company of master practitioners (teachers, instructors, coaches, mentors and so on) who pass on the knowledge that they have gained over many years of immersion in their domain, learning and experience. As noted in the previous chapter, tacit knowledge is knowledge that cannot easily be put into words and is teachable to others largely through practice and social interactions in the workplace. In this sense it is, metaphorically, knowledge that is in one's 'fingertips' (though there are cognitive explanations for the acquisition by deep immersion, storage in highly complex schemas and retrieval on the basis of contextual cues and the execution of action scripts; see for example, Klein 2003). As a result of their sharing and interacting through narratives, artefacts, metaphors and so forth the master and the apprentice may develop a shared mental model comprising both declarative and procedural elements for the task. The process is interactive and reciprocal in that the dialogue may change the master performer's mental model also.

Hodgkinson and Sparrow argued that whilst the concept of the knowledge-based economy and knowledge-based work is not new, the management of knowledge has assumed heightened importance over recent decades for a number of reasons:

1. The bulk of the fixed costs associated with knowledge are associated with its creation rather than its sharing (hence the costs are 'up-front').
2. The rapid branching and fragmentation of knowledge (especially with the advent of information and computing technologies) calls for some form of harnessing of this resource to avoid its uncontrolled dispersion, proliferation (2002: 72–3) and replication (resulting in wasted effort).

It is interesting to note that in our global economy there exist significant differences with regard to the ways different cultures interpret knowledge. For example, in the West the interpretation is often an explicit-rational conceptualization, whilst in non-Western cultures interpretations may include the tacit-intuitive also. The effective management of knowledge and L&D in a global economy calls for a more eclectic interpretation of knowledge and learning beyond the rational, and for some acknowledgement of the validity of different ways of knowing. A corollary of this is that researchers and practitioners need to explore the ways in which the different interpretations of knowledge and how it may be acquired can be reconciled, accommodated and integrated into L&D practice.

Action and Reflection in Learning

In their different ways reflection and action are each concerned with the ways in which managers can engage more directly and effectively with their worlds. Two action-based approaches will be examined: the reflective practitioner model of Donald Schön and Chris Argyris in the USA, and the action learning approach of Reg Revans in the UK. Each in its own way is concerned with similar fundamental issues, although the emphasis in each approach is somewhat different. Both are concerned with how to understand and narrow the gap between managers' thoughts and their actions. Action and reflection are pervasive to the extent that they occur across different L&D contexts and hence are relevant to the issue of collective learning but also individual learning, especially in the areas of leader and manager development (see Chapter 7).

L&D FACTS & FIGURES

Donald A. Schön was born in Boston in 1930, graduated from Yale in 1951 and went on to postgraduate studies at Harvard (incidentally he was also a highly accomplished and prize-winning musician, having studied clarinet at a conservatoire in Paris). His book *The Reflective Practitioner: How Professionals Think in Action* and other related works have been immensely influential in management and other professions. His argument (like Polanyi and others) was that professionals know more than they can put into words and come to rely upon improvisation learned in practice (thinking on their feet) as much as on the technical rationalist models learned in graduate schools and professional education. Schön died in 1997. (*Source*: M. K. Smith, 2001. *Donald Schön: Learning, Reflection and Change*, www.infed.org/thinkers/et-schon.htm)

The process of reflection (defined by Senge as slowing down our thinking processes to become aware of how we form our mental models of the world) is inextricably linked to the process of inquiry (holding 'conversations' where we openly share views and develop knowledge about the sharedness of assumptions) (Senge et al. 1994: 237). Hence reflection-and-inquiry may be considered a means for collective learning in terms of both its process and its outcomes. Herein lies a distinction between it and some interpretations of social forms of learning such as the observational learning involved in human modelling – the latter process may be in a sense collective but the outcome is more likely to be an individual one (such as the adoption of a model behaviour).

The Method of Action Science

Argyris and Schön's method of action science is a body of theory and research for exploring the reasoning that underlies our actions. This involves inward reflection and analysis about the way in which problems are defined. Two concepts are crucial in understanding the action science approach:

1. Espoused theories; these are the personal assumptions that managers may subscribe to and claim that they use.
2. Theories-in-use; these are the assumptions and beliefs that are used to guide action but which managers are very often not aware of, although they can be inferred from behaviour.

Argyris himself was surprised to find that there were often 'fundamental systemic mis-matches between an individual's espoused and in-use designs' (1995: 20), and the dynamic between an espoused theory and a theory-in-use means that managers may unwittingly screen out certain information. This information, if taken heed of, may have helped to define the problem being confronted in a different and potentially more effective way (Woodall and Winstanley 1998: 155). One effect of this is that managers may trap themselves in defensive routines that insulate their mental models from critical examination. A result of this may be the development of a skilled incompetence that is used as a shield from the 'pain and threat posed by learning situations'. It is a defence but a dysfunctional one in that by exercising skilled incompetence managers also protect themselves from getting the results that they want to achieve (Senge 1990: 182). The practice of action science in the hands of a skilled facilitator draws out and exposes to scrutiny the subtle and potentially erroneous assumptions and patterns of reasoning that underlie behaviours. This insight can be a profound one because it may reveal that our thoughts and actions are based upon tenuous sets of assumptions and incomplete mental models. Raelin describes action science as allowing learners to:

> engage in an emancipatory discourse, thus testing their mental models, especially their inferences and assumptions about others and their own behaviour. Co-workers come to understand the embedded cultural myths that underlie their felt needs and wants expressed in their relationship with others. (2000: 91)

Argyris and Schön (1974) identified two distinct patterns of behaviour based on the fact that people's goals appear sometimes to be built upon unquestioned assumptions about the world and in particular about the behaviour and thoughts of others (hence the relevance to collective learning). These two patterns of behaviour are referred to as Model I behaviour and Model II behaviour. In Model I behaviour the following precepts underlie thought and action:

1. Define and achieve set goals.
2. Maximize winning and minimize losing.
3. Minimize generating or expressing negative feelings.
4. Be rational. (Argyris and Schön 1974)

The result is that managers delude themselves into believing that the assumptions underlying their espoused theories (based upon goals and rational processes) are actually guiding their behaviour in the right direction. Such a train of events is distinctly unreflective and at a deeper level can be 'self-sealing'. Senge cites the example of the ladder of inference (see Figure 5.1), which is based upon self-generating beliefs that assume that our beliefs are true, that the truth is obvious, that our beliefs are based on real data and that the data we select are the real data. These beliefs remain untested but guide our actions in ways that can profoundly affect personal outcomes. On the other hand, Model II behaviour encourages the testing of underpinning assumptions, the public testing of 'theories-in-use' and the collective surfacing of mental models by:

1. Providing others with directly observable data and honest reports about one's thoughts and feelings.
2. Allowing individuals free and informed choice.
3. Commitment to a course of action that is internally driven and maximal, not a commitment in response to threats, coercion or the fear of punishments or being penalized. (Argyris and Schön 1974)

L&D FACTS AND FIGURES

Chris Argyris was born in Newark, New Jersey in 1923. He went to university at Clark, where he came into contact with Kurt Lewin. He went on to gain a PhD in Organizational Behaviour from Cornell University. Chris Argyris has been a faculty member at Yale University (1951–71) and at the time of writing is the James Bryant Conant Professor Emeritus of Education and Organizational Behaviour at Harvard University. One of his major areas of research and theorizing (undertaken with Donald Schön) was around the extent to which human reasoning, not just behaviour, can become the basis for diagnosis and action. As well as writing and researching, Chris Argyris has been an influential teacher of, amongst others, Peter M. Senge. (*Source*: M. K. Smith, 2001. Chris Argyris: theories of action, double-loop learning and organizational learning, *The Encyclopaedia of Informal Education*, www.infed.org/thinkers/argyris.htm)

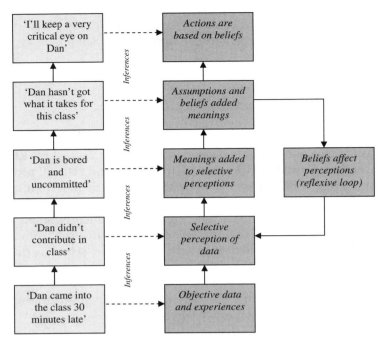

Figure 5.1   The ladder of inference (adapted from Senge et al. 1994: 243)

Senge has further developed the action science principles of his teachers Argyris and Schön and applied them to the discipline of 'mental models' (one of the disciplines or 'thinking technologies' expounded in his best-selling book *The Fifth Discipline* – see below). He identifies four tools for developing the skills of reflection and inquiry:

1.   The ability to notice our leaps from observation to generalization.
2.   Being able to articulate what normally goes unsaid.
3.   Blending advocacy (promoting an idea) and inquiry (honest reflection on the idea) to promote collaborative learning through 'honest investigation' (1990: 186).
4.   Facing up to the gap between what we say (on the face of it) and what we do (based upon our deeper-seated beliefs).

In addition to the techniques outlined by Argyris, Schön and Senge, Raelin suggested that cognitive mapping might also be a useful tool that could help individuals to reflect critically in groups on assumptions, beliefs, inferences and actions. Cognitive mapping is a technique for identifying the concepts and the links between them and the ways in which these represent a manager's beliefs concerning a particular domain (Axelrod 1976). The map is represented visually and may be able to capture perceptual filters and idiosyncratic views (Allard-Poesi

et al. 2001: 352). The method allows individual managers to order their perceptions but also gives those responsible for the formulation of strategy a way
to understand the perceptions of others (Easterby-Smith et al. 1991: 95). Many of
these techniques require the skilled assistance of another person whom Senge
recommends should be 'ruthlessly compassionate' (1990: 202), since in a world
where we cannot 'see our own eye', a constructive, compassionate critic may be
a valuable learning resource.

PERSPECTIVE FROM PRACTICE: ARGYRIS'S LEFT- AND RIGHT-HAND COLUMN CASE METHOD

Based on the following source: C. Argyris, 1995. Action science and organisational learning, *Journal of Managerial Psychology*, 10(6): 20–6.

There are several techniques available to the action science practitioner.
Argyris describes the left-hand/right-hand column case method as having
the advantages that it produces concrete data (in the form of a 'conversation') in ways such that the actors are responsible for the meanings produced
and cannot blame the instrument or the data. Furthermore it is conducted
under circumstances that are potentially harm-free. The instructions to participants are to:

1. Describe a key organizational problem (for example, by writing one
    paragraph on the subject).
2. Think of a person with whom you could talk to solve the problem.
3. Write down the strategy you would use in the meeting with this person
    (write one paragraph).
4. Split a page into two columns.
5. In the right-hand column write out the imaginary conversation with the
    person with whom you were having the conversation (two pages).
6. In the left-hand column write down any idea or feeling that you would
    have but which you would not communicate to the other person.

   Argyris sees the cases that this reflective dialogue produces as providing
managers with vivid examples of their own skilled incompetence in which
they try not to upset the other person and persuade them to change their
position. The cognitive load that this kind of interaction can impose in real
time may mean that it is difficult to slow down the skilled incompetence.
One result can be that the skilled incompetence and its thought processes
may run away with the situation, leaving the manager to struggle and eventually succumb to it. Examples of a left-hand column sequence (that is, the
thoughts and feelings not communicated) include: 'She's not going to like

Continued

this, but we have to discuss it'; 'I better go slow; let me ease in'; 'This is beginning to **** me off'.

Following reflection on the cases, participants are invited to redesign them. One of the first realizations many participants have is of the need to slow things down beyond the millisecond responses that typically govern our interactions and that life in an organization often demands. Practice is also important and about as much is needed as is required to play a 'not-so-decent' game of tennis, according to Argyris (1995: 25). Argyris argued that there are several consequences of this technique:

1. Members of the group experience each other as more supportive and constructive.
2. Crises are reduced.
3. Behavioural change leads to new values, which lead to more effective problem solving and decision making.

The ultimate aim of the process is to develop actionable generalizations that help users to diagnose, invent, produce and evaluate the impact of what they have produced in order to identify patterns of causal reasoning that in turn impact on learning at the individual, group and organizational levels (1995: 26).

The Method of Action Learning

A different form of action-related inquiry was advocated by Reg Revans in the UK in the 1960s. He called his approach 'action learning' and based it on the argument that in a turbulent, fast-moving and uncertain business environment the rate of learning must exceed the rate of change if an organization is to stay ahead and remain competitive and effective. The approach embodies a very specific technique for facilitating learning and should not be confused either with experiential learning or any other general 'learning by doing' approach. One of its direct antecedents is the humanistic approach of Carl Rogers, where true learning and development is achieved by helping individuals to help themselves (Woodall and Winstanley 1998: 193). Revans established a clear set of guiding principles and processes for facilitating learning by managers acting on real-world problems.

The approach is now an established L&D technique. It was conceptualized over half a century ago (between 1947 and 1950) by Revans at the newly nationalized National Coal Board in the UK. The approach might be seen as a reaction against the prevailing educational model of the day, which tended to produce what might be termed 'clever' managers (technical specialists with convergent thinking styles) rather than 'wise' managers (those with divergent thinking styles who are able to see a bigger picture and ask probing questions) (Garrett 2000: 52). Revans's approach might be seen as a reaction against a set of educational (in effect pedagogical) principles that over-relied upon pre-programmed knowledge that was by definition in the past and which, once it had been written down, might not be as useful for solving 'here-and-now' problems. What is likely to be much more effective is the ability to ask penetrating, meaningful and insightful questions (here it overlaps with the processes of action science in which managers are encouraged to ask questions about their assumptions and beliefs). Revans was, by training, a physicist (he reportedly worked with Ernest Rutherford), as well as being an Olympic-standard athlete. His natural science background shows through in the way he expressed some of the principles of action learning, for example in two famous 'equations'. The first equation relates learning (L) to the rate of change in the environment (C):

$$L \geq C \qquad \text{(Equation 1)}$$

The second equation relates recorded knowledge (A) and our ability to use it (p), and the set of questions that the new situation poses (Q) and our individual ability to pose them (q):

$$L = pA + qQ \qquad \text{(Equation 1)}$$

Action learning relies on facilitating inquiry that enables managers to ask insightful questions (content) and also to develop the ability or skill to ask insightful questions (process) (Equation 2) in order to keep up with or stay ahead of change (Equation 1). The ability to ask insightful questions may be blocked by managers idealizing those solutions that worked well in the past, being charmed by the charisma of other perhaps more powerful managers, by acting impulsively rather than reflectively and by belittling subordinates (Revans 1983).

L&D FACTS AND FIGURES

Reginald W. Revans was the originator of the method of action learning. He was an Olympic long-jumper and Cambridge physicist. He worked for Essex Education Authority and the National Coal Board in the UK. He visited India and in his work he was struck by the similarity between Buddhism and action learning. He is also quoted as saying that 'intuition, the unremembered urges of the past, must always be the first weapon of the manager, he [or she] must be able to grasp the underlying structures of situations that challenge him [or her]' (1982: 10). (*Source*: R. W. Revans, 1982. *The Origins and Growth of Action Learning*. Bromley: Chartwell-Bratt.)

The process of action learning is organized on the basis of groups of learners known as action learning sets. A set usually comprises between six and ten participants and is facilitated in its content and process issues by a skilled set adviser. In the spirit of skilled inquiry and a focus upon practice it is important that the

Table 5.2 Types of action learning based upon permutations of task and context (adapted from Garrett 2000: 59)

		Task	
		Own job	*Other job*
Context	*Own organization*	*Own job projects*: effective as induction and personal development activities.	*Internal exchange projects*: effective for establishing links between different parts of an organization.
	Other organization	*Technical expertise exchanges*: effective for horizontal transfer of best practice and benchmarking.	*External exchanges*: highly effective for personal development, broadening of one's perspective and valuing diversity.

adviser is not seen to be, or indeed acts as, an expert. The experts are the participating managers themselves both individually and collectively; they are 'comrades in adversity' (to use a well-worn Revans phrase). The content of the learning are live projects (usually a complex organizational problem that cannot be answered using solely pre-existing knowledge). The live projects are ones that each individual participant is confronted with in their job role (note the connection to andragogical learning principles). The advantages of working on real problems may be self-evident:

- participants have to find workable solutions;
- leadership and other facilitative skills are developed in the process;
- the organization is likely to benefit from the outcomes;
- the learning transfers to the work context immediately and learning of process skills is likely to be more widely applicable beyond the immediate project. (Raelin 1999)

An additional dimension may be added to action learning by the various permutations of task and context, as outlined in Table 5.2.

PERSPECTIVE FROM PRACTICE: IMPLEMENTING ACTION LEARNING

Based on the following source: M. Pedler, J. Burgoyne and T. Boydell, 1997. *The Learning Company: A Strategy for Sustainable Development*, London: McGraw-Hill.

Action learning aims to provide an externally imposed structure (i.e. from the method and the adviser) but with internally driven content and direction (i.e. from the participants) (Woodall and Winstanley 1998). Although in practice the method is complex and highly interactive, it is possible to boil it down to a number of steps (see Pedler et al. 1997: 171). The process Pedler et al. suggest is summarized below:

1. Recruit the set members: about six is an optimum number of managers who wish to develop themselves and their organization by tackling an appropriate live issue (for example, improving service quality, enhancing internal communication, etc.).
2. Specify the problem: describe the problem and what the outcome and benefits will look like.
3. Find a sponsor: identify within each of the members' organization a sponsor who can advise, comment and help to implement any proposed solution that the set identifies.
4. Agree a programme: arrange a series of meetings with the adviser (for example, a day a month) and commit to these.
5. Facilitate the meeting of the set: at the set meeting each member should be prepared to report on the problem, describe their efforts, explain their actions, invite questions, accept feedback and reciprocate with other set members. The meeting should conclude with the setting of goals to be attained by the next meeting.

Pedler et al. note that the process looks simpler than it actually is in practice and that 'only people prepared to give it a go and take a risk will be able to act and learn in this way' (1997: 171). The success depends in large part upon the commitment of the action learning set members and the facilitative skills of the action learning set adviser.

Action Science and Action Learning

A question that is sometimes asked is: What is the difference between Revans's action learning and Argyris and Schön's action science? Raelin concedes that there is a good deal of similarity between them since they both aim to improve collective learning processes, emphasize the use of knowledge in the service of action, are participatory and collaborative, employ experimental (that is, not pre-set) and experiential methodologies, promote reflection and critical self-reflection and encourage the use of a process facilitator (1997: 22). However, for Raelin the question of where action learning ends and action science begins is a crucial matter. He identifies a number of important differences that facilitators need to be aware of. In its emphasis on inquiry into one's own reasoning processes and underlying beliefs and those of others, Raelin argued that action science goes deeper than action learning. The latter is more concerned with surface practicalities and behavioural change through public reflection (1997: 23). Raelin described the aspiration of action science as aiming to develop an intrapersonal cognitive awareness (another term for this might be meta-cognitive awareness). A further important source of difference is that action learning is satisfied with contextualizing the learning (a concern for here-and-now problems) in a rational way; action science, on the other hand, seeks to decontextualize it in order to distil from practice more deep-seated generic assumptions and beliefs that underpin specific actions (a concern for here-and-now reasoning) in an emancipatory fashion (1997: 32). In one sense the action science approach may, according to Raelin, be at a higher level of learning and abstraction, and it is important that facilitators recognize the differences in order that they can know 'whether and how to shift gears [from action learning to action science] in the midst of an [learning] intervention' (1997: 33). Because of their emphasis upon process both methods represent tried and tested techniques for managers who wish to develop the capability to learn-how-to-learn.

PERSPECTIVE FROM PRACTICE: APPLYING ACTION LEARNING IN A SMALL/MEDIUM-SIZED ENTERPRISE IN THE UK

Based on the following source: C. L. Davey, J. A. Powell, J. E. Powell and I. Cooper, 2002. Action learning in a medium-sized construction company, *Building Research & Information*, 30(1): 5–15.

Action learning is an approach that has typically been used with self-selecting groups of senior managers in large organizations (such as GEC, W.H. Smith and Lever Brothers in the UK). As with much of L&D, there has been comparative paucity of research (both independent and action-based) in small and medium-sized enterprises (SMEs). Hence this example of action learning in an SME is relevant in helping to fill that gap; it is also interesting for the fact that the company chairman, although not a participant, took an active role in the project by identifying a broad aim and sub-goals in relation to the company strategy, and also in nominating participants (small works managers and a site manager from different divisions of the company, George & Harding Ltd., based in southern England).

The aim of the project was to improve in both technical and management areas in order to give the company an 18-month lead over its competitors by moving the company away from traditional contract management systems. The latter were perceived as being inefficient because they drew managers' attentions away from projects and clients and into peripheral administrative and financial matters. The chief executive wanted a reorientation so that '100 per cent' of managers' efforts would be directed at projects that delivered bottom-line results for clients.

The action learning set comprised six managers and met for three to four hours every month over a 12-month period under the guidance of a set adviser. Data were collected by the researchers from the set meetings – in the form of written accounts and observations of verbal and non-verbal behaviours – in order to identify issues relating to content, process (for example, engagement and openness), actions and the role of the set adviser. In addition an independent consultant attended some of the meetings to evaluate the extent to which the implementation corresponded to action learning 'best practice' for a task-focused group (hence the criteria included efficient use of time, topic focus and articulation). Objective performance data were not collected.

The project was a means by which the managers gained time to think, and to develop new ideas and test out the viability of these ideas amongst colleagues in a safe and structured environment. Some problems were encountered from the rest of the organization (the 'out group') in the form of scepticism and potential alienation from those who were not involved directly. The managers who participated felt empowered to solve problems. The set's activities had spin-outs into other parts of the organization (for example, through the identification of needs that could be met through conventional training). The fact that the chairman appeared to have 'bought in' to the project meant that the highest possible profile sponsor and champion was available to the project. In spite of some tensions, the dynamic of involving the chairman appears to have been mutually beneficial. The technical process of lean production was a specific issue that the set addressed and their learning revealed a number of deep-seated and unfounded misconceptions in the organization about lean production. The project was useful in correcting misunderstandings that were not apparent beforehand and also in overcoming internal barriers to lean production. In terms of the action learning *process* the researchers concluded that:

1. It is important that the stages of group development be recognized and accommodated in the formation and working of the set.
2. The relationship between the set members and the chairman was crucial to the implementation and success of the project.
3. It appears that action learning can work to create the cultural change required in organizations of this type (small firms involved in the construction business).

Perceived potential difficulties in applying the technique included the action learning project becoming an end in itself rather than a means to an end; its appearing less significant from the outside than from the inside; and the imposition of 'hard' performance targets which might undermine the learning process.

Team Learning

A team may be defined as a task-oriented formal group. Theories of team development propose that in order to achieve an effective level of functioning, a group of individuals (who will eventually constitute a team per se) pass through a dynamic process of team development over a period of weeks, months or even years. The best-known description of this process is the model proposed by Tuckman (1965), who argued that a group passes through four stages of formation and development on its way to being an effective unit:

1. The first stage is forming; here the group is no more than a collection of individuals with a greater or lesser sense of purpose but without a clear view on how the group's goals will be achieved (see Rollinson and Broadfield 2002: 326–7). Collective learning is likely to be ad hoc, fragmentary and uncoordinated. The interpersonal processes will involve trying to understand each other's background, skills, motives and the potential roles that each may ultimately occupy in pursuit of the group's goal.
2. The second stage is referred to by Tuckman as 'storming'. Here the interpersonal processes that began in the first stage begin to become more explicit and conflict may surface, sometimes even in a forceful way as individuals bid for power, roles and territory. This potentially conflictual stage is a vital catharsis if the group's formation is to proceed. Hence the storming stage should not be viewed negatively – it may be a temporal space for constructive conflict to occur (see Rollinson and Broadfield 2002). Collective learning in this stage is likely to be centred on the surfacing of assumptions and mental models and the beginnings of the development of a shared understanding (perhaps based on the realization that members do not see things in the same way.
3. In the subsequent stages ground rules that have been emergent to this point crystallize and a task focus surfaces with informal rules for cooperation and interaction (this is the 'norming' stage). The collective learning will be based upon the development of a shared understanding of the different perspectives that each member brings, an acceptance, and an accommodation of these into the group's working methods based upon the commonly understood and accepted ground rules.
4. A shared understanding allows the basis for coordinated and collective action and learning. In the final stage the team is able to begin performing in a mutually supportive and effective way. This may involve, at this point, questioning of the common assumptions and shared mental models that have evolved through stages 1 to 3, with new routines, procedures and rules being established and owned by the group in a spirit of collective inquiry, learning and action.

L&D FACTS AND FIGURES

Richard Hackman and his colleagues provide a number of L&D-related lessons that they have learned from their research into teams and team learning: (a) training intact teams is crucial; (b) learning experiences should be spread out over weeks or months to enable the teams to apply their newly learned skills; (c) allowing managers to experience working in teams themselves increases their coaching capabilities. (*Source*: R. J. Hackman, R. Wageman, T. M. Ruddy and C. L. Ray, 2000. Team effectiveness in theory and in practice. In C. L. Cooper and E. A. Locke (eds), *Industrial and Organisational Psychology*. Oxford: Blackwell.)

Tuckman's model is useful from an L&D perspective because it can alert us to some of the potential problems that may exist in building a new team and also it can provide guidelines for how L&D can contribute to the team development process. L&D practitioners may be charged with the responsibility for team building and it is important to have a model or theory upon which L&D activities for team development can be built over and above generic issues of communication and interpersonal skills development. This has been taken a stage beyond the Tuckman model by Carew et al. (1986), who fused the situational leadership model (Hersey and Blanchard 1988) with Tuckman's model to suggest appropriate facilitator behaviours for each of the four stages. The Hersey and Blanchard situational leadership model contends that the behaviours that leaders should deploy are contingent upon the context. Their team leader behaviour framework was based on two dimensions of 'supportive' and 'directive', thus creating the following four behaviours:

1. Directing (high directive, low supportive): Carew et al. suggest that this is the appropriate style for the forming stage.
2. Coaching (high directive, high supportive): appropriate for the storming stage when the leader/facilitator may have to coach the team members in the knowledge required for the completion of the task whilst engaging in supportive behaviours such as active listening, empathizing and so forth.
3. Supporting (low directive, high supportive): aligns with the norming stage as the facilitator encourages the members to take on more and more of the group and task functions (Raelin 2000: 154).
4. Delegating (low directive, low supportive) in the performing stage allows the team to take full responsibility with the leader/facilitator as a monitor and resource to be called on when needed.

Like mental models, team learning is one of Senge's five disciplines for organizational learning. His starting point is the notion of the dysfunctionality of wasted energy, which he contends is a product of a misalignment amongst team members. Realignment is a necessary precondition before delegation and empowerment can occur. If alignment can be achieved this endows the team with the capabilities to think insightfully and synergistically, using the power of many minds (rather than a collection of single minds) acting in spontaneous yet coordinated ways and informing and being informed by other teams (Senge 1990). Senge's discipline of team learning has two main elements:

1. The first element is dialogue and discussion: in a dialogue there is free and creative expression of ways to address complex issues. In a discussion different views are presented and defended in search of the 'best' decision, and the 'trick' is to distinguish between these two complementary activities (1990: 236).
2. The second component of team learning is learning to deal creatively with negative forces, for example those forces that may oppose dialogue and discussion, including the defensive routines that are a manifestation of Argyris and Schön's Model I behaviour (such as 'smoothing over' and 'win-lose' as opposed to 'win-win' scenarios) (Senge 1990).

To avoid lapsing continually into defensive routines, team learning requires regular practice so that a team can develop its 'joint skill in fostering a team IQ that exceeds individual IQs' (1990: 259). From a cognitive perspective, an outcome of team learning is a shared mental model. But if this is the case, what does this sharedness look like?; and what is it that teams need to share (Hodgkinson and Sparrow 2002: 80)? Salas and Cannon-Bowers (2001) argue that teams need to develop:

1. A sharedness with respect to a common knowledge about task-related processes such as team working itself.
2. Knowledge of team members' individual expertise and skills (thus enabling individuals to adjust their own behaviours commensurate with their perceptions of those of the other members of the team).
3. Shared beliefs that may or may not lead to the cognitive consensus necessary to reach decisions (Hodgkinson and Sparrow 2002).

Of course, as well as formal teams there are in all organizations informal groupings of individuals that serve to meet social and emotional needs, and membership of such groups is a powerful mechanism whereby learning can occur.

PERSPECTIVE FROM RESEARCH: CREATING CARDIAC SURGERY TEAMS THAT LEARN IN THE USA

Based on the following source: A. Edmondson, R. Bohmer and G. Pisano, 2001. Speeding up team learning, *Harvard Business Review*, October, 79(9): 125–32.

Edmondson et al. (2001) researched the ways in which cardiac surgery teams (typically comprising a surgeon's assistant, scrub nurse, anaesthetist and a technician) learned how to use a new surgical procedure called minimally invasive technology. This new surgical procedure has the major advantage that the surgeon can work on the heart through an incision between the ribs rather than making a major incision through the patient's breastbone. They collected data from 16 medical centres on procedures involving 660 patients. They were able to single out three factors that were associated with success in learning how to use the new procedure:

1. Designing a team for effective learning: Edmondson et al. identified two critical aspects of team design. The first of these was the extent to which team leaders choose particular individuals to fill the required specialisms within the team. For example, some teams selected their members in a collaborative way and based the selection decision not only on technical competence but also on the individual's ability to work with others, deal with new and ambiguous situations and their preparedness to offer suggestions to team members of higher status (Edmondson et al. 2001).

2. Framing the challenge: teams that were more successful in implementing the new technology framed the surgical problem less as a technical one and more as an organizational one (for example, creating new ways of working together as a team rather than simply acquiring new technical skills) (Edmondson et al. 2001).

3. Creating psychological safety: as Edmondson et al. noted, individual learning is a private affair; team learning, on the other hand, occurs in public and individuals risk appearing foolish or incompetent if their experiments do not work out. For trial-and-error learning to occur successfully the fear of embarrassment has to be neutralized if the necessary 'robust back-and-forth communication amongst team members required for real-time learning' is to occur (Edmondson et al. 2001: 131). One of the chief factors in creating a safe environment in which individuals felt comfortable in making suggestions was through the actions and attitudes of the surgeon who led the team. It is he or she who would be looked to in the first instance for cues about how team members were expected to behave.

Communities of Practice and Activity Theory

When considering collective learning one is by definition concerned with social processes. Bandura's social learning theory was encountered in a previous chapter in an attempt to understand and explain the learning of an individual in a group; in the present context the concern is with the learning of the group (as well as the individuals within it). Theories of collective and organizational learning have drawn upon models of individual cognition, but alongside this in the 1990s there was a growing interest in a different perspective on learning. This view was of learning as situated in social practice. In the eyes of some it developed in opposition to the psychological and cognitive view of learning since it is concerned not with the processing of information but with the 'metaphorical world' of interpretation where social structures are continuously being produced, reproduced, interpreted and reinterpreted (Elkjaer 1999: 78). It contrasts with entity-based theories, such as cognitivism (Barab and Plucker 2002), which place knowledge in the head of the learner rather than viewing cognition as being distributed amongst individuals and socially constructed as information processed between individuals (Salomon 1993).

In a management context it relates closely to a social constructionist perspective that draws upon the interpretavist paradigm of Karl Weick and others; it is concerned with the ways in which organizational 'realities' are socially constructed. In a different field (that of organizational and managerial cognition) Hodgkinson and Sparrow argue that theories and models from cognitive psychology, viewing organizations as systems of information, may be contrasted with the Weickian perspective that views organizations as systems of interpretation and meaning. An important question is, 'Are these two perspectives incommensurate?' Hodgkinson and Sparrow argue that in the context of organizational and managerial cognition both perspectives are 'ultimately required if we are to develop adequate theoretical accounts of the way strategic competence is developed and utilized in organisations' (2002: 27). The same could be argued for L&D: if we are to develop a broadly based and comprehensive understanding of L&D in the workplace, both the cognitive and the social perspectives are needed. Without this dual perspective we run the risk of limiting our understanding to a partial view gained through one particular lens and of ignoring any potentially valuable insights that perspectives other than our own may provide.

The two fundamental concepts from the perspective of learning as being situated in a context, affected by and affecting the context (a situated view of learning) are communities of practice (CoPs) and legitimate peripheral participation (LPP). Lave and Wenger define a community of practice as:

> a set of relations among persons, activity and the world, over time and in relation with other tangential and overlapping communities of practice. A community of practice is an intrinsic condition for the existence of knowledge, not least because it provides the interpretive support necessary for making sense of its heritage. (1991: 98)

This notion takes us back to a question posed earlier in the book regarding the distinction between learning and working. From a social constructivist perspective Gerhardi and Nicolini provide us with one answer to our query when they claim that working and learning are not distinct activities, instead they are closely bound up with each other in a local practice and a local context. Many of these debates in this realm place much emphasis upon the role of language as a medium of social construction, hence within this purview learning is a label that both produces a socially constructed reality and is produced by that reality (Gerhardi and Nicolini 2001: 43).

The second important concept of the situated learning perspective is that of legitimate peripheral participation (LPP). It describes the process whereby newcomers become included in a community of practice through:

Peripherality (an approximation to full inclusion), which gives access and exposure to real-world practice from its edge and a sense of how the community operates. The curriculum or content of the shared endeavour is not a written-down scheme but is in the community itself (Wenger 1998).

Legitimacy, in that those individuals chosen to participate may be treated as potential members of the community. The lessons 'given' are not about practice but are part of practice and take place within practice (Wenger 1998: 100–1). The term is seen as deriving from an interpretation of learning in traditional apprenticeships (Elkjaer 1999), wherein the sponsorship of a 'master' is required for apprentices to have access to the practice. A similar relationship may be observed in universities today where potential doctoral students gain legitimacy by being 'taken on' by a professor or other experienced researcher who is already a legitimate member of the community of practice.

The starting point for some discussions of the perceived gap between learning and working appear to be based upon a view of L&D (or more correctly 'training') as an 'educational' process that is divorced from the real world and concerned with content more than process. For example, Seely-Brown and Duguid (1991) argued that much conventional learning theory, including that found in most training courses, tends to endorse the value of abstract knowledge over actual practice, resulting in a separation of learning from working. However, it is precisely this separation between learning and working that many of the widely endorsed and well-practised models, systems and techniques of individual and collective learning attempt to overcome. For example, the experiential learning model examines the ways in which individuals may grasp and transform their real-world experiences to create knowledge. The model is as much concerned with process as it is concerned with content. Another example is the andragogical theory of Knowles; it is rooted in the needs and experiences of the adult learner.

An argument that the learning models that underpin much L&D practice privilege abstract and decontextualized knowledge over a concern for a contextualized view of learning and working (and of these things as being intimately related) is open to question and challenge. The corpus of mainstream L&D theory and practice jettisoned educational models many decades ago in attempts to situate learning in a work-related context. Revans's action learning concept is a good case in point: programmed knowledge (p) is seen as necessary but insufficient in itself; it must be complemented with the disposition and ability on the part of managers to conduct their own inquiries (Q) into their beliefs, actions and outcomes.

L&D FACTS AND FIGURES

In EU member states on average more than two-thirds of participants in VET (vocational education and training) programmes attend an education or training establishment. Only in Italy (and Ireland) are there programmes that take place almost exclusively in the workplace – for example, the Apprendistato scheme in Italy. (Source: CEDEFOP, 2003. *Key Figures on Vocational Education and Training*, http://www.cedefop.eu.int)

Orr carried out ethnographical research in the 1980s on working and learning practices amongst a group of service technicians. The research related a 'thick' detailed description of the work as it is actually carried out (non-canonical practice), in comparison to the same way the work is 'thinly' described in manuals and training courses (canonical practice). (Canonical in this sense refers to practice as decreed by a written set of rules – the origin of the term relates back to the authority vested in written texts such as biblical scriptures.) The perceived gap in adequacy between the canonical and non-canonical practices was wide to the extent that if the service technicians in the company concerned had adhered to the canon (the written rules), the company's services would have been in chaos (Seely-Brown and Duguid 1991). From an L&D perspective the problem may have stemmed from the organization's faith in 'formal training and canonical practice' (Seely-Brown and Duguid 1991: 62) rather than any intrinsic worthlessness of planned L&D per se. Seely-Brown and Duguid's discussion is instructive in this regard since the theories of learning implicated in the service technicians' documentation and training appear to view learning from the abstract stance of pedagogy. Perhaps a more experiential, andragogical or action-based perspective in the design of the training programmes themselves might have obviated some of the negative views that the technicians seemed to express regarding the practical value of the training provided. The way in which training is described may belie a particular perception of L&D as 'the transmission of explicit, abstract knowledge from the head of someone who knows to the head of someone who does not in surroundings that specifically excludes the complexities of practice' (1991: 68) in the training room. Such models of learning have been under attack not only from situated learning theorists, but, as we have already seen, from within the L&D community itself for many decades.

PERSPECTIVE FROM RESEARCH: DUALITIES IN THE CONTEXT OF A COMMUNITY OF PRACTICE IN THE USA

Based on the following source: S. A. Barab, M. Barnett and K. Squire, 2002. Developing an empirical account of a community of practice: characterising the essential tensions, *The Journal of the Learning Sciences*, 11(4): 489–42.

Dualism is the view that in any domain there may be two independent underlying principles (for example, good and evil, mind and matter, form and content and so forth). In the context of L&D, content and process is an example of a duality that underlies the domain of practice. An instance of such a duality may be found in the Community of Teachers (CoT) programme as described by Barab et al. (2002). The CoT programme is a preparation programme for pre-service teachers working towards secondary teacher certification in the USA. Participants join the community and remain a part of it for between two and four years. The learning proceeds in a collaborative and reflexive way between school practice and university seminars. The CoT is based on the assumptions that a strong sense of community is important for learning, learners are equals in defining the programme, intensive fieldwork is essential and performance should be as authentic as possible. The study reported by Barab et al. is a lengthy and rigorous exemplar of an empirical account of a CoP; it is only possible here to focus on one aspect of it in order to illustrate some of the dynamics and dualities of learning in context.

In traditional accounts it is often tempting to place action and reflection as opposites. However, Wenger replaced the notion of a dichotomy with the concept of a duality wherein the 'process of engaging in practice always involves the whole person, both acting and knowing at once' (1998: 48). This renders neither the concrete solidly self-evident nor the abstract transcendentally general; instead they are paired needs and both gain their meaning in the context of practice, in relation to each other and in a constant interaction (Wenger 1998).

How does this look in reality? In keeping with Engstrom's work (see below), Barab et al. treat tensions as conflicting needs that drive a system of activity and they use the example of the teacher's portfolio to illustrate this. The portfolio is an assessment instrument used to capture the dynamic of practice as it unfolds. Keeping a portfolio is based upon the stages of: developing the portfolio purpose; collecting the portfolio of evidence; comparing the portfolio of evidence to the assessment criteria. Participants are encouraged to weigh evidence and be strongly reflective in their portfolios; hence the portfolio in the CoT context has a strong self-determining function. However, there is ostensibly a tension in the portfolio device: reflectivity and accountability coexist in it at one and the same time; these roles are con-

Continued

stantly present with its accountability promoting reflection and vice versa. The notion of a duality leads to the insight that reflecting on the constant interplay of these functions is much more fruitful than trying to understand each in isolation. The accountability and reflective function are an example of a paired need (an essential tension) that is 'dialectically co-constitutive' (2002: 526).

Discussion Point

Can you recognize any other 'essential tensions' in L&D practice? What about dualities – where are other dualities in L&D theory and practice? (Look for things that are less well understood in isolation and better seen in terms of their interplay.)

'Knowing' within the situated learning paradigm is an activity rather than a thing; it is contextualized rather than abstract and reciprocally constructed in an individual–environment interaction (Barab and Duffy 2000). From this perspective Engstrom's activity theory uses the term 'knowing' (to signify an active achievement), as opposed to 'knowledge' (a commodity), as a vehicle for exploring how people do their knowing within a community that has shared concepts, tools, technologies, rules and norms (Blackler et al. 1999: 208). Within Engstrom's theory an activity system is defined as consisting of:

- a subject or agent (individuals or groups that act and whose agency is selected as the point of view for the analysis);
- an object or actions (that which is acted upon);
- the components or tools that mediate the relationships between subject and object (such as conceptual and physical tools, community rules and divisions of labour).

Barab and Plucker use the examples from the course activities of a group of students to illustrate these concepts: an example of an object would be the students' understanding, a subject would be the students themselves and the mediating elements of the system the tools such as textbooks, lectures and other instructional tools (2002: 172). In contrast to the cognitive approach, activity theory holds that consciousness and meaning are formed in a collective activity (Leont'ev 1981) and the study of activity in a social system ceases to be the psychology of the individual but instead focuses on the interaction between an individual, systems of artefacts and other individuals in historically developing institutional settings (Miettinen 1999: 174). Hence further questions that activity theory seeks to answer are: who do people 'do' their knowing with and under what circumstances do they learn to collaborate with people from different communities of knowing (Blackler et al. 1999)? Activity theory also connects with issues of identity. Blackler et al. cite the example of medical doctors who, on the basis of the interpretation that they have for the role of medical activity, can choose to enact their individual knowing in a variety of contexts (such as somatic, psychosomatic, economic or community health). The role of L&D practitioners could be similarly analysed in this regard by asking the question, 'How do they enact their knowing: as an agent of change, as an upholder of the organizational status quo?' The responses to these questions will have significant implications for how and with whom the L&D practitioner does her or his knowing, how they engage with learning and how they relate to others from different communities of knowing.

Coaching, it may be argued, is one way in which an individual can begin to be assimilated into a community of practice through engaging with the coach (who is likely to be a legitimate member of the community). Coaching can be given by the manager, another colleague or other competent person and the coach helps learners to improve their task performance by allowing for practice, evaluating and monitoring performance, asking searching questions, actively listening and giving encouragement. Buckley and Caple (1992: 175) identify the advantages of coaching as:

- meeting individual needs in terms of pace and content;
- constant interaction between the learner and the coach;
- opportunities for continuous feedback;
- reduced downtime (since the job may continue albeit at a reduced pace during coaching);
- direct transfer of learning to the job.

The learner can, by observation and guidance, respond to the coach's actions, and begin to understand the nature of practice as it unfolds and discover how to engage in it – learn what behaviours and other factors help or hinder this engagement, establish what one is good at and have the opportunity to produce outcomes and artefacts (Wenger 1998: 95). The everyday practical drawbacks of intensive coaching, from an L&D perspective, are that:

- time spent in preparation for a coaching session for an individual may be the same as for a group of learners;
- the coaching may be subject to interruptions as a result of operational requirements;
- the coach must be skilled in instructing as well as being an expert in the relevant element of the job or task (and not pass on bad habits or incompetent performance);
- the coach and learner must be compatible (Buckley and Caple 1992: 175–6).

Coaching is, in a sense, the epitome of on-the-job learning since (as Reid and Barrington 1999: 90 noted) it has the advantage 'that the question of learning transfer to the actual job does not arise'. With the cascading of L&D responsibilities (including coaching) to line mangers, it is important to consider how this one-time poor relation of L&D can be understood and planned more effectively in order to give more structure to on-the-job learning.

PERSPECTIVE FROM PRACTICE: STRUCTURED ON-JOB TRAINING (OJT)

Based on the following source: J. A. de Jong and B. Versloot, 1999. Job instruction: its premises and its alternatives, *Human Resource Development International*, 2(4): 391–404.

de Jong and Versloot (1999) give a useful historical account of the way in which job instruction training developed in the twentieth century, and attribute its formalization to the First World War when the US shipping industry had the challenge of training almost half a million employees in a very short time. A simple four-step job instruction method was developed, to be carried out by supervisors: preparation (show); presentation (tell); application (do); inspection (check). This method has been formalized by Jacobs and Jones as structured on-job training (OJT), in which there are four sequential events:

1. Prepare the learner and present the instruction.
2. Require a response.
3. Provide feedback.
4. Evaluate performance. (Jacobs and Jones 1995).

In a further elaboration de Jong and Versloot (1999) suggest three types of on-site learning:

1. *On-site instruction*: the systematic passing on of skills on the basis of an identified task.
2. *On-site study*: the learner explores the tasks to be learned in an active way.
3. *On-site practice*: a form of 'learning-by-doing' in which the learner works with an experienced worker and takes over increasingly large parts of the job as her or his skill level increases.

Structured OJT provides invaluable opportunities for stimulating the flow of organizational knowledge through problem identification, learning cooperatively through inquiry and reflection (de Jong and Versloot 1999: 401) and the engagement of learners in reflection upon their experience and their own problem-solving processes (Raelin 1999: 137). Instead of taking it for granted that such a process will occur naturally and successfully it may be necessary, where increasing reliance is being placed upon workplace learning, to formalize and manage OJT in order that the learning transfer gains that it promises can be delivered.

Failure to do so may represent an inefficient waste of a potentially valuable learning resource.

Organizational Learning

Organizational learning, alongside the concept of the learning organization, was one of the most important management issues of the 1990s. As an illustration of this Crossan and Guatto (1996) searched a number of the main management publications databases (including the *Social Sciences Citation Index*, *ABI/Inform* and *Psychinfo*) and noted an almost exponential growth in publications on the subject. For example, in the years 1980–9, whilst there was a 37 per cent growth in general publications, there was a 636 per cent growth in organizational learning publications! The reasons for this explosion in interest have been attributed to the fact that scholars from a wide range of disciplines became more involved in theorizing and researching collective learning and also that many consultants and companies caught on to the commercial significance of organizational learning (Easterby-Smith and Araujo 1999). Although organizational learning as a topic of research had been around for decades, the heightened interest in the 1990s could be attributed to a management fashion (some might say 'fad'). Alternatively, it is often argued that one of the main reasons for the growth in the theoretical and practical significance of the concept of organizational learning was because of increased competitive pressures on organizations. As competition became more intense and technology evolved rapidly, markets were deregulated and became more global, and organizations were forced to respond to these changes. Innovative and entrepreneurial capabilities were increasingly important attributes and learning came to be seen as a lasting and non-imitable source of innovative capacity and hence competitive advantage.

The term 'organizational learning' has been traced back at least as far as Cyert and March in 1963, and there are almost as many definitions of it as there are books and articles on the subject. One problem of this fragmentation and multiplicity of perspectives is that in spite of the widespread acceptance of the notion of collective learning, there is no widely accepted model or theory of organizational learning (Fiol and Lyles 1985). The following definitions are illustrative of the variety of perspectives on what learning per se is:

Action-science: 'A process of detecting and correcting error' (Argyris 1977).
Performance-enhancement: 'The expansion of an organisation's capacity to create its own future and the results it truly desires' (Senge 1990).
Knowledge-creation: 'The creation of new knowledge (making tacit become explicit), dissemination of it throughout the whole organisation and the embodiment of it into new technologies, products and services' (Nonaka 1991).

Definitions of organizational learning in the literature are equally diverse. A selection of these is shown in Table 5.3.

Table 5.3 A selection of definitions of organizational learning (adapted from Spicer 2000: 331–3)

Source	Definition
Cangelosi and Dill (1965: 200)	'A series of interactions between adaptation at the individual or sub-group level and adaptation at the organisational level. Adaptation occurs as a result of three kinds of stress, one of which stimulates subsystem learning, one total system learning and one both subsystem and total system learning.'
Simon (1969: 26)	'. . . the growing insights and successful re-structuring of organizational problems by individuals reflected in the structural elements and outcomes of the organization itself'.
March and Olsen (1975: 168)	'Organizations and the people in them learning from their experience. They act, observe the consequences of their action, make inferences about those consequences, and draw implications for future action. The process is adaptively rational.'
Argyris and Schön (1978: 116)	'. . . when individuals, acting from their own images and mental maps, detect a match or mismatch of outcomes to expectation which confirms of disconfirms organizational theory-in-use.'.
Fiol and Lyles (1985: 803)	'Organizational learning means the process of improving actions through better knowledge and understanding.'
Levitt and March (1988: 320)	'Organizations are seen as learning by encoding inferences from history into routines that guide behaviour. The generic term "routines" includes the forms, rules, procedures, conventions, strategies and technologies around which organizations are constructed and through which they operate.'
Stata (1989: 64)	'Organizational learning occurs through shared insights, knowledge and mental models . . . [and] builds on past knowledge and experience – that is memory.'
Huber (1996: 822)	'An organization learns when, through its processing of information, it increased the probability that its future actions will lead to improved performance.'
Nicolini and Meznar (1995: 727)	'. . . a social construction which transforms acquired cognition into accountable abstract knowledge'.
Hayes and Allinson (1998: 12)	'Organizational (collective) learning involves sampling the environment, including the effects of past behaviour, and using the information made available by this process to codify the mental models, schema or cognitive maps that guide behaviour.'
Snyder and Cummings (1998: 875)	'Learning is organizational to the extent that: (a) it is done to achieve organization purposes; (b) it is shared or distributed among members of the organization; (c) learning outcomes are embedded in organization systems, structures and culture.'

Defining and Describing Organizational Learning

The definitions in Table 5.3 and the concept of organizational learning in itself beg a number of questions:

1. How may an entity such as an organization learn, and can an organization have the analogue of a cognitive system?
2. Where is organizational knowledge created, and how does organizational learning differ from individual learning?
3. Can organizational learning be measured or researched in a scientifically rigorous way, and how is organizational learning relevant to management and L&D practice?

These questions are all part of an ongoing debate. One of the simplest and most clear-cut descriptions is that provided by Senge, who described organizational learning as an increased capacity for effective action. This may be contrasted with the elaborate definition provided by Argyris and Schön (notice the links with the reflection-in-action concept of action science):

> Organisational learning occurs when individuals within an organisation experience a problematical situation and inquire into it on the organisation's behalf. They experience a surprising mismatch between expected and actual results of action and respond to that mismatch through a process of thought and further action that leads them to modify their images of organisation or their understanding of organisational phenomena and to restructure their activities so as to bring outcomes and expectations into line, thereby changing organisational theory in use. In order to become organisational, the learning that results from organisational inquiry must become embedded in the images of organisation held in its members' minds and/or in the epistemological artefacts (the maps, memories and program) embedded in the organisational environment. (1996: 16)

These various perspectives on the nature of organizational learning allow a number of features of organizational learning to be distinguished: organizational learning is the development of new knowledge, understanding or skills that become embedded in the organization's shared mental models and that have the potential to influence behaviour in ways that can lead to enhanced performance in response to internal or external disequilibria.

Argyris and Schön distinguish between two different types or levels of organizational learning (in much the same way as they distinguished between Model I and Model II learning in our discussion of action science) – single-loop learning and double-loop learning (see Figure 5.2).

Single-loop learning occurs when an organization deals with discontinuities in the internal or external environment without changing the underlying model that guides its actions (Argyris 1976). The result is an adjustment of established

Single-loop learning

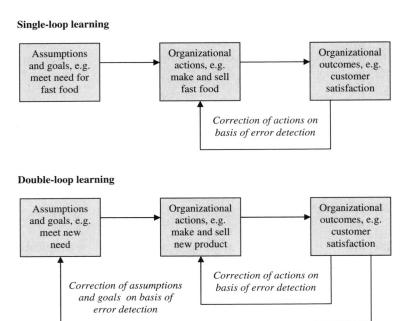

Figure 5.2 Single- and double-loop learning (based on Argyris and Schön 1978; Slater and Narver 1995; Probst and Buchel 1997: 33–4)

ways of working in pursuit of goals under existing sets of assumptions. The stimulus might be a gap between desired objectives and actual outcomes and existing theories of action. An analogy is of a heating system of a house controlled by a thermostat set to 17 °C:

1. The goal is to keep the room temperature at 17 °C.
2. The function of a thermostat is to detect error (i.e. any gap between the actual temperature in the house and the desired temperature of 17 °C).
3. The action is that the heating is turned on or off automatically to raise or lower the temperature in the house to 17 °C.

The crucial point is that the goal is to maintain the house at a temperature of 17 °C, based on the assumption that keeping a house at a certain temperature (i.e. 17 °C) is a desirable state of affairs (a value); this value is satisfied on the basis of a set of assumptions and through the action of turning on or off a heating system.

To translate these ideas to a business context, consider the following. A shortfall from a given level of production of a particular product might be addressed by introducing overtime working to produce more of the product (this, it is assumed, is a desirable goal for the organization). The organization adjusts to environmental factors (the shortfall in production), but existing norms and values are not questioned and remain directed towards the extant purpose of the company (such as 'meet need for fast food' in Figure 5.2).

Single-loop (or adaptive) learning is the process of adjusting effectively to given goals under existing norms by mastering the environment (Probst and Buchel 1997: 33). Single-loop learning can lead to the dominant logic; for example, the tyranny of the currently served market (Prahalad and Hamel 1990) within an organization being unquestioned and, concomitantly, the development of core capabilities that may, if taken for granted as an unquestionable assumption or a 'given', become core rigidities (Leonard-Barton 1992). One of the effects of single-loop learning is that it may encourage convergent thinking (as opposed to more creative divergent thinking) and hence it may inhibit innovation.

Double-loop learning occurs when an organization responds to discontinuities in the internal or external environment by modifying the assumptions that guide behaviour. These assumptions are reframed and a result might be an overhaul of established ways of working in pursuit of perhaps radically different goals under new sets of norms that are based on different sets of assumptions about the organization's mission, customers, capabilities or strategy. The assumptions may be unknown or known to the members of the organization but are likely not to be articulated and may even be undiscussable.

To return to the analogy of the heating system: in the single-loop learning system the focus was on the action of maintaining the room's temperature at 17°C. Under double-loop learning conditions the question might arise of whether a particular set temperature is the appropriate way to deal with the discontinuity, which may lead to alternatives being explored – such as asking the inhabitants of the house to wear thicker clothes, redesigning the house, not living in a house but some other form of dwelling that would ensure their comfort.

In the business context, the example of a shortfall in production might be addressed by asking deeper questions about why a shortfall exists, how this relates to the organization's goals, whether the mission itself is valid, and a possible redefining of why business is conducted in the first place. Hence, double-loop (or generative) learning is the process of questioning organizational norms and values, and building a new frame of reference (Probst and Buchel 1997: 35).

One inference that may be drawn from this is that double-loop learning is superior to single-loop learning, especially in times of radical change. However, this is not always necessarily the case and there are definitely associated risks with double-loop learning in certain situations. For example, in the case of the Chernobyl nuclear disaster the engineers departed radically from existing routines and standard operating procedures (SOPs) in what could be seen as a double-loop learning exercise that failed to pay off (Easterby-Smith and Araujo 1999: 3).

Facilitating Organizational Learning

As noted earlier, one of the attractions of – and reasons for – the explosion of interest in organizational learning in the 1990s was the perception that it had considerable potential as a management tool for the leverage of competitive advantage through, amongst other things, enhanced creativity, organizational change and innovation. When viewed in simple processual terms, organizational learning can be seen to involve a number of stages that share some of the features of the articulation and codification of tacit knowledge discussed in the previous chapter. The stages proposed by Slater and Narver are summarized thus:

Acquisition: the first stage is the acquisition of information beyond that contained in the organization's formal information systems. This may be obtained through benchmarking, joint ventures, networking, strategic alliances and working more closely with customers and so forth.

Encoding and storage: the second stage is that of the encoding and storage of new knowledge into a collective organizational memory. This can be as simple as documenting explicit knowledge in information systems, standard operating procedures (SOPs), mission statements, procedures and protocols. These elements may be considered to be part of a 'hard' storage system for organizational learning. Much organizational learning is not so explicit as to be codifiable in these hard forms but relies much more for its transmission and storage on social interactions, participation in a community of practice and so forth (there is not necessarily any implication here that a CoP can be synthesized or 'created' by management).

Sharing: a cognitive perspective would suggest that the products of individual learning are stored in an individual's schemas or mental models (for example, as declarative and procedural knowledge) and that these encompass basic beliefs and assumptions which may aid or restrict understanding (Kim 1993: 39). From this viewpoint organizational memory may be said to comprise the total of the individual mental models of the members of an organization. By making individual mental models explicit it is possible to create shared mental models and it is these that make the organizational memory usable.

Interpretation and incorporation: the sharing stage, as well as requiring dissemination, also leads to the interpretation of the new information and its incorporation into extant schemas. It may be recalled from our examination of implicit learning and of the cognitive explanations of learning at the individual level that were offered at the individual level, that the degree of fit between the new information and the extant schema can result in the simple accommodation of the new information. Alternatively it may involve some reconceptualization of existing frameworks in order that the discontinuity or ambiguity presented by the new information may be assimilated into a modified cognitive structure. At an organizational level this may entail minor adjustments to routines and procedures (actions) in a single loop or adaptive manner, or it may entail some more profound and wider-ranging modification of mission and goals (through double-loop or generative learning). Without a shared interpretation and the wider dissemination of new information the learning may remain embedded in the separate mental models of a collection of individuals without the question of, 'What does this mean for us (collectively)?' being asked (Slater and Narver 1995).

At a collective level the public reflection upon new information and its reinterpretation may serve to bring to the surface tension, conflicts and disagreements: crises may be precipitated; some individuals may even be unable to continue in the organization under a new shared set of meanings. Slater and Narver (1995) noted that the effective resolution of conflicts may require the use of structured facilitation for the surfacing of potential disagreements. Allowing the process free reign may unleash dysfunctional behaviours and destructive emotions that might create long-term and unbridgeable rifts. As noted above, Slater and Narver (1995) modelled organizational learning in processual terms (acquisition, dissemination and interpretation), whilst Nevis et al. (1995) identified a number of factors that may facilitate organizational learning (scanning imperative, performance gap, concern for measurement, experimental mind-set, continuous education [sic], multiple advocates, involved leadership and systems perspective). A synthesis of their approaches is presented in Figure 5.3.

The perspectives considered thus far view organizational learning largely from a cognitive perspective. However, to understand organizational learning it is important to consider how emotions are sometimes ignored or avoided in organizations, and also to consider what role organizational power and politics play in this dynamic over and above cognition (Vince 2001: 1338). The dynamic observed and interpreted by Vince in an action-based research project in a large public utility company in the UK identified relationships between the development of strong emotions in different sub-systems of the organization. This fed the development of ways of avoiding communication between the sub-systems of the organization, which itself then protected and justified the separateness of the different parts and counteracted learning. Principles of action science lead one to the inevitable conclusion that the concomitant effect upon learning of such a dynamic is likely to be detrimental. Even when new shared interpretations have the potential to inform actions it may not be reasonable to expect direct and immediate behaviour change on the basis of the new collective knowledge since the opportunities for application may not present themselves immediately (Slater and Narver 1995: 66). It may be concluded that the development of shared mental models can be facilitated in a number of ways:

- by having a climate of openness with accessibility of information, sharing of problems, errors and lessons, and debate and conflict being seen as constructive ways to foster learning;
- by a shared perception of the performance gap with an emphasis on measurement in an attempt to identify the sources of disequilibria;
- by multiple perspectives, involving individuals from all levels of the organization in advocating new ideas and new methods of working (Nevis et al. 1995).

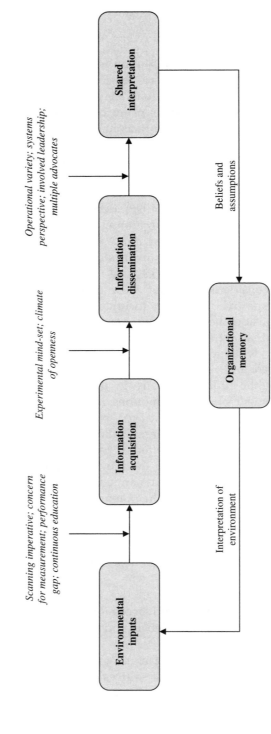

Figure 5.3 A model of the organizational learning process (adapted from: Nevis et al. 1995; Slater and Narver 1995)

In considering how organizational learning (or, more correctly, double-loop learning) may be managed and facilitated we begin to venture into the domain of prescription and the concept of the 'learning organization'.

PERSPECTIVE FROM PRACTICE: KNOWLEDGE SHARING AT SHELL INTERNATIONAL EXPLORATION AND PRODUCTION (SIEP)

Based on the following source: http://www.sitescape.com/next/test_shell.html

Shell International Exploration and Production (SIEP) is that part of the global oil and gas company Royal Dutch Shell which is responsible for the company's oil and gas exploration worldwide. Arguably it is the foundation (almost literally) upon which the rest of the business is built. The SIEP division has 30,000 employees and because of the nature of its business its employees – though they may work in similar functional areas (for example, well engineering, corrosion engineering and so forth) – are dispersed across the globe often in remote and inaccessible locations, sometimes offshore (on oil and gas platforms). This creates obvious difficulties for the sharing of information and transferring of new knowledge between employees since they may be thousands of kilometres apart and in different time zones. The problem is exacerbated by the turnover rate because employees typically move jobs within three to four years after an assignment in one location has been completed.

In order to enable knowledge sharing to take place within these constraints SIEP developed a knowledge-sharing intranet based on a system called Site Scape Forum, which formed a global network of electronic discussion groups. These e-groups provide a forum for asking questions and providing answers on topical issues and problems. Questions are posted onto a 'high traffic' area and, once posted, a question usually generates between three and four responses in the first 24 hours. After 30 days the questions and the answers are archived to create a knowledge base that users are encouraged to search before posing a question (as there is a good chance that the problem may already have been posed and solved). According to Shell, many SIEP employees spend between one and two hours per week on the forum.

Examples of the problems solved on the forum include stand-by online help for a team undertaking a particularly taxing and difficult drilling process, and the results of experimental horizontal drilling techniques posted and shared to promote best practice across the division. SIEP's aim was to produce electronic 'communities of practice' in which employees would be motivated to participate by the intrinsic interest that these professionals had in their own discipline and their inquisitiveness about related

Continued

areas. One positive outcome of this is that there is cross-fertilization and sharing of mental models between pipeline engineers and corrosion engineers, creating a synergy that would not otherwise have happened.

The estimated 'bottom line' benefit of the system is US$200 million. Other benefits include the speeding-up of the learning of new recruits with reduced 'time to competence'. The project had relatively small beginnings in SIEP, with a few thousand members spread across 100 communities. These were later merged to give three large communities in core businesses of SIEP (sub-surface, well and surface) and 10 smaller communities in supporting areas such as finance, IT, HR and safety. In total there are estimated to be about 15,000 users of the forum.

Although the evaluation of the project is not independent (http://www.sitescape.com/next/test_shell.html), the principle of creating electronic communities of practice is an exciting and interesting application of technology in pursuit of collective learning. The contextual factors for SIEP make it especially vulnerable to some of the barriers to organizational learning that have been identified (like fragmented and pooled learning – see below). By facilitating, surfacing and disseminating knowledge, along with collective inquiry, SIEP appears to have recognized the potential benefits of collective learning and has made conscious efforts to manage the process to make it more effective and efficient.

Incomplete Learning

As well as looking at how learning is happening, one further way to deepen our understanding of organizational learning is to look at how it does not happen, i.e. where it fails, is incomplete or where there are barriers and blockages to the acquisition, sharing and actioning of new knowledge. One of the problems of this line of argument, though, stems from the different ways in which success may be interpreted. For example, different groups in an organization may have different agendas and targets and perceive and evaluate the same outcome in different ways. For political reasons new leaders may evaluate outcomes in different ways than their predecessors, and individuals opposed to an action may not recognize a positive outcome. Hence the interpretation and evaluation of outcomes is likely to be heterogeneous at the organizational level (Levitt and March 1988). Organizations may also develop superstitious misunderstandings: an over-inflated self-confidence amongst executives on the basis of past performance may lead them to over-estimate the extent to which they can actually control situations, for example (March and Shapira 1987). One of the drawbacks of this superstitious learning is that it can reinforce routines that are perceived as leading to success, but this action may be based on premature commitment to particular routines and their subsequent reinforcement by inaccurate learning. More seriously still, this may act to the exclusion or inhibition of other more effective routines. An individual's job role may also constrain learning when he or she is unable to exert any major effect upon the shared mental model or to influence organizational action. Kim (1993) identified three other ways in which learning can be incomplete:

1. Situational learning: a problem is encountered, solved on the spot, and then the individual moves on to the next task but forgets or omits to codify the new knowledge (Kim 1993). The Shell project discussed previously is an example of how to combat this incompleteness.
2. Fragmented learning: here the individual may learn but the organization does not. Organizations that are decentralized and without strong internal networks are susceptible to this problem (Kim 1993). For example, managers who are geographically or organizationally isolated from others may create new knowledge but the organization cannot benefit because the learning is fragmented.
3. Opportunistic learning: here an individual, group or part of an organization takes unilateral action and bypasses the organization's widely shared mental models as embodied in routines, organizational norms or culture. Opportunistic learning can be highly productive, as in the case of the teams in IBM that were involved in the development of the PC in record time by bypassing the company's normal bureaucracies (Kim 1993: 46).

PERSPECTIVE FROM RESEARCH: MEASURING ORGANIZATIONAL LEARNING IN US MANUFACTURING FIRMS

Based on the following source: M. J. Tippins and R. S. Sohi, 2003. IT competency and firm performance: is organisational learning a missing link? *Strategic Management Journal*, 24: 745–61.

One of the perennial criticisms of organizational learning research has been the relative dearth of empirical studies. For example, Easterby-Smith and Araujo (1999) observed that out of 150 published papers on the subject in 1997 only 15 of these were based on new empirical data, ten of which were intervention-based studies, leaving a paltry five studies out of 150 (just over 3 per cent) that were based on independent non-action-based methods. Easterby-Smith and Araujo describe this pattern as 'worrying' (1999: 11). Recent years have witnessed an increase in the number of studies that have attempted to measure organizational learning, and an example of this line of research is the study by Tippins and Sohi (2003) which set out to explore the relationships between information technology, organizational learning and organizational performance.

Information technology (IT) provides members of an organization with quick and effective access to information; hence an organization's IT competence can contribute to the currency of organizational knowledge and provides one way of developing a knowledge consensus (shared mental model) through dissemination. Tippins and Sohi postulated that there would be a

Continued

link between a firm's IT competency and its abilities to acquire and dissem-
inate information. They argued that for this to occur, the IT system in terms
of knowledge of it, its objects and operations must serve both storage and
dissemination functions and must also be accessible to organizational
members. The researchers also aimed to address what might be seen as the
'holy grail' for organizational learning research: the link between organizational learning and performance. The study undertaken by Tippins and Sohi
is reported at some length here as an example of cross-sectional research
design and the subsequent analyses.

Hypotheses: the two hypotheses from the Tippins and Sohi study relevant
to our discussions were:

H1: IT competency is positively related to organizational learning.
H2: There is a positive relationship between organizational learning and firm
    performance.

Research Design and Measures: Tippins and Sohi opted to use a cross-
sectional survey design to address their research hypotheses and operationalized the various constructs via a series of measures in the form of
Likert-scaled statements:

1. IT competency consisted of three facets: IT knowledge (four items: for
    example, how knowledgeable they are about new computer-based inno-
    vations); IT operations (six items: for example, use of computer-based
    systems to analyse customer and market information); IT objects (five
    items: for example, whether the company has a formal MIS – manage-
    ment information systems – department).
2. Organizational learning consisted of a number of facets: information
    acquisition (six items: for example, asking customers what they want or
    need); information dissemination (six items: for example, the extent to
    which sharing customer information is the norm); shared interpretation
    (five items: for example, the extent to which managers agree on how best
    to serve customers); declarative ('what') memory (seven items: for
    example, how much is known about customers' sales goals); procedural
    ('how') memory (five items: for example, the extent to which experience
    has taught managers what to ask our customers).

These questions were each scored on a seven-point Likert scale. Firm performance was also measured, using a self-report format: respondents were
asked to rate their firm in terms of its profitability, customer retention and
sales growth over the past three years relative to their direct competitors.

Sample and Procedure: the survey was mailed to 524 senior executives of a
sample of US manufacturing firms. Non-response bias can be a potentially
serious problem in studies of this nature. It is defined as the refusal of some
subjects to participate in the study. Non-response may be connected to the
characteristics of the study and the higher the non-response the greater the

bias might be (Royer and Zarlowski 2001: 156). In order to address this Tippins and Sohi decided to re-mail non-respondents a month after the initial survey was sent out and in both mailings a dollar bill was included as an incentive. The mailings yielded a total of 271 responses (the final 52 per cent response rate compares very favourably with other surveys of this nature). They assessed non-response bias by comparing respondents and non-respondents on a number of demographic and firm characteristics variables. They found that there were no differences between respondents and non-respondents, suggesting that non-response bias was not likely to be a problem with these data.

They also tested for common method variance (because all the measures were in self-report Likert-scaled format) by submitting their data to a factor analysis. If common method variance is present in the data a single general factor might be expected to emerge (this is often referred to as Harman's single factor test and is widely used to screen data for a common method factor). Two factors rather than a single general factor emerged, which the authors took as an indication that their data set was relatively free of common method bias.

Results: the scales that Tippins and Sohi used demonstrated content validity (through interviews with subject experts) and reliability (Cronbach α's were in the range 0.78 to 0.91; it may be recalled that the recommended minimum is 0.70 – see Nunally 1978). Results from multiple regression analyses (using structural equation modelling, SEM) indicated:

1. A statistically significant relationship between IT competency and organizational learning ($\beta = 0.504$; $t = 4.94$; $p < 0.01$), thus lending support to H1.
2. A statistically significant relationship between organizational learning and firm performance ($\beta = 0.371$; $t = 4.03$; $p < 0.01$) and therefore supporting H2.
3. That the effect of IT on firm performance was through organizational learning, i.e. the effect of IT is mediated through organizational learning. A mediator is one form of an intervening variable (the other form is the moderator – not considered in detail here, but shown in Figure 5.4). A mediator variable (C) intervenes in the direct causal relationship between an independent variable (A) and a dependent variable (B) (Mbengue and Vandangeon-Duremez 2001: 269). The association is of the form that A influences C, which in turn influences B (Baron and Kenny 1986). In the context of Tippins and Sohi's study this means that IT (A) influences organizational learning (C) which in turn influences firm performance (B) – see Figure 5.4.

These findings suggest that IT only enhances firm performance when it is complemented by the necessary organizational learning capabilities (such as

Continued

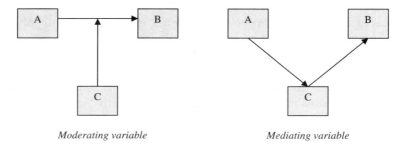

Moderating variable   Mediating variable

Figure 5.4 Effects of moderating and mediating variables (C) in a causal relationship between independent variable (A) and dependent variable (B) (adapted from Thietart 2001: 270)

the various facets of learning specified in Tippins and Sohi's model). IT by itself is not effective in this regard; it needs to be harnessed with and through organizational learning to influence performance. IT and organizational learning in combination are related to firm performance. Investment in IT *alone* is unlikely to solve organizational problems. The research is limited by the fact that:

- it is cross-sectional, and therefore it is effectively a snapshot at one moment in time;
- the measures used are all self-report and can therefore only be subjective assessments of learning, competence and performance;
- the findings are of limited generalizability.

Nevertheless this study goes some way to making a significant contribution to the growing body of organizational learning research by providing what appear to be reliable and valid measures and showing some, albeit limited, evidence of a link between organizational learning and the performance of manufacturing firms in the USA.

PERSPECTIVE FROM PRACTICE: THE SELF-REPORT ASSESSMENT OF ORGANIZATIONAL LEARNING

Based on the following source: E. Sadler-Smith, D. P. Spicer and I. Chaston, 2001. Learning orientations and growth in smaller firms. *Long Range Planning*, 34: 139–58.

One of the potential problems in a field that is theoretically quite disparate is the danger that constructs and measures may begin to proliferate as each group of researchers bases their assessment instruments on particular theories. It is also important that measurement tools are used that are reliable and valid. Table 5.4 presents a measure of organizational learning that has demonstrated some evidence of reliability and validity. For example, Cronbach α is 0.79 and statistically significant positive correlations have been observed between organizational learning and entrepreneurial management style and job complexity ($p \leq 0.05$) – see Sadler-Smith et al. 2001.

Critical Perspectives

Organizational learning has been criticized conceptually and as a field of academic inquiry on a number of grounds. For example, organizational learning is concerned with enhancing organizational performance (an improvement bias). The difficulty with the improvement bias is that it can lead to a definition of learning not so much in terms of its process but in terms of outcomes and therefore can conceal the dynamics of the process (Huysman 1999). Moreover, learning about the process of learning may be obscured over a concern with learning and performance improvements (for example, the Tippins and Sohi study discussed above). The emphasis on increased performance is a strong attribute of the learning organization movement and hence may be extrapolated as a weakness of the organizational learning field also (see below). Huysman argues that to counteract the improvement bias researchers should concentrate on the process of learning and reserve the issue of outcomes for further investigation. An assumption of a performativity perspective is that learning is a 'good thing'; however, some authors have argued, from a critical perspective, against learning. Contu et al. (2003) identify the stance of 'no alternative to learning' that is woven into much of the management and learning discourse (we have met some of these in this chapter; for example, 'learning as the *only* sustainable source of competitive advantage'). This assertion with its underpinning values and assumptions makes it difficult to be or appear to be 'against learning', but at the same time the 'no alternative' stance glosses over potentially contradictory and antagonistic organizational practices. We have already met in Chapter 1 Antonacopoulou's research (2001), which discussed the paradoxical nature of the relationship between learning and training. A more radical perspective is presented by Ortenblat, in which he argues for the emancipation of employees so that they are no longer socialized into an existing shared mental model. Within his radical utopia individuals will be in control of their own learning and knowledge, whilst efforts to make the organization independent of any one individual will be resisted by employees; there will be a formal system of democratic norms; all employees will be guaranteed permanent appointments; work time is 'strictly restricted'; and people see their organization as part of a bigger whole and are not afraid of 'killing' their organization to give space for a more healthy alternative (Ortenblat 2002: 96).

Table 5.4 A short questionnaire for the assessment of organizational learning (note that Questions 4, 6 and 7 are reverse scored). (*Source*: Sadler-Smith et al. 2001)

	Strongly agree	Agree	Neither agree nor disagree	Disagree	Strongly disagree
1. This is an open organization and as much information as possible is made available to employees.	☐	☐	☐	☐	☐
2. Ideas from all employees are listened to and acted on to change company policy even if they challenge senior managers' views.	☐	☐	☐	☐	☐
3. There is two-way communication between employees of all levels about what this company's doing and where it's going.	☐	☐	☐	☐	☐
4. Company strategy and policy is prescribed by senior managers.	☐	☐	☐	☐	☐
5. We actively encourage employees and customers to let us know if we're going wrong in the way we do things and to let us know how we can improve.	☐	☐	☐	☐	☐
6. We're reluctant to try out new ways of working because we're not the sort of company that can take risks.	☐	☐	☐	☐	☐
7. Employees are discouraged from experimenting with new and novel ways of working.	☐	☐	☐	☐	☐
8. We do have set working practices, but we can change these in pursuit of greater efficiency if need be.	☐	☐	☐	☐	☐
9. We try to promote risk taking and experimentation in our working methods.	☐	☐	☐	☐	☐

The Learning Organization

The concept of the learning organization is sometimes perceived as being difficult to disentangle from the related concept of organizational learning. Several authors have clarified the distinction (for example, Tsang 1997). Easterby-Smith and Araujo (1999) describe the differences thus:

1. The learning organization is most often the concern of consultants (or academics in a consulting role) who are interested in developing normative models and prescribing methods of organizational change concerned with improving learning processes.
2. Organizational learning is more within the purview of management and organization researchers and is concerned with describing, explaining and attempting to understand the processes of learning as they occur in originations.

That said, the two fields overlap and interrelate; for example, learning organization prescriptive frameworks are often based upon the assumption that the double-loop type of organizational learning is superior to single-loop learning and attempts are made to describe tools and techniques for facilitating double-loop organizational learning.

The norms towards which an aspirant learning organization might aim depend upon how it is defined. For example, Pedler et al. describe the learning organization thus: 'a learning company [organization] is an organisation that facilitates the learning of all its members and consciously transforms itself and its context' (1997: 3). Senge's description demonstrates the ways in which the concept of the learning organization draws upon organizational learning theory: 'an organisation that is continually expanding its capacity to create its future'. For such an organization it is not enough merely to survive. 'Survival learning', or what is more often termed 'adaptive [single-loop] learning', is important – indeed it is necessary. But for a learning organization, 'adaptive learning' must be joined by 'generative [double-loop] learning', 'learning that enhances our capacity to create' (1990: 14).

Senge's definition retains a subtlety of the organizational learning theory that is sometimes overlooked or glossed over, namely that double-loop and single-loop learning are not mutually exclusive and that both may be needed. It is often taken for granted that an organization will engage in single-loop learning; the challenge is how can double-loop learning be fostered and developed? Some of the responses to this question were addressed earlier when the concept of organizational learning itself was examined. However, we will now consider in more detail some of the prescriptive models of what it means to be a learning organization and the ways in which the concept has been applied.

Poell (1999) identified a number of recurring themes in the learning organization literature and many of the features he and his colleagues singled out have clear theoretical antecedents in areas that have been considered in relation to knowledge and learning at the individual and collective learning levels, namely:

- single- and double-loop learning processes (as in the work of Argyris and Schön);
- creation and distribution of knowledge (as in the work of Nonaka);
- collective dialogue and inquiry (as in the work of Revans and Argyris and Schön);
- learning-to-learn (as in the work of Kolb);
- integration of learning and working (as in the work of Lave and Wenger);
- strategic integration of HRM (as in the work of Schuler and Jackson);
- shared vision, empowerment, continuous learning and coaching.

One of the most widely cited models of the learning organization is that of Senge and the associated notion of the five disciplines (as in the title of his 1990 book, *The Fifth Discipline*). What does Senge mean by a 'discipline' in this context? First of all, he does not mean any kind of enforced order; instead he is referring to a body of theory (perhaps better described as a set of principles) that must be studied and mastered in order to be put into practice. In a paradoxical way the disciplines are never fully acquired but instead a lifetime is spent in mastering them and as one learns more one becomes more aware of one's ignorance. An implication of this is that the learning organization is not a destination ever to be arrived 'at' but is a state of 'being', which continuously unfolds one's understanding of oneself, one's organization, the world and one's place in it. The five disciplines (or 'component technologies') for learning are:

1. Personal mastery: the ability to continually clarify and deepen our personal vision.
2. Mental models: unearthing our internal pictures of the world and opening them to others.
3. Shared vision: developing a shared picture of the future and fostering genuine commitment to this.
4. Team learning: attaining the capacity to 'think together' and make synergies that work.
5. Systems thinking: the discipline that integrates the others into a coherent body of theory and practice (Senge 1990).

An alternative view is provided by Pedler et al. (1997), who specify eleven characteristics of a learning company. Their model shares some commonality of content with the eleven attributes of a global learning organization described by Marquardt and Reynolds (1994). The eleven characteristics of Pedler et al. cluster into five super-ordinate groups, summarized in Table 5.5. Readers are referred to Pedler et al.'s book for comprehensive descriptions of the model and its application (numerous case studies are presented). As an example, the 'enabling structure' characteristic has a number of component features, which prescribe organizational structural arrangements and processes that are hypothesized as enabling learning, including the flexible structuring of job roles to allow for experimentation and growth, rules that are flexible enough to be changed on the basis

Table 5.5 Characteristics of the learning company (*Source*: Pedler et al. 1997: 15–17)

Looking in	Informating, i.e. IT is used to 'make information widely available to front line staff in order to empower them'
	Formative accounting and control helps employees know how money works in the company
	Internal exchange, i.e. departments contract with and learn from others in the internal supply chain
	Rewarding employee flexibility
Strategy	Learning approach to strategy, i.e. strategy is emergent and to some extent seen as experimental
	Employee participation in policy making
Learning opportunities	Learning climate, i.e. a culture of questioning, feedback and support fosters learning
	Self-development opportunities and the resources to support this are available to employees
Structures	Enabling structures, i.e. organizational design is a means to an end not an end in itself
Looking out	Employees who have contact with customers and suppliers (i.e. boundary workers) scan the environment and bring the information back into the company
	There is inter-company learning through joint ventures, benchmarking, etc.

of inquiry and performance appraisals that are geared to an L&D purpose rather than sanctions. The characteristics and their component features have high face validity and the model of Pedler et al. is explicitly designed as an intervention tool for organizational learning and development. The book contains a diagnostic instrument that enables a company to map:

- where it currently stands with respect to these eleven characteristics;
- where it would like to be in some desired future state.

Through this 'gap' analysis it is possible to identify areas for action and to assign priorities to these. Each organization is able to devise an organizational learning and development action plan that is relevant both to its current deficiencies but also to its desired future state. A 'dissatisfaction index', which can have values in the range 100 (very dissatisfied) to 0 (completely satisfied), can be calculated thus, on the basis of employee responses to the survey:

$$\text{Dissatisfaction index} = \frac{\text{How it should be} - \text{how it is}}{\text{How it should be}} \times 100$$

This diagnosis is the first stage in a generic 'plan–do–check' cycle common in so many rational planning processes in organizations. In the context of the learning company the model is articulated thus: diagnosis ('how do you measure up?'), action ('creating the learning company') and reflections ('further thoughts and directions') (Pedler et al. 1997). There are a number of other models of the learning organization, a selective comparison of which is presented in Table 5.6. The various characteristics of the different models have been subjectively grouped together.

Discussion Point

What are the essential differences between the 'organizational learning' and the 'learning organization' perspectives? Why do L&D practitioners need these concepts as part of their professional knowledge and practice? Justify your assertions.

Poell (1999) criticizes the concept of the learning organization on two principal grounds: (a) the neglect of issues of organizational power; (b) a restricted view of learning and work. The former has been dealt with elsewhere (Ortenblat 2002; Contu et al. 2003). Poell drew specific attention to the view that within the learning organization field the notion of working that lends itself most easily to the prescription is that of team working, but clearly work is organized in other ways (individual, inter-organizational and so forth), hence there may be an assumption that most work is team-based. Also it is not always clear exactly how the laudable aspirations contained in the prescriptions might be implemented. The learning organization ideal assumes that all workers will be able and willing to find their own learning route and will be self-motivated self-developers. The question is what to do if workers are not willing to learn continuously, to innovate and double-loop learn on an ongoing basis, to be responsible for their own development and share their knowledge (which may be their own source of competitive advantage in the internal labour market) with colleagues (Poell 1999). Individuals' knowledge assets may be organization specific and person specific. So in times of uncertainty and downsizing individuals may take decisions about the extent to which they are willing to surrender these assets. This may be influenced by the employment relationship. For example, where there is a strong reciprocal alignment of organizational and employee interests this may create the motivational basis for employees to learn in ways that play an role in the longer-term development of the business (see Boxall and Purcell 2003: 146). By way of a conclusion, some of the limitations of the learning organization concept may be summarized as follows:

1. There is reinvention and duplication across models with no real attempt at theoretical convergence.
2. The prescriptive nature of the discourse means that it may be seen as a recipe for success and, on the basis of much of the rhetoric, a panacea for a wide range of organizational problems and development issues.

Table 5.6 Learning organization characteristics

Super-ordinate category	The learning company *Pedler et al. (1997)*	Global learning organization *Marquardt and Reynolds (1994)*	Essence of a learning organization *Gephart et al.(1996)*	The five disciplines *Senge (1990)*
Participation and strategic learning	Learning approach to strategy	Strategy Vision		Shared vision
Knowledge acquisition	Participative policy making Boundary worker as environmental scanners Inter-company learning	Empowerment Environmental scanning		
Knowledge dissemination and sharing	Informating Formative accounting and control Internal exchange	Teamwork and networking Knowledge creation and transfer	Continuous learning at the systems level Knowledge generation and sharing	Team learning Mental models
Adaptability	Reward flexibility		Spirit of flexibility and experimentation	
Organizational structure and culture	Enabling structures A learning climate	Appropriate structures Corporate learning culture Supportive atmosphere	Culture of learning People-centred	
Learning and development	Self-development opportunities for all	Learning technology		Personal mastery
Integrated thinking *Continuous improvement*		Quality	Critical systemic thinking	Systems thinking

3. Employee relations issues have tended to be somewhat side-stepped in some of the rhetoric that surrounds the learning organization.

4. Its action-basis and consultancy-driven approach may have concomitant effects upon its theoretical utility, scientific rigour and generalizability.

PERSPECTIVE FROM PRACTICE: STRONG CULTURE VERSUS THE LEARNING ORGANIZATION IN A US ENGINEERING FIRM

Based on the following source: D. N. Ford, J. J. Voyer and J. M. Gould-Wilkinson, 2000. Building learning organisations in engineering cultures: case study, *Journal of Management in Engineering*, July/August: 72–83.

What is sometimes lost sight of in discussions of the learning organization and its implementation is the role – and in some cases the debilitating nature of the role – that the internal context can play in determining the success or otherwise of planned interventions designed to foster organizational learning. For example, 'engineering cultures' are often perceived to have more of a 'harder' technology focus than a 'softer' people focus. Furthermore, the balance amongst the various competing cultures within a single organization can also play an important role and create tensions in the arena of organizational learning. In this regard Ford et al. report attempts to transform a high-technology engineering company in the USA into a learning organization.

The case study department was the Data Shaping Division (DSD) of a manufacturer of semi-conductors (under the fictitious name of Computer Chips International) which employed 1,800 workers. The company mission was the development of new products and the redesign of existing products to meet new market needs. Engineers played a leading role in the organization and determined its dominant culture. This was driven by an optimism based on faith in science and technology, a 'can do' attitude allied to a problem-solving and pragmatic bent. The company had low turnover (although it had recently downsized from 3,000 employees) with a strong work ethic amongst employees (partly as a result of a wish to avoid being laid off). A principal issue that DSD had to address was that of cycle time (development project durations). A project team concluded that the concepts and tools of the learning organization as embodied in Senge's work could, by transforming DSD into a learning organization, substantially reduce product cycle times (Ford et al. 2000: 74).

A sub-unit of the DSD, the Progressive Logic Department (PLD), with 100 employees, was chosen as a pilot site prior to the planned implementation across the whole of the DSD. The Implementation Team was supported by researchers from the Organisational Learning Center at Massachusetts Institute of Technology (MIT). Ford et al. claimed that because the only challenge that existed in the organization to building a learning organization related to culture (for example, senior manager support was taken as a given), this acted effectively as an experimental 'control' enabling the effect of culture to be singled out for study. The research adopted an action-based approach and members of the Implementation Team themselves were trained in qualitative research methods (such as participant observation). Observation is a method by which researchers collect data by directly observing processes in an organization over a period of time (Ibert et al. 2001: 183). Participant observation involves an internal viewpoint and in this case the researchers were complete participants (other lesser degrees of participation include the participant as observer, observer as participant and non-participant observation – see Ibert et al. 2001). The issue of measurement and validity in the research was addressed through the use of multiple methods (for example, interviewing and observation) and triangulation, using the Implementation Team as multiple analysts (this tests whether or not the findings are merely a product of the methodology used, Ibert et al. 2001).

Competencies in the five disciplines of the learning organization as defined by Senge (systems thinking, personal mastery, mental models, shared vision and team learning) were chosen as evaluation criteria for the project. These disciplines were seen as enabling skills for the three steps in the process of organizational learning proposed by Nevis et al. (1995), namely: knowledge acquisition, knowledge sharing and knowledge utilization. The latter was modelled in a virtuous cycle as leading to performance improvement, recognition of the benefits of learning, commitment to organizational learning, effortful learning and positive feedback into enhanced competence in the five disciplines. Ford et al. describe in depth the ways in which the five disciplines were implemented and their attempted integration with the Nevis et al. process against the ever-present background of a strong engineering culture. They identified a number of constraints on the project's success, but principal amongst these were the knowledge sharing and knowledge utilization stages of the process. Whilst readers are referred to the full article for the details, the researchers' overall assessment of the project's attempts to transform the DSD into a learning organization was that it had failed.

The project's 'failure to transform the DSD into a learning organisation' (2000: 81) was hypothesized as being for three possible reasons:

1. The first of these is attributed to the lack of an experimental mind-set in the DSD's engineering culture; failures were seen less as a source of learning and more as a high risk for the experimenter with high potential costs (it should be remembered that this is set in a context of low job security).
2. The second possible factor was the lack of organizational and physical infrastructure for organizational learning.

Continued

3.   The third possible explanation, and related to (1) above, was the strength of the engineering culture and, arguably, an intrinsic dysfunctionality from a learning perspective.

Ford et al. are consistent with Schein's characterization of an engineering culture in which the preference is for automatization and 'designing people out' of the system. The risk averseness and general anxiety with regard to job security compounded created a resistance to learning that was impossible for the Implementation Team to penetrate. The Implementation Team became isolated, acting in effect as an ad hoc executive, which exacerbated the perceived threat from organizational learning. The research presents an honest and frank exposition of the difficulties of implementing the concept of a learning organization in a culture that is inherently technocratic and risk averse. The authors argue that, to be successful, the potential negative effects of this culture should have been recognized earlier and the necessary infrastructures for learning put into place in an environment that might come to embrace experimentation and learning. The extent to which these are incommensurate with the dominance of a learning-averse culture (in this case an engineering culture) remains an open question on the basis of this research.

Discussion Point

What would your response, as an L&D practitioner, be to an enthusiastic Chief Executive who tasks you with the project of turning her organization into a learning organization? How might you frame your response?

Summary: the Competent Organization

So where does a discussion that has ranged through collective learning, to organizational learning and the learning organization leave us at this point in the first decade of the twenty-first century? Strategy has been emphasized throughout much of our discussions, as has the notion of learning as a core competence of a dynamic and agile company that faces environmental turbulence and uncertainty. One potential way forward is by bringing theories of managerial and organizational cognition and learning to bear upon the notion of strategic competence as manifested in the concept of the competent organization (Hodgkinson and Sparrow 2002). Although similar sounding to 'the learning organization', seekers of normative descriptions and prescriptive solutions may be disappointed with Hodgkinson and Sparrow's concept of the competent organization. However, what is to be found instead is:

1. A scientifically rigorous exploration of a wide spectrum of psychological theory applied to the strategic management process.
2. A critical appraisal of the potential value of this for enhancing individual and organizational performance through 'strategic competence'.

The latter is defined as 'the ability of organisations (or more precisely their members) to acquire, store, recall, interpret and act upon information relevant to the longer-term survival and well-being of the organisation' (Hodgkinson and Sparrow 2002: xv). A strategically competent organization equates in Hodgkinson and Sparrow's view to a learning organization but not in any narrow or prescriptive sense. For Hodgkinson and Sparrow the learning organization field of study and practice amounts to little more than a repackaging of old established ideas. Instead, strategic competence is a manifestation of the organization's ability to learn through the processes of managerial and organizational cognition. But what characterizes a strategic competence in Hodgkinson and Sparrow's approach?

1. Firstly, the ability to detect signals, especially weak signals, in the environment that may presage a need for the organization to change.
2. Secondly, data that is gathered from the environment has to be filtered, stored, recalled at the appropriate times and interpreted in actionable ways.
3. This leads to the third issue, that of knowledge management – a central process in a competent organization.
4. Fourthly, the development of strategic competence is itself self-reinforcing since it enables an organization to proactively develop additional competencies and move into new markets.

By contrast, a lack of strategic competence may mean that the organization is trapped in a viscous circle of reactive behaviour in defending weaker and weaker existing markets, products and services (Hodgkinson and Sparrow 2002).

Hodgkinson and Sparrow's competent organization (see Figure 5.5) is based in part upon recognition of the limits of rationality and calls into question long-held assumptions that underpin much of managerial thought and action. For example, the axioms that strategic decision makers are inherently rational, that business environments are objective entities out there waiting to be discovered through rational analyses and that successful strategy is a result of deliberate planning are questioned (2002: 2). Instead, their arguments are rooted in a perspective founded upon precepts from managerial and organizational cognition which contend that:

1. Managers have limited information processing capacity, an issue compounded by the fact that the world is becoming more complex and data rich.
2. Managers employ various strategies to reduce the information processing load that is placed upon them.
3. Managers develop a simplified understanding of the world to guide their actions and this understanding is encapsulated in their individual schemas.

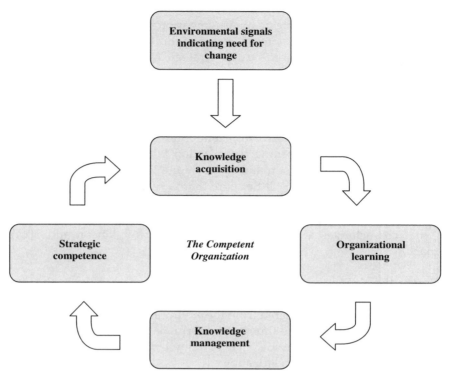

Figure 5.5 Relationship between strategic competence, information acquisition, organizational learning and knowledge management (after Hodgkinson and Sparrow 2002)

4. Individual schemas act as filters that can lead to errors and biases and inappropriate and ineffective decisions (Hodgkinson and Sparrow 2002).

From an L&D perspective one of the attractions of this viewpoint is that is raises much broader possibilities for managers to develop a personal understanding of their own learning processes and those of their organizations. Hence, through the application of the body of theory that underpins Hodgkinson and Sparrow's work and its translation into actionable knowledge, L&D in general and management development in particular is presented with a very powerful set of scientifically rigorous tools for the development of individual and organizational meta-cognition (i.e. the capacity to think-about-thinking at the organizational and individual levels). This follows in the long tradition of cognitive research that has attempted to understand learning-how-to-learn, but takes a much broader multi-level approach in that it goes beyond the confines of individual cognition and into the realm of collective cognition.

Concept Checklist

Can you now define each of the Key Concepts listed below, and are you now able to achieve the other Knowledge Outcomes specified at the beginning of the chapter?

- Collective learning
- Knowledge creation
- Action and reflection
- Action science
- Action learning
- Espoused theories
- Theories-in-use
- Model I behaviour
- Model II behaviour
- Ladder of inference
- Team learning
- Communities of practice (CoP)
- Legitimate peripheral participation
- Activity system
- Organizational learning
- Single-loop learning and adaptive learning
- Double-loop learning and generative learning
- Shared mental models
- Incomplete learning
- Learning organization
- The Competent Organization

CHAPTER 6
Planning Learning and Development

Key Concepts

Needs assessment; needs identification; sources of performance problems; analysis of L&D needs; individual, job and organizational analyses; performance appraisal; 360° feedback; personal development plans; hierarchical task analysis; cognitive task analysis; critical incident technique; concept analysis; functional analysis; competence; occupational standards; NVQs; needs prioritization; organizational-level analysis; SWOT analysis; PESTLE analysis; integration and alignment

---

Knowledge Outcomes

After studying this chapter you should be able to:
- define each of the key concepts listed above;
- distinguish between needs identification and needs analysis;
- describe how a needs assessment may be carried out at the individual, job or organizational levels;
- compare, contrast and critically evaluate the various methods that are available for the assessment of L&D needs;
- explain the significance of integration and alignment in the L&D planning process.

Introduction

If you're not sure where you're going, you're liable to end up some place else.
Robert F. Mager, *Preparing Instructional Objectives*, **p. v**

The L&D function in exists in organizations to support and enable learning. One of its roles is to serve as a business tool whose purpose is to enhance individual and organizational performance and thus contribute to the achievement of strategic goals. From this strategic business perspective L&D practitioners may be seen as being business partners with managers with a shared responsibility for maximizing the impact of L&D. Against this rational backcloth the planning and the practice of L&D is an integrated systematic process (for example, based upon the identification and analysis of needed performance and any associated knowledge and skill requirements), which, through alignment, may help to ensure that the impact of L&D reaches beyond the scope of the individual employee to the collective levels (i.e. the team, department and organization). The foundation of L&D planning is the accurate assessment of learning needs and the integration of the needs of the employee with those of the team, department and organization of which he or she is a member. If organizations undertake L&D without first conducting an accurate needs assessment they run the risk of over-doing L&D, doing too little L&D or 'missing the point completely' (Brown 2002: 596). Furthermore, if L&D practitioners fail to integrate the various stages of the planning process or align their L&D efforts between the individual and collective levels, they run the risk of duplication, wasting resources and missing out on valuable opportunities for synergies to be created within and across levels.

The 'assessment of learning need' refers to two related and sequential activities: firstly, the identification of the learning need (i.e. whether a need actually exists or not) and, secondly, the analysis of the learning need (i.e. what the precise nature of the identified need is). The needs assessment phase of an L&D project serves a diagnostic purpose and Boydell and Leary (1996) argued that the needs assessment phase must be done properly as it is the basis for many subsequent L&D activities – otherwise L&D may end up being ill-directed and inadequately focused. At the individual level an L&D need is defined as the gap between the level of performance that is desired or required of the employee and the employee's actual level of performance:

L&D need = (Desired or required level of performance) minus
(Actual level of performance)

The performance requirements should have links to critical success factors (these may be in specific areas, as in the balanced scorecard approach, or not confined to particular categories). The performance requirements and critical success factors may then be used as indicators of the employee's or organization's developmental trajectory (which may range from minimal developmental activity with a focus on maintaining specific skill levels to more ambitious performance and career development targets). The developmental trajectory itself should be translatable into specific L&D needs that have to be met. The articulation of needs is not enough, however, and there must be a viable action plan that indicates the targets, the means by which they will be met, what the time-line is and how the evaluation of the outcomes will be conducted.

PERSPECTIVE FROM PRACTICE: COMMITMENT SETTING AT MICROSOFT

Based on the following source: K. N. Shaw, 2004. Changes to the goal-setting process at Microsoft, *Academy of Management Executive*, 18(4): 139–42.

Microsoft has a performance-based culture and central to this is the setting of individual goals as part of a performance management system. The practice is built upon goal-setting theory, which amongst other things asserts that:

1. People who have specific hard goals ('stretch goals') perform better than those with easy, vague or 'do your best' goals.
2. The more goal successes a person has, the higher their levels of satisfaction (Latham 2004: 126).

Latham argued that the reasons that goal setting is successful in enhancing performance are fourfold: firstly, commitment to a goal entails diversion of attention and resources away from goal-irrelevant activities; secondly, challenging goals energize people; thirdly, goals affect persistence, for example in terms of effort and efficiency; and finally, goals motivate people either to use the knowledge they have or to get the knowledge that is needed to solve the goal.

According to Shaw, past experiences at Microsoft suggested that goals tended to be 'aspirations and hopes' rather than genuine commitments. Therefore it was decided to change the language (but not the underlying principles) and the emphasis in the performance management system from 'goals' to 'commitments'. At the apex of a pyramid of commitments were the Microsoft Commitments themselves, i.e. 'driving shareholder value through innovation, customer responsiveness, and the development of talent' (2004: 141). Running as a thread through the various levels of commitment was the aspiration to get alignment between individual, team and organizational commitments. In practice this translated into an annual performance review, which covered three issues:

1. Commitments: identifying between five and seven high-level commitments for individual employees and ensuring they are aligned with the business commitments.
2. Execution Plan: identifying how the employee will deliver on their commitments and including significant milestones. The Execution Plan may also be used as a coaching tool for managers to use with employees in order to monitor progress and give feedback.
3. Accountabilities: identifying success measures and metrics that can be used to evaluate the extent to which the commitments have been realized.

The key features of the commitments as specified on the Microsoft Review Form are that they should be: specific, measurable, achievable, results-based and time specific; aligned with the other commitments of the employee's manager, the organization and Microsoft Commitments (see above); supported with customer-centric actions and aligned with divisional business plans (Shaw 2004: 142).

If, in a performance-based culture, a performance requirement or learning need is incorrectly identified (for example, a performance deficit is attributed to an employee's lack of skill whereas the actual problem lies in the design of the job) or poorly analysed (for example, the wrong content is specified for a training programme), a number of consequences may follow:

• learners may not acquire the appropriate knowledge or skill;
• performance may not be enhanced;
• scarce and valuable resources may be wasted;
• the image and credibility of the L&D function may suffer;
• L&D will not contribute to meeting the organization's strategic objectives.

Similar problems may also be encountered if generic (i.e. not specific or special) L&D is offered that is not based upon anything other than a cursory check of its relevance to individual, job or organizational requirements. If the identification and analysis of L&D needs is of prime importance in the management of performance, from a practical point of view it begs the question of 'How might L&D needs be identified and analysed?' The main purpose of this chapter will be to explore a framework for such analyses and examine the various tools and techniques that are available to the L&D practitioner in the assessment of learning needs (see Figure 6.1).

Levels of Needs Assessment

A useful way of approaching the issue of needs identification and analysis is by examining learning needs at a variety of different levels. The needs analysis model

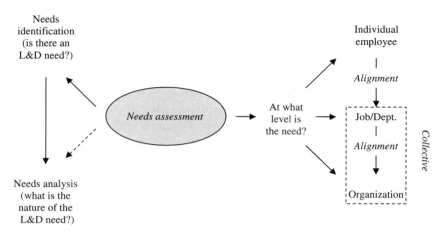

Figure 6.1 Conceptual framework for needs assessment

of McGehee and Thayer (1961) suggests that researching L&D needs can be conducted at three successive levels that are themselves not mutually exclusive:

Individual level: for example, by asking the question, 'What are the learning needs of each individual employee?'
Job level: for example, 'What are the learning needs of a specific job or the tasks that go to make up a job?'
Organizational level: for example, 'What are the learning needs for an organization at a particular time and under particular sets of circumstances?'

The second and third of these levels may be considered as a collective level of analysis since they do not focus on the individual per se; their concerns are the requirements of the job (irrespective of the individual) and the collection of individuals who make up the organization (and therefore may include the team and the department levels) – see Figure 6.1.

L&D FACTS AND FIGURES

The concept of identifying and analysing training needs at multiple levels was first explicitly advocated by McGehee and Thayer in 1961 in their book *Training in Business and Industry*. Since then the idea has appeared in many different guises and, like many of the taxonomic approaches to L&D, still provides a useful framework for analysis to this day. Their three levels were: organization analysis: identifying where training can and should be used in the organization; operations analysis: the collection of data about a specific job in order to identify the knowledge and skill required to carry out the job satisfactorily; person analysis: identifying how well each employee is performing.

As well as being concerned with conceptual issues, our discussion will also focus on practical issues since it is the assessment of needs using valid and reliable tools which is of direct concern to the L&D practitioner on a day-to-day basis. How and where the emphasis is placed within needs assessment may vary according to the role that is being assumed by the L&D practitioner. For example, from a 'provider' role perspective L&D is more likely to be concerned with analysing the gaps in performance between current and desired results and, once they have been identified, placing the needs in some form of priority order. From a 'change agent' role perspective L&D may be more concerned with systemic issues that may translate into broader problems relating to organizational development as well as L&D per se. The latter is more likely to emphasize organizational learning and the management of knowledge as opposed to an emphasis upon individual learning and training. The overarching purposes of needs assessment and L&D planning are to ensure that L&D interventions:

- address priority learning needs that can enable individuals, departments or organizations to meet their goals and commitments;
- are aligned between the individual's goals and commitments and the collective (i.e. team or department and the organization) goals and commitments (this issue of alignment will be returned to at the end of the chapter).

PERSPECTIVE FROM PRACTICE: 'ONE SIZE DOES NOT FIT ALL' – LEARNING NEEDS ASSESSMENT AT TRANSPORT FOR LONDON

Based on the following source: T. Harlow and A. Smith, 2003. Necessary measures, *People Management*, November: 48.

One of the assumptions of providing generic L&D programmes is that they will meet individual learners' requirements; this is a somewhat 'broad brush' approach. Giving all learners the same L&D content via the same method runs a risk of providing learning that may be largely irrelevant to their individual job or personal development needs and that may be incongruent with their learning preferences or learning styles. Such an approach is likely to be a hit-and-miss affair in all but those few cases where all learners need exactly the same content and method (as may be the case with an organization-wide performance problem, but even then different methods might be required for different learners). These were problems that Transport for London anticipated when it introduced a new IT database package for over 1,000 of its employees. Rather than provide the same generic training approach for all 1,000 learners, the company decided to carry out a *learning needs analysis*, by means of an e-questionnaire, to identify each individual employee's personal needs. Once the needs had been identified (and they varied in terms of the

Continued

content and depth of learning required as well as the preferred learning methods), they were met using the most appropriate means for the individual (for example, workshops, 'email tips', coaching and so forth). The analytical technique used was deemed successful enough to be rolled out to other IT L&D projects. Amongst the reported benefits were:

1. Individual employees learned only person-relevant or job-relevant information.
2. L&D was more efficient; for example, employees spent less time out of the office (time to competence was shorter).
3. L&D was more effective; for example, employees acquired knowledge and skills that were directly linked to business and job needs.
4. Employees who needed to attend formal group-based training courses each all had similar needs. It should be noted that often a source of frustration for participants and course leaders is that the individuals within a group have different needs and expectations – this potential problem appears to have been ameliorated in this case.

The assessment of learning needs is based upon a number of assumptions, including:

- planned L&D is not a panacea for all organizational ills;
- there are many problems within organizations that are not solvable by L&D alone;
- it is the responsibility of the L&D practitioner to try to distinguish between performance problems over which L&D can have leverage and those problems where L&D can have little or no influence or power.

If poor individual, job or organizational performance is evident and the symptoms have been clearly identified, the next step is to track down the cause of the problem (Herbert and Doverspike 1990). Poor performance may be the result of a number of factors including:

1. Lack in the work environment, for example because employees may not have the right tools and equipment to do the job to the required standard.
2. Lack of motivation and incentives, for example because payment systems and jobs may be poorly designed or badly implemented.
3. Lack of knowledge and skills, for example, because no training has been provided, training is substandard, employees' skills are becoming outdated (skill obsolescence) and so forth (Roscoe 1995).

Roscoe (1995: 61–2) presented a checklist of questions that the L&D practitioner may ask at this stage of the planning process as one means of identifying the source of the problem at hand; these are summarized in Table 6.1.

Table 6.1 Checklist of sources of ineffective performance (from Roscoe 1995: 61–2; Boxall and Purcell 2003: 137–8)

Lack in organizational environment (Does the organization make it possible to perform?)	Yes	No
1. Are job holders' roles clear?		
2. Is there role conflict?		
3. Is there role ambiguity?		
4. Are lines of reporting clear?		
5. Are systems and procedures clear?		
6. Are adequate resources available?		
7. Is equipment suitable for the job?		
8. Are performance targets clearly articulated?		
9. Is there integration between L&D activities and HR activities?		
10. Is there alignment between individual responsibilities, job roles, departmental performance and organizational goals?		

Lack of motivation and reward (Do employees have the will to perform?)	Yes	No
1. Are learners choosing to perform well or badly?		
2. Are efforts exercised consistently and at an appropriate level?		
3. Is the effort required greater than the reward?		
4. Are there positive consequences for performing well and/or negative consequences of not performing?		
5. Are there rewards for non-performance?		
6. Is the task distasteful or unpleasant?		
7. Does the culture of the organization support performance and commitment?		
8. Does the individual employee have the incentive to contribute to the team, department or organization's performance?		

Lack of knowledge and skills (Do the employees have the 'can do?' to perform?)	Yes	No
1. Are learners new to the organization or the task?		
2. Do learners know how to perform a particular task (do they have the procedural knowledge)?		
3. Do the learners know why they perform a particular task (do they have the declarative knowledge)?		
4. Do learners know the standard to which they are expected to perform?		
5. Do learners and managers agree on the level of performance required?		
6. Do learners get feedback on performance?		
7. Has there been opportunity to practise newly acquired skills in the workplace?		

Cause and effect in L&D may not always be linked in a simple linear fashion and what may appear to be a problem deriving from one source may in fact be linked to another one (Senge 1990: 70). Figure 6.2 illustrates two causal chains that can in fact be amalgamated and thereby reinforce each other through feedback to exacerbate an unsatisfactory situation.

This discussion illustrates two important points:

1. Firstly, a system perspective can bring insights by facilitating an overall view in which sets of cause-and-effect relationships may be identified. It enables interrelationships and changing patterns to be seen rather than 'things' and 'snapshots' (Senge 1990: 68).
2. Secondly, it raises issues about the role of the L&D practitioner and how she or he is designated with the organization, or indeed how they see themselves. For example, do they consider themselves to be passive providers of L&D

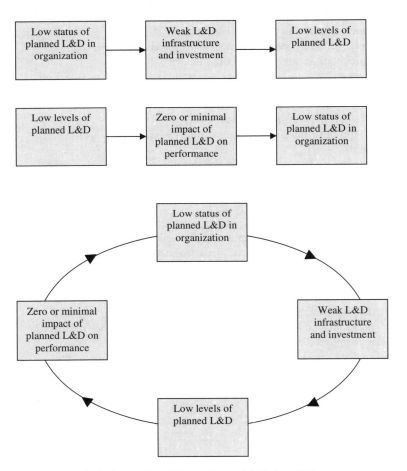

Figure 6.2 Two causal chains and a vicious circle of L&D inactivity

solutions (such as training courses) or proactive seekers of organizational problems and facilitators of change who are prepared to break into cycles and disrupt any negative feedback loops that may be precluding L&D having an impact?

PERSPECTIVE FROM PRACTICE: 'NO-NONSENSE' NEEDS ANALYSIS FOR PERFORMANCE PROBLEMS AT GENERAL MOTORS, USA

Based on the following source: K. Finson and F. Szedlak, 1997. General Motors does a needs analysis, *Training & Development*, May: 103–4.

The General Motors (GM) metal fabrication plant uses what Finson and Szedlak termed a 'giant cookie cutter' that presses the shape of a part (a blank) out of a coil of sheet metal. The performance problem was that the blanker department was not achieving the desired levels for its production schedules, efficiency or cost competitiveness. The analysts went in with an open mind and not with a view to analysing any potential L&D need; rather their aim was to identify the symptoms and causes of the perceived problem:

1. The symptoms were decreased efficiency, increased transition times to change cutting tools (dies) and increased downtime (due to lack of steel and the need to repair cutting dies).
2. The causes were identified as frequent changes to schedules, poor communication between departments, inventory errors as a result of inefficient storage methods and poor scheduling of maintenance and production.

Once the problems had been identified the team used a variety of data collection methods for the analysis phase (including interviewing a wide range of employees and administering a questionnaire survey). Their analysis and interpretation of the data revealed L&D and non-L&D solutions to the identified performance problems:

Non-L&D solutions: Have an organized floor plan for the storage room, colour code the dies and have service departments give higher priority to the blanker area.

L&D solutions: Use a computer program for scheduling and provide training in the use of computer programs for inventory control and statistical process control (SPC).

The intervention that had greatest impact was the last one, and SPC was taught by in-house instructors (thus reducing the cost of training and having the added benefit of a company-specific input). This resulted in a 30 per cent

Continued

reduction in scrap rate and gave over half a million US dollars' saving in year one alone. The example illustrates a number of important points: firstly, L&D analysts should approach problems in an open-minded way without any preconceived ideas; and secondly, L&D analysts should be prepared for the need to recommend a mix of L&D and non-L&D solutions if a comprehensive answer to a complex problem is to be found.

L&D FACTS AND FIGURES

The Investors in People (IIP) is a government-sanctioned national standard in the UK awarded to companies who can demonstrate that amongst other things: (a) they have a strategy for improving performance through planned L&D; (b) managers' capabilities to lead, manage and develop employees are clearly defined and that they are effective in this; (c) employees' contribution to the organization is recognized and valued and that employees take ownership of the L&D process; (d) L&D is effective and promotes improved performance; (e) L&D is continuously improved. According to Investors in People, over 37,000 organizations in the UK have IIP recognition. (*Source*: http://www.investorsinpeople.co.uk)

Needs Assessment at the Individual Level

It is at the individual level of analysis where we often see the strongest degree of horizontal integration between general HR processes and L&D activities. Two methods of analysis at the individual level will be considered: traditional performance appraisal and 360 degree feedback.

Performance Appraisal

Appraisal (and the associated personal development planning needed to achieve set targets and to improve competencies) is at the heart of an integrated approach to HR management and is crucial for L&D at the operational level (Harrison 2002). Performance appraisal is defined as a system of formal methods for planning and evaluating individual performance. It usually involves employee interviewing (typically on an annual basis) and commonly includes some element of development needs analysis (Boxall and Purcell 2003: 144). Woodall and Winstanley (1998: 112) described the appraisal interview as being for many organizations the 'mainstay of their approach to identifying individual development needs'. Guidelines for 'best practice' in performance appraisal are to be found in many HR student texts and in the professional HR arena (for example: http://www.cipd.co.uk). Assessment criteria for appraisal may include inputs and outputs:

Inputs or behaviours might include, for example in a salesperson's appraisal, product knowledge, initiative, communication skills and appearance.

Outputs or performance might include, in a salesperson's appraisal, volume of sales, attitude and selling skills (Pettijohn et al. 2001: 139).

In spite of attempts to objectify appraisal it is nonetheless a contentious area, not least because many of the difficulties associated with appraisal stem from the:

- level of skill required to carry out the process effectively;
- commitment to the process of the appraiser (who is usually the line manager);
- appraisee's own commitment to the process.

The difficulties might manifest themselves as line managers carrying out the process who are themselves not well informed about how to do it and who also may lack a personal belief in and commitment to the process. This might be especially true in turbulent times; for example, if there is organizational restructuring that paradoxically may involve cutbacks at middle management levels, which may in turn increase the pressure on managers to the extent that they may not be able to find the time and the motivation to carry out appraisal (Woodall and Winstanley 1998). In terms of the role of performance appraisal in identifying and analysing L&D needs, some of its main potential drawbacks are bias, error and subjectivity in appraisals. Again, these issues may be linked to a lack of necessary knowledge and skills, but also perhaps to more deeply entrenched issues of bias and prejudice.

In addition to methodological issues Harrison (2002: 260–1) identified the organizational context and its receptivity to appraising employee performance, broader issues of organizational culture and values as well as power and politics as presenting further practical problems. Newton and Findlay (1998) argued that the assumption that an organization's members have shared interests, perceptions and expectations (i.e. that the organizational system is a unitary one in this regard) is problematical because in any organization there will be a multiplicity of interests and power groups each with their own agendas. The integrity of performance appraisal is vulnerable in this respect since it forms a high-profile platform for the acting out of any possible divisions and agendas.

Based upon her own experience with managers, Harrison argued that the appraisal process cannot resolve deep-rooted problems related to an organization's culture, strategy, effectiveness and HRM policy: 'at best it can expose them, at worst it will be destroyed by them' (2002: 264). This is further illustration that it is the interaction between HR, L&D and the context that is likely to exert the strongest effect upon the efficacy of planned L&D activities (including the assessment of learning needs). Appraisal systems that are used for salary administration purposes may not be appropriate for developmental purposes since the appraiser's reward and development roles may come into conflict. Hence there may be good reasons for separating them out them out in time or having different individuals take on the respective roles. Similarly, Woodruffe (1993) argued that rather than treating them as unified outcomes of the appraisal process there should be a clear separation between:

- determination of reward (in which the appraiser is required to act as judge);
- identification of L&D needs (in which the appraiser is required to act as coach and mentor).

Over and above issues relating to lack of knowledge and skills and the potential conflict of appraiser roles, a number of writers also allude to the possibility of dysfunctional, biased and even prejudicial behaviours on the part of some managers. This may involve the conscious act of not giving accurate appraisals, or conscious or unconscious acts of error and bias through being perversely motivated, 'powerholic' and 'workaholic' tendencies or even simple 'infantile jealousies' (Boxall and Purcell 2003: 145). In addition to these individual and contextual issues Harrison also identified some additional practical difficulties such as:

1. Appraisees not admitting to and concealing failings (an instance of training needs analysis not leading to learning, see Antonacopoulou 2001).
2. Hostility; over-rating or under-rating of performance on the basis of the appraisee's level of self-esteem and self-confidence.
3. Appraisers' lack of interpersonal skills or understanding of the appraisee's job role.

Herbert and Doverspike (1990) suggested that organizations considering using performance appraisal as a means to identify needs should be cautious for a number of reasons. For instance, it is likely to be costly and complex at an organization-wide level; the ability of managers to make accurate judgements is questionable due to errors and biases; the intention to use the system for appraisal should be specified before the system is designed; managers must be motivated to make accurate ratings; and a developmental solution should be available for an identified need (1990: 265). Harrison (2002: 261–2) suggested that some of the problems can be overcome by:

1. A 'genuinely collaborative approach to the setting of individuals' targets' in order to exploit mutuality of interests.
2. The use of competencies as a framework for appraisal and discussion; avoiding rating systems in appraisal that has an L&D focus.
3. Appraiser training (for example in assessment methods, avoidance of bias and discrimination).

One might add to this list: the need to have clear performance criteria; using valid and reliable instruments for the assessment and recording of the process and the outcomes; and finally, the appraiser having accurate and comprehensive information on the appraisee's job role and their levels of performance. Efforts to overcome the difficulties may be worthwhile since the effects of a well-designed appraisal system can be far-reaching and go beyond its L&D purpose. For example, there is a positive relationship with job satisfaction when appraisals do provide clear criteria, the criteria meet with the appraisee's approval, are perceived as fair and are used in determining rewards (Pettijohn et al. 2001: 127).

PERSPECTIVE FROM RESEARCH: GUIDELINES FOR BEST PRACTICE IN PERFORMANCE APPRAISAL

Theorizing, research and practice suggest that performance appraisal systems can play a valuable part in the way individual performance is managed if 'they [the systems] are managed astutely' (Boxall and Purcell 2003: 144). Theories of goal setting and its underpinning empirical base also provide a useful source of practical guidance for the L&D practitioner. If we acknowledge the potential problematic issues (such as bias, error, levels of commitment and so forth) it is still possible to distil some pointers for the L&D practitioner who may wish to employ this potentially powerful technique in needs assessment:

1. Determination of reward and remuneration through appraisal should be treated separately from the identification of learning needs (Woodruffe 1993).
2. False or unrealistic expectations should not be raised with respect to training provision and developmental opportunities within the organization (Boxall and Purcell 2003).
3. Appraisers should not assume that employees and employers have shared interests (Newton and Findlay 1998).
4. Appraisers should be well briefed and understand the appraisee's job role (Mabey and Salaman 1995: 160).
5. Appraisers should have some knowledge of the concept of L&D needs and their identification.
6. Line managers need to be committed to the notion of appraisal generally and for L&D purposes in particular.
7. Latham (2004: 127) summarized the conditions for effectiveness in goal setting: the employee must have the knowledge and skills to attain the set goal; the employee must be committed to the goal especially if it is difficult; employees need feedback on their progress towards the goal; complex tasks should be broken down into sub-goals; any situational constraints to achieving the goal should be ameliorated by managers.
8. Line managers should be willing to engage in the facilitation and support of the implementation of L&D plans that flow from appraisals (Woodall and Winstanley 1998).

360° Feedback

This method of analysis involves obtaining feedback on an employee's performance from multiple sources: for example, from their line manager, peers, subordinates, internal customers and sometimes external customers as well. The process
tends to be a structured one with feedback sought in the form of ratings across a
range of competencies, often through the use of formal instruments to ensure a
consistency of approach. The administration, analysis and interpretation of the
instruments used is a specialized task for which sophisticated software packages
are available. Giving feedback is best achieved by using a skilled facilitator or
coach. Cook and Macauley (cited in Torrington et al. 2002) suggested that the
benefits of the 360 degree approach, if implemented effectively, are likely to
include:

- improved communications and continuous feedback;
- contribution to a climate of constructive criticism and debate;
- a stronger ownership of performance and development goals.

Attention to detail in the design and the implementation of 360 degree systems
is important and steps have to be taken to ensure clarity of purpose, confidentiality of raters and the avoidance of collusion between the parties (Torrington et
al. 2002: 309). The process may also be the subject of some of the problems identified in relation to performance appraisal. 360 degree assessments are used in particular for the identification and analysis of L&D needs for manager and leader
development purposes and will be discussed further in Chapter 7.

The purpose of learning needs assessment at any level is in order that some
statement of needs, based upon the collection and analyses of data, may be formulated. This forms an input into the next stage of the L&D process (the setting
of learning goals – or objectives – and the designing and planning of L&D). One
outcome of the individual-level needs assessment may be a Personal Development Plan (PDP). A PDP might, for example, consist of a specification of:

1. An individual's development objectives, their links to the business plan, the
   HR plan and their personal development need.
2. The proposed developmental actions with specified time-scales and a recording and monitoring of L&D activities (both formal and informal) engaged in
   to support the plan (see Woodall and Winstanley 1998: 147–8).

Harrison (2002: 262–3) suggested that to be effective a PDP should also draw a
clear distinction between job-related L&D and longer-term career or personal
development related L&D activities. One precept that underpins PDPs is that of
self-development. It may be recalled that one of the assumptions of Knowles's
andragogical learning model is that adults have a need for and the ability to be
self-directing. One implication of this is that part of the manager's and the L&D
practitioner's role is to facilitate learning though a process of self-directed inquiry
rather than via a pedagogically driven, didactic approach. In linking these notions

of personal responsibility, planning and performance, PDPs have been described by Floodgate and Nixon as a 'critical document' in L&D because they provide a means of:

1. Encouraging individual responsibility for learning.
2. Supporting workplace-based learning more explicitly and overtly.
3. Highlighting the role and opportunities for managers to be involved in L&D through needs assessment, coaching and so forth.
4. Emphasizing the link between personal L&D and performance and also the management of performance.
5. Reinforcing continuous improvement principles in relation to L&D.
6. Translating learning needs into meaningful and measurable action plans (Floodgate and Nixon 1994: 43).

It is atypical for PDPs to be compulsory (although they may in reality be so when integrated into a mandatory appraisal process). In a study of the mandatory implementation of PDPs amongst teachers in Alberta, where PDPs became compulsory in 1998, Fenwick (2003) identified some reported benefits in the areas of greater employee commitment to learning, increased focus on purposes of development, increased collegiality and learners' sense of self-affirmation. The main problem appeared to be the tension between the need to control the mandatory system and professionals' need to exercise autonomy. Fenwick's conclusion was that with sufficient employee–supervisor trust, dialogue, flexibility and patience, PDPs can enhance a process of dialogue and questioning that not only promotes professional practice but can also 'energise collective learning' (2003: 59). There is no 'one best way' for PDPs to be designed or implemented; furthermore, a personal development plan is but one tool (alongside, for example, action plans, learning logs and learning contracts) for the management of the individual L&D process.

PERSPECTIVE FROM PRACTICE: PDPS IN A RETAIL BANK IN THE UK

Based on the following sources: J. F. Floodgate and A. E. Nixon, 1994. Personal development plans: the challenge of implementation – a case study, *Journal of European Industrial Training*, 18(11): 43–7; M. Higson and J. P. Wilson, 1995. Implementing personal development plans: a model for trainers, managers and supervisors, *Industrial and Commercial Training*, 27(6): 25–9.

Floodgate and Nixon presented a case study of the ways in which PDPs were implemented in a retail bank in the UK against the background of a traditional 'training' culture. Performance management processes in the organization encouraged personal development; however, the uptake of learning

Continued

and development opportunities was variable and 'passively compliant' rather than self-initiated because of a lack of perceived intrinsic benefit of L&D to the individual (1994: 43). The culture in the bank up to this point was one in which employees were reactive rather than proactive, and the concept of training was embedded in a procedurally based training course delivery model. The model that the organization wanted to move towards was one in which individuals took responsibility for learning through self-management of the process. This was seen as being more congruent with the way in which the organization was developing, from being sales-focused and bureaucratically controlled towards being customer-focused and cross-functional. The PDP model was used to enable individuals to:

- analyse their strengths and L&D needs in structured ways;
- articulate their L&D needs to managers in order that their needs be met;
- record L&D achievements against learning targets (a critical success factor in the performance review process);
- express themselves in terms of the knowledge, skills and abilities they had (and not be seen simply as a person with a job title and grade).

The bank provided written guidance on how to produce a PDP and also face-to-face sessions so that employees could explore the concept in greater depth and so that managers could answer questions and provide reassurance. The PDP itself covered:

1. Job requirements: current strengths that needed to be maintained, weaker areas of performance that needed improvement and new areas of performance that had to be learned from scratch.
2. Personal development: transferable skills that would enhance current performance and improve internal marketability.
3. Career development: preparing for different, bigger and broader roles (Floodgate and Nixon 1994).

The plans themselves varied between individuals, with some identifying 'small scale', quite specific L&D needs (for example, training in a particular skill) whilst others charted out three-year career paths. Buy-in by the various stakeholders was crucial to success: 'it is pointless trying to implement PDPs by mandate and even more pointless when local personnel and training staff are not sold on their use' (1994: 46). Furthermore, managers' performance in this regard was judged on how well they helped the individual to take responsibility in the process (Floodgate and Nixon 1994).

A study of a similar issue by Higson and Wilson examined the introduction of PDPs in a retail financial organization (a building society). Their starting point was a number of perceived difficulties with on-the-job L&D; for example, many people simply did not know how to learn, they lacked confidence and had low self-esteem (self-efficacy) in this area. These issues can be further compounded if organizations provide unstructured and hap-hazard 'training', do not have a structured career planning process, over-rely on generic qualifications (such as NVQs) and utilize training courses as the main form of L&D (for example, by drawing upon 'menus' of training courses from providers' catalogues). In the organization studied by Higson and Wilson the aim was to keep the PDPs as simple as possible. They con-sisted of:

1. Statement of job: definition of role and constituent tasks with assessment of performance (by learner and manager) in order to identify perform-ance gaps (and hence learning needs).
2. Learning plan: to avoid overload three high-priority learning needs from the preceding stage were transferred to the learning plan, which also stated how the needs would be met (for example, through coaching, job rotation, training courses or distance learning packages).
3. Learning log: this was a simple document that was completed each week to demonstrate what had been learned and was monitored by the line manager.

As far as implementation was concerned, employees were allowed one hour per week protected time for learning. PDPs were part of the performance appraisal process and the aim was for managers' appraisal to cover how well they managed the PDP process for learners.

Needs Assessment at the Collective Level: the Job

One purpose of needs assessment at the job level is to identify the knowledge, skills and attitudes that are likely to be required by a job holder in general (as opposed to a specific individual) to perform effectively. A job may, for the pur-poses of some of the analytical techniques outlined here, be considered to com-prise a set of tasks. A task in this context may be behavioural (that is, based on observable actions) or cognitive (based on thinking operations). It should be borne in mind, however, that this simple categorization is something of a simplification. We will consider one behavioural method of analysis (hierarchical task analysis, HTA) and one cognitive method of analysis (cognitive task analysis, CTA). As we shall see, the two approaches are complementary to the extent that CTA builds upon some of the perceived limitations of HTA. Hierarchical task analysis and cognitive task analysis are often based upon the identification of how an expert performer might complete the task. They involve the elicitation of how an expert might behave (their exemplary performance) or think (their cognitive processes) respectively. The other methods that are discussed subsequently are broader in that they relate to the analysis of a specific job (as a collection of tasks).

Hierarchical Task Analysis (HTA)

Hierarchical task analysis is a method by which a task can be broken down into the various operations and sub-operations of which it is composed. The analysis may be represented in a format that resembles a tree diagram or dendrogram (Buckley and Caple 1992: 82). Tasks are expressed as:

Goals, which are comprised of a hierarchy of operations indicating what a person should be expected to do in carrying out their role.
Plans indicating when subordinate tasks should be carried out (Shepherd 1998).

HTA was an approach that was developed in the 1950s, 1960s and 1970s in the UK by Annett et al. (1971) and further developed by Shepherd (1976). It draws upon *logical* rather than psychological principles for the identification and analysis of L&D needs, specifying learning objectives and defining the content of a learning programme (Patrick 1992: 169). One of the central issues with this approach is how the term 'task' is defined. Shepherd defined a task as 'a problem facing an operator' (the person responsible for carrying out the task of interest is called the operator). Task analysis is one way of identifying strategies for solving the problem; moreover, Shepherd argued that the approach is relevant to the analysis of cognitive as well as behavioural tasks (1998: 1538).

The process of HTA begins with the analyst stating the overall goal which is then *redescribed* (broken down) into a set of *subordinate* operations and their *plan* (essentially the order of the tasks). Plans represent the sequence and conditions under which operations are carried out satisfactorily and are a useful analytical tool when describing complex tasks. The outcome of the analysis is a comprehensive statement of what an operator should be seeking to achieve. The results of the HTA can be used to draw up a specification of the objectives, content or assessment for a training programme. It is a way for L&D practitioners and sponsors of planned L&D to specify with precision what is required in the job and what will be achieved through the planned training.

In the trivial example shown in Figure 6.3 the task is broken down into its various operations (only one of which is shown here: 'boil kettle') and the associated plans (1, 2, 3, etc.). Operations that are <u>underlined</u> are not redescribed (this is the technical term in HTA for not being broken down any further) and there are further guidelines that can be applied in HTA for stopping rules (knowing when the redescription, or breaking down, has gone far enough). Readers are referred to the work of Annett, Duncan, Shepherd and others for a more detailed consideration of this and other technical matters. The outcome of the analysis specifies precisely what a competent performer should do ('add water to kettle', 'apply heat to kettle' and so forth). It is statements such as these that could form a set of learning objectives (in this case for a not-much-needed course on making tea) that indicate what the learner should be able to do once they have been trained ('By the end of the training the learner will be able to heat water in a kettle to a temperature suitable for the making of tea'). The statements also provide a basis for

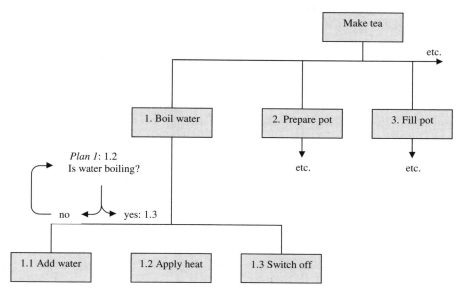

Figure 6.3 Part of a simplified HTA for making a cup of tea

assessment. HTA is often perceived as being most applicable to behavioural tasks. However, it is a complex technique and its proponents have argued a strong case for its utility in cognitive tasks since all performance entails an interaction between cognition (thinking) and action (behaviour). For a detailed discussion of the case for HTA in the cognitive domain readers should consult Shepherd (1998). HTA is consistent with goal-setting theory (Latham 2004), and in particular the efficacy of identifying sub-goals as a means to facilitating the achievement of more complex higher-order goals.

Patrick (1992: 183–4) summarized the advantages and disadvantages of the approach thus:

Advantages: it is flexible and economic; it has general applicability to a wide range of tasks; the results are immediately translatable into learning needs and objectives; it is logically exhaustive; it provides a structure for the content of a learning programme.

Disadvantages: HTA can be a difficult and complex cognitive task for the analyst; it relies heavily on the skill and ingenuity of the analyst and different analysts may produce different results.

Cognitive Task Analysis (CTA)

Cognitive task analysis is a method for eliciting knowledge from subject experts. CTA aims to identify the requisite knowledge and skills needed to perform a task along with the cues and cognitions that enable an expert to perform these tasks effectively (Salas and Cannon-Bowers 2001). CTA outputs can include templates for complex decision skills and experts' mental models. These maps and protocols can then be used as frameworks for developing scenarios and simulations for use in planned L&D as well as to develop job aids to supplement L&D activities. As was noted in Chapter 3, expert performance can include cognitions that are performed without much conscious awareness (when an expert is, so to speak, on 'auto-pilot'). This level of performance may distinguish the expert from the non-expert and novice. Experts' knowledge (which is often held tacitly) is developed as a result of continued practice and experience, and its automatic or semi-automatic execution frees up much-needed cognitive resources for other aspects of thinking and doing (Salas and Cannon-Bowers 2001). As well as being a means of defining expert performance CTA can also be used to diagnose individual performance deficiencies (hence CTA can work at both the job and the individual levels).

Unfortunately CTA does not have one single and well-accepted definition and, to complicate things further, the knowledge elicitation techniques used in CTA vary somewhat. The most frequently used of these include structured and semi-structured interviews, group interviews, verbal 'think aloud' protocols, retrospective verbal protocols, analysis of previous incidents and observation of task performance. From an L&D perspective one of the key concerns is that CTA methods are often seen as being difficult to use and time-consuming. Some of the limitations of conventional CTA prompted Klein and his colleagues to develop a more user-friendly approach, which they called 'applied cognitive task analysis' (ACTA). One of their aims was to make CTA more accessible to L&D practitioners and to instructional designers in particular and managers in general. Like CTA, the ACTA technique is intended to assist the identification of the key cognitive elements required to perform a task proficiently. The cognitive requirements that ACTA addresses are:

1. The task's difficult judgements and decisions.
2. The attentional demands placed upon the individual.
3. The identification of critical cues and patterns.
4. Experts' problem solving strategies.

ACTA includes knowledge elicitation and knowledge representation techniques. Knowledge elicitation techniques involve the use of interviews (and sometimes observation), whilst knowledge representation techniques are a means to depict cognitive information (for example, by cognitive mapping). Various ACTA methods were developed by Klein and his colleagues to complement each other, and are designed to tap into and represent different aspects of cognition. The ACTA process is a logical sequential one (see Figure 6.4):

1. The first step in the process is the production of the task diagram (usually by means of interview). This gives an overview of the task and highlights any

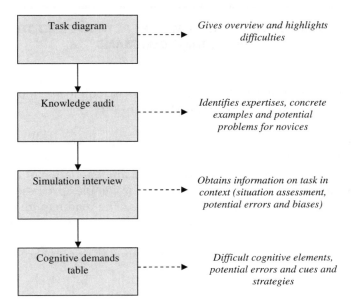

Figure 6.4 Klein's ACTA process

cognitive difficulties, which may be explored in greater detail later in the analytical process (Militello and Hutton 1998).

2. The second step, the knowledge audit, reviews the aspects of expertise required for the effective execution of a task. As the various aspects of expertise are elicited from the expert they are probed to elicit further details. Concrete examples associated with the task are identified and investigated. This technique also encourages the interviewee (usually a subject expert) to identify why elements of the task may present a problem to inexperienced individuals (Militello and Hutton 1998).

3. The third step, the simulation interview or scenario, obtains information on the task in context. It allows the interviewer to explore and probe issues such as situation assessment, potential errors and biases, and how a novice would be likely to respond to the same situation (Militello and Hutton 1998).

4. In the final step, the production of a cognitive demands table (CDT) is a means of merging and synthesizing data. The CDT is the 'deliverable' of the ACTA for the practitioner use in the design of training. It allows them to focus in on specific outcomes of the analysis that are pertinent to problem solving and decision making and hence is a potentially powerful means for aiding the design of L&D (Militello and Hutton 1998).

PERSPECTIVE FROM PRACTICE: ACTA APPLIED TO FIRE-GROUND COMMAND

Based on the following source: L. G. Militello and R. J. B. Hutton, 1998. Applied cognitive task analysis (ACTA): a practitioner's toolkit for understanding cognitive task demands, *Ergonomics*, 41(11): 1618–41.

Some of the applied research reported by Klein and his co-workers was conducted in the context of the emergency services, and fire-fighting in particular. This research helped in the development and validation of the method as well as providing a cognitive roadmap of the complex processes involved in dealing with specific emergency situations. The roadmap gives a broad overview of the task and also identifies the difficult cognitive elements. For fire-ground command Militello and Hutton first of all described a surface-level view of the cognitive elements involved and their sequence as follows:

1. Initial assessment of the situation.
2. Primary search and rescue.
3. Secondary search and rescue.
4. Critique and debrief on performance.

They noted that at this stage one of the skills of the analyst is to not be 'sucked into' a detailed assessment of the minutiae of every step and not be seduced by the mass of detail inside the subject-matter expert's head. They based the knowledge audit process upon those categories of knowledge that research and theory suggest are among the important characteristics of expertise. For example, expertise in general might include things like one's perceptual skills, and therefore in this case the analyst might ask the interviewee: 'Have you had experiences where part of a situation just popped out at you; where you noticed things going on that others didn't catch? What is an example?' (Militello and Hutton 1998: 1622). An example cited by Militello and Hutton is that of noticing sounds of a victim's breathing. In this situation a strategy used by an expert might include holding one's own breath. This task might be difficult for a novice because he or she may not know what kind of sounds to listen for, may not be able to distinguish them from breathing apparatus or fire noises and may not think to hold their own breath.

The technique as described by Militello and Hutton also involves presenting the subject-matter expert with a challenging scenario and asking him or her to identify events (for example, on-scene arrival), actions (such as accounting for people), assessment (sheltering people who have been evacuated), the critical cues in the situation (for example, type of building, temperature, weather and so forth) and the potential errors (such as searching for people who are not in the building). The outcome of the analysis is the cognitive demands table, which Militello and Hutton described as consisting of:

1. Difficult cognitive elements, for example finding victims in a burning building.
2. Reasons why these are difficult, for example, where there are lots of distracting noises.
3. Common errors, for example, novices sometimes do not recognize their own breathing sounds.
4. Cues and strategies used by experts, for example: 'stop, hold your breath and listen'.

Klein's research suggested that in actual fire-ground situations intuitive or expert decision making such as that executed by experienced fire-fighters occurred through a complex and integrative process of consciously imagining what would happen when a particular action was carried out (2003: 16). He called this 'mental simulation'. The visual picture gives a whole view of the situation and experts appear to observe this whole view. They then 'see' what happens (sometimes several times) and if they 'like what they see' they will respond; if they don't like it they will alter the action script or jettison it and look for another option.

Critical Incident Technique

This method was devised by Flanagan in the 1950s and aims to identify either outstandingly effective or outstandingly ineffective behaviour in pursuit of the general aim of an activity. By 'incident' Flanagan was referring to observable human activity that is 'sufficiently complete in itself to permit inference or prediction to be made about the person performing the act' (Easterby-Smith et al. 1991: 83). By 'critical' Flanagan was referring to incidents where the purpose, consequences and effects are likely to be clear to the observer. A famous example is the moment (critical incident) at which some US Army helicopter pilots appeared to lose control of their aircraft when landing in groups (Easterby-Smith et al. 1991). The approach enables the analyst to single out the important tasks or components of behaviour and also those that may be performed ineffectively and hence are likely to represent a high-priority learning need (Patrick 1992). In the helicopter example the critical incident was when the pilot viewed the ground through another helicopter's rotor blades (Easterby-Smith et al. 1991). The critical incident technique itself typically consists of a number of steps:

1. Determination of the general aims of the job or tasks to be investigated.
2. Preparing a method (i.e. plans and instructions) for data collection.

3. Collection of data pertaining to critical incidents from interviews and observations (for example, by asking a respondent a question of the form: 'Think of an occasion on which . . .').
4. Analysis and categorization of data.
5. Interpreting and reporting of results.

Patrick (1992) cited some examples from Kirchner and Dunnette's 1957 study in which 135 incidents were collected from 85 sales managers, and from Kay's 1959 study of 74 employees of a wire and cable company, which generated 691 incidents. In the sales manager study incidents of effective performance included environmental scanning, which resulted in the identification of new customers, whilst ineffective performance included failing to follow up customer complaints, which resulted in long-term customer dissatisfaction. The approach does have some drawbacks, for example incompleteness (since by definition the collection of critical incident data leaves additional data to be collected to give a complete picture of the job and its context), and the need for expert analysts to judge what constitutes effective or ineffective behaviour (Patrick 1992: 189).

PERSPECTIVE FROM PRACTICE: CRITICAL INCIDENTS AS A MEANS TO IDENTIFYING SERVICE PROBLEMS IN THE AUSTRALIAN RETAIL WINE INDUSTRY

Based on the following source: L. Lockshin and G. McDougal, 1998. Service problems and recovery strategies: an examination of the critical incident in a business-to-business market, *International Journal of Retail & Distribution Management*, 26(11): 429–38.

The aim of Lockshin and McDougal's project was to understand the types of service problems encountered between businesses involved in distributing wine to retail outlets, restaurants and hotels in Australia. Data were collected via telephone interviews using a pre-tested structured questionnaire. The questionnaire aimed to allow participants to describe a specific incident where they had a critical problem with a wine supplier and to explain what happened as a result of that incident. Following the description of an incident, other more specific questions (rated on a scale of one to 10) were asked by Lockshin and McDougal, including:

1. How big a problem was the incident?
2. How well did the supplier handle the incident?
3. How often does this happen?
4. How important is the product line involved to your business?
5. How satisfied are you with the supplier concerned?

In total 75 respondents participated in the study. A classification scheme was established based upon outcome components such as delivery timeliness, availability, system error, personnel behaviour and 'promise not met'. A second dimension to the classification was whether the incident was a routine matter (for example, to do with a weekly delivery) or a non-routine matter (for example, a special order). A matrix was produced of incident type and whether it was routine or non-routine and incidents were classified or coded by two researchers. The latter raises questions of the extent to which their analyses concurred to produce similar results. Where this is a question it is important that the level of consistency between the coders is established. The inter-coder reliability of the classifications was assessed by the researchers and deemed acceptable at 85 per cent.

Although the authors' prime concern was with the operational and logistical issues, it is possible to infer a number of L&D-related issues from this simple example. In situations where problems do occur suppliers often try to recover the problem through normative recovery strategies. The incidents provided enough detail to identify the source of the incidents and to examine the recovery strategies used by respondents. This then enabled:

1. Sources of performance problems to be identified; for example, packing procedures themselves might be flawed or individual packers may not have the knowledge or skill to pack according to the required procedure.
2. Effective recovery strategies to be singled out (that is, not necessarily the predetermined ones) and form the basis of further L&D.

Notice that the source of the performance problem and the proposed solution may or may not have an L&D component. Either way the knowledge created through the research could form a useful input into the collective store of knowledge in this organization. The knowledge thus created would need to be managed effectively using the appropriate information and knowledge management systems if its utility is to be maximized (see Shell's SiteScape system in Chapter 5, for example).

Competence-based Analyses

Boyatzis defined competence as an underlying characteristic of a person which can be a motive, trait, skill, aspect of one's self-image or social role, or a body of knowledge that the individual uses. His book of 1982 entitled *The Competent Manager* is considered one of the seminal works in this area. In it a set of management competencies were identified that appeared to predict 'excellence' in managerial work. The research sample for the study consisted of over 2,000 managers in 12 different organizations and across over 40 different types of jobs in the USA. The competencies revealed by these data were grouped into a number of clusters:

1. Goal and action: for example, concern with impact and pro-activity.
2. Leadership: for example, self-confidence.
3. HRM: for example, managing group processes.
4. Focus on others: for example, self-control and perceptual objectivity.
5. Directing subordinates: for example, use of unilateral power.

Boyatzis' approach centred on the identification of the attributes of successful performers (i.e., it is a 'bottom-up' approach). However, it is also possible to take the perspective from the top-down by examining the role, tasks and duties of an occupation or job role through functional analyses (Woodall and Winstanley 1998: 81). By its nature functional analysis, like HTA, demands a reductionist approach to the description of job roles. One of the first systematic attempts in this regard was devised by Fine in the 1970s, whose format for analysis was based upon the following questions:

1. Who performs the task?
2. What actions do they carry out?
3. What results are they expected to accomplish?
4. What tools, equipment or other work aids are necessary for effective performance of the task?

This line of enquiry results in an identification of the primary functions that need to be carried out for competent performance. The emphasis is on process and observable outcomes (i.e. actions and results). The method has been refined over the years and has formed bases for approaches for the identification of competence standards across a whole range of jobs. The UK's National Vocational Qualifications (NVQ) framework has drawn heavily upon functional analysis to identify the required roles, tasks and duties of job incumbents (Woodall and Winstanley 1998: 81). The analysis is at the job level but the outcomes (competence statements, standards or frameworks) may be applied at the individual level; they can, as was noted earlier, provide a basis for appraisal. Competence-based analysis aims to produce:

1. A statement of the role or purpose of the job.
2. A breakdown of the job into areas of competence.
3. Statements of the competencies needed to perform in each of the areas.
4. Criteria for the assessment of competence.

L&D FACTS AND FIGURES

The UK's Chartered Institute of Personnel and Development's (CIPD) Annual Training Survey 2004 found that a majority (65 per cent) of the organizations that they surveyed were involved with National Vocational Qualifications in some way. (*Source*: Training and Development 2004: Survey Report (April 2004). London: CIPD.)

PERSPECTIVE FROM PRACTICE: L&D PRACTITIONER COMPETENCE STANDARDS

Competence standards exist in many occupational areas including L&D. Here are two examples of L&D competence statements, one more at the operational level and the other more at the strategic level. Note that they are expressed in performance terms and hence provide criteria for the assessment of successful performance in these tasks in the L&D job role:

1. At the operational level being able to identify and analyse learning needs is expressed as follows: (a) review how capable the whole organization is of meeting its development needs; (b) develop a learning and development programme for the organization.
2. At the strategic level being able to establish an organizational strategy to guide the organization is expressed as: (a) define values and policies to guide the work of your organization; (b) formulate objectives and strategies to guide your organization; (c) gain support for organizational strategies (Employment National Training Organisation 2004).

Discussion Point

How might you assess whether or not an individual L&D practitioner is competent in the areas described in the examples above?

PERSPECTIVE FROM PRACTICE: THE VOLVO PERSPECTIVE ON COMPETENCE AT WORK IN SWEDEN

Based on the following source: J. Sandberg, 2001. Understanding competence at work, *Harvard Business Review*, March: 24–8.

It was noted above that the derivation of competence statements demands an analytical and reductionist approach; however, it was this reducing of a job role to a standardized checklist of skills that did not sit well within Volvo. When they examined what it was in the eyes of engineers themselves that distinguished the skills needed by a good testing engineer – although it was generally agreed who the best engineers were – there was disagreement on why they were the best. The source of the differences seemed to be to do with the ways in which the job was understood by the engineers, as mani-

Continued

fested in the way they described the skills needed (there was general agreement on what the skills themselves were). Three types of competent performer were described.

1. Sequential optimizers defined the job in terms of the competence of being able to make the engine perform according to specifications. In order to achieve this the engineers focused upon individual performance categories in a sequential problem-solving manner (the perspective was analytic).
2. The second group, interactive optimizers, understood the job in terms of the resolution of trade-offs between different performance categories which involved a focus on all performance categories simultaneously (the perspective was holistic).
3. The final group described the job in terms of making the engine provide the customer with a good driving experience, hence their main perspective was customer-based; these were described as customer optimizers (the perspective was external and customer-focused).

These differences explained many of the observed variations in the ways competent engineers carried out their jobs. The general implications drawn from this by Sandberg are that if it is not easy to identify objectively and unequivocally the attributes required for success (apart from in simple, routine and repetitive tasks), it is correspondingly difficult for these attributes to figure in selection and L&D in a meaningful way. He argued that the way forward is to shift the emphasis away from 'flawed attribute checklists' towards identifying and understanding what complex jobs entail, even when these qualities cannot be expressed in simple and unambiguous terms. The identification of what a complex job entails is likely to encompass tacit knowledge and skills that have been acquired through implicit learning. This presents real challenges to the L&D practitioner from an analytical perspective. Techniques such as Klein's ACTA go some way towards tapping into the expertise that experienced performers bring to bear upon complex tasks. Nonaka's SECI-*ba* theory of knowledge creation also presents ways in which expertise can be codified and articulated.

Harrison (2002: 277) argued that the conventional competence-based approach tends to be best suited to those situations in which there is a need to:

- develop clearly defined standards of performance, perhaps because of a lack of any such standards previously, or because of a drive towards the measurement of performance and its improvement;
- link L&D within the organization to nationally recognized standards; for example in the UK there are National Vocational Qualifications (NVQs) for many different occupations and at a variety of levels.

The national standards that are produced by competence-based analyses are usually generic rather than organization specific and it may be that that the organization's own jobs have to be 'shoe-horned' to fit a general framework. This has been one of the main criticisms of the competence-based approach, with the corollary that organizations may be better off developing their own standards. However, in many situations it actually may not be necessary to 'reinvent the wheel' by developing company-specific standards; it may be better for a generic competency approach to be used with flexibility and discretion. Mumford (1993: 103) argued that this is preferable to simply doing nothing. The competencies developed by Boyatzis have, for example, been used beyond the USA in a variety of ways. Harrison (2002) reported a case study of Manchester Airport in the UK where company directors used them as a basis to develop their own organization-specific set of competencies in three clusters: firstly, understanding what needs to be done (for example, critical reasoning, visioning and business 'know-how'); secondly, getting the job done (for example, achievement drive, control and flexibility); and thirdly, taking people with you (for example, motivation, interpersonal skills and influence) (Harrison 2002). In doing so the company did not have to start from scratch and also overcame one of the principal limitations of generic competence frameworks – their lack of organizational specificity. Currie and Darby (1995) suggested that there are a number of other weaknesses of generic competencies:

1. The first of these is the definition of competence, especially at a managerial level. The competence-based approach tends to make the assumption that managerial skills are of a general nature, but it is argued by many that this is by no means the case. Managerial and other professional jobs will differ from one organization to the next (see the Perspective from Practice on accountants below). Furthermore, definitions often fail to make distinctions between high and low performers and may not be particularly effective in assessing the 'softer' skills such as assertiveness, creativity, sensitivity and intuition (Currie and Darby 1995: 14).
2. A second problem in Currie and Darby's view is the over-emphasis placed upon assessment (often in terms of practical workplace outcomes), which means that there may be concomitantly less emphasis upon learning (hence subordinating knowledge, understanding and higher-order cognitive skills in favour of that which is observable).
3. A third problem with the competence-based approach in their view is in terms of assessment, and in particular that there may not be any discrimination between high and low performers. Using threshold competencies (basic requirements to carry out a job) and performance competencies (which differentiate between levels) can obviate this problem.
4. Finally, a practical problem that is often encountered is the complexity and bureaucracy involved in administering the standards and their assessment (Currie and Darby 1995: 15).

Sims and Veres (1989) argued that the content of planned L&D for new entrants to a job or present incumbents of a given job role is best determined by an analysis that identifies what is required of that particular position. Moreover, this should go beyond the simple identification of the knowledge, skills and attitudes required and ought to include an individual's values, critical thinking patterns and judgement processes. This is important if L&D is to enable learners to apply integrated knowledge in a practical job-related manner (1989: 103). Thus competencies should embody a desired behavioural outcome based upon the job requirements, with an emphasis upon performance and the context and conditions under which this will occur (Sims and Veres 1989).

Clearly the notion of competency and its operationalization in L&D is not unproblematic and it has been hotly debated in academic circles for many years (see, for example, Burgoyne 1993). Moreover, in practical settings the ways in which competencies are interpreted and applied can be the subject of a wide degree of variability (as we saw with the example of Volvo and Manchester Airport). Perhaps the greatest value of generic standards lies in their utility in two areas:

1. Firstly, to professional bodies and educational institutions in order that they may ensure consistency and coherence in education, qualifications and certification.
2. Secondly, in the control and management of L&D, especially for those jobs that may be specified in performance terms, for example when designing L&D interventions, and in appraising and evaluating individual job performance (for which they provide an agreed standard).

So where does this leave the practitioner who has to judge if, when, where and how to use competencies? The questions posed by Woodall and Winstanley provide a useful set of prompts for the manager who may be considering embarking on the path of competence-based L&D. He or she may like to consider:

1. What is the purpose of defining competence?
2. To what use will defined competencies be put?
3. How will competencies be identified?
4. Who should be involved in developing a competence-based approach?
5. How will the competencies be used and implemented in the organization? (Woodall and Winstanley 1998: 86–7).

In Australia, for example, the National Training Board went some way to answering the important questions about the practical implications by specifying the key features that competencies in their national context should exhibit. Pickett (1998) argued that if competencies are to be valid and useful they should be:

- realistic to work practices;
- expressible as an outcome;

- be capable of demonstration, observation and assessment;
- be intelligible to learners, managers and L&D practitioners;
- be general enough to describe activities that have the potential to transfer to other organizations (Pickett 1998: 111–12).

PERSPECTIVE FROM PRACTICE: PRODUCING OCCUPATIONAL STANDARDS FOR PROFESSIONALS

Based on the following source: G. Hardern, 1995. The development of standards of competence in accounting, *Accounting Education*, 4(1)17–27.

Because of the nature of expert and professional performance, perhaps some of the greatest difficulties in producing occupational standards are encountered in the domain of professional work. The professions (i.e. those job roles that involve some branch of advanced learning) typically are founded upon a large and complex domain of knowledge and its interpretation and application in real-world contexts. Because of the importance of knowledge in professional work the latter has been the source of a number of difficulties when it comes to the functional analysis of a professional's job role. However, for the reasons alluded to above (for example, the management of professionals' education and for ensuing consistency) the notion of competence has been attractive to a number of professional bodies. Hardern (1995) examined these issues from the point of view of the accountancy profession and he argued that the application of functional analysis to the professional occupation of accountancy raises a number of important issues:

1. Firstly, because of the breadth and depth of the competencies required in the accounting profession a complete and detailed specification is likely to be voluminous and unwieldy. On the other hand, producing a workable standard may yield something that is too bland for practical use; hence a middle course between these two extremes needs to be found.
2. Secondly, any professional standards for accounting expressed in outcome terms need to be supplemented with extensive statements of underpinning knowledge if they are to be of use in the education and training of professionals.
3. Thirdly, the actual definition of the professional level of competence (for example, Level 5 in the UK's NVQ system) is problematic and, furthermore, how to make this specific to a profession is often difficult because of the wide variety of strategic and contextual issues affecting an organization. It is dealing precisely with these complex issues that singles out the expert and professional performer from the novice.

Continued

4.   Finally, some aspects of a professional's job role – such as exercising pro-
     fessional judgement, organizational and political skills, adaptability and
     flexibility and the contingent nature of these – may be too elusive to catch
     in outcome terms (Hardern 1995).

Functional analysis of a professional role must, in Hardern's opinion, look
beyond the narrow task requirements and attempt to define the softer
aspects of competence (1995: 21). Hardern also alerts us to the problems
associated with the assessment of performance and points to the potential
value of well-designed and -implemented appraisal systems and assessment
centres in this regard.

It was noted at the outset than an important aspect of L&D needs assessment is
the assignation of priorities such as 'high', 'medium' or 'low' to identified learning needs. This can then make the outcome of the needs assessment phase more
manageable because some of the analytical techniques discussed are highly reductionist and may lead to the identification of a large number of potential L&D
needs. The L&D practitioner must have some way of sorting the wheat from the
chaff. Identified needs should be prioritized in order that resources and effort may
be focused appropriately. Bramley (1989) described a useful addendum to the
concept of job-level analysis that was developed by the Armed Forces in the UK.
By eliciting information relating to the difficulty (is the task difficult, 'yes' or 'no'?),
importance (is the task very important, moderately important or not important?)
and frequency (is the task performed very frequently, moderately or infrequently?) an algorithm may be produced that assigns 'training levels' (i.e. levels
of priority) to a particular identified need.
    In this difficulty, importance and frequency (DIF) protocol individual tasks are
judged firstly according to whether or not they are difficult, then according to their
degree of importance to the job and finally tasks are rated according to how frequently they are performed (Bramley 1989: 11). The various permutations of these
judgements are then used in the algorithm to determine the 'training level' or priority that can range from the highest Level 1 (over-train and reinstate at regular
intervals), through Levels 2 (train to job proficiency level) and 3 (train to 'need-
to-be-aware' level) to Levels 4 and 5 (do not train). For example, a task that is very
difficult, very important and very infrequently performed might be assigned an
L&D priority of 'very high' to the extent that job incumbents should be over-
trained with respect to the specific task. One might speculate that performing an
emergency landing of an aircraft would fall into this category; hence there may
be a need to over-train pilots in the simulated emergency landing procedure. The
dangers are that the procedure may become mechanistic and also that the judgements and ratings involved can be somewhat subjective. Some measure of inter-
rater agreement might be needed if the prioritization exercise is seen as being
critical to the effectiveness of L&D. An alternative is to bear some of these ques-

tions of difficulty and importance in mind as subjective judgements when assigning priorities to specific L&D projects. Such an exercise is likely to be a useful way of directing resources to the most important and pressing L&D needs (Figure 6.5).

L&D FACTS AND FIGURES

The UK's Chartered Institute of Personnel and Development's (CIPD) Annual Training Survey 2004 found that the types of training rated as most important amongst respondents were induction, health and safety and technical skills. (*Source*: Training and Development 2004: Survey Report (April 2004). London: CIPD).

Learning objectives or training objectives (the term 'outcomes' is also sometimes used) are a deliverable from the needs assessment phase. Objectives translate the outcomes of the preceding analyses into usable statements for the design of L&D activities (for example, training courses, on-job instruction, etc.). They may also form the basis for assessment and evaluation. Objectives may be derived from any

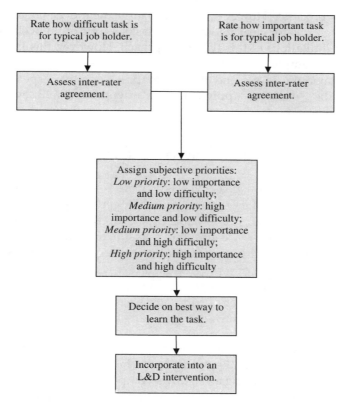

Figure 6.5   Prioritizing L&D needs

of the three levels of analysis; we will confine our consideration here to the job level as it is often the case that the analytical approaches such as HTA yield formal and precise statements of learning outcome or terminal behaviour (i.e. performance). Objectives-based analyses traditionally involve comprehensive statements of:

Performance: what the learner is expected to be able to do after L&D has occurred (for example, 'compile a spreadsheet').

Conditions: the important conditions under which performance is expected to occur (for example, 'using MS Excel on a PC').

Criteria: the level of acceptable performance (for example, 'to 100 per cent accuracy').

Each of the elements identified by Mager can be further unpacked. Performance as a statement of what a learner will be able to do indicates that the underlying philosophy is arguably behaviourist (indeed some people refer to these types of statements as behavioural objectives). So by definition a performance statement must comprise a verb: 'By the end of the learning the employee will be able to word process a document'. Here the verb is 'process'; it is an observable action (one could watch someone do this and judge whether or not they had learned how to word process). However, this emphasis on the behavioural element, powerful though it is for clearly identifiable tasks, is one of the well-documented criticisms and limitations of this type of approach. However, this limitation need not be fatal; for example, it is entirely feasible to construct objectives that are less precise in behavioural terms and that encompass cognitive aspects of learning such as 'describe', 'explain', 'apply', 'analyse', 'synthesize' and 'evaluate' (these are all 'doing words').

L&D FACTS AND FIGURES

The classic L&D text on objectives is Robert F. Mager's book *Preparing Instructional Objectives* (1984), from where we get the quote: 'If you're not sure where you're going, you're liable to end up some place else.' As well as being an authoritative account and a useful practical guide to writing behavioural objectives, the book is also interesting because of the way it is written. It is in the form of a programmed text with questions and routing to different parts of the book depending upon one's responses to the questions – arguably a forerunner of computer-based training.

As noted above, in this performance-based approach two other components of an objective are often employed: the conditions, which in the case of the word processing example might be 'using a Windows-compatible word processing package installed on a standard office personal computer'; and the criteria (or standards), which in the case of the word processing example might be 'to 95 per cent accuracy at the rate of 100 words per minute'. This type of approach is especially useful for skills learning and assessment where precision and the quantification of performance is important. Its use is most often confined to learning for such tasks and under such circumstances.

The concept of a learning objective as an outcome or a goal is commensurate with theories of motivation and performance and the supporting empirical research. For example, in goal-setting theory a goal is defined as a desirable level of achievement and the theory is based upon a number of principles:

1. Challenge: individuals who are given complex and challenging goals perform better than those given no goals or simple and unchallenging ones.
2. Specificity: goals are more effective in eliciting performance when they are specific rather than vague.
3. Suitability: to maintain or enhance an individual's self-efficacy the goal should be commensurate with the individual's ability to successfully accomplish the set goal.
4. Involvement: learners' participation in goal setting can enhance performance (the individual has to accept the goal that has been set).
5. Feedback: for goal setting to be effective individuals need to be aware of the extent to which they are achieving the goal. (See Latham 2004.)

The implications of goal-setting theory for learning are that learning targets should be clear, challenging and achievable; ideally they should have been agreed with learners, and facilitators should give feedback on the extent to which targets are likely to be met. Objectives present a structured (some would argue too structured) format for the development of statements of learning outcome. The main criticisms include the argument that they are too difficult to formulate, they put too much stress on trivial and easily measured behaviours (thus rendering important those things that happen to be easily measurable but which may be inconsequential), it is dangerous to put too much emphasis on behaviours and not all desirable results can be specified in advance (Rowntree 1982: 51–2). Like many tools, objectives can be a 'good slave but a bad master' and the use of the conditions and standards elements is perhaps best restricted to the more mechanistic, behavioural or competence-based tasks. However, the use of performance statements is fairly ubiquitous in L&D practice and has made its way into the mainstream of learning design in both in industry and education and arguably is of central importance in the L&D process.

Discussion Point

What in your view are the strengths and weaknesses of the objectives-based approach? Does it have any place in modern L&D with its emphasis upon learning rather than training?

Collective Needs Assessment: the Organization

Collective L&D needs can manifest themselves in a number of ways, for example:

1. Common needs across teams or groups of employees in the organization in response to an internal or external jolt, for example if a new IT system is to be introduced company-wide or if the legal framework in which the company operates changes.

2. A performance gap afflicting the organization as a whole as revealed by aggregate measures of performance (such as turnover, sales, productivity, customer satisfaction and so forth), for example, the need to reverse a declining market share (Gibb 2002: 41).

L&D FACTS AND FIGURES

Over three decades ago Richard Morano, then of the Xerox Corporation, argued that the most important task of the training department is that of determining the training needs of the organization, since this 'not only shows us the direction that we should take, but also provides justification to management that the courses being offered meet the 'real' needs of the organisation' (1973: 26). Putting aside the terminology of the age (the emphasis upon 'training' and 'courses'), the sentiment that Morano voices is very much one ahead of its time in stressing the strategic role that L&D should play in developing knowledge and skills that can support the direction that the organization should take.

Assessing L&D needs at the organizational level is an integrative exercise requiring a whole view. Two key issues at this level are the extent to which L&D is seen as a strategic activity and, related to this, the extent to which the culture of the organization supports L&D. How then at this organizational level might the L&D practitioner identify and analyse the knowledge and skills that the workforce needs to have in order that they may support the achievement of organizational objectives? Salas and Cannon-Bowers (2001) described the intrinsic purpose of an organization-level analysis as being focused upon those system-wide components (such as the congruence of L&D with the organization's objectives, the available resources, constraints and support for transfer of learning) that may affect the impact of L&D. Learning needs assessment at the organization level is by definition a strategic task in that by looking at the organization's needs one inevitably asks questions relating to the overall mission, goals and objectives. Moreover, in strategically driven models of HRM the fit between strategy and the configuration of the organization's human resources is seen as being a means to the mobilization of people in achieving goals. This was one of the bases of some of the early models of HRM (for example, Fombrun et al. 1984). The so-called 'fit' approach is predicated on the rational model, where the business goals are set, and forces are mobilized to secure the achievement of the set goals. The assumption is that performance will improve when human resources (including L&D) are configured to support the firm's predetermined choice of strategy.

Boxall and Purcell (2003: 54) identified a number of problems with the 'fit' approach; for example, it tends to overlook employee interests by ignoring the need to align in a reciprocal fashion the employees' interests with those of the organization. It may therefore fail to integrate business needs and employee needs. This is especially important in the area of L&D because learner motivation is a crucial determinant of how an employee engages with L&D. Boxall and Purcell argued that managers must give thought to how they can meet the baseline needs of employees whose knowledge and skills are crucial to the firm's survival. With the shift in many Western economies to service and knowledge-based work this becomes even more pressing and may represent a fundamental shift in power relations within organizations.

A further limitation of older models such as the fit model is that the rationalist assumptions may not always hold and a more realistic state of affairs may be one in which there is a dialogue between what can be achieved in HR terms and what the organization wants to achieve. Through such a dialogue alternative possibilities may be explored and new avenues opened up. As noted, some would even go so far as to argue that the HR strategy may in fact be the prime mover in this relationship, and if 'people are the key to competitive advantage, then we need to build [the organization] on our people strengths'; therefore the people within the organization (and they way they are managed and the knowledge and skills that they have or may acquire) become less the implementers of strategy and more the driving force behind strategy (Torrington et al. 2002: 33).

The SWOT analysis is a general problem-solving and decision-making tool that is part of rational approaches to strategic management. Even though the limits of rationality and rationally based techniques are well documented, the identification of weaknesses (which may then be transformed as opportunities for development) or perceived threats (the learning implications of which might translate into current shortfalls in knowledge and skills) are legitimate techniques for helping to identify general organizational issues which may have L&D implications. As a technique SWOT (Strengths, Weaknesses, Opportunities and Threats) analysis is both highly adaptable and comprehensive in that it looks internally (at strengths and weaknesses) and externally (at threats and opportunities). From an L&D perspective SWOT-type approaches are potentially useful because they focus on needs in terms of:

Strengths to be capitalized upon, and whether further development of these is needed.

Weaknesses in the organization's knowledge and skill base and the identification of the knowledge and skill that need to be addressed through L&D or other HR-related practices.

Opportunities to be exploited and the knowledge and skills needed to do so.

Threats that may be counteracted by development.

The information required for each cell in a SWOT analysis can be acquired by a variety of means including surveys, interviewing, brainstorming, group discussions and so forth (Boydell and Leary 1996).

PERSPECTIVE FROM PRACTICE: USING SWOTS TO IDENTIFY ORGANIZATIONAL L&D NEEDS

Based on the following source: E. Sadler-Smith, P. Gardiner, B. Badger, I. Chaston and J. Stubberfield, 2000. Using collaborative learning to develop small firms, *Human Resource Development International*, 3(3): 285–306.

The aim of this action-based project was to identify individual and organization-level L&D needs in a sample of small firms in the UK. The needs assessment served two purposes:

1. A content purpose: to specify the content for organization-specific L&D programmes.
2. A process purpose: using the L&D cycle (including the needs assessment) as a vehicle to develop individual and collective learning competencies within the participating organizations.

The authors used an integrated model for learning needs assessment with a view to designing a learning programme, the implementation of which was facilitated by an external learning adviser. The adviser worked in a consultative capacity with the company. For the organizational level of analysis Sadler-Smith et al. used a modified version of the traditional SWOT framework in a workshop environment (Table 6.2). The SWOT covered three functional areas, which were predetermined from an examination of the small firm and strategy literature as being critical to firm success. The three areas were marketing, finance, and people and planning.

The composition of the group for the needs assessment exercise varied between organizations; sometimes it was virtually the whole company, in other cases it was the management team only. An experienced facilitator led the group-based SWOT analyses, the aim of which was to identify across the three functional areas:

- those issues which were important to the development of the company;
- the relative priority of the identified needs;
- the content of a learning programme for the company that met the higher priority needs.

For example, one of the identified needs at the organizational level was 'learning about new markets'. In this case a learning adviser with expertise in market research worked with the project team in the organization to enable them to conduct market research. Not only did the team develop within the firm the competence to conduct market research (content skills), they also developed skills in working and learning together as a project team (learning process skills). The ultimate aim was for the learning adviser to be able to step back, having embedded the learning process competence within the organization.

Another example of organization-level needs dealt with in this way was understating customer expectations of service quality; in this case the learning adviser was experienced in the hotel sector and was able to enable managers in the organization to develop the capabilities to design, implement and act upon customer satisfaction surveys. The research suggested that the process of needs assessment had at least two important effects:

1. It revealed knowledge that was latent within the organizations and enabled the surfacing and sharing of this knowledge to take place.
2. It enabled the individual and organizational competencies for enhanced performance to be collaboratively identified by managers, advisers and researchers.

Gibb (2002) identified other sources of information that might provide useful data for an organization-level L&D needs assessment:

1. HR plans: for example, future demands for staff and their levels of knowledge and skill, the need for induction programmes, etc.
2. Succession planning: for example, in determining senior management L&D needs.
3. Review of critical incidents: for example, in order to learn from mistakes and other experiences.
4. Management information systems: for example, in order to make 'real time' performance and accounting data available to managers.
5. Organization-wide collation of data from performance appraisal and performance management systems (Gibb 2002: 43).

One might add to this list two more techniques. The first of these is *scenario planning*, with its emphasis on developing successful strategies, enabling creative thinking, resolving organizational flaws and enhancing strategic conversation (Van der Heijden et al. 2002). All of these are likely to have some implications for planned L&D across the organization as well as at the individual level. Furthermore scenario planning itself is also likely to be an important element of an L&D programme for firms concerned with longer-term survival and growth (see Chapter 5). The second technique is the traditional PESTLE (political, economic, social, technological, legal and ecological) analysis (see Walton 1999: 41).

Table 6.2 Sample SWOT framework for organizational learning needs identification (adapted from Sadler-Smith et al. 2000)

Strengths	Weaknesses
Typical Prompts	*Typical Prompts*
What is this company good at?	Are there any obvious lacks in knowledge and skills?
Who are your customers?	Do you suffer from poor marketing?
What are the skills of your employees?	What are your disadvantages in the marketplace?
Sample Outcomes	*Sample Outcomes*
Breadth of product range	Lack of peak-time capacity
Design standards	Lack of strategic perspective
Customer loyalty	Reliance on old outmoded PR
Quality of products and services	'Fire fighting'
Opportunities	**Threats**
Typical Prompts	*Typical Prompts*
What are the new markets you could move into?	Where is the new competition?
What new products or services could you offer?	Which are the declining markets?
Are there any favourable changes in consumption patterns that might benefit the company?	Are there any unfavourable changes in consumption patterns?
Sample Outcomes	*Sample Outcomes*
European markets	Global recession
Digital technology	Need to keep growing to offset ever-rising costs
New distribution channels	Changes in legal requirements

Conclusion: Integrated Framework for L&D Needs Assessment

Needs assessment may be seen as an important part of a performance planning process that consists of the identification and specification of:

1. Performance requirements.
2. Critical success factors.
3. Developmental trajectory.
4. L&D needs.
5. L&D action plan.

This process may operate at the individual and the collective (i.e. departmental and organizational levels). Needs assessment by its nature relies upon analytical techniques (for example, HTA) in which attention to the fine detail of the problem to hand and the proper execution of the specific method are both essential if the findings are to be reliable and valid. One of the downsides to this is that the analyst may find him- or herself 'sucked in' to a specific performance issue and the mass of detail that this may yield from its analysis. This is inevitable since being analytical involves the identification and logical examination of the elements of a problem. One result of this may be that the L&D practitioner (in an analyst role) may not be able 'to see the forest for the trees'; the concern for accuracy allied to the potential for overload in terms both of volume and complexity of information may result in a myopia in which the bigger picture is lost sight of. This applies to the analysis at any level of resolution, be it the individual employee's needs, those of a department or work group or of the whole organization. Hence the L&D practitioner may find it useful to use a framework into which the various elements of the planning process can be placed and which can:

1. Serve as a framework that integrates the performance requirements, metrics, trajectories, needs and action plans, and aligns the interests of the individual employee, the team or department and the organization.
2. Provide the basis for a checklist of actions for integration and alignment.

A suggested framework is shown in Figure 6.6; the checklist of actions is shown in Table 6.3. Together these may provide the L&D practitioner with a means by which they can examine closely the relationships between the various stages in an L&D planning process, but also keep a check on the ways in which the actions that occur at each stage can be cross-mapped to the superordinate level (for example, from employee to department) or subordinate level (for example, from

Table 6.3 Checklist for the needs assessment framework

Employee to department	Department to organization
Q1: What are the individual's key *performance requirements* and how do they support the performance requirements of the department?	Q2: What are the department's key *performance requirements* and how do they support the goals of the organization?
Q3: Based upon the developmental trajectory what are the individual's *L&D needs* that need to be met? How do these support the department's developmental trajectory?	Q4: Based upon the developmental trajectory what are the department's *L&D needs* that need to be met? How does this support the organization's developmental trajectory?
Q5: Based upon the specified needs what are the individual's L&D *action plans* for meeting their needs and how do they fit with the departmental action plan?	Q6: Based upon the specified needs what is the department's L&D *action plan* for meeting its needs and how does this fit with the organization's action plan?

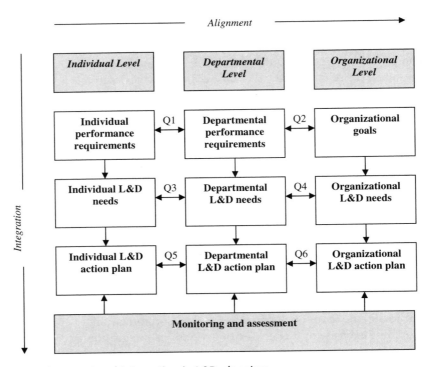

Figure 6.6 Alignment and integration in L&D planning

organization to department). Conducting the analysis in this way may enable the L&D practitioner to see the whole and the parts simultaneously through integration and alignment.

Concept Checklist

Can you now define each of the Key Concepts listed below, and are you now able to achieve the other Knowledge Outcomes specified at the beginning of the chapter?

- Needs assessment
- Needs identification
- Sources of performance problems
- Needs analysis
- Individual, job and organizational analyses
- Performance appraisal
- 360°/multi-rater feedback
- Personal development plans

- Hierarchical task analysis
- Cognitive task analysis
- Critical incident technique
- Concept analysis
- Functional analysis
- Competence
- Occupational standards
- NVQs
- L&D needs prioritization
- Organizational-level analysis
- SWOT analysis
- PESTLE analysis
- Integration and alignment

CHAPTER 7
Management and Leadership Learning and Development

Key Concepts

Leader and manager; leadership; management; manager in learning; manager as learner; national frameworks; 360 degree feedback; assessment and development centres; manager competence; action-based methods; coaching; mentoring; leaders and leadership; transactional-transformational leaders; WICs model; leadership development methods; team building; outdoor development; emotional intelligence; succession planning; learning leader

Knowledge Outcomes

After studying this chapter you should be able to:

- define each of the key concepts listed above;
- explain how managers' learning and development (L&D) needs may be identified and analysed;
- suggest appropriate ways by which managers and leaders may be developed;
- explain the theoretical bases of management and leadership development;
- critically evaluate the methods of management and leadership development described in the chapter;
- explain the meaning and significance of the concept of the learning leader for L&D.

Introduction

The best of all leaders is but a shadowy presence to his followers. When his task is accomplished and his work done the people all say 'It happened to us naturally'.

From the *Tao te Ching*, **Book 1, Verse XVII**

The learning and development of managers and leaders is a crucial element of L&D practice in modern organizations for two reasons: firstly, because many more individuals are now being expected to take on a managerial role, a leadership role or to embrace a managerial function as part of their job; and secondly, because managers and leaders, by virtue of their positions in organizations, have a key role in facilitating collective learning (i.e. of their team or the whole organization). In this chapter we will consider management and leadership L&D in terms of what it should try to achieve and how it might be facilitated. However, it will be useful to begin by considering some of the differences between leaders and managers and by examining the nature of the relationships involved in each case (see Table 7.1).

Table 7.1 Some definitions of leadership and management

Author	Description
Bennis and Nanus (1985: 21)	These authors summarized their perception of the distinction in simple terms when they said that 'managers do things right; leaders do the right thing'.
Kotter (1988)	Kotter argued that managing is to do with planning, organizing and controlling, whereas leading is more to do with visioning, networking and building relationships.
Bass (1990)	Managers must be able to lead and leaders must be able to manage, hence the term manager may be seen as a *role label* whilst leader is a *role function* (see also Sternberg 2003).
Boyatzis (1993)	A manager is someone whose concept of the organization is rooted in competitive advantage, whose work is based on planning to produce predictable results and solve problems through the allocation of organizational resources. The leader, on the other hand, is someone who may be seen as having a concept of the organization rooted more in its philosophy and mission, and whose work is to stimulate change, motivate and inspire (1993: 6).
Dansey-Smith (2004)	Management is concerned with 'doing', is shorter-term and transactional with a specific task focus and with a concern for controlling, monitoring and supervising; leadership, on the other hand, is concerned with 'being', is longer-term focused, transformational, builds relationships and fosters creativity and innovation.

L&D FACTS AND FIGURES

Manager: A person who manages (a department of) a business, organization, institution, etc.; a person with an executive or supervisory function within an organization, etc.

Leader: One who guides others in action or opinion; one who takes the lead in any business, enterprise, or movement; one who is 'followed' by disciples or adherents; the chief of a sect or party. (Definitions from: *Oxford English Dictionary* http://dictionary.oed.com)

Are all leaders managers? Clearly not – leaders may lead but without fulfilling the formal role of a manager. Are all managers leaders? Not necessarily – a manager may manage but he or she may not be seen by those whom they manage as being the leader. Whilst many have attempted to delineate the role of manager from that of leader it should be noted that there are dissenters to the distinctions that some have drawn between leaders and managers. For example, Raelin (2004: 132) attributed the sometimes pejorative nature of the distinction to a *Harvard Business Review* article by Zaleznik (published in 1977), in which he claimed that 'a bureaucratic society which breeds managers may stifle young leaders who need mentors and emotional interchange to develop' (1977: 67). In Raelin's view this is something of a false distinction since managers are not excluded from leadership, and in his view there is the potential for leadership to emerge from any individual under the right sets of circumstances (a view with which not all commentators would agree). Mumford argued that to attribute only the most routine and least exciting parts of the organizational tasks to the manager whilst attributing the stimulating, exciting and direction-changing aspects to the leader 'demeans the managerial process itself' (1993: 105–6).

PERSPECTIVE FROM PRACTICE: LEADER OR MANAGER? – SPORTING EXAMPLES FROM THE UK AND THE USA

Kousez and Posner defined a leadership relationship as a reciprocal one between those who choose to lead and those who choose to follow, in which there is a two-way accountability (Dansey-Smith 2004). Managerial relationships, on the other hand, are often ones in which a group is controlled and coordinated by a formally sanctioned superior; there may be less of an element of choice. By way of illustration, consider the relationships involved in the following two contrasting examples of a team manager (American football coach) and a team leader (English cricket captain):

Manager: the NFL Football Coach, Bill Parcells. The manager's or coach's role differs from that of the leader in the football context since the manager or coach is external to the team itself. The American football coach Bill Par-cells described it thus: 'My challenge as a coach is to organise it, structure it, give the team a good enough design and the motivation to allow the team to play to its potential' (Fagenson-Eland 2001: 48).

Leader: the former English Cricket Team Captain Nasser Hussain. In this context the captain's role is an internal team leadership one whereby a team member is assigned or assumes responsibilities related to morale, motivation and conflict (Day et al. 2004). Cowley described the former England cricket captain Nasser Hussain thus: 'What I liked most about him as captain, apart from his determination, was his honesty . . . he blamed nobody but himself for the failings of his team . . . Even when events turned against him he never missed a press conference or evaded difficult questions' (Cowley 2003: 13).

In these examples the sports team captain has an authority to lead a team towards a common goal (winning the game) by virtue of being nominated as the leader, but also through the credibility, standing and respect accorded him or her by the other team members. The captain's formal authority is augmented by the informal authority vested in him or her through a par-ticular type of relationship with the team's members. Contrast the role of the captain with that of the team manager; here the role is a formal one where he or she exercises prescribed authority through control, coordination, plan-ning and monitoring.

A further distinction also exists between 'a manager' and 'management' (and sim-ilarly between 'a leader' and 'leadership') in the L&D context. The term 'manager' is concerned with an individual and a role and hence is at a micro level, whereas 'management', on the other hand, is more concerned with a process and or a set of social relationships (Day 2001) and hence is at a macro level. For example, manager development might include the education and training of an individual where the emphasis is on he or she acquiring specific types of knowledge and skills in order to enhance task performance in an existing, new or impending man-agement role. Kamoche (2000) argued that the dominant theme in management development is the development of management expertise as a source of strate-gic value that can enhance organizational functioning. Management development is concerned with the development of the management process within an organ-ization, which encompasses the development of individual managers and hence may include manager development but has broader implications in terms of developing the organization collectively. Similarly leadership development might encompass expanding the collective capacity of organizational members to engage effectively in leadership roles and processes and 'learn' their way out of situations that could not have been foreseen (Day 2001: 582). What constitutes successful management and leadership development may also be contested and problematic. Mabey (2002: 1155) identified a number of competing views: for example, from a managerialist and functionalist perspective 'success' might mean the development of capable and committed managers who are able to contribute to organizational learning and performance. For others, 'success' might be conceptualized as a fairer distribution of knowledge and power in an organization. The theme in much of management and leadership L&D practice is one of the appropriation of learning and development in pursuit of enhanced individual and organizational performance.

L&D FACTS AND FIGURES

Ram Aditya and his colleagues have argued that one of the most useful formulas in the world is:

$$Ability \times Motivation = Performance$$

In other words, 'if you want someone to do something they're not doing now you've got to make them able (guidance), make them want to (good feelings). To [me] this is the closest we're likely to get to any universal truth about leadership'. (*Sources*: R. N. Aditya, R. J. House and Kerr, S. 2000. Theory and practice of leadership: into the new millennium. C. Fletcher and C. Baldry. 1999. Multi-source feedback systems: a research perspective. In C. L. Cooper and I. T. Robertson (eds), *International Review of Industrial and Organisational Psychology*, 14: 130–65.)

Leader development and manager development are each subsets of leadership development and management development respectively. Furthermore, since the role of leader and manager are to an extent overlapping there are shared elements of each. Many of the theories of leadership which we will meet originated in the USA and, as Rollinson and Broadfield (2002: 365) noted, whilst they do not state that leader and manager are synonymous, they often focus on the manager as leader and as someone who occupies a position of leadership. The relationships between manager development and management development, and between leader development and leadership development, are summarized in Figure 7.1. For the purposes of the chapter the terms 'management learning and development' and 'leadership learning and development' will be mostly used and it should be assumed that they encompass manager and leader development respectively.

Management Learning and Development

Management L&D includes personal development and the design and application of competencies to improve behavioural outcomes, as well as broader issues

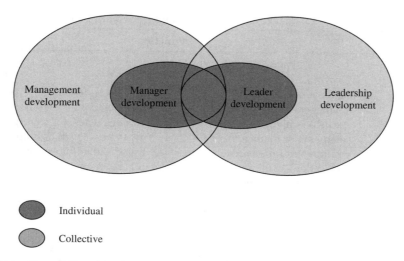

Figure 7.1   The relationships between manager and leader development and management and leadership development

of socialization, organizational change and organizational learning (Kamoche 2000). Management development is concerned with the development of:

1. Individual managers and their careers: it is likely to include elements of management training and management education, in an organizational context (Burgoyne 1988). Manager L&D is at the micro level and is concerned with building individual capability.
2. Management processes within an organization: it may include manager development but has broader implications in terms of developing the organization collectively. Management L&D is at the macro level and is concerned with building management capability across the organization. Similar observations apply to leader and leadership L&D.

This is presented in Table 7.2.

In order to understand what management L&D should address, it is first necessary to consider the role of the manager (there is ongoing debate regarding this issue, including Mintzberg's work of several decades ago to more recent contributions by Hales 1999 and others). In simple terms, the role of the manager may be considered to have two facets: firstly, the 'what' or the content of management, for example, planning, organizing, controlling and leading; secondly, the 'how' or the process of management, encompassing, for example, Mintzberg's informational, interpersonal and decisional roles. Management content and process interact in, and with, the features of the manager's environment, including the business processes, technology, financial systems, organizational culture and structure and the power and politics issues in the organization. This interaction confers a uniqueness upon the process of management in different organizational contexts

Table 7.2 Manager and management and leader and leadership L&D (*Source*: Day 2001)

		Function	
		Manage	*Lead*
Level	*Micro*	*Manager L&D* The development of individual managers and their careers (which is likely to include elements of management training and management education) in an organizational context. Emphasizes developing an intrapersonal competencies.	*Leader L&D* Emphasizes developing interpersonal leadership competencies, for example social awareness (such as empathy), social skills (for example, conflict management) and self-motivation.
	Macro	*Management L&D* The development of the management process within an organization and which may include manager development but has broader implications in terms of developing the organization collectively.	*Leadership L&D* Expanding the collective capacity of organizational members to engage effectively in leadership roles and processes and 'learn' their way out of situations that could not have been foreseen.

and between individual managers. Management L&D is therefore likely to be context specific and present problems in the specification of generic role descriptors and likely behaviours.

Two additional dimensions may be added to these perspectives that also have important implications for L&D. The first is, as noted at the outset, the blurring of the boundaries that surround management; in a sense the job of managing has expanded beyond the formal role label and many non-managerial jobs have management functions within them. The second point is that of the relationship between managers and management and learning which may manifest in two ways: firstly, managers are involved in learning as gatekeepers, champions, promoters, sceptics, facilitators and so forth; and secondly, managers are implicated as learners themselves in any involvement they have in manager development, management development or organizational learning. Hence any consideration of management L&D should concern itself both with the manager-in-learning and the manager-as-learner.

The Manager in Learning

Managers are key players in the learning process within organizations and have a number of L&D roles in this respect (aspects of which were alluded to in the discussion of the strategic and organizational contexts of L&D in an earlier chapter):

1. Managers as sponsors of learning: managers may sponsor learning in the sense of sanctioning or initiating its occurrence by formal means such as a request for training for a member of staff or in response to meeting the L&D needs identified during the appraisal process. The reverse may also be true; managers might need to be convinced of the benefits and value of L&D. The failure of managers to 'buy in' to the L&D concept may present considerable, if not insurmountable, barriers to the implementation of effective L&D. This adds further emphasis to the importance of marketing L&D within organizations, and especially amongst key stakeholder groups.

2. Managers as clients of the L&D function: managers may be clients of L&D in at least two ways. Firstly, they may sponsor L&D by committing resources to it, for example through expenditure on a training course or learning materials and equipment (such as computers), commitment to a bespoke L&D project and so forth. Secondly, managers themselves may also be clients of L&D in their capacity as learners (see below).

3. Managers as facilitators of individual and organizational learning: managers (especially in a line manager role) may act as instructors, coaches or mentors to other learners. Managers have a crucial facilitatory role to play in the L&D process. This may take the form of assisting in or supporting the identification of employees' learning needs (for example, through appraisal), creating the conditions whereby new learning may be applied in the workplace (thus aiding the transfer of learning) and at the end of the process in contributing their views as to the effectiveness of L&D (thus being part of its validation and evaluation). Managers may also be agents of change in their organizations and through their own L&D facilitate the learning of the organization itself. The manager-in-learning and the manager-as-learner overlap in this respect.

The Manager as Learner

The issue of the manager as learner is concerned with the questions: 'What management L&D should take place?' (i.e. the need that must be met) and 'How should it happen? (i.e. the method or approach to be adopted). Wexley and Baldwin (1986) drew a simple distinction between management education (activities traditionally conducted by colleges of business and universities and which may have a longer-term impact), management training (activities designed to impart specific managerial skills and whose impact needs to be more or less immediate), and on-the-job experiences (with the acknowledgement that most of management development may occur on the job itself) (see Figure 7.2).

As a learner the manager is a client of the L&D function and as such the planning of management L&D involves a number of systematic activities based upon the generic L&D cycle including:

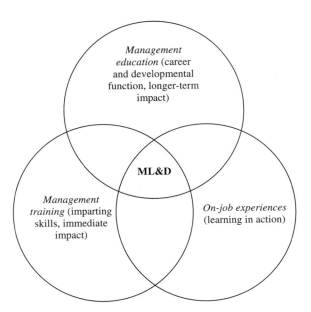

Figure 7.2   Management learning development (ML&D) (after Wexley and Baldwin 1986)

1. Analysing and auditing present and future management L&D needs in the organization, both in terms of what knowledge and skills individual managers will require but also in terms of what the pool of management skills required by the organization are now and are likely to be in the future.
2. An assessment of the existing and potential capabilities of managers against the level of performance required of them (perhaps in terms of predefined competencies).
3. Producing and implementing management L&D policies, plans and practices in order to meet the identified needs through education, training and on-job learning (Harrison 2002: 361).

With respect to the first activity this is essentially a matter of needs assessment at the individual or collective levels. There have been numerous attempts at defining the job role of a manager in order to come up with a definitive set of competencies (the knowledge, skills and personal attributes needed to fulfil the manager's job role). The issue of job-level analysis and the notion of competence have both been discussed in a previous chapter, but it is worth noting that the issue of management competence and management development has a special significance for a number of reasons. Firstly, the job role of a manager is ubiquitous and generally perceived to be of high significance in determining the effectiveness and efficiency of organizational processes. The second reason relates to the sometimes-perceived inadequacies in the performance of this significant group of employees. In the UK in the 1980s there were a series of reports and publications that highlighted the L&D needs of British managers (see, for example, Constable and McCormick 1987; Handy 1988). Mumford (1987), in commenting on these two reports, made three salient points that are still relevant to this day: firstly, that management L&D should aim to create more effective managers (and not merely provide training and education opportunities for them); secondly, that management L&D should involve the whole process and most particularly learning from experience; and finally, where formal L&D is made available to managers it should be integrated with on-job learning.

PERSPECTIVE FROM PRACTICE: THE UK'S COUNCIL FOR EXCELLENCE IN MANAGEMENT AND LEADERSHIP

Based on the following source: http://www.managementandleadership council.org/

The Council for Excellence in Management and Leadership (CEML) was appointed by the UK government's Secretaries of State for Education and Employment and for Trade and Industry in April 2000 with the objective 'to develop a strategy to ensure that the UK has the managers and leaders of the future to match the best in the world'. CEML conducted research into the quantity and relevance of, and level of demand for, management and leadership development in the UK. From this it then developed some specific proposals. The main findings of their research were that:

1. Even though there has been a growth in the provision of management development over the last decade, there still appeared to be skill shortages in this area and especially in terms of leadership abilities.
2. Demand for management training, particularly in smaller firms, was low and was not being adequately met either by the range of formal opportunities or by subsidized initiatives from government.
3. Larger organizations preferred to develop their own company specific (i.e. bespoke) management and leadership development programmes, but these initiatives should not stand in isolation and larger organizations required more flexibility from providers of management and leadership L&D.
4. Finally, despite the recognition by professionals of the importance of management and leadership development, few professional associations required any management learning prior to membership and even fewer of these required management and leadership L&D as part of their Continuing Professional Development (CPD) requirements.

In response to the issues identified in their research CEML made some specific proposals in a number of what were seen to be key areas (small firms, larger organizations and the professions):

Continued

Small and Medium-sized Enterprises (SMEs): There has been a confusing array of support and advice initiatives available to SMEs. CEML deemed that what was required was a coherent approach, building on the creation of a unifying Small Business Service (http://www.sbs.gov.uk/) in order to bring some order to the confusing plethora of management and leadership development initiatives coming from different government departments and agencies and also from the European Union. CEML also proposed that schemes should be introduced that 'join entrepreneurs in their world and tap seamlessly into the activities that they undertake as a normal part of running their businesses'. In other words, there was a call for SME management learning to be situated in practice. In order to meet this need for more workplace and small company-specific learning, CEML developed the Business Improvement Tool for Entrepreneurs (BITE) to signpost clients to a range of solutions that 'work with the grain and mimic their [the SME's] informal processes', for example through self-managed mentoring within the firm, entrepreneurial networking and skills sharing within and between firms – see http://www.managementandleadership-council.org/bite/.

Larger Organizations: CEML recognized that there was much good practice in management and leadership development both in the UK and overseas, underpinned by a body of academic research. CEML's strategy was to try to improve the spread of this best practice by developing a Leadership Development Best Practice Guide. (http://www.managementandleader-shipcouncil.org/GPG/).

Professional associations: CEML's view was that an 'irreducible core of management and leadership development' should be introduced into the professions' pre-qualification and Continuing Professional Development (CPD) programmes. The improvement in management and leadership skills in the professions would be likely to lead to better performance across the economy as a whole (CEML).

In the UK and other nations management development assumes a policy (and political) and national significance to the extent that the UK government has taken considerable interest in the L&D of this group of employees. Hence alongside the more recent efforts in the UK at intervention in management and leadership L&D by government, there have been a number of attempts to define the content as well as the level of competence required of a manager (which may be used as the basis for management L&D needs assessment, qualification structures, performance assessment, etc.). There currently is a UK government-sanctioned body, the Management Standards Centre (MSC), which is the latest in a line of policy bodies charged with the responsibility for defining management competence. However, it should be noted that there is a potential problem in this regard since arguably there is a tension between the defining of the job role in general terms (generically) and its operationalization in individual work contexts (locally) and, furthermore, there are practical L&D ramifications of this. The issue of generic-versus-specific management competence is one to which we will return shortly.

L&D FACTS AND FIGURES

The 2004 American Society for Training and Development (ASTD) survey revealed that managerial and executive development combined were allocated the most learning in 2003 and 2004 across a broad cross-section of US organizations. (*Source*: ASTD State of the Industry Report 2004.)

Assessing Managers' Learning Needs

The methods for L&D needs assessment at the individual level outlined in previous chapters (for example, performance appraisal) apply to the manager's job role in the same way as they do to other types of job role. However, because of the functional relationship between managers and other employees (for example, superior, peer and subordinate relationships) there is a need to employ additional methods that take into account these hierarchical relationships as part of the assessment of management L&D needs. At a more strategic level Mabey (2002: 1143) argued that the means by which an organization conducts its needs assessment for management development is a 'meaningful litmus test' of an organization's attitude towards management development.

Multi-rater Feedback

The basic premise of multi-rater feedback (MRF) is that the people best suited to judge the performance of others are those who work most closely with them (Peiperl 2001: 143). MRF can be from 180° or full 360° perspectives and usually involves ratings from oneself, direct reports, the boss, peers, and may include others such as suppliers. It is an important diagnostic and learning tool in manager and leader development. At the heart of the process is the comparison of different ratings from external sources (peers, subordinates, customers, etc.) and internal sources (self-ratings), which can be used to give a 'circle' of relevant viewpoints (Day 2001: 587). Ratings are given against job-relevant competencies and skills and may be used to facilitate a learning needs assessment exercise (usually in the form of a discussion) between the ratee and her or his line manager (or an L&D practitioner) in order to draw up individual L&D action plans or personal development plans (PDPs). Sophisticated computer-based and online systems are now widely available that enable responses to be elicited by email and allow managers to aggregate scores across teams or departments. Other approaches employ a less structured method by using more informal question formats (Redman and

Wilkinson 2002). 360° feedback's principal advantages are that it reduces the reliance upon a single or small number of sources of data for the rating of individuals' performance (Harrison 2002: 260) and it gives an all-round perspective that enables managers to see themselves as others see them. Research by Fletcher and Baldry (1999) suggested that subordinate ratings improve in reliability when the number of subordinates is increased, and Wexley and Klimoski (1984) found that peer ratings are potentially amongst the most accurate judgements of employee behaviour (Tyson and Ward 2004). Comparison of an individual's self-appraisal with the ratings offered by others is essential because accurate self-perception is an important prerequisite for effective management and leadership (Conger and Toegel 2003) and is a starting point for a self-reflective developmental process. 360° or multi-rater methods have a number of additional advantages:

Precision: advantages recognized by Conger and Toegel (2003) include the fact that multiple ratings give a much more precise picture than single source ratings.

Perceptions: 360° feedback is anonymous and reduces the defensiveness of ratees because it is perceived as being more objective.

Reliability: from a psychometric perspective, using multiple raters and multiple sources of data makes good sense in terms of enhancing the overall reliability of feedback (Day 2001: 589).

One drawback is that its use may be extended beyond its applications for development and into other areas, such as appraisal, for which it was not intended (i.e. the temptation for efficiency and 'killing two birds with one stone'). One of the problems in doing so is that it may violate the psychological safety of the rating process. A further practical difficulty arises when attempts are made at minimizing variations in ratings; for example, by discarding discrepant ratings or sanctioning discrepant respondents, and over-quantifying the method. Doing so may throw away valuable and meaningful data on variations in response patterns and also in the meanings contained within written comments and examples (Conger and Toegel 2003). Toegel and Conger (2003: 297) noted that its uses have been extended beyond its original developmental purposes and that it shows signs of replacing traditional performance appraisal. Goodge (2005) concurred with this view when he stated that more and more companies are using 360° feedback to support the appraisal process. Toegel and Conger argued that the use of 360° feedback for performance appraisal purposes can lead to it losing its potency as a process for honest and constructive feedback and that the time has come for its reinvention as two distinct tools, one for management development (qualitatively based) and one for performance feedback (quantitatively based). Goodge argued against hard links between 360° feedback and appraisal (for example, unscrupulous employees may collude if ratings are linked to hard rewards) and, where it is used, making the MRF results available only after the appraisal has decided upon performance and rewards.

**PERSPECTIVE FROM PRACTICE: 'BEST PRACTICE' CLAIMS
IN 360° FEEDBACK**

Based on the following sources: E. Rogers, W. Rogers and W. Metlay, 2002. Improving the payoff from 360 degree feedback, *Human Resource Planning*, 25(3): 44–54.

The authors of this 'best practice' article offered a series of guidelines for managers for how to maximize the benefits of the 360° approach (Rogers et al. 2002). The prescriptive guidance offered by Rogers et al. is based upon their 'in-depth research study of 43 global organisations' (including BP Amoco Group, Citigroup, Ford Motor, Kellogg's and Rockwell International). They drew from this work a number of critical success factors (CSFs) for implementing 360° feedback, including:

- confining the process to individual development rather than being linked to performance and reward issues;
- linking the assessment framework to business-focused competencies which themselves should be linked to strategic imperatives;
- subjecting the system and process to a high degree of administrative control;
- providing training in advance for all those involved, and using internal coaches to help managers understand and develop plans from the feedback results and the process.

Organizations involved in the study appeared to be of the view that the process improved job performance, but participants were less convinced of the benefits in strategic and profitability performance terms for the whole organization. In spite of this there appeared to be an overall feeling that the 360° feedback process was worth the resources committed to it. Rogers et al. concurred with the views expressed by a number of previous researchers when they argued that the inclination to link 360° assessment with compensation or performance appraisal should be avoided unless the organizational culture can sustain and support such activity (2002: 54).

Peiperl suggested that the process of peer feedback can be potentially problematic because of four paradoxes:

1. Paradox of roles: it is hard to be a peer and a judge because as colleagues we may find it difficult to give forthright and candid feedback for fear that it might strain or damage working relationships. One result of this paradox is that the feedback that is given may be conservative, and even 'distorted, overly positive, and, in the end unhelpful to managers and recipients' (2001:

143) This source of conflict needs to be addressed at the outset by clear demarcation of roles and being clear that participants are ready to give candid assessment and feedback.

2. Paradox of group performance: Pierperl noted that much of the work that goes on in organizations is team-based. Individual and team performance is the outcome of a complex interaction of individuals, roles, task and context. Consequently, peer feedback programmes that focus upon the individual may miss these aspects of performance; moreover peer feedback within a team may be seen as a threat to the relationships in a close-knit group (Peiperl 2001).

3. Paradox of measurement: quantification of ratings makes the management and aggregation of performance scores administratively less difficult; however, such approaches (which are characterized by a comparative ease of measurement) often fail to yield 'the detailed, qualitative comments and insights that can help a colleague improve performance' (2001: 144). In other words, Peiperl argued that administrative simplicity of measurement and the developmental utility of results are not necessarily related.

4. Paradox of rewards: when peer feedback is linked to financial or other rewards individuals will tend to focus their attention upon the reward outcome (for example, a pay rise) and overlook the more constructive and developmental feedback that the process may generate (Peiperl 2001).

Discussion Point

From an L&D perspective, how might Peiperl's four paradoxes of peer feedback be managed?

Assessment and Development Centres

An assessment or development centre is based upon a systematic approach to identifying precisely what is required for success in a particular job (for example, leadership, integrity, tenacity and team-building skills), then labelling these attributes in terms of a short list of tightly defined criteria and providing a forum where they can be reliably assessed (Harrison 2002: 335). Assessment centres (where the prime aim is assessment) or development centres (the prime aim being development) are important career and organizational development tools since they can be used to identify individuals who may be fast-tracked immediately, those who have the potential to aspire to senior management positions or who can fill new positions within a redesigned organizational structure.

An assessment centre provides a more rigorous and comprehensive assessment of development potential than does appraisal on its own. An assessment centre process itself might consist of a series of exercises designed specifically to capture and simulate multiple aspects of the job (Woodruffe 1993). The intention is to identify individuals' capabilities in relevant job areas (for example, group working and problem solving) and highlight any associated development needs of the individuals concerned. As with appraisal, it is important that facilitators, observers or assessors should be trained in the requisite observational and assessment skills. The type of exercises used may typically include interviews, psychometric tests, tests of verbal and critical reasoning, presentations, in-tray exercises (a paper-based simulation), case study analyses, problem solving and decision-making scenarios and role-playing exercises (one-to-one or group-based) (Woodall and Winstanley 1998: 127–8). Woodruffe (1993) cited the following advantages and disadvantages of assessment centres:

Advantages: generally better reliability and validity in the methods employed (although this course depends upon how well they are designed and implemented). They are perceived to be fair, have high face validity, generate greater acceptance of outcomes, and enable self-reflection and ownership of development issues (Woodruffe 1993).

Disadvantages: they are complex to design, time-consuming and resource-intensive to administer, hence they may be unsuitable where the expertise or resources are not available or if the costs outweigh the benefits. For these reasons they are often reserved for use with senior managers and executives, where the payoffs of making the right career development decisions are likely to be high (Woodruffe 1993).

As with any L&D needs assessment process there are practical problems that need to be addressed if assessment and development centres are to be effective. Exercises need to be well designed (i.e. reliable and valid), assessors need to be qualified and trained and management should show commitment to the process. The assessment of manager L&D needs is a crucial first step in the planning process for management L&D. The nature of managers' learning needs is likely to be dependent upon context, and moreover that context is likely to have a number of different dimensions (including the organizational and national dimensions), which the L&D practitioner will need to accommodate when designing and delivering management L&D. In the next section we will consider an example from practice where organizational context (the public sector in the USA) played an important role in determining the type, level and content of management L&D.

PERSPECTIVE FROM PRACTICE: ASSESSING THE L&D NEEDS OF PUBLIC-SECTOR MANAGERS IN IDAHO, USA

Based on the following source: P. W. Patton and C. Pratt, 2002. Assessing the training needs of high-potential managers, *Public Personnel Management*, 31(4): 465–84.

The problems faced by the organizations involved in Patton and Pratt's study are familiar ones: the promotion of technically competent non-managerial employees to management positions and the need to succession plan in the light of retirement and other factors. This requires an analysis of L&D needs in relation to the issues shown in Figure 7.3.

To assess these needs the researchers chose to use focus group interviews in order to determine where current and potential supervisors and managers experienced gaps in their own knowledge and skills. One of the advantages of the focus group approach is that it enables feelings and opinions on causes of problems and solutions to be solicited. This type of end-user involvement may open up a broader range of options for management of L&D delivery than a closed questionnaire, survey-type approach might yield. Interview-type approaches also involve stakeholders more closely than less personal approaches, such as surveys, by informing them and gaining their support for the project. The participants in Patton and Pratt's study were employees in the state of Idaho in the north-west USA. They were asked to respond to a number of issues including:

1. What training topics would be most useful for new managers, what education or training do you wish that you had received and what was the most important experience that you have had that taught you about management?
2. What skills, abilities and personal characteristics would you look for in a new hire to a management position?
3. What skills, abilities and personal characteristics single out the best manager that you have had in your career and the worst manager that you have had in your career? (Patton and Pratt 2002)

Analysis, integration and synthesis of participants' responses enabled four clusters of knowledge, skills and personal attributes to be identified that could be used as the content for a management development programme for this particular organization:

General administration and organization: manager role, function, responsibility and skills; ethics and professionalism; planning and goal setting; organization design and performance assessment and evaluation.

Technical and quantitative: accounting, budgets, technology, legal and regulatory frameworks.

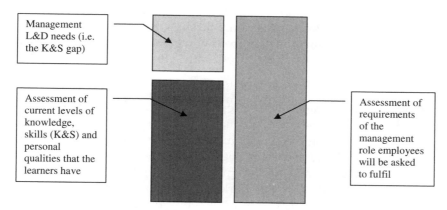

Figure 7.3   Management L&D needs assessment (based on Patton and Pratt 2002)

Analytical and conceptual: problem solving, decision making, research skills, planning tools and techniques.

Human skills: interpersonal and organizational communication, leadership styles, motivation, performance management, feedback, grievance and conflict management.

These clusters of knowledge, skills and personal attributes are organization specific and hence are likely to have high job relevance, content validity and face validity amongst participants. One of the drawbacks of this highly company-specific approach is that it is likely to identify only issues relevant to job incumbents. What it may not achieve is the identification of latent or future needs. For this reason a more comprehensive and external perspective (which some customization of a generic management competence standard might provide) may also be helpful as an input to the definition of programme content.

Competence-based Approaches

The definition of management competence is concerned with identifying the knowledge, skills, attitudes, behaviours and traits (such as personal drive) that lead to effective behaviour in the manager role. Woodall and Winstanley suggest that a competence-based management L&D paradigm assumes that:

- management may be seen as a skill and a behaviour that can be developed (rather than being innate);
- the focus is upon work-related knowledge and skills practised and applied in real-world settings (rather than formal 'pre-programmed' knowledge and skills);

- management L&D should be delivered through the most appropriate range and mix of methods (rather than only through formal courses);
- assessment and evaluation can be by means of portfolios of evidence, practical demonstrations and so forth rather than by means only of formal examination (1998: 75).

Competencies in management development provide a clear set of performance criteria and fit well in a performance management framework in which the aim is to apply set criteria to the description of a job role in order to enable standardization and comparability of assessment. Woodall and Winstanley made the distinction between the UK-type approach based upon what managers do, and the US-type approach (typified by the work of Boyatzis) which focused upon what singled out superior performance from merely satisfactory performance. In the UK management competence standards have been classified at three levels (3–5), each corresponding to an appropriate National Vocational Qualification (1997) – see Table 7.3.

The development of generic national standards at these levels is typically achieved through functional analyses of the manager's job role and sometimes in conjunction with wider consultation with employers, individual managers and other stakeholders. For example, in the UK this process has led to the identification of six functional areas of management and leadership and is embodied in the

Table 7.3 UK's NVQ-level descriptors for management competence (*Source*: www.management-standards.org.uk)

Level	Descriptor
Management Level 3	Managers operating at this level have a tightly defined area of responsibility; some limited opportunity for taking decisions and managing budgets; responsibility for achieving specific results by using resources effectively; responsibility for allocating work to team members, colleagues or contractors.
Management Level 4	Managers operating at this level have responsibility for allocating work to others, achieving specific results by using resources effectively, carrying out policy in their defined area of authority, controlling limited financial budgets, and contributing to broader activities, such as change programmes and recruitment.
Management Level 5: Operational	Managers operating at this level have operational responsibility for substantial programmes and resources, have a broad span of control, proactively identify and implement change and quality improvements, negotiate budgets and contracts, and lead high-level meetings.
Management Level 5: Strategic	Managers operating at this level have responsibility for substantial programmes and resources, the strategic development of their organization and have a broad span of control, proactively identify and implement change and quality improvements, negotiate budgets and contracts and lead high-level meetings.

UK's National Occupational Standard for Management and Leadership (see below).

PERSPECTIVE FROM PRACTICE: THE UK'S NATIONAL OCCUPATIONAL STANDARD FOR MANAGEMENT AND LEADERSHIP

Based on the following source: Management Standards Centre. 2004. National Occupational Standard for Management & Leadership, www.management-standards.org.uk

We will examine the UK's National Occupational Standard (NOS) with a view to highlighting some of its key features in terms of the performance it describes and some of the related underpinning factors (such as knowledge and understanding). The Management Standards Centre (MSC) is the UK government-recognized standards-setting body for management and leadership. The standards are designed to act as a benchmark of best practice and were designed on the basis of:

1. Review of the pre-existing 1997 standards was undertaken with end-users 'to understand what they liked and disliked about them' and to identify areas of change in management since 1997.
2. Benchmarking against other, more recent, types of occupational standards from both the private, public and voluntary sectors and against other international standards.
3. Occupational and functional mapping exercise in terms of numbers of managers in the UK across various industry sectors, the functions that managers undertake in the workplace and the behaviours that underpin effective performance (the latter was included in an attempt to recognize those 'soft skills' which managers bring to their role; see: www.management-standards.org.uk).

The NOS is composed of six functional areas of management:

1. Managing self and personal skills: for example, managing one's own resources and professional development.
2. Providing direction: for example, developing and implementing operational plans for one's own area of responsibility.
3. Facilitating change: for example, encouraging innovation in one's team.
4. Working with people: for example, developing productive working relationships with colleagues.
5. Using resources: for example, managing a budget.
6. Achieving results: for example, managing a project (see: www.management-standards.org.uk).

Continued

Table 7.4 Sample breakdown of the 'manage a project' aspect of 'achieving results' area (*Source*: www.management-standards.org.uk)

Element	Description
Main *generic skills*	For example evaluating, delegating, communicating, setting objectives and decision making in managing a project.
Specification of *outcomes*	What the manager must be able to do, for example, discuss and agree the key objectives and scope of the proposed project and the available resources with the project sponsor(s) and any key stakeholders.
Behaviours that underpin effective performance	For example, the capability to recognize changes in circumstances promptly and adjust project plans and activities accordingly.
Three categories of *knowledge and understanding*	*General* knowledge and understanding (for example, the fundamental characteristics of projects as opposed to routine management functions/activities). *Industry/sector*-specific knowledge and understanding (for example, project management tools and techniques commonly used in the industry or sector). *Context*-specific knowledge and understanding (for example, the project sponsor(s) – the individual or group for whom the project is being undertaken.)

> If we take the 'manage a project' aspect of 'Achieving results' as a convenient example it reveals a number of more detailed aspects, which gives some indication of the level of exhaustive analyses that have been undertaken in order to develop the standard (readers are referred to www.management-standards.org.uk for the full and voluminous documentation of the UK's NOS and further background information) – see Table 7.4.

As noted previously, there have been concerns expressed about competency frameworks in general and especially when applied to the manager's role. For example, Mumford (1993) was unconvinced by these approaches since in his view the contingent and situational nature of management make the relevance and utility of national standards dubious. Harrison argued that functional approaches do not necessarily take local conditions and context into account and hence are subject to drawbacks (although the latest standards to recognize context, see Table 7.4). Her main criticisms were that:

1.   The managers' job is fluid and dynamic (as well as flexible) and hence once a set of competencies have been identified they may be superseded in part by changes in the internal and external business environment and the expectations that this places upon managers.

2. They may serve a narrowing and constraining function upon managers' thinking and behaviour, becoming part of a dominant logic in the organization perhaps at the very time when creativity, innovation and initiative are needed, and therefore may serve as a strait-jacket which stifles innovation and creativity (Harrison 2002).

A number of authors have attempted to define performance in ways that do not fall foul of the contingent nature of management. For example, Schroder (1989) argued that there are four groups of high-performance competencies covering the cognitive (for example, conceptual flexibility), motivational (for example, interpersonal search), directional (for example, self-confidence) and achievement (for example, proactive orientation) domains (Woodall and Winstanley 1998: 82).

Discussion Point

To what extent has the UK's NOS for Management and Leadership addressed some of the problematic issues associated with generic standards and the underlying approaches to competence development? Justify your reasoning.

Management L&D Methods

The discussion so far has focused upon the foundational stages of the management L&D process (the identification and analysis of learning needs). We will now turn our attention to how these needs may be met. It should be noted, however, that although the various methods will be discussed in the context of management L&D many of the approaches might also be employed effectively in leadership learning and development (given that leadership is one functional aspect of a manager's role) and their separating-out is to an extent arbitrary. When viewed from a traditional educational and training perspective management L&D includes activities that are designed to develop individuals for a management role and are delivered through academic, consultancy, institutional (professional) and organizational provision (Cannon 1994). Such activities are likely to rely upon more-or-less traditional delivery methods (for example, through case study, lectures, discussion, simulation, role play and so forth). Similarly, training courses delivered through academic and other organizations or institutions may rely on broadly similar techniques. Rather than concern itself with the traditional and educationally based methods, the main concern in this chapter will be with methods that are delivered in the workplace or in close proximity to it and which take complex 'real life' work problems and issues as their starting point. Raelin (2004: 131) articulated a view that appears to be prevalent amongst many writers; namely, that one of the main problems of management L&D (and arguably L&D

in general) is the transfer of learning issue. The context in which new skills will be practised is crucial, and in this regard Raelin cited Steve Kerr (then of GE's Leadership Development programme): 'You should never send a changed person back to an unchanged environment.' For this reason the discussion of management L&D will focus on a number of approaches where the transfer of learning is less likely to problematic because of the 'situatedness' of the learning that these approaches are designed to engender. At this point it may be worth reiterating the point made by Mumford over a decade ago, which was referred to earlier: learning from work experiences and learning from formal education and training activities must be integrated rather than separate activities (1987: 19).

The two principal groups of methods that will be examined and revisited are action-based methods (action science and action learning) and coaching and mentoring. Hill (2004: 121) argued that becoming a manager was largely a process of newly appointed managers learning from experience by action (and not merely contemplation) in order to transform themselves in terms of their understanding of what it means to be a manager; their interpersonal judgment, their self-knowledge and coping with stress and emotions. McCall concurred with this view when he stated that the primary source of learning to lead is experience and 'the role played by training and other formal programs is relatively modest in comparison to other kinds of experiences' (2004: 127). These various approaches may be seen to be aligned theoretically with the experiential and andragogical learning principles (as exemplified in the models of Kolb and Knowles), the social and situated learning theories of Bandura, Lave and Wenger, and the notion of cognitive constructivism proffered by Cobb, Yackel and others (see Chapter 2).

Action-based Methods for Management L&D

One of the perceived difficulties with a number of management L&D methods, such as simulations or games, is that they may be seen as replacing 'reality with fantasy' and hence run the risk of being perceived by managers as 'unreal' (Mumford 1993). More specifically, Mumford argued that simulation exercises (such as 'build a tower out of Lego bricks') may be used to promote reflection about teamwork, but one of the principal problems with such techniques is that they are *not* managerial reality and therefore have three attendant problems:

1. Control: they are designed by, and under the control of, the tutor with 'rules of the game' that are not set by the participating managers.
2. Purpose: they may sometimes be used just to give variety and activity in a long programme.
3. Learning preferences: different individuals may respond to them in different ways (Mumford 1993: 153).

An important question, therefore, is: 'Can we use reality (in a safe way) as the basis for managerial learning rather than use tasks that might have low face validity for participants, could even be seen as trivial and hence may lack credibility?' One way to obviate this potential problem is by basing learning in work itself through the use of the action-based methods. Action-based approaches are based upon the principles of surfacing, sharing and collective dialogue and reflection of the manager's own and other's understandings and of the impact of these understandings on subsequent individual and collective action. As noted previously, there are two main traditions from the USA and the UK respectively.

Action science (Argyris and Schon): the aim is for the manager to go beyond problem solving and experiential learning and into the realm of questioning how the problem is defined and why it is defined in a particular way. On a practical level the method concerns itself with the ways in which managers may screen out certain information in an attempt to control their environment through what may often turn out to be defensive routines (Woodall and Winstanley 1998: 155). In practical terms the methods used often involve inward reflection and analyses about the way in which problems are defined and the comparative roles played in thought and action by:

- espoused theories: these are the personal assumptions that a manager will subscribe to and claim to use;
- theories-in-use: these are the assumptions and beliefs that are used to guide action, which managers are very often not aware of but which may be inferred from behaviour.

Managers may trap themselves in defensive routines that insulate their mental models from critical examination with the result that a skilled incompetence is developed. This may be used as a shield from the 'pain and threat posed by learning situations' and can be dysfunctional to the extent that it can protect and prevent managers from getting the results that they want to achieve (Senge 1990: 182).

Action learning (Revans) is based on the argument that in a turbulent, fast-moving and uncertain business environment the rate of learning must exceed the rate of change if an organization is to stay ahead and remain competitive and effective (see Chapter 5). Action learning relies on facilitating inquiry that enables managers to ask insightful questions (content) and also to develop the ability or skill to be able to identify and ask those insightful questions (process). The ability to ask insightful questions may be blocked by idealizing solutions that worked in the past, being charmed by the charisma of other managers and by acting impulsively rather than reflectively (Revans 1983). Revans had reservations about the value of what he termed 'programmed knowledge' (a term he used to refer to the content of formal taught management training courses), a view echoed more recently by McCall when he argued that formal educational programmes should not be the centrepiece of development for practising managers but used to supplement and facilitate properly managed and effective learning through experience (McCall 2004: 129).

Discussion Point

What in your view are the main strengths and weaknesses of action-based approaches to management L&D? How realistic is it in busy workplaces to ask managers to make time and space for reflection? What are the consequences of not doing so?

Developmental and Executive Coaching

Thach and Heinselman distinguish between content coaching, feedback coaching and in-depth development. Content coaching tends to be short-term, providing learners with knowledge and skills in specific areas (for example, strategic decision making and global marketing). Feedback coaching typically lasts over a period of months and its purpose is to give feedback on performance and create a development plan. In-depth development is even longer term (maybe six to 12 months) using multiple methods of data collection (including multi-rater feedback) with the aim of constructing a personal development plan that is based upon extensive feedback and the use of projects for learning as an ongoing process that may go beyond a year (Thach and Heinselman 1999). The second and third of Thach and Heinselman's functions serve a developmental purpose, the first serves an instructional purpose – hence it is possible to distinguish between:

1. Coaching that serves primarily a task function and which is employed in order to improve an individual employee's proficiency in a job or task through informal help or instruction from a more skilled colleague. This will be referred to as instructional coaching and the activities he or she engages in are similar to job-instruction training Much informal coaching goes on all the time in organizations as senior employees help more junior ones (Johnson 2001). An instructional coach is usually internal to the organization.
2. Coaching can also serve more of a developmental function with a longer-term and growth focus, especially when applied to manager, leader or executive development. This will be referred to as developmental coaching (and includes executive coaching). A developmental (or executive) coach is usually external to the organization. The process is more formal and lasts over a period of months or even longer.

Recent years have seen the rapid development of the practice of executive coaching (and in parallel even the so-called 'whole life' coaches) to the extent that in the USA executive coaching is the fastest-growing area of consultancy (Jayne 2003). In the UK a survey by the Chartered Institute of Personnel and Development found that 80 per cent of the HR practitioners sampled use coaching (Jarvis 2004). In response to this rapid expansion the UK's CIPD has developed a set of professional standards, which aims to provide accreditation of suppliers of coaching products and services (*People Management*, September 2004).

L&D FACTS AND FIGURES

In the USA it has been estimated that the costs of executive coaching can range from $1,500 for a single day to $100,000 for a longer-term programme over a number of years for a single executive (Day 2001: 591). Users of one-on-one executive coaching include American Express, AT&T, Citibank, Levi-Strauss and Proctor & Gamble (Olivero et al. 1997).

Developmental coaching goes beyond instruction in tasks and can help learners to define their needs and values ('what's important to them?') within a process based upon trust, mutual respect, honesty and openness. Developmental coaching can, if executed well, produce a synergy between an individual's professional and personal lives that can be motivating and fulfilling. It is a means by which management L&D can be made highly personalized and individually focused. To be comprehensive and integrated developmental coaching might encompass content, learning process and underlying beliefs and assumptions (see Mezirow 1991). A developmental coach differs from a mentor in that he or she has not necessarily trodden the same path as the learner, but the skill of the coach is to provide help along the way. Hence, coaching should not be confused with mentoring (a way to share experience and fast-track technical and other skills) nor should it be confused with counselling either (which deals with emotional states in a therapeutic or clinical setting).

L&D FACTS AND FIGURES

The UK's Chartered Institute of Personnel and Development's (CIPD) Annual Training Survey 2004 found that the largest net increases in training provision were in the areas of coaching (51 per cent), e-learning (47 per cent) and mentoring and buddy systems (42 per cent). (*Source*: Training and Development 2004: Survey Report (April 2004). London: CIPD.)

The benefits of developmental coaching are that it gives the one-on-one assistance that may be essential for the realization of personal and career goals; moreover, it can be flexible and hence can be tailored to fit in with work schedules and can give 'quick wins' which may improve individuals' self-efficacy, continuance motivation and commitment to the process. Pitfalls may be encountered when it is not integrated with other aspects of L&D, if the coach and the learners are not well matched, if the wrong type of coaching is being provided (for example, it is being confused with counselling), if the coach is unskilled or if one or more of the parties is not wholly committed. The question may also be asked about which executives are most likely to benefit from executive coaching and hence be worth what may turn out to be a substantial investment. Wasylyshyn (2003) suggests that the executive's motivation, whether or not there are performance problems, the executive's trust in coaching and the likelihood of the executive forming a solid working alliance with the coach should all be taken into account.

PERSPECTIVE FROM PRACTICE: FACILITATING TRANSFER OF LEARNING THROUGH EXECUTIVE COACHING IN THE USA

Based on the following source: G. Olivero, D. K. Bane and R. E. Kopelman, 1997. Executive coaching as a transfer of training tool, *Public Personnel Management*, 26: 461–9.

The authors aimed to explore the ways in which coaching could assist in the transfer of learning from a conventional course to the workplace. They conducted their study in two stages. Participants were 31 top and middle managers and supervisors in a health agency in a city in the north-east of the USA. The first stage consisted of classroom-style three-day interactive workshops, which covered various aspects of the managerial role. Participants were asked to complete a knowledge pre-test and a post-test, as well as a questionnaire to gauge their reactions to the programme. In stage two, eight managers from the group were trained as one-on-one executive coaches and provided coaching for the remaining 23 participants on implementing the new managerial competencies learned in stage one. Each coach provided feedback and guidance during one-hour, weekly coaching sessions over a period of two months (Olivero et al. 1997).

The evaluation of the programme revealed post-test scores to be higher than pre-test scores and the difference was statistically significant. Participants' job performance was measured in terms of the timeliness and correctness of the completion of patient evaluation forms (PEFs). After training the average increase in participants' productivity was 22.4 per cent; when training was augmented by coaching the average increase in productivity was 88 per cent. The authors claimed that these results demonstrated 'the dramatic effects of one-on-one executive coaching as a transfer of training tool' through its effects on goal setting, collaborative problem solving, practice, feedback and supervisory involvement in learning. The coaching also may have had a positive impact upon perceived self-efficacy (widely acknowledged as a key influence upon learning performance in training settings – see Salas and Cannon-Bowers 2001). As a practical tool this form of peer coaching may provide a useful bridge between the learning situation and the work situation and the application of new knowledge and skills (widely acknowledged as an inhibitor in the effectiveness of L&D in general). It can help to change some attributes of the work environment (such as peer support) into which the changed manager is re-immersing him- or herself.

Discussion Point

What are the main threats to the internal validity (see Chapter 9) of the Olivero et al. (1997) study as summarized above? How might the issues you identify have been resolved in the research design phase?

Mentoring

The word 'mentor' is a noun meaning 'an experienced and trusted adviser' (*Oxford Encyclopedic English Dictionary* 1991). Treating it as a verb has led to the term 'mentoring' and also to a new noun 'mentee' (the latter will be avoided here in preference to the term protégé). Mentoring involves the help of an expert and/or experienced senior employee to provide, in a one-to-one relationship, guidance and advice in order to help a less experienced colleague (who may be a newcomer or be experiencing a change in role) cope and grow with relevant aspects of their job role. Coaching and mentoring differ in terms of the nature of the interaction and the skills employed and in terms of the employment relationship (a developmental coach is often external to the organization). Jayne (2003: 37) described a mentor as being someone who has 'already walked the path that their protégé is about to tread – they've been there, done that, and have the [business experience] to prove it'. The differences between a mentor and a developmental coach may be explained in terms of a sporting analogy (Johnson 2001): the coach is usually 'off the court', helps you to play but is not in the team; a mentor is someone who is 'on the court' and can help you develop your game from within. As Johnson also noted, a mentor may have power within the organization and sponsor the protégé into opportunities, and the role may be taken on spontaneously or as a part of a formal system. Instructional and developmental coaching and mentoring are all compatible; they simply serve different functions and are usually provided by different individuals.

The mentor role usually fulfils a number of functions (Kram 1985): psychosocial functions: role modelling, friendship, counselling, acceptance and affirmation; career development functions: including task-related coaching, sponsorship, exposure, visibility, protection and provision of challenging assignments. Gibb and Megginson (1993) further distinguish between a mainstream role – traditional activities of providing induction and development for new employees – and a learning support role – activities that are geared towards specific vocational goals. Research suggests positive relationships between the functions provided by a mentor and a protégé's career progression (for example, Fagenson 1989; Arnold and Johnson 1997).

L&D FACTS AND FIGURES

The term 'mentor' is derived from a character in Homer's *Odyssey*. The story goes that as a result of Odysseus' travels, Telemachus (son of Odysseus and Penelope) had been deprived of a father figure to serve as a role model. The goddess Athena intervened in Telemachus' life as part of her felt obligation to Odysseus and set out in the guise of Mentor to educate, support and develop Telemachus. Telemachus grew physically and mentally, and by giving him new challenges of increasing complexity Mentor's role transformed from instructor and trainer to supporter and enabler. As Telemachus gained in confidence Mentor's support was reduced, and he was eventually left to carry on without Mentor's support, making the transformation from 'timid youth to self-confident and resourceful man' (Gibb 2002: 270). (*Source:* S. Gibb, 2002. *Learning and Development: Processes, Practices and and Perspectives at Work*, Basingstoke: Palgrave Macmillan.)

Hegstad (1999) argued that the processes involved in the mentor–protégé relationship may be explained in terms of social exchange theory, which hypothesizes that such relationships are an exchange of social performances and that the motivation to enter into a relationship is the expectation of obtaining a reward of some sort. There is reciprocity to the extent that all parties will expect to derive benefits and both will incur costs (Rollinson and Broadfield 2002: 323). The exchange can go beyond the individual: for example, an individual who has received the benefits of a mentor–protégé relationship may serve to mentor another person or repay the organization in some way (via continuance commitment, for example) (Hegstad 1999), giving a multiplier effect. In her application of social exchange theory to the mentor-protégé relationship, Hegstad hypothesized that the relationships between the antecedents (individual demographics, previous experience of mentors, career stage, job level) and outcomes (psychosocial and career development benefits, organizational commitment, motivation, performance, retention) are moderated by several factors. For example, feedback and communication between mentor and protégé, reward systems (which can either help or hinder) and the organizational systems or policies whereby mentors and protégés are selected and matched. A moderator variable modifies the intensity (higher or lower) and/or the sign (positive or negative) of the relationship between an independent and a dependent variable (Mbengue and Vandangeon-Derumez 2001: 269). The moderated relationship as hypothesized by Hegstad is shown in Figure 7.4.

The benefits of mentoring to protégés and their organizations are well documented (for example, rewards, promotions, satisfaction and commitment), but according to Hegstad both mentors and protégés stand to gain from the exchange. Mentors may benefit from enhanced professional and psychosocial development, increased visibility, more respect, and power and enhanced professional identity and networking opportunities. On the other hand, failure is also possible as a

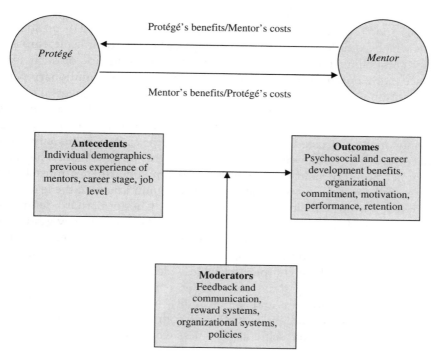

Figure 7.4 Social exchange in mentoring (adapted from Rollinson and Broadfield 2002: 323) and a model of the mentoring process based on Hegstad (1999)

result of cultural and structural factors in the organization. Harrison (2002) argued that the success of any mentor programme depends upon its active support by senior managers, the setting of clear objectives, monitoring and evaluation of the programme, and sufficient level of resources to support mentors and protégés. To be effective as a mentor an individual needs to be a good listener, confident and clear about their own position, senior enough to be well informed, knowledgeable in relevant areas, supportive of the objectives of the mentor programme, accessible and accepting of their mentor role (Walton 1999: 194–195).

Discussion Point

Can the various management L&D methods outlined above be justified on theoretical grounds? In other words, what are the theoretical bases for their use in management L&D? Explain your reasoning.

Leaders and Leadership

Leaders have been seen as crucial players in human endeavour throughout history and the term 'leader' has valiant, just and heroic connotations. In Ancient Greece the leader was often portrayed as a noble individual who was only interested in what was good for Athens, and not in increasing his own wealth or prestige. Individuals who become leaders often earn their place because their leadership is emotionally compelling (Goleman et al. 2003) and the influence of such leaders' influence many not, of course, always be benign. From an evolutionary perspective Nicholson (2000) argued that 'dominance is a biological universal among all social mammals' and that, as such, human beings 'demand' leaders. In classical times Plato attempted to persuade his fellow Greeks that the 'captain of the boat' is the only one to be trusted with its control, since the captain is the only one with the necessary expert knowledge (Grint 1997) . In ancient China the military philosopher Sun Tzu held that commitment from subordinates must be based upon perceived justice and reasonableness, not a commitment to the leader's goal through fear (Grint 1997). In the twentieth century Chester Barnard defined leadership as the 'quality of the behaviour of individuals whereby they guide people or their activities in organised effort' (1948: 91). For Barnard the effectiveness of the leader–follower relationship was, in quasi-mathematical language, a function of the interaction of three complex variables – leader, follower and conditions. Barnard also argued that some of a leader's most effective behaviours (for example, vitality, decisiveness and responsibility) are not to any great extent intellectual; rather they are largely a 'matter of course', they are unconscious and responsive to the extent that self-consciousness would 'check their force, speed or accuracy' (ibid.: 100).

In modern businesses leadership is increasingly appealed to and sought after as a means to pull organizations through crises, to lead them into new and uncharted territory and to reinvent and revitalize corporations. In early work in the UK by Adair, it was argued that effective leadership is a function of the interaction between the leader, the situation and the team, and that the overlapping needs of the task (achievement), the team (building) and the individual (developing) have to be focused upon at all times. In the USA Moss-Kanter made the point that people want to believe that there are leaders who can 'walk on water' but we should be aware that beneath the surface there are 'large boulders holding up each individual, such as past experience and mentors' (Hill 2004: 122). Leaders have great responsibility thrust upon them and they are often seen as the panacea for social and organizational problems (Bolman and Deal 2003: 336). Indeed recent decades have, if anything, witnessed an increasing reliance upon leaders with the emphasis in organizations changing from administration, to management, to leadership (Stewart and McGoldrick 1996: 15). Strategic leadership is receiving increased attention, given the observations that strategic leaders and executive succession practices have significant effects on the overall performance of an organization (Aditya et al. 2000). Leadership has become one of the most topical issues in management practice and it is a vibrant and lucrative element of the management and executive education market (Ready and Conger 2003). Ashkanasy (2004: 165) has argued that it is hard to overstate the importance of leadership in today's corporate environment, especially in the light of business failures and the critical role that leadership can play in almost every aspect of corporate and communal life. Leaders are critical to organizational success and so their learning is also a crucial aspect of L&D, but as with many other aspects of L&D, it is crucial that efforts at leadership L&D are directed in the right way. In the remainder of this chapter we will begin by revisiting the concept of the 'leader', examine the importance of their learning and development and explore some of the ways in which it may be facilitated. The chapter will end with a consideration of the concept of the 'learning leader'.

L&D FACTS AND FIGURES

The significance that organizations attach to leadership is perhaps reflected in the levels of expenditure on leadership education and development, estimated at $50 billion in the USA in 2000 (Ready and Conger 2003). Such levels of expenditure are only worthwhile if leadership L&D is effective. Other research has suggested that US corporations may waste between $5.6 and $16.8 billion each year on ineffective leadership development (Connaughton et al. 2003: 46).

Rollinson and Broadfield (2002: 357) summarized many of the salient issues in leadership theory and research when they made the following observations:

- a leader's influence is non-coercive;
- leadership is goal-directed;
- leadership authority is conferred by others from below;
- followers confer leadership upon an individual whom they perceive has the capacity to attain a specific goal;
- leaders may satisfy group members' socio-emotive as well as their task needs;
- leadership is a two-way reciprocal process in which leaders' and followers' needs are satisfied in the relationship;
- leader–follower relationships are dynamic and fragile.

Leadership does not necessarily stem from formal hierarchies (a person can be a leader without a position of formal authority); rather leadership is exercised through a subtle process of mutual influence to produce a cooperative effort (Bolman and Deal 2003). Rollinson and Broadfield offer the following definitions:

Leadership: 'a process in which leaders and followers interact in a way that enables the leader to influence the actions of followers in a non-coercive way, towards the achievement of certain aims of objectives' (2003: 357).

Leader: 'a person who occupies a role which involves conforming to a set of behavioural norms and expectations emanating from followers, in return for which they confer on the leader a degree of power which allows the leader to influence their actions' (2003: 361).

Leadership research has been a vibrant area of management scholarship over the past half century and even the briefest consideration of this is beyond the present scope. A concise summary is to be found in Aditya et al. (2000). One of the most recent and influential theories is the full-range leadership model of Bass and Avolio (1994). Their theory draws upon a distinction between transactional leadership (most suited to stable situations in which the leader diagnoses the followers' needs and adopts an appropriate style) and transformational leadership (most suited to changing environments and where the leader communicates to followers what needs to be done to cope with the change and rise to the challenge). Dvir et al. (2002) argued that the final two decades of the twentieth century witnessed some convergence in leadership theories around the concepts of the 'transformational', charismatic' and 'visionary' leadership. The four key characteristics of the transformational leader originally suggested by Bass and Avolio are: charisma (comprising expertise, articulateness, trustworthiness and sensitivity), vision (sensitivity and foresight), intellectual stimulation of followers and, finally, individualized consideration of followers and the taking of their needs into account and providing them with recognition and opportunities for achievement (Dvir et al. 2002). But, as with earlier models of leadership, the transactional–transformational model is not without its difficulties:

1. The attributes of the transformational leader arguably are difficult to define, and hence from an L&D point of view may be difficult to develop.
2. Leader charisma is particularly difficult one since it is often viewed as the vital prerequisite but may in fact not be a necessity to shape a visionary company (Collins and Porras 2000; Sadler 2001).
3. The transformational style is sometimes glorified and the transactional style denigrated whereas in reality they may be mutually reinforcing components of effective and efficient leadership (Rollinson and Broadfield 2002: 395).

L&D FACTS AND FIGURES

The Greek word *kharisma* is from *kharis* meaning 'favour' or 'grace'. Charisma is defined as: (a) the ability to inspire followers with devotion and enthusiasm; (b) an attractive aura or great charm. (*Source*: *Oxford Encyclopedic English Dictionary*, 1991).

On the basis of a review of the leadership literature and the insights from their own consulting practices, Goffee and Jones (2000: 64) argued that inspirational leaders appear to share a number of unexpected qualities: they selectively show their weaknesses and their differences; they manage their followers with 'tough empathy'; and they 'rely heavily on intuition to gauge the appropriate timing of their actions'. More recently still Bolman and Deal (2003) have attempted to reconceptualize leadership in terms of four metaphorical frames through which organizations may be viewed: a structural frame (organizations as 'factories'); a human resources (HR) frame (organizations as 'families'); a political frame (organizations as 'jungles'); and a symbolic frame (organizations as 'theatres' or 'temples'). In Bolman and Deal's model an effective leader, when viewed within each frame, has number of characteristics (see Table 7.5). An alternative approach to the concept of leadership, from a cognitive perspective, is offered by Sternberg as a response to the perceived criticism that traditional models of leaderships are too narrow. Sternberg's model is based on the argument that an individual needs to synthesize three key cognitive and behavioural components in order to be effective as a leader. The three components are wisdom, intelligence and creativity (WICs) – see Figure 7.5.

Before considering how leadership development should occur, we must ask what it should set out to achieve. In terms of 'what' leadership L&D should attempt to accomplish, as in the case of management competence, certain professional institutes and other bodies have attempted to formulate their own definitions. For example, the UK government, through the Management Standards Centre and professional bodies such as the Chartered Institute of Personnel and Development (CIPD), have developed their own sets of leadership standards. In the USA the Academy of Human Resource Development (AHRD) has developed its own leadership competency model.

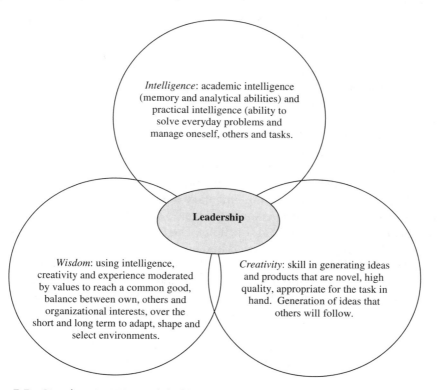

Figure 7.5   Sternberg's WICs model of leadership (adapted from Sternberg 2003: 387)

Table 7.5   Four images of leadership (adapted from Bolman and Deal 2003)

Frame	Description
Structural leaders	'Analysts and architects'; they do their 'homework', focus on implementation, and experiment, evaluate and adapt; however they become ineffective if they behave as 'petty tyrants' (Bolman and Deal, 2003: 349).
HR leaders	'Catalysts and servants'; they believe in people (and they let them know), are visible and accessible, and empower others; they are ineffective if they become 'weaklings or pushovers' (ibid.).
Political leaders	'Advocates and negotiators'; they clarify what they want and what they can get, they assess the power bases, they build linkages to key stakeholders and prefer to persuade and negotiate and coerce only if they have to; they are ineffective if they become 'con artists or thugs' (ibid.).
Symbolic leaders	'Prophets and poets'; they lead by example, they use visible and dramatic symbols to capture attention, communicate a vision and tell stories, show respect and use history; they are ineffective when they become 'fanatics or fools' (ibid.).

PERSPECTIVE FROM PRACTICE: LEADERSHIP COMPETENCY FROM A US L&D PERSPECTIVE

Based on the following source: E. F. Holton and S. S. Naquin (eds), 2000. Developing high-performance leadership competency, *Advances in Developing Human Resources*, Monograph 6.

The purpose of the AHRD's high-performance leadership competency model was to merge leadership research with performance improvement theory by drawing upon multiple leadership perspectives. The approach acknowledges a distinction between management and leadership skills and functions, but sees them as complementary to the extent that there are probably few instances where a person can develop leadership skills without also being competent at managerial functions. The AHRD model is based around three leadership performance levels and six competency domains (see Table 7.6). The model does not adhere strictly to the transactional/transformational model of leadership (though this is acknowledged), rather it attempts to be integrative. The model is comprehensive in its coverage and is reductionist and functionalist in its approach; visioning, for example, is broken down to include performance statements such as 'creates a shared vision of the organization' and 'specifies the future state of the organization's core processes'. How these might be operationalized and measured is perhaps an area for debate.

Table 7.6 AHRD's high-performance leadership competency framework. (*Source*: Holton and Naquin 2000)

Performance level	Competency domain	Competency group
Organization level	Strategic thinking	Organizational analysis Visioning Strategy formulation Organizational design
	Strategic stewardship	Performance management Goals management Interface management Resource management Change management
Process level	Process management	Understanding and identifying Establishing goals Team management
	Process planning	Improvement Development Measurement system design
Individual level	Employee performance	Goal setting Rewards and coaching Motivating commitment Assessment
	Employee potential	Employee development Suportive environment HR systems Job and work redesign

In terms of what leadership development should set out to achieve, Day (2001) argued that a distinction exists between leader and leadership development on the basis of the relational aspects of the competencies involved. Leader development emphasizes the development of individual knowledge and skills associated with a formal leadership role (an intrapersonal competence base). In leadership development, on the other hand, the primary emphasis is on building and using an interpersonal competence base (2001: 585). Examples of the intrapersonal skills of a leader might include self-awareness, self-regulation and self-motivation, whereas interpersonal leadership skills might include social awareness (such as empathy) and social skills (for example, conflict management) (Day 2001). Leadership L&D assumes that leadership itself is a function of the social resources embedded in relationships, for example, 'How can we participate productively and collaboratively in the leadership process' (see Drath and Palus 1994; Day 2001: 605).

One of the functions of leadership is an alignment of a group of individuals towards the achievement of a common goal. This alignment has technical and intellectual components, but it also has an emotional component that is arguably crucial to the synergy of the group's efforts in relation to the goal. Goleman et al. (2002: 270) suggested that the leader's 'attunement' to a vision in a way that motivates enthusiasm and arouses a passion requires a 'direct connection with peoples' emotional centres' (271) via emotional intelligence. In an earlier work Goleman (1998: 187) argued that for high-performance leadership the emotional, as opposed to technical or cognitive, competencies 'make up 80 to 100 percent' of those needed for success. An effective CEO in these terms might have three main clusters of competencies – one cognitive and two in the domain of emotional intelligence:

1. Cognitive: thinking strategically, broad scanning, seeking out information and application of conceptual thinking.
2. Personal competencies: achievement, self-confidence and commitment (similar to the intrapersonal domain).
3. Social competencies: influence, political awareness and empathy (the interpersonal domain).

These emotional competencies are both intrapersonal (for example, self-confidence) and interpersonal (influence) aspects of leader and leadership learning and development (leadership L&D) – see also Day (2001). Emotional competencies manifest themselves in prescriptive models of leadership development. For example, the US Army's Be-Know-Do (BKD) model specifies the emotional attributes of self-control, balance and stability alongside mental attributes (such as will and self-discipline) and physical attributes (such as health and physical fitness) (see Campbell and Dardis 2004).

Leadership L&D Methods

There is an aphorism that leaders are 'born and not made' and if this is true it raises a number of questions, potential contradictions and tensions for the practice of leadership L&D. The question of whether leaders are born or made is frequently asked. Kouzes and Posner (2002: 386) expressed the view that leadership is an 'observable set of skills and abilities . . . and any skill can be strengthened, honed and enhanced, given the motivation and desire, the practice and feedback, and the role models and coaching'. The question was explored in some detail by Doh (2003), who examined four important questions for leadership L&D. Can leadership be learned? Can leadership be taught? How can leadership be taught? To whom and by whom can it be taught? In endeavouring to find answers to these questions Doh interviewed a number of leading US scholars in the field of leadership theory and research. Some of the views expressed by the Doh's 'gurus' are summarized in Table 7.7. One of the main implications for leadership L&D, as revealed by Doh's questioning, is that whether or not the necessary leader and leadership skills can be developed in the classroom is an open question (there is variability in the responses given). But what does not appear to be in doubt is that when leadership L&D does take place it should rely on what Doh termed 'heuristics' (a better term might be workplace-relevant practices), such as coaching, mentoring, looking for patterns and experience-based approaches (2003: 66). Conger expressed the view that leaders are 'born and made', by which he meant that some of the leadership qualities, such as self-confidence and drive, may be formed early on in life but, more importantly, later life experiences (often in times of hardship and intense challenge) can account for successful leadership performance (2004: 136). The notion of hardship and adversity in leader development also emerged in the concept of 'crucibles of leadership' as advanced by Bennis and Thomas (2002). Their argument was that one of the most reliable indicators of leadership is an individual's ability to construct meaning from negative events and learn from them under the most trying of circumstances (2002: 39). A crucible literally means a 'small melting pot' and the trying circumstances that Bennis and

Table 7.7 Experts' views on the learning and teaching of leadership (*Source*: Doh 2003)

Question	Summary of selected reponses
Can leadership be learned?	'Some managers have a head start . . . but everyone can improve.' (Useem)
	'Not everyone can become an outstanding player . . . yet most will benefit and improve their "game".' (Conger)
	'If you don't focus your efforts and work at it you won't be an effective leader.' (Stumpf)
Can leadership be taught?	'There is a critical contextual dimension . . . which is the product of immersion in one's field . . . [this] is difficult to teach.' (Conger)
	'Of course. But the methods need to focus on creating meaningful experiences . . . what is taught – to be useful – must be learned in personal, applicable and more intuitive way.' (Stumpf)
	'Some of the tacit dimensions may be conveyed through experiential teaching.' (Hitt)
How can leadership be taught?	Synthesizing lessons from own experiences
	Coaching and mentoring
	Practice with feedback in realistic, rich environments (simulations, internships, role plays, etc.)
	Case studies and action learning for strategic thinking
	Experiential exercises for behavioural skills
	Discussing leadership failures as well as successes
To whom can leadership be taught?	Individuals with high achievement and ambition needs, capacity for strategic thinking, pragmatism, minimum level of persuasive and inspirational communication skills, emotional intelligence, learning orientation and desire to lead (Conger)
	Motivation to lead and interpersonal maturity based on experience (Stumpf)
	Emotional intelligence (Useem)

Thomas' interviewees cited included negative experiences of prejudice, illness and violence, as well as positive experiences of challenging and demanding assignments under the guidance of a powerful mentor. They suggested that great leaders possess four essential skills:

1. Engaging others in shared meaning.
2. Exercising a distinctive and compelling voice.
3. Exhibiting one's sense of integrity and strong value set.
4. Adaptability which can transcend adversity (Bennis and Thomas 2002: 45).

PERSPECTIVE FROM RESEARCH: DEVELOPING TRANSFORMATIONAL LEADERSHIP SKILLS

Based on the following source: T. Dvir, D. Eden, B. J. Avolio and B. Shamir, 2002. Impact of transformational leadership on follower development and performance: a field experiment, *Academy of Management Journal*, 45(4): 735–44.

This research further explored the question of the trainability of leadership and its concomitant effects down the line upon followers. The aim of this experimental study was to test the impact of transformational leadership, enhanced by training, upon follower development and follower performance. The study involved two groups of leaders from the armed forces (comprising 54 leaders who had 90 direct followers and 724 indirect followers), who were randomly assigned either to a treatment condition in which they received transformational leadership training ($N = 32$) or a control group where they received routine eclectic leadership training ($N = 22$). The workshops both for experimental and control groups employed role play, group discussions, simulations, presentation, videos, and peer and trainer feedback. There were several measures used in the study that are pertinent to our discussions:

1. Transformational leadership was measured using the Multifactor Leadership Questionnaire (MLQ) 5X (Avolio et al. 1999).
2. Development of followers was assessed using self-report measures of a number of variables including self-efficacy, collectivistic orientation, critical-independent approach and active engagement .
3. Performance of followers was measured by means of a written test and a number of practical tests (including use of equipment, physical fitness and obstacle course).

The analysis of the results revealed statistically significant differences between the treatment and control groups in terms of the effects upon direct followers' self-efficacy ($p < 0.05$), collectivist orientation ($p = 0.06$) and critical-independent approach ($p < 0.01$) and upon indirect followers' perform-ance on the written ($p < 0.05$), practical ($p = 0.08$) and obstacle course tests ($p < 0.01$). These results suggested that leaders in the experimental group (i.e. who had undergone transformational leadership training) had a more pos-itive impact on direct followers' development and on indirect followers' per-formance than did the leaders in the control group (i.e. who had undergone routine leadership training). The research may be taken as indicating that providing individuals with the knowledge and skills of transformational leadership can have a positive knock-on effect upon important areas of direct follower development (thus initiating a cascade effect), and further down the chain an effect upon the performance of indirect followers may also be wit-nessed. It appears therefore that not only can transformational leadership be taught, but also that it may have a real impact upon those not directly involved in the learning.

Leadership development is a high-profile L&D activity and one which has a high payback potential. From an L&D perspective there are a number of implications that may be drawn from the various leadership models, theories and research con-sidered thus far:

1. Leaders need to be sensitive to the readiness of followers to behave in partic-ular ways.
2. Leaders should have or acquire the skills of being able to identify followers' readiness.
3. Leaders must be aware of their own leadership style and have the capacity to vary their style in accordance with the circumstances.
4. Leaders must be attentive to the context in which they operate and their capa-bilities to lead within that context; for example, the leadership qualities required in a business start-up are different from those required for sustain-ing success (Conger 2004: 138).
5. Leaders must be responsive to the dynamics of the leader–follower relation-ship and the extent to which followers are developing new skills and compe-tencies. Leader behaviour should reflect these changes.
6. Leaders must exhibit modesty to the extent that they are prepared to relin-quish their leadership role and hand over authority to others more suited to the task or context; hence for leadership development to be effective there needs to be succession planning.

In our consideration of leadership L&D we are concerned with the attributes of a leader that are worthwhile attempting to develop; however, given the complex and contingent nature of leadership, specifying a 'recipe' is not only chal-lenging, but also arguably inappropriate. Indeed it is unsurprising that it has been argued that there is no universal leadership approach that should be taught and learned by all. One alternative is to outline some broad principles and then examine practical examples of leadership development in action.

PERSPECTIVE FROM RESEARCH: THE SEARCH FOR BROAD PRINCIPLES FOR LEADERSHIP L&D

Based on the following source: S. L. Connaughton, F. L. Lawrence and B. D. Ruben, 2003. Leadership development as a systematic and multidisciplinary enterprise, *Journal of Education for Business*, September/October: 46–51.

Connaughton et al. (2003), whilst noting that there is no shortage of leadership models or popular guides to developing leadership, identified a number of principles that might inform L&D practice. These have been described and reinterpreted below to develop some assumptions upon which leadership L&D might be based:

1. Leadership is complex and there are many factors associated with the individual, the context and their interaction. Leadership is contextual to the extent that it is difficult to treat it in a decontextualized and abstract way. Indeed, 'the very meaning of leadership may depend upon the kind of institution in which it is found' (Bass 1995: 38). Prescriptive approaches to leadership L&D are unlikely to be effective.
2. Leadership is other-oriented in terms of serving followers, influencing them, understanding and inspiring them as well as coordinating and directing them. Leadership L&D should include these competencies.
3. Leadership is not a static phenomenon but involves interactive and dynamic interplay between individuals and their contexts. Leader–member relations are crucial in this interplay. Leadership L&D should include interpersonal competencies.
4. Leadership is emergent over time in terms of the role of leader, the influence of leaders, and who the leaders are. Leadership L&D should take cognizance of the medium to longer term both in relation to whom it targets and the likely outcomes and payback.
5. Leadership is an art as well as a science, to the extent that social scientific principles in the abstract must be interpreted and applied by each individual in ways that are commensurate with her or his own personality, skills, experience, values, capabilities, goals and contextual assessments. Leadership L&D should acknowledge and attempt to accommodate individual differences in styles and preferences.
6. Leadership is enacted through communication since leaders should not only conceive a vision but articulate it to others and enact it through

others. This communication and enactment occurs through verbal, non-verbal and symbolic means (Witherspoon 1997). Leadership L&D should encompass reflection and dialogue.

7. Leadership is becoming increasingly mediated and virtual in its nature in a world where organizations and individuals' interactions and cognitions are distributed spatially and temporally. Leaders may find themselves interacting with individuals in other parts of the world through networked computers; followers may be in other time zones (Connaughton et al. 2003). Leadership L&D should recognize the role that technology plays in leadership per se and the potential that it may offer for developmental activities.

Connaughton et al. also asserted that leadership can be learned and taught, but if it is to be successful the methods used must relate to desired outcomes; learners must have the opportunities to apply lessons learned; learners must be able to reflect with peers and experts; and finally, learners must have the opportunity to learn from experienced leaders through observing, listening and interacting with them.

Hernez-Broom and Hughes (2004), in observing the trend in leadership L&D over the past few decades, noted that classroom-type leadership training and development is now often complemented or even supplanted in some cases by a whole range of alternative approaches. This change in emphasis parallels a similar transformation in L&D more generally as experientially, andragogically and action-based methods have penetrated practice over the past two decades and more. Coaching, mentoring, action learning, outdoor development, reflective journaling and 360° feedback are all examples of methods that are increasingly used in leadership development (Hernez-Broom and Hughes 2004).

Conger and Fulmer (2003) concurred with the view that one-off educational experiences are often insufficient, and that it is far better to pair classroom 'training' with real-life exposure to a variety of jobs and bosses through job rotation, special projects and action learning. This aligns well with the emergent view in L&D in general that the 'blending' of appropriate methods is potentially one of the most effective ways of enhancing the impact that L&D can have upon performance. We will now consider some of the methods that may used to facilitate leadership L&D, with two provisos: firstly, that none of these is likely to be effective on its own, and secondly, that although considered under the heading of leadership development some of them could equally also be used for management development purposes (indeed some have argued that there may be little point in practice in separating out leaders and managers when it comes to development – see Campbell and Dardis 2004: 27). Gist and McDonald-Mann (2000) distinguish between skills-based leadership L&D (including lecture, case study, role play, behavioural modelling and simulation), feedback-intensive L&D (including group discussions, 360º feedback), distance learning and executive education. We will examine team building, outdoor leadership development, emotional intelligence and succession planning as examples of leadership development tools.

Team Leadership and Team Building

Recent decades have witnessed pressures for decreased product development times, increased process efficiency, better functional integration and more adaptability and flexibility in order to respond to changed market conditions. Companies are required to respond speedily and effectively to customer demands, changes in requirements and new and novel business problems. This has meant that job design and work systems in many organizations have had to be reconfigured, often alongside far-reaching reductions in the numbers of job levels, reduced bureaucracy and decentralization (Boxall and Purcell 2003). There have been concomitant increases in employee empowerment that have meant that individuals and teams interface directly with customers and suppliers and are also involved in making decisions for themselves under new forms of management and leadership. The need for integration of organizational processes has meant that activities that were previously separate both in space and time now need to be tightly coupled. Many of these moves are linked to the development of teams and team working, seen by some managers as the 'fundamental building block of the organisation' (Boxall and Purcell 2003: 105).

L&D FACTS AND FIGURES

In the UK in the 1970s and 1980s R. Meredith Belbin established the concept of team roles on the basis of research carried out at the Industrial Training Research Unit (ITRU) in Cambridge and during management development work at Henley Management College. In group syndicate exercises Belbin observed that some teams functioned better than others and attributed this to the teams' compositions. Belbin developed the *Belbin Team-Role Self-Perception Inventory (BTRSPI)* as a means by which L&D practitioners can identify individuals' preferences for particular team roles (of which there are nine). This diagnosis can then be used as a basis for group exercises or to identify work teams' learning needs. Similar approaches have been adopted in the USA by Glenn Parker, with his concept of 'team player'.

Self-directed teams or self-managed teams have the delegated leader or manager responsibility that previously would have been held by a higher level or levels of managerial hierarchy (for example, for budgets, selection, planning, scheduling, control and deployment of resources). Self-directed teams are not the only type of work group; other types of teams include cross-functional management teams (Torrington et al. 2002: 323), which may have been put together for the purposes of a particular project (as in the case of new product development). In this case each member of the team brings with them the expertise from their own function (for example, technology, marketing, finance or human resources). Other types of team include functional teams (made up of members from within a function, for example, the HR team or L&D team) and problem-solving teams (coming-together of individuals from within or across functions) (Torrington et al. 2002).

Integral to the process of team working is the learning of the members of the team, including the development of leader–follower relationships. Teams are both a way of meeting organizational objectives (for example, in terms of production targets, enabling work schedules and so forth) and also a powerful means by which new knowledge can be created within the community of the team to the extent that they may form a 'focal point for learning' (Boxall and Purcell 2003: 107). The keys to effective team performance lie in how well the team is led, how members of the team relate to and interact with each other and the extent to which the team learns collectively. A crucial role for the L&D function in this regard is enabling effective team leadership and promoting team development in order that the team can become the focal point for organizational learning. According to Dyer, to function effectively a team and its leadership needs to be developed to the extent that the members of the team are able to:

- engage in face-to-face interaction so that the members can influence each other in productive ways;
- exhibit interdependence through structured relationships;
- have a sense of identity to the extent that individuals perceive themselves to be a member of the team;
- aspire to commonly held goals through interdependent tasks (Dyer 1995: 24–5).

To this list can be added the need to have clearly delineated roles and responsibilities, foremost amongst which is the role of the leader. The issue of identifying team member contributions as a way of selecting teams or identifying team development needs is well documented in the work of Belbin and others. But what are the downstream activities from this team needs assessment that may be implemented in order to improve team effectiveness, and in particular through leadership L&D? Torrington et al. identified three potential areas of need:

1. Team leader and manager training: newly nominated team leaders (and team managers) are being required to take on a new role (including by taking on more responsibility or giving up control); hence team leader L&D is likely to encompass both the skills of delegation and management as well as the attitudinal aspects of the changing philosophy of working practices in the organization, for example through increased involvement, empowerment and participation.

2. Team member training: all members of teams (followers and leaders) are likely to need some L&D input with respect to their new team role, which may include general skills such as problem solving, communication and time management.
3. Team development: this is the broadest and most important area of team learning and members need to come to a joint understanding of the core purpose of the team, to visualize the team's future role and develop their roles and ways of working for the team. The way in which this aspect of team L&D is configured is likely to depend to some extent upon the stage of development that the team is at.

Dyer (1995) offered a 'top-down' approach as one way of developing a team. He argued that the critical shift is away from power being located in 'the boss' to a situation in which goals and decisions are made jointly by the members and the leader. As a result communication channels are opened up, team members (formerly 'subordinates') initiate actions and plans, and differences and conflicts are worked through rather than being smoothed over. From a collective learning perspective this can involve a transition in the role of the team leader from educator to coach to facilitator (as part of a team development process – Dyer 1995: 49). Dyer's model is summarized in Table 7.8. Within this model the leader is seen as the prime mover of team development and one of her or his functions is to facilitate the movement of the team through the natural stages of development by assuming a number of leader roles. The actual process can take place in formal settings (for example, the classroom) or informal workplace settings (such as meetings and in the course of projects) and can comprise whatever activities are appropriate to the learning and the team's stage of development. The actual activities may include group discussions, cognitive mapping exercises to surface and share mental models, public reflection and dialogue, role playing, case study, scenario analyses, simulations and so forth.

Table 7.8 Dyer's staged model of team leader development (*Source*: Dyer 1995: 49–58)

Stage	Leader role	Description
1	*Leader as Educator*	Developing the team's understanding of the characteristics of a team and the roles involved (for example: sharing power, sharing leadership, developing working guidelines, identifying key roles and individual skills).
2	*Leader as Coach*	Intervening at appropriate points to draw attention to team processes and how these may need to be adjusted, reclarification of roles, guidelines and so forth. Passing on through social interaction relevant aspects of process and content.
3	*Leader as Facilitator*	Intervening only when there is a matter that is not dealt with collaboratively and cooperatively within the team. The team works organically and largely autonomously with minimal directive input from leader.

PERSPECTIVE FROM PRACTICE: A 'CULINARY' APPROACH TO TEAM DEVELOPMENT IN ILLINOIS, USA

Based on the following source: H. Prager, 1999. Cooking-up effective team building, *Training & Development*, December: 14–15.

The search for increasingly innovative and more effective team-building methods continues unabated in an L&D market that seems to have an insatiable appetite for novel solutions. The Lake Forest School of Management, Illinois has developed this to new extremes with 'team banquets'. The concept is based on the assertion that some of the 'most effective and efficient teams in the world are to be found in the kitchens of fine restaurants' (1999: 14). The programme was developed with an internationally known chef and involved 25–30 employees, divided into teams, with a head chef and five assistant chefs chosen at random (for example, a clerk could be the head chef and the manager one of the five assistants).

The overall task was for the participants to prepare a gourmet banquet within two hours using the raw ingredients and equipment provided. Each team was assigned a particular part of the banquet to prepare. The results were judged by the teams in terms of the leadership and team working (as well as the culinary) results. Anecdotal reports by one participant claimed parallels to her own industry (printing) in the following ways: effective communication and following procedures were essential, as were cooperation and the analogy for the workplace provided by the kitchen. Although the kitchen was far removed from participants' workplaces, the analogical value is that it provides a means for dialogue and reflection about real-world practices.

On the basis of these experiences in implementing the team banquet Prager suggested some general guidelines for choosing a team development programme:

1. Use an approach that fits with the organizational culture.
2. Ensure that the outcomes of the exercise match the learning and development needs of the participants.
3. Use a scenario that will translate into skills and learning in the participants' workplace.
4. Stretch people by placing them outside of their comfort zones (but not too far) and outside of their familiar physical work environment.

Discussion Point

Given the views expressed by Mumford regarding the use of certain types of simulations (recall that in his view they may be seen as replacing 'reality with fantasy' and hence may run the risk of being perceived by managers as 'unreal'), to what extent do you think it is valid to use the techniques such those outlined from Lake Forest? Justify your reasoning.

Outdoor Development

Outdoor development is a set of techniques in which structured (often physical) activities are used in an out-of-doors environment to help individuals (often leaders or managers but also whole teams as well) to learn and develop. In the UK the direct antecedents of outdoor development are youth organizations, the military and the Outward Bound Trust (Badger et al. 1997). In the 1980s government training programmes in the UK often advocated outdoor development as a vehicle for personal development and it appears to have been a significant growth area in the UK during the 1990s (Woodall and Winstanley 1998). The activities that are used in outdoor development often centre upon projects based around physical activities, which are designed to develop and challenge individuals' skills in areas such as decision making, team working, leadership, problem solving and communication. Its potential benefits are that:

1. Tasks can be designed to mimic organizational structures, processes and hierarchies and hence their outcomes have real and immediate consequences.
2. It affords a safe environment and may provide opportunities for the pace of learning to be accelerated and experiment beyond the bounds of what may be acceptable in the workplace (Badger et al. 1997).

The theoretical basis that is usually offered is the ubiquitous experiential learning cycle whereby the activities are based upon an experience, followed by reflection, drawing conclusions and action planning. The types of experiences used in outdoor development activities are often in the form of physical problem-solving exercises. These are sometimes disparagingly referred to as 'planks and oil drums' exercises since in the past a typical exercise might have been to lead the team across a river using the wooden planks and empty oil drums provided. Outdoor development has moved on, but where the traditional 'planks and drums'-type exercise is used nowadays it has to be strongly justified (Woodall and Winstanley 1998: 177). The intention is to offer opportunities for development in various management and leadership skills as well as providing a forum for self-analysis and reflection (Reid and Barrington 1999: 349). Most programmes offer a mixture of outdoor and classroom-based activities as well as opportunities for self-diagnosis and feedback. An outdoor development event (or indeed any L&D activity) should not be seen as self-contained, since it must encompass an element of action planning for the transfer and application of the learning to the workplace. Outdoor development can have a number of leadership development purposes, some of which are also related to team building (see above):

1. Developing a newly formed team: it can be used in an attempt to bind individuals together into a close-knit group as a precursor to longer-term team development through work assignments or at various crucial milestones in a group's development (Harrison 2002: 290).

2. Developing an existing team: this provides the opportunity for a whole workgroup from an organization to spend time away from the workplace in a structured and challenging environment.

3. Identifying, practising and developing leaders' skills: outdoor development activities may be used to identify the extent to which particular individuals already have leadership skills. It can also be used to develop leadership skills by allowing space for simulation and practice in a structured and safe environment.

As Woodall and Winstanley noted, the process needs to be handled carefully as there can be a number of complications. For example, when developing an existing team, if participants are not all of the same status there may be some disruption to group dynamics. Enhancing group solidarity through team building away from the workplace may create a 'them and us' attitude when the group returns to the workplace (Woodall and Winstanley 1998). One further problem pertains to some of the physical exercises that may be used in that they may favour younger and fitter individuals and may even be discriminatory (Truelove 1995: 302). An increased use of such programmes in the UK in the 1980s led to a growth in the number of providers, who were of varying quality (Woodall and Winstanley 1998: 177). In recent years the emphasis in many of these programmes has shifted from activities that require physical fitness and good psychomotor skills to activities that might be seen as more realistic and worthwhile, such as environmental and community projects (Irvine and Beard 1999: 368).

PERSPECTIVE FROM RESEARCH: END-USER PERCEPTIONS OF OUTDOOR DEVELOPMENT IN THE UK

Based on the following source: B. Badger, E. Sadler-Smith and E. Michie, 1997. Outdoor management development: use and evaluation, *Journal of European Industrial Training*, 21: 318–25.

The effectiveness of outdoor development is, in the view of Truelove (1995: 300), a 'matter of opinion' and it ultimately may produce better 'canoeists and abseilers' than it does better managers. One problem is the transferability of the knowledge and skills gained from the outdoor situation to the work situation. Some L&D activities may be viewed positively in terms of participants' immediate reactions but their value to the job in the longer run may be less clear. Badger et al. (1997) used questionnaire data from 54 organizations in the UK (35 of whom were users of outdoor development) in an attempt to explore the attitudes of end-users. They found that organizations that had used outdoor development felt that it was an effective part of their overall management development programme and yielded benefits in the areas of personal development, team development, leadership and commu-

Continued

nication. The overwhelming majority of users (95 per cent) felt that the learning was transferable to the workplace and 79 per cent felt that it had enhanced workplace effectiveness for the participants. However, the extent to which these participating organizations were committed to realizing or perceiving these benefits from the outset is not clear from this research. Badger et al. (1997: 325) argued that it is essential that outdoor development has:

- learning objectives that pertain to a real need, that are clearly specified at the outset and are linked to corporate goals;
- a strategy for measuring the impact of the programme in place so as to give 'as clear and unambiguous a view as possible of the ultimate effect'.

They concluded with the view that without these preconditions being met there is the danger that the use of outdoor development may be more as a result of fad, fashion, perceived wisdom and anecdote, rather than hard evidence.

Emotional Intelligence and Its Development

The role of emotions in management generally and in leadership in particular has gained greater salience in recent years. This development may be reflected in the ways in which leadership theory has evolved; for example, the transformational leader is characterized by their emotional impact upon others and the emotional connectedness to followers (Hernez-Broom and Hughes 2004). Goleman et al. (2002: 5) argued that the emotional task of the leader is both the original and most important task of leadership and in this sense is 'primal'. The emotional states of leaders and their followers are reciprocal and hence how leaders manage their emotional states can affect the mood of followers.

L&D FACTS AND FIGURES

One of the very first scientific papers on the construct of emotional intelligence (EI) was by Peter Salovey and Jack Meyer in 1990 and since then EI has, through its appeal to the popular imagination (in the popular view it is most often associated with the work of the Daniel Goleman, whose book *Emotional Intelligence* was a best-seller in 1996), become one of the most widely known and discussed aspects of psychology in both the popular press and the management field, to the extent that its impact has achieved 'epic' proportions.

Certain L&D activities can assist with the deepening of one's emotional resonance with oneself and with others. For example, 360° feedback can deepen a leader's understanding of how their mood is perceived, the role it may play in their performance and the emotional state which they may engender in others. Multi-source and multi-rater feedback can be a useful way for individuals to build the intrapersonal competencies demanded of the leader's role. Kets de Vries (Couto 2004) singled out emotional intelligence (in terms of self-reflectivity and how comfortable followers feel with a leader) as being of crucial importance in leadership. The arguments relating to emotional intelligence underline the significance of the development of intra- and interpersonal competencies in any leadership L&D programme.

PERSPECTIVE FROM RESEARCH: DEVELOPING EI – SOME EVIDENCE FROM THE USA

Based on the following source: R. E. Boyatzis, E. C. Stubbs and S. N. Taylor, 2002. Learning cognitive and emotional intelligence competencies through graduate management education, *Academy of Management Learning and Education*, 1(2): 150–62.

Boyatzis and his colleagues investigated the assertion that manager or leader performance is predicted both by individuals' cognitive competencies and their emotional intelligence. The work was based on the view that there is a compelling need to integrate the development of emotional competencies into management education. Boyatzis et al. used cross-sectional and longitudinal designs employing samples of MBA students from the Weatherhead School of Management at Case Western Reserve University in the USA (1987 to 2001). Participants' competencies were assessed using self-report and direct-observation measures of management and leader competencies (namely, leadership, relationship, helping, sense-making, information gathering and analysis, theory building, quantitative and technology skills, goal setting, action and initiative).

Boyatzis and his colleagues claimed that the Weatherhead programme demonstrated significant improvements in participants' cognitive and emotional intelligence competencies. They compared also the full-time and part-time programmes and found that the part-time programe did not have the same degree of impact on competency improvement as the full-time programme, but nonetheless there were strong improvements for part-time participants in a significant number of cognitive and emotional competencies. According to Boyatzis et al., the improvements were not possible through traditional management education methods ('lecture and discussion'), where the half-life of the knowledge acquired might be as low as six weeks; instead it is crucial to employ more 'holistic' approaches (2002: 161). More-

Continued

over the improvements in emotional intelligence did not detract from the improvement in cognitive abilities. Boyatzis et al. suggested that it is as though emotional intelligence and critical thinking abilities develop hand in hand. Interestingly, these views are supported to some extent by Mintzberg and Gosling (2002), who suggested that a holistic management education curriculum might include experiential and self-expressive (unusual or unexpected) activities, incorporating methods as diverse as drama workshops and discussions of ethics and spirituality. Such activities might give participants the opportunity to focus on themselves, their lives, their work and their world in order to get a better feel for managing the self and others.

Succession Planning

An important factor in leadership development, but one which may sometimes be overlooked, is that of succession planning. Leadership succession planning and its L&D ramifications demands horizontal integration between the activities of the L&D function and the HR function more generally. Developing an individual into a competent leader can take years or even decades, and for this reason McCall (2004: 128) expressed the view that, paradoxically, it makes little sense to begin executive development at senior levels, and that it is much better to start the process lower down and pay particular attention to role and career transition points. Conger and Fulmer argued that leadership development actually begins at the middle management levels by identifying and focusing upon what they term 'linchpin' positions. These are management jobs that are essential to the long-term health of the organization (for example, the plant manager in a manufacturing firm) and for which there needs to be alignment to the extent that there is a management or leadership 'pipeline' that takes a longer-term perspective rather than concentrating on quick fixes or 'fighting fires'. As well as focusing on developing individuals for key positions, a succession management system should also be:

- transparent so that people have some idea about their status in the succession plan;
- monitored in order that the company knows if the right people are moving through the system at the right pace;
- adapted as the people and the context change and evolve (Conger and Fulmer 2003).

It was noted earlier that Sternberg offered a tripartite wisdom-intelligence-creativity (WICs) model in response to some of the perceived weakness of traditional models of leadership. The WICs model begs the question of whether some or all of its elements can be developed in leaders though planned interventions. Sternberg's answer to this question is in the affirmative and he offers the following general guidelines, although no concrete suggestions are made as to how the guidelines themselves might be operationalized in a planned L&D programme:

1. Intelligence: can be thought of as having two components – the analytical and the practical. For the analytical element this involves making serious efforts to be a critical thinker and hence may include the thinking skills of reflection, evaluation and enquiry. For the practical element it involves convincing others of the value of one's ideas and demonstrating their viability and practicability, and hence might include communication and persuasion skills.
2. Creativity: defying the crowd, perseverance in the face of obstacles and taking sensible risks.
3. Wisdom: using one's intelligence, creativity and experiences for the common good, balancing one's own and others' interests over the long and short term and making genuine efforts to understand others' points of view and incorporating them into one's own perspective.

Discussion Point

Can the various leadership and leader L&D methods outlined above be justified on theoretical grounds? In other words, what are the concepts and theories that could be used to argue in favour of their use in a leadership or management L&D programme? If a method has no obvious theoretical basis can it ever have a place in L&D practice? Explain your reasoning.

PERSPECTIVE FROM PRACTICE: LEADERSHIP DEVELOPMENT AT 3M IN THE USA

Based on the following source: M. Alldredge, C. Johnson, J. Stolzfus and A. Vicere, 2003. Leadership development at 3M: new process, new techniques, new growth, *Human Resource Planning* 26(3): 45–55.

The authors described an ambitious initiative to reinvigorate leadership development at 3M following the appointment of a new CEO, who set out clear and challenging expectations of 3M's leaders (including the capability for a stronger execution of strategy, delivery of results, flexibility, urgency and accountability). As part of this initiative the company converted an existing R&D facility that was in close proximity to executives' offices into a new Leadership Development Institute (LDI) at a cost of $3.2million. The CEO and his direct reports created a set of leadership attributes that were to be the focus of the LDI's activities. The attributes were: 'chart the course'; 'raise the bar'; 'energize others'; 'resourcefully innovate'; 'live 3M values'; and 'deliver desired results'.

Continued

In order to develop the capabilities of leaders to meet these challenges the company created a 17-day Accelerated Leadership Development Programme (ALDP), which consisted of:

1. A five-day leader-led classroom component. The 'teachers' for this were 3M leaders themselves along with some assistance from selected outsiders (i.e. academics and consultants). The aim was for the teachers to provide theory and best practice from within 3M and from outside the company. The leaders who acted as teachers were coached on how to do so by external academics and consultants.
2. Ten days of action learning during which participants tackled important business issues selected by the CEO. The aim of the action learning component was to allow participants to develop team skills, address complex and challenging real-world issues (such as R&D productivity and global business development), develop self-awareness and link the learning back to workplace issues.
3. Two days of presentations and debriefings to share and reflect on the content and process.

A further dimension to the ALDP is what 3M termed 'Personalized Learning', which aimed to accommodate the fact that each leader's learning style and leadership development opportunities and needs were different. The personalized element consisted of an up-front 360° assessment, a half-day personal objective-setting exercise, one-to-one meetings with each leader and coaches (from HR) prior to the programme to review the diagnostics, and the assignment to small groups that formed the action learning sets. The small groups created a safer environment for sharing, feedback and support. The authors reported qualitative evaluatory data in terms of the leadership attributes referred to earlier and readers are referred to the original source for a full discussion of the impact.

Discussion Point

What features of the 3M project do you feel may have made the greatest contribution to its apparent success?

Not all efforts are as successful as the 3M programme described above appears to have been. Ready and Conger attributed some of the lack of success in leadership development to the prevalence of what they termed three 'pathologies', namely: 'ownership is power' (manifested as fragmented ownership of leadership L&D with little coherence); 'productization' of leadership development (manifested as an emphasis on the product, referred to disparagingly as 'edutainment', rather than a focus on the organizational problem per se); 'make-believe metrics', for example by measuring success in terms of the utilization rates of leadership programmes (such as 'backsides on seats'), unit costs and simple take-up measures of new products such as 'e-learning for leadership skills'. Ready and Conger (2003) argued that to counteract these problems leadership development should:

1. Share ownership and demand accountability: leadership L&D should have shared accountability and ownership amongst the CEO, the top team, senior line managers, HR (we might add including the L&D function) and the learners themselves.
2. Invest in process, not products: leadership L&D should focus squarely on the problems to be solved rather than a series of disconnected programmes and 'rush to action' packages promulgating the latest trend in popular management thinking.
3. Measure what matters: the philosophy that 'initiatives that cannot be measured have no value' does not apply to leadership L&D. The evaluation of leadership development should ask the right questions about the development of skills in areas such as thinking strategically, working cooperatively and the cross-company coordination of efforts.

Discussion Point

How would you respond to a sceptical senior executive who challenges your proposals for a leader development programme and the whole ethos of leadership development with the view that leaders are 'born not made'?

Conclusion: the Learning Leader

The concept of the learning leader has two facets: one focuses upon individual learning and the personal outcomes of this process; the second focuses upon what he or she may do to facilitate collective learning and the organizational outcomes associated with this process. The former is the subject of traditional leader L&D, and it is to the latter (i.e. the role of the leader in collective learning) that we now turn our attention. Many of the changes in management and organization in recent years have redefined old paradigms. Organizations appear to be in a constant state of flux against a backcloth of a dynamic and fast-moving business environment. For example, the learning organization challenged older administratively driven structures; collective learning is seen as overcoming the weakness of decisions taken by 'too few brains'; and developments in work design and organizational design allied to technological change have led to a realization of the distributed nature of working and knowing.

The learner (broadly conceived) now takes centre stage in much of organizational life. Leadership as a 'primal' (Goleman et al. 2002) process in organizations has not escaped these developments and in a learning environment, leaders, rather than providing answers, need to be able to 'reinforce others and join with them in their quest for answers' (Raelin 2000: 45). Organizations in the modern world demand leaders who are learners. Learning leaders are less defined by the skills and styles that they have than they are by individual characteristics such as the ability to communicate and argue, by an orientation to process rather than structure, and with a curiosity and sensitivity supported by a strong self-confidence (Krebsback-Gnath 2001: 899). Learning leaders are individuals who help followers to create meaning through engagement in a mutual learning enterprise, and Meisel and Fearon (1994) suggested that this search for meaning has a number of identifiable attributes:

- seeing doubt, uncertainty and ambiguity as opportunities for learning and not just a state of anxiety that needs to be remedied;
- being prepared to stop, think and question and run the risk of experimentation that may overhaul old established ways of working and using paradigm shift as a source of creativity;
- organizing the search for new information, its acquisition, articulation and sharing and converting new learning into actionable knowledge.

Sadler (2001) argued that the interest in the role of the leader and in leadership in organizations and learning stems from two sources. The first of these is the importance that processes of influence (such as that exercised by a leader) have upon the achievement (or performance) and adaptation of an organization in response to environmental uncertainty and turbulence. The second reason, he argued, is because employees are more sophisticated and educated than they were in the past and therefore the heroic and charismatic style of leadership is likely to hold less sway than is an approach that encourages teamwork, participation and learning. Learning leaders who can fulfil the role of steward, designer and teacher are needed at all levels, from the Board to the shop floor (Sadler 2001: 423).

In contrast to this idea is the reality that leadership can sometimes also be a barrier to learning, especially when there are not enough leaders and when those who are available block learning by treating 'knowing' as a greater virtue than 'learning', thus curtailing the opportunities of followers to contribute to the generation and acquisition of new knowledge (Berthoin et al. 2001; Sadler 2001). According to Berthoin et al. (2001: 882–3), learning leaders have a responsibility to ensure that the cultural factors that may impede learning are surfaced and that people are able to avoid colluding with the dominant and culturally acceptable definition of the organizational problem. Hence leaders can be seen potentially both as facilitators of learning and barriers to learning; a learning leader is able to recognize the blockages (and the possibility that he or she may also be contributing to them), and, through public scrutiny and reflection, surface and share assumptions and values in order that a more explicit and commonly held understanding may be achieved. Child and Heavens (2001: 312–13) described the contribution of leaders to learning as having three dimensions:

- establishing a culture conducive to learning that breaks down barriers, where these exist, by the communication of a vision from the top and frame-breaking moves where barriers prove to be insuperable;
- supporting the culture with a set of practices that permit autonomy, which will lead to the creation of insights and new knowledge in pursuit of present effectiveness and future opportunities for the organization;
- enabling boundary-spanning communication across three channels between higher management and other groups in the organization, differing specialisms within the organization and the organization and other organizations including customers, suppliers, competitors and research institutions (Child and Heavens 2001).

As well as learning through planned and formalized activities, learning leaders (and others) can develop the capacity to learn through 'off the job' experiences in work and everyday life more generally. Ruderman et al. (2002) suggested that there are a number of ways in which this may occur; for example, the skills of handling multiple tasks in non-work settings (such as the home) can be good practice for doing so at work. Personal interests and the pursuit of these can also contribute to job performance since they may give knowledge about a location, an industry type or a customer's perspective. Learning to lead in home or non-work organizations can yield valuable lessons that may translate to a job role (Ruderman et al. 2002). But what might we look for in our efforts to recognize a leadership that is conducive to learning? According to Drath, the attributes of learning leadership might include:

1. Shared sense making: leading a process of reflection and questioning, paying attention to the parts and the whole of a problem simultaneously, and asking questions not just about 'what change is needed?' but 'why is change needed?'.
2. Connection: leading a process of enriching the forms of connections within an organization between different functional silos and getting relationships to work in new ways that foster learning and confront and explore root causes of challenges.
3. Navigation: leading with a sensitivity to the forces of change as they happen and steering a course in response to the dynamics of the internal and external environments (see Drath 2001).

We began our discussion of the learning leader by drawing a distinction between the individual learning of the leader and the collective learning that he or she may facilitate. The two are inextricably linked and, under a virtuous set of circumstances, developing the leader can also lead to the development of the organization through establishing, supporting and fostering the culture for learning and the associated mind-sets and processes (see Child and Heavens 2001). Similarly, the development of an organization of itself demands the development of its leaders through tough assignments and by motivating, challenging and provoking them to learn. Gosling and Mintzberg (2004: 21) argued that leadership development should result in organizational development. Moreover, they argued that where the L&D has taken place in an educational context (for example in an MBA programme), there should be an obligation on the individual to diffuse her or his learning into the organization in order to maximize its collective impact. Such an approach may be founded on a partnership between organizations and educational establishments (such as business and management schools) through a commitment to the continual acquisition and diffusion of learning throughout organizations as a matter of company philosophy and practice (Gosling and Mintzberg 2004: 22). A virtuous circle of leadership and learning is illustrated in Figure 7.6.

The complexity and the dynamism of modern business environments are often cited as reasons why it is essential that organizations and individuals learn to change and adapt to changed conditions. In our earlier discussions of collective learning and action learning we encountered the maxims that learning is 'the only sustainable source of competitive advantage' and that managers' learning must be equal to or greater than the rate of change in their environment. Drawing together the various strands that have emerged in the course of these discussions it is possible to propose a profile for a learning leader and for learning leadership. The characteristics of a learning leader include:

1. A commitment to their own and others' learning-in-action and learning-from-action.
2. An intrapersonal awareness that values reflexive self-knowledge and the capability to recognize those defensive reactions that may inhibit learning.

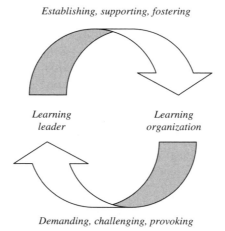

Establishing, supporting, fostering

Learning leader   *Learning organization*

Demanding, challenging, provoking

Figure 7.6 A virtuous circle of leader learning and organizational learning

3. An ability to make judgements that take account of context; in this sense such judgements may exhibit some of the features of expertise (see Dreyfus and Dreyfus 1986) or the unconscious and responsive leader behaviours described by Barnard (1948).
4. An interpersonal awareness to the extent that they extend time and suspend their own beliefs to empathize with others.
5. A systemic mind-set that enables them to see organizations from an integrated and holistic viewpoint (Raelin 2004: 134).

How does a leader become a learning leader? In their research into leadership and learning in cardiac surgery teams in the USA, Edmondson et al. (2001) argued that creating the environment for learning is not that difficult but time is of the essence. It is crucial that leaders act quickly since it is to them that followers look for the cues about how they are expected to behave. In order to set the right tone from the outset leaders need to: be accessible rather than aloof; ask for and value the input of followers: and, finally, admit their mistakes and serve as a 'fallibility model' in order to provide witness to the fact that errors can be discussed without fear of retribution (Edmondson et al. 2001: 132) and that in real-world practice authentic leadership and authentic learning are inextricably interconnected.

Discussion Point

How would you respond to the view that it is impossible to develop an organization without also developing its leaders? Justify your response.

Concept Checklist

Can you now define each of the Key Concepts listed below, and are you now able to achieve the other Knowledge Outcomes specified at the beginning of the chapter?

- Leader and manager
- Leadership and management 360°
- The manager in learning and the manager as learner
- National frameworks
- 360° feedback
- Assessment and development centres
- Manager competence
- Action-based methods
- Coaching
- Mentoring

- Leaders and leadership
- Transactional-transformational leadership
- WICs model
- Leadership development methods
- Team building
- Outdoor development
- Emotional intelligence
- Succession planning
- Learning leader

CHAPTER 8
Technology, Learning and Development

Key Concepts

Technology of L&D; technology in L&D; instructional design; varieties of learning; Bloom (knowledge, comprehension, application, analysis, synthesis, evaluation); Gagné (intellectual skill, motor skill, verbal information, cognitive strategy, attitude); internal conditions; external conditions; instructional media; concept analysis; distance learning; open learning; flexible learning; programmed learning; computer-based learning; modes of computer-based instruction (tutorial, drill, simulation, assessment); e-learning; networked/non-networked; synchronous/asynchronous; learning communities; collective cognition; e-learning organization

---

Knowledge Outcomes

After studying this chapter you should be able to:

- define each of the key concepts listed above;
- distinguish between technology of learning and development (L&D) and technology in L&D;
- explain the benefits and drawbacks of instructional systems design models;
- distinguish between open and distance learning and describe the features of flexible learning;

- explain how individual differences in styles and preferences may be acknowledged and accommodated through learning and support strategies;
- describe and critically evaluate the concept of e-learning.

Introduction

The learning effectiveness of media for the delivery of instruction can be assured when consideration is given to the prescriptions of instructional theory.
Robert Mills Gagné, *The Conditions of Learning and Theory of Instruction,* **p. 300**

'Technology' comes from the Greek words *tekhne* meaning an art or craft, and *tekhnologica* meaning a systematic treatment. The more familiar modern interpretation refers to the practical application of knowledge (usually scientific knowledge) within a selected field. The term is widely used in common parlance to refer to a diverse collection of tools, instruments, machines, organizations, methods, techniques, systems and so forth. Technology often looms large in L&D as practitioners attempt to harness the latest inventions in order to deliver and facilitate learning. This chapter is not concerned with information and computing technology's latest inventions and gadgets but with the role that technology (as broadly conceived above) has played and currently has to play in L&D. The question that we must begin by asking is: 'What do we mean by technology in the L&D context?' The nexus of technology and L&D manifests itself in two ways (as illustrated in Figure 8.1):

1. Firstly, and most commonly, as technology in L&D, such as the use of computer and information technologies to deliver information, enable communication between learners, record and assess progress and so forth. This is an explicit and tangible use of technology in L&D.
2. Secondly, technology manifests itself as the technology of L&D; by this we mean the application of scientific knowledge from various fields (such as cognitive psychology) to solve practical L&D problems (and often supported by technology in this process as described in (1) above). This is a more implicit use of technology (in the sense of the application of scientific principles) and represents a technical-rationalist approach to the design of L&D.

The role of technology is important because facilitating effective and efficient planned L&D entails making informed decisions, firstly about which of the available methods to use, and secondly how to deploy them in order to ensure they are executed effectively. This process involves making fine judgements about how to balance out the various competing demands placed upon time and resources for both the L&D function and learners in order to arrive at an optimum decision

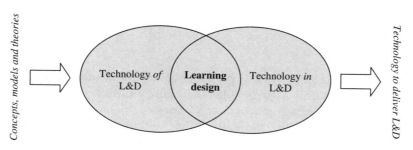

Figure 8.1 Technology and L&D

that meets stakeholders' needs. This decision process is compounded by at least two factors:

1. The first is the plethora of methods that are now available. Choosing the wrong method can be costly both in terms of the effort and resources that may be needlessly expended, but also in terms of the impact that a poor decision (for example, choosing the wrong technology) may have upon L&D's professional reputation and credibility within an organization.
2. The second reason is the rapid pace of technological change. Today's state-of-the-art learning technology may quickly become tomorrow's museum piece. Inevitably, therefore, the market for L&D methods can be prone to the vagaries of trends and styles and, allied to this modern computer-based technology, can be seductive both in its potential and its promises.

Choice over L&D method has to be exercised in a skilful way which takes into account what theory, research, practice and common sense has to tell us. This chapter is therefore concerned with how the practitioner can better understand L&D methods in order that he or she can make as informed a decision as possible so that individual and collective learning in the workplace may be facilitated. This immediately raises an important question about the manageability of learning in the workplace. Some would argue that learning is a process that is by its nature undeterministic, and the processes by which it occurs and its outcomes are difficult to predict.

PERSPECTIVE FROM PRACTICE: CHOOSING LEARNING TECHNOLOGY WISELY

Based upon the following source: C. A. Mellon, 1999. Technology and the great pendulum of education, *Journal of Research on Computing in Education*, 32(1): 28–35.

Continued

Mellon identified a number of lessons from the educational sector in the USA that L&D practitioners more generally might benefit from applying to the workplace:

1. Forcing technology upon practitioners without adequate training, support and within a reasonable time-frame is unlikely to improve learning and performance or win over sceptics.
2. There needs to be the recognition that within the population of L&D practitioners there will be a wide spectrum, from enthusiastic technophile to Luddite technophobe, with most practitioners likely to fall somewhere in the middle. Implementation strategies for technology-based learning need to take this into account.
3. For technology-based learning to be effective L&D practitioners must select materials and resources that help to meet the carefully defined learning objectives and also blend these into a broader spectrum of learning experiences.
4. Practitioners should be cognizant of the differences in learning styles and learning preferences that may exist in a given group and they should consider having alternatives to technology available or not having too much technology as this may demotivate and alienate some learners.

L&D to an extent is an uncertain process and we have to accept that rational decision models when applied to L&D have their limits. However, attempts can be made to guide the process towards particular outcomes that we see as desirable (indeed this is the essence of the L&D practitioner's role), otherwise we abandon the process to chance and serendipity, and potentially to chaos. However, this also means being comfortable with a level of ambiguity. Ultimately, in spite of our best efforts, the outcomes that transpire from L&D may be novel and unexpected and over and above (i.e. incidental learning) or instead (i.e. unplanned learning) of those that were intended. This is not necessarily a negative aspect of L&D: some of the most valuable learning experiences in our lives can be those that we did not anticipate or plan for. Being part of L&D either as a practitioner or as a learner may surprise us in sometimes exhilarating and unexpected ways.

Against this backcloth and from the perspective of the L&D practitioner (whose role it is to plan, guide and facilitate learning), there needs to be some means by which:

- outcomes can be specified that meet the identified learning and growth needs of individuals and organizations (and we have already met the concepts of needs assessment, objective setting and development planning);
- learning processes can be directed in such a way as to maximize the likelihood of the desired outcomes being achieved (the various theories of learning offer some help in this regard).

A fundamental distinction that was drawn in a previous chapter was between explicit learning (where the outcomes are often predetermined in advance) and implicit learning (where the outcomes are largely undetermined). This chapter will be concerned with planned learning; however, given the view that much of human learning does not occur in formal contexts (Eraut 2000), we must bear in mind the potential for unintended outcomes. The chapter's main concern is explicit learning (i.e. learning that is open to introspection both in terms of its content and process) on the assumption that we can often tell (i.e. verbalize) both what we know and how we came to know it. Explicit learning may take place in a formal and planned way or through experiences that have occurred in a non-formal, serendipitous fashion. Usually, explicit learning is a deliberative activity for which time has specifically been set aside for that purpose (Eraut 2000: 115). The chapter will explore how the technology of learning and technology in learning can be used to plan, implement and manage learning in organizations in order that L&D meets identified needs at the individual and collective levels.

Discussion Point

Weick and Westley (1999) expressed the view that 'organizational learning' might be considered an oxymoron. An oxymoron is a figure of speech in which two ideas of opposite meaning are combined together, like 'act naturally', for example. 'Organization' with its connotations of order, and 'learning' with its connotations of creating a new way of seeing the world might be considered contradictory. In your view is 'managing L&D', like 'organizational learning', an oxymoron? Justify your reasoning.

L&D FACTS AND FIGURES

The 2004 American Society for Training and Development (ASTD) survey revealed that the use of technology for delivering learning has continued to increase, with 29 per cent of respondents across a broad cross-section of US organizations using technology to deliver learning, more than half of which was online learning. (*Source*: ASTD State of the Industry Report 2004)

Technology of Learning: Instructional Design Theories

The design and implementation of L&D is based upon the accurate identification and analysis of learning needs. It may be recalled that at the individual level the outcomes of the identification and analysis stages are likely to include learning objectives, personal development plans (PDPs) and other formalized statements of intent. The information contained within these expressions of learning needs will provide considerable guidance to the L&D practitioner as to what the content of a programme, appropriate learning design and subsequent implementation might look like. One of the key issues here is the type of learning that should take place in order to meet the need (as expressed in the objective). We will examine various models (or taxonomies, i.e. a classification scheme) of learning and consider how these can help to guide design decisions. From a historical perspective this work may be set within a long tradition of instructional design (or, as it is sometimes referred to, instructional systems design, ISD) theory. The theory is a useful one when attempting to design L&D that requires a high degree of structure, as in the case of distance learning or e-learning, where there is a need to 'automate' the process in the absence of direct contact with an instructor. The term 'instructional design' is perhaps an unfortunate one at the present time because it has connotations of learning as a mechanistic and behaviouristic process. A better alternative might be 'learning design theory' since this in effect is what the various ISD models refer to.

Gagné and Briggs's Contribution

Instructional design theory (IDT) is most often associated with the work of Gagné and Briggs. Their approach represented an attempt to integrate a wide range of knowledge from various learning theories into a model of how to design learning. The model has a breadth of applicability (across the cognitive, psychomotor and affective domains) but is most widely used for designing learning for the acquisition of intellectual skills. The model has been developed and built upon subsequently (see for example Gagné et al. 1992) but its fundamental principles present a robust guide for the development of particular types of structured L&D (see Figure 8.2). The main elements of the model that will be considered here are the concepts of varieties of learning, the conditions which support learning, the sequencing of learning activities and the role of learning media in the design process.

L&D FACTS AND FIGURES

Robert Mills Gagné was a graduate of Yale. He became Professor of Educational Research at Florida State University and served as an aviation psychologist during the Second World War and held posts at Penn State and Princeton. Leslie J. Briggs was a graduate of Ohio State and, along with Gagné, may be considered one of the co-founders of the field of instructional systems design (ISD). Briggs was a Professor in this field at Florida State University. Gagné's classic text in the field is *The Conditions of Learning and Theory of Instruction* (1965, 1970, 1977, 1985). Gagné and Briggs's major joint work is *Principles of Instructional Design* (1979) and revised in 1992 with W. W. Wager.

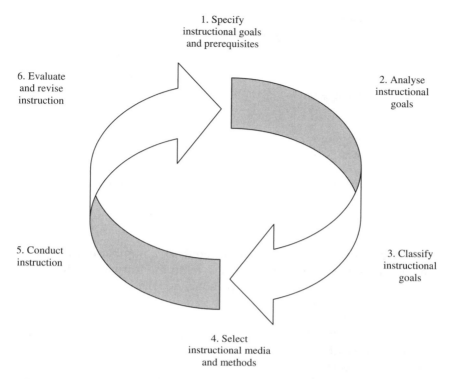

Figure 8.2 Basic instructional systems design framework (adapted from Gagné et al. 1992; Bonner 1999)

Varieties of Learning: Many different taxonomies of learning have been proposed over the years. These are essentially statements of what the categories of human learning (or, to put it another way, the types of learning) are that may be planned for when designing L&D interventions. There are clear links to objectives, and more recent variants of ISD such as Merrill's component display theory which links together types of learning with prescribed outcomes. One of the most widely known taxonomies is that for the cognitive domain produced by Bloom and his colleagues in the USA in the 1950s (taxonomies were also developed for the affective and psychomotor domain).

Bloom and his co-workers specified six categories consisting of knowledge, comprehension, application, analysis, synthesis and evaluation (Table 8.1). Gagné, on the other hand, classified human learning into five categories or domains consisting of intellectual skill, motor skill, verbal information, cognitive strategy and attitude (see Table 8.2). Gagné's focus was upon what is actually learned, and in focusing upon this he specified the types of learning outcomes involved. In the cognitive domain these are expressed as learned capabilities, which in themselves are not observable and so we have to rely on other indirect evidence to assess if the capability has been acquired. In the motor skill domain, for example, the

Table 8.1 Comparison of the different taxonomies of learning (adapted from Driscoll 1994; Bonner 1999)

Bloom	Gagné
Knowledge	Verbal information
Comprehension	Intellectual skills
	• Discriminations
	• Concepts
Application	• Rules
Analysis	• Higher-order rules
Synthesis	
Evaluation	Cognitive strategies

learner will have learned to execute movements in a number of motor acts (like throwing a ball), whilst in the attitudinal domain the learner will have acquired mental states that influence choices of personal actions which are expressions of tendencies (Gagné 1985: 48).

In the cognitive domain the capability that is acquired when learning verbal information (such as 'the date the Second World War ended'), for example, is the capacity to state this information (for example 'the year 1945'). This type of knowledge, as was noted earlier, is also known as declarative knowledge (the ability to 'declare' something) and is distinct from procedural knowledge (i.e. the rules for carrying out a particular operation, for example the ability to do something, like making a cup of tea). In addition to the affective and motor skills the remaining three types of learning may be grouped under the heading cognitive (verbal information, intellectual skill and cognitive strategy). Each differs in terms of the information processing demands they make on the cognitive system. The cognitive strategies are equivalent to an executive function which, amongst other things, determines when and how to choose intellectual skills and verbal information (Goldstein 1993: 102) as appropriate responses.

Conditions for Learning: As well as comprising the taxonomy, the model also specifies the conditions under which each type of learning may take place. There are two kinds of conditions necessary for each type of learning to occur:

Internal conditions are the previously acquired capabilities (the prerequisites) that are essential to, or provide support for, the acquisition of the new capability (in a sense they include the extant schemas that need to be in place and into which new knowledge will be assimilated).

External conditions: these are the instructional events and circumstances beyond the learner that activate and support the acquisition of the capability (for example, the instructional methods that should be used).

Different sets of conditions are required for each type of learning to occur.

Table 8.2 Gagné's five varieties of learning, the conditions and sample tasks (based on Gagné 1985)

Type of learning	Conditions		Sample task
	Internal	External	
Verbal information	Recall of larger meaningful context	Present new information in broader context	States the main types of evaluation methods and their uses
Intellectual skill	Various for the five sub-categories of intellectual skill (discrimination, concrete concept, defined concept, rule and higher-order rule). (See Gagné 1985: 89–137.)		Distinguishes between a PC and Mac (discrimination) Calculates return on investment of an IT project (application of a rule) Develops a protocol for the selection of job candidates (generating a higher-order rule)
Cognitive strategy	Recall of relevant rules and concepts	Successive presentation of novel problems with solution unspecified	Anticipate future scenarios for organization and produce appropriate strategic responses
Attitudes	Recall of information and intellectual skills relevant to targeted personal actions	Establishment or recall of respect for source (usually a person) Reward for personal action of observation of respected person	Chooses to behave towards customers in a specific manner
Motor skills	Recall of component motor chains	Establishment of executive sub-routine Practice of total skill	Executes an emergency stop in a vehicle travelling at speed

Sequencing Learning Events: Learning events are the activities that take place in a particular learning situation. The events that are planned to take place should be sequenced in an appropriate way and configured so as to support the acquisition of the specific learned capability. Gagné provides detailed guidance on how this may be achieved.

Learning Media: Within the theory these are also referred to as 'instructional media' and are the means by which stimuli are presented to provide the events of instruction (or learning). Instructional or learning media include the full range of audiovisual, print and electronic media available. The model provides a logic for decision making; for example, a medium should only be selected after the learned capabilities, instructional events and instructional sequences have been determined. This is a useful piece of general practical advice for the L&D practitioner, who may be pressured by internal clients to provide a particular type of learning solution before the precise nature of the learning need has been revealed by the analysis.

Strengths and Weaknesses of the Approach: Gagné and Briggs's model may be seen as being too prescriptive and individual-focused and not taking into account the social context within which much learning takes place. Following the system slavishly may reduce learner choice and autonomy since goals and activities are set by instructional designers, may emphasize content at the expense of process and may oversimplify things to the extent that the learning does not reflect the complexities of the real world (Alessi and Trollip 2001: 35). The criticisms are acknowledged; however, the theory is valid and relevant in the design of self-instructional materials such as distance learning packages and computer-based learning materials. One of the reasons for this is the fact that where learning proceeds in the absence of an instructor or teacher, materials need to be designed in such a way as to present a coherent structure and logical sequence with appropriate feedback (probably decisions that an experienced and expert teacher would do rapidly and almost unconsciously in a face-to-face situation). In a way the ISD model, especially when applied to learning media such as computers, provides a way of 'automating' learning, and this is necessary in the absence of a teacher since when a teacher is on hand he or she is able to answer questions, change direction and provide feedback. In self-instructional situations no such immediate response is readily available. The model is useful beyond the design of self-instruction and in Harrison's view Gagné's *Conditions of Learning* 'not only offers excellent practical advice about the design of learning events but illuminates it at the scholarly level with a discussion of the psychology of learning' (2002: 309).

PERSPECTIVE FROM PRACTICE: SELECTING LEARNING METHODS ON THE BASIS OF OBJECTIVES

Based upon the following source: S. Bonner, 1999. Choosing teaching methods based on learning objectives: an integrative framework, *Issues in Accounting Education*, 14(1): 11–39.

Bonner's primary concern was with the way in which the methods for accounting education may be chosen on the basis of the learning objectives and the type of learning (in terms of the categories of verbal information, intellectual skills and cognitive strategies). However, the process she suggests is a clear application of Gagné's work and is also generic to the extent that it may be used in the design of structured learning experiences more generally. The process consists of a number of steps:

1. Specify learning objectives (and any prerequisite skills – and add objectives for these if needed): for example, in the accounting field it might be for the learner to be able to 'classify a transaction as being a revenue or an expense'.
2. Classify learning objectives by type of learning (in terms of the various categories outlined above): the above is an example of the learning of a defined concept (a type of intellectual skill).
3. Choose learning methods (taking into account learning styles, motivation, costs and so forth): a defined concept can be taught by first of all describing and demonstrating the classification of items into conceptual categories, secondly by facilitating the recall of previously learned relevant concepts, thirdly by supplying a definition of the concept, fourthly by giving the learner examples and non-examples of the concept, and finally by asking the learner to classify examples.
4. Select learning media: each of the five steps in (3) above may be accomplished via different media; for example, read text (1), listen to a lecture (2 and 3), watch a demonstration of discrimination (4) and answer short objective questions (5).

Bonner suggested the use of a simple matrix of media × conditions for each of the types of learning as a potentially useful tool for designers of structured learning materials. She argued that the important insights that the approach reveals are that a single teaching method cannot be sufficient and the higher-order, more complex skills require active involvement on the part of the learner.

Concept Analysis

Sometimes the needs identification stage of the planning process reveals that there may not actually be any new task in the sense of an observable skill to be learned, but rather the L&D need is for the acquisition of a body of knowledge that can be subsequently applied to the job or task. In this case a behaviourally fixated L&D practitioner may be perplexed since there is quite possibly no tangible outcome in terms of motor, interpersonal or other observable skill to be aimed at in the analysis process. Instead there may be a rather more intangible body of knowledge consisting of facts, concepts and theories, which are the basic building blocks of any particular subject domain. This has clear links to Gagné's taxonomy, the notions of cognitive tasks and cognitive maps (since these will be based upon a body of expert knowledge) and the cognitive operations associated with a body of knowledge. In addition to the techniques that are available and are being developed for the identification of managers' cognition and cognitive processes (such as cognitive mapping), it is also possible to analyse a particular subject domain conceptually in terms of the over-arching topics and sub-topics in order to produce a conceptual taxonomy (in a 'tree' or hierarchical form) or a concept map (a 'web' akin to a 'mind map') showing a less hierarchical set of interrelationships. In order to produce such a conceptual taxonomy or map Rowntree (1990) identified a number of stages:

1. Identify and define each concept.
2. Identify examples and counter-examples as illustrative of the concept.
3. Examine the links to related concepts.
4. Explicate the nature of the links between concepts and related concepts (for example, in the form of rules, theories, generalizations).
5. Substantiate the conceptual analysis with reference to contexts and empirical research.

Different subject matters can have different conceptual structures and even the same subject can be represented and 'taught' in different ways by arranging the structure and sequence of the concepts in particular ways. Integration of new learning into extant conceptual structures (mental models) is important if learning is to be meaningful. Over three decades ago Ausubel (1968) proposed that meaningful learning occurs when new ideas are incorporated into an already existing conceptual structure. As we have noted elsewhere, our mental models are often simplifications of realities; they will sometimes encompass heuristics or rules of thumb that enable us to solve problems and make decisions quickly and with cognitive economy. The problem with these conceptual frames is that they may become deeply entrenched, so much so that they may even outlive their usefulness and sometimes persist in the light of contradictory evidence. The constraints imposed by our mental models may be such that we are simply not aware of them any more and our mode of thinking becomes a filter that restricts the information we able to receive (Van der Heijden et al. 2002: 2). In a business context this kind of constrained thinking can be a threat to the perception of environmental threats and can also inhibit creativity and innovation; therefore managers need tools to enable them to break out of rigid patterns of thought. Cognitive mapping is one way in which managers' mental models may be surfaced and made more explicit in an attempt to facilitate reflection and analysis and hence avoid cognitive inertia and 'grooved thinking' (see Hodgkinson and Sparrow 2002).

Technology in Learning: Distance Learning, Computer-based Learning and e-Learning

Having explored some of the issues relating to the technology of learning (for example, in instructional design) we can now turn our attention to the role of technology in learning. As noted previously, technology in learning is most often applied in those situations where the learner and the tutor are separated spatially (i.e. they are distant from each other) and temporally, which usually suggests an open learning, distance learning and, more recently, e-learning-type approach.

Distance and Open Learning

The terms 'open learning' and 'distance learning' are often used interchangeably although the two concepts are not necessarily related. Stewart and Winter (1995) distinguished between them thus:

Distance learning: here the learner is not continuously and immediately supervised by another person (for example, a tutor); he or she does usually benefit from the services of an organization or institution who are able to provide support where necessary, and uses materials in a variety of formats usually provided by the institution or the organization.

Open learning: here the learner has autonomy over learning in terms of what, how, when, where and at what pace learning takes place.

These two dimensions may be conceptualized as being independent (as is illustrated in Figure 8.3) and the various permutations are associated with differing degrees of flexibility. The alternative term 'flexible learning' is sometimes used when discussing learning that offers choice over time, place, pace, content and level of delivery. Our immediate discussions will focus upon what might be termed 'low technology' distance learning methods, i.e. those that are based around text or print-based resources. These are usually configured in a self-

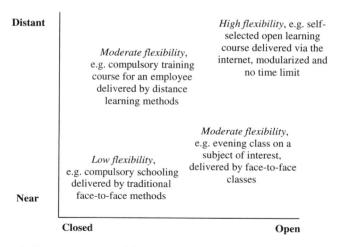

Figure 8.3   Proximity, openness and flexibility of L&D

instructional format where the use of instructional design principles (a technology of L&D) enable the learner to work through materials at a time, place and pace that is convenient to them and their work or personal circumstances.

L&D FACTS AND FIGURES

The roots of distance learning and self-instruction may be traced back to the influence of behaviourism on the design of learning and its specific application in the development of 'programmed learning'. The latter was seen as a means to improve the effectiveness and efficiency of training through making learning quicker, cheaper and more participative. Writing in the general management journal *California Management Review* almost four decades ago, Buckley described programmed learning or programmed instruction as a learning experience in which there is close interaction between the student and subject matter without the contiguous intervention of a teacher or instructor (Buckley 1967).

The role of technology in this type of system came to the fore with the use of programmed texts and even 'teaching machines' as a substitute for a conventional face-to-face interaction or a traditional textbook. The role for the teacher, instructor or subject expert lay in the careful design of the learning material in terms of its level, sequence and mode. The typical features of programmed learning included:

1. Explicit objectives which state what the learner will be able to do after learning has taken place.
2. 'Chunking' of knowledge such that the learning is designed as 'bite-sized' pieces arranged as small steps (or 'frames') which the learner can assimilate without being overwhelmed.
3. Learner participation by giving their response to specific learning activities or questions at an appropriate point in the sequence.
4. Reinforcement whereby the student can check the answers to their response immediately, thus getting direct feedback on whether their answers are right or wrong – and, if they are wrong, why they are so.
5. Self-pacing whereby the student progresses through the material at a pace that is commensurate with her or his ability to absorb the information and deal with the learning tasks as well as the impact of local contextual factors on the learning process (such as location and personal or work circumstances).

Many of the contemporary claims on behalf of learning technologies – such as e-learning – that enable the learner to learn at a place, pace and time that is convenient to her or his needs, are directly traceable to similar claims made for programmed learning (PL). PL is the antecedent of much of what has gone under the various banners of distance learning, open learning, computer-based training and technology-based learning. The programmed learning approach gave way to an educational technology approach derived from ISD theory, which has a number of sequential and interdependent elements, for example:

- identify purposes: usually in terms of objectives for learning;
- develop the appropriate learning experiences that are commensurate with the objectives and the type of learning;
- evaluate the effectiveness of the learning experiences in achieving the set purpose;
- improve the learning experiences in the light of the evaluation (Rowntree 1982).

Discussion Point

What are the features of programmed learning that may be singled out as behaviourist?

There was a rise in the popularity of open and distance learning for L&D purposes in business in the 1980s. Stewart and Winter (1995) attributed this rise to a concern for acquiring new methods that could help L&D become more responsive to the needs of organizations and as a means to enhance the effectiveness of L&D. In the UK, open and distance learning was heavily promoted by government (for example, by the Manpower Services Commission). Whilst much open and distance learning (ODL) was text-based, stakeholders were keen to grasp the potential offered by computers and used computer-based training (CBT). Hence, the continuing development of technology and its application in L&D also fuelled the rise of ODL and has continued to do so. The attempts at applications of ODL for in-company L&D raised a number of important issues for L&D practitioners and managers in general. Firstly, Stewart and Winter argued that one of the mistakes made by many organizations who took up ODL as part of their approach was to fail to appreciate the level of support needed by learners. Whilst there are always going to be individuals who may be considered autodidacts (able to teach themselves) most people require some form of support from a tutor or their manager. Moreover, not all types of learning lend themselves to an autodidactic approach. Secondly, much valuable learning takes place through interactions with other learners and through the sharing of information, assumptions beliefs and values; hence much of learning is to an extent a collective process. Thirdly, a further problem came with the implementation of ODL, because sometimes there was the implicit assumption that learners could or would undertake the learning out of working hours in their own time and that learners and L&D practitioners would embrace the technology.

L&D FACTS AND FIGURES

Many large organizations in the UK invested heavily in the distance learning approach, with some even going as far as to establish their own in-house distance and open learning production and management facilities (for example, British Telecom and British Gas). These were often corporate (i.e. HQ) functions serving a regional structure which, as well as providing company-wide learning materials, were also in the vanguard of organizational change in these formerly publicly owned organizations, which had been privatized under the government headed by Margaret Thatcher in the 1980s.

Many organizations were quickly dissuaded of the latter because learners needed the time to complete ODL packages just as much as they needed the time to attend a conventional training course, and there was a need for protected time. This obviated many of the advantages in terms of reduced down-time, although one of the principal advantages of ODL remained intact, namely that there were reduced training costs in terms of direct costs of travel and subsistence if sufficient numbers of learners were involved to justify the return on investment (ROI). But if individuals are to undertake ODL (or any other form of L&D) there usually has to be a payback for them. This raises another point made by Stewart and Winter: that learner motivation is a critical matter in open learning, as evidenced by low take-up rates and high drop-out rates in many ODL programmes. Hence the benefits of ODL have to be sold to the learners (and not only the benefits to the business) – the learner him- or herself has to be able to see some reward, be it in the form of better performance, a qualification etc.

Stewart and Winter also highlighted the management and the resource implications. Managing ODL in a business context is no easy task. The programme needs to be thoroughly researched, well designed, integrated with other L&D initiatives, programmed-in with work schedules, monitored and evaluated. The buy-in of the L&D practitioners themselves also has to be secured, otherwise the stakeholders who potentially are its main ally could perceive it as a threat to their job roles. Any unitarist assumption of shared values and perceptions between management and L&D practitioners in this or other arenas is open to question.

L&D FACTS AND FIGURES

Gibb (2002) quoted some 'ball park' figures for the development of IT-based ODL. For example, developers' costs per hour in the year 2000 were about £100 and it took about 300 hours to develop one hour of learning content; hence the total cost for one hour's learning could be around £30,000.

The resource impact sometimes came as a surprise to many of those involved in ODL. The assumption was that it would save money through being a more efficient use of learners' time, being better integrated into work schedules and so forth. The reality is that to develop cost-effective programmes that are specific to the organization's needs is often expensive – and sometimes prohibitively so. The result may be a 'Catch 22' situation in which bespoke materials are needed because generic materials do not fit the L&D need; but generic materials are all that can be afforded because the cost of 'going bespoke' may be too high. The costs for low-technology distance learning is likely to be somewhat less than for e-learning, but the same argument applies in that to be efficient the costs often need to be spread across a large number of learners who have a common learning need that promotes a consistency of content and message. Hence the effectiveness of ODL is often predicated upon economies of scale, for example where large numbers of employees need to undertake a common programme (perhaps over a short time period and where learners are geographically spread out). Under these circumstances the payback can be substantial. Where there are smaller numbers of learners it may not be cost effective to develop bespoke materials for one's own organization. Hence, 'off-the-shelf packages' may need to be used. As noted earlier, one problem can be that generic packages may not meet the specific needs of the individual or the organization (unless they are aimed towards some standard curriculum or content as in the case of an NVQ or educational qualification).

The rapid developments in information and computing technologies (ICT), and particularly the networking of computers within and beyond organizations, gave a boost to the concept of ODL during the 1990s and opened new and exciting avenues for the management of learning and knowledge within organizations. Building upon the model of Shale and Garrison (1990), a model of the relationships between the elements directly involved in an ODL system are shown in Figure 8.4. Distance learning enabled some of these interactions to be non-contiguous (spatially) and also asynchronous (i.e. not conducted in 'real time' with instructors or other learners).

PERSPECTIVE FROM PRACTICE: SUPPORTING FLEXIBLE LEARNING BY DESIGN

Based upon the following source: E. Sadler-Smith and P. J. B. Smith, (2004). Strategies for accommodating individuals' styles and preferences in flexible learning programmes, *British Journal of Educational Technology*, 35(4): 395–412.

It is beyond doubt that there has been a considerable growth in the use of flexible methods of delivery for workplace learning and development. However, in designing learning generally there is often the assumption that

Continued

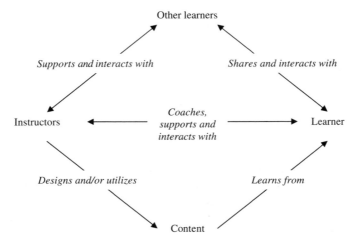

Figure 8.4 The elements of an ODL system (after Shale and Garrison 1990)

learners will exhibit uniformity in the ways in which they process and organize information (cognitive style), in their predispositions towards particular learning formats and media (instructional preferences) and the conscious actions they deploy to deal with the demands of specific learning situations (learning strategies). These issues are of particular importance in programmes of flexible learning in particular, not least because there may not be an instructor or other learners around provide assistance if a mode or structure of presentation is posing difficulties for an individual learner; in short, there maybe no one to ask. In adopting such a stance one runs the risk of ignoring important aspects of individual differences in styles, preferences and strategies. Hence, in flexible programmes there is an even greater need to take care over issues of learning design, and to anticipate difficulties and build in support structures and strategies as far as is practicable.

Sadler-Smith and Smith argued that there are a number of dimensions that need to be considered in such an approach. The first of these is the question of, 'Who is involved?' (i.e. who are the actors in the process – designer, learner or supporter?); the second is: 'What aspect of individual difference needs to be accommodated? (i.e. what is the construct – cognitive style, learning style or instructional preference?). Each of the latter may be defined as follows:

Cognitive style (sometimes referred to as a thinking style): an in-built and automatic way of organizing and processing information during learning (for example, thinking in 'words' or 'pictures', 'parts' or 'wholes', 'rational' or 'intuitive', etc.).

Learning style: an individual's habitual way of engaging in or approaching the learning process (for example, as in the Kolb or Honey and Mumford learning cycles).

Learning preference: an individual's actual or declared choice of one method of learning over another. A learning preference is often manifested as observed behaviour and should theoretically be related to style and strategy (Riding and Rayner 1998: 12).

Sadler-Smith and Smith mapped out some of the possible ways in which each of these constructs could be accommodated by the each of the stakeholders. Their suggestions are summarized in Table 8.3.

Computer-based Learning

Technology in L&D usually refers to the use of 'hard' electronic technologies, as opposed to the 'softer' technology of print. The past three decades have witnessed the widespread application of electronic technology and associated media to deliver and support L&D. The most recent manifestation of instructional technology is the combined use of computing and information technologies in the form of a worldwide web of computers (the internet) as a means to access and deliver large volumes of information quickly and synchronously across geographically disparate areas.

When new technologies are developed their application to support L&D is often eagerly exploited (Gibb 2002: 181). And so it was with the advent of the micro-computer in the 1970s, when the principles of programmed learning, which heretofore had been confined in the main to programmed texts (and which was sometimes cumbersome), were applied to computer-based learning. The opportunities afforded by the computer to branch, give feedback and present information in textual and graphical form in colour (albeit in a limited way in the early days) built upon the principles developed in the 1960s and 1970s for programmed learning. So in effect what one witnessed with early computer-based learning materials was programmed learning 'on screen'. This was a laudable and legitimate application of the technology. The use of the printed page for programmed learning was cumbersome – indeed one might argue that programmed learning was a soft technology ahead of its time. The computer provided the flexibility needed in order that the benefits (such as interactivity, remediation, feedback, diagnosis and analysis of performance) of programmed learning could in fact be realized. Some of the benefits of computer-based learning replicate the features of distance learning and open learning; for example, learners are freed from time and geographical constraints, they can interact with the computer programme, they have access to a wide array of resources and are able to exercise greater control over the level, pace and sequence of the learning (Piccoli et al. 2001).

Table 8.3 Stakeholder–construct matrix for customizing flexible delivery of L&D

Stakeholder	Construct		
	Cognitive style	**Learning style**	**Instructional preference**
Instructional/ learning designers' strategies (i.e. before learning takes place)	Giving structured route through the learning and/or giving global perspective of the content. Verbal presentation of information and/or visual presentation of information. Presentation of information dual mode (i.e. pictorial and textual). Making structure and scope of content explicit as well as its relationship to other topic areas. Translating pictorial presentation into verbal presentation.	Grounding new learning in a context of experience. Providing opportunity for deliberation, reflection, and articulation of knowledge. Access to additional information for in-depth pursuit of conceptual/theoretical bases of taught content. Clear articulation of potential application of new learning Integration of reflection and theory (off-the-job learning) with experience and application (on-the-job learning).	Exposure to a diversity of experiences and problem-solving situations to allow learners to sense their preferences. Identification and accessing of others who can provide demonstration, discussion and guided practice. Making a wider range of learning methods available for learners to sample and gain experience and confidence in using.
Learners' strategies (i.e. during learning)	Translating verbal presentation into pictorial/diagrammatic presentation.	Predisposition to becoming more self-aware. Acknowledgement of individual strengths and weaknesses in learning style. Development of action plan to enhance weaknesses.	Predisposition to becoming more self-aware. Acknowledgement of individual preferences and biases. Commitment to exposure to wider range of learning methods.
Supporters' strategies (e.g. L&D practitioner, instructor, manager, coach, mentor, tutor, etc.)	Identification and understanding cognitive style. Exposition of learning strategies to accommodate cognitive styles. Integration of cognitive styles awareness into a learning contract. Identification of tasks and resources to support learning contract.	Negotiation of learning contracts that integrate reflection and theory (off-the-job learning) with experience and application (on-the-job learning). Counselling learners in exploring realms outside their habitual learning style.	Making available wide range of alternative delivery mechanisms. Counselling of learners as to value of methods that may not match their preferences.

One criticism levelled at computer-based learning was that it often appeared to be no more than 'electronic page turning', whereas the computer should in theory be a highly effective medium for certain forms of learning because it can store a vast amount of information, it can present information in variety of modalities, it can branch, provide immediate feedback and remediation and it has a very fast processing speed. When these capabilities are used to their fullest extent the computer offers huge potential as a medium of instruction, and especially as a medium for self-instruction. But, like any other medium, computers in learning should be used for what they are good at and to this end Allesi and Trollip (2001) identified a number of possible modes of computer-based instruction:

1. Tutorial mode (including hypermedia): here the computer takes on a teaching role in presenting information and guiding the learner and providing for learner control, questioning, response judging, feedback and remediation.
2. Drill mode: this engages learners in practising new knowledge or skills as a means to aiding retention and the assimilation of knowledge into long-term memory.
3. Games and simulations: these allow learners to operate freely in an 'exploration mode' within a structured environment (see later section).
4. Assessment: computers can be used in a number of ways, for example in constructing a test (by composing it from a question bank) and also in administering a test and recording the results (in terms of numbers of items correct, time taken, wrong answers chosen and so forth).

Computers can also be used in the collation, analysis and presentation of test or performance data. These modes of instruction can be administered across a network or on a stand-alone personal computer, and they can be delivered to learners on disk storage or downloaded. Gibb (2002) identified a number of issues that surfaced as the technology developed and was applied in the development of computer-based training (CBT) or computer-based learning (CBL), which latterly became known as 'multi-media':

1. The use of multimedia (text, graphic, animation, audio and video) provided a means to 'turbo-charge' learning (note the hyperbole) but in practice technical problems surfaced with different delivery platforms and operating systems.
2. Learning design problems also were evident with material being produced that was 'deadly dull', with content almost indistinguishable from textbooks (the 'electronic book syndrome') and interactivity confined to exposition-and-answer (tutorial mode), 'drill and practice' or crude and unconvincing attempts at simulation.
3. The validity, relevance or currency of the content often proved to be short-lived, which was at odds with the long lead-in times and high development costs for CBT (Gibb, 2002).

e-Learning

With the advent of networked computers and the 'dot com' revolution of the 1990s, the language and hyperbole surrounding technology-based learning shifted again and a new term was born – 'e-learning'; in common parlance it appears to have superseded CBT, CBL and multi-media. One of the principal sources of ambiguity in terminology (see Facts and Figures below) is the extent to which computer-based applications are networked or non-networked. The term 'e-learning' will be used henceforth to encompass both networked and non-networked applications as opposed to the stand-alone non-networked use of computers for L&D purposes. The use of synchronous networked applications opens up new possibilities for virtual classrooms, streaming of video and interactive 'chat' sessions over and above web-based training and online information sources available with asynchronous networked applications (Naish 2004). With the emergence of the internet there are far-reaching social, organizational and educational implications since the connectivity this technology offers makes possible shared activity in an organized and sustained way (Sloman and Reynolds 2003).

L&D FACTS AND FIGURES

A UK definition of e-learning: The Chartered Institute for Personnel and Development (CIPD) defined e-learning as 'learning that is delivered or mediated by electronic technology for the explicit purpose of training in organisations' (www.cipd.co.uk/elearning).

An EU definition of e-learning: Learning that is supported by information and communication technologies (ICT). E-learning is therefore not limited to digital literacy (the acquisition of IT competence) but may encompass multiple formats and hybrid methodologies, in particular, the use of software, internet, CD-ROM, online learning or any other electronic or interactive media. (CEDEFOP http://www.cedefop.eu.int).

A US definition of e-learning: The American Society for Training and Development defined e-learning in its 2001 survey of the field as the delivery of content via the internet, intranet/extranet, audio- and video-tape, satellite broadcast, interactive TV or CD-ROM.

Information and communication technology-based media have features that are unique in the history of learning technologies (increased speed of communication, reduced costs of communication, increased connectivity between people, increased communication bandwidth and the integration of the various technologies; see Buchel and Raub 2001: 521). This has opened up the possibility for an e-learning that is a quantum leap away from the stand-alone CBL of the 1980s and 1990s. The notion of stand-alone CBL where learning was delivered from a non-networked PC quickly gave way in the late 1990s to the concept of the networked PC as a learning medium either as part of an intranet or the internet. This connectivity opened the way for what some have termed virtual learning environments (VLEs) and which are often referred to as e-learning. The advent of networked computers meant that learners were able to interact with other learners and instructors in an open-system environment and have access to a vast array of resources available from a global web of computers (see Naish 2004 above).

The field of e-learning is emerging and, not surprisingly, terminologies are often confusing and overlapping: terms such as 'synchronous e-learning', 'live e-learning' (Salopek 2002), 'web-based learning', 'virtual learning environments' (VLEs) are sometimes used interchangeably. In general they all rely upon the combination of information and communication technologies into a single integrated system (or medium), which is used to deliver and facilitate learning. In terms of a classification, the systems can be:

Synchronous networked: learners and tutors interact in real time and in effect participate in a live electronic classroom. Learners may listen to an instructor via an audio connection (over the internet or via a telephone line) while seeing visual material on screen (Salopek 2002). Learners are able to ask questions, be questioned, and enter into discussions with other learners.

Asynchronous networked: learners are able to interact with other learners and tutors but not in real time; for example, this might be by means of emails, bulletin boards, and so forth. Real-time interaction is not always essential and the synchronous capability of e-learning is probably best reserved for those situations where it is really needed (such as brainstorming, demonstration and feedback, discussion and debate) (Salopek 2002: 18).

Synchronous networked e-learning differs from stand-alone computer-based learning in that the latter does not possess the capability for learners to communicate and interact with others with comparative ease (stand-alone is an individual medium). Networked computer-based learning goes beyond a computer-to-learner self-instructional format (which was one of the drawbacks of CBT in that the isolation and auto-didacticism required did not suit all learners) to encompass the collaborative and group elements of learning (with their personal, social and interactive features). Moreover, the rapid advances in technology have meant that the processing speed and storage capacities of computer systems mean that it is possible to use extremely complex and elaborate designs that may draw upon high-fidelity video and audio representations within a synchronous or asynchronous environment.

The economies-of-scale arguments apply equally to e-learning methods as to traditional print-based distance learning methods. As Rushby (2003: 545) noted, there are important differences in this regard between what he termed 'educational e-learning' and 'corporate e-learning'. The learner populations in the educational sector (especially for the compulsory schooling years) are likely to number many thousands and yield economies of scale that are much larger than in most corporate e-learning ventures. Gibb concluded that e-learning may only be useful 'in [those] circumstances where many people needed instructing in a short time in something with a short shelf life' (2002: 182). Such methods have the potential, if used appropriately, to respond to many new and emerging challenges that face organizations – such as knowledge management and the maintenance of corporate memory. These are issues that are important in the area of collaborative learning, and the unique contribution that networked computers can offer in this regard is considerable (see below).

PERSPECTIVE FROM PRACTICE: e-LEARNING – FROM HYPE TO HANGOVER?

Based upon the following sources: A. Schafter, 2001. An e-learning survey, *T&D*, November: 74–7; M. Sloman, 2004. No pipe dream, *People Management*, 10 (23): 38–9.

In 2001 the ASTD conducted a brief web-based survey to investigate how readers of its magazine *T&D*, aimed at L&D practitioners, saw e-learning (as defined above) in their companies. Their sample comprised 671 responses and included a wide spread of companies, with training budgets ranging from under US$10,000 (18 per cent) to over $1 million (22 per cent). The main findings of the ASTD survey were that:

1. Only a very small minority of respondents had no involvement in e-learning (less than 6 per cent).
2. Almost 20 per cent of respondents were at the stage of exploring the options and a further 20 per cent were at the stage of planning, selecting, designing or piloting programmes.
3. Sixteen per cent of respondents were beginning implementation.
4. Just over one-quarter of respondents had been using e-learning for some time.

In the UK the Chartered Institute of Personnel and Development (CIPD) conducted a very small-scale ($N = 100$) online survey to monitor progress, identify problems and offer some thoughts for the future of e-learning. The overall finding was that e-learning is 'still very much a work in progress' (2004: 38), following the initial optimism and sometimes overselling that took place in the 'dot com' boom. In terms of actual usage stand-alone CD-ROM was the most frequently used e-learning method. The mean figure for the amount of L&D that is actually delivered through e-learning was a mere 9 per cent. The overall conclusion was that e-learning is a potentially important means for delivering learning but it must be combined with other types of delivery to form an effective package of resources. As one of the respondents in the CIPD survey put it: 'e-learning in its early years suffered from being over-hyped . . . now it is suffering from a hangover from this phase' (2004: 39).

Modern networked learning systems present a very powerful L&D platform and the use of intranets and the internet – with their capabilities of communication (one-to-one and one-to-many, etc.), rapid searching and fast and flexible publication – has the changed the face of technology-based learning and allowed the emergence of new forms of learning communities. Sloman and Reynolds distinguish between two types of learning communities that are made possible through the medium of e-learning:

Formal e-learning community: a group of learners who interact, communicate and share knowledge under the guidance of an e-moderator. This is a more complex and advanced form of supported online learning.

Informal e-learning community: a learner employs ICT to communicate with and learn from individuals inside or outside the organization during the normal course of work (2003: 260–1).

Web-based environments may be configured to facilitate and support both these kinds of learning communities because they are multi-media; can integrate information in a variety of forms; support interactive communication; support networks to access information in non-linear ways; provide cross-platform environments that work between different computer operating systems using a common script language (for example, HTML, JavaScript) and a standard internet address (such as an IP address) (Liaw and Huang 2002). There are security implications in both cases but especially with the informal community. E-learning is a step-change from old-fashioned CBL through the potential that is offered by features such as web browsers, search engines, hyperlinks, e-mail, news groups, online conferencing, as well as the benefits of flexibility, synchronous and asynchronous communication, interactivity and control.

PERSPECTIVE FROM RESEARCH: LEARNER SATISFACTION IN WEB-BASED MANAGEMENT LEARNING COMMUNITIES IN THE USA

Based upon the following source: J. B. Arbaugh and R. Duray, 2002. Technological and structural characteristics, student learning and satisfaction with web-based courses: an exploratory study of two on-line MBA programs, *Management Learning*, 33(3): 331–47.

Arbaugh and Duray asked the question, 'What are the factors that predict learning and satisfaction in web-based management education?' They conducted their research in two business schools in the west and mid-west of the USA whose internet-based delivery programmes included a variety of standard self-instructional features (such as study guide, orientation, tests and help), along with more socially oriented features such as 'forum' (a dis-

Continued

cussion platform for the class), 'chat' (a chat room for student use) and 'profiles' (personal information including profiles, hobbies and 'things most important to me'). They explored the relationship between usefulness, ease-of-use and flexibility of the online learning materials and environment and student learning and satisfaction (quality, satisfaction with the internet medium and likelihood of taking future courses in this way). In terms of learner satisfaction, the most important features of online delivery were course flexibility and programme flexibility. This underscores the flexibility of time, place and pace argument that has been offered many times as a justification for learning-at-a-distance. Class size (bearing in mind this was a business school programme with built-in social interaction facilities) showed a negative relationship with student learning and satisfaction. In terms of learning and satisfaction it might be better for online courses to have fewer rather than more students in internet 'forums' or 'chat rooms' than would be the case in traditional classes. This militates against mass online instruction in favour of smaller online learning communities.

Arbaugh and Duray argued that one implication of this is that the perceived use of the online medium as a cost reduction tool for delivering learning may be unfounded. Neither perceived usefulness nor perceived ease of use of the technology were associated with learning or satisfaction (nor were age or gender). The technological aspects of online delivery may be akin to learning 'hygiene factors' and only noticed if they are sub-standard. The authors argued that online courses could actually be more expensive than traditional methods, but this does not mean online courses will automatically be less profitable – they might, due to their inherent flexibility and appeal to busy managers, be able to command a premium price in time-pressured environments. Increasing the degree of social interaction in a web-based environment, where the learning community provides the opportunity to 'network' within a fairly exclusive group, might further enhance its appeal to managers and leaders.

The issue of learner control over content, sequence and pace of learning is a central feature of much e-learning (as it was with programmed instruction). This is based on the premise that it will relate in a positive way to motivation, the more effective and efficient processing of information, better learning performance and higher levels of learner satisfaction. Learner control allows individuals to express their individuality (in terms of the rate at which they process information, their preferences for particular modes of presentation and so forth) which, it is assumed, will affect performance in a positive fashion. However, it is arguable whether the learner is the best judge of the instructional strategy to be adopted, and hence there is a fine line to be trodden having a programme that is robust in design terms and which gives enough choice and control for learners without losing structure and coherence. Alessi and Trollip (2001) recommend that the most important control is that of sequence, forward progression, backward reviewing and the ability to pause, continue or skip video or audio sequences.

L&D FACTS AND FIGURES

The ASTD's E-learning Trends 2004 Survey revealed that 38.4 per cent of respondents used e-learning for IT end-user and desk-top training, 35.7 per cent for general business skills (ranging from leadership to sexual harassment) and 30.4 per cent for customer service training and task specific skills. (*Source*: ASTD Learning Circuits E-learning Trends 2004.)

One of the fundamental questions that surrounds any new medium is, 'What value does it add over existing approaches?' especially where there is a significant investment decision to be made. The notion of 'value' in this context can have a number of connotations and can refer to many things including reduced costs, enhanced flexibility and improved learning effectiveness. Over the decades each new learning technology has been accompanied by a certain amount of 'hype' regarding its 'revolutionary' potential, and how it might be able to change the face of learning for ever. Unfortunately the level of rhetoric is not usually accompanied by a similar level of rigorous scientific research into the impact that such technologies can have upon learning. Hence, the question of how effective the new technologies are is a crucial one in validating their effectiveness. One of the problems in conducting research that will provide unequivocal answers to these questions is that it often requires experimental and longitudinal research designs that can be complex and difficult to implement. An experimental study is one in which the researchers attempt to systematically manipulate relevant variables and to examine the effect of this upon the outcome variables (Haslam and McGarty 1998: 38).

PERSPECTIVE FROM RESEARCH: THE EFFECTIVENESS OF WEB-BASED LEARNING

Based upon the following source: G. Piccoli, R. Ahmad and B. Ives, 2001. Web based virtual learning environments: a research framework and preliminary assessment of effectiveness, *MIS Quarterly*, 25(4): 401–26.

In the USA Piccoli et al. examined the effectiveness of e-learning (they termed it a 'virtual learning environment' or VLE) for basic IT training in undergraduate education. They define a VLE as a computer-based environment that is a relatively open system; it allows interactions with other participants and provides access to a wide range of resources and may be

Continued

distinguished from computer-based learning (in which learners individually enter a self-contained computer-based learning environment) and classroom-based learning (where technologies may be used in support of classroom activities). The distinction is that the VLE adds a communication dimension to the previously individualized learning experience (person-to-computer) thus fostering the creation of communities of learners and encouraging electronic interaction and discussion (person-to-computer-to-many).

The researchers developed a web-based VLE to teach introductory-level IT skills to a group of 146 business undergraduates at an American university. They aimed to test the following hypotheses:

1. Hypothesis 1 (H1): students in the VLE will achieve higher test scores than their counterparts in the traditional learning environment.
2. H2: students in the VLE will report higher levels of computer self-efficacy that their counterparts in the traditional environment.
3. H3: students in the VLE will report different levels of satisfaction from students in the traditional learning environment.

Two instructors were involved in the experiment, each teaching one section of the course in the VLE (the treatment group) and the other section in the traditional way (lecture, demonstration and practice assignments). In the VLE learners connected to the online classroom at a time convenient to themselves, they worked independently, used online teaching materials, communicated through email and discussion boards, accessed online materials through a web browser and were free to skip, review and repeat materials at will. Grades on mid-term and final examinations were used as a measure of achievement, and grading was by a pool of experts who were blind to the research. Since gender has been shown to impact upon the use of technology in learning this was included as a control variable in the analysis, as was the variable 'instructor' in order to take account of any potential effects of the idiosyncrasies of the two instructors. Analysis of variance (ANOVA) is a statistical technique that is often used to determine the probability that differences in means across several groups are due solely to sampling error (Hair et al. 333). The examination of group means, the F statistic and the probability level (p) allow the researcher to draw conclusions about the nature of the group differences. ANOVA also allows the researcher to examine the joint effects of two treatment variables (for example, job level and gender). ANOVA was used to identify any effects of type of learning environment on performance (H1), self-efficacy (H2) and satisfaction (H3):

1. H1 was not supported: although the scores for VLE students (82.5) were higher than for those in the traditional environment (79.4) the results were not large enough to be statistically significant ($F = 1.442$; df = 1, 141; $p = 0.232$).
2. The students in the VLE environment reported higher levels of computer self-efficacy (7.17) than did those in the traditional environment (6.53)

and the results were statistically significant at the 1 per cent level ($F = 7.498$; df = 1, 141; $p = 0.007$), thus supporting H2.

3. Similarly, there was a main effect of learning environment on student satisfaction with those in the traditional classroom reporting higher satisfaction scores (4.02) than those in the VLE (3.70) and again the results were statistically significant, this time at the 5 per cent level ($F = 6.23$; df = 1, 141; $p = 0.014$), thus supporting H3.

Some of the findings were ambivalent and even negative regarding the relative benefits of the VLE. The conclusions that Piccoli et al. drew were that learners of basic IT in a VLE or traditional classroom environment achieve comparable levels of mastery. Many of the students were only accustomed to traditional methods and they reported that they found the shift to self-direction, autonomy and control a difficult transition. The control and novelty of the VLE was frustrating for many. Not surprisingly the engagement with the VLE increased learners' computer self-efficacy through their own efforts and ability. Levels of satisfaction with the traditional environment were consistent across the time period; however, satisfaction with the VLE broke down in the second half of the semester, perhaps due to accumulated frustration with lack of familiarity and the novelty of the system, which led to isolation and anxiety. The researchers conclude that previous experience with the domain of VLEs is necessary to avoid these problems happening (some of which may be attributable to technical issues).

Discussion Point

In research designs the issue of internal validity is concerned with the question: 'Did the treatment make a difference in this particular situation?' Unless the internal validity of an experiment has been established the interpretation of any effects of an experimental manipulation is not possible (Goldstein 1993: 191). From the evidence provided are there any internal validity issues in the above study? What implications for practice are there?

Many of the documented problems relating to the implementation and diffusion of e-learning may be related to difficulties of interaction between users and technologies, as well as the resistance of some of the stakeholders to challenges in traditional means of learning (Gnisci, Papa and Spedaletti 1999). For example, usability (which typically refers to satisfaction towards the system, ease of use of equipment and effective use by users) can be a serious impediment to the success of computer-based learning. One problem that confronts organizations who come to rely increasingly upon technology are these important end-user issues; for example, the failure of non-computing specialist end-users (be they learners or

L&D practitioners) to extract the maximum benefit from the technology may have a longer-term impact upon the viability of the medium. The main practical findings from the Piccoli et al. (2001) study are that:

1. e-learning can help new learners develop the confidence necessary to make them successful computer users.
2. It may be necessary to let learners self-select into the learning environment that is most suitable to their skills and preferences.
3. The real benefits of e-learning may come from the blending of the desirable features of e-learning with the personal contact elements of a traditional environment.

If the benefits of e-learning are to be fully maximized end-users need to learn how to use the medium in a way that adds value for them (i.e. that meets their needs and gives a payback, preferably quickly). One of the paradoxical questions, of course, is whether or not e-learning is the best means to teach people how to use e-learning. The development of end-user competence is crucial if learners are not to become frustrated and disillusioned by a lack of skill in dealing with the very technology that is supposed to enhance their learning. End-user training may be seen therefore as a crucial foundation and prerequisite for effective and efficient e-learning. The technical complexities can be compounded when, as with e-learning, the networked dimension is added. Many of the problematic aspects of usability (in the form of end-users' awareness and skills of the technology) may evaporate as a younger generation of learners who are familiar with ICT from school and college enter the workforce. In this situation it is likely to be the older workers who may need end-user computer training if e-learning is to benefit them.

L&D FACTS AND FIGURES

The ASTD's E-learning Trends 2004 Survey revealed that 25.9 per cent of respondents were aware of e-learning and 50.6 per cent were interested in using it. Employees' main concerns were the time commitment (30.2 per cent), technical competency required (24.4 per cent) and the level of self-discipline required (20.9 per cent). (*Source*: ASTD Learning Circuits E-learning Trends 2004.)

PERSPECTIVE FROM PRACTICE:
IMPLEMENTING e-LEARNING EFFECTIVELY

Based upon the following source: M. Gold, 2003. Eight lessons about e-learning from five organisations, *Training & Development*, August, 54–7.

The author offered a number of solutions to some of the more mundane problems that may be encountered when trying to implement a learning management system (LMS). For example, in spite of the claims that equipment compatibility is beginning to be achieved, Gold noted that a lack of compatibility required most of the organizations studied to adjust their selection of courseware to fit with their technology platforms. This meant that sometimes learning design features came second to the question of, 'Will it work with minimal intervention?' The example of Lucent technology was cited, which has its own team of e-learning specialists who write 'wrap-arounds' in order that third-party courseware works on its LMS. Companies like Kodak chose to work with just a few e-learning providers to minimize this potential problem. In Gold's research Kodak also found that a 'build it and they will come' expectancy did not work, and paradoxically the benefits to the organization of flexibility and reduced downtime were seen by some employees as disadvantages since they sometimes enjoyed the respite and stimulus that being in the classroom with others, and hence away from work, gave them. The process of making potential learners aware of the e-learning resource that is available and building in and publicizing the potential payoff to them is important (Gold 2003).

E-learning technology should be used only if it meets the L&D needs per se and not purchased because of its technical elegance and complexity. For example, the system needs to be simple enough for end-users to navigate and use without becoming frustrated. All of the available features that technologists and vendors can offer may not actually be needed and might even get in the way of the learning by confusing and overloading users. The freedom offered by the internet can also bring with it security problems, especially for financial organizations – for this reason many organizations limit access to the e-learning campuses only via the same security system that is used for the company system (Gold 2003). The problems of identifying the bottom-line dollar impact of any L&D project are well documented. Some of the organizations that Gold described referred to the broader and 'softer' factors that e-learning can impact upon. For example, in Deloitte it would have been impossible to introduce e-business without the associated learning programme, but to attribute the subsequent expansion in business to the L&D would be fallacious; instead it pays to look at the whole picture and make a sensible and subjective judgement about the contribution that L&D has made (Gold 2003).

If an e-learning organization is ever going to be possible the technological foundations have to be in place. Based upon the foregoing research and examples of practice (see Gold 2003), the following recommendations for the successful implementation of an e-learning infrastructure are offered:

1. Try to balance technological and learning design issues in the selection of optimum and workable platforms for e-learning.

2.　Promote the availability of e-learning opportunities – don't expect learners to 'walk through the door'.

3.　Don't get seduced by the complexity, sophistication and elegance of the technology – judge it on its efficacy for learning.

4.　Have an e-learning security policy and system in place.

5.　Try before you buy.

6.　Don't be naïve in expecting or committing L&D to simplistic notions of dollar bottom-line paybacks from e-learning investments – learning is more complex than that.

7.　Have a senior sponsor or champion.

8.　Chunk and protect learning time.

9.　Choose from the best and blend to give the best mix of learning methods.

10.　Don't assume computer literacy – invest in end-user training.

Discussion Point

Do you think that it would ever be possible to create an 'e-learning organization'? If so, what would it look like? Explain the reasoning behind your views. You may wish to go back and take a look at some of the salient features of a learning organization and the concepts of organizational learning as outlined in a previous chapter. How can ICT add value to these processes?

Conclusion: Collective Cognition and the Creation of an e-Learning Organization?

Organizations do not have cognitive systems in the way that human beings do. Therefore it is not organizations that learn, it is people; hence cognition in organizations is a distributed phenomenon (Simon 1991). Boland et al. argued that the process of distributed cognition occurs when autonomous individuals make interpretations of their situation; groups of individuals amongst whom there is an interdependency share interpretations to develop a collective understanding; or managers' individual actions take interdependencies into account to yield a coordinated outcome (1994: 457). In this situation the activities can persist despite changes in personnel, and hence the knowledge that sustains the activities is not purely personal but is distributed (Eraut 2000: 130). IT can support distributed cognition by enabling individuals to make richer representations of their understandings of their actions and their consequences through reflection and dialogue and hence inform their subsequent actions (Boland et al. 1994). Collaborative and collective learning is made viable through e-learning platforms, which can make possible a distributed cognition, and in which ICT is used to enable the acquisition, distribution, interpretation, storage and sharing of knowledge. E-learning is one technologically mediated means by which an organization can enhance its corporate memory through collective or organizational learning. These ideas suggest an alternative and perhaps broader definition of e-learning: 'Learning that is enabled by ICT for the purposes of enhancing the knowledge and skill base of individuals and the organizations of which they are a part in order that they may solve problems in more effective ways.' This definition takes the concept of e-learning beyond networked CBL and into the arena of knowledge elicitation and sharing at the collective level as a means by which an individual and the organization can self-reflect, surface assumptions and values (i.e. its shared mental model), and open these up to critical public scrutiny by members of the organization through dialogue in order to inform subsequent actions. A number of organizations have attempted to use ICT for the purposes of e-learning as broadly defined above, for example Shell's Site Scape was examined in some detail in the discussion of collective learning in a previous chapter. The interplay of these elements of self-reflection, dialogue and action may, according to Boland et al., lead to a richer representation of understanding (see Figure 8.5).

An important feature of e-learning when defined more broadly than the facilitation of instruction by computers is that it opens up many more possibilities for e-learning as an integrated system for L&D, knowledge management and knowledge creation. This becomes all the more feasible when one considers, firstly, the ubiquity of the PC and networked PCs in organizations and, secondly, that this type of learning may take place inevitably and informally but which may be managed more effectively. The features of speed, economy, connectivity, bandwidth and integration raise the question for organizations: 'To what extent do they value these capabilities, do they need to take advantage of them and how can they manage the system and its processes more effectively?'

One of the advantages of the use of any storage medium, and electronic media in particular, is that when the memory of an individual fails as a resource (because he or she does not encode the information, forgets, does not yield up information

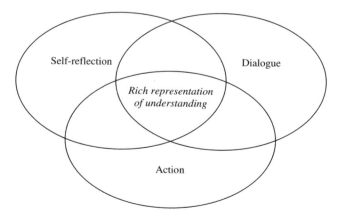

Figure 8.5   Self-reflection, dialogue and action in distributed cognition (after Boland et al. 1994)

or leaves the organization) other organizational members can turn to stored sources of data for retrieval. Buchel and Raub noted that the archival storage of information can enable organizational members to review and interpret patterns of communication and negotiation over time and to engage in dialogue. This can lead to jointly arrived-at solutions to organizational problems and shared understandings. The crucial element in the process is not the richness or the technical elegance of the information storage and retrieval system per se, rather it is in the shared meanings that are derived through communication and dialogue.

Child (2001: 676) described how PepsiCo uses ICT to promote learning within the company and its joint ventures. The company circulates information within its corporate network to the point of redundancy through its email system, which permits simultaneity of communication, is fast, overcomes time differences and allows for the open and shared expression of views. PepsiCo also circulates consolidated reports for different countries and regions. The learning and transfer of beneficial practices between different countries has resulted in, for example, knowledge about how to curb thefts on distribution runs (this was transferred from the company's Hungarian operation to its Chinese joint venture; Child 2001). One of the problems associated with the 'writing down' (as electronic practices) of these behaviours is that it reifies the activities for consumption outside of the practice but leaves out much of what may have happened. In the words of Wenger: 'a whole day of work, negotiation of meaning, boredom, inventiveness, rebellion, conversation and community building [may be] reified into a number which is a very restricted representation of that day' (1998: 132). These are the types of challenges to which L&D and knowledge management practices in organizations need to respond.

Concept Checklist

Can you now define each of the Key Concepts listed below, and are you now able to achieve the other Knowledge Outcomes specified at the beginning of the chapter?

- Technology of L&D
- Technology in L&D
- Instructional design
- Bloom's taxonomy
- Gagné's varieties of learning
- Internal conditions and external conditions
- Instructional media
- Concept analysis
- Distance learning, open learning and flexible learning
- Programmed learning
- Computer-based learning
- Modes of computer-based instruction

- e-learning (networked/non-networked and synchronous/asynchronous)
- Learning communities
- Collective cognition
- e-Learning organization

CHAPTER 9
Evaluating Learning and Development

Key Concepts

Evaluation; internal validation; external validation; validity; content validity; balanced scorecard; purposes of evaluation; pragmatic purpose; research purpose; professional-political purpose; reaction level; summative; formative; affective reactions; utility reactions; learning level; behaviour level; results level; context-input-reaction-outcome (CIRO); return on investment (ROI); alternatives to taxonomic approaches; evaluating reactions; evaluating knowledge; evaluating skills; simulations; evaluating attitudes; evaluating changes in job behaviour; learning transfer; evaluating results; benefit–cost ratio; L&D's ultimate contribution; flow; signature strengths; meaningful work

---

Knowledge Outcomes

After studying this chapter you should be able to:

- define each of the key concepts listed above;
- describe the purposes of evaluation;
- describe the various levels in the augmented evaluation taxonomy;
- explain the bases of criticisms of taxonomic approaches to evaluation and describe possible alternatives and their potential value;

- explain how you would evaluate learning and development (L&D) at each of the levels in the taxonomy;
- explain some of the difficulties of evaluating L&D;
- describe what an L&D practitioner might do in order to facilitate the transfer of learning;
- explain what you understand to be the ultimate contribution of learning and development from the standpoint of individuals and organizations.

Introduction

Each of us has a picture, however vague, of what we would like to accomplish . . . How close we get to attaining this goal becomes the measure for the quality of our lives. If it remains beyond reach, we grow resentful or resigned; if it is at least in part achieved, we experience a sense of happiness and satisfaction.

Mihaly Csikszentmihalyi, *Flow: The Classic Work on How to Achieve Happiness*

That L&D 'pays' rather than 'costs' is a view that many L&D and HR practitioners might intuitively subscribe to. Unfortunately other stakeholders, who may be more interested in the bottom-line payback, often need a good deal more convincing in terms of the return-on-money-spent. Evaluation is the final and arguably the most exacting stage of the L&D cycle, and pinpointing its contribution can often be a significant technical and practical challenge. Indeed the perceived difficulties, especially at the higher levels, often render it the subject of much rhetoric but considerable neglect – a custom sometimes 'honour'd more in the breach than in the observance'. In the view of Warr et al. (1999) there is a widespread need to improve the evaluation of L&D. The evidence supports this. For example, in a review by Collins (2002) only 16 out of 54 management development studies they looked at evaluated the impact of L&D on organizational performance. In a study of firms in the UK who were committed to L&D per se it was found that just over half of the respondents carried out evaluation to justify expenditure on L&D, whereas almost 90 per cent evaluated in order to see if the learning objectives had been met (Sadler-Smith et al. 1999). Canning argued that evaluation has become a tedious ritual performed half-heartedly at the end of an L&D event; he went on to suggest that 'if the human resource development [L&D] function has grown in stature over the last ten years, then it has little to do with the body of knowledge that has become known as training evaluation' (1996: 3).

Any tedium may be due in no small part to an over-reliance on cursory end-of-training course 'happiness sheets' that allow us to tick the box, close the lid and move on to the next project. In a hurried and time-pressured business environment there are often strong temptations and good practical reasons to behave in this way, but to do so is ultimately self-defeating. Such an approach may belie a tokenism that adds little to L&D practice in the longer term; nor does it enhance the accountability or credibility of the L&D function. This is a pity since evaluation is an inherent and indispensable part of a strategic approach to L&D. Phillips has argued that rather than reacting to the demands of others, or simply in order to meet an expectation or duty, there is a need for L&D practitioners to move towards a more proactive posture regarding evaluation (see Stoel 2004: 47). Kirkpatrick's (1996) view that the L&D field has not provided the type of evaluation that clients seek most – namely, measures of training's effect on the organization – adds fuel to the debate over the status, practice and value of evaluation. Not only do we need more evaluation; we need better evaluations and we need a clearer view of what we are evaluating and why.

Evaluation is paradoxical; it has until recently been comparatively uncontested terrain with most of the theory and practice converging around frameworks of levels of analysis, which yield what are in essence taxonomies of outcomes (for example, knowledge or skills gained). This is no bad thing. The approach was pioneered by Donald L. Kirkpatrick and it became almost a mantra for evaluation in the 1960s through to the 1990s (and indeed takes up a good proportion of this chapter), but it has now itself come under critical scrutiny. Dionne (1996: 279–80) has noted that although the question of how best to evaluate training is not a new one, our ability to assess the impact of training has to make huge strides if we are to meet managers' needs for simple and inexpensive methods. He identified the lack of a unifying *model* for theory and research as a principal barrier in this regard. This view is echoed by Holton (1996), who attributed the lack of progress to an over-reliance on taxonomies of outcomes as the bases for evaluation. One of the most exciting developments in the field of evaluation in recent years has been the attention accorded by researchers to constructing valid theoretical frameworks for evaluation over and above the solid foundation provided by older taxonomic approaches.

L&D FACTS AND FIGURES

In England *Learning and Training at Work 2000* estimated that the total costs to employers in England of providing training over the previous 12 months consisted of off-the-job training, £14.6 billion (course-related, £11.8 billion; other, e.g. seminars, workshops, £2.8 billion) and on-the-job, £9.0 billion (http://www.skillsbase.dfes.gov.uk).

Evaluation is concerned with the total worth or value of L&D in monetary and non-monetary terms for employees and the organizations of which they are apart. It is all the more important when one considers that American industries, for example, annually spend billions of dollars on training and development, and if previous estimates are to be believed, not more than 10 per cent of these expenditures may actually result in transfer to the job (Baldwin and Ford 1988: 63). Hence doing evaluation in a meaningful way and getting it right are all the more important when one considers the potential value that L&D has to enhance individual and organizational performance – and, conversely, the potential waste of resources if L&D is misdirected.

Historically there may have been a philanthropic attitude that did not require the same justification of returns from learning and development in organizations as was required of other functional activities (Kirkpatrick 1979: 78). However, it is becoming more and more important, in a world where organizational activities, systems and processes are required to be accountable for the value that they add, for L&D to demonstrate its contribution to the development and growth of individual employees and the organizations of which they are a part. Nonetheless, evaluation is problematic perhaps because it is perceived as being difficult to do well. It is unfortunate that simplistic practices sometimes appear to dominate the field, often performed perhaps out of some sense of duty rather than as a means for learning and continuous improvement. Evaluation is crucial if L&D is to promote the demonstrable value of learning to an audience of senior managers and other key stakeholders who have competing demands placed upon their time and energy and the resources they have at their disposal.

L&D FACTS AND FIGURES

A survey by the ASTD published in 2004 examined the proportion of time (as a percentage) that a sample of L&D practitioners in the USA spent on various activities. The findings revealed that L&D practitioners in the sample on average spent only 7.6 per cent of their time on measuring and evaluating L&D. (*Source*: P. Davis, J. Naughton and W. Rothwell, 2004. New roles and new competencies for the professional, *Training and Development*, 58(4): 26–36.)

Evaluation and Validation

Goldstein defined evaluation as:

> The systematic collection of descriptive and judgmental information necessary to make effective decisions related to the selection, adoption, value and modification of various instructional activities. (1993: 181)

In this sense evaluation subsumes validation (both internal validation and external validation) (Stewart 1999: 183). Sanderson (1995: 114–15) defined validation as follows:

Internal validation was described by the training policy arm of the UK government back in the 1970s as a series of 'assessments designed to ascertain whether a training programme has achieved the behavioural objectives specified' (Department of Employment 1971). Internal validation is concerned with whether L&D has met the objectives that were set.

External validation is concerned with whether the objectives for the L&D are realistically based upon an accurate initial identification of the learning needs. It consists of a series of assessments to 'ascertain whether the [behavioural] objectives of an internally valid training programme were realistically based on an accurate identification of training needs' (Department of Employment 1971: 32).

Logically, and in practice, it is entirely possible for an L&D activity (for example, a training course) to be internally valid (that is, it meets the objectives as set) but externally invalid (the objectives that were set did not meet the identified needs). The optimum situation, of course, is where the objectives that have been set are valid in relation to the identified need and the L&D is executed in such a way as to meet these objectives. To be of value to individuals and organizations L&D should meet the criteria of internal and external validity. The worst of all possible worlds is where the L&D is invalid both internally and externally (that is, it does not meet a need in terms of its defined objectives and the L&D also did not meet the defined objectives). External validity imposes an upper limit on the value of L&D; if external validity is lacking the ultimate worth of the learning, no matter how well executed, will be constrained because the needs that have been identified are themselves not an accurate reflection of the organizational problem.

PERSPECTIVE FROM RESEARCH: INTERNAL AND EXTERNAL VALIDITY

Based upon the following source: I. L. Goldstein, 1993. *Training in Organisations: Needs Assessment, Development and Evaluation.* Pacific Grove, CA: Brooks/Cole Publishing.

It should be noted that in conventional psychological interpretations the terms 'internal validity' and 'external validity' have slightly different meanings from the way we have discussed them above. The internal validity of an experiment refers to the extent to which the effect of an independent variable on a dependent variable has been correctly interpreted (Haslam and McGarty 1998: 46). Goldstein distinguished between them thus: internal validity refers to the basic question of, 'Did a treatment (an L&D intervention such as a course) make a difference in this particular situation?' External validity, on the other hand, refers to the generalizability or representativeness of the findings and is always a matter of inference since it cannot be expressed with complete confidence (1993: 191). Goldstein gives a succinct discussion of the various threats to internal validity. In answer to the question, 'Did the L&D make any difference?', for example, factors might include participants' history, their maturation, the effects of testing, and so forth. Similarly there are a number of potential threats to external validity, i.e. the generalizability of the results of the experiment; for example, if there were other treatments that might have had an effect, such as participants being exposed to multiple methods of learning – hence the effect of one of these alone cannot be isolated (Goldstein 1993: 195). Some of the threats to internal validity as identified by Goldstein are summarized below.

History: events other than the experimental treatment that occurred between pre-test and post-test.

Maturation: biological (such as tiredness) or psychological effects (such as boredom) that occur between pre-test and post-test.

Testing: pre-tests can sensitize participants as to what to look for in the treatment in order to answer questions on the post-test.

Instrumentation: changes in grading standards (perhaps because of different raters) may affect pre-test and post-test scores.

Selection of participants: biases in choosing groups (for example, volunteers for the treatment group and random selection for the control group) can affect results.

The notion of validation (internal and external) should not be confused with the term validity when the latter is used in connection with the design of evaluation studies (Patrick 1992: 523).

Evaluation is concerned with what effects L&D has had and whether or not the organization was right to try to solve the problem through L&D in the first place (Sanderson 1995: 124). Evaluation runs as a thread from the L&D event itself back to the identification and analysis of the learning needs. In this regard the flows within the L&D cycle should be seen as being iterative rather than as a 'purely mechanistic clockwork rotation' (Anderson 1993: 166). This discussion again illustrates the interrelated nature of the L&D cycle and the extent to which each stage depends upon the others. It emphasizes the fact that a weak needs identification and analysis can be a quicksand for the subsequent stages in the process. Evaluation is also concerned with the extent to which learning transfers from the learning situation to the job, and how this has affected performance and eventually (but perhaps not ultimately) whether or not the benefits outweighed the costs. These questions could be put more bluntly: 'Did the organization need L&D?', 'Did the L&D work in practice?', 'Did the L&D improve employee performance?' and 'Was there a payback from the costs involved?' The relationships between these various aspects of evaluation are shown in Figure 9.1.

The validity of the content of L&D can be examined critically by means of an importance/emphasis matrix (Goldstein 1993), based upon the premise that if the needs assessment is carried out effectively and the L&D is designed to reflect these needs the content of the L&D will be valid, i.e. it will have content validity. It should be emphasized that the concept of content validity by itself in evaluation

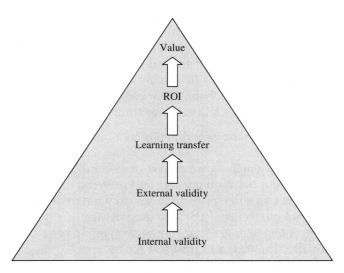

Figure 9.1 The relationships between validity, transfer of learning, return on investment (ROI) and the value of L&D

Table 9.1 The importance/emphasis matrix illustrating the content validity of L&D (adapted from Goldstein 1993: 213)

| | | Content's importance in relation to identified L&D needs | |
		Important	*Not important*
Content's emphasis in L&D programme	*Emphasized*	Content valid (relevant)	L&D is not job-related (irrelevant material included). Perceived irrelevance by learners. Likely wasted investment.
	Not emphasized	Needs unmet by L&D (relevant material not included) Opportunity missed. Likely wasted investment.	Content valid (by omission)

is a problem because a programme may well be content-valid but that does not guarantee that the learners learned the material or that they were able to apply it to their jobs (Goldstein 1993: 215). The various permutations are illustrated in Table 9.1.

Content validity of L&D is an important predictor of learning performance. Bates et al. (2000) explored the impact of the content validity of L&D (along with opportunity to use learning and four interpersonal support factors) on supervisors' ratings of workplace application of learning from a computer-based learning package. The content validity of the L&D was assessed by means of three questions within a longer questionnaire (for example: 'Skills and knowledge taught in the training are the same skills and knowledge needed to do a good job'). The research found that the perceived validity of the content of L&D (along with supervisor sanctioning for the L&D, peer support for the new learning and change resistance) were statistically significant predictors of supervisory ratings of performance post-training and accounting for 44 per cent of the variance in these non-self-report performance ratings.

PERSPECTIVE FROM PRACTICE: QUALITY AND CONTINUOUS IMPROVEMENT IN L&D

Evaluation in L&D is at the heart of a process of continuous improvement that aims to deliver quality to stakeholders. Quality is a critical competitive dimension to the extent that organizations or functions that cannot deliver products or services that meet the needs of internal or external clients cease to add value or be serious competitors. The issue of quality has grown to the extent that it has almost become a hygiene factor; clients now take for granted that a supplier will execute according to product and service specifications (Kaplan and Norton 1996: 87). Within the 'quality' movement the focus is on the client, who in the case of the L&D function might be learners, line managers, departmental managers, senior managers, the CEO, customers or shareholders. The client in this respect is anyone who receives the services of the L&D function (the supplier) and the evaluation of the supplier takes place by the immediate client. A generic quality cycle is depicted in Figure 9.2. The research, specification and planning, delivery and review and monitoring (i.e. evaluation) are centred upon meeting the needs of the client or clients (Hannagan 2002: 183).

One of the potential difficulties with this cycle is that review and monitoring (i.e. evaluation) are depicted as the final stage in the process; indeed Gibb (2002: 107) noted that evaluation is often the weakest link in the whole L&D process since it is the step that is most likely to be neglected or underdone. As was argued previously, treating evaluation in this way is problematical in both the short and the long term. One danger of treating evaluation as the final stage in the process is that it may be overlooked, postponed or ignored because of a lack of resource, effort or simply because of fatigue. A further danger is that evaluation may be seen as being solely concerned with the preceding delivery (i.e. implementation) stage of the process. However, whether or not the earlier research (i.e. needs identification and analysis) and planning stages have been executed successfully is also one of the principal questions that evaluation should seek to address. The L&D cycle is better conceived as an integrated process that does not treat the evaluation stage as a discrete entity at the end; rather it should be thought about

Continued

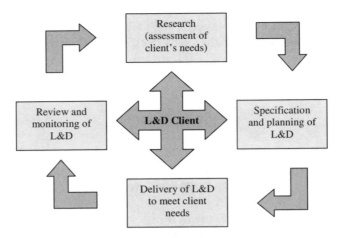

Figure 9.2 Quality cycle (adapted from Hannagan 2002)

and planned for during the application of the other stages (Stewart 1999: 178). But what does this mean in practice?

1. Firstly, it means that there should be continuous monitoring and checking at all stages and a preparedness amongst L&D practitioners to be adaptable and flexible.
2. Secondly, if new information comes to light during the specification and planning stage (i.e. design) stage with respect to the L&D needs, these should wherever possible be taken into account during the design process.
3. Thirdly, it means accepting that L&D is an uncertain process and treating it as iterative, for example by pilot-testing and being prepared to accommodate feedback and criticisms.
4. Fourthly, it means that the review and monitoring of L&D should ask questions about the validity of each of the preceding stages, not just about the implementation and delivery.

The Purposes of Evaluation

If one accepts that evaluation is an attempt to judge the value that L&D adds to an organization and its individual members, it is perhaps important to step back at this point and examine the fundamental question: 'Why evaluate L&D?' Doing so reveals some of the more subtle and political aspects to evaluation that may have a 'knock-on' effect upon the practical matters, such as who should carry out the evaluation of L&D, when it should take place, how the results may be used, interpreted and so forth. Bramley (1991) argued that evaluation has five main purposes:

1. Feedback as a form of quality control over the design and delivery of L&D and as means of improving the professional competence of the reflective L&D practitioner. This means creating a feedback loop as part of a self-correcting system (Hamblin 1974).
2. Research into the effectiveness of the various approaches to L&D and adding to the stock of professional knowledge. Such knowledge needs to be generalizable.
3. Evaluation is an intervention and as such changes the process by its mere presence – a fact that the L&D practitioner needs to be cognizant of when evaluation is being conducted.
4. Control in the sense of assessing the value added by the L&D function within the organization. In this regard Hamblin described the purpose of evaluation as control, which is 'in effect the management of training: the process of collection, analysis, and evaluation of information, leading to decision making and action' (1974: 11).
5. Evaluation can be used in political ways and as part of a power game within an organization. This has ramifications for the role of the various stakeholders and their interests, agendas and perceptions and the way in which evaluations are communicated, interpreted and acted upon.

The purposes are interrelated, but the control and power purposes are especially significant since they have implications for the ways in which evaluation is carried out and by whom. An arena where this issue manifests itself is in the presentation and interpretation of evaluation results. Egan and Beis (2001: 44) present a hypothetical case in which a client manager insists that negative feedback be expunged from an evaluation report. They commented upon the dilemma faced by the L&D practitioner in this example (in this case an external consultant). The authors suggested that in dealing with such situations ethical standards of behaviour are crucial to integrity. In their illustrative example the L&D practitioner: (a) established a basis of informed consent in the evaluation process of all participants; (b) retained responsibility for the interpretation of the results and did not bow to pressure to misrepresent; (c) protected the confidentiality of sources of negative feedback; (d) sought out advice from a group of peers to clarify and resolve the conflict. Further ethical dilemmas may confront L&D practitioners in the areas of the interpretation and explanation of results of evaluations (Russ-Eft 2001; Zukerman and Preskill 2001).

Easterby-Smith (1986) identified three purposes of evaluation, some of which overlap with those put forward by Bramley:

1. Proving the value of investing in L&D, i.e. by demonstrating that something positive has happened as a result of training or developmental activities.

2. Improving L&D, i.e. trying to ensure that current or future programmes become better than they are at present.
3. Learning and recognizing that evaluation cannot be separated out from the process on which it focuses; for example, a pre-test is a form of evaluation which of itself informs the learning process (Stewart 1999: 183–4).

Newby also presented a similar list, which couches the purposes of evaluation in terms of the benefits to be accrued. This includes: control of quality, improving L&D design, enhancing professional self-esteem of L&D practitioners, demonstrating a 'track record', articulation of appropriate and relevant criteria against which L&D may be judged and as an intervention strategy whereby L&D practitioners and managers can reappraise their roles (which may open the door to better needs identification, implementation and support for L&D). Gibb, on the other hand, summarizes five somewhat different facets of evaluation's purposes:

1. Pragmatic evaluation, which is concerned with identifying what is bad and eliminating costs and waste.
2. Ethical evaluation, which attempts to maximize the good service and justice for those involved in L&D.
3. Intellectual evaluation, which constructs valid tools and exposes prejudices.
4. Social and business evaluation, which directs effort at the point where it is most needed.
5. Personal evaluation, which through a process of self-reflection may provide a basis for those involved in L&D to convince themselves that 'what they do works' (2002: 113).

A summary of some of the various views on the purposes of evaluation is presented in Table 9.2.

Evaluation is a form of reflection. Learning and the process of reflection are inextricably linked. Learning is a means by which organizations can create new knowledge. Evaluation therefore may be a process of questioning, reflection and inquiry and hence a means by which organizations can learn. We have already

Table 9.2 Summary of the purposes of evaluation

Source	Purposes
Bramley (1991)	Feedback, research, intervention, power, control
Easterby-Smith (1986)	Proving, improving, learning
Gibb (2002)	Pragmatic, ethical, intellectual, social, business, personal
Newby (1992)	Quality control, efficient L&D design, professional self-esteem, track record, identification of assessment criteria, intervention
Reid and Barrington (1999)	Investment appraisal, feedback, improvement, learning, achievement of objectives
Stewart (1999)	Promoting (in addition to proving, improving and learning)

met the concept of reflection in earlier chapters. It is important to note that reflection can be focused upon content (the subject), process (methods used to resolve the problem) and the premises (the underlying beliefs and assumptions) (Mezirow 1991). Note that if reflection itself is a process it may also be possible to reflect upon how the reflective process itself has been engaged with. Preskill and Torres (1999) argued that evaluation as an 'evaluative enquiry' may serve as a vehicle for organizational learning. Evaluative inquiry may encompass a number of related activities, the underlying principles for which were summarized by Preskill and Torres (1999) as:

1. Asking questions: developing a spirit of curiosity that acts as a catalyst for learning through inquiry ranging from the broad and diagnostic (interpretative) to mundane factual questions.
2. Identifying and challenging values, beliefs and assumptions: these are the taken-for-granted behaviours and dispositions that may have been developed over long periods of time. For organizational learning to occur these assumptions need to be questioned in a public way.
3. Reflection: enabling L&D practitioners to reflect upon what happened and why it happened in that way that it did. Reflection can be during the process (to learn lessons for here-and-now improvements, a kind of formative inquiry) or after the process (to learn lessons for future use, a kind of summary inquiry).
4. Dialogue: sustained collective inquiry into shared meanings to understand wholes and uncover assumptions by asking for reasons that underpin statements or answers, thus making errors, biases and distortions more public.

The notion of evaluative inquiry has implications for the L&D practitioner and their role since to engage in evaluative inquiry as a means for evaluation involves much more than the technicist stance of asking whether a project worked or not, how it might be changed and whether more resources should be put into it. It implies a role for L&D practitioners that is different from the traditional technical one and that is more akin to the role of a catalyst, change agent or facilitator of organizational learning (Preskill and Torres 1999: 111).

What is clear from these discussions is that evaluation can serve multiple purposes, which range from the purely technical (for example, 'Did this intervention achieve its aims?') to the political (for example, 'How might these findings be interpreted in this organization at this time?'). Stewart raised another interesting possible role for evaluation that is connected to the political purpose outlined by Bramley, which he refers to as a 'promoting purpose' in which the results of an evaluation are used to provide marketing information for L&D within the organization. The promoting role of itself raises ethical issues that are themselves tied up with notions of objectivity and subjectivity in the interpretation of the results of evaluation and the extent to which an L&D practitioner, as one of the principal stakeholders, ever can be 'objective' in these circumstances. Stewart highlights the importance of recognizing the degree to which the evaluation process itself can be considered entirely objective and he objects to claims of objectivity on the grounds that the establishment of criteria is itself a subjective act. Any criterion can have multiple meanings to different stakeholders and furthermore the learners themselves may have no role in negotiating the criteria and hence may be disenfranchised by attempts to objectify the process (Stewart 1999: 181). Gibb (2002: 110) concurred with this view by drawing our attention to the extent to which the problem of defining standards in a reductionist and objective way is compounded by the very act of evaluation being a political and potentially threatening process. Stewart argued that the promoting role is an inevitable and implicit process that can be legitimized and served more effectively by being made explicit (perhaps through evaluative inquiry). Anderson (1993: 178–9) elaborated upon the notion of the promoting role for evaluation when he discussed its 'marketing' function, which from an evaluation perspective entails a coherent 'brand' being set out by the L&D function and a careful consideration being given to marketing the L&D concept to the main 'buyers', seen by Anderson and others as the senior management in the organization, although the client base may be broader than this.

Notwithstanding the substantive point being made by Stewart, it is clear that the process of evaluation is reducible to a technical level. This needs to be seen against the background of an organizational context in which power and politics can render the process fraught with difficulty. National context can add additional layers of complexity, for example by the need to evaluate L&D in terms of politically desirable, externally imposed or externally driven frameworks and goals (such as the Investor in People standard in the UK). This should not be taken as an encouragement for the L&D practitioner to shy away from evaluation, quite the reverse. One focus of this chapter is to explore how a comprehensive and effective evaluation founded on sound social scientific principles can be achieved that takes into account the social and political context in which the act of evaluation is situated (as well as its moral and ethical dimensions).

Acknowledgement of the difficulties posed by evaluation in a real-world organizational context places one in a position somewhere between those referred to by Goldstein as 'negativists', who feel that evaluation of L&D is unnecessary or impossible, and the impassioned positivists, who believe that only a rigorous scientific evaluation using pre-test, post-test, experimental and longitudinal research designs will suffice (Goldstein 1993: 183–4). Adopting a middle way places one in the position of being an activist (Goldstein 1993) or – better still – a realist in terms of what is desirable and achievable with respect to the evaluation of L&D. This stance places one in a position where the difficulties are acknowledged, and an optimum approach is adopted that balances as much scientific rigour and practical relevance as possible with what is achievable in an organization that must continue to function alongside the efforts of L&D practitioners to conduct interventions and evaluate them.

To summarize the arguments, evaluation may be seen as serving at least four non-mutually exclusive purposes in organizations (see Figure 9.3):

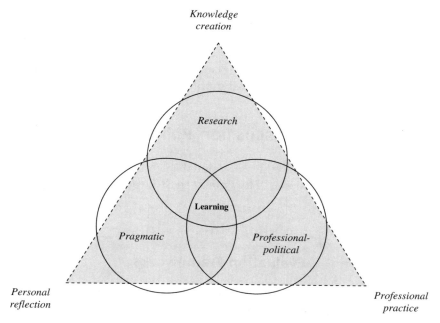

Figure 9.3 Four purposes of evaluation (research, pragmatic, professional-political and organizational learning)

1. A pragmatic purpose, in which it provides feedback for L&D practitioners and other stakeholders on how effective a particular L&D project, intervention or activity has been. This information may then be used for continuous improvement purposes in a specific context, the results of which are likely to be of limited generalizability but which nevertheless constitute reflection upon individual and organizational practice.
2. A research purpose, in which it helps, through an intellectual endeavour, to shed light upon the processes of L&D in organizations, and may be concerned with questions regarding why some methods are more effective than others, how specific methods and approaches might be improved upon and how this is informed by and informs extant theories of learning and instructional design. The results of evaluations within this purpose are likely to be more generalizable than (1). The questions raised from this perspective may be of interest not only to the ongoing continuous development of the individual L&D practitioner but also to the evolution of the field of L&D (and HR) as a profession that is based upon evidence-based practice.
3. A professional-political purpose within a specific occupational, organizational and societal context. Here deeper questions of purpose and meaning must be confronted regarding for whom evaluation is being conducted, to what purpose the results will be put, what is the degree of objectivity and subjectivity involved, and what counts as valid knowledge. The ethics of the eval-

uation in the context of the L&D practitioner as a professional marketer of learning and principal stakeholder in the process are also raised.

4. An organizational learning purpose: whereby L&D practitioners assume the role of change agent or facilitator of organizational learning by engaging in the processes of reflection and dialogue, asking questions, and identifying and challenging values, beliefs and assumptions (see Preskill and Torres 1999).

Discussion Point

What are the likely ethical and professional dilemmas that evaluation may raise for the L&D practitioner? How might these be addressed or overcome?

Evaluation Frameworks

The perception of 'how to' evaluate has over the past half century converged around a classic framework put forward by Donald L. Kirkpatrick in the 1950s. Like the systematic approach to L&D, the Kirkpatrick framework has within it a simplicity and an inherent logic that has made it difficult to surpass as a taxonomy. However, after almost half a century of pre-eminence the approach is now being questioned on theoretical grounds. In this chapter we will examine some of the various taxonomic frameworks upon which evaluation can be based; we will then go on to explore some of the critiques that have been made of this family of approaches and consider some alternatives.

The Kirkpatrick Framework

The most influential contribution to evaluation theory and practice has come from Kirkpatrick's 1959 framework for the evaluation of training; it appears to have generated a great deal of subsequent interest and related work from authors in the UK such as Warr et al. (1970), Hamblin (1974), and Bramley (1991). The Kirkpatrick framework has been similarly influential in the USA (see, for example, Dixon 1996; Phillips 1996). Like the systematic approach itself, the logic of Kirkpatrick's framework has ensured its durability. The assumption of Kirkpatrick's original work was that 'one training director cannot borrow evaluation results form another; he/she can however borrow evaluation techniques' (1979: 78). In other words, Kirkpatrick proposed a generic framework and associated set of techniques that were applicable in a wide variety of settings; for example, the approach has been applied in education as well as industry. Whilst intrinsically the four levels are not qualitatively different (although it is possible to argue that the higher levels are of greater overall significance), in practical terms real differences have emerged in empirical studies of what organizations typically evaluate in practice (Alliger et al. 1997; Sadler-Smith, Down and Field 1999). For example, the Alliger et al. (1997) study suggested that the majority of organizations (72–89 per cent) depend upon evaluations of what learners' views were (their reactions), whilst the involvement at other levels (for example, learning, behaviour and results) decreased monotonically the higher up the levels we move (29–40 per cent measure what was learned, 11–12 per cent measure transfer to the job and 2–7 per cent measure impact on the business). We will now consider these four levels in more depth with a view to understanding their significance for L&D practice.

L&D FACTS AND FIGURES

Donald Kirkpatrick's 'Techniques for Evaluating Training Programs' first appeared in a four-part series in the *Journal of the American Society of Training Directors* in November 1959. Kirkpatrick's framework has had widespread and enduring popularity as a result of its simplicity and ability to help L&D practitioners think about training evaluation criteria in a systematic way. Kirkpatrick based it on four simple questions: what were the learners' views on the L&D; what did they actually learn; did the L&D transfer to their job; and what was the impact of the L&D on the business? These questions then translated into four levels of evaluation.

Reaction level: this level of evaluation is most typically applied in the case of formalized L&D experiences – for example, a training course, workshop or other event – and hence it is most easily understood in this context. In its simplest interpretation an evaluation at the reaction level refers to 'how well the trainees liked a particular training program' (Kirkpatrick 1979: 78). The reaction of learners can be assessed with respect to:

1. Content of the programme, such as its relevance to their job, the level of interest or motivation it aroused in them (how much motivation they came to it with might also be a factor here) and so forth.
2. Objectives of the programme: how relevant were they, were they achieved?
3. Methods used to deliver the programme: were they appropriate, were they executed well, and so forth?
4. Resources and environment: what was the quality of the visual aids used, was the physical environment conducive to learning?
5. Personal effectiveness of the trainer or instructor.

Evaluation at this level is necessarily and inevitably highly subjective since it is concerned with learners' opinions and feelings. Nonetheless, the latter are likely to be important determinants of how learners engage with a learning event and the extent to which they may undertake formalized learning in the future. Hence, even though they may only be opinions they can be important predictors of current and future learning behaviours. Reactions are not, however, necessarily related to eventual learning and job performance since it is entirely possible for an individual to enjoy a training course, for example, but not learn from it (Goldstein 1993: 161). Learners' reactions are seen by some (for example, Hamblin 1974) as the first point in a causal chain that can affect learning, transfer to job and ultimately results.

PERSPECTIVE FROM RESEARCH: ARE LEARNERS' REACTIONS RELATED TO LEARNING OUTCOMES?

Based upon the following source: G. M. Alliger, S. I. Tannenbaum, W. Bennett, H. Traver and A. Shotland, 1997. A meta-analysis of the relations among training criteria, *Personnel Psychology*, 50: 341–58.

Alliger et al. (1997) explored the correlations between learners' reactions and other aspects of evaluation. Correlation is a means by which the relationship between two variables can be described and quantified. Two variables are said to be correlated if changes in one variable are associated with changes in the other variable (Hair et al. 1998: 151). Note the use of the term 'association'; there is no logical inference of cause-and-effect that can be inferred from a simple association between two variables. The correlational method does not make any inferences about causes. The strength of the relationship can be quantified using the correlation coefficient, the most commonly used of which is the Pearson product-moment correlation (Pearson's r) (Haslam and McGarty 1998). The value of r indicates the strength of the association, -1.00 indicating a perfect negative correlation, $+1.00$ indicating a perfect positive correlation. In L&D research values approaching 1.00 are very rare indeed. According to Haslam and McGarty, values of r near to zero indicate no correlation; 0.10 to 0.30 is an r which may be described as 'small' (and with a sample size of $N = 100$ a correlation of 0.30 should be apparent in the scatter-plot); $0.30 \leq r \leq 0.50$ is 'moderate'; $r > 0.50$ may be described as 'large' (see Haslam and McGarty 1998: 232). The correlation coefficient can also tell us something about the size of the overlap between the two variables (i.e. the amount of common variance). For example, if there is a correlation of 0.50 between learners' reactions to training and their subsequent job performance, there is 25 per cent (r^2 or $(0.50 \times 0.50) \times 100$ per cent) common variation between the two variables (reaction and performance). The remaining 75 per cent is not associated with reactions. If the value of r is low, for example 0.30 (common variance in this case is 9 per cent), this means that 91 per cent of the variation in one variable is associated with things other than the variation in the other variable (Haslam and McGarty 1998: 234) (see Figure 9.4).

Continued

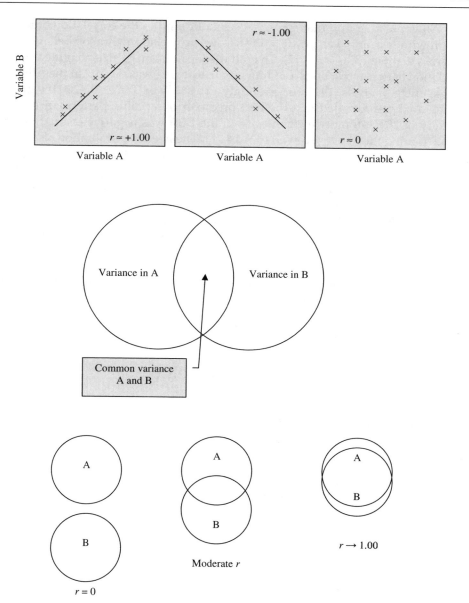

Figure 9.4 Schematic representations of correlation coefficients and common variance (adapted from Burroughs 1975; Haslam and McGarty 1998)

Alliger et al. found that across six scientific studies the correlation of reaction with learning was low ($r = 0.14$), as was correlation with job behaviours across eight studies ($r = 0.12$). Overall the mean (sample-size weighted) correlation between reactions and immediate learning was on 0.07 in the Alliger et al. meta-analysis (1997). Interestingly, in a study by Tan et al. (2003) regression analyses revealed that the best predictor of learning performance in a study of 283 automotive technicians in the USA was negative evaluation of the training they have received ($\beta = 0.41**$). The negative evaluation also correlated with pre-training knowledge. They explained the counter-intuitive finding by arguing that trainees who were already knowledgeable may have evaluated it negatively because it failed to live up to their expectations; this is, however, a quite speculative assertion. The conclusion that they draw from this is that equating the value of L&D with positive learner evaluations may not be the best way of judging success. The overall conclusion we can draw is that to attribute learning performance to favourable reactions is likely to be an erroneous inference, and to expect learning to take place simply because learners reacted favourably is an unrealistic expectation. This does not mean, however, that learners' reactions are unimportant, they are crucial in other ways.

Discussion Point

To what extent do you agree with the assertion that learners' reactions are important in L&D practice? Justify your reasoning.

Reaction evaluation need not be conducted only at the end of a learning event; making reaction evaluation a part of the ongoing process (i.e. formative) can be a valuable way to influence the direction of a learning event, and to shape content and process to meet the needs of the learner. Hence reaction evaluation itself can be:

Summative: the gathering of learners' views at the end of an event.
Formative: the gathering of learners' views during the event.

Reaction evaluation as a summative event informs future L&D practice, but if only conceived in these terms it may overlook valuable ongoing learning experiences for the reflective L&D practitioner. Indeed, such reaction evaluation need not be formalized as such but may involve simply canvassing the opinions of learners in situ. Typically, however, the reaction evaluation is usually summative and most often in the form of an end-of-event questionnaire (sometimes referred to disparagingly as a 'happy sheet'). Indeed the tone of much of the discussion of reaction-level evaluation is sometimes disapproving. One danger is that reaction-level evaluation may end up being treated as a duty and not taken seriously as a learning opportunity for the practitioner as part of a continuous improvement process.

Whilst empirical evidence and logic suggest that it is not necessary for learners to have a favourable reaction in order to learn, it may be difficult to argue that so long as the learning objectives were achieved the learners' views are irrelevant. Perhaps a better way to think about reactions is to further unpack them in terms of two possible dimensions that evaluation practice often fails to discriminate adequately between:

Affective reactions: the extent to which the learners found the programme to be enjoyable.

Utility reactions: the learners' views on the extent to which the programme may affect the capability to perform their job (Alliger et al. 1997).

When using questionnaires in order to assess constructs that are not amenable to direct measurement, single questions (items) are sometimes used and although they are easy to formulate, they are sometimes problematic in terms of their measurement properties. In order to overcome the limitations of single items researchers often develop multi-item scales (i.e. a series of questions on the same theme). For example, when assessing learners' reactions to L&D through questionnaire it is often the case that a number of items are written and included in a questionnaire survey that is administered to participants in an L&D programme or event (usually at the end). The extent to which these questions will each be tapping into different aspects (dimensions) of learners' reactions is often overlooked; however, as we noted above, some researchers have unpacked the subdimensions of the reaction construct. But how do we decide which items group together? How do we know if the items we design to assess a particular dimension of learners' reactions actually do behave in a consistent way? How do we uncover the underlying features of learners' reactions in an empirical way? Factor analysis provides one way of addressing these questions.

Factor analysis is a means by which correlational techniques are applied to complex data sets in order to simplify them (Kline 1994). It does this by analysing the interrelationships (correlations) among a large number of variables to define a smaller number of underlying dimensions known as factors (Hair et al. 1998: 90). Factor analysis is based upon the degree of association between variables expressed as the correlation coefficients in the form of a matrix that shows this relationship between all the variables in a set. As a measure of association the correlation matrix is amenable to visual inspection and even to the identification of patterns when the number of variables is small (for example, a five by five matrix would include ten unique intercorrelations, excluding the diagonal elements). However, with large numbers of scores the correlation matrix quickly becomes complex and the identification of even simple patterns by eye is difficult. Factor analysis simplifies a matrix of correlations by identifying a smaller number of latent variables (factors) and providing a loading for each variable (analogous to the correlation of a variable with a factor) on each factor. The factor itself is defined by the loadings of each individual variable on it (Kline 1994). Hair et al. (1998: 92–3) provided a useful example from the marketing area, where three underlying variables ('in-store experience', 'product assortment and availability', and 'product quality and price') were identified from a much larger group of variables. As well as simplifying interpretation these factors can then be used as summary variables in further analyses (such as group comparisons and regressions), whereby the scores for individual variables may be summed and divided by the number of variables loading on the factor to give a mean score. As a very simple rule of thumb, sample sizes of a least 100 are required for factor analysis and usually more participants than this are necessary (see below and also Kline 1994 for more detailed guidance).

PERSPECTIVE FROM RESEARCH: THE USE OF EXPLORATORY FACTOR ANALYSIS TO UNCOVER THE DIMENSIONALITY OF PARTICIPANTS' RESPONSES TO L&D

Based upom the following source: R. B. Morgan and W. J. Casper, 2000. Examining the factor structure of participant reactions to training: a multidimensional approach, *Human Resource Development Quarterly*, 11(3): 301–17.

In their research Morgan and Casper used a data set comprising 9,128 questionnaires from employees of a government agency in the USA covering learners' reactions to 800 different classes on 400 different L&D events. The questionnaire was a standard one used by the organization and consisted of 32 questions (items), the majority of which were scored on a five-point satisfaction scale (from very satisfied to very dissatisfied); three items were scored on a three-point scale. Morgan and Casper randomly split the data set into two sub-samples (A and B) with sub-sample B as a 'hold-out' for further confirmatory factor analysis (a more sophisticated multivariate technique not discussed here and implemented in statistical computer packages such as LISREL and AMOS).

Recall that the purpose of factor analysis is to reduce the original items (32 in this case) to a smaller, more manageable group that may reflect underlying dimensions of learners' reactions. The factor analysis revealed that there appeared to be six underlying dimensions to learners' reactions and these accounted for 63.5 per cent of the variance in scores. Morgan and Casper employed principal axis factoring and used Cattell's (1966) scree test as the means to decide how many latent groupings there were; they rotated their solution to simple structure to allow for correlations between the factors (which one might expect in this instance) and took the criterion of salient loading as 0.40 (loadings of less than this being treated as 'non-significant'). Although the latter value (0.40) is often taken as a convenient rule of thumb, some factor analysts prefer to use a value that is commensurate with the sample size. For example, Hair et al. suggest that 0.40 is appropriate for a sample size of 200. With larger samples a lower value is needed for significance (for example, where $N = 350$ the criterion of salient loading may be taken as 0.30), whilst for samples of 100 participants 0.55 is an appropriate threshold value for the factor loadings. Furthermore, with respect to sample size Comrey and Lee (1992) offered the following guidance on sample size for factor analysis: $N = 50$, very poor sample size; $N = 100$, poor; $N = 200$, fair; $N = 300$, good; $N = 500$, very good; $N = 1,000$, excellent. The reason for this is that correlation coefficients tend to be less reliable when estimated from small samples; hence it is important for the sample size to be large enough to enable correlations to be reliably estimated (Tabachnik and Fidell 1996: 640). Kline (1994: 73) argued that to insist on a minimum N of 200 is pessimistic and that in data with a clear factor structure an N of 100 may be sufficient.

The factors that emerged from Morgan and Casper's data were named (labelled) on the basis of the individual items that loaded on each of them. Hence, the six factors that made up learners' reactions were satisfaction with: (1) instructor (six items, for example: 'how satisfied were you with the instructor's knowledge of the course material and subject matter?'); (2) management and administration process (seven items, for example, 'how satisfied are you with the availability of training courses for individuals in your job classification?'); (3) testing process (three items, for example, 'how satisfied are you with the fairness of the course exam?'); (4) utility of training (seven items, for example, 'how satisfied are you with the relevance of the course content to you job?'); (5) materials (four items, for example, 'how satisfied are you with the audio and visual aids used by the instructor?'); (6) course structure (two items, for example, 'how satisfied are you with the length of the training course?').

The most important finding from this research is that it provides support for the view that a multi-dimensional approach is needed when considering learners' reactions. To simply use the term 'reaction' in a global (unidimensional) and indiscriminate way begs the question of 'reaction to what?' The research by Morgan and Caspar has gone some way to identifying the facets of learners' reactions to L&D. They call for a taxonomy of participant reactions to L&D which may also be of value in researching training effectiveness, for example by enabling the question of 'which dimensions of learners' reactions are associated with effective L&D?' to be asked. The empirical findings also concur with the hypothesized 'utility factor' suggested by Alliger et al. (1997). Clearly there is an upper limit on the validity of Morgan and Casper's findings since the items themselves may not be exhaustive of all potential dimensions of reaction (the domain may be restricted). The generalizability of the findings is also open to question given the use of a sample from a single organization. Nonetheless their research illustrates the value of going not just beyond single-item measures of reaction, but also by going beyond unidimensional measures.

Learning level: it will be recalled from Chapter 6 that within a systematic approach to L&D the specification of learning objectives is a key milestone in the process. Evaluation at the learning level is concerned with the extent to which the pre-specified objectives have been met. Learning-level evaluation can be concerned with any of the various forms of learning – for example, knowledge, skills and attitudes. The form that the evaluation takes and the techniques used will depend to a large extent upon the type of learning being assessed. As with reaction, the temptation is to see learning-level evaluation as purely summative; however, much is to be gained by evaluating learning in a formative fashion in order that:

1.   Learners may become more aware of their progression towards the goals.
2.   L&D practitioners may become more aware of whether the learning process is being effective or not.

This may prompt L&D practitioners to make changes or provide remediation in the light of emerging evidence in order to promote more effective and efficient learning. Interestingly, one potential benefit of reaction-level evaluation (especially as a formative process) is that it may reveal the accuracy or otherwise of the objectives themselves and may therefore function as a check on the external validity of the L&D event as it has been predefined (for example, by asking the question: 'How relevant is what is being covered to your work?'). This does therefore give scope, of course, for the external validity to be enhanced in the light of the learners' views.

The question of the content validity also raises interesting questions with respect to any learning that takes place that was unplanned and not pre-specified in the learning aims or objectives. On the basis that L&D can be uncertain, a more flexible approach than that intimated by a strict adherence to the systematic approach is required since much useful learning may take placed that was unplanned for. In the evaluation of learning it may be advisable to build in some mechanism whereby this unplanned learning can be articulated and recognized. Goal-free evaluation is a more open-ended approach in which the focus is not upon what the learners achieved in a predetermined sense but what emerged for them in the experience.

Bramley (1991) argued that in one sense the evaluation of knowledge, skills and attitudes cannot be complete until it is followed back and assessed in the workplace in order to discover to what extent the learning is useful for the job and has transferred from the learning situation to the workplace. A corollary of this point is that the learning level of evaluation may be decomposed into at least three sub-levels: knowledge, skills and attitudes. A further distinction that may be mapped onto these levels is that of planned versus unplanned learning outcomes (each of these may yield gains in knowledge, skill or attitude). Again, as with the reaction level, the Kirkpatrick framework is revealed as having more levels than meets the eye. The assumption in some interpretations of Kirkpatrick – and subsequent frameworks that build upon Kirkpatrick – is that if the learning transfers from the learning situation to the job situation, learning outcomes are causally connected to job behaviour outcomes. It is to the issue of changes in workplace behaviour and performance that we will now turn our attention.

Behaviour/performance level: this level of evaluation is concerned with any effect that L&D may have in the workplace upon learners' behaviour and performance. It is concerned with the extent to which learning has transferred to the job and the extent to which the changed behaviours result in enhanced performance. The latter is a subtle but important distinction to which Stewart (1999: 187) draws our attention, since it is entirely feasible for a learner to demonstrate changed behaviours in the workplace as a result of L&D, but whether or not this results in enhanced individual performance is a different matter. Stewart cites the example of a salesperson whose behaviour (for example, attitudes towards the customer) may change through learning; this may or may not, however, have a concomitant effect upon sales performance. A distinction may be drawn therefore between these two facets of workplace outcome.

In point of fact the latter issue to which Stewart refers (which is in effect performance) is arguably situated in the next level ('results') of the Kirkpatrick framework and does illustrate that the boundaries in the Kirkpatrick framework may not be as clear-cut as they at first seem. Another distinction may be drawn between individual performance (to which Stewart is referring) and organizational performance, which is the interpretation often attached to the Kirkpatrick results level (see next section). For present purposes and for the sake of clarity the behaviour level will be considered as being concerned with how the job is being carried out differently by an individual as a result of L&D and in the sense of 'behaviour' as specified originally by Kirkpatrick. An important feature is the transition between levels from learning to behaviour; hence just as it was the case that a favourable reaction does not imply better learning, so learning does not necessarily imply enhanced behaviours in the workplace (Goldstein 1993: 165) nor do they imply improved performance. The methods that may be used to assess behaviour will be considered in more detail below.

Results level: Kirkpatrick originally used this level of evaluation to refer to the effects of L&D in terms of organizational objectives. In this sense it transcends the individual and the job level and is more akin to the strategic level of analysis, for example as alluded to in the previous discussions of the application of a balanced scorecard-type approach in L&D. Traditionally such results-level outcomes have been seen in terms of costs, turnover, absenteeism, grievances, workforce satisfaction and commitment (Goldstein 1993: 166). This assumes that the planning for the L&D was cognizant of the organizational-level issues in the first place; however, if these were absent in the planning process then results are difficult to assess, except through some post hoc or retro-fitting of actual outcomes to presumed organizational-level needs. Thus if a customer-care training programme is introduced in an organization with a view to enhancing levels of customer satisfaction, the up-front analyses may require quite careful specification of intended or anticipated gains. It is at this level also that issues of benefit–cost analyses are important, where the aspiration is often to balance the quantifiable gains made through L&D against the costs of the programme (both the direct costs and indirect costs such as downtime, etc.). As might be expected, this is one of the most difficult levels at which to conduct quantitative analyses because the benefits that may transpire (such as increased sales) may not be directly attributable to L&D since there may be a whole set of confounding factors (such as changes in demand, competitor behaviour, buyer behaviour and so forth). Some commentators suggest that in the absence of experimental designs this level of analysis is very difficult to execute in a rigorously scientific way.

One approach to tackling these difficult issues lies in further subdivision into departmental- and organizational-level benefits (Stewart 1999: 188) wherein the former might include departmental output, waste material costs, absenteeism, staff turnover or accident frequency, and the latter might encompass cultural changes, labour flexibility, amenability to change and enhanced ability to recruit and retain skilled workers (Harrison 2002: 316). What is clear from this discussion of the Kirkpatrick framework is that the notion of levels is not as unambiguous as many interpretations of it suggest. As noted above, there are sub-levels within the levels and there are also interrelationships between the levels, which mean that they are not as discrete as they may at first appear; here we begin to see some opportunities to unpack the Kirkpatrick framework. Before we examine some of the criticisms that have been levelled, it will be useful to examine other approaches that take a similar perspective but which have different or supplementary levels to those of Kirkpatrick (or at least different names for the same levels).

L&D FACTS AND FIGURES

During its 2004 International Conference the American Society for Training and Development (ASTD) presented Donald L. Kirkpatrick with the Lifetime Achievement in Workplace Learning and Performance Award. The highly prestigious ASTD award recognizes an individual for a body of work that has had significant impact on the field of workplace learning and performance. Kirkpatrick's name is permanently etched in the history of the field of workplace learning and performance and has become synonymous with evaluation, a cornerstone of the practice. (*Source*: http://www.astd.org).

Other Evaluation Taxonomies

The Hamblin (1974) framework (Figure 9.5) is similar to Kirkpatrick's with the additional feature that it emphasizes hypothetical cause-and-effect relationships wherein one level (for example, reactions) impacts upon the succeeding level, in this case learning; the effect of the reaction becomes an 'ingredient of the new level of causation' in the learning level (Anderson 1993: 171). The precept is that the act of training causes a series of interlinked effects (reaction effects, E1; learning effects, E2; job behaviour effects, E3; organization effects, E4; ultimate value

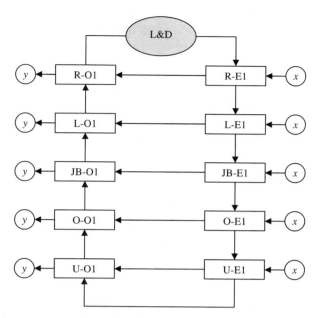

Figure 9.5 Hamblin's evaluation framework (adapted from Hamblin 1974). *Notes*: E, effects; O, objectives; R, results; L, learning; JB, job behaviour; O, organization; U, ultimate; *x*, input factors extraneous to L&D itself; *y*, outputs extraneous to L&D)

effects, E5). Patrick is of the view that this idea of a chain of causal links is 'quite neat' (1992: 517) but that it breaks down for the hypothesized E1–E2 link between the reaction effects of training and the learning effects of training (as we learned from our previous discussions). Hamblin also built in a corresponding objective for each level against which the effects may be evaluated (O1–O5).

Hamblin also included additional factors, which may be outside of the L&D practitioner's control, that may influence effects. In this way Hamblin's framework is more like a model (in the sense that Holton and others refer) than is Kirkpatrick's because Hamblin is more explicit about some of the hypothesized relationships between the elements of the model and other extraneous factors. In terms of the internal–external validation distinction, E2 is concerned with internal validation, whilst E3 to E5 are concerned with external validation (Patrick 1992: 523). One problem with the way in which the Hamblin framework may be interpreted is that the ultimate value level may be easily couched in terms of the dollar value or cost of learning. However, the ultimate value of learning may be something that goes beyond E1 through E4 (the latter arguably could encompass the return on investment) and be personal, transforming and life-changing, and hence may be difficult to value in monetary or performance terms (for example, the 'human good' of L&D as perhaps the ultimate level).

Like Kirkpatrick before them, Warr et al. (1970) also adopted a series of levels of outcomes as the basis of their framework but the approach is subtly different and, like Hamblin's approach, augments the original Kirkpatrick levels in a significant way. Warr et al.'s framework has four levels, each of which is concerned with the acquisition of information upon which L&D decisions may be based:

1. Context: evaluation of learning needs and objectives.
2. Input: evaluation of possible resources and choice between alternative L&D inputs.
3. Reaction: evaluation of learners' immediate or delayed reactions to the L&D.
4. Outcome: evaluation of the changes as a result of L&D in learning, job behaviour, job performance.

The approach goes under the acronym of CIRO, standing for context, input, reaction and outcome. The third and the fourth levels correspond to the Kirkpatrick framework, with a correspondence of the reaction level in both frameworks. Warr et al.'s outcome level encompasses the second through fourth levels of Kirkpatrick but is termed slightly differently: immediate outcome (learning level); intermediate outcome (on job behaviour level); and ultimate outcome (effects of enhanced job performance on the organization). The major difference between this approach and the Kirkpatrick one comes with the context and input levels that precede the reaction and outcome levels. The context level examines 'what it is that needs to be changed' and is concerned with questions such as 'Is L&D an appropriate solution?', 'Are the objectives appropriate?', 'Do they relate to the needs analysis in a logical and consistent manner?', 'Are the objectives unambiguous, measurable and achievable and how will outcomes be assessed?' (Sanderson 1995: 127). These should be familiar questions to L&D practitioners who have considered the issue of needs identification and analysis, and indeed the context level is in effect a needs analysis phase. It differs slightly in that it infers a continuous monitoring and reappraisal; hence it depicts evaluation as an ongoing and iterative process. Similarly, the input level in the CIRO framework is concerned with issues of learning design (what methods should be used, who should provide the L&D, how should the L&D be organized and so forth).

The final Kirkpatrick-type approach to be considered (albeit briefly) is that expounded by Phillips. The significant addition in his framework is the explicit consideration of return on investment (ROI), which he adds as a fifth and final level over and above the business results level. His justification for this is that if too much money is spent on a specific L&D project performance might increase but 'you can end up with a negative ROI' (Stoel 2004: 47). Phillips also has alternative labels to the some of the other levels:

Level 1: Reaction, satisfaction, planned action.
Level 2: Learning.
Level 3: Application.
Level 4: Business impact.
Level 5: ROI.

Phillips has written extensively on ways in which this fifth level of evaluation may be approached and we will consider this further in the section on 'Methods'.

The relationship between the original Kirkpatrick framework and the later but related approaches are shown in Table 9.3. Note that the table attempts to emphasize the value added by the different authors. For example, it does not imply that Bramley ignores the reaction level, for example – simply that his major contribution is with respect to the evaluation of the different levels of learning (indeed most of his book is a very thorough treatment of this issue). As may be seen, one might suggest that when compared and analysed there are multiple separate levels at which evaluation can be conducted. Table 9.3 represents an augmented taxonomy. Each of the levels requires specific approaches to its assessment. Before we turn to the various techniques and methods that may be applied in evaluating at each of the levels, we will briefly examine some of the critiques of the various Kirkpatrick-type frameworks.

L&D FACTS AND FIGURES

The 2004 American Society for Training and Development (ASTD) survey of a broad cross-section of US organizations revealed that 74 per cent of respondents evaluated L&D at the reaction level, 31 per cent at the learning level, 14 per cent at the performance level and 8 per cent at the results level. (*Source*: ASTD State of the Industry Report 2004).

Critiques of Evaluation Taxonomies

Taxonomic approaches specify the criteria against which the worth or value of L&D may be assessed; for example, learner reactions are a set of criteria based around favourable and unfavourable views of learners within an implicit set of values in relation to, for example, the usefulness of the learning for them. The same line of reasoning may be applied to the other levels. It is the most widely applied framework, providing a simple taxonomy of outcomes that enables the complex empirical and methodological issues associated with evaluation to be approached logically and coherently and with reduced complexity. However, some have argued that the simplicity of the approach may also be a liability (Alliger et al. 1997). Alliger and Janak (1989) identified and critically assessed three assumptions, which, they argue, underpin the Kirkpatrick framework.

1. The first weakness in the assumptions of the Kirkpatrick framework is that each succeeding level is more informative than the preceding one. This may be questioned on the grounds that not all L&D aims to effect change at all four levels and that it is not necessarily the case that the dollar estimation of L&D's contribution is more important than the lower levels. There are occasions when a more qualitative evaluation (Alliger and Janak 1989), perhaps

Table 9.3　The augmented L&D taxonomy

Kirkpatrick (1979)	Warr, Bird & Rackham (1970)	Hamblin (1974)	Bramley (1991)	Phillips (1996)	Summary	
	Context				1.	Context
	Input				2.	Input
Reaction	Reaction	Reaction		Reaction and planned action	3.	Affective reaction
					4.	Utility reaction
Learning	Immediate outcome	Learning	Changes in knowledge	Learning	5.	Knowledge gained
			Changes in skill		6.	Skills gained
			Changes in attitude		7.	Attitudinal change
Behaviour	Intermediate outcome	Job behaviour		Applied learning on the job	8.	Job behaviour
Results	Ultimate outcome	Organization		Business results	9.	Organizational results
				Return on investment	10.	Return on investment
		Ultimate value			11.	Ultimate

embodying a more inductive, goal-free methodology, would be more appropriate than a deductive approach.

2.　The second assumption that may be inferred is that each level is caused by the preceding level. Reaction may not be expected to cause learning: for example, a learning experience may be somewhat unpleasant but effective; similarly, reaction measures and learning measures are often administered at the same time and there are no grounds to assume that the former causes the latter (Alliger and Janak 1989).

3.　The third assumption is that each succeeding level is correlated positively with the preceding level. As noted previously, Alliger and Janak examined this assertion by analysing the correlation amongst the levels that were reported in published studies. They found that correlations between reaction and learning were of the order of 0.07, and those between reaction and behaviour were 0.05. The correlations between the other levels were higher but modest nonetheless. This seems to argue against the causal chain that Hamblin postulated in his framework (from the learning level upwards).

As has been noted, a number of variants of the framework have been presented that go beyond four levels into five and more (indeed in the preceding discussion an augmented eleven-level framework was offered based on a synthesis of these various frameworks). Note that the term 'framework' has been used throughout in preference to the term 'model'. In general terms the latter refers to a group of elements or concepts that are linked together in some relational or functional way and that may enable predictions to be made about the system under consideration. The Kirkpatrick approach is not a model in this sense (which he himself admits openly – see below); rather it is a framework, a set of criteria or taxonomy (a classification) of outcomes. It does not attempt to explain cause-and-effect relationships between the different elements of the framework. This leads us to a recent debate regarding the validity of the four-level approach.

Trenchant and fundamental criticisms of the Kirkpatrick framework have been voiced by Holton (1996) and his co-researchers. One major aspect of the critique offered by Holton is that the four-level evaluation framework does not meet the criteria for a theory or a model, which then raises the need for a fully specified model for L&D evaluation that does contain distinct concepts between which relationships are hypothesized and which enable predictions to be made about the system and the associated cause-and-effect relationships. As part of a critique of Kirkpatrick's framework Holton proposed a model in which there are a number of important differences between his work and that of Kirkpatrick:

1. The significance of reactions is downplayed.
2. There are three outcome measures: learning, individual performance and results.
3. Influences on outcomes are specified.

So, for example, learning is affected by motivation, ability and perceptions of L&D; individual performance, as well as being related to learning, is affected by motivation to transfer, the transfer climate and the transfer design (i.e. the features of the learning design that promote transfer). Organizational performance (related to individual performance) is affected by links to organizational goals, expected utility (given that L&D that has low expected utility it will be less able to demonstrate results) and ROI and external events (i.e. those factors that are extraneous to training but that may affect the organizational results, for example equipment failures) (see Figure 9.6).

A detailed discussion of the model and the accompanying debates is beyond the present scope; however, Holton has argued that L&D practitioners who use the four-level framework are likely to arrive at erroneous conclusions about their programmes and that what is needed is a model such as that the one that he and his co-researchers have proposed, which can be used as a diagnostic tool for the identification of critical influences on outcomes and which may help L&D practitioners to arrive at valid explanations for the outcomes obtained (Holton 1996: 18). Theoretically and conceptually this is a strong position. It is still necessary, however, to specify outcomes – but important to treat them only as such. As a footnote to this brief discussion it is insightful to consider Kirkpatrick's response to these criticisms (which were typically pragmatic): 'when I read [Holton's] article, I thought: I don't think I ever called it a model. I just called it the four levels. So someone criticized me and said, 'It's not a model, it's a taxonomy'. I thought to myself, so what? I don't care if it's a taxonomy or a model. It's four levels and people find it useful' (Stoel 2004: 46).

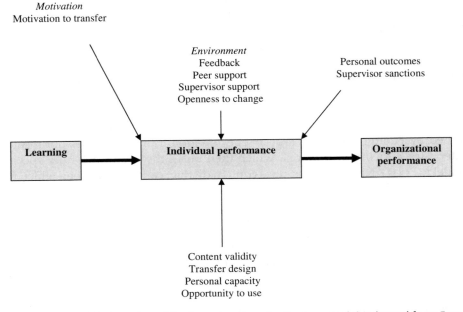

Figure 9.6   Simplified version of the Learning Transfer System model (adapted from Ruona et al. 2002)

Evaluating L&D

The levels (whether it is four, five or eleven) at which the evaluation is conducted and the research approach adopted when evaluating L&D depends upon a number of factors. For example, it may depend upon the knowledge and skills of the evaluator (since some methods are likely to be technically more complex than others), the resources available to support the evaluation (some methods are more resource intensive than others) and so on. Easterby-Smith (1986) identified a number of approaches, each of which is distinct in its methodological stance:

1. The scientific method: for example, using deductive approaches and experimental designs to test hypotheses and answer research questions like 'Is distance learning more effective for the acquisition of facts, concepts and principles than is classroom-based instruction?'
2. The systems approach, which examines the inputs to the L&D system and the way in which they are translated into identifiable outcomes.
3. The goal-free approach that in effect takes a bottom-up, inductive approach in examining what the outcomes turned out to be in practice, and illuminative approaches in which the evaluation focuses progressively on interesting ideas and aspects of practice rather than preconceived issues.

4. The responsive method in which the various stakeholders have their own unique input into setting the evaluation agenda (see Woodall and Winstanley 1998: 29).

Which approach is taken is a matter for the individual L&D practitioner to decide in terms of the aims of the evaluation, the organizational context and the resource constraints under which she or he may be required to operate. We will now examine some of the principal levels identified in Table 9.3 in order to explore the ways in which the practice of evaluation might be conducted (Table 9.4).

Evaluating Context

Evaluating context is concerned with the identification and analysis of the learning needs and the setting of objectives or goals. A previous chapter gave some consideration to methods of learning needs analysis. Learning theory is also relevant when considering the context since, as may be recalled from the setting of appropriate and challenging goals, it is an effective means by which learning and achievement can be fostered. Traditionally the setting of goals is seen as part of the L&D cycle, with the prime responsibility as that of the L&D practitioner who effectively crafts and synthesizes the issues raised in the needs analysis stage into effective and appropriate learning designs. However, Baldwin et al. (2000) caution against making such an activity the sole responsibility of the L&D function since in their view the issue of setting goals (and the concomitant issues of design) need to take cognizance of the views of managers. They argue that managers should work with learners prior to L&D taking place in order to set goals for learning that are commensurate with likely transfer. One reason for this is that the most powerful source for transfer in the organizational context may be the learner's manager since the review and rewards controlled by one's boss are likely to be very powerful influences on employee learning and behaviour. Baldwin et al. also argue that a further element of the pre-training context is the creation of a sense of personal ownership of the learning and the goals for transferring the learning to the workplace (embodying a commitment to apply learning): 'the more we can make transfer of learned knowledge and skills part of the learner's felt need to be consistent with an earlier commitment, the higher the probability is that we will see motivated behaviour in that direction' (2000: 33).

Evaluating Inputs

Inputs may be evaluated during the design stage, at the pilot-testing stage or during the implementation stage. At the design stage this evaluation can take a number of forms. For example, it can involve continuous checking against the identified needs in order to ensure that the project does not drift away from the findings of the needs identification and analysis. This keeps a check on the external validity issues provided that the identification and analysis of learning need

Table 9.4 Some suggested methods of evaluation for the augmented taxonomy of L&D outcomes

Category	Timing	Level	Principal methods of evaluation
Needs identification	Pre-L&D	Context	Needs assessment tools
Needs analysis		Input	
Satisfaction	Immediate	Affective reaction	Questionnaires and interviews with learners
		Utility reaction	
	Delayed	Affective reaction	
		Utility reaction	Questionnaire and interviews with learners and managers
Learning gain	Immediate	Knowledge gained	Tests, observations, assessments
		Skills gained	
		Attitudinal change	
	Delayed	Knowledge gained	Tests, observations, assessments, work sampling, manager assessments
		Skills gained	
		Attitudinal change	
Job performance	Post-L&D	Job behaviour	
Organizational non-financial performance		Organizational results	Performance indices, non-financial cost–benefit analysis
Financial performance		Return on investment	ROI calculation
Personal growth		Ultimate	Career and life trajectory

was itself accurate. This stage can also involve pilot testing of designs (for example, workshop design, materials design, assessment design and so forth) in order to check the internal validity (that the learning will achieve what it set out to do). A complementary approach is to anticipate learning transfer issues at the input stage and design the project in such a way that the chances of learning transfer may be maximized.

Evaluating Learners' Reactions

The evaluation of learners' reactions can take a number of forms. Typically it comprises the use of a questionnaire, often administered at the end of a learning event. As discussed earlier, the aim of the exercise is likely to be some assessment of the opinions and feelings of the learners with respect to the content of the programme, the learning objectives, the method of delivery, the strengths and weaknesses of the L&D practitioner, the physical environment and so forth. A number of approaches are available to assess these various factors: for example, Likert-scaled questions are quick and easy for the learner to complete and also enable quick and easy quantification of results, thus enabling ease of comparison between different events, locations, methods and so on. What these methods offer in terms of ease and accuracy of measurement they lose in terms of the depth of meaning that can be elicited. In order to assess learners' unique opinions and feelings it may be necessary to adopt more open types of question or to avoid the use of questionnaires altogether and use some form of one-to-one or group interview. Recall that this type of approach is often used only to provide information as to the internal validity of the event, but it has the potential to offer a much richer picture with regard to the external validity and may serve as a check on the input and context levels of evaluation discussed previously.

Reaction evaluation is most often conducted immediately after the L&D event has ended (referred to as 'immediate reaction evaluation'); however, it is entirely possible to delay the evaluation of learners' reactions until they have returned to the workplace. This type of delayed reaction evaluation has the advantage that it serves to allow the learner to consider the learning that has taken place in relation to the workplace and its demands so they may be better placed to judge its utility. Delaying may help to avoid any post-event euphoria or halo effect associated with a charismatic facilitator. In the cold light of day back at the workplace the learners may be able to give a more sober and objective view of the event itself and, more importantly, its relevance and potential application in the workplace. Delayed evaluation is administratively more difficult and response rates are likely to be lower.

PERSPECTIVE FROM PRACTICE: EVALUATING LEARNERS' REACTIONS

Goldstein (1993: 161) suggested the following guidelines for evaluation at the reaction level:

1. Base reaction questionnaires on the content and objectives derived from the needs identification and analysis phase.
2. Design the questionnaire so that responses can be easily quantified, analysed, tabulated and compared.
3. Provide for participant anonymity in questionnaire responses.
4. Provide space for items that are not covered in the standardized closed questions.
5. Pre-test the questionnaire and modify as appropriate.

Continued

As a further aid to the design of instruments (questionnaires or interview schedules) for evaluation at the reaction level, Table 9.5 contains some potential questions, some of which are amenable to open or closed (yes/no or Likert scales) format. Recall that evaluation of learners' reactions may occur at two levels: their affective reaction (this may include factors such as their satisfaction with the learning methods, materials, location, facilitator and so forth) and their utility reaction (their views on the extent to which the learning is relevant to their work and the extent to which it may contribute to enhanced job performance). The research by Morgan and Casper (2000) utilized a seven-item utility reaction scale that has shown initial evidence of reliability (Cronbach $\alpha = 0.91$) and construct validity.

Evaluating Knowledge

The knowledge that is embodied in the learning objectives will differ in terms of its level of complexity and the cognitive operations that it demands of the learner. In a previous chapter we came across the concept of taxonomies of learning outcomes, and one example that was considered, albeit briefly, was that devised by Bloom and his colleagues in the 1950s for the cognitive domain. The cognitive domain in Bloom's taxonomy comprised knowledge, comprehension, application, analysis, synthesis and evaluation. Each of these levels demands a different form of assessment. For example, at the level of knowledge the learner may be required simply to recall an item of verbal information (such as 'Define the term "validation"'), whilst at the level of evaluation the learner might be required to give a critical evaluation of the systematic approach to L&D (evaluation is being used in a different sense here to mean the ability on the part of the learner to make informed, integrated and critical judgements). Evaluation as a form of learning is a more complex cognitive operation than recall and will involve knowledge, comprehension and analysis; it is most likely to include elements of synthesis and application as well. This is more than a classificatory exercise since the measures employed at the evaluation of learning level should fit the predefined learning objectives (which themselves are likely to have been derived from a needs identification and analysis).

There are a variety of objective tests of knowledge that can be used to test the different levels of the cognitive domain, including true/false questions, multiple-choice questions, free-response questions, completion/deletion statements, matching pairs, short-answer questions (Bramley 1991: 40–2; Buckley and Caple 1992: 197–200). Depending on how they are applied, objective tests (or any other form of test) can have a formative role (informing students of their progress and diagnosing weaknesses to be addressed during the learning) or a summative role as an end-of-event final assessment and grading. Pre-testing and post-testing are an objective way of quantifying the learning gain or gain ratio defined in percentage terms (see Bramley 1991: 43), as follows:

Table 9.5 Possible questions for immediate and/or delayed reaction evaluation

Examples of open questions

Which part of the course was *most* valuable to you?
Which part of the course was *least* valuable to you?
If you could make *one* change to the course what would it be?
What other topics would you like to have seen included? (please list)

Examples of Likert-scaled questions (with supplementary open questions)

How effective was this course in meeting the objectives that were set? (please tick)	*Very effective* ☐	*Effective* ☐	*Neither* ☐	*Ineffective* ☐	*Very ineffective* ☐
Please suggest any ways that it could be made more effective in meeting the objectives.					
How effective was the facilitator in delivering the course?	*Very effective* ☐	*Effective* ☐	*Neither* ☐	*Ineffective* ☐	*Very ineffective* ☐
Please suggest any ways that the facilitator could be more effective.					
How would you rate the facilities and resources for learning?	*Very good* ☐	*Good* ☐	*Neither* ☐	*Poor* ☐	*Very poor* ☐
Please suggest any ways that the facilities and resources could be improved to support learning.					
There was an appropriate balance of facilitator input, learner involvement and practical exercises.	*Strongly agree* ☐	*Agree* ☐	*Neither* ☐	*Disagree* ☐	*Strongly disagree* ☐
Please suggest any ways that the balance between the different elements could be redressed.					
How relevant do you think the course will be/has been to your job?	*Highly relevant* ☐	*Relevant* ☐	*Neither* ☐	*Irrelevant* ☐	*Highly irrelevant* ☐
Please suggest any ways that the job-relevance of the course could be enhanced.					

Examples of yes/no closed questions

Would you recommend this course to others in your position?	*Yes*	*No*
Do you consider this course value for money?	*Yes*	*No*

Gain ratio (%) = ((post-test score – pre-test score)/(maximum possible score – pre-test score))/100 %)

Learning gains may also go beyond the mechanistic, immediately quantifiable and objective approaches. For example, individuals may have highly individualized learning programmes in the form of personal development plans (PDPs) that may be being met through self-development, action learning and so forth. This type of approach is likely to call for less rigid approaches to the assessment of progress. Subjective assessment of knowledge gained can be obtained through self-assessment by means of diaries or learning logs; these can be especially useful if the learner is being encouraged to reflect upon the process as well as the content of learning. This type of approach is especially beneficial when the learning encompasses personal development and the acquisition of relevant skills – see below. Learning logs can also be used as a way for learners to record their views on how well a particular method is working for them. Figure 9.7 shows an example of a workshop evaluation form that could be adapted to suit a variety of purposes.

The evaluation of knowledge and skill lends itself to the use of experimental research designs. These are useful when the aim is to explore the relative benefits of different learning methods (i.e. different treatments) in an experimental setting. Burroughs (1975) outlined the various permutations of experimental designs available to the researcher (Figure 9.8). A strict experimental design utilizes one or more treatment groups (i.e. the group that receives the L&D intervention such as a course or package) and one more control groups (who receive no such treatment). Individuals are randomly assigned to the treatment or control groups. Such an approach requires the control of a range of extraneous variables in order that the effects of different types of learning method (treatment) may be isolated in the analyses (often utilizing analysis of variance, ANOVA). Such approaches potentially have a high level of scientific rigour but are not always straightforward to implement in organizational settings. It is often the case that management researchers working in the positivistic paradigm have to recognize the practical difficulties, which may mean using quasi-experimental designs in which pre-testing and post-testing is conducted on two groups, one of which might attend a course whilst the other group do not (Easterby-Smith et al. 1991: 37); there are, however, a number of important validity issues associated with their use.

Evaluating Skills

As with the evaluation of knowledge, the assessment of changes in levels of skill is dependent upon the type of skills that are embodied in the learning objectives. Skills themselves may be divided into intellectual skills (such as 'analysis' and 'application'), manual and psychomotor skills, and social and interpersonal skills. The intellectual skills have been discussed previously in the consideration of evaluation of knowledge. In this section we will discuss the various ways in which

WORKSHOP		
Personal Reflection Form		
List the exercises from the workshop that you used.	*Rate the usefulness of exercise to you for your learning and its likely impact upon your work (1, low; 5, high).*	*Why did you apply the particular rating? What did you like/dislike about it? Why did you think it was useful or not to your work? How could it be improved?*
	Usefulness for learning	
	Usefulness to work	
	Usefulness for learning	
	Usefulness to work	
	Usefulness for learning	
	Usefulness to work	
	Usefulness for learning	
	Usefulness to work	

Write a personal statement on the overall usefulness of the workshop to you in your work.

How might the workshop overall be improved for future participants?

Thank you for your comments and cooperation; they will be invaluable in helping us to improve the workshop for future participants. All information provided will be treated anonymously.

Figure 9.7   Sample workshop evaluation form

Design	Random selection	Observation 1	Treatment	Observation 2
1st poor design: one-shot case study	None	None	Treatment	Post-test
2nd poor design: one group, before and after	None	Pre-test	Treatment	Post-test
3rd poor design: static group comparison	None	None	Treatment	Post-test
	None	None	None	Post-test
1st good design: before and after control group design	Random assignment to treatment group	Pre-test	Treatment	Post-test
	Random assignment to control group	Pre-test	None	Post-test
2nd good design: four-group design	Random assignment to treatment group	Pre-test	Treatment	Post-test
	Random assignment to control group	Pre-test	None	Post-test
	Random assignment to treatment group	None	Treatment	Post-test
	Random assignment to control group	None	None	Post-test
3rd good design: post-test only, control group	Random assignment to treatment group	None	Treatment	Post-test
	Random assignment to control group	None	None	Post-test

Figure 9.8   Experimental designs. (*Source*: Burroughs 1975: 49–54)

some of these other skills can be assessed. It should be noted that it is not necessarily a straightforward matter to isolate a skill such as intellectual (cognitive), manual or social since in practice human behaviour may contain elements of each. For example, manual skills and social skills are each likely to have underpinning knowledge upon which skilled performances in manual and social domains draw. There are other specific categories of skill such as decision making and planning that make demands upon an individual's cognitive and interpersonal resources and have to be treated in an integrated manner. Note also that the experimental research design discussed briefly in the preceding section can also be applied in the evaluation of skills learning.

Manual skills are normally assessed in a workplace context; however, there are certain types of skill that cannot be practised 'live', so to speak – the emergency landing of a passenger aircraft is one example. In such situations L&D relies upon the use of simulated conditions (in this example the flight simulator) in order to assess performance. That said, there are practical tools and techniques that are especially relevant to the assessment of manual skills learning and that are equally useful in work and non-work settings; it is to these that we now turn our attention.

It may be recalled from our discussion of learning objectives that the specification of performance, conditions and standards may be of particular benefit with respect to manual skills learning. They enable the L&D practitioner and the learner to be aware of what is required, to what standards (for example, what the tolerances of a finished job might be, what the sequence of events might be, and so on) and under what conditions (for example, what equipment is to be used and so forth). The link back to hierarchical task analysis should be clear here – HTA enables the precise actions and their sequence to be identified and specified in advance and hence used to define the end point of the learning. An example might be the changing of a wheel on a car: this consists of a series of discrete steps (for example: stop on hard level surface, switch of engine, apply handbrake, etc.) that must be performed to a certain standard (for example, the wheel nuts have to be tightened sufficiently) and in a particular sequence (for example, the car must be 'jacked up' before the wheel is removed) (Bramley 1991: 47; Buckley and Caple 1992: 202). It would be inappropriate to test an individual skill in this task in anything other than a simulated or real situation; any other form of assessment, such as a written test or a computer simulation, would be ineffective (especially since to set up the live situation in this case is relatively inexpensive and fairly risk free). A written test might be used in such situations to assess the underpinning knowledge but would not be sufficient of itself.

The issue of cost and risk is an important one with respect to skills assessment. Where the costs of learning in a live situation are expensive and/or of high risk (for example, emergency shut-down of a nuclear power station) then there are few alternatives other than simulation; however, under these circumstances the fidelity of the simulation to reality needs to be high. This has cost implications – the cost of a typical flight simulator for training is estimated at $500/hour and millions of dollars to develop and produce, for example, but this needs to be balanced against the potential cost to individuals, organization and society of poor performance (for example, in the case of flying an aircraft or running a nuclear power station). The level of an employee's skills can be assessed in a number of ways: for example, by examining the finished piece of work for quality, tolerances, dimensions, utility and so on or by an assessment of the performance itself. The latter is often undertaken by an assessor, who may observe and question the learner to test their performance against a predetermined set of criteria. The role of the assessor in the assessment of skilled performance will be discussed more fully in the subsequent section on evaluating job behaviour.

Evaluating Attitudinal Change

An attitude may be defined as a mental state of readiness, organized through experience, which exerts a directive or dynamic influence on an individual's response to objects and situations with which it is related (Allport 1954). Attitudes are often thought of as having three components:

Cognitive component: the ideas and propositions that express the relationships between situations and attitudinal objects (Gagné 1985); for example, 'people watch too much TV'.
Affective component: the emotional or feeling aspect that accompanies an idea, for example a feeling of frustration that people don't spend more time on other things rather than TV.
Behavioural component: the predisposition or readiness to act towards an object or situation in a consistent way, for example, not to own a TV set (Gagné 1985: 221–2).

The consistency principle states that people attempt to maintain consistency between these three components (Rollinson and Broadfield 2002); thus if one component changes individuals can either reverse the change in this component or change the other two to align with the change in the first. Attitudes affect performance both during L&D and subsequently in the job (Patrick 1992: 201), hence they are important because they underpin and inform changes in behaviour. Consider the case of an employee's attitudes towards customers and, for example, whether the employee exhibits a positive and caring attitude towards customers. This attitude is likely to inform and determine to a large extent the way the employee behaves in the workplace when dealing with customers. A positive attitude towards an object (for example, customers) predisposes an individual to behave in a positive way towards the object. Clearly, it is possible for an employee to hold negative and uncaring attitudes towards customers and still exhibit positive behaviours. However, the consistency principle would lead us to question the extent to which such a stance could be maintained. Two further complicating factors are the role of:

*   beliefs about outcomes of behaviour: people usually have positive attitudes about behaviours that they believe will help them to achieve their goals;
*   subjective norms: if socially accepted rules conflict with an individual's attitude and the associated behaviours the intention to behave in that way will be weakened (Rollinson and Broadfield 2002: 146).

Attitudinal change may therefore be seen as a key aspect of workplace behaviour and performance. According to Rollinson and Broadfield the consistency principle underpins most serious attempts to change peoples' attitudes and a reliance upon the creation of *dissonance* (when the behaviour towards an object is not consistent with the attitude towards the object) through persuasion (2002: 143).

The use of techniques such as role play, simulations and so forth may be seen as attempts at persuasion (not in the sense of merely persuasive passive communication, for example, by just saying 'TV is bad for you'), which seeks to activate cognitive dissonance that the individual will then attempt to reduce. The effectiveness of persuasion depends upon the source of the message (the credibility, for example), the nature of the message (whether it is perceived as balanced and unbiased) and the nature of the recipients (Rollinson and Broadfield 2002). One approach to attitude change that is based upon some of these precepts, and which we have already met, is human modelling, which draws upon Bandura's social learning theory. Human modelling works by establishing the model's credibility and appeal, the model communicating or demonstrating the desired choice of personal action, and further and ongoing reinforcement of this by additional communication or demonstration (Gagné 1985: 232, 238). One unintended side-effect of attempts at attitudinal change can be the 'boomerang effect', which may occur when a message of low persuasiveness in comparison to the perceived threat to one's personal freedom induces a retrenchment of the attitude as an assertion of individuality and resistance to change (Rollinson and Broadfield 2002: 144).

PERSPECTIVE FROM PRACTICE: ATTITUDINAL CHANGE

The learning or modification of an attitude is a complex phenomenon. It depends upon previously acquired learning; thus attempts to develop positive attitudes towards customers could not proceed without some knowledge of concepts such as internal and external customers, customer expectations, quality and so on. The following process, based upon Bramley (1991) and Gagné et al. (1992: 91), is offered as a simple checklist-type approach for L&D in which attitudinal change is a component:

1. Assess where the learner is with respect to the values that make up the attitude (perhaps by means of an inventory, interview, group discussion).
2. Identify desirable attitudes (for example, valuing participative management) and possible alternative choices so that learners know what the alternatives available to them are (middle managers cannot 'buy into' participative management if they don't know what it is or if they have misconceptions about it).
3. Provide the learner with pros and cons and long-term benefits of the desired behaviour (for example, the benefits for themselves and other stakeholders of participative management).
4. Attempt to change or develop what are seen as desirable attitudes through appropriate learning experiences (such as discussions, role play, simulations, group working, etc.).

Continued

5. Provide relevant models for the desired behaviour (for example, managers who have themselves been through a change process and embraced the concept in question, say, 'participative management') and give exposure to a credible source who themselves exhibit behaviours consistent with the attitude ('do as I do' not 'do as I say').

6. Ensure that the workplace environment supports the desired choice of behaviour (for example, that learners do have the opportunity for greater involvement in decision making and that the organization itself is willing to empower them).

7. Provide an action plan whereby the learner can express the ways in the new attitude can be applied and further developed in a workplace which itself acknowledges how the desired behaviour fits into a larger framework of organizational change (for example, increased customer focus).

8. Assess the extent to which the desirable attitude has been exhibited in the workplace, for example through self-, customer, subordinate and peer ratings.

9. Recognize and reward the desired behaviour when it is exhibited. For example, if managers want employees to embrace participative management and engage with it they must recognize and reward the behaviours that are evidence of this attitude.

Where quantifiable assessment of attitudes is necessary a number of approaches are possible. Remenyi et al. (1998: 154–5) suggest that single items (where a single question is used to measure the construct of interest) or multiple items (where two or more questions are used to measure a construct) may be used. Typically such items are scored on an ordinal scale (for example, from 'strongly agree' to 'strongly disagree'). Multiple items have the advantage that they are better able to provide a sufficient working definition of the attitude or construct in question and the assumptions of interval-level measurement are more tenable (Remenyi et al. 1998: 155). A typical scale for the measurement of a construct would comprise a minimum of three questions. Bramley also suggests the use of semantic differential items. A crucial issue for the evaluation of L&D in general is that to be of value data should not only be meaningful to decision makers and able to be collected within typical organizational constraints, but it should also be based on psychometric principles (Tannenbaum and Woods 1992). Simple factual questions of a type requiring yes/no, categorical or ratio-scale responses are comparatively simple to design and analyse; for example, sex, job level or number of years' tenure. Here a single response may do the job; however, complex and abstract phenomena, such as attitudes, are more problematic to assess using single items (Wilson 1996: 109).

PERSPECTIVE FROM RESEARCH: THE INTERNAL CONSISTENCY OF MULTIPLE-ITEM SCALES

'Attitudes to L&D' exist as a continuum. When relying upon a single-item measure, the chances of locating an individual accurately on such a continuum are low. Multiple-item scales offer the opportunity of more accurate assessment and also are amenable to more rigorous examinations of their reliability and validity. A key concept in terms of reliability is the internal consistency of a scale, defined as the extent to which a set of variables is consistent with what it aims to measure. Based upon the correlations between items in the scale, the parameter known as Cronbach's α is a commonly used measure of reliability and its value ranges from zero to one (Hair et al. 1998: 88). Nunally (1978) suggested that the minimum value for Cronbach's α should be 0.70, although marginally lower values sometimes appear in published studies. In tests used for selection and assessment it is generally accepted that α should be considerably higher, perhaps 0.90 or higher.

Computer programs such as the Statistical Package for the Social Sciences (SPSS) now make scale development and refinement much easier than in the past since such packages will not only compute the value of α for the scale but will help to identify any items that may be inconsistent with the other items in the scale. This enables the researcher to spot those items that can be eliminated in order to enhance the internal consistency of a multiple-item measure. Such items can often be identified by their lower item-total correlations ($r < 0.30$ is a rule of thumb that is sometimes used) and also by the 'alpha-if-item-deleted' statistic which packages such as SPSS will calculate. Multiple-item scales can be successfully refined through pilot testing in order to enhance their internal consistency to an acceptable level. The use of multiple-item scales is in many ways superior to the use of single items for the measurement of attitudes (and other constructs).

There are other related methods that may also be used when designing and developing measures of attitudes and other abstract constructs. For example, the underlying structure of a composite scale that aims to measure several different facets of learners' attitudes towards L&D might be disentangled using exploratory and confirmatory factor analysis (EFA and CFA). The use of EFA was discussed previously and a detailed treatment of these issues is beyond the present scope, but a useful introduction may be found in Kline (1994). Scale development is a complex process demanding much scientific rigour: a useful summary of the process is to be found in de Vellis (1991).

Another technique highlighted by Bramley for the assessment of attitudes is the use of repertory grid. In this technique the researcher asks an individual to consider a number of examples of a concept and to say what criteria he or she would use to distinguish between the examples of the concept (for example, 'a participative manager'). Bramley used the concept of 'good interpersonal skill' and described how the process can be used to derive constructs that describe this concept, for example 'supportive vs. not supportive', 'listens to what I have to say vs. has preconceived ideas'. For a detailed description of the method readers should consult Bramley (1991: 53–7) or Easterby-Smith et al. (1991: 84–7). The method is especially useful for surfacing constructs that may otherwise remain unarticulated. The conceptualizations are not externally imposed; rather they are derived from participants' own perceptions. One of the drawbacks of the method is that it requires a fair amount of knowledge, skill and practice to be executed effectively.

Evaluating Changes in Job Behaviour

The difference between this level of evaluation and the preceding level relates to context, because job behaviour level changes are situated in the context of the workplace and are therefore concerned with the key issue of the transfer of learning. The transfer of learning was discussed in some detail in a previous chapter. Once the transfer of learning occurs from the learning situation to the job situation, the question then turns to a consideration of how changes in job performance may be assessed. Buckley and Caple suggested a range of methods that can be used, including follow-up interviews, observation, monitoring of action plans drawn up during learning, performance appraisal and self-assessment, and an examination of employee output and results (1992: 209). Follow-up (delayed) evaluations in order to explore the usefulness of L&D can be valuable, firstly as an assessment of the individual's performance, but secondly they can assist in the evaluation of the L&D itself (vis-à-vis continuous improvement). Bramley (1991: 45) suggested that delayed evaluation of L&D might be undertaken by asking learners and line managers:

- how useful the knowledge or the skills learned has been in the job;
- whether they have actually used the knowledge and skills in the job situation;
- what difficulties they might have had in applying the new knowledge;
- whether the learner can perform the necessary skills to the manager's satisfaction (Bramley 1991: 51).

The assessment of competence is a further way in which L&D may be assessed at the behaviour level. In the UK this most often is tied to a National Vocational Qualification (NVQ) and the assessor is either the learner's own supervisor or an equivalent person from another workplace. The advantages are that the supervisor has an in-depth knowledge of the job, is situated in the workplace and is ideally placed to try to ensure that the validity of the assessment is high (Edwards 1999: 390). The usual caveats apply, of course, with regard to observational rating of performance (for example, bias and so forth). Edwards also highlighted other potential problems, such as the time-consuming nature of the process of collecting evidence to be used as the basis for assessment, the lack of opportunity to display all the competencies in a workplace for a complete range of skills and also corner-cutting and even corruption in the assessment process (Edwards 1999: 391). As was noted in our earlier discussion of competence, competency profiles are often developed for particular jobs or roles and these can have a number of applications in areas such as recruitment, appraisal and the evaluation of learning at the performance level. A competence profile (or job description) may be useful for the evaluation of learning and performance.

PERSPECTIVE FROM PRACTICE: NATIONAL VOCATIONAL QUALIFICATIONS (NVQS) IN THE UK

Based upon the following source: I. Grugulis, 2003. The contribution of National Vocational Qualifications to the growth of skills in the UK, *British Journal of Industrial Relations*, 41(3): 457–75.

The vocational qualification system in the UK was for decades in need of a radical overhaul. A national system was needed as a means by which the skills in the workforce might be increased and credited. A further pressing reason was the need to rationalize the system; for example, in 1990 there were 279 different qualifications for secretaries (Keep 1994: 311), whilst other occupational areas did not have any (Grugulis 2003). NVQs are means to demonstrate occupational proficiency and their focus is on assessment not training. In 1996 the government set up the National Council for Vocational Qualification (NCVQ) to oversee a process in which the aims were to set national standards; these would be set by lead bodies that had a significant involvement of employers to represent the needs of industry. The system is overseen by: the assessor, who helps the candidate record his or her evidence of performance and achievement in terms of the component tasks; the internal verifier, who is responsible for ensuring consistency of procedures and so on; and the external verifier, who is responsible for ensuring consistency and comparability between different assessment centres.

A radical departure for the time was the fact that NVQs did not specify a course or curriculum but instead specified terminal performance that a competent employee should be able to display, thus enabling experienced and skilled employees to become qualified without having to undertake additional training (Grugulis 2003). Levels of achievement range from Level 1 (roughly equivalent to the UK's General Certificate of Secondary Education) through to Level 5 (roughly equivalent to postgraduate degree level) (Reid

Continued

and Barrington 1999: 337). There are many hundreds of qualifications available in the scheme across a wide range of occupational areas and they encompassed 47 per cent of vocational qualifications awarded in 1999–2000. NVQs have been successful in many ways: they are a performance-based and independent of mode of study; they have a practical emphasis; and they enable flexibility of learning and assessment (Grugulis 2003). Grugulis, however, also argued that they have failed to set out what they aimed to achieve for a number of reasons:

1. The emphasis is behavioural with little technical or academic elements and performance is defined in narrow terms with little recognition of the complexities of real work.
2. Assessment may lack consistency and the systems of recording and monitoring are seen by many as bureaucratic and complex.
3. They are focused on performance in the current job, which makes it difficult to assess the extent to which they have actually raised skill levels (they could conceivably merely have recorded the skill level that already existed).
4. The employer-led aspiration may also be fallacious since many organizations 'have little idea of how training might be implemented effectively' (2003: 470) and may respond to L&D in an ad hoc, reactive and short-term way.
5. There is a unitarist assumption that employers can and do articulate the demands of work to satisfy not only their own interests but those of their employees. The workplace is, however, a contested terrain and the unitarist assumption is highly questionable (Grugulis 2003).

Grugulis concludes by comparing her perceptions of the weaknesses of the UK system with the German system in which the design of vocational qualifications is derived from a synthesis of expertise from employers' associations, regional governments, trade unionists and educationalists.

L&D FACTS AND FIGURES

In the UK in 2002 just over half (52 per cent) of employers reported that training was leading to a formal qualification, and two out of five employers (38 per cent) offer NVQs to one or more of their employees. (*Source*: Learning and Training at Work 2002, Department for Education and Skills SFR 02/2003.)

Performance appraisal and other forms of evaluation of behaviour are conducted by collecting primary data via observation. However, the validity of observational data can be compromised from a number of possible sources. For example, reactivity may occur – where the observations may be accurate but subjects are not behaving in the way they normally behave. This may perhaps be because of the personal characteristics of the observer (personal reactivity) or because of the very fact that they are being observed (procedural reactivity) (Foster 1996: 88–9). Another potential problem may arise because of observer bias, which can affect which actual behaviours are selected for observation and recording, and also the observer's misperception or misinterpretation of the behaviour he or she has witnessed. These are all issues that L&D practitioners need to be aware of and guard against in the evaluation of job behaviour. One way around such problems is to use multiple-raters; however, this is resource intensive and itself presents some methodological difficulties. When two raters are used to assess performance it is important to recognize that there are likely to be differences in the scores that they assign to the same performance. The reliability of the ratings given by the different raters can be found by correlating sets of scores using the Pearson product-moment correlation coefficient (Rust and Golombok 1989: 72–3) to give inter-rater reliability.

It may be recalled that Stewart (1999) drew a useful and important distinction between behaviour and performance at the individual level. His argument was that even though an individual may change her or his behaviour as a result of L&D this may not translate into enhanced performance in the workplace. A number of factors can impinge upon this, including issues relating to the transfer climate within the organization (and general cultural factors of which the transfer climate may be one indicator), as well as other extraneous factors that an individual may not have control over (for example, if she or he is member of a team where performance is contingent upon the collective efforts of the individuals who make up the team). Bates et al. (2000) singled out the crucial role that supervisors, managers, peers and workgroup members can play in the success or failure of applying new learning to the job; hence these social factors are an important element of the transfer climate. They suggest that to maximize transfer individuals need to partner with each other to identify critical learning needs; managers need to prepare learners for learning and transfer prior to L&D taking place; and to motivate, coach and provide the opportunities needed to apply and reinforce new learning after formalized L&D has taken place.

Evaluating L&D's Impact on Organizational Results

The effects of L&D become more difficult to assess at the organizational level because there are a whole host of factors in the internal and external environment of the organization that impact upon performance. Isolating the effects of L&D in these circumstances to provide a convincing argument of value added is not always an easy thing to do. Traditional approaches to the problem of evaluating L&D's impact on the performance of the organization have typically specified a set of outcomes upon which L&D might be expected to impact. Jacobs and Washington (2003: 348) argued that although business and financial outcomes are important, other performance measures should be included such as retention, promotion rates and task flexibility. This is important for two reasons: firstly, it acknowledges that there is a broader span of outcomes that L&D might impact upon beyond the financial; and secondly, it recognizes L&D and performance as being implicated in a complex and dynamic chain of inputs and outputs. For example, L&D may be linked to promotion, which may be linked to individual performance, which itself can be linked to business unit outcomes and so forth (Jacobs and Washington 2003). To expect simple cause-and-effect relationships in complex organizational systems may be over-optimistic. Some of the approaches are summarized in Table 9.6. As may be seen, an analysis of the approaches offered by Bramley, Buckley and Caple, and Reid and Barrington yields six categories of potential outcome as a result of L&D:

- *Quantity outcomes*: for example, sales.
- *Quality outcomes*: for example, customer complaints.
- *Business process outcomes*: for example, machine downtime.
- *Resource outcomes*: for example, reduced materials wastage.
- *Stakeholder perception outcomes*: for example, enhanced employee relations.
- *HR outcomes*: for example, greater diversity of skills in the workforce.

Each of these various outcomes may be quantified by different means; for example, at the 'hard' end the quantity of sales is concrete and measurable in an objective manner, whilst at the other extreme perceptions and attitudes are more abstract and require different approaches (for example, the scaling techniques discussed in relation to learner reactions). The categories presented here may provide a variety of outcomes for which L&D interventions may be designed in the first place and measured against on completion. These may also be integrated with a balanced scorecard-type approach (Table 9.7), discussed previously, in which a specific L&D need and the associated inputs (for example, the training provided) are then evaluated in terms of outcomes in the areas of quantity, quality, business processes, resources, stakeholder perceptions and HR issues. The outcomes may be specified in advance in order to serve as criterion measures for the L&D and which represent expectations and embody commitments from the various stakeholders. Such an approach requires a partnership between the L&D function and clients in order that outcomes that are specified are relevant and realistic.

The problem remains of isolating the effects that a specific L&D programme may or may not have had upon these outcomes. In the absence of evaluations that stick closely to experimental designs, the evaluation of L&D at the organizational level becomes a matter that involves a considerable amount of interpretation and judgement requiring skill, experience and expertise. An additional factor

Table 9.6 Suggested criteria for evaluation of organizational-level impact of L&D

Bramley (1991: 72–3)	Buckley and Caple (1992: 212–13)	Reid and Barrington (1999: 260–1)	Summary criteria
Units produced; tasks completed; turnover; units sold; money collected; on-time deliveries; etc.	Goals and targets achieved (quality, quantity, etc.)	Overall profitability	*Quantity outcomes*
Defects; failure rate; error rates; reworking; scrap; waste; shortages; etc.		Lack of customer complaints	*Quality outcomes*
System and work process goals (processing time, productivity, operating costs, running costs, performance–cost ratio, time needed to train new employees, downtime, accident rate, etc.)			*Business process outcomes*
	Resource acquisition (ability to attract and retain new market, people, finance, etc.)		*Resource outcomes*
	Client and stakeholder satisfaction (as evidenced in loyalty, feedback, survey results, attitudes, etc.)		*Stakeholder perception outcomes*
	Internal processes (indicators may include satisfaction, commitment, grievances, attitudes of staff, turnover, conflict, climate, communication, etc.)	Favourable attitude to L&D proactive labour force that will accept change; requests for L&D from managers; availability of suitable people to promote from within the organization	*HR outcomes*

Table 9.7 Balanced scorecard-type approach for the evaluation of L&D (adapted from Kaplan and Norton 1996; Walton 1999)

Organizational L&D (context) need						
L&D measures (input) to meet the need						
Outcomes	Quantity outcomes	Quality outcomes	Business process outcomes	Resource outcomes	Stakeholder perception outcomes	HR outcomes
Critical success factors						
Critical measurements						
Criterion indicators						

that is often overlooked in the evaluation of L&D at all levels, but at the organizational results-level especially, is that of time. The effects of L&D are likely to take weeks, months or even years to translate into enhanced performance for the organization. As Holton and Baldwin (2000: 4) noted, the learning transfer literature has focused on what they term near transfer (that is, short-term results), whereas what may be required is a better balance of evaluation of outcomes from both near transfer and far transfer perspectives (i.e. the longer-term transfer and the generalization of the learning to new situations). Hence, when evaluating organizational performance outcomes the researcher needs to try to ensure a longer-term commitment to observing the payoff (Collins 2002: 101). This raises problems in itself, since it is unlikely that an organization could commit, for example, to a three-year project to examine the impact of L&D. However, if organizations are to understand the ways in which their investment in L&D is impacting upon performance, and if scholars are to increase their knowledge of the effects of L&D on organizations, more longitudinal studies are required. A paradox is that results are perceived as the most important outcome when judging L&D's success, but in a sense may be distal from the L&D event itself (occurring in parts of the organization and at times that may be far removed from the L&D function that initiated the effect). In this regard, sponsors of L&D who have unrealistic expectations in terms of what can be evaluated in a scientifically rigorous way (and not necessarily what can be achieved in evaluation terms) may need to have their expectations managed early on in the process (see Alliger et al. 1997).

L&D FACTS AND FIGURES

In a survey published in 2002, 66 per cent of employers in the UK who had provided any training over the previous 12 months reported that this had led to an increase in labour productivity. (*Source*: Learning and Training at Work 2002, Department for Education and Skills SFR 02/2003.)

Questions are also raised about who should undertake evaluations, and when. There are trade-offs between evaluators internal to the organization (for example, managers or L&D practitioners) and external agents (such as consultants). The former have the benefit of having the insider knowledge that may endow greater efficiency with regard to the design and execution of evaluation (since these groups are likely to have quicker and easier access to information, dissemination, communications within the organization) but may be less able to bring as much objectivity to the process. External agents, on the other hand, may have fewer issues of subjectivity to contend with, and although they may bring a fresh external perspective they are likely to have to climb a steeper learning curve with respect to understanding local issues and concerns. A middle way is for a combination of internal and external evaluators to undertake the project, each bringing with them strengths that can offset the weaknesses of the other group. Collins is in no doubt: in her view L&D practitioners in organizations must take the lead both in addressing the lack of results-level evaluation and in linking L&D to organizational strategy. This will involve combining robust evaluation theory (not just appropriate taxonomies of outcomes) with performance-based theories to create an appropriate system for the measurement of organizational-level improvements as a result of L&D (Collins 2002: 106).

L&D FACTS AND FIGURES

The UK's Chartered Institute of Personnel and Development's (CIPD) Annual Training Survey 2004 found that the three most important items covered by the training budgets amongst respondents were external courses and conferences (92 per cent), hiring external consultants and trainers (85 per cent) and books and training manuals (82 per cent). (*Source*: Training and Development 2004: Survey Report (April 2004). London: CIPD.)

Evaluating the Return on Investment

The quantifiable 'cash' returns from L&D are of particular relevance to practice since it is often the case that senior managers and other stakeholders within organizations expect some 'bottom line' quantification of the benefits that have accrued from the costs of L&D. The costs of L&D may be substantial and can include such items as fees, materials, travel and accommodation, design and development costs, L&D department overheads, downtime, replacement costs and so forth. Gibb (2002: 121) noted that the idea of returns on these costs as an absolute number that can give an exact value returned for an exact value invested is a seductive idea and is seen as the 'Holy Grail' for many L&D practitioners. In the simplest terms, the benefit–cost ratio (BCR) and payback period may be calculated as in the example that follows, which is based on Gibb (2002).

1. Assume an L&D project that will cost £50,000 to design, develop, implement and evaluate and that will have a shelf life of two years and will over that period produce £100,000 of savings in increased efficiency and effectiveness.
2. Benefit–cost ratio: benefits/costs = benefit–cost ratio (BCR) (where: BCR < 1 = loss on the L&D project; BCR = 1 means a break-even on the project; BCR > 1 = positive return on the L&D project):

$$BCR = £100,000/£50,000 = 2.0$$

3. Payback period: this is the time taken to recoup the costs of a project; the payback period = total investment/annual savings:

$$Payback\ period = £50,000/£50,000 = 1\ year$$

A number of alternative approaches to examining the relationships between the costs and the benefits of L&D are outlined in Table 9.8. It should be noted that these are fairly crude measures but can be used to give an indication of the way the investment and the benefits accrued may be weighed up. Phillips outlined an approach to addressing the thorny issue of how the benefits from training might be addressed in return-on-investment (ROI) calculations. He suggests five steps for converting hard data (for example, components produced on an assembly line) or soft data (for example, safety rule violations) to monetary values:

1. Focus on a single unit of improvement in output (for example, one component failure or one safety rule violation).
2. Determine the value of each unit (for example, the value of a single component or the potential cost of a safety rule violation).
3. Calculate the change in performance as a result of L&D after factoring in other potential influences on the change.
4. Obtain an annual amount for the monetary value of the changes performance.
5. Determine the annual value (the product of the unit value and the annual performance change). (See Phillips 1996.)

This figure can then be used in the relevant calculation. He acknowledged that it is the softer aspects of performance, such as customer dissatisfaction, that are the most difficult to quantify but urges L&D practitioners not to be perturbed. Estimates from a number of sources, such as learners, supervisors and senior managers, may be a helpful way to get convergence on an agreeable estimate for the

Table 9.8 Some simple approaches to quantifying the relationships between the costs and benefits of L&D. (*Source:* Phillips 1996)

Method	Calculation	Example	Meaning
Benefit–cost ratio (BCR)	(Monetary benefits of L&D project)/(Costs of L&D project)	The ABC company has measured the impact of its latest marketing training project over the past three years as £600,000 in increased sales. The project cost £120,000 to implement over that same period. $BCR = £600,000/£120,000 = 5.0$	At ABC for every £1 spent on the marketing training project £5 in benefits were returned.
Cost–benefit ratio (CBR)	(Costs of L&D project)/(Monetary benefits of L&D project)	The XYZ company has measured the impact of its latest marketing training project over the past three years as £600,000 in increased sales. The project cost £120,000 to implement over that same period. $CBR = £120,000/£600,000 = 0.2$	At XYZ every £1 accrued in benefits from the marketing training project cost the company 20p.
Payback period	(Costs of L&D project)/(Annual savings)	The ABC's marketing training project had a shelf life of three years. Over that time it accrued £600,000 in increased sales and cost £120,000 to implement over that time. $Payback\ period = £120,000/(£600,000/3) =$ $£120,000/£200,000 = 0.6$	The marketing training project at the ABC company broke even after 0.6 years (i.e. 7.2 months).
Return on investment	(Monetary benefits of L&D project – Costs of L&D project)/(Costs of L&D project)	The overall financial benefit from the ABC company's marketing training project was £600,000 in increased sales. The costs over the three-year period over which the project ran were £120,000. $ROI = (£600,000 - £120,000)/(£120,000) = 4.0$	For every £1 invested in the ABC company's marketing training project there was a return of £4 in net benefits. (This could of course be turned on its head and interpreted as every £1 accrued in net benefits actually cost the company 25p in the costs of the project).

less tangible aspects of performance. Hence there is perhaps a need for partnership between the relevant stakeholders if evaluation is to produce meaningful results.

L&D FACTS AND FIGURES

The payback from L&D when designed and implemented under the right sets of circumstances can be substantial. Phillips cited a number of case studies of American evaluation projects in which the ROI varied between 215 per cent for a 15-hour supervisory skills L&D programme in a bakery, to 2000 per cent for a two-day sales training programm for a large commercial bank (Phillips 1996: 45).

PERSPECTIVE FROM RESEARCH: IN SEARCH OF THE 'HOLY GRAIL' OF L&D?

Based upon the following sources: L. J. Bassi, J. Ludwig, D. P. McMurrer and M. van Buren, 2002. Profiting from learning: firm level effects of training investments and market implications, *Singapore Management Review*, 24(3): 61–75; J. A. Molina and R. Ortega, 2003. Effects of employee training on the performance of North American firms, *Applied Economics Letters*, 10: 549–52.

If L&D investment does create value for businesses it is logical and legitimate to expect above-average financial performance from those firms that invest in L&D. Bassi et al. accessed a large data set collected by the ASTD and based their analysis on 575 US-based firms for whom they were able to link information on training with publicly reported financial performance data for the years 1996 through 1998. The performance index they used was the total stockholder return (TSR), which is defined as the change in stock price plus any dividends in a given year. It represents the 'best measure of the return that would be experienced by an individual investor' (Bassi et al. 2002: 65). Through correlational, sub-group and regression analyses they found that:

1. Firms in the top quartile for L&D investment have higher median TSRs than firms in the lower quartiles. However, as the authors noted, such a relationship may be spurious because, for example, riskier and inherently more productive industries are also more likely to need to provide L&D.
2. Even when taking into account extraneous factors such as industry type, size, prior financial performance and earnings (to address the limitation noted in (1) above), a significant positive relationship was observed between L&D investments and TSRs.

The authors consider the magnitude and implications of this as substantial – for example, a one standard deviation's increase in a firm's annual per-employee investment in L&D (about $680 in the mid- to late 1990s in the firms studied) generated about '6 per cent improvement in next year's TSRs'. Positive relationships were also observed between L&D investment and gross profit margin, return on assets and income per employee (see Bassi et al. 2002: 67).

Molina and Ortega's research aimed to analyse the impact of L&D on the performance of North American firms in terms of TSR also. They found that higher levels of training were associated with significant benefits that can increase firm performance. Their findings are commensurate with Bassi et al. In addition to the financial indicators used (including TSR) they also examined the differences between high-training firms (HTFs) and low-training firms (LTFs) in terms of a number of HR-related outcomes. They observed that HTFs outperformed the LTFs in terms of:

1. Voluntary turnover: 13 per cent in HTFs vs. 23 per cent in LTFs.
2. Involuntary turnover: 4 per cent versus 11 per cent.
3. Desirability as a place to work: 4.21 mean score versus 3.65.
4. Percentage reporting high employee satisfaction: 70 per cent versus 37 per cent.
5. Percentage reporting high customer loyalty: 59 per cent versus 47 per cent.

L&D FACTS AND FIGURES

Evaluation is a key aspect of the UK's Investors in People standard. To be an Investor in People organizations must take evaluation of L&D very seriously. Amongst other things, an Investor in People is able to describe the organization's overall investment of time, money and resources in L&D, and can explain and quantify how L&D has improved the performance of the organization. (*Source*: http://www.investorsinpeople.co.uk)

The task of evaluation is a daunting one – theoretically, methodologically and logistically. Given that the typical US organization spent $2 million on L&D in 1998, according to the ASTD, and worldwide business and governments spend many billions of dollars per annum, L&D clearly is important from a financial perspective and its impact is crucial from the point of view of the well-being, fulfilment and personal growth of individual employees. Evaluation is as critical an activity in L&D practice as needs identification, needs analysis, design and implementation. Without evaluation the value-added contribution of L&D remains untested and anecdotal. L&D as a function within organizations, along with mainstream HR, is attempting to enhance its professional reputation; evaluation has much to contribute to this particular endeavour. Evaluation is a way to promote L&D (Stewart 1999), generate buy-in (Collins 2002) and continuously improve the body of professional knowledge that L&D practice is based upon and may ultimately contribute to the extension of the concept and remit of L&D itself. L&D practitioners must take the lead in this by using evaluation tactics and strategies that are specific, reliable, valid and focused whilst also being broad enough to satisfy the evaluation needs of a broad range of stakeholders and organizations in rigorous but relevant and meaningful ways. The limitations of the Kirkpatrick framework are acknowledged and the ongoing theoretical and empirical development to build a coherent theory of learning transfer and evaluation are to be welcomed. Alongside this there is more to the Kirkpatrick framework than meets the eye. As we have discovered, the original four levels may in fact be disaggregated in order to give a more detailed and comprehensive picture. This, along with a balanced scorecard-type approach, may provide practitioners with tools that can be used to answer some of the 'what?' and 'how?' questions associated with the implementation and continuous improvement of L&D. The 'why?' question is a little more elusive.

Conclusion: L&D's Ultimate Contribution?

Having reached the lofty heights of ROI we might expect the journey to be over since for many the dollar return is often considered to be the end of the story – the ultimate value and the 'Holy Grail' of evaluation and L&D. However, we may recall that at the beginning of this chapter it was stated that evaluation is concerned with the total worth or value of L&D in monetary and non-monetary terms for employees and the organizations of which they are a part. Whilst evaluation embraces questions of learning for performance enhancement, it also encompasses broader issues such as personal development and growth. If we take as an example the Phillips framework discussed earlier, the highest (ultimate) level of L&D's value within this perspective is L&D's effect upon the organization's performance and profitability. Hamblin posed the question, 'What are the valued ends towards which training and other activities are ultimately directed?' Much of the discussion of the 'ultimate' nature of L&D's contribution is often concerned with the techniques of ROI calculation, on the assumption that the 'value' is exclusively a monetary one. It should be remembered that the foundations for modern L&D theory and practice were laid in a post-Second World War era of technological advancement both in society in general and the workplace in particular (for example, Dooley 1945). Worth and value were then – and still are – often couched in terms purely of performance enhancement. That said, Hamblin himself, writing in the early 1970s, argued that the 'hard-headed' view that would automatically equate 'ultimate value' with 'costs' may be quite mistaken (1974: 22).

As noted earlier in Chapter 1, it has been argued that philosophy is one of the underpinning disciplines of human resource development (see Weinberger 1998), and it can provide insights for the L&D practitioner with respect to evaluation. For example, virtue ethicists such as MacIntyre have argued that business and management appears to have formed its ethical base almost exclusively in the concept of effectiveness and 'doing a good job', and where what is earned (individually or corporately) is the measure of success. However, as MacIntyre noted, people can be effective at doing a bad job (MacIntyre 1984). From the perspective of virtue ethics Horvath (1995) has argued that what may be lacking in business is a meaningful definition of what is 'good' and 'right'. As a result of this, businesses may be without an internal standard of what constitutes good (or worth or value) by which they can evaluate their acts or enable employees to develop or express those dispositions that will sustain right practices. Furthermore, they may be without a clear definition of what constitutes 'meaningful work' in terms of what is good or right; if 'meaningful work' is not defined or understood then concomitantly neither is 'meaningful L&D'. Arguably, one of ultimate aims of the organization and L&D in addition to, or over and above, performance and ROI might be to support and enable individuals in achieving a 'meaningful' working life.

Seligman (2002), the founder of the positive psychology movement, defined a 'meaningful life' as one in which an individual uses her or his 'signature strengths' in the service of that which is larger than the individual. He defined the 'good life' as using one's signature strengths to obtain gratification in the main realms of one's life. Gratifications are 'activities we very much like doing but they are not necessarily accompanied by any raw feelings [such as the pleasures associated with senses and emotions] at all. Rather the gratifications engage us fully, we become immersed in them, and we lose self-consciousness' (2002: 102). Gratifications are about enacting signature strengths. The latter are, according to Seligman, strengths of character that a person owns and celebrates and exercises every day in many aspects of life, including work. They include things such as wisdom and knowledge, courage, justice, temperance and transcendence – issues which leadership research and practice is beginning to address (see, for example, Bolman and Deal 2003; Sternberg 2003). Seligman further argued that to maximize work satisfaction individuals need to be able to use their signature strengths every day if possible, and moreover he recommends that individuals should identify their signature strengths and choose work that meshes with them or re-craft their present job to fit their strengths. As far as employers go, they should choose employees whose signature strengths mesh with their work and they should make space for employees to 're-craft' their work to suit their strengths within the bounds of the organization's goals. Seligman is making a plea for congruence between the fundamental signature strengths of the individual and the demands made by and opportunities provided by their job role. If one accepts Seligman's arguments then perhaps an important role for L&D is to enable individuals to embark upon developmental trajectories that capitalize upon their signature strengths.

Alongside emerging questions of 'good', 'purpose' and 'meaning' the notion of performance enhancement has not gone away, indeed it is perhaps stronger than ever. However at the beginning of the twenty-first century the notions of 'worth' and 'value' are being reinterpreted and rediscovered and this is adding a new dimension to questions about the meaning of working and learning and their interconnectedness. For example, Leigh (1997) argued that it is not impossible to envisage a new corporate paradigm which is concerned with producing a quality service or product that promotes more general well-being and which provides occupation that is conducive to employees' personal growth and happiness. Since the workplace occupies many people for a good proportion of their lives, logically it should present, or aim to present, opportunities for personal growth in relation to the issue of the meaningfulness of the occupation. Chalofsky (2003: 56–7) has developed a construct of 'meaningful work' that reflects work as an expression of our inner being. His construct consists of a number of facets that embody self, work and balance and which align the purposes, values and relationships that make up our lives:

Self: the sense of the self and bringing one's whole self (mind, body, emotion and spirit) to the workplace.

Purpose: the sense of purpose in one's life and having a positive belief system about achieving one's purpose.

Potential: the acknowledgement of one's potential for learning and growth and the capacity to seek challenges and aspire.

Balance: the achievement of centredness and a balance within one's work and between one's work and the other aspects of one's life (Chalofsky 2003).

An L&D based on the values of self, purpose, potential and balance would, firstly, have the potential to facilitate learning, creativity and productivity and the personal growth of employees; secondly, would be located in organizations where individuals have the opportunity to enhance the quality of their lives; and finally, would be incommensurate with those organizations that are a source of dissatisfaction, alienation and apathy for their employees. An interpretation of what L&D's ultimate contribution might be in the context proposed by Leigh, Chalofsky and others is radically different and perhaps utopian; it goes beyond, but does not reject, ROI as the only level to which L&D can aspire. The value of L&D encompasses issues of organizational well-being (for example, survival and profitability), but also inevitably and necessarily encompasses individual well-being (for example, meaningful work, personal growth and happiness). L&D may therefore be judged by the ultimate contribution that it can make to the well-being, personal growth and happiness of individuals and the organizations of which they are a part. The evaluation of L&D's ultimate contribution in these terms may raise questions about what has been the worth and value of L&D to the individuals who make up an organization in terms of their own:

1. Personal well-being: how has L&D contributed to individuals' well being?
2. Satisfaction with working life: how has L&D helped to add meaning to the jobs that employees perform?
3. Work–life balance: how has L&D enabled employees to create an appropriate balance of work and non-work activities?
4. Self-expression: how has L&D contributed to employees expressing their individuality, talents and abilities?

5. Personal growth: how has L&D contributed to employees identifying and further developing their innate talents, to acquiring new ones and to their growth both as employees and as human beings?
6. Happiness: how has L&D contributed to the happiness of employees?

These are perhaps controversial questions. But such an interpretation of the ultimate level is arguably the most intangible, most important and currently least acknowledged aspect of L&D's evaluatory framework. Scholars such as Chalofsky and writers such as Leigh (1997) have initiated an important L&D debate, in parallel with which others are drawing our attention to the issues of ethics, values and integrity (Beattie 2004; Russ-Eft 2004). Bates et al.'s value matrix encompasses 'meaning' as an outcome of a learning and development that creates 'workplaces that enable people to fulfil important inner needs' (2002: 232). These things are not incompatible with performance; indeed they may benefit performance through enhanced loyalty, satisfaction and self-efficacy. The theory and practice of L&D is searching for a basis upon which these issues can be articulated, acknowledged and addressed in order that its mission can be expanded beyond performance enhancement (whilst not rejecting it) to encompass a concern with human needs and values in the workplace. Moves are being made in that direction; for example Russ-Eft (2004) has made the plea for the recognition that the practice of L&D ultimately is concerned with human beings and human values, as well as the processes, systems and organization created by them. The Academy for Human Resource Development has developed a set of guiding principles for values in the professional and ethical conduct of L&D (Aragon and Hatcher 2001). The trends may be towards the emergence of an authentic and values-based L&D the shape of which is as yet unclear. The challenge with be achieving a reciprocity between a values-based L&D (self, purpose, potential and balance) and its performance-enhancement mission (return on investment). All of this represents an important stage in the evolution of the field (see Woodall et al. 2004).

Handy (1994) argued that in order to counteract the excessive trends of working life which can lead to isolation, fragmentation and reductionism, employees need to cultivate a sense of continuity, connection and direction by integrating the past, present and future and their place within it. To this end one purpose of L&D may be to provide employees with a means of finding their own anchorage amidst the changes of modern organizational life (Barnett 1997; Johnston 1999: 485). The ultimate goal of L&D might be to offer the opportunity for individuals to develop, grow or even undergo transformation. Can L&D contribute to transforming working lives that may be boring and meaningless into working lives that embody elements of meaning and enjoyment, and perhaps ultimately where creativity and total involvement combine? Taken to its logical conclusion, this calls for a reframing of L&D in order that it may add value at the ultimate level for the individuals who are the embodiment of the organization. The technical, professional, ethical and moral challenge is to explore the commensurability of this with the needs of modern organizations. Csikszentmihalyi noted that conformity is often welcomed in some organizations, but also that in rapidly changing and dynamic

business environments more than mere conformity is needed. Employees, especially knowledge workers, need autonomy, scope for initiative, creativity and personal growth. He argued that as individuals mature physically and mentally they
may come to feel that their talents remain dormant or unacknowledged, crushed
by the demands of the mundane and everyday (Csikszentmihalyi 2003: 69). The
state of being that Csikszentmihalyi refers to as 'flow' is a state of joy, creativity
and total involvement in which problems seem to disappear and there is an exhilarating feeling of transcendence. This is more likely to occur for employees in
those organizations where work is more than 'occupation', where an employee
can feel both challenged and nurtured, and where there are increased opportunities to use one's strengths, talents and capabilities to their fullest extent, and where
learning is at the *heart* of organization.

Concept Checklist

Can you now define each of the Key Concepts listed below, and are you now able
to achieve the other Knowledge Outcomes specified at the beginning of the
chapter?

- Evaluation
- Internal validation and external validation
- Content validity
- Balanced scorecard
- Purposes of evaluation
- Reaction level
- Summative and formative evaluation
- Affective reactions and utility reactions
- Learning level
- Behaviour level
- Results level
- Context-input-reaction-outcome (CIRO)
- Return on investment
- Alternatives to taxonomic approaches
- Evaluating reactions
- Evaluating knowledge
- Evaluating skills
- Simulations
- Evaluating attitudes
- Evaluating changes in job behaviour
- Learning transfer
- Evaluating results
- Benefit–cost ratio and ROI
- L&D's ultimate contribution
- Flow, signature strengths and meaningful work

References

Aditya, R. N., House, R. J. and Kerr, S. 2000. Theory and practice of leadership: into the new millennium. In C. L. Cooper and I. T. Robertson (eds), *International Review of Industrial and Organisational Psychology*.

Agor, W. H. (ed.). 1989. *Intuition in Organizations: Leading and Managing Productively*. Newbury Park, CA: Sage.

Alessi, S. M. and Trollip, S. R. 2001. *Multimedia for Learning: Methods and Development*. Boston, MA: Allyn & Bacon.

Allard-Poesi, F., Drucker-Godard, C. and Ehlinger, S. 2001. Analysing representations and discourse. In R. A. Thietart (ed.), *Doing Management Research: A Comprehensive Guide*. London: Sage.

Alldredge, M., Johnson, C., Stolzfus, J. and Vicere, A. 2003. Leadership development at 3M: new process, new techniques, new growth. *Human Resource Planning*, 26(3): 45–55.

Alliger, G. M. and Janak, E. A. 1989. Kirkpatrick's levels of training criteria: thirty years later. *Personnel Psychology*, 42: 331–42.

Alliger, G. M., Tannenbaum, S. I., Bennett, W., Traver, H. and Shotland, A. 1997. A meta-analysis of the relations among training criteria. *Personnel Psychology*, 50: 341–58.

Allinson, C. W. and Hayes, J. 1996. The Cognitive Style Index: a measure of intuition-analysis for organizational research. *Journal of Management Studies*, 33: 19–135.

Allport, G. W. 1954. Attitudes in the history of social psychology. In G. Lindzey and A. Aronson (eds), *Handbook of Social Psychology*. Reading, MA: Addison Wesley.

American Society for Training & Development. 2004. *State of the Industry Report*. www.astd.org

Anderson, A. 1993. *Successful Training Practice: A Manager's Guide to Personnel Development*. Oxford: Blackwell.

Anderson, J. R. 1990. *Cognitive Psychology and Its Applications*. New York: Freeman.

Anderson, J. R., Reder, L. and Simon, H. 1996. Situated learning and education, *Educational Researcher*, 25(4): 5–11

Anderson, N., Herriot, P. and Hodgkinson, G. P. 2001. The practitioner–researcher divide in industrial, work and organisational (IWO) psychology: where are we now and where do we go from here? *Journal of Occupational & Organizational Psychology*, 74(4): 391–411.

Andrews, D. H. and Goodson, L. A. 1980. A comparative analysis of models of instructional design, *Journal of Instructional Development*, 3: 2–16.

Annett, J. and Sparrow, J. 1985. The transfer of training: a review of research and practical implications, *PLET*, 22(2): 116–24.

Annett, J., Duncan, K. D., Stammers, R. B. and Gray, M. J. 1971. *Task Analysis*. Training Information Paper No. 6. London: HMSO.

Antonacopoulou, E. P. 2001. The paradoxical nature of the relationship between training and learning, *Journal of Management Studies*, 38(3): 328–50.

Aragon, S. R. and Hatcher, T. 2001. Ethics and integrity in HRD: case studies in research and practice, *Advances in Developing Human Resources*, 3(1): Monograph.

Arbaugh, J. B. and Duray, R. 2002. Technological and structural characteristics, student learning and satisfaction with web-based courses: an exploratory study of two on-line MBA programs, *Management Learning*, 33(3): 331–47.

Argyris, C. 1976. Single-loop and double-loop models in research on decision making, *Administrative Science Quarterly*, 21: 363–77.

Argyris, C. 1977. Double-loop learning in organisations, *Harvard Business Review*, 55(5): 115–25.

Argyris, C. 1995. Action science and organisational learning, *Journal of Managerial Psychology*, 10(6): 20–26.

Argyris, C. and Schön, D. A. 1974. *Theory in Practice*. San Francisco: Jossey-Bass.

Argyris, C. and Schön, D. A. 1978. *Organisational Learning*. Reading, MA: Addison Wesley.

Argyris, C. and Schön, D. A. 1996. *Organisational Learning II: Theory, Method and Practice*. Reading, MA: Addison-Wesley.

Arnold, J. and Johnson, K. 1997. Mentoring in early career, *Human Resource Management Journal*, 7(4): 61–70.

Ashkanasy, N. M. 2004. Book review: Leader development for transforming organisations, *Academy of Management Executive*, 18(4): 165–6.

Atkinson, T. 2000. Trusting your own judgment (or allowing yourself to eat the pudding). In T. Atkinson and G. Claxton (eds), *The Intuitive Practitioner: On the Value of Not Always Knowing What One Is Doing*. Buckingham: Open University Press.

Atkinson, T. and Claxton, G. (eds), 2000. *The Intuitive Practitioner: On the Value of Not Always Knowing What One Is Doing*. Buckingham: Open University Press.

Austin, J. H. 1999. *Zen and the Brain: Toward an Understanding of Meditation and Consciousness*. Cambridge, MA: MIT Press.

Ausubel, D. 1985. Learning as constructing meaning. In Entwistle, N. (ed.), *New Directions in Educational Psychology, 1: Learning and Teaching*. London. The Falmer Press.

Ausubel, D. P. 1968. *Educational Psychology: A Cognitive View*. New York: Holt, Rinehart and Winston.

Avolio, B. J., Bass, B. M. and Jung, D. I. 1999. Re-examining the components of transactional and transformational leadership using the Multifactor Leadership Questionnaire, *Journal of Occupational and Organizational Psychology*, 72: 441–62.

Axelrod, R. (ed.) 1976. *Structure of Decision: Cognitive Maps of Political Elites*. Princeton, NJ: Princeton University Press.

Baddeley, A. D. 1997. *Human Memory: Theory and Practice*. Hove: Psychology Press.

Baddeley, A. D. and Hitch, G. J. 1974. Working memory. In G. Bower (ed.), *Recent Advances in Learning and Motivation* (8). New York: Academic Press.

Badger, B., Sadler-Smith, E. and Michie, E. (1997). Outdoor management development: use and evaluation, *Journal of European Industrial Training*, 21: 318–25.

Baldwin, T. T. and Ford, J. K. 1988. Transfer of training: a review and directions for future research, *Personnel Psychology*, 41: 63–105.

Baldwin, T. T., Ford, K. J. and Naquin, S. S. 2000. Managing transfer before learning begins: enhancing the motivation to improve work through learning, *Advances in Developing Human Resources*, 8: 23–35.

Bandler, R. and Grinder, J. 1975. *Structure of Magic: A Book about Language and Therapy.* London: Science & Behaviour Books.

Bandura, A. 1977. *Social Learning Theory.* Englewood Cliffs, NJ: Prentice Hall.

Bandura, A. 1996. Social learning. In A. S. R. Manstead and M. Hewstone (eds), *The Blackwell Encyclopaedia of Social Psychology.* Oxford: Blackwell.

Bandura, A. 2003. On the psychosocial impact and mechanisms of spiritual modelling, *International Journal for the Psychology of Religion*, 13(3): 167–73.

Barab, S. A. and Duffy, T. 2000. From practice fields to communities of practice. In D. Janssen and S. M. Land (eds), *Theoretical Foundations of Learning Environments.* Mahwah, NJ: Lawrence Earlbaum Associates, 25–56.

Barab, S. A. and Plucker, J. A. 2002. Smart people or smart contexts: cognition, ability and talent development in an age of situated approaches to knowing and learning, *Educational Psychologist*, 37(3): 165–83.

Barab, S. A., Barnett, M. and Squire, K. 2002. Developing an empirical account of a community of practice: characterising the essential tensions, *The Journal of the Learning Sciences*, 11(4): 489–542.

Barnard, C. 1948/1997. The nature of leadership. In K. Grint (ed.), *Leadership: Classical, Contemporary and Critical Approaches.* Oxford: Oxford University Press.

Barnett, R. 1997. *Towards a Higher Education for the New Century.* London: Institute of Education.

Barney, J. B. 1991. Firm resources and sustained competitive advantage, *Journal of Management*, 17(1): 99–120.

Barney, J. B. 1999. Looking inside for competitive advantage. In R. S. Schuler and S. E. Jackson (eds), *Strategic Human Resource Management.* Oxford: Blackwell.

Baron, R. M. and Kenny, D. A. 1986. The moderator–mediator variable distinction in social psychological research: conceptual, strategic and statistical considerations, *Journal of Personality and Social Psychology*, 51(6): 1173–182.

Bass, B. M. 1990. *Bass & Stodgill's Handbook of Leadership: Theory, Research and Managerial Applications.* New York: Free Press.

Bass, B. M. 1995. The meaning of leadership. In J. T. Wren (ed.), *The Leader Companion: Insights on Leadership through the Ages.* New York: The Free Press.

Bass, B. M. and Avolio, B. J. 1994. *Improving Organisational Effectiveness through Transformational Leadership.* Thousand Oaks, CA: Sage.

Bassi, L. J., Ludwig, J., McMurrer, D. P. and van Buren, M. 2002. Profiting from learning: firm level effects of training investments and market implications, *Singapore Management Review*, 24(3): 61–75.

Bastick, T. 1982. *Intuition: How We Think and Act.* New York: John Wiley.

Bates, R., Chen, H. C. and Hatcher, T. 2002. Value priorities of HRD scholars and practitioners, *International Journal of Training and Development*, 6(4): 229–39.

Bates, R. A., Holton, E. F., Seyler, D. L. and Carvalho, M. A. 2000. The role of interpersonal factors in the application of computer-based training in an industrial setting, *Human Resource Development International*, 3(1): 19–42.

Bateson, G. 1972. *Steps to an Ecology of Mind*, Northvale, NJ: Aronson.

Beattie, R. S. 2004. Line managers, HRD, ethics and values: evidence from the voluntary sector. In J. Woodall, M. Lee and J. Stewart (eds), *New Frontiers in HRD*. London: Routledge.

Behling, O. and Eckel, N. L. 1991. Making sense out of intuition. *Academy of Management Executive*, 5: 46–54.

Bennett, R. and Leduchowicz, T. 1983. What makes an effective trainer? *Journal of European Industrial Training* (Special Issue), 7(2).

Bennis, W. and Nanus, B. 1985. *Leaders: The Strategies for Taking Charge*. New York: Harper and Row.

Bennis, W. and Thomas, R. J. 2002. Leadership crucibles, *Executive Excellence*, 19(11): 3–4.

Berthoin Antal, A., Lenhardt, U. and Rosenbrock, R. 2001. Barriers to organisational learning. In M. Dierkes, A. Berthoin Antal, J. Child and I. Nonaka (eds), *Handbook of Organizational Learning and Knowledge*. Oxford: Oxford University Press.

Blackler, F., Crump, N. and McDonald, S. 1999. Organisational learning and organisational forgetting. In M. Easterby-Smith, L. Araujo and J. Burgoyne (eds), *Organisational Learning and the Learning Organisation: Developments in Theory and Practice*. London: Sage.

Boerner, C. S., Macher, J. T. and Teece, D. J. 2001. A review and assessment of organisational learning in economic theories. In M. Dierkes, A. Berthoin Antal, J. Child and I. Nonaka (eds), *Handbook of Organizational Learning and Knowledge*. Oxford: Oxford University Press.

Boland, R. J., Tenkasi, R. V. and Te'eni, D. 1994. Designing information technology to support distributed cognition, *Organization Science*, 5: 456–75.

Bolman, L. G. and Deal, T. E. 2003. *Reframing Organisations: Artistry, Choice and Leadership*. San Francisco: Jossey-Bass.

Bonner, S. 1999. Choosing teaching methods based on learning objectives: an integrative framework, *Issues in Accounting Education*, 14(1): 11–39.

Borthick, A. F., Jones, D. R. and Wakai, S. 2003. Designing learning experiences within learners Zone of Proximal Development (ZPDs): enabling collaborative learning on-site and on-line, *Journal of Information Systems*, 17(1): 107–34.

Bowers, K. S., Regher, G. and Balthazard, C. 1990. Intuition in the context of discovery, *Cognitive Psychology*, 22(1): 72–110.

Boxall, P. and Purcell, J. 2003. *Strategy and Human Resource Management*. Basingstoke: Palgrave Macmillan.

Boyatzis, R. E. 1982. *The Competent Manager: A Model for Effective Performance*. Chichester: John Wiley.

Boyatzis, R. E. 1993. Beyond competence: the choice to be a leader, *Human Resource Management Review*, 3(1): 1–14.

Boyatzis, R. E., Stubbs, E. C. and Taylor, S. N. 2002. Learning cognitive and emotional intelligence competencies through graduate management education, *Academy of Management Learning and Education*, 1(2): 150–62.

Boydell, T. and Leary, M. 1996. *Identifying Training Needs*. London: Institute for Personnel and Development.

Bramley, P. 1989. *Evaluating Training*. London: Kogan Page.

Bramley, P. 1991. *Evaluating Training Effectiveness: Translating Theory into Practice*. London: McGraw-Hill.

Branson, R. K., Wager, B. M. and Rayner, G. T. 1977. *Inter-service Procedures for Instructional Systems Development*. Tallahassee, FL: Centre for Educational Technology, FSU.

Briggs, L. J. and Wager, W. W. 1981. *Handbook of Procedures for the Design of Instruction*. Englewood Cliffs, NJ: Educational Technology Publications.

Broadbent, D. E. 1958. *Perception and Communication*. London: Pergamon.

Brown, J. 2002. Training needs assessment: a must for developing an effective training program, *Public Personnel Management*, 31(4): 569–78.

Bruner, J. S. 1957. *Contemporary Approaches to Cognition*. Cambridge, MA: Harvard University Press.

Buchel, B. and Raub, S. 2001. Media choice and organisational learning. In M. Dierkes, A. Berthoin Antal, J. Child and I. Nonaka (eds) *Handbook of Organizational Learning and Knowledge*. Oxford: Oxford University Press.

Buckley, J. W. 1967. Programmed instruction in industrial training, *California Management Review*, 10(2): 71–9.

Buckley, R. and Caple, J. 1992. *The Theory and Practice of Training*. London: Kogan Page.

Burgoyne, J. 1988. Management development for the individual and the organisation, *Personnel Management*, June: 40–4.

Burgoyne, J. 1993. The competence movement: issues, stakeholders and prospects, *Personnel Review*, 22(6): 6–13.

Burke, L. A. and Miller, M. K. 1999. Taking the mystery out of intuitive decision-making. *Academy of Management Executive*, 13: 91–9.

Burke, L. A. and Sadler-Smith, E. 2006. Instructor intuition in the educational setting, *Academy of Management Learning and Education* (in press).

Burroughs, G. E. R. 1975. *Design and Analysis in Educational Research* (Educational monograph number 8). Birmingham: Faculty of Education, University of Birmingham.

Campbell, D. J. and Dardis, G. J. 2004. The 'be, know, do' model of leader development, *Human Resource Planning*, 27(2): 26–39.

Cangelosi, V. E. and Dill, W. R. 1965. Organisational learning: observations towards a theory, *Administrative Science Quarterly*, 10: 175–203.

Canning, R. 1996. Enhancing the quality of learning in human resource development, *Journal of European Industrial Training*, 20(2): 3–10.

Cannon, T. 1994. *Management Development for the Millennium: Working Party Report*. London: Institute of Management.

Carew, D. K., Parisi-Carew, E. and Blanchard, K. H. 1986. Group development and situational leadership: a model for managing groups, *Training & Development Journal*, 40(6): 46–50.

Carliner, S. 2004. Business models for training and performance improvement departments, *Human Resource Development Review*, 3(3): 275–93.

Carney, R. N., Levin, J. R. and Levin, M. E. 1994. Enhancing the psychology memory by enhancing the memory of psychology, *Teaching of Psychology*, 21(3): 171–4.

Cattell, R. B. 1966. The scree test for the number of factors, *Multivariate Behavioral Research*, 1(April): 245–76.

CEDEFOP, 2003. *Key Figures on Vocational Education and Training*, http://www.cedefop.eu.int).

Chalofsky, N. 2003. *Meaningful Work*, Training and Development, December: 52–8.

Chartered Institute for Personnel and Development. 2004. *Training and Development 2004: Survey Report*. London: CIPD.

Child, J. 2001. Learning through strategic alliances. In M. Dierkes, A. Berthoin Antal, J. Child and I. Nonaka (eds), *Handbook of Organizational Learning and Knowledge*. Oxford: Oxford University Press.

Child, J. and Heavens, S. 2001. The social constitution of organisations and its implications for organisational learning. In M. Dierkes, A. Berthoin Antal, J. Child and I. Nonaka (eds), *Handbook of Organizational Learning and Knowledge*. Oxford: Oxford University Press.

Claxton, G. 1997. *Hare Brain and Tortoise Mind: Why Intelligence Increases When You Think Less*. London: Fourth Estate.

Claxton, G. 2000. The anatomy of intuition. In T. Atkinson and G. Claxton (eds), *The Intuitive Practitioner: On the Value of Not Always Knowing What One is Doing*. Buckingham: Open University Press.

Cobb, P. and Bowers, J. 1999. Cognitive and situated learning perspectives in theory and practice, *Educational Researcher*, 28(2): 4–15.

Cobb, P. and Yackel, E. 1996. Constructivist, emergent, and socio-cultural perspectives in the context of developmental research, *Educational Psychologist*, 31: 175–90.

Cole, R. E. 1998. Introduction to special issue on knowledge and the firm, *California Management Review*, 40: 15–21.

Collins, D. B. 2002. Performance level evaluation methods used in management development studies from 1986 to 2000, *Human Resource Development Review*, 1(1): 91–110.

Collins, J. C. and Porras, J. I. 2000. *Built to Last: Successful Habits of Visionary Companies*. London: Random House Business.

Comrey, A. L. and Lee, H. B. 1992. *A First Course in Factor Analysis*. Hillsdale, NJ: LEA.

Conger, J. A. 2004. Developing leadership capability: what's inside the black box? *Academy of Management Executive*, 18(3): 136–9.

Conger, J. A. and Fulmer, R. M. 2003. Developing your leadership pipeline, *Harvard Business Review*, December: 76–84.

Conger, J. A. and Toegel, G. 2003. Action learning and multi-rater feedback as leadership development interventions, *Journal of Change Management*, 3(4): 332–49.

Connaughton, S. L., Lawrence, F. L. and Ruben, B. D. 2003. Leadership development as a systematic and multidisciplinary enterprise, *Journal of Education for Business*, September/October: 46–51.

Constable, J. and McCormick, R. 1987. *The Making of British Managers*. London: British Institute of Management/Confederation of British Industry.

Contu, A., Grey, C. and Ortenblat, A. 2003. Against learning, *Human Relations*, 56(8): 931–53.

Couto, D. L. 2004. Putting leaders on the couch: a conversation with Manfred F. R. Kets de Vries, *Harvard Business Review*, January: 65–71.

Cowley, J. 2003. O captain, my captain! *New Statesman*, 4 August 2003: 13.

Cronbach, L. J. 1951. Coefficient alpha and the internal structure of tests, *Psychometrika*, 31: 93–6.

Crossan, M. M. and Guatto, T. 1996. Organisational learning research profile, *Journal of Organisational Change Management*, 19(1): 107–12.

Csikszentmihalyi, M. 1992/2002. *Flow: The Classic Work on How to Achieve Happiness*. London: Rider.

Csikszentmihalyi, M. 2003. *Good Business: Leadership, Flow and the Making of Meaning*. London: Hodder and Stoughton.

Currie, G. and Darby, R. 1995. Competence-based management development: rhetoric and reality, *Journal of European Industrial Training*, 19(5): 11–18.

Cyert, R. M. and March, J. G. 1963. *A Behavioural Theory of the Firm*. Oxford: Blackwell.

Dansey-Smith, F. 2004. Why 'soft' people skills are the key to leadership development, *Strategic HR Review*, 3(3): 28–31.

Davenport, T. H. and Prusak, L. 1998. *Working Knowledge – How Organisations Manage What They Know*. Boston: Harvard Business School Press.

Davey, C. L., Powell, J. A., Powell, J. E. and Cooper, I. 2002. Action learning in a medium-sized construction company, *Building Research & Information*, 30(1): 5–15.

Davis, L. N. and Mink, O. G. 1992. Human resource development: an emerging profession – an emerging purpose, *Studies in Continuing Education*, 14(2): 187–202.

Davis, P., Naughton, J. and Rothwell, W. 2004. New roles and new competencies for the professional, *Training & Development*, 58(4): 26–36.

Davis, S. H. and Davis, P. B. 2003. *The Intuitive Dimensions of Administrative Decision-making.* Lanham, MD: Scarecrow.

Day, D. 2001. Leadership development: a review in context, *Leadership Quarterly*, 11(4): 581–613.

Day, D., Sin, H.-P. and Chen, T. T. 2004. Assessing burdens of leadership: effects of formal leadership roles on individual performance over time, *Personnel Psychology*, 57: 573–605.

Delery, J. 1998. Issues of fit in strategic human resource management: implications for research, *Human Resource Management Review*, 8(3): 289–309.

Department of Employment. 1971. *Glossary of Training Terms.* London: HMSO.

Department for Education and Skills. 2002. *Learning and Training at Work, SFR 02/2003.* London: Department for Education and Skills.

Derry, S. 1996. Cognitive schema theory in the constructivist debate, *Educational Psychologist*, 31(3/4): 163–74.

Despres, C. and Chauvel, D. 2000. A thematic analysis of the thinking in knowledge management. In C. Despres and D. Chauvel (eds), *Knowledge Horizons: The Present and the Promise of Knowledge Management.* Boston: Butterworth Heinemann.

Dewey, J. 1916. *Democracy and Education.* New York: Macmillan.

Dewey, J. 1938. *Experience and Education.* New York: Macmillan.

DeWolfe-Waddill, D. and Marquardt, M. 2003. Adult learning orientations and action learning, *Human Resource Development Review*, 2(4): 406–29.

Dionne, P. 1996. The evaluation of training activities: a complex issue involving different stakes, *Human Resource Development Quarterly*, 7(3): 279–86.

Dixon, N. M. 1996. New routes to evaluation, *Training and Development*, 50(5): 82–6.

Doh, J. P. 2003. Can leadership be taught? Perspectives from management educators, *Academy of Management Learning and Education*, 2(1): 54–67.

Dooley, C. R. 1945/2001. The Training within Industry report, *Advances in Developing Human Resources*, 3(2): 127–289.

Downs, S. 1995. Learning to learn. In S. Truelove (ed.), *Handbook of Training and Development.* Oxford: Blackwell.

Drath, W. 2001. *The Deep Blue Sea: Rethinking the Source of Leadership.* San Francisco: Jossey Bass.

Drath, W. H. and Palus, C. J. 1994. *Making Common Sense: Leading as Meaning Making in a Community of Practice.* Greensboro, NC: Center for Creative Leadership.

Dreyfus, H. and Dreyfus, S. 1986. *Mind over Machine: The Power of Intuition and Experience in the Era of the Computer.* Oxford: Blackwell.

Driscoll, M. P. 1994. *Psychology of Learning and Instruction.* Needham Heights, MA: Allyn & Bacon.

Dubin, R. 1978. *Theory Building.* New York: Free Press.

Dvir, T., Eden, D., Avolio, B. J. and Shamir, B. 2002. Impact of transformational leadership on follower development and performance: a field experiment, *Academy of Management Journal*, 45(4): 735–44.

Dyer, W. G. 1995. *Team Building: Current Issues and New Alternatives.* Reading, MA: Addison Wesley.

Easterby-Smith, M. 1986. *Evaluation of Management Education, Training and Development.* Aldershot: Gower.

Easterby-Smith, M. 1997. Disciplines of the learning organisation: contributions and critiques, *Human Relations*, 50(4): 1085–113.

Easterby-Smith, M. and Araujo, L. 1999. Organisational learning: current debates and opportunities. In M. Easterby-Smith, L. Araujo and J. Burgoyne (eds), *Organisational Learning and the Learning Organisation: Developments in Theory and Practice*. London: Sage.

Easterby-Smith, M., Thorpe, R. and Lowe, A. 1991. *Management Research: An Introduction*. London: Sage.

Edmondson, A., Bohmer, R. and Pisano, G. 2001. Speeding up team learning, *Harvard Business Review*, (October) 79(9): 125–32.

Edwards, C. 1999. Evaluation and assessment. In J. P. Wilson (ed.), *Human Resource Development: Learning and Training for Individuals and Organisations*. London: Kogan Page.

Egan, T. M. and Beis, A. L. 2001. Managing client reactions to evaluation results, *Advances in Developing Human Resources*, 3(1): 44–7.

Elkjaer, B. 1999. In search of a social learning theory. In M. Easterby-Smith, L. Araujo and J. Burgoyne (eds), *Organisational Learning and the Learning Organisation: Developments in Theory and Practice*. London: Sage.

Employment National Training Organisation, 2004. Full unit and element summary for learning and development, http://www.ento.co.uk/standards/

Engle, R. W., Kane, M. J. and Tuholski, S. W. 1999. Individual differences in working memory capacity and what they tell us about controlled attention, general fluid intelligence and functions of the prefrontal cortex. In A. Miyake and P. Shah (eds), *Models of Working Memory: Mechanisms of Active Maintenance and Executive Control*. Cambridge: Cambridge University Press.

Eraut, M. 2000. Non-formal learning and tacit knowledge in professional work, *British Journal of Educational Psychology*, 70(2): 113–36.

Eysenck, M. W. 1996. *Simply Psychology*. Hove: Psychology Press.

Fagenson, E. A. 1989. The mentor advantage: perceived career/job experiences of protégés versus non-protégés, *Journal of Organizational Behavior*, 10(4): 309–20.

Fagenson-Eland, E. 2001. The NFL's Bill Parcells on winning, leading and turning round teams, *Academy of Management Executive*, 15(3): 48–55.

Fenwick, T. 2003. Professional growth plans: possibilities and limitations of an organisation-wide employee development strategy, *Human Resource Development Quarterly*, 1491: 59–77.

Finson, K. and Szedlak, F. 1997. General Motors does a needs analysis, *Training & Development*, May: 103–4.

Fiol, C. M. and Lyles, M. A. 1985. Organisational learning, *Academy of Management Review*, 10(4): 803–13.

Fletcher, C. and Baldry, C. 1999. Multi-source feedback systems: a research perspective. In C. L. Cooper and I. T. Robertson (eds), *International Review of Industrial and Organisational Psychology*, 14: 149–93.

Floodgate, J. F. and Nixon, A. E. 1994. Personal development plans: the challenge of implementation – a case study, *Journal of European Industrial Training*, 18(11): 43–7.

Fombrun, C. J., Tichy, N. and Devanna, M A. 1984. *Strategic Human Resource Management*. New York: John Wiley.

Ford, D. N., Voyer, J. J. and Gould-Wilkinson, J. M. 2000. Building learning organisations in engineering cultures: case study, *Journal of Management in Engineering*, July/August: 72–83.

Foster, P. 1996. Observational research. In R. Sapsford and V. Jupp (eds), *Data Collection and Analysis*. London: Sage.

Freedman, R. D. and Stumpf, S. A. 1980. Learning style theory: less than meets the eye, *Academy of Management Review*, 5: 445–7.

Fulmer, R. M., Gibbs, P. and Keys, J. B. 1998. The second generation learning organisations: new tools for sustaining competitive advantage, *Organisational Dynamics*, 27(2): 6–21.

Furnham, A. 1997. Fire the training department, *Across the Board*, 34(3): 9–10.

Gagné, R. M. 1985. *The Conditions of Learning and Theory of Instruction*. New York: Holt, Rinehart and Winston.

Gagné, R. M. and Briggs, L. J. 1979. *Principles of Instructional Design*. New York: Holt, Rinehart and Winston.

Gagné, R. M., Briggs, L. J. and Wager, W. W. 1992. *Principles of Instructional Design*. Fort Worth, TX: Harcourt Brace Jovanovich.

Gainey, T. W. and Klaas, B. S. 2002. Outsourcing the training function: results from the field, *Human Resource Planning*, 25(1): 16–22.

Garavan, T. 1991. Strategic human resource development, *Journal of European Industrial Training*, 15(1): 17–30.

Garavan, T. N., Costine, P. and Heraty, N. 1995. The emergence of strategic human resource management, *Journal of European Industrial Training*, 19(10): 4–10.

Garcia, M. U. and Vano, F. L. 2002. Organisational learning in a global market, *Human Systems Management*, 21(3): 169–81.

Garrett, B. 2000. *The Learning Organisation: Developing Democracy at Work*. London: Harper-Collins.

Gendlin, E. T. 1981. *Focusing*. New York: Bantam.

Gephart, M. A., Marsick, V. J., Van Buren, M. E. and Spiro, M. S. 1996. Learning organizations come alive, *Training and Development*, December: 35–45.

Gerhardi, S. and Nicolini, D. 2001. The sociological foundations of organisational learning. In M. Dierkes, A. Berthoin Antal, J. Child and I. Nonaka (eds), *Handbook of Organizational Learning and Knowledge*. Oxford: Oxford University Press.

Gibb, S. 2002. *Learning and Development: Processes, Practices and Perspectives at Work*. Basingstoke: Palgrave Macmillan.

Gibb, S. and Megginson, D. 1993. Inside corporate mentoring schemes: a new agenda of concerns, *Personnel Review*, 22(1): 40–54.

Gist, M. E. and McDonald-Mann, D. 2000. Leadership training and development. In C. L. Cooper and E. A. Locke (eds), *Industrial and Organisational Psychology*. Oxford: Blackwell.

Gnisci, A., Papa, F. and Spedaletti, S. 1999. Usability aspects, socio-relational context and learning performance in the virtual classroom: a laboratory experiment, *Behaviour & Information Technology*, 18(6): 431–43.

Goffee, R. and Jones, G. 2000. Why should anyone be led by you? *Harvard Business Review*, September/October: 62–70.

Gold, J., Rodgers, H. and Smith, V. 2003. What is the future of the human resource development professional? A UK perspective, *Human Resource Development International*, 6(4): 437–56.

Gold, M. 2003. Eight lessons about e-learning from five organisations, *Training & Development*, August, 54–7.

Goldstein, I. L. 1993. *Training in Organisations: Needs Assessment, Development and Evaluation*. Pacific Grove, CA: Brooks/Cole Publishing.

Goleman, D. 1996. *Emotional Intelligence: Why It Can Matter More Than IQ*. London: Bloomsbury.

Goleman, D. 1998. *Working with Emotional Intelligence*. New York: Bantam.

Goleman, D., Boyatzis, R. and McKee, A. 2002. *The New Leaders: Transforming the Art of Successful Leadership into the Science of Results*. London: Time Warner.

Goodge, P. 2005. How to link 360° feedback and appraisal, *People Management*, January, 11(2): 46–7.

Gosling, J. and Mintzberg, H. 2004. The education of practicing managers, *MIT Sloan Management Review*, Summer: 19–22.

Gourlay, S. 2001. Knowledge management and HRD, *Human Resource Development International*, 4(1): 27–46.

Grant, R. M. 2000. Shifts in the world economy: the drivers of knowledge management. In C. Despres and D. Chauvel (eds), *Knowledge Horizons: The Present and the Promise of Knowledge Management*. Boston: Butterworth Heinemann.

Gregory, R. L. 1987. *The Oxford Companion to the Mind*. Oxford: Oxford University Press.

Grieves, J. and Redman, T. 1999. Living in the shadow of OD: HRD and the search for identity, *Human Resource Development International*, 2(2): 81–102.

Grint, K. 1997. Classical leadership. In K. Grint (ed.), *Leadership: Classical, Contemporary and Critical Approaches*. Oxford: Oxford University Press.

Grugulis, I. 2003. The contribution of National Vocational Qualifications to the growth of skills in the UK, *British Journal of Industrial Relations*, 41(3): 457–75.

de Gues, A. 1997. *The Living Company, Growth, Learning and Longevity in Business*. London: Nicholas Brearley.

Hackman, R. J., Wageman, R., Ruddy, T. M. and Ray, C. L. 2000. Team effectiveness in theory and in practice. In C. L. Cooper and E. A. Locke (eds), *Industrial and Organisational Psychology*. Oxford: Blackwell.

Hair, J. F., Anderson, R. E., Tatham, R. L. and Black, W. C. 1998. *Multivariate Data Analysis*. Upper Saddle River, NJ: Prentice Hall.

Hales, C. P. 1999. Why do managers do what they do? Reconciling evidence and theory in accounts of managerial work, *British Journal of Management*, 10(4): 335–50.

Hamblin, A. C. 1974. *Evaluation and Control of Training*. Maidenhead: McGraw-Hill.

Hamel, G. and Prahalad, C. K. 1994. *Competing for the Future*. Boston, MA: Harvard University Press.

Handy, C. 1988. *Making Managers*. London: Pitman.

Handy, C. 1994. *The Empty Raincoat*. London: Hutchinson.

Hannagan, T. 2002. *Management: Concepts and Practices*. Harlow: FT Prentice Hall.

Hardern, G. 1995. The development of standards of competence in accounting, *Accounting Education*, 4(1): 17–27.

Harlow, T. and Smith, A. 2003. Necessary measures, *People Management*, November: 48.

Harrison, R. 2002. *Learning and Development*. London: CIPD.

Hartog, D. N. and Verburg, R. M. 2004. High performance work systems, organisational culture and firm effectiveness, *Human Resource Management Journal*, 14(1): 55–78.

Haslam, S. A. and McGarty, C. 1998. *Doing Psychology: An Introduction to Research Methodology and Statistics*. London: Sage.

Hayes, J. and Allinson, C. W. 1998. Cognitive style and the theory and practice of individual and collective learning in organisations, *Human Relations*, 51(7): 847–71.

Hegstad, C. D. 1999. Formal mentoring as a strategy for human resource development: a review of research, *Human Resource Development Quarterly*, 10(4): 383–90.

Heraty, N. and Morley, M. 1995. Line managers and human resource development, *Journal of European Industrial Training*, 19(10): 31–7.

Herbert, G. R. and Doverspike, D. 1990. Performance appraisal in the training needs analysis process: a review and critique, *Public Personnel Management*, 19(3): 253–70.

Hernez-Broom, G. and Hughes, R. L. 2004. Leadership development: past, present and future, *Human Resource Planning*, 27(1): 24–32.

Hersey, P. and Blanchard, K. H. 1988. *Management of Organisational Behaviour*. Englewood Cliffs, NJ: Prentice-Hall.

Higson, M. and Wilson, J. P. 1995. Implementing personal development plans: a model for trainers, managers and supervisors, *Industrial and Commercial Training*, 27(6): 25–9.

Hill, L. A. 2004. New manager development for the 21st century, *Academy of Management Executive*, 18(3): 121–7.

Hodgkinson, G. P. and Sadler-Smith, E. (2003). Complex or unitary? A critique and empirical reassessment of the Allinson–Hayes Cognitive Style Index, *Journal of Occupational and Organizational Psychology*, 76: 243–68.

Hodgkinson, G. P. and Sparrow, P. 2002. *The Competent Organization*. Buckingham: Open University Press.

Hogarth, R. M. 2001. *Educating Intuition*. Chicago: University of Chicago Press.

Holman, D., Pavlica, K. and Thorpe, R. 1997. Rethinking Kolb's theory of experiential learning: the contribution of social constructivism and activity theory, *Management Learning*, 28: 135–48.

Holton, E. F. 1996. The flawed four-level evaluation model, *Human Resource Development Quarterly*, 7(1): 5–21.

Holton, E. F. 2000. On the nature of performance and learning in HRD. In W. E. A. Ruona and G. Roth (eds), *Advances in Developing Human Resources* (Advances 7). San Francisco, CA: Berrett-Koehler.

Holton, E. F. and Baldwin, T. T. 2000. Making transfer happen: an action perspective on learning transfer systems, *Advances in Developing Human Resources*, 8: 1–4.

Holton, E. F. and Naquin, S. S. (eds). 2000. Developing high-performance leadership competency, *Advances in Developing Human Resources*, Monograph 6.

Holton, E. F., Bates, R. A. and Ruona, W. E. A. 2000. Development of a generalised learning transfer system inventory, *Human Resource Development Quarterly*, 11(4): 333–60.

Honey, P. and Mumford, A. 1992. *A Manual of Learning Styles*. Maidenhead: Peter Honey Publications.

Horvath, C. M. 1995. Excellence v. effectiveness: MacIntyre's critique of business, *Business Ethics Quarterly*, 5(3): 499–532.

Horwitz, F. M. (1999). The emergence of strategic training and development: the current state of play, *Journal of European Industrial Training*, 23(4/5): 180–90.

Huber, G. 1996. Organisational learning: a guide for executives in technology critical organisations, *International Journal of Technology Management*, 11(7&8): 821–32.

Huber, G. P. 1996. Organisational learning: the contributing process and the literatures. In M. D. Cohen and L. S. Sproull (eds), *Organisational Learning*. Thousand Oaks, CA: Sage.

Huczynski, A. and Buchanan, D. 2001. *Organizational Behaviour: An Introductory Text*. Harlow: Pearson.

Hull, C. L. 1943. *Principles of Behaviour*. New York: Appleton-Century-Crofts.

Huselid, M. A., Jackson, S. E. and Schuler, R. S. 1997. Technical and strategic human resource management effectiveness as determinants of firm performance, *Academy of Management Journal*, 40(1): 171–88.

Huysman, M. 1999. Balancing biases: a critical review of the literature on organisational learning. In M. Easterby-Smith, L. Araujo and J. Burgoyne (eds), *Organisational Learning and the Learning Organisation: Developments in Theory and Practice*. London: Sage.

Ibert, J., Baumard, P., Donada, C. and Xureb, J. M. 2001. Data collection and managing the data source. In R. A. Thietart (ed.), *Doing Management Research: A Comprehensive Guide*. London: Sage.

Irvine, D. and Beard, C. 1999. Management training and development. In J. P. Wilson (ed.), *Human Resource Development: Learning and Training for Individuals and Organisations*. London: Kogan Page.

Isenberg, D. J. 1984. How senior managers think, *Harvard Business Review*, November/December: 81–90.

Jacobs, R. L. and Jones, M. J. 1995. *Structured On-the-job Training: Unleashing Employee Expertise in the Workplace*. San Francisco, CA: Berrett-Koehler Publishers.

Jacobs, R. L. and Washington, C. 2003. Employee development and organisational performance: a review of literature and directions for future research, *Human Resource Development International*, 6(3): 343–54.

Jarvis, J. 2004. Get the right coach, *People Management*, 10(13): 49–52.

Jayne, V. 2003. Coaches, mentors and you, *New Zealand Management*, 50(1): 34–9.

Johnson, L. D. 2001. Coaching and mentoring, *Manage*, May: 10–12.

Johnson-Laird, P. N. 1988. *The Computer and the Mind: An Introduction to Cognitive Science*. London: Fontana.

Johnston, R. 1999. Supporting learning in the third millennium. In J. P. Wilson (ed.), *Human Resource Development: Learning and Training for Individuals and Organisations*. London: Kogan Page.

de Jong, J. A. and Versloot, B. 1999. Job instruction: its premises and its alternatives, *Human Resource Development International*, 2(4): 391–404.

Jung-Beeman, M., Bowden, E. M., Haberman, J., Frymiare, J. L., Arambel-Liu, S., Greenblatt, R., Reber, P. J. and Kounios, J. (2004). Neural activity observed in people solving verbal problems with insight. *Public Library of Science – Biology*, 2(4): 0500–0510. http://biology.plosjournals.org

Kamoche, K. 2000. Developing managers: the functional, the symbolic, the sacred and the profane, *Organization Studies*, 21(4): 747–74.

Kaplan, R. S. and Norton, D. P. 1996. *The Balanced Scorecard: Translating Strategy into Action*. Boston, MA: Harvard Business School Press.

Kaplan, R. S. and Norton, D. R. 1996. Using the balanced scorecard as a strategic management system, *Harvard Business Review*, January/February.

Kaplan, R. and Norton, D. 2001. *The Strategy Focused Organisation*. Boston, MA: Harvard Business School Press.

Kaufmann, G. (2001). Creativity and problem solving. In J. Henry (ed.), *Creative Management*. London: Sage.

Kayes, D. C. 2002. Experiential learning and its critics: preserving the role of experience in management learning and education, *Academy of Management Learning & Education*, 1(2): 137–49.

Keep, E. 1994. Vocational education and training for the young. In K. Sisson (ed.), *Personnel Management*. Oxford: Blackwell.

Kim, D. H. 1993. The link between individual and organisational learning, *Sloan Management Review* (Fall): 37–50.

Kirkpatrick, D. L. 1967. Whose responsibility is training: the relationship between line and staff training roles, *Training and Development Journal*, March: 22–5.

Kirkpatrick, D. L. 1979. Techniques for evaluating training programmes, *Training and Development Journal*, June: 78–92.

Kirkpatrick, D. L. 1996. *Evaluating Training Programs: The Four Levels*. San Francisco, CA: Berrett-Koehler Publishers.

Kirsch, I., Lynn, S. J., Vigorito, M. and Miller, R. R. 2004. The role of cognition in classical conditioning, *Journal of Clinical Psychology*, 60(4): 369–92.

Klein, G. 2003. *Intuition at Work: Why Developing Your Gut Instincts Will Make You Better at What You Do*. New York: Currency Doubleday.

Kline, P. 1994. *An Easy Guide to Factor Analysis*. London: Routledge.

Knowles, M. S. (1968). Androgogy, not pedagogy! *Adult Leadership*, 16: 350–2, 386.

Knowles, M. S. 1990. *The Adult Learner: A Neglected Species*. Houston: Gulf Publishing Company.

Knowles, M. S., Holton, E. F. and Swanson, R. A. 1998. *The Adult Learner: The Definitive Classic in Adult Education and Human Resource Development*. Woburn, MA: Butterworth-Heinemann.

Kolb, D. A. 1984. *Experiential Learning: Experience as the Source of Learning and Development*. Englewood Cliffs, NJ: Prentice-Hall.

Kotter, J. 1988. *The Leadership Factor*. New York: Free Press.

Kouzes, J. M. and Posner, B. Z. 2002. *The Leadership Challenge*. San Francisco: Jossey Bass.

Kraack, T. 2003. Turning the aircraft carrier, *Training & Development*, November 2003.

Kram, K. E. 1985. *Mentoring at Work: Developmental Relationships in Organisational Life*. Glenview, IL: Scott, Foresman.

Kransdorff, A. 1999. Applying experiential learning to work, *Knowledge Management Review*, 9: 12–15.

Krebsback-Gnath, C. 2001. Applying theory to organisational transformation. In M. Dierkes, A. Berthoin Antal, J. Child and I. Nonaka (eds), *Handbook of Organizational Learning and Knowledge*. Oxford: Oxford University Press.

Kuchinke, K. P. 2000. Debates over the nature of HRD: an institutional theory perspective, *Human Resource Development International*, 3(3): 279–83.

Kuchinke, K. P. 2001. Why HRD is not an academic discipline, *Human Resource Development International*, 4(3): 291–4.

Lapre, M. A. and Van Wassenhove, L. N. 2002. Learning across lines: the secret to more effective factories, *Harvard Business Review*, October: 107–11.

Latham, G. P. 2004. The motivational benefits of goal-setting, *Academy of Management Executive*, 18(4): 126–9.

Lau, D. C. 1963. *Lao Tzu: the Tao Te Ching*. London: Penguin.

Lave, J. and Wenger, E. 1991. *Situated Learning: Legitimate Peripheral Participation*. New York: Cambridge University Press.

Le Doux, J. 1996. *The Emotional Brain: The Mysterious Underpinnings of Emotional Life*. New York: Touchstone.

Lee, M. 2004. A refusal to define HRD. In J. Woodall, M. Lee and J. Stewart (eds), *New Frontiers in HRD*. London: Routledge.

Leigh, P. 1997. The new spirit at work, *Training & Development*, March: 26–33.

Leonard, D. 1998. An organic learning system at Chaparral Steel, *Knowledge Management Review*, 1(3): 10–11.

Leonard, D. and Sensiper, S. (1998). The role of tacit knowledge in group innovation, *California Management Review*, 40: 112–30.

Leonard-Barton, D. 1992. The factory as a learning laboratory, *Sloan Management Review*, Fall: 23–38

Leont'ev, A. N. 1981. *Problems of the Development of the Mind*. Moscow: Progress.

Levitt, B. and March, J. G. 1988. Organisational learning, *Annual Review of Sociology*, 14: 319–40.

Liaw, S. and Huang, H. 2002. How web technology can facilitate learning, *Information Systems Management*, Winter: 56–61.

Lim, D. H. and Johnson, S. D. 2002. Trainee perceptions of factors that influence learning transfer, *International Journal of Training and Development*, 6(1): 36–48.

Lindeman, E. C. 1926. *The Meaning of Adult Education*. New York: New Republic.

Locke, E. A. and Latham, G. P. 1990. *A Theory of Goal Setting and Task Performance*. Englewood Cliffs, NJ: Prentice-Hall.

Lockshin, L. and McDougal, G. 1998. Service problems and recovery strategies: an examination of the critical incident in a business-to-business market, *International Journal of Retail & Distribution Management*, 26(11): 429–38.

Loo, R. 2004. Kolb's learning styles and learning preferences: is there a linkage? *Educational Psychology*, 24(1): 99–108.

Lynham, S. A. 2000. Theory building in the human resource development profession, *Human Resource Development Quarterly*, 11(2): 159–78.

Lynham, S. A. 2002. The general method of theory-building research in applied disciplines, *Advances in Developing Human Resources*, 4(3): 221–41.

Lyon, U. 1996. Influence, communication and neuro-linguistic programming in practice. In J. Stewart and J. McGoldrick (eds), *Human Resource Development: Perspectives, Strategies and Practice*. London: Pitman Publishing.

Mabey, C. 2002. Mapping management development practice, *Journal of Management Studies*, 39(8): 1139–160.

Mabey, C. and Salaman, G. 1995. *Strategic Human Resource Management*. Oxford: Blackwell.

Mabey, C., Salaman, G. and Storey, J. 1998. *Human Resource Management: A Strategic Introduction*. Oxford: Blackwell.

MacIntyre, A. 1984. *After Virtue*. Notre Dame, IN: Notre Dame Press.

Mager, R. F. 1984. *Preparing Instructional Objectives*, Belmont, CA: David S. Lake Publishers.

Mainemelis, C., Boyatzis, R. E. and Kolb, D. A. 2002. Learning styles and adaptive flexibility: testing experiential learning theory, *Management Learning*, 33(1): 5–33.

March, J. G. and Olsen, J. P. 1975. The uncertainty of the past: organisational learning under ambiguity, *European Journal of Political Research*, 3(2): 147–71.

March, J. G. and Shapira, Z. 1987. Managerial perspectives on risk and risk taking, *Management Science*, 33(11): 1404–418.

Marquardt, M. J. and Reynolds, A. 1994. *The Global Learning Organisation*. New York: Irwin.

Maul, G. P. and Spotts, D. S. 1993. Developing computer-based instructional courses, *Information Management*, November/December: 9–11.

Maurer, T. J. 2002. Employee learning and development orientation: toward an integrative model of involvement in continuous learning, *Human Resource Development Review*, 1(1): 9–44.

Mayer, R. E. 1995. The search for insight: grappling with Gestalt psychology's unanswered questions. In R. J. Sternberg and J E. Davidson (eds), *The Nature of Insight*. Cambridge, MA: MIT Press.

Mayer, R. E. and Moreno, R. 2003. Nine ways to reduce cognitive load in multimedia learning, *Educational Psychologist*, 38(1): 43–52.

Mbengue, A. and Vandangeon-Derumez, I. 2001. Causal analysis and modelling. In R. A. Thietart (ed.), *Doing Management Research: A Comprehensive Guide*. London: Sage.

McCall, M. W. 2004. Leadership development through experience, *Academy of Management Executive*, 18(3): 127–30.

McDonald, D. and Smith, A. 1995. A proven connection: performance management and business results, *Compensation and Benefits Review*, 27: 59–64.

McGehee, W. and Thayer, P. W. 1961. *Training in Business and Industry*. New York: John Wiley.

McGoldrick, J., Stewart, J. and Watson, S. 2001. Theorising human resource development, *Human Resource Development International*, 4(3): 343–56.

McLean, G. N. and McLean, L. 2001. If we can't define HRD in one country how can we define it in an international context? *Human Resource Development International*, 4(3): 313–26.

Megginson, D., Joy-Matthews, J. and Banfield, P. 1993. *Human Resource Development*. London: Kogan Page.

Meisel, S. L. and Fearon, D. S. 1994. Leading learning. In S. A. Cavaleri and D. S. Fearon (eds), *Managing in Organisations that Learn*. Cambridge, MA: Blackwell.

Meister, J. C. 2005. Learning that leads to high performance, *Chief Learning Officer*, January: 58.

Mellon, C. A. 1999. Technology and the great pendulum of education, *Journal of Research on Computing in Education*, 32(1): 28–35.

Mezirow, J. 1991. Transformative dimensions of adult learning. San Francisco: Jossey-Bass.

Miettinen, R. 1999. The riddle of things: activity theory and actor-network theory as approaches to studying, *Mind, Culture and Activity*, 6(3): 170–95.

Militello, L. G. and Hutton, R. J. B. 1998. Applied cognitive task analysis (ACTA): a practitioner's toolkit for understanding cognitive task demands, *Ergonomics*, 41(11): 1618–641.

Miller, G. A. 1956. The magical number seven, plus or minus two: some limits on our capacity for processing information, *Psychological Review*, 63: 81–97.

Mintzberg, H. and Gosling, J. 2002. Educating managers beyond borders, *Academy of Management Learning and Education*, 1(1): 64–76.

Mitroff, I. 2003. Do not promote religion under the guise of spirituality, *Organization*, 10(2): 375–82.

Molina, J. A. and Ortega, R. 2003. Effects of employee training on the performance of North American firms, *Applied Economics Letters*, 10: 549–52.

Morano, R. 1973. Determining organizational training needs, *Personnel Psychology*, 26: 479–87.

Morgan, G. 1997. *Imaginization*. San Francisco: Berrett-Koehler Publishers.

Morgan, R. B. and Casper, W. J. 2000. Examining the factor structure of participant reactions to training: a multidimensional approach, *Human Resource Development Quarterly*, 11(3): 301–17.

Mosher, B. 2003. Marketing enterprise learning, *Chief Learning Officer*, November 2003: 24–8.

Mumford, A. 1987. The education and training of British managers, *Industrial and Commercial Training*, September/October: 19–20.

Mumford, A. 1993. *Management Development: Strategies for Action*. London: IPM.

Myers, D. G. 2002. *Intuition: Its Powers and Perils*. New Haven, CT: Yale University Press.

Nadler, J., Thompson, L. and van Boven, L. 2003. Learning negotiation skills: four models of knowledge creation and transfer, *Management Science*, 49(4): 529–40.

Nadler, L. 1970. *Developing Human Resource*. Houston, TX: Gulf.

Nadler, L. 1979. *Developing Human Resources*. Austin, TX: Learning Concepts.

Naish, R. 2004. Avoid deep fried camembert: how blended learning can avoid the high-fat option, *E-learning Age*, November: 24–5.

Neisser, U. 1976. *Cognition and Reality*. New York. W. H. Freeman.

Nevis, E. C., DiBella, A. J. and Gould, J. M. 1995. Understanding organisations as learning systems, *Sloan Management Review* (Winter): 73–85.

Newby, A. C. 1992. *Training Evaluation Handbook*. Aldershot: Gower.

Newton, T. and Findlay, P. 1998. Playing god? The performance appraisal, *Human Resource Management Journal*, 6(3): 42–58.

Nicholson, N. 2000. *Managing the Human Animal*. London: Texere.

Nicolini, D. and Meznar, M. B. 1995. The social construction of organisational learning: conceptual and practical issues in the field, *Human Relations*, 48(7): 727–46.

Nonaka, I. 1991. The knowledge creating company, *Harvard Business Review* (November/December): 96–104.

Nonaka, I. 1994. A dynamic theory of organisational knowledge creation, *Organization Science*, 5: 14–37.

Nonaka, I., Toyama, R. and Byosiere, P. 2001. A theory of organisational knowledge creation: understanding the dynamic processes of creating knowledge. In M. Dierkes, A. Berthoin Antal, J. Child and I. Nonaka (eds), *Handbook of Organizational Learning and Knowledge*. Oxford: Oxford University Press.

Nonaka, I., Toyama, R. and Konno, N. 2000. SECI, ba and leadership: a unified model of dynamic knowledge creation, *Long Range Planning*, 33(1): 16–17.

Norman, D. A. 1968. Toward a theory of memory and attention, *Psychological Review*, 75: 522–36.

Norman, D. A. and Bobrow, D. G. 1975. On data-limited and resource limited processes, *Cognitive Psychology*, 7: 44–64.

Nunnally, J. C. 1978. *Psychometric Theory*. New York: McGraw-Hill.

Nye, M. J. 2002. *HYLE-International Journal for Philosophy of Chemistry*, 8(2): 123–7.

O'Connor, J. and Seymour, J. 1990. *Introducing NLP: Psychological Skills for Understanding and Influencing People*. London: Element.

O'Driscoll, M. P. and Taylor, P. J. 1992. Congruence between theory and practice in management training needs analysis, *The International Journal of Human Resource Management*, 3(3): 593–603.

Olivero, G., Bane, D. K. and Kopelman, R. E. 1997. Executive coaching as a transfer of training tool, *Public Personnel Management*, 26: 461–9.

Ortenblat, A. 2002. Organisational learning: a radical perspective, *International Journal of Management Reviews*, 4(1): 71–85.

Oxford Encyclopaedic English Dictionary. 1991. Oxford: Oxford University Press.

Paas, F., Renkel, A. and Sweller, J. 2003. Cognitive load theory and instructional design: recent development, *Educational Psychologist*, 38(1): 1–4.

Patrick, J. 1992. *Training Research and Practice*. London: Academic Press.

Pattanayak, B. 2003. Gaining competitive advantage and business success through strategic HRD: an Indian experience, *Human Resource Development International*, 6(3): 405–11.

Patton, P. W. and Pratt, C. 2002. Assessing the training needs of high-potential managers, *Public Personnel Management*, 31(4): 465–84.

Pedler, M., Burgoyne, J. and Boydell, T. 1997. *The Learning Company: A Strategy for Sustainable Development*. London: McGraw-Hill.

Peiperl, M. A. 2001. Getting 360° feedback right, *Harvard Business Review*, January: 142–7.

Penrose, E. 1959. *The Theory of the Growth of the Firm*. Oxford: Blackwell.

Pettigrew, A., Jones, E. and Reason, P. 1982. *Training and Development Roles in Their Organisational Setting*. Sheffield: Manpower Services Commission.

Pettijohn, C. E., Pettijohn, J. S. and d'Amico, M. 2001. Characteristics of performance appraisals and their impact on sales-force satisfaction, *Human Resource Development Quarterly*, 12(2): 127–46.

Phillips, J. J. 1996. ROI: the search for best practice, *Training & Development*, February: 42–7.

Piccoli, G., Ahmad, R. and Ives, B. 2001. Web-based virtual learning environments: a research framework and a preliminary assessment of effectiveness in basic IT skills training, *MIS Quarterly*, 25(4): 401–26.

Pickett, L. 1998. Competencies and managerial effectiveness, *Public Personnel Management*, 27(1): 103–15.

Pinker, S. 1997. *How the Mind Works*. New York: W. W. Norton.

Pinto, P. R. and Walker, J. W. 1978. What do training and development professionals really do? *Training and Development Journal*, July: 58–64.

Poell, R. 1999. The learning organisation: a critical evaluation. In J. P. Wilson (ed.), *Human Resource Development: Learning and Training for Individuals and Organisations*. London: Kogan Page.

Polanyi, M. 1966. *The Tacit Dimension*. London: Routledge & Kegan Paul.

Porter, M. 1985. *Competitive Advantage: Creating and Sustaining Superior Performance*. New York: Free Press.

Porth, S. J., McCall, J. and Bausch, T. A. 1999. Spiritual themes of the learning organisation, *Journal of Organizational Change Management*, 12(3): 211–20.

Prager, H. 1999. Cooking-up effective team building, *Training & Development*, December: 14–15.

Prahalad, C. K. and Hamel, G. 1990. The core competence of the corporation, *Harvard Business Review*, May–June: 79–91.

Preskill, H. and Torres, R. T. 1999. The role of evaluative enquiry in creating learning organisations. In M. Easterby-Smith, L. Araujo and J. Burgoyne (eds), *Organisational Learning and the Learning Organisation: Developments in Theory and Practice*. London: Sage.

Probst, G. and Buchel, B. 1997. *Organisational Learning – the Competitive Advantage of the Future*. London: Prentice-Hall.

Raelin, J. 1997. Action learning and action science: are they different? *Organizational Dynamics*, 26(1): 21–34.

Raelin, J. A. 1999. The design of the action project in work-based learning, *Human Resource Planning*, 22(3): 12–28.

Raelin, J. A. 2000. *Work-based Learning: The New Frontier of Management Development*. Upper Saddle River, NJ: Prentice-Hall.

Raelin, J. A. 2004. Don't bother putting leadership into people, *Academy of Management Executive*, 18(3): 131–5.

Ready, D. A. and Conger, J. A. 2003. Why leadership development efforts fail, *MIT Sloan Management Review*, Spring: 83–8.

Reber, A. S. 1989. Implicit learning and tacit knowledge, *Journal of Experimental Psychology: General*, 118: 219–35.

Reber, A. S. 1993. *Implicit Learning and Tacit Knowledge: An Essay on the Cognitive Unconscious*. New York: Oxford University Press.

Redman, T. and Wilkinson, A. 2002. *The Informed Student Guide to Human Resource Management*. London: Thomson Learning.

Reger, R. K., Gustafson, L. T., Demarie, S. M. and Mullane, J. V. 1994. Reframing the organisation: why implementing total quality is easier said than done, *Academy of Management Review*, 19(3): 565–84.

Reid, M. A. and Barrington, H. 1999. *Training Interventions: Promoting Learning Opportunities*. London: Chartered Institute of Personnel and Development.

Remenyi, D., Williams, B., Money, A. and Swartz, E. 1998. *Doing Research in Business and Management: An Introduction to Process and Method*. London: Sage.

Revans, R. W. 1982. *The Origins and Growth of Action Learning*. Bromley: Chartwell-Bratt.

Revans, R. W. 1983. *The ABC of Action Learning*. Bromley: Chartwell-Bratt.

Reynolds, M. 1997. Learning styles: a critique, *Management Learning*, 28(2): 115–33.

Riding, R. J. and Rayner, S. 1998. *Cognitive Styles and Learning Strategies*. London: David Fulton.

Rogers, C. R. 1969, 1983. *Freedom to Learn*. Columbus, OH: Merrill.

Rogers, C. R. 1980. *A Way of Being*. Boston, MA: Houghton Mifflin.

Rogers, E., Rogers, W. and Metlay, W. 2002. Improving the payoff from 360-degree feedback, *Human Resource Planning*, 25(3): 44–54.

Rollinson, D. and Broadfield, A. 2002. *Organisational Behaviour and Analysis: An Integrated Approach*. Harlow: FT Prentice Hall.

Roscoe, J. 1995. Analysis of organisational training needs. In S. Truelove (ed.), *Handbook of Training and Development*. Oxford: Blackwell.

Rosenshine, B. V. and Meister, C. 1992. The use of scaffolds for teaching less-structured cognitive tasks, *Educational Leadership*, 49(7): 26–33.

Rothwell, W. and Wellins, R. 2004. Mapping your future: putting new competencies to work for you, *Training & Development*, 58(5): 1–8.

Rouillier, J. Z. and Goldstein, I. L. 1997. The relationship between organisational transfer climate and positive transfer of training. In D. Russ-Eft, H. Preskill and C. Sleezer (eds), *Human Resource Development Review: Research Implications*. Thousand Oaks, CA: Sage.

Rowntree, D. 1982. *Educational Technology in Curriculum Development*. London: Paul Chapman Publishing.

Rowntree, D. 1990. *Teaching through Self-instruction: How to Develop Open Learning Materials*. London: Kogan Page.

Royer, I. and Zarlowski, P. 2001. Sampling. In R. A. Thietart (ed.), *Doing Management Research: A Comprehensive Guide*. London: Sage.

Ruderman, M. N., Ohlott, P. J., Pazner, K. and King, S. N. 2002. Benefits of multiple roles for managerial women, *Academy of Management Journal*, 45(2): 369–87.

Ruona, W. E. A. 2001. The foundational impact of the Training within Industry project on the HRD profession, *Advances in Developing Human Resources*, 3(2): 119–26.

Ruona, W. E. A., Leimbach, M., Holton, E. F. and Bates R. 2002. The relationship between learner utility reactions and predicted learning transfer among trainees, *International Journal of Training & Development*, 6(4): 218–28.

Rushby, N. 2003. Editorial, *British Journal of Educational Technology*, 34(5): 545–7.

Russ-Eft, D. 2001. Interpretation and explanation of research and evaluation results: a case study in use and misuse, *Advances in Developing Human Resources*, 3(1): 51–4.

Russ-Eft, D. 2002. A typology of training design and work environment factors affecting workplace learning and transfer, *Human Resource Development Review*, 1(1): 45–65.

Russ-Eft, D. 2004. In search of ethics and integrity in HRD. In J. Woodall, M. Lee and J. Stewart (eds), *New Frontiers in HRD*. London: Routledge.

Rust, J. and Golombok, S. 1989. *Modern Psychometrics: The Science of Psychological Assessment*. London: Routledge.

Sadler, P. 2001. Leadership and organisational learning. In M. Dierkes, A. Berthoin Antal, J. Child and I. Nonaka (eds), *Handbook of Organizational Learning and Knowledge*. Oxford: Oxford University Press.

Sadler-Smith, E. and Shefy, E. 2004. The intuitive executive: understanding and applying 'gut feel' in decision-making, *Academy of Management Executive*, 18(4): 76–91.

Sadler-Smith, E. and Smith, P. J. B. (2004). Strategies for accommodating individuals' styles and preferences in flexible learning programmes, *British Journal of Educational Technology*, 35(4): 395–412.

Sadler-Smith, E., Down, S. and Field, J. (1999). Adding value to HRD: evaluation, Investors in People in small firm training, *Human Resource Development International*, 2: 369–90.

Sadler-Smith, E., Gardiner, P., Badger, B., Chaston, I. and Stubberfield, J. 2000. Using collaborative learning to develop small firms, *Human Resource Development International*, 3(3): 285–306.

Sadler-Smith, E., Spicer, D. P. and Chaston, I. 2001. Learning orientations and growth in smaller firms. *Long Range Planning*, 34: 139–58.

Salas, E. and Cannon-Bowers, J. A. 2001. The science of training: a decade of progress, *Annual Review of Psychology*, 52(1): 471–99.

Salomon, G. 1993. *Distributed Cognitions: Psychological and Educational Considerations*. Cambridge: Cambridge University Press.

Salopek, J. J. 2002. Virtually face to face, *e-learning*, February: 16–19.

Sandberg, J. 2001. Understanding competence at work, *Harvard Business Review*, March: 24–8.

Sanderson, G. 1995. Objectives and evaluation. In S. Truelove (ed.), *The Handbook of Training and Development*. Oxford: Blackwell.

Scarborough, H., Swan, J. and Preston, J. 1999. *Knowledge Management: A Literature Review*. London: Institute of Personnel and Development.

Schafter, A. 2001. An e-learning survey, *T&D*, November: 74–7.

Schroder, H. 1989. *Managerial Competence: The Key to Excellence*. Iowa: Kendall Hunt.

Schuler, R. S. and Jackson, S. E. 1987. Linking competitive strategies with human resource management practices, *Academy of Management Executive*, (1)3: 207–19.

Schwartz, B. and Reisberg, D. 1991. *Learning and Memory*. New York: W. W. Norton.

Seely-Brown, J. and Duguid, P. 1991. Organisational learning and communities of practice: toward a unified view of working, learning and innovation, *Organisation Science*, 2(1): 40–57.

Seligman, M. E. P. 2002. *Authentic Happiness: Using the New Positive Psychology to Realise Your Potential for Lasting Fulfilment*. New York: Free Press.

Senge, P. M. 1990. *The Fifth Discipline: The Art and Practice of the Learning Organisation*. London: Doubleday.

Senge, P. M., Kleiner, A., Roberts, C. B., Ross, R. B. and Smith, B. J. 1994. *The Fifth Discipline Fieldbook*. London: Nicholas Brealey Publishing.

Shale, D. and Garrison, R. 1990. *Education at a Distance*. Malabar, FL: Krieger.

Shapiro, S. and Spence, M. T. (1997). Managerial intuition: a conceptual and operational framework, *Business Horizons*, 40: 63–73.

Shaw, K. N. 2004. Changes to the goal-setting process at Microsoft, *Academy of Management Executive*, 18(4): 139–42.

Shepherd, A. 1976. An improved tabular format for task analysis, *Journal of Occupational Psychology*, 49: 93–104.

Shepherd, A. 1998. HTA as a framework for task analysis, *Ergonomics*, 41(11): 1537–552.

Shirley, D. A. and Langan-Fox, J. 1996. Intuition: a review of the literature. *Psychological Reports*, 79: 563–84.

Simon, H. 1991. Bounded rationality in organisational learning, *Organization Science*, 2: 125–39.

Simon, H. A. 1969. *Sciences of the Artificial.* Cambridge, MA: MIT Press.

Simon, H. A. 1987. Making management decisions: the role of intuition and emotion. *Academy of Management Executive*, February: 57–64.

Simon, H. A. 1989. Making management decisions: the role of intuition and emotion. In W. H. Agor (ed.), *Intuition in Organizations: Leading and Managing Productively.* Newbury Park, CA: Sage.

Sims, R. R. and Veres, J, G. 1989. Training for competence, *Public Personnel Management*, 18(1): 101–7.

Skinner, B. F. 1938. *Behavior of Organisms.* New York: Appleton-Century-Crofts.

Slater, S. F. and Narver, J. C. 1995. Market orientation and the learning organisation, *Journal of Marketing*, 59(3): 63–74.

Sloman, M. 2004. No pipe dream, *People Management*, 10(23): 38–9.

Sloman, M. and Reynolds, J. 2003. Developing the e-learning community, *Human Resource Development International*, 6(2): 259–72.

Smith, M. K. 2001. Chris Argyris: theories of action, double-loop learning and organizational learning, *The Encyclopaedia of Informal Education*, www.infed.org/thinkers/argyris.htm).

Smyth, M. M., Morris, P. E., Levy, P. and Ellis, A. W. 1987. *Cognition in Action.* London: LEA Associates.

Snyder, W. M. and Cummings, T. G. 1998. Organisation learning disorders: conceptual model and intervention hypotheses, *Human Relations*, 15(7): 873–95.

Spicer, D. P. 2000. Mental models, cognitive style and organisational learning: the development of shared understanding in organisations. Unpublished PhD thesis, Plymouth Business School, University of Plymouth.

Stafford, T. 2005. White hot route: the brain can be very responsive to emotion information, *The Psychologist*, 18(2): 97.

Starbuck, W. H. and Hedberg, B. 2001. How organisations learn from success and failure. In M. Dierkes, A. Berthoin Antal, J. Child and I. Nonaka (eds), *Handbook of Organizational Learning and Knowledge.* Oxford: Oxford University Press.

Stata, R. 1989. Organisational learning – the key to management innovation, *Sloan Management Review*, 30(3): 63–74.

Sternberg, R. J. 1999. *Cognitive Psychology.* Fort Worth, TX: Harcourt Brace College Publishers.

Sternberg, R. J. 2003. WICS: a model of leadership in organisations, *Academy of Management Learning and Education*, 2(4): 386–401.

Stewart, J. and McGoldrick, J. (eds). 1996. *Human Resource Development: Perspectives, Strategies and Practice.* London: Pitman Publishing.

Stewart, J. 1999. *Employee Development Practice.* London: FT Pitman Publishing.

Stewart, J. and Winter, R. 1995. Open and distance learning. In S. Truelove (ed.), *Handbook of Training and Development.* Oxford: Blackwell.

Stoel, D. 2004. The evaluation heavyweight match, *Training and Development*, 58(1): 46–8.

Sugarman, B. 2001. A learning-based approach to organisational change, *Organisational Dynamics*, 30(1): 62–76.

Swanson, R. A. 1995. Human resource development: performance is the key, *Human Resource Development Quarterly*, 6(2): 207–13.

Swanson, R. A. 2000. Theory and other irrelevant matters, *Human Resource Development International*, 3(3): 273–8.

Swanson, R. A. 2001. Human resource development and its underlying theory, *Human Resource Development International*, 4(3): 299–332.

Sweller, J. and Chandler, P. 1994. Why some material is difficult to learn, *Cognition and Instruction*, 12(3): 185–233.

Sweller, J., van Merrienboer, J. J. G. and Paas, F. G. W. C. 1998. Cognitive architecture and instructional design, *Educational Psychology Review*, 10(3): 251–96.

Tabachnick, B. G. and Fidell, L. S. 1996. *Using Multivariate Statistics*. New York: HarperCollins.

Taggart, W. 1997. Discovering and understanding intuition. *Exceptional Human Experience: Studies of the Unitive, Spontaneous Imaginal*, 15: 174–88.

Tan, J. A., Hall, R. J. and Boyce, C. 2003. The role of employee reactions in predicting training effectiveness, *Human Resource Development Quarterly*, 14(4): 397–412.

Tannenbaum, S. I. and Woods, S. B. 1992. Determining a strategy for evaluating training: operating within organisational constraints, *Human Resource Planning*, 15: 63–81.

Tennant, M. 1988. *Psychology and Adult Learning*. Routledge: London.

Thach, L. and Heinselman, T. 1999. Executive coaching defined, *Training & Development*, 53(3): 43–9.

Thietart, R. A. (ed.) 2001. *Doing Management Research: A Comprehensive Guide*. London: Sage.

Thorndike, E. L. 1928. *Adult Learning*. New York: Macmillan.

Tippins, M. J. and Sohi, R. S. 2003. IT competency and firm performance: is organisational learning a missing link? *Strategic Management Journal*, 24: 745–61.

Toegel, G. and Conger, J. A. 2003. 360 degree assessment: time for reinvention, *Academy of Management Learning and Education*, 2(3): 297–312.

Torraco, R. J. 1997. Theory building research methods. In R. A. Swanson and E. F. Holton (eds), *Human Resource Development Research Handbook: Linking Research and Practice*. San Francisco: Berrett-Kohler Publishers.

Torraco, R. J. 1999. Research methods for theory building in applied disciplines: a comparative analysis, *Advances in Developing Human Resources*, 4(3): 355–76.

Torrington, D., Hall, L. and Taylor, S. 2002. *Human Resource Management*. Harlow: FT Prentice-Hall.

Tosey, P. and Mathison, J. 2003. Neuro-linguistic programming and learning theory: a response, *The Curriculum Journal*, 14(3): 371–88.

Tranfield, D. and Starkey, K. 1998. The nature, social organisation, and promotion of management research: towards policy, *British Journal of Management*, 9: 341–53.

Truelove, S. 1995. Developing employees. In S. Truelove (ed.), *Handbook of Training and Development*. Oxford: Blackwell.

Tsang, E. W. K. 1997. Organisational learning and the learning organisation: a dichotomy between descriptive and prescriptive research, *Human Relations*, 50(1): 73–89.

Tuckman, B. W. 1965. Developmental sequence in small groups, *Psychological Bulletin*, 63(6): 384–99.

Tulving, E. 1972. Episodic and semantic memory. In E. Tulving and W. Donaldson (eds), *Organisation of Memory*. New York: Academic Press.

Tyson, S. and Ward, P. 2004. The use of 360 degree feedback technique in the evaluation of management development, *Management Learning*, 35(2): 205–23.

Ulrich, D. 1997. *Human Resource Champions: The Next Agenda for Adding Value and Delivering Results*. Boston, MA: Harvard Business School Press.

Van der Heijden, K., Bradfield, R., Burt, G., Cairns, G. and Wright, G. 2002. *The Sixth Sense: Accelerating Organisational Learning with Scenarios*. Chichester: John Wiley.

Van Merrienboer, J. J. G., Kirschner, P. A. and Kester, L. 2003. Taking the load of a learner's mind: instructional design for complex learning, *Educational Psychologist*, 38(1): 5–13.

de Vellis, R. 1991. *Scale Development*. Newbury Park, CA: Sage.

Vince, R. 1998. Behind and beyond Kolb's learning cycle, *Journal of Management Education*, 22: 304–19.

Vince, R. 2001. Power and emotion in organisational learning, *Human Relations*, 54(10): 1325–351.

Vince, R. 2003. The future practice of HRD, *Human Resource Development International*, 6(4): 559–63.

Vroom, V. 1964. *Work and Motivation*. New York: John Wiley.

Wagner, R. K. 2002. Smart people doing dumb things: the case of managerial incompetence. In R. J. Sternberg (ed.), *Why Smart People Can Be So Stupid*. New Haven, CT: Yale University Press.

Wagner, R. K. and Sternberg, R. J. 1985. Practical intelligence in real-world pursuits: the role of tacit knowledge, *Journal of Personality and Social Psychology*, 49: 436–58.

Wagner, R. K. and Sternberg, R. J. 1990. *Street Smarts*. In K. Clark and M. Clark (eds), *Measures of Leadership*. Greensboro, NC: Centre for Creative Leadership.

Wallas, G. 1926. *The Art of Thought*. New York: Harcourt Brace.

Wally, S. and Baum, J. R. (1994). Personal and structural determinants of the pace of strategic decision making, *Academy of Management Journal*, 37: 932–56.

Walton, J. 1999. *Strategic Human Resource Development*. London: FT Prentice Hall.

Warr, P., Allan, C. and Birdi, K. 1999. Predicting three levels of training outcome, *Journal of Occupational and Organisational Psychology*, 72: 351–75.

Warr, P., Bird, M. and Rackham, N. 1970. *Evaluation of Management Training*. Aldershot: Gower.

Wasylyshyn, K. M. 2003. Executive coaching: an outcome study, *Consulting Psychology Journal: Practice and Research*, 55(2): 94–106.

Weick, K. E. and Westley, F. 1999. Organisational learning: affirming an oxymoron. In S. R. Clegg, C. Hardy and W. R. Nord (eds), *Managing Organisations: Current Issues*. London: Sage.

Weinberger, L. A. 1998. Commonly held theories of human resource development, *Human Resource Development International*, 1(1): 75–93.

Wenger, E. 1998. *Communities of Practice: Learning, Meaning and Identity*. Cambridge: Cambridge University Press.

Wexley, K. N. and Baldwin, T. T. 1986. Management development, *Journal of Management*, 12(2): 277–94.

Wexley, K. N. and Klimoski, R. 1984. Performance appraisal: an update. In K. M. Rowland and G. R. Ferris (eds), *Research in Personnel and Human Resources Management*, 2: 35–79.

Wiig, K. M. 2000. Knowledge management: an emerging discipline rooted in a long history. In C. Despres and D. Chauvel (eds), *Knowledge Horizons: The Present and the Promise of Knowledge Management*. Boston, MA: Butterworth Heinemann.

Wilson R. 1996. Asking questions. In R. Sapsford and V. Jupp (eds), *Data Collection and Analysis*. London: Sage.

Wind, J. and Crook, C. 2005. *The Power of Impossible Thinking*. London: Wharton School Publishing.

Winn, W. 2002. Current trends in educational technology research: the study of learning environments, *Educational Psychology Review*, 14(3): 331–51.

Witherspoon, P. D. 1997. *Communicating Leadership: An Organizational Perspective*. Boston, MA: Allyn and Bacon.

Wittrock, M. C. 1989. Generative processes of comprehension, *Educational Psychologist*, 24: 345–76.

Wognum, A. A. M. 2001. Vertical integration of HRD policies within companies, *Human Resource Development International*, 4(3): 407–21.

Wognum, I. and Fond Lam, J. 2000. Stakeholder involvement in strategic HRD aligning: the impact on HRD effectiveness, *International Journal of Training and Development*, 4(2): 98–110.

Woltz, D. J. 2003. Implicit cognitive processes as aptitudes for learning, *Educational Psychologist*, 38(2): 95–104.

Wood, R. and Bandura, A. 1989. Social cognitive theory of organizational management, *Academy of Management Review*, 14(1): 361–84.

Woodall, J. and Winstanley, D. 1998. *Management Development: Strategy and Practice*. Oxford: Blackwell Publishers.

Woodall, J. Lee, M. and Stewart, J. (eds). 2004. *New Frontiers in HRD*. London: Routledge.

Woodruffe, C. 1993. *Assessment Centres: Identifying and Developing Competence*. London: IPM.

Xie, J. and Wu, G. 2001. Training and development in the People's Republic of China, *International Journal of Training and Development*, 5(3): 223–32.

Zaleznik, A. 1977. Managers and leaders: are they different? *Harvard Business Review*, (May/June) 55(3): 67–77.

Zambarloukos, S. and Constantelou, A. 2002. Learning and skills formation in the new economy: evidence from Greece, *International Journal of Training and Development*, 6(4): 240–53.

Zeinstra, B. 2004. Converting from a training department to a profit centre, *Chief Learning Officer*, December: 32–7.

Zukerman, B. and Preskill, H. 2001. Throwing a curveball in the game of evaluation: deception and the misuse of findings, *Advances in Developing Human Resources*, 3(1): 55–7.

Subject Index

Author Index